# Great Film Directors
## A CRITICAL ANTHOLOGY

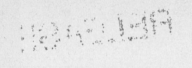

# Great
# Film Directors

## A CRITICAL ANTHOLOGY

edited by

### Leo Braudy
*The Johns Hopkins University*

and

### Morris Dickstein
*Queens College of the
City University of New York*

199452

NEW YORK · OXFORD UNIVERSITY PRESS · 1978

Library of Congress Cataloging in Publication Data
Main entry under title:

Great film directors.

  Bibliography: p.
  1.  Moving-picture producers and directors—Biography
—Addresses, essays, lectures.  I.  Braudy, Leo.
II.  Dickstein, Morris.
PN1998.A2F38     791.43'0233'0922     76-42668
ISBN 0-19-502312-9

Printed in the United States of America

*With thanks to the Yale Film Society, 1961–1968,
where we first saw so many of the movies*

# Contents

# Acknowledgments

For their help in fashioning this anthology we would like to thank Jonathan Baumbach and Michael Wood, who wrote essays especially suited to our needs; Richard Corliss and Robin Wood, who helped smooth the way through a tangle of permission-gathering; Ron Gottesman, who contributed ever-flowing bibliographical aid; Mary Ellen Evans, our manuscript editor; Sallie Iannotti, who translated several vital pieces; and Laurence Holder and Robert Klein, who helped us in the job of proofreading. Most of all, we owe our appreciation to John Wright, the ideal editor, at once supportive and cajoling, and to Jean Shapiro, who so greatly eased the burdens of the whole process.

L.B.
M.D.

# Introduction

Most film courses are structured historically or focus on the careers of directors, while most film anthologies are organized around theories and theoreticians or along the lines of the evolution of film criticism. Our first goal was therefore to assemble an anthology whose structure corresponded to the usual route by which a student enters the advanced study of film, as well as an anthology that could be used in conjunction with one of the many histories of film that have appeared in recent years. We have chosen to emphasize the individual director and to concentrate on the shape of individual careers and the special qualities of the most important films.

The first contact one has with any art involves an introduction to its special materials, its angle of vision, and its way of organizing the world. All of us have come into contact with film long before we took any formal course; our memories are crowded with individual films that were important to us long before we knew there were directors. Only later do we come to a sense of the film as a creative art.

Whatever we take to be the best avenue of approach to this special art—and critical beliefs will no doubt change with the same speed that they have in the more established arts—those beliefs will always grow from and be tested against individual films. Furthermore, our aesthetic judgments will be developed in terms of the careers of those artistic creators who are in English called directors. So long as one responds to individual films, and that response modifies one's ideas of what is possible for film to do, one must also, if only for shorthand, attribute the shaping of that film to a primary creative force, the director.

The career of a film director—the foundation and elaboration of his favorite techniques, images, stories, and performers—offers a unique opportunity to study the interaction of personal, social, historical, and formal causes in the creation of art. To understand the role of the director becomes the first step toward an examination of the relative contribution of the scriptwriter, the cameraman, and the producer. Only the actor or actress has the same kind of continuity from film to film as the director. To the director's unseen shaping power, which varies drastically from film to film, from studio to studio, from one personality to another, we might compare the star's more visible continuity, which sustains in one person a variety of separate roles, much as a director's career might run from musicals to mysteries to costume drama. But, while stars often exist independently of the film that gives them definition, and have more meaning as popular icon or social myth, an appreciation of the work of a particular director can be the first step toward a wider understanding of film itself.

Auteur theory, as the argument for a critical emphasis on the director has been called, was first discussed extensively in the French film magazine *Cahiers du Cinéma* in the 1950s by soon-to-be filmmakers like François Truffaut, Jean-Luc Godard, Claude Chabrol, Jacques Rivette, and Eric Rohmer, as well as the magazine's founder, André Bazin. Auteur theory in its first incarnation was not rarefied and abstract, but polemical and immediate; Truffaut called it a *"politique"* or polemic, not a *théorie*. Its principal aim was to rescue the artistry of the director from the heavy hand of studios and producers, and it directed its strongest attack against the "quality" films that sacrificed creative energy for smooth production values. In the first extensive article supporting an auteurist point of view, Truffaut praised as great directors solitaries like Jacques Tati, poets like Jean Cocteau, "non-commercial" humanists like Jean Renoir, and rebels against studio authority who produced their own films, like Howard Hawks.

In fact, as we look back on the history of film, two major traditions have almost from the first days determined the public image of the film director: the flamboyant genius, founded in Georges Méliès' magical short films of the late 1890s but most definitively shaped by D. W. Griffith in America twenty years later; and the retiring professional craftsman, whether they were American action directors like Hawks and John Ford, who shunned personal publicity, or intense creators devoted solely to their art, such as Carl Dreyer and Robert Bresson. Griffith's legacy appeared strongly in directors such as Josef von Sternberg, Erich von Stroheim, Cecil B. DeMille, and Orson Welles—the directorial myth that threatens to become more important than any creation; at the other extreme, especially in Hollywood, the evasive director disappears behind his work until each film has the appearance of a found object, a necessary part of the landscape, created by no one or by everyone.

Both extremes of course involve the interaction of publicity and personal temperament at a particular stage of film history. The categories are further complicated by the overlapping myth of commercial pressure, a tyranny exerted on genius and professional alike—the conformist studios, the doltish producers, the struggle to achieve great projects that should have found funding immediately. Only the hack, goes the story—the director on studio contract—is immune from such pressure, because he has no art in his soul.

Later refinements of the auteur theory, as it has become more theoretical, have tried to rescue the studio director as well, by proclaiming the aesthetic gold to be distilled from working against pressure. Frank Capra, whose films are an excellent argument for what can be accomplished in a studio setting, has pointed out that experimentation was easier when there was guaranteed work and a guaranteed number of films to be turned out than it is today, when every film has to justify itself individually. Highbrow fear of the distorting effect of commercialism can sometimes lead to preciosity, excessive intellectuality, or a desperate quest for singularity, as many recent off-beat film projects testify. Though film is no longer as much a mass medium as it once was, it still is a commercial presentation of one's work. The most obscure independent filmmaker (whether obscure in renown or in message) wants to find or invent an audience for his work. So too then, the pressures of commercialism, of collective creation, must be considered as one of the necessities of craft and even of art—the vital slip between intention and attainment, the need to grapple with and integrate the talents of others, the ability to take advantage of opportunity, deprivation, and excess. Too often in film criticism a particular effect is "explained" by a material problem: subdued lighting, for example, is "caused" by lack of money. But it is precisely such adaptations of circumstance into significance that are the heart of the film-making process. And the principal adapter, the crucial improviser and controller, is the director.

Still another variety of director, often related to the self-publicizing genius, yet frequently akin to the more unassuming directors as well, is the film theoretician. Viewed in retrospect, Truffaut, Godard, and the other *Cahiers* critics were creating in the auteur theory a justification for their own personal style. Such interaction between theory and practice had begun as early as the 1920s, principally among Soviet directors such as Sergei Eisenstein, V. I. Pudovkin, and Dziga Vertov—the most prominent conceptual critics of the early years of film. In the 1930s their central position was taken over by non-directing critics whose background was often in art history; such were Rudolf Arnheim, Bela Bálasz, and Parker Tyler. Such writers and the directors who sympathized with them—often men of the Left—were usually committed to a particular definition of art, often social in nature, in which film was a notable but by no means the only mode of expression. But more and more theoreticians were turning to exclusive theories of film, fed in part by the English documentary school of the 1930s and the tradition of experimental film beginning in the 1920s, which argued the absolute difference between film and the other arts.

With the Italian neo-realist directors who came to prominence after World War II, most notably the director Roberto Rossellini and the scriptwriter Cesare Zavattini, there came a belief in the special ability of film to transmit day-to-day reality. The other arts might be invoked, but more for contrast than for similarity. The personal vision praised by the auteur critics synthesized such divergent tendencies by stressing those exemplary creators who represented the most complete form of each film possibility. Thus, in the movement of the critical dialectic, the recent semiotic and structuralist approaches to film, which emphasize the special ways in which films create patterns of significance, represent a return to the emphasis on form over content.

In contrast to such explicit statements about what film is or is not, what it can or cannot do, should or should not do, most American directors maintained a strong silence. Emerging less from the other arts than from the entrepreneurial and immigrant world of the early twentieth century, such directors, if asked why certain choices were made in their films, tended to answer—if they answered at all—that "it felt right." Richard Koszarski has collected in *Hollywood Directors, 1914–1940* (New York, 1976) an impressive body of statements and articles by some of the most important directors of the period. But most of them either tell the details of production, relate personal autobiography and reminiscence, or make a plea for the importance of film directors instead of delivering theoretical statements or even hearty generalizations about film. These directors were self-conscious without being self-aware. The style of directorial personality they embodied, before the 1960s brought a more often college-trained, more self-consciously "cultural" group into Hollywood, stood in direct contrast to the familiar type of European director—the instinctual American versus the conceptualizing, theorizing European. In part, these were stereotypes that reflected both the different social status of film audiences in Europe and America and the different social origins of film directors.

The *Cahiers* adoption of the auteur theory helped facilitate the development of a history of film through a history of approved "great names." In part, it brought the possibility of Romantic notions of individual creativity into a medium that had often been dismissed for its collectivity and anonymity. Aesthetic respectability demanded identifiable artists, and the promise of self-conscious art offered by the auteur theory accorded nicely with the readiness of an international film public in the 1960s to believe that their pleasures and their tastes might coincide. Truffaut had been as concerned to develop a theory of film creation as a theory of film criticism, and in practice it often had less to do with rethinking or redefining the special aesthetics of film than with the effort to make filmmakers as acceptable as writers, painters, sculptors, playwrights, and composers.

André Bazin complained that the search for the auteur too frequently ignored the crucial question, Auteur of what? The worthy and the unworthy were lumped together as content was ignored in favor of recognizable style. To the extreme auteurists no great director could make a bad film, and every man with a movie camera wanted his name above the title. In this uncritical rampage the interest in the film director had become just another item in the armory of "taste," suitable for pompous statements in movie lobbies and helpful for deciding which movies to watch on television.

Talking theoretically and creating a body of artistically valuable work have not always been complementary talents, although they have not proved to be as contradictory as some would like to think. Some interplay is therefore necessary between the great director and the great work—the coherent personal vision and the ability to embody it in a powerful creation. The twenty-three directors we have chosen for inclusion in this anthology are so diverse in their careers—and all of distinguished stature in their achievement—that no model film director could be drawn from them, just as no model film could be fitted together from their best works. Nor do we assume that the auteurist perspective is necessarily the best way to understand their works. Many of the critics we have included, such as Andrew Sarris on Antonioni, Roy Armes on Robert Bresson, and Robin Wood on Howard Hawks, take up what might be called an auterist point of view. But many articles are also roundly anti-auteurist, such as those of Susan Sontag on Bergman, Parker Tyler on John Ford, and Manny Farber on Howard Hawks.

The essays are not exhaustive so much as indicative of the kind of attention, both scholarly and popular, immediate and meditated, that has been paid to the major directors in the history of film. Our inclination has in general been toward essays that describe, analyze, and evaluate individual films and careers, and we have sought to give some sense of the variety of critical approaches and the different critical moods: the poeticizing of the French, the allusiveness of the English, the pugnacity of the Americans. We have included reviews that respond immediately to the experience of a film, articles that survey an entire career, and essays that consider particular films or directors in the light of a larger aesthetic theory or method. Sometimes a particular film, like Welles's *Citizen Kane* or Fellini's *8¹/₂*, offers a chance to observe these various approaches as they intersect.

We have also chosen essays that avoid isolated analysis and see works in terms of other films and directors. This overlap of reference itself should help convey the texture and solidity of film as art. It seems hardly possible, for example, to speak of Chaplin or Keaton, Ford or Hawks, without at least referring to the other. So, too, we have been moved to include comments by one director on another: Buñuel on Dreyer and Lang, Truffaut on Lang, Ray on Renoir, Rivette on Hawks.

Our frustrations in compiling this volume have been of two kinds:

paucity of certain kinds of essays to represent some directors, and the absence of any essays at all to do justice to others. Our ideal was to have both a concise overview and a specific focus on one or two major films for each director. But for many of the great directors whom we have had to exclude—such as Stroheim, F. W. Murnau, Ernst Lubitsch, Kenji Mizogu- chi, Yasujiro Ozu, Satyajit Ray, and Max Ophuls—the amount of distin- guished criticism so far published has been meager indeed, while for others—notably Renoir, Hitchcock, Welles, and Bergman—the critical literature, of varying quality, is dauntingly extensive. This situation reflects in part the polemical urges of film criticism, which has repeatedly gravitated to certain "problem" directors to be attacked or defended, sometimes for contemporary cultural reasons rather than for the innate qualities of their work. Much of the motivation for praising (or condemning) Soviet directors in the 1930s was ideological as well as aesthetic; Italian neo-realism in the late 1940s represented the resurgent moral conscience of Europe; and the enthusiasm for Alfred Hitchcock in the 1950s and 1960s carried the implicit belief in the complexity of popular culture and the importance of affective style.

The most valuable criticism of the arts may gather its energy from such seeming non-artistic urges, without much care for the future needs of the anthologizer. But film is also beginning to behave like one of the more venerable arts, and previously established reputations will no doubt move up and down with the times. Keaton is now up, while Chaplin is down, and the public accolades he received were those of a survivor rather than an artist, at least until the wave of renewed attention that followed his death in 1977. Welles is down and Hitchcock is up, although beginning to surfeit. Will Griffith's "sentimentality" soon no longer be an obstruction to our ap- preciation of his work, as that same problem has so recently disappeared from our reading of Dickens? In the future will the now-admired severity of Bresson seem an excess and the now-deplored flamboyance of Fellini seem austere?

The future of film criticism promises to be very different from its past, although with obvious continuities. Our selections here have often been made more for coverage than for depth, as much to suggest as to define—a look backward on a very fruitful period of writing about film, yet one with many bare spots as well. Film criticism and theory in recent years have moved away from an emphasis on the single film and the single creator to an interest in larger patterns, whether the sociological patterns of genre and studio production, the anthropological patterns of structural analysis, or the perceptual patterns of signs and significance. Broader views of the many factors contributing to the creation of a film and the audience's response also involve problems beyond that of the director's personal vision.

But our experience of film, like our experience of any art, will always be mediated by our experience of the work and our curiosity about its creator, whether single or collective, conscious, unconscious, or self-conscious. As this anthology looks back on an important period in the history of film criticism and appreciation, we hope that it also looks forward into a future where film critics and filmgoers alike will respond with greater flexibility to the variety of great achievements already accomplished and the new ones to come.

# Michelangelo Antonioni

*MICHELANGELO ANTONIONI was born in 1912 in the northern Italian city of Ferrara. He began to write for the theater and for newspapers as an undergraduate at the University of Bologna, and started working in films as a scenarist and assistant director in the early 1940s. During the heyday of neo-realism in the late 1940s, he worked as a film critic and screenwriter and made a number of distinctive short documentaries. He began to depart from the neo-realist style in his first feature,* Cronaca di un amore *(Story of a Love Affair, 1950). Not only did he use professional actors in middle-class settings, he also portrayed his characters with less social emphasis, in a manner more personal and psychological, stressing what he later described as their "spiritual aridity" and "moral coldness."*

*Instead of pursuing a documentary interest in society's problems, Antonioni's films give an inward and existential turn to neo-realism, emphasizing not the privations of the poor but the boredom and sterility of the lives of the rich. The nuance and feeling of his depiction of women is surpassed only by that of Ingmar Bergman among modern directors; starting with* Le amiche *(The Girl Friends, 1955), and especially in four films with Monica Vitti made between 1960 and 1964, he was able to give full expression to his sense of their restlessness and dissatisfaction. In these same films men are invariably weak and vacillating, but also exploitative: they are professionals compromised in their professions, moral cowards pathetically dependent on strength of the women they use and neglect.*

*In his best films of the mid-1950s,* Le amiche *and* Il grido *(The Outcry, 1957), which still have a residue of structured plot and dramatic dénouement, the unhappiness of the characters culminates in suicide. The weaker of these films,* Il grido, *with its male protagonist, is close to conventional neo-realism, but the malaise of* Le amiche *strongly anticipates the mood and rhythm of* L'Avventura *(1960), first of a trilogy and Antonioni's masterpiece.* Le amiche *was adapted from* Among Women Only, *the final novel by the great Italian writer Cesare Pavese, himself a suicide and an obsessive student of suicide, whose work explores the kinds of ennui and emotional malaise that Antonioni made central to his films; even Pavese's tone, a Hemingway-like style of emotional disjunction and flat understatement, strongly influenced Antonioni.*

L'Avventura, *the first film to bring Antonioni's themes and narrative techniques to full expression, also brought him international acclaim. It was followed in quick succession by the second and third parts of the trilogy,* La notte *(1961) and* L'Eclisse *(Eclipse, 1962), and by his first color film,* Red Desert *(1964). Antonioni repeats himself in these films, and the last two are weakened by a certain narrowness of vision; they pull away from experience toward a metaphysical assertion about modern life, one already overworked by the existentialists in the 1940s and 1950s.*

*L'Avventura, however, remains a fresh and shocking film statement. One of its novelties is an open-ended plot, in which a major character unaccountably disappears halfway through the film, as though to bring film narrative closer to reality than dramatic convention will allow. Although the dialogue is deliberately banal, strong undercurrents of feeling and atmosphere build up between the lines, through long, uneventful sequences and striking shots of the natural setting, which subtly contrast with the boredom, aimlessness, and shallow hedonism of most of the characters. L'Avventura is notable also for its narrative rhythm, which, like Ray's Pather Panchali, distressed early reviewers by its casual pace; to them the film seemed pointlessly drawn out. Antonioni builds meaning through oblique suggestion and a gradual heightening of atmosphere. His narrative mixed significant images and objects with exceptionally long takes, quite unlike the tradition of montage descending from Griffith and Eisenstein.*

*Antonioni's feeling for milieu extends not only to the natural landscape but also to the man-made environment, especially the sleek and angular surfaces of modern architecture, art, and interior decoration. Eclipse and Red Desert focus on these geometrical forms, conveying a sense of joyless luxury and sterile abstraction that comments obliquely on the characters' inner life. After Red Desert, however, Antonioni worked abroad, where his sense of milieu was less secure and more programmatic. Blow-Up (1966) is brilliantly energetic in its portrayal of every facet of swinging London in the mod sixties; yet, in succeeding viewings, its sensibility seems more rigid and abstract, more of an outside imposition on the milieu. It breaks new ground for Antonioni, however, with its photographer-hero, who is not only a committed professional, in a special sixties style, but also something of an artist: a man with a camera, who, through repeated visual framing, fuses art and detection like the filmmaker himself.*

*Antonioni's attempt to "do" the political and cultural upheaval in America in Zabriskie Point (1970) was far less successful, but he recovered considerably in The Passenger (1975). There he was best at what he had always done best—the silences between people, the dissonances and distances in their relationship—and his treatment of locale remained beautifully effective. But he handles the thriller plot and the script's identity theme ineptly and mechanically, and makes only perfunctory use of Jack Nicholson's estimable acting gifts: Nicholson, like most American actors, is not a "cool" performer in the mode of Monica Vitti. In sum, Antonioni's work has yet to recover the élan it had when he burst on the international scene in 1960. Despite the success of* Blow-Up, *the film did not presage the sort of renewal and redirection we find in Bergman's work after* Persona.

*Ian Cameron and Robin Wood are authors of a critical study,* Antonioni *(1968).* *Roy Huss has compiled the collection* Focus on Blow-Up *(1971). Published scripts include* Four Screenplays *(1963),* L'Avventura *(1969),* Blow-Up *(1970), and* The Passenger *(1976).*

# "L'Avventura"

## Ian Cameron

The story of *L'Avventura* is extraordinarily simple—during a yacht cruise, a girl disappears on a lonely island; her girlfriend and her lover search for her and begin an unstable relationship. Structurally the film is remarkable for its almost complete lack of resolution—particularly in the case of Anna, who is, after all, one of the two leading characters in the first part of the film. Little explanation is given for her disappearance, and none at all of what she has done. A few hints are planted that she might have gone away (sounds from unseen motor boats) or committed suicide (a dissolve from Claudia calling her name to waves crashing between two rocks, and a cut from Claudia holding Anna's blouse to a stormy sea), but nothing more. When Antonioni was in London in 1960, he was asked what happened to Anna. He replied, "I don't know. Someone told me that she committed suicide, but I don't believe it." That sums up Antonioni's whole attitude to plots and construction in films. As he is concerned with exploring situations rather than with tailoring neat plots, Anna is of no further interest to him after she has broken with Sandro—whatever the means she has used—and so she does not reappear. In 1960, most other writers or directors would, I think, have brought her back at the end to give a "neat" construction and a "dramatic" resolution.

Antonioni has called the story "a detective story back to front." Like the two protagonists we lose interest in the search for Anna as our attention is diverted to Sandro's affair with Claudia. Our experience of the events parallels the characters' experience in the film. We are never put in the position of knowing more facts than Claudia and Sandro. Because they never find out what happened to Anna, the director does not tell the audience.

We receive information as it is presented to the characters, in the wrong, or rather "illogical," order. Example: we are not actually told until near the end of the film, when she mentions it to Patrizia, that Claudia comes from a poor family. In retrospect one can find sufficient evidence of her social position earlier in the film, but one realizes its significance only after one has been told—Antonioni relies heavily on the audience's power of recollection. The jumbled order in which we receive facts and the elimination of what Antonioni calls ''unnecessary technical baggage... logical narrative transitions'' are motivated by his belief that ''cinema today should be tied to the truth rather than to logic.'' In life one does not get to know people in a logical way, and he does not see any reason for making things easy for his audience by changing this in his films.

Similarly, the length of each scene is dictated by the time it would take to happen. Antonioni avoids the sort of unreal screen time where crafty cutting is used to speed up the ''slow'' bits of the action. If it takes a character ten seconds to walk across a courtyard, he will take ten seconds on the screen in *L'Avventura,* even though there is a cut from one camera position to another in the middle. Others might remove a second or two at the cut to prevent the film from dragging. But to Antonioni these seconds are just as important as the ones on either side. He subjects his audiences to real time as his characters would experience it: he would not sacrifice that to maintain a ''good'' (i.e., brisk or at least steady) pace.

Although our experience may parallel that of the protagonists, we are not invited to identify with them. The method of acting and filming is designed positively to discourage it. In place of subjective camerawork Antonioni favors deep not-quite-subjective shots with the camera close behind one of the characters who is visible in the frame. We observe more or less from his viewpoint without being sold the idea that we are looking through his eyes. In the earlier films, intimate scenes were normally shown in straight two-shot, which automatically places the camera even further outside the action as an observer. The method of *L'Avventura* still does not allow identification, but involves the camera more closely with the action.

As we are shown what the characters see, and learn what they learn without identifying with them, our appreciation of their feelings must be primarily intellectual. We are therefore more conscious than the characters of the meaning of their behavior (as we would not be if we started identifying with them). This places us in a position to correlate our observations of all the characters and reach the general conclusions which Antonioni expects us to draw.

Antonioni's concern with behavior rather than storytelling shows in the treatment of the minor characters. Apart from Claudia, Anna, and Sandro, only Ettore, the architect for whom Sandro works, and Gloria Perkins, the starlet, are essential in advancing the plot—and Ettore need never have appeared on screen (indeed his part was heavily cut in filming).

The others, Corrado and Giulia, Raimondo and Patrizia, the chemist and his wife, Anna's father, the old fisherman and the princeling painter, are given much more weight than their contribution to the "action" demands. They mostly serve an altogether different purpose: to provide an environment within which the situations can develop, and which heightens the effect of the main action by making us aware of its implications or by contrasting with it. . . .

The first part of the film and particularly the island sequences, then, are used to fill in the necessary background to the action (here again there is rigorous exclusion of the unnecessary—for example, we never learn much about Claudia's antecedents). In the foreground, Antonioni relies on our minute observation of what the characters are doing or saying. Every gesture has a precise significance and every technical device Antonioni can muster is used to help us see it. We have to observe for ourselves the build-up of the relationship between Claudia and Sandro; it is not explained to us. Socially, Claudia is an intruder from a lower class. She is given a lift to the yacht in Anna's car, and elsewhere Anna treats her in a slightly patronizing way—having her wait outside while she makes love with Sandro or offering to give her a blouse which she likes. Claudia is embarrassed by Raimondo's grotesquely half-hearted attempts to seduce Patrizia, and offers to leave them alone. She is the only one to derive any spontaneous enjoyment from the cruise; a particular gesture makes this clear—her delight when one of the yacht crew comes ashore with a bowl of fruit.

Before Anna's disappearance, there is virtually no contact between Claudia and Sandro. Claudia is the first to wonder where Anna is. As she says "*Anna dov'è?*" she looks at Sandro. She is the only one of the group who feels much responsibility for Anna's disappearance. Sandro's first reaction is irritation—"Anna is full of ideas." Giulia at first enjoys the search as a new diversion, but soon she is absorbed in her own problems— "Did you see how Corrado treats me? He does everything to humiliate me." Such selfishness shocks Claudia. Already isolated from the rest by her position—her only link with them was Anna—Claudia soon comes into conflict with them when she insists on remaining on the island. Antonioni brings out the conflict by having her walk away from the camera and from the rest of the group before she says "I'm staying." Then he cuts to a full-face shot of her showing determination, with the others behind her while Sandro urges her to leave. As he is staying because he feels that he should, Sandro is disturbed by Claudia's genuine feeling of responsibility. He tells her that she will be in the way—the lamest of excuses for getting rid of her. Corrado is staying to get away from Giulia—

CORRADO: I'm staying too.

GIULIA: Why? What if it rains?
CORRADO: If it rains, I'll buy an umbrella.

Throughout the subsequent scene in the fisherman's hut, the tension between Claudia and the men, particularly Sandro, is conveyed through a favorite Antonioni device—she avoids looking at them. Even the least perceptive critics noticed without help that on the whole, people didn't look at each other in *L'Avventura*. What they failed to see was the expressive use that Antonioni makes of the direction in which his characters are looking. If they look each other straight in the eye, there is an emotional reason for it; if they don't, there's a reason for that too.

The conflict between Sandro and Claudia eventually becomes explicit when the old man asks what has happened:

SANDRO: Nothing . . . nothing.
*Claudia turns, amazed, to look at him.*
CLAUDIA: Why not tell him?
*Then, to the old man—*
CLAUDIA: A girl who was with us has disappeared.
*The old man seems frankly surprised at this.*
OLD MAN: How do you mean disappeared? . . . Drowned?
CLAUDIA: Not drowned . . . Disappeared, we don't know where she is.
SANDRO: And it's my fault. Say that as well. You're thinking it.
CLAUDIA: Rather than minding so much about my thoughts, you would have done better to try to understand what Anna was thinking.

Claudia looks at Sandro only when she is outraged enough to clash with him. When she runs out into the rain, calling for Anna, her action is an expression of her feelings of responsibility for Anna. Sandro's part in the whole scene reflects his inability to appreciate spontaneously the feelings of other people. . . .

Sandro on the make for his fiancée's best friend is a spectacle which would, by Hays Code morality, mark him down for summary retribution—particularly as he's doing this when his fiancée might have committed suicide.

But Antonioni does not condemn Sandro or invite us to do so. He has even gone so far as to say that Anna's disappearance creates a gap that is immediately filled by other factors. . . .

Sandro's yen for Claudia derives partly from his insecurity: he needs comforting as well as the boost to his ego that would come from her seduction. He finds refuge from his troubles in his overriding impulse—desire is only part of it—for Claudia. Antonioni sees this as a general condition: the world is sexually awry because men have found in a compulsive eroticism some diversion from their problems. "Why do you think that eroticism has flooded into literature and entertainment? It is a symptom (perhaps the easiest one to perceive) of the emotional sickness of our time . . . man is uneasy . . . so he reacts, but he reacts badly, and is unhappy."

Antonioni sets out to show us that the urge that has taken hold of Sandro is not something particular and therefore significant only on a personal level. Throughout the film we are presented with sexual behavior that is silly, lewd, or grotesque. On the yacht there is Raimondo greedily caressing various items of a resigned Patrizia's anatomy. There are the young men of Messina, induced to riot as a publicity gimmick for a well-stacked starlet. She appears in a dress that is distended slightly past bursting point so that a torn seam on her thigh proffers the repressed locals a calculatedly arousing peep at her underclothes. Equally grotesque are the comic efforts of the little gardener in the train to get into conversation with a servant girl. And when Claudia finally goes to Sandro there is the chemist at Troina whose surliness is suddenly dropped as she appears: he becomes friendly so that he can have more time to admire her legs, to the fury of his young wife. The peasants in the market place at Noto who gather round to gape at Claudia are possessed by the same sad compulsion as Sandro: sex in Antonioni's eyes has degenerated from a joyful expression of emotion into a gloomy means of escape.

When Sandro grasps Claudia's hand for the first time, her look as she gazes down at him (he is a little downhill from her) is sufficient to indicate her determination to resist and not to be distracted from the search. At their next encounter, her resolution falters. In this scene, as often with Antonioni, the leading part is taken not by either of the characters but by the setting. The embrace is provoked by their sudden proximity to each other, which in turn is a direct result of the confined space in the yacht cabin.

If it is the product of an environmental accident, the responsibility of the characters is diminished. In Antonioni's world, actions are often determined as much by the surroundings as by the people themselves—either in an immediate and physical way by the setting or by conditioning from the environment which tends to limit their choice. At times Claudia and particularly Sandro seem to be activated more by social and environmental forces than by their own decisions. Thus placed outside the area of individual moral judgments, their actions take on a wider significance. Claudia's action in kissing Sandro goes against everything she has previously felt (remember her horror at Giulia's concern with her own situation during the search). Antonioni makes his characters retain a human unpredictability. They do not perform actions worked out to be consistent with a thesis. In fact this sort of unreasoned but not gratuitous action is of the greatest importance to Antonioni. "I wanted to show that sentiments which convention and rhetoric have encouraged us to regard as having a kind of definite weight and absolute duration, can in fact be fragile, vulnerable, subject to change. Man deceives himself when he hasn't courage enough to allow for new dimensions in emotional matters—his loves, regrets, states of mind—just as he allows for them in the field of technology." In this light Claudia's action in the cabin scene is not at all a matter for condemnation. She is beginning to face up to the new emotional situation of her desire for Sandro. But her spontaneous action lasts only until she has had time to realize what she is doing. Then she breaks away from Sandro and goes ashore. . . .

In *L'Avventura* there are two main elements which provide the environment for the action: the sexual looseness of the secondary characters, and the barrenness and/or solitude of the locations—the island, the deserted village, the train without passengers, and the hotel on the morning after the party.

"In this film," said Antonioni, "the landscape is a component of primary importance. I felt the need to break up the action by inserting, in a good many sequences, shots which could seem banal or of a documentary nature (a whirlwind, the sea, dolphins, etc.). But in fact these shots are essential because they help the idea of the film: the observation of a state of affairs. We live today in a period of extreme instability, as much political, moral, and social as physical. I have made a film on the instability of the emotions, on their mysteries." So the instability of the elements provides a visual parallel.

Throughout the film, the locations and even the climatic conditions play a crucial part in its development. Anna's home, which is glimpsed in the opening sequence, and Sandro's rather precious flat help to characterize them. In addition to its function as a symbol of barrenness, the island location allows us to see the characters separated from the *milieu* in which they are accustomed to operate. In this setting we are able to see them deprived of their normal time-occupying routine. The storm which gathers as the search progresses contributes to the increasing seriousness of the situation. In one shot—Claudia on a rocky promontory with waves crashing around it—the location is used to show us the desperateness of Claudia's isolation, another factor which drives her toward Sandro. . . .

The relevance of the background to the foreground becomes crucial in the Noto sequences. We learn from Sandro's monologue on the bell tower that he is an architect who has given up his creative ambitions for the easy money he could make by the purely mechanical job of estimating. The reawakening of these ambitions is connected with his feelings for Claudia. The first time we were aware that architecture had any particular signifi-

with the help of Claudia, Sandro will somehow find the strength to give up his comfortably lucrative job and resume his vocation.

Sandro may not be any less weak than he was previously but at least he has found some feeling of responsibility for the way his actions affect others or, at any rate, Claudia. Sandro's irresponsibility, his lapsed vocation and his unsatisfactory love affair at the beginning of the film are all bound up together and related to the weakness of his social environment. As Chiaretti says in his introduction to the script, "*L'Avventura* could not have taken place except in an anaemic *milieu* like that of the Italian bourgeoisie."

This, I think, is the core of the film: on a general level, the connection between the condition of a society and its morality; individually the integration of sexual behavior with the rest of the personality—for instance, the relevance of Sandro's emotional life to his work. Sartre has expressed a similar view, talking in a newspaper interview about the necessity of building a bridge between Marx and Freud: "Freud was the first to say something that seems to me of capital importance: that everything which makes a man has meaning. . . . What matters is his demonstration that sexual desire is not simply sexual desire, but something that will encroach on a man's whole personality, even affecting the way he plays the piano or the violin."

# From A to Antonioni

## Jonathan Baumbach

The subject of Antonioni's films, of the trilogy [of *L'Avventura, La notte,* and *L'Eclisse*] in particular, is nostalgia—our uses and abuses of the past—while the style is abrasively un-nostalgic. It is one of the reasons—there are others—that his films are so much less ingratiating than the cinema of his contemporaries, of, say, Godard and Fellini. Antonioni's films are beautiful in a style uncompromisingly hard-edge, are unparaphrasable, elude patterns of interpretation, and frustrate conventional expectations of plot and theme. One admires Antonioni's films without feeling fond of them, or one resists them, turns blind to avoid seeing their beauty. The technique is alienating—shocking. The tension the films create is formal and grows out of the kind of risks Antonioni takes at the expense of conventional expectation. *Red Desert,* his first color film, has the most conventional narrative; the risk it takes is (1) in the color, and (2) in dealing with what is essentially trite subject matter—it attempts to intensify the expected (the platitudinous) into mystery. All of the films are mysteries.

All of the films are love stories. In each of the narratives, love or what passes as love turns out to be insufficient or a sham; love is dead, dying, in the death throes of willful pretense. In *L'Avventura,* Anna, the apparent heroine, wanders off from her fiancé—they have stopped off at an island during an excursion—and disappears. We are concerned, by habit of response, from years of going to movies, with the mystery of her disappearance. The film frustrates us: we never find out what's happened to Anna, she never appears again, which is disorienting and shocking. Antonioni's films teach us to see, as if we've never used our eyes before, by not allowing us our old ways of seeing. (I am speaking now primarily of the trilogy and of *Red Desert. Il grido* and *Le amiche* are good films, but they are not, like the later ones, revolutionary.)

Anna's fiancé and a friend, Sandro and Claudia, search for her. In the process they find themselves drawn to each other. The more they resist whatever it is between them—their affection for Anna perhaps—the more intensely involved they become. They become lovers. The romantic aspect of their relationship is intensified because it seems doomed, or at least endangered, by the eventuality of Anna's return. From moment to moment, with a kind of tragic forboding, we expect Anna to reappear. Her shadow, the potentiality of her presence, haunts the lovers, seems to. The ending is a revelation. Claudia, searching for Sandro who is not in his room at the hotel, obsessively afraid that he is with Anna, discovers him making love to another girl altogether—a shock for her and, given the conventional expectations of the film, for us. As Claudia is stripped of her illusions, so in effect are we. What we must admit to ourselves is that what has passed for love between Sandro and Claudia, what they've experienced as love, has been a fraud all along, a mutual self-delusion made possible by the occasion of Anna's disappearance. Sandro is a hollow man, apparently incapable of deep feeling. Claudia has been foolishly romantic, in love with a man she has willfully failed to see. At the end, in the early morning street, Claudia cries for the death of her idea of Sandro—the death of illusion, the death of love. Sandro cries. For a moment they experience themselves and perhaps each other without illusion. Without his asking Claudia forgives him. It is a terrible and touching moment. The experience of the film is cathartic, an exorcism of romantic illusions, of old ways of seeing. As metaphor Anna's disappearance is irrevocable. The form of the film is its message.

More, of course, can be said about *L'Avventura;* but I'd like to concentrate my discussion on *Red Desert* and talk about the trilogy only insofar as it looks forward to the later film. The films of the trilogy are increasingly bleak. In each, under the pressure of crisis—a dim awareness of some kind of internal dying—Antonioni's characters resort to patterns of nostalgia to revive their lives. *La notte* is about a husband and wife, once in love, now numb to each other (and to themselves), sleepwalkers, living the death of boredom. In terms of conventional expectation, predicated on the kind of nostalgic wistfulness we bring to bear habitually as an audience, the film moves—all the romantic portents are there—toward the resurrection of their dead love. Giovanni and Lidia (Mastroianni and Moreau) move through the movie like sleepwalkers, awaiting hopefully, without the energy of hope, awakening. At the start they go to an elegantly sterile modern hospital to visit a close friend, Tomasso, who admires Giovanni and is in love with Lidia, a good-natured and gentle man who is dying of cancer. Romantic anticipation: as a result of Tomasso's death, as in effect a legacy of his devotion to Lidia, Lidia might again experience herself as someone capable of being loved; and Giovanni, when he learns of Tomasso's love, might rediscover his wife, fall in love with her again, be renewed as a man and as a writer, etc. Just below the surface of our awareness these are the expectations the film sets up. Giovanni and Lidia seek for themselves what we as an audience want for them, what we want, by habit of empathy, for ourselves. All of the forms of nostalgia are brought to bear. Lidia takes a long walk in which she encounters, as in a dream, a place where she and Giovanni used to go as lovers. Moved by nostalgia, she phones Giovanni and asks him to meet her there. Nothing comes of it. We experience a succession of factitious rebirths. Illusions fall away like dead skin. Nothing comes of nothing. The dead feelings remain. At an all-night party at the estate of a wealthy industrialist who wants to hire Giovanni (as a kind of intellectual-in-residence, a surrogate penis—a further irony, since Giovanni feels impotent as a writer), the guests in a manic mood jump into the swimming pool with their clothes on and come out, one suspects, unregenerated. Giovanni seeks renewal through a love affair with the industrialist's daughter, Valentina (Monica Vitti), a sensitive and creative girl alienated from her parents' world. Nothing comes of it.

The ending is typically and masterfully audacious. The sun is coming up. Giovanni and Lidia leave the party as disconsolate and bored apparently as they were at the beginning, yet there is the spark of something between them. What will happen has been prophesied to some extent in an earlier dialogue between Lidia and Valentina.

LIDIA: . . . Tonight I only feel like dying . . . It would at least put an end to all this agony. At least something new would begin.
VALENTINA: Or maybe nothing.
LIDIA: Yes, maybe nothing.

The setting is ambiguously romantic: the golf course on the industrialist's estate, a piece of artificial nature, though it is as beautiful in its way as real country. Lidia and Giovanni sit on the edge of a sand trap and talk openly—she tells him that Tomasso has died. Giovanni laments that he has been selfish and blind, insists to Lidia that he loves her. Lidia reads her husband a letter—a love letter—that Giovanni had written to her some years back. He listens, uncomprehending—one wonders how Antonioni dared use a device so apparently sentimental—unable to recognize the subject of the letter or its author. It is for both not a renewal, as we had hoped, but an inescapable recognition that love is dead between them. All illusions of hope have been destroyed. In an agony of lust, a kind of death throe, they make love as the dawn rises—the scene visually reminiscent of an earlier scene in which a mad girl at the hospital attacks Giovanni. A new days begins. The ending is painful, terrible, but also exhilarating in that, like the characters, we are able to see things finally as they are, unmuddied by romantic illusion. To see is a beginning, is the end of the night.

What other illusions are left us? *Eclipse* deals with unromantic love, love without illusions, between two modern, well-adjusted people, and is the bleakest of the three films. I have avoided so far talking about images which, ideally, is the way films should be talked about. In each of Antonioni's films there is a central image—what I like to think of as the essential setting of the action—which adumbrates the experience of the characters. I mention it now because it seems to me the most striking thing about *Eclipse*, that objects, institutions, places, have more weight and life in this film than the characters.

The island, where Anna disappears, where an extended and frustrating search for her takes place, is the central image-as-metaphor of *L'Avventura*. The island is magnificent, desolate, mysterious, a lonely and barren place surrounded by the sea—a natural universe divorced from the affairs of men. The deserted country town where Sandro and Claudia make love for the first time is an extension (metaphorically) of the same image. It is similarly a place of loss. In *La notte* the modern hospital, where Tomasso lies dying under anesthetic, is the central image—the film opens with an abrasive shot of its contour. The frigid elegance of that palace of death and convalescence, a metaphor for the world of the film—no births take place in that hospital, only madness and convalescence and death—haunts our awareness throughout. Giovanni's and Lidia's modern apartment is an extension for us (as image) of the hospital. As Tomasso is incurable, so in a different way are Giovanni and Lidia. The sterility of the architecture suggests the sterility of the characters: Giovanni and Lidia are childless, Giovanni feels he can no longer write, their feelings are moribund, etc.

In *Eclipse* the Stock Exchange, where the passions of birth and death are enacted through the making and destroying of fortunes, is the central image. It is an emblematic place, a microcosm of the world. The hero (or anti-hero) Piero, a young man of exceptional vitality and emptiness, works on the Exchange as a broker. Antonioni films the frenetic activity of the market—another kind of death throe—with extraordinary vividness. The most remarkable scene in the movie, much more interesting and passionate than the love scenes between Vittoria and Piero, is the performance of a ritual minute of silence during a busy time on the Exchange in commemoration of some official's death. The frenzy of activity stops, its energy in tense suspension, as if everyone had suddenly died. And then, with increased momentum—the tension released—the activity starts again like an explosion. Ends and beginnings become one, as in the momentary darkness of an eclipse.

*Eclipse* goes against the grain of our expectations even more radically than *L'Avventura* and *La notte*. The love story of Piero and Vittoria, which is the central narrative concern of the film, is dropped in apparent midstream—the relationship neither alive nor dead, unresolved. We move away from the lovers, who have in effect disappeared (like Anna), into a series of images which exist not as correlatives of the characters' feelings but as objects, as realities, independent of the characters. Antonioni's comment is implicit: there is no more to be said about Vittoria and Piero—their souls are dying, they have died. The world goes on without them, though their absence from the last shots has a foreboding quality as if the end of something—of life as we know it perhaps—is approaching. The images form a kind of metaphorical history (and pre-history) of the world. The last image is a close-up of a modern street lamp, a man-made sun, its light blanking the screen. An ambiguous prophecy. The end and the beginning, the light and the darkness, as one.

*Red Desert* opens with a burst of yellow flame. A stunningly beautiful color film—the most beautiful of color films—about an excruciatingly neurotic woman's alienation from an ultramodern (apparently dehumanized) world. I say apparently dehumanized. When I first saw *Red Desert* I felt, beautiful as it was, it was a failure—the beauty of the color at odds with the nightmare of its theme. Bringing to bear my own prejudices against machines and factories, I had misconceived the experience of the film. What makes Antonioni a major artist is that he creates apparently insurmountable obstacles for himself and almost, mostly, surmounts them. The result is a disorienting and transcendently original work of art. The power of an Antonioni film is derived from the formal risks it takes, from the tension of going against the expected current of its own conventions. It strikes me that the greatest art is the transcendent (and flawed) solution of an apparently impossible problem.

*Red Desert* is a profoundly disturbing film. Giuliana's neurosis seemed to me an outgrowth of her struggle to survive, to become wholly alive and human in a world which derives its rhythm, its money and goods, from electronics. This world is not so much the cause of Giuliana's neurosis, as I was quick to believe, as the catalyst of its intensification. As Antonioni tells us in an interview in the *Cahiers,* his heroine is "tied to life rhythms that are now out of date." Our lives have been in the process of extraordinary change in the past twenty years, and we're feeling it—the fallout of what has been an explosive mutation in the rhythms of our lives—most intensely at the present. Change, even when less revolutionary, is frightening, and we struggle (out of old habits of survival) to retain the old ways. Antonioni is a modernist. *L'Avventura, La notte,* and *Eclipse* are exorcistic films about dead feelings, about boredom and apathy, about the painful inadequacy of our old ways of solving problems. *Red Desert* is the next logical step—a film about the beauties (and horrors, of course, too) of the new world. The story of Giuliana's struggle to renew herself as a woman, the agony of her dislocation, is set against a background of factories, of machinery that spits flame and belches smoke like some mythological monster.

*Red Desert* is conceived as if no one had ever made a color film before.

If *Eclipse* is a prophecy of the end of the world, *Red Desert* is a vision of the new world to come, of the world that is apparently in the process of becoming. It is a film about—much of it projected through the disoriented psyche of Giuliana—the loss of old values and the inability to adapt to new ones. Giuliana's husband and child are at home in their world, without passion or desperation—in the modern sense, cool. That they love her is not enough. Giuliana (Monica Vitti) needs to be needed, to be loved romantically—it seems to her the only salvation.

The story Giuliana makes up for her son when the boy is in the hospital, his legs apparently paralyzed, is one of the texts of the film. The story is about a young girl, almost but not quite a woman, living an Edenic existence on a deserted island, content and lonely. One day a sailboat approaches her island and (with undefined expectancy) she swims out to it. To her surprise she discovers that no one is aboard. Before she can inspect it further the boat leaves, disappearing over the horizon. She is disappointed, though only for a moment. Then she hears someone singing, as if to her. Again there is no one there. The sound is coming from a cove of rocks—she swims over to it—the rocks like flesh. "Who was singing?" the boy asks. "Everyone," Giuliana tells him. "Everyone was singing."

It is of course the story of her life she is telling the boy, a romanticized version of it. The island is a metaphor for her isolation. The boat is an opportunity, though as it turns out an illusory one, to escape her loneliness. In that the boat is empty it suggests another kind of escape, suicide perhaps—we know that she has made an attempt in the past. There are several boats in the film—a central and recurring image—suggesting travel, change, the possibilities of a new life—in one case, where the yellow flag is raised, plague and death. It is also the symbol of Corrado (Richard Harris), who, out of romanticized restlessness, is perpetually traveling from one place to another. The singing is coming from those who love her, the fleshly forms not quite human, a kind of divine womb. She tells Corrado in the next scene, before they go to bed, that what she wants is all the people who ever loved her around her like a wall.

It turns out that the boy was pretending to be paralyzed, acting out, insofar as he understands it, his mother's sense of him. It is also conceivable that in the desperation of her need to be needed Giuliana prefers him helpless. And perhaps, if we view the episode of the boy as a paradigm, the deadness of feeling that Giuliana perceives around her is an indication of her failure to see the real life that's there. After the boy begins to walk again Giuliana runs to Corrado, who seems, in her romantic sense of him, the only one left who can help her, a last hope. Corrado's room is dark brown paneled wood, the color of earth, when Giuliana comes in. After they make love—the sex scene as nightmarish as any ever filmed—the room appears pink (flesh-colored), almost like a baby's room. Where she had seen Corrado as a strong, masculine figure, he seems to her like a child after her disillusion with him—the color, when Antonioni wants it that way, a correlative of his heroine's sense of things.

The ending of the film is inconclusive. Giuliana is with her son again as at the beginning (Antonioni likes to end as he began) in a subdued mood—calm or inert? She has learned, like the bird she tells her son about, to avoid the poisonous yellow smoke, a step toward learning how to live in the world, a beginning. And one suspects, at the same time, something of an end. Giuliana has learned how to survive, but at what expense, and to what purpose?

*Red Desert* is the first color film, the most beautiful color film. To make such a film is in itself an affirmation.

An Antonioni movie presents us with a new way of seeing—that is, forces us to see against our preconception of the way things are. No other artist deals with the hang-ups and delusions and possibilities of love, which is to say life, in our time as profoundly and truthfully as Antonioni. So even if we have to give up our old myths about movies—the nostalgia that things were simpler and therefore better in the old days—it may even be worth it. Maybe not. Nostalgia dies hard: old dreams have their pleasure. In any event, resist it or not, we shall never again be as we were, which is what Antonioni has been telling us. In black and white. In films of luminous beauty. In color.

With a residual pang of nostalgia, I suppose I prefer the new days to the old. As a movie lover only, however. The world Antonioni celebrates is damned hard to live in.

# No Antoniennui

## Andrew Sarris

Michelangelo Antonioni's *Blow-Up* is the movie of the year, and I use the term "movie" advisedly for an evening's entertainment that left me feeling no pain (or Antoniennui) whatsoever. It is possible that this year's contributions from Ford, Dreyer, Hitchcock, Chabrol, and Godard may cut deeper and live longer than Antonioni's mod masterpiece, but no other movie this year has done as much to preserve my faith in the future of the medium. If you have not yet seen *Blow-Up,* see it immediately before you hear or read anything more about it. I speak from personal experience when I say it is better to let the movie catch you completely unawares. One of its greatest virtues is surprise, and the last thing you want is to know the plot and theme in advance. Unfortunately, most of the reviewers have given the show completely away. Judith Crist coyly conceals the plot gambit in *Gambit,* but she spills the beans on *Blow-Up* with no qualms whatsoever. Why? I suppose she considers *Blow-Up* too esoteric for audiences to enjoy in the course of mindless moviegoing. It's a pity since, purely on a plot level, *Blow-Up* provides more thrills, chills, and fancy frissons than any other movie this year.

The excitement begins with the opening credits which are stenciled across a field of green grass opening into a pop blue rhythm and blues background of dancing models perceived only partially through the lettering which, among other things, implicates Antonioni in the script and heralds Vanessa Redgrave, David Hemmings, Sarah Miles, and a supporting case of unknowns. The billing is misleading. Miss Redgrave and Miss Miles make only guest appearances in what amounts to a vehicle for David Hemmings and Antonioni's camera. *Blow-Up* is never dramatically effective in terms of any meaningful confrontations of character. The dialogue is self-consciously spare and elliptical in a sub-Pinteresque style. Fortunately, the

24-hour duration of the plot makes it possible for Antonioni to disguise most of the film as a day in the life of a mod photographer in swinging London town. What conflict there is in *Blow-Up* is captured in the opening clash between vernal greens on one plane and venal blues, reds, yellows, pinks, and purples on another. The natural world is arrayed against the artificial scene; conscience is deployed against convention.

The film itself begins with more obvious contrasts. A lorry loaded with screaming revelers made up in garishly painted mime faces. Cut to derelicts trudging silently out of flophouse with bundles and belongings. One would suspect Antonioni of facile Marxist montage in his cross-cutting between mimes and derelicts, between noisy merriment and quiet morning afterment, but one would be wrong. The mimes are merely an Italianate mannerism in London, and the derelicts are simply the grubbier side of a photographer's visual concerns. Nevertheless, the cross-cutting functions by itself without any explicatory dialogue or commentary. Even the protagonist is identified for us only by degrees. Antonioni can afford a leisurely exposition for two reasons. First, we are going to be looking at Hemmings all through the movie, and a slightly mysterious materialization will not hurt him at the outset. Secondly, the emphasis throughout is not so much on the protagonist himself as on what he and his camera see and on how well he blends in with the background. Gradually we are filled in not so much with a plot as with a routine—a day in the life of a candid cameraman.

*Blow-Up* abounds with what Truffaut calls "privileged moments," intervals of beautiful imagery while nothing seems to be happening to develop the drama or advance the narrative. Very early in the film, the camera confronts the photographer's long black convertible head-on at a crossroads. Suddenly the entire screen is blotted out by a blue bus streaking across from right to left, followed by a yellow truck. That sudden splash of blue and yellow defines Antonioni's mood and milieu better than any set of speeches ever could. Wherever Antonioni's camera goes, doors, fences, poles, even entire buildings seem to have been freshly painted for the sake of chromatic contrast or consistency. Part of Antonioni's ambivalence toward his subject in *Blow-Up* is reflected in the conflicting temptations of documentary and decoration. After painting the trees in *The Red Desert* a petrified gray, Antonioni feels no compunctions about painting an outdoor phone booth in *Blow-Up* a firehouse red. If reality is not expressive enough, a paint brush will take up the slack. This theory of controlled color is carried about as far as it can go in *Blow-Up* before its artistic limitations become too apparent. Antonioni is heading in a dangerous direction, but the Pirandellian resolution of the plot saves him on this occasion from the stylistically bloated decadence of *The Red Desert*.

The ultimate beauty of *Blow-Up* is derived from the artistic self-revelation of the director. *Blow-Up* is to Antonioni what *Lola Montes* was to the late Max Ophuls, what *Ugetsu* was to the late Kenji Mizoguchi, what *Contempt* was to Godard, what *French Can-Can* was to Renoir, what *Limelight* was to Chaplin, what *Rear Window* was to Hitchcock, what $8\,^1/_2$ was to Fellini—a statement of the artist's life. As David Hemmings moves gracefully through off-beat sites in London, his body writhing to meet the challenge of every new subject, we feel that Antonioni himself is intoxicated by the sensuous surfaces of a world he wishes to satirize. Curiously, he is more satisfying when he succumbs to the sensuousness than when he stands outside it. The unsuccessful sequences—the rock 'n' roll session, the marijuana party, the alienation conversations between Hemmings and Vanessa Redgrave in one scene and Sarah Miles in another—all suffer from the remoteness of cold chronicles recorded by an outsider. Antonioni is more successful when he forgets his ennui long enough to photograph a magnificent mod fashion spectacle which transcends the grotesquely artificial creatures that lend themselves to the illusion. Even more spectacular is the teenybopper sandwich orgy which digresses from the main plot. An entire generation of mini-teasers and inhibited exhibitionists are divested of their defenses in a frenzied choreography of bold beauty and heart-rending contemporaneity. The stripping away of pink and blue leotards may explain why the Metro lion has decided to skulk away from the opening credits like a timid pussy cat scared of the Production Code.

The fact that Antonioni can be entertaining even when he is not enlightening makes the eruption of his plot all the more stunning. It starts simmering in the midst of apparent aimlessness. The photographer-protagonist wanders out of an antique shop, drifts by chance into a park where he ignores a grotesquely sexless park attendant jabbing trash with her pike, passes by a tennis court where two children are playing a clumsy brand of tennis, photographs pigeons afoot and in flight, then stalks a pair of lovers up a hill. At a distance, it looks like a tall girl pulling at an older man in what later will be recalled in retrospect as a spectacle of carnal Calvary. Here Hemmings becomes a weak-kneed voyeur as he scurries behind fences and trees with his telescopic lens. This is raw, spontaneous Life in an ominously leafy setting. Vanessa Redgrave, she of the incredibly distracting long legs and elongated spinal column extended vertically through an ugly blue-plaid mini-suit making her look at a distance like a seven-foot girl guide, in short, Vanessa Redgrave via Antonioni rather than Karel (*Morgan!*) Reisz, runs up to Hemmings to plead for the pictures, but everything in the movie has been so fragmented up to this time that we accept her trivial invasion of privacy argument at face value. Hemmings refuses to return the negatives, and later tricks her into accepting bogus negatives while he develops and "blows up" the real ones. What seemed like a tryst in a park is magnified into a murder. Death which has hovered over Antonioni's films from the very beginning of his career makes its grand entrance in a photographer's studio through the eyes of a camera which sees truth whereas the eyes of the photographer see only reality. This then is the paradox of Antonioni's vision of art: The further we draw away from reality, the closer we get to the truth. Vanessa Redgrave, an irritating, affected personality in her "live" scenes, comes to life with a vengeance in the "blow-up" of her photos.

From the moment of his artistic triumph, the protagonist becomes morally impotent. He has discovered truth, but is unable to pass judgment or secure justice. He returns to the scene of the crime that night and finds the corpse of the murdered man. He visits a neighboring artist and mistress only to find them furiously flagrante delicto. He returns to his studio and discovers the theft of his blow-ups. He is physically frightened when he hears footsteps and begins to cower in a corner of his decor. It is only the artist's mistress (Sarah Miles) treading as beautifully as ever on her cat feet and in her transparent dress. He tells her about the murder, but she is too preoccupied with her own problems to give him much help.

The rest of the film threatens to degenerate into one of Antonioni's shaggy dog Odysseys to futility when the photographer returns to the scene of the blown-up crime. The wind is blowing. The body is gone. The leaves flutter with chilling indifference. Then suddenly the mime revelers from the opening sequence reappear in their loaded lorry and disembark at the tennis court. Two mimes play an imaginary game with somewhat clumsy gestures while the others watch with silent, swivel-headed concentration. Antonioni's camera begins following the action of the imaginary ball back and forth across the net until it is "hit" over the fence near where the photographer is standing. He walks back to the spot where the "ball" has landed, and throws it back. He then begins swiveling his head back and forth, and even hears the ball bouncing. He smiles at his own susceptibility, but suddenly an expression of pain flashes across his face. The camera cuts to an overhead shot of the photographer, a self-judgment of both contempt and compassion. Antonioni, the ex-tennis player who once sold his trophies to live, has come out in the open with a definitive description of his divided sensibility, half Mod, half Marxist. Unlike Fellini, however, Antonioni has converted his confession into a genuine movie which objectifies his obsessions without whining or self-pity. As befits the classical tradition of moviemaking, *Blow-Up* can be enjoyed by moviegoers who never heard of Antonioni.

# "Blow-Up": From the Word to the Image

## John Freccero

The quality of Antonioni's films was a subject of heated debate long before the appearance of *Blow-Up,* the film which both intensified the debate and shifted it to a more popular forum. All the critics agreed that the film marked a radical departure from Antonioni's previous idiom, both visually and thematically. For one thing, Monica Vitti was missing. For another, swinging London seemed to lend more visual movement to this film than to any of his others. Finally, perhaps most startling, this film seemed to have a plot, or almost, and the first half of it prompted some to speak of it as though it were alienated Hitchcock. Put most simply, while nothing ever seemed to happen in *L'Avventura, La notte, L'Eclisse,* or *Il deserto rosso,* here at least something had indeed happened, although it was difficult to say with any assurance what it was. For the film theorist, the radical change in subject matter marked a thematic change of great importance. Because the leading character is a photographer who attempts to interpret his own work, it appeared that the director had left off his exploration of neurosis and alienation in order to make his own entry, however oblique, into the debate about the nature of his own medium.

*Blow-Up* is in fact a series of photographs about a series of photographs and so constitutes what might be called a metalinguistic metaphor, a highly self-conscious and self-reflexive meditation on its own process. Because it is a discourse about discourse, it is subject to all the charges of ambiguity that are usually levelled at such self-contained messages, even when they occur in everyday speech. At the same time, however, that ambiguity places it within a literary tradition, founded perhaps by Petrarch, in which literature's subject is itself and the portrait of the artist is his act.

There can be no doubt that Antonioni's mod photographer, Thomas, is in fact an artist—primarily a visual artist. Early in the film, a scene at the

Excerpted from the article of the same title in *Yale/Theater* 3 (Fall 1970). Reprinted by permission of the author.

house of his painter friend establishes a symbolic equation between their respective techniques. Bill is contemplating one of the paintings that differs markedly from all his other work in that it contains a figurative element, or what seems to be one:

> While I'm doing them, they don't say anything to me—just one big mess. After a while I find something to hang onto. Like that leg there. Then it comes through by itself. It's like finding the key in a mystery story.

For those who fail to recall those lines when the photographer examines his own work, Antonioni has Patricia, the painter's companion, restate the equation when she sees the photographic blow-up: "It looks just like one of Bill's paintings." When he is first introduced, Bill would seem to be the photographer's antitype, a loser trying desperately to keep his painting, which Thomas jocularly threatens to steal, and his woman, who wants desperately to be stolen. By the film's ending, it becomes evident that the parallel is exact, for Thomas too has lost both his work of art, which is stolen, and the woman he coveted who is somehow responsible for its loss.

As a visual artist, however, Thomas differs markedly from the painter and even from his fellow photographers in that he aspires to totality. He seeks to transcend time and to achieve the self-containment and the autonomy of a world created by his camera rather than illustrated by it. This, I take it, is the sense of a detail which most critics of the film have overlooked but which seems to me essential. One of the first things we learn about Thomas and the reason why he finds himself in the park, at the scene of the crime where he makes his discovery, is that he is putting together, structuring, a *book* of photographs. Thomas differs from his photographer colleagues, whose craft is documentary, in that his gaze transforms the representation of reality into its image, an interpretive act resembling that of the painter. He differs from the painter, however, in that he introduces the temporality of syntax into his art, juxtaposing images into a structure along a syntagmatic axis, which is the essence of language or, for that matter, of montage. Had he succeeded in putting together his book of images and achieving a real simulacrum of time, he would have come very close to resembling the film maker who has been accused of excessively literary preoccupation.

However veiled the allegory and however arch the transposition, the confessional suggestiveness of the story is the unmistakable consequence of the metalinguistic metaphor. As long as one remains within a narrative structure, then the story that tells its own story is perfectly self-contained. When stories are great art, however, and not myth, they come into existence through a consciousness that exists as story-teller: to tell the story of how the story came into existence is necessarily to portray the storyteller, no matter how metaphorically, just as the storyteller's autobiography, as storyteller, is the story he tells. So with Antonioni's meditation on his own art: Thomas is perhaps the portrait of the director as a young director and his failure is Antonioni's subsequent triumph.

The structure is familiar in literature, from Dante to Proust, and was recently introduced into the film by Federico Fellini, the title of whose cinematic autobiography, $8\frac{1}{2}$, points unmistakably to the fact that it is a retrospective attempt to understand his own work. The story is of a director who, while fearing that he is washed up after what seems to him to have been a fragmentary career, nevertheless is filming a film that is in fact the film we view. Most interesting from our standpoint, however, is the conclusion of $8\frac{1}{2}$, where the director is called upon to sum it all up, both as character and as director, and to give significance to all that went before. Finding himself unable finally to do this, he crawls under the banquet table where he is being honored and shoots himself, whereupon he is immediately resurrected in time to conduct his band of mimes and *pagliacci* in the parade that is Fellini's trademark, the *Trionfo,* so to speak, of illusion over reality.

Fellini the *magus* hides his human despair, just as do his characters, behind the mask of the lie; in this case, the phony suicide, which both gives a conclusiveness to his life story and grants him, author and *persona,* the leisure and the Archimedean point outside of time from which to tell it. It is this compromise with authenticity, the willing embrace of the lie inherent in the medium itself, that Antonioni has always refused. Fellini perhaps set up the problematic, the cinematic code, and Antonioni perhaps assumes it, for film makers, no less than writers, must work within a tradition; nevertheless, the bittersweet of Fellini's lie is rejected and the code is assumed only to be destroyed. In his preface to a collection of six screen plays, Antonioni had written: "The greatest danger for the film maker consists in the extraordinary means the medium provides in order to lie." *Blow-Up* is the dramatic refutation of Fellini's make-believe and its bleakness consists in the fact that the only alternatives it offers to the lie are the search or silence.

To make the point about the metaphoric relationship between the director and his protagonist a little more convincingly, I should like for a moment to go outside the "text." In an interview on Italian television, Antonioni was asked why, when he knew it would cost him ecclesiastical approval in Italy, he included in the film the photographer's orgy with a pair of teeny-boppers. He replied that while he was not at all averse to incurring the displeasure of the censors, he really had something else in mind. In a world as notoriously alienated and neurotic as his own, he felt the need to provide some relief with an episode of good clean fun. The television interviewer was an ideal straight-man, since he had not seen the film and therefore could not catch the irony. Even the most casual viewing of the film would have revealed that it is precisely for the same reason, to find some erotic relief from a gloomy world, that Thomas goes into the park in the first place. His book of photographs includes a series of portraits of derelict old men in a public dormitory, most of them more or less close to death. In order to relieve the grimness of his photographs, which he senses with some detachment, he goes into an Arcadian scene, a park with an enclosed garden, where he photographs a pair of lovers. It is only later that he discovers, with the retrospective gaze of the artist interpreting his own work, that he has in fact portrayed not the embrace of lovers, but the death of an older man. In short, the fact of death which he had been seeking to evade. Had he seen Poussin or read Panofsky, he would have known that this disillusionment awaits all attempts at pastoral evasion: "Et in Arcadia ego." Death resides even in Arcady.

What makes the photographer symbolically capable of making that discovery is of course a discovery about himself. The interpretive act of the artist does not depend so much on the physical evidence as on the construct which one is ready to bring to it and before Thomas can understand, his own authenticity must be questioned. This occurs in his orgy with the aspiring models, who stand chronologically in relationship to him as does the girl, Vanessa Redgrave, to the older man for whose death she is somehow responsible. By a cinematic tour de force, Antonioni presents us with the visual equivalent of one of the oldest *double-entendre* of erotic poetry: to die, the orgasm as the moment of death. Lying prostrate on the floor of his studio after his debauch, the photographer looks up and discovers, or thinks that he discovers, the erstwhile older lover lying in the photograph in precisely the same position. He does not as yet suspect what the audience has already grasped: just as Thomas is the metaphoric embodiment of Antonioni's art, so the older man is the metaphoric embodiment of Thomas's art. The dead man is the dead-end conclusion of Thomas's book and thus, symbolically, an all too definitive portrait of the artist which cannot be revived by cinematographic sleight-of-hand. . . .

Vanessa Redgrave is the first woman whom the photographer seems genuinely to desire and whom he treats, almost, as another human being. Until her appearance in the film, Thomas's sexuality seems as dehumanized as his art, the sexuality of the voyeur (a metaphor for novelistic detachment at least as old as Chaucer), who so transcends his own mortality that he can achieve satisfaction merely by observing, like some

God, from a privileged perspective. So he makes love to the model Verushka with his camera or, alternately, frolics with the little girls wrapped in the purple paper he uses for his back-drop. So too, he looks at the pleading eyes of Patricia while she somewhat distractedly allows Bill to make love to her. This last scene is virtually a literary topos: in Chaucer's *Troilus and Criseyde,* when the loving couple are finally in bed together, Pandarus keeps them company while he retires to the fireside to read his old romance. Here, while Patricia and Bill are making love, Thomas turns to look once more at Bill's nearly figurative painting to see what it reveals. The technology may differ somewhat, but the mechanism is the same.

With Vanessa Redgrave, on the other hand, he finds a kindred spirit whose identity and past are as mysterious as his own. Antonioni underscores their complementarity even by their dress, for in the scene that provided the publicity stills, the whiteness of her bare flesh and her blue skirt are the colors, symmetrically reversed, in which he is dressed—blue shirt and white slacks—while both she and Thomas are wearing identical belts. As they stand in the doorway of the bedroom, the scene seems to be set for what might have been the only completely human encounter of the film, but they are interrupted in a moment that, in another cinematic atmosphere, might have provided comic relief—the delivery of the propeller which Thomas had purchased at the antique store. The almost funny moment marks the intrusion of Thomas's vocation and the evasion of reality that it represents. By the parallelism that the film has established between the artist's sexuality and his art, the failure of human love, or at least human contact is exactly equivalent to the failure of his work to achieve humanity.

The meeting with Vanessa Redgrave proves to be an amorous disillusion, so that once she disappears from the studio, she no longer has any part to play in the film. After Thomas's discovery that the story was not quite as he had envisioned it, the audience discovers that the plot of the film is not the suspense story *it* had been led to expect. The object of Thomas's search is not the killers or the perpetrators of the plot, but the body itself, the authenticity of which he had caught a glimpse in the park. The search is a familiar one in the artistic work of which Thomas is the metaphor, the search of the heroine in *L'Avventura,* the spiritual odyssey of *Il grido,* but in this film, the truth of Antonioni's revelation is briefly revealed in the moment when the photographer touches the body, as if to feel the point of tangency between reality and his art. Antonioni's sociological indictment finds expression again in the photographer's frantic search for some solidarity in order to sustain him in his investigation. As the revelation had been achieved by a kind of bracketing, so he turns to society in the same order, first to the young, who are drugged joylessly by their music, and then to the older, drugged by their cocktails and marijuana. In each of these episodes, the photographer is momentarily taken in by the collective, conditioned desires of the society around him and each time, rediscovering himself as alone in his knowledge, he moves away from his surroundings in despair and disgust. The guitar, smashed by the musician, becomes valorized by the frenzy of his young fans and the photographer joins in the struggle to possess it. Once free of the mob, he throws the worthless bits away. Like the airplane propeller, the intrinsic worth of the object is nil, but it is given value by the collective desire imposed on the crowd by image peddlers. This analysis of London night life, which dismayed English audiences, is the image of a world possessed by a kind of madness that seems to blind it to the fundamental fact of death, in art as in life. The demons of this evasion inhabit the entire world of mass media, they are its spirits, and so they begin and end Antonioni's film.

The film opens at dawn with a group of students, extravagantly dressed, presumably for Rag Week, their faces painted white, who descend from their jeep and scatter to inhabit the whole of the city. Like the *Untorelli* of Manzoni's *Promessi sposi,* their mission seems to be to spread the plague whose name is perhaps best established by the strange protest sign GO AWAY, that one of them gives to the photographer as he speeds away from the desolation of the public dormitory. The same students close the film in the famous and problematic ending, again at dawn, where some watch and others play a phantom tennis match without a ball. Thomas watches the students, at first with amusement, as they follow with dead seriousness and the same joyless and empty look that he had previously seen at the rock session, the flight of an imaginary ball. When the phantom ball seems to have gone outside the court, presumably at his feet, they plead with him with their eyes to return it. He hesitates, finally stoops as if to pick something up, weighs it in his hand and finally throws it back, thus collaborating in their phantom game. As he walks slowly away, the sound of a tennis ball against a racket can clearly be heard, and the camera moves slowly away from the minute figure of the photographer until he quite literally disappears before our eyes.

The demonic character of the students can scarcely be doubted. Their fantastic dress, their appearance at dawn, their white faces, their station in life and weird behavior mark them clearly as what anthropologists would call ''marginal'' figures, the demons of tradition, who mediate between the world of the spirit and the world of matter. Their appearance in the stark world of Antonioni's film is inexplicable until one realizes that they are not meant to appear in *his* kind of film at all. They are Fellini characters, the clowns and fantastically attired circus people, whose joy is gone and whose magical illusion is unmasked as the lie that Antonioni takes it to be.

Thomas's collaboration is the sign that he has joined the ranks of the talented perpetrators of illusion, and that he disappears both as person and artist, leaving Antonioni to his lonely search for the truth.

... Antonioni's film makes the point that the recognition in art of human mortality can be evaded but never superseded. His critique of the medium and of its capacity to lie, at the very inception of a new technological era, is reminiscent of the critique of the new printing medium launched by Cervantes at the beginning of this (now dying) linear age. In the second part of *Don Quixote,* Altisidora has a dream which symbolizes the disenchanted view of the new cultural revolution. She describes her dream:

> The truth is, I arrived at the gate of Hell, where something like a dozen devils were playing tennis, all in their breeches and doublets, with their collars trimmed with Flanders lace and with ruffles of the same which served them as cuffs with four inches of arm bare to make their hands look longer. They were holding rackets of fire and what most astonished me was that instead of balls they used what looked like books, stuffed with wind and fluff . . .

Technology has been refined to the point that the message has lost even the physical reality still represented by the book, the word has turned to image, while sender and receiver stare blankly as though their transaction at some point still touched the solidarity of the ground. Their game, in which everyone loses, is one that Antonioni refuses steadfastly to play. In his own terms, he can hope for no greater victory.

# Ingmar Bergman

INGMAR BERGMAN *was born in 1918 in the medieval university town of Uppsala, Sweden, the son of a Lutheran minister. While studying at the University of Stockholm, he staged amateur plays; later he directed productions at several local theaters and acted both in contemporary works and in classics by Shakespeare and Strindberg. During World War II, Swedish neutrality ushered in a period of anxious intensity among Swedish intellectuals. The young Bergman played an important role in this unsettled time, writing several novels, plays, and a script that was made into a very successful film by Alf Sjöberg* (Torment, *1944).*

*The next year Bergman wrote the script for and directed his first film,* Crisis, *which explored the problems of adolescents in an oppressive adult society, and he pursued this theme in several succeeding films. Meanwhile, as director of the municipal theaters of Hälsingborg and Göteborg, he staged such works as Camus'* Caligula, *Tennessee Williams's* A Streetcar Named Desire, *and several of his own plays. With the film* Prison *(1948), made under the immediate influence of Sartre's* No Exit *and the plays of Luigi Pirandello, Bergman first showed his characteristic double interest in both the social and the personal reality of his story and the aesthetic medium in which it is expressed. This led to films about artists as well as films that contain plays or other films (as in* Prison*), or fragments of both. To this almost classic theme of artistic self-consciousness Bergman added his special sensitivity to the potentially inhuman detachment of the artist who uses human suffering as the materials of his art.*

*Bergman's next few films dealt extensively with what might be defined as his solution to artistic inhumanity—the nature and experiences of women. In his career as both stage and film director, Bergman, like John Ford and Jean Renoir, usually depends on a stock company of actors and actresses who give his films an ongoing, family-like feeling, despite their separate stories. Both men and women contribute to this ambiance, among them Harriet Andersson, Bibi Andersson, Gunnar Björnstrand, Eva Dahlbeck, Ingrid Thulin, Liv Ullmann, and Max von Sydow. But the women are more often the central characters; their lives and feelings are the mystery the film attempts to probe, while the men tend to be observers or self-involved performers, sometimes empty and unrealized as characters, as in* The Touch *(with Elliot Gould, 1971).*

*The great work of this period (before Bergman achieved international recognition with* The Seventh Seal, *1957) is* Sawdust and Tinsel *(also known as* The Naked Night, *1953), in which Bergman adopts the expressionist motif of the world as circus, and the artist as performer. In the United States,* The Seventh Seal *appeared at a time when the general public was beginning to look at film directors as legitimate artists, and Bergman swiftly became the definition of the great director. This acclaim was in great part a tribute to the obvious seriousness of his films, although* Smiles of a Summer Night *(1955), a virtuoso combination of Mozart and Shakespeare, had already announced the light touch with sex comedy that lay beneath the heavier films and gave them substance.* Wild Strawberries *(1957),* The Magician *(1958), and* The Virgin Spring *(1960) further solidified the public impression of Bergman as the gloomy realist of the North, and the trilogy of* Through a Glass Darkly *(1961),* Winter Light *(1963), and* The Silence *(1963) continued to explore the existentialist and religious themes that had marked his earlier career.*

The Silence—*with its plot centering on two women and a young boy in a mysterious city, its collage of often surrealist images and incidents— served moreover as prelude to a Bergman masterwork,* Persona *(1966), a new fusion of his double interest in psychology and aesthetics, in which self-awareness and artistic awareness test the limits of identity itself.* Hour of the Wolf *(1968),* Shame *(1968),* Passion of Anna *(1969), and* Cries and Whispers *(1973) further explored the connected problems of the artist in society and the individual in relationship, although increasingly without the visual and structural fragmentation of some of the earlier films.* Scenes from a Marriage *(1974) added a new dimension through Bergman's adaptation of a documentary television method to the ongoing minutiae and crises of a relationship;* The Magic Flute *(1975), the record of a Bergman-directed performance of the Mozart opera, comments brilliantly on both media at once;* Face to Face *(1976) seems much too detached and clinical in its exploration of the breakdown of a woman psychiatrist.*

*Bergman's voluntary exile from Sweden as a result of income tax problems leaves in some doubt his future as a filmmaker, seemingly so deeply indebted to his native setting, although he continues to work with many of the same actors and actresses, as well as his long-time cameraman, Sven Nykvist. His first foreign production (shot principally in Bavaria) was* The Serpent's Egg, *a film about an American trapeze artist in Nazi Germany.*

*The following Bergman scripts are available in English in book form:* Smiles of a Summer Night, The Seventh Seal, Wild Strawberries, The Magician *(1960);* Through a Glass Darkly, Winter Light, The Silence *(1967);* Persona, Shame *(1972). Critical works dealing with Bergman include those by Birgitta Steene (1968), Robin Wood (1969), Vernon Young (1971), and John Simon (1972). A collection of essays on Bergman has been edited by Stuart M. Kaminsky (1975). Narrative versions of* Cries and Whispers, The Touch, The Hour of the Wolf, *and* The Passion of Anna *appear in Bergman:* Four Stories *(1976).*

# Ingmar Bergman in the 1950s

## James F. Scott

During the last two decades filmmaker Ingmar Bergman has been busily making his name one of the best known in Europe and America. No doubt there is a trace of faddishness in his success, since certain idiosyncrasies of his vision have endeared him to those who luxuriate in their own neuroses. Whatever his limitations, however, his accomplishments are genuine. Most obviously, he has brought to the cinema a sense of form which is exceptionally acute. It is of more particular significance, though, that Bergman's very specialized talent—his capacity to bring fantasy, dream, and myth once again within the area of major cinematic interest— constitutes a valuable counterpoise to the dominantly realistic, socially oriented film of Western Europe.

The long-standing sociological bias of European cinema makes Bergman's subjectivist style crucially important to the further development of film technique. Premature in their technical aspirations, the early expressionist ventures of France and Germany, epitomized in *The Cabinet of Dr. Caligari,* gave way in the middle twenties to the meticulous realism which has since dominated the work of Europe's best-known directors, Cocteau and Dreyer perhaps excepted. While the stark detail of Pabst's *The Joyless Street* caught the imagination of depression-ridden Europe, several distinguished Soviet directors were showing how well the film would adapt to convey the content of dialectical materialism. During the thirties, moreover, the influence of Eisenstein and Pudovkin loomed steadily larger, not only because of their penetrating writings upon cinematography but equally as a result of the growing collectivist tendencies of Western culture. In the era of fascist challenge and socialist response, the director followed the lead of the philosopher in sensitizing his audience to the realities of mass movement, as maturing techniques of editing made montages and dissolves

This essay is a slightly revised version of the author's "The Achievement of Ingmar Bergman" in *The Journal of Aesthetics and Art Criticism* 24, no. 2 (December 1965). Reprinted by permission of the author.

the ideal means to catch the fury of a street riot, the deployment of battalions, the squalor of a famine-haunted village.

These emphases, of course, were accelerated by World War II and its aftermath, as the haggard honesty of Italy's *neo-realismo* reminds us. In their work of the postwar decade, Rossellini and de Sica, as well as Antonioni and Visconti, took their inspiration from the public world of burned cities and displaced masses, the shattered landscape where ignorant armies clashed by night. And though these artists have given most polished utterance to the upheaval of European reconstruction, their material differs only in degree from the works of lesser Continental directors who have addressed themselves to essentially the same phenomena. Nearly all have concentrated upon the response of the individual to some realistically rendered environment, the shaping of spirit accomplished within some institutional frame. Only quite recently has the drama of psychic reality begun to regain prestige.

Both tradition and disposition, however, have inclined the Swedish director to resist the idiom of documentary realism. Temperamentally introspective and the product of a prosperous, relatively static, politically neutralist culture, he has found little to excite him in *cinema engagé*. His inspiration derives instead from earlier achievements of his native Svensk Filmindustri, from the gothic world of Sjöström's *The Phantom Coach* and the psychoanalytical orientation of Sjöberg's cinematic *Miss Julie*. Bergman's theater is the inner world of the psyche, where need engenders desire or fear enervates will, where memory beclouds sight and reason struggles against madness. As would be expected, his apprenticeship to filmmaking has assumed the form of a continuing experiment with means to bring the revelations of the analyst's couch and the magician's stage convincingly before the camera.

It was during the 1950s that Bergman established himself as a major director and first found a mode acceptable to his subjectivist vision. This involved launching his career as a scriptwriter, recruiting his basic production team, and learning how to extract consistently expert performances from a choice ensemble of actors. Bergman wrote his first original screenplay in 1948, for *Port of Call*,[1] though it was not until 1952 that he abandoned his off-and-on collaboration with Herbert Grevenius. *Port of Call* also occasioned Bergman's first contact with two key members of his technical staff, photographic director Gunnar Fischer and film editor Oscar Rosander. Fischer shot almost every Bergman picture of the next decade,

1. Throughout the essay I will employ the American titles of Bergman's films, on the assumption that these are the most familiar. My citations of dialogue are from *Four Screenplays of Ingmar Bergman* (New York, 1960) and *The Virgin Spring* (New York, 1960), both translated by David Kushner and Lars Malmström.

while Rosander handled much of the cutting. The look of Bergman's films in the 1950s owes a great deal to the artistic preferences of these men, especially the photography of Fischer. The cadre of actors varies more widely, but typically includes Eva Dahlbeck, Harriet Andersson, and Gunnar Björnstrand (each making his first appearance with Bergman in 1952) as well as Max von Sydow, Bibi Andersson, and Ingrid Thulin, all of whom joined the troupe in the middle fifties. Although Bergman never reduces these actors to stereotypical presences (von Sydow, for instance, plays everything from a questing knight to a gas station attendant), he tends to cast them in somewhat predictable roles, as if to make them enflesh certain aspects of his private world. The mobile features and deep-set eyes of von Sydow ideally qualify him as the soul-searching Bergmanian hero, while the angular face and stiff carriage of Björnstrand turn him towards colder, more skeptical, more cynical roles. Harriet and Bibi Andersson tend to personify the distinction between sensuous and spiritual youthfulness, while Dahlbeck and Thulin provide Bergman with complex versions of feminine maturity. In the company of these technicians and performers, Bergman perfected the style which sets off his films of the fifties from those he would make in the following decade.

In technical terms, this style is disarmingly simple. Range and angle are supremely important, because Bergman uses gradual movements of the camera to exclude unwanted background material from his shots, thus allowing the changing composition of successive frames to define the shifting emotional responses of his characters. Montage also figures in the projection of the inner life, but not so prominently. Single inserts are much more common than elaborate optical mosaics. For his most sophisticated effects he prefers the dissolve, especially a very slow dissolve which retains the displaced image long enough to make its force operative in the new frame.

In transacting this interior revelation, Bergman has always depended heavily upon a small store of cinematically compelling images, remarkable both for the frequency with which they occur and for the variety amid sameness achieved in their use. The natural world in its seasonal changes; the stage or arena; the mirror or glass: these are the basic visuals of Bergman's films. Laden with traditional associations yet always reshaped by immediate dramatic contexts, these deceptively simple details define the various expressions of selfhood in its continuous encounter with nature and society. These images are truly symbols, for repetition invests them with more than literal expressiveness.

Few shots figure so prominently in Bergman's films as those of water, which through its power to reflect both form and light typically serves to control a larger body of outdoor imagery. The water image is central because it mediates between the phenomenal and the psychic world, suggesting not only the endless flux of experience but also the tendency of such experience to take color from the mental complexion of those undergoing it. Nearly always ambivalent, the image is both a natural absolute and a psychic variable. Hence in the last scene of *Secrets of Women* (1952), the open and expansive surface of the lake spread before the eloping lovers naturalistically represents the fluid possibilities of life available upon their escape from a restrictive environment. At the same time, however, the delicate moonlight silhouetting these exuberant innocents symbolizes their own naive infatuation, as is borne out in a bystander's comment upon the charming impermanence of romantic affection. A similar mergence of sea and skyscape operates to define the relationship between the young lovers of *Illicit Interlude* (1950). As their liaison develops, Bergman's camera hovers over scenes in which moving waters flash brilliantly with the glint of noonday sunshine, blinding and evanescent as the passion of the lovers it iconically resembles. And while the rhythm builds towards the accident which robs the heroine of her lover, the motif of quenched fire is extended in the blazing skyrockets whose downward trajectory is towards extinction in the sea. In cooperation with various seasonal backdrops, the water image continues to function in Bergman's later films. Witness the frozen landscape of *Winter Light* (1963).

Another metaphor to which Bergman shows great partiality is that of the stage. Even when his protagonists are not professional actors, they continue to be players of roles. This point is frequently emphasized in photography which concentrates attention on some kind of enclosed area. Here the frail self seeks to assume some acceptable public posture, largely in the interest of its own psychic survival. The importance of role-playing is underscored in a sequence from *The Naked Night* (1953), which uses the circus arena as the stage for a fight between the clumsily candid circus-master and the wily thespian who has stolen his mistress. With his calculatedly graceful movements, the actor outmaneuvers and humiliates his adversary, not because he is the better man but because he is the better performer. Though the role he plays is knavish, it equips him to live successfully, if not honorably, in a world where personal identity is constantly threatened by the intrusive demands of others. One's public stance need not be perverse, though, as is shown in *The Magician* (1958) when Vogler triumphs over Vergérus. In the famous attic scene from this film, victory again lies with the actor, the showman who has planned his performance supremely well. But Vogler's sleight-of-hand is fundamentally a moral act, in that it explodes the cocksure positivism of his antagonist. When the man he supposed a corpse rises to life before his blurred vision, Vergérus finds his scientific posture crushed as completely as the broken spectacles Bergman's tracking camera picks up. At the moment of crisis, Vogler has played the role of conjurer more effectively than Vergérus the role of rational skeptic, and in this case the vanquished player is the less humanly admirable of the two. If these sequences make the significance of the stage metaphor seem ambiguous, the matter is appreciably clearer in *Winter Light*. From this film we understand that man constructs his various masks not so much to defeat others as to save himself. Indeed, he must strut and fret his hour upon the stage, whether or not his performance is even worthy of an audience. Thus it is with Parson Tomas, whose desperate effort to find spiritual insulation brings him finally to conduct a solemn vesper service within the sanctuary of his empty church. Like so many Bergmanian characters, doubting Tomas ritualizes his behavior as stage play and thereby reveals the strategy of personal defense embodied in its formalized pattern.

To the images of nature and art should be added the mirror or glass, for Bergman employs this visual detail to further the analysis of private emotions—sometimes to suggest the achievement of self-knowledge, more often to explore, ironically, its absence. The thematic metaphor of *Through a Glass Darkly* (literally translated, "as if in a mirror") is photographically central to all Bergman's work. Its operation is well illustrated in *Dreams* (1955), a film in which reflecting images objectify contrasting motifs of innocence and experience. For the giddy young model, Doris, whose journey to the city betokens complete commitment to her career, a short pause before the window of a jewelry shop perfectly reveals her sensuous ardor, a precondition of the gusto with which she faces the opening up of life. As she savors the array of precious stones, facial gestures caught in the glass fuse with the elegant display itself, creating an image which identifies her enthrallment with the plush expectations of a successful career. But the aging fashion designer who makes the trip with Doris entertains no such romantic illusion about herself. The elder woman's resignation to life's hopelessness is framed in a mirror image which superimposes her expressionless features upon a rain-spattered window, the droplets both visually and psychologically analogous to human tears. The image also projects her future, which, like the accidental splash of water, may promise much random motion but little significant change of pattern. The kind of camera work we see here is transparently simple, yet the more effective for its unpretentiousness. While dramatic realism places a mirror in the roadway, Bergman's mirrors stand before the human soul.

Of course, isolated details never make a great film, and Bergman's stature depends ultimately upon his ability to incorporate expressive images into larger dramatic patterns. When he is most successful, this rhythm is neither theatrical nor painterly, but arises from a grasp of the unique ontology of cinema: action is progressively interpreted and resolved in symbols of psychic life which develop naturally from the photographic surface. First attaining the proportions of greatness in *The Seventh Seal* (1956) and culminating in the masterful effects of *The Virgin Spring* (1959), Bergman's experiments in symbolic drama exemplify both the trials and the triumph of a director determined to harmonize graphic values and dramatic movement, visually projecting the spiritual energy of his protagonists while faithfully rendering the successive occasions which call it into being.

After achieving unqualified success with the stylized realism of *The Naked Night,* Bergman turned in the middle fifties to the more explicitly symbolic mode of *The Seventh Seal.* Developed from his own play, *Wood on Painting,* the film would seem foredoomed to be excessively theatrical. And it does, in fact, lean too heavily upon the static iconography of expressionist drama. In spite of Bergman's effort to create fluidity, the symbolic chess match remains slightly intrusive, occasionally interruptive of the action. The remarkable feature of *The Seventh Seal,* however, is the degree to which the director overcomes the implicit tendencies of his material. Throughout the film the physical texture of life surrounds us with oppressive density, almost demanding the soritical gamesmanship by which Antonius Block in his match with Death strives to master the chaos of experience. Nor do the several appearances of Death stand in frozen isolation from the human drama. Solid and imposingly alive (he even wields a saw), this allegoric figure is drawn into the natural landscape, while the apocalyptic tempest gathers in storm clouds whose substance seems perfectly tangible. Furthermore, Bergman minimizes the intrusiveness of directly expressionistic scenes through a careful modulation of tonal rhythm which prepares us for these exceptional chords. This results in interplay between the concrete visuals of camera reality and the symbolically staged mental processes of the doubt-haunted hero.

With praiseworthy neatness, Bergman immediately relates the expressionistic dimension of the film to dramatic action and scenic detail. The opening frames vividly portray the disenchanted Crusader who can no longer maintain his spiritual poise in a world limitlessly drab and relentlessly fluid, like the wash of the surf beside which he tries to pray. When saluted by Death, however, Block refuses to surrender until his mind has wrested some meaning from the purposeless flux of experience. There follows the beginning of the chess match, whose symbolic import is defined through superimposition. As the two players advance their king's pawns, the dissolve impresses the geometrically exact patterns of the chessboard upon the plastic, asymmetrical surface of the sea, thereby suggesting Block's eleventh-hour search for a logically structured philosophy to refurbish his shattered faith. The match with Death, we thus realize, will progress in a manner directly analogous to Block's heroic struggle against the spirit of negation that threatens his moral universe.

Having established his basic symbol, Bergman wisely refrains from further appeals to the chessboard until the intensity of the action has been permitted to mount, climax, and fade in a delicate decrescendo at the center of the film. We are reminded of the game when Block informs his confessor that he will defeat Death with "a combination of the knight and the bishop"—a plan illustrative of the protagonist's continuing loyalty to the feudal mystique. But while this allusion impresses its import upon us, we are carried forward to a crisis of action so powerful as to efface all sense of contrivance or artifice. Sound, timing, and pictorial composition cooperate to make Block's meeting with the self-torturing flagellants one of the most memorable in Bergman's films, the more so because it effectively alters the direction of the hero's quest for certitude. As this sequence begins, the gay song of dancers is drowned in the fearful chant of plague-stricken marchers, a counterpointing which leads naturally to the expressions of terror frozen into the faces of those awestruck by the grotesque procession. The chilling sound of whips and scourges is hushed during the oration of the sadistic monk who leads the penitents, but the horrific snap of the lash is again heard as the congregation resumes its pilgrimage amid swirls of incense which suffocates as many as it sanctifies. Before the marchers vanish, a long-range shot from high angle appropriately signifies a new perspective, the one Block has attained now by detaching himself intellectually from the company of the orthodox. Explosive action thus begets new perception, which leads, after a parallel climax in the subplot, to a gradual calming of the dramatic rhythm. Frenzied shrieks give way to pastoral hospitality as Block enters into a new covenant of friendship with the traveling performers. And at this moment the return to the static world of the chessboard comes as a dying fall which reverberates in solemn stillness.

Unfortunately, this rising and falling rhythm is not so well suited to the latter part of the film, since completion of the chess match necessitates interruption of the mounting pressure of catastrophe. Confronted with this problem, Bergman handles his material knowingly, but not quite successfully. To emphasize continuity, he omits the dissolve we expect as Block, after witnessing the deaths of Tyan and Raval, returns to the chessboard for the misplay which symbolically represents the spirit of hubris dramatized in scenes immediately preceding. There is also an attempt to make the symbolic interlude itself suspenseful, for Block's toppling of the chessmen is a stratagem to cover the escape of Jof and Mia. Skyscape montage interpolated as this pair leaves Block's company restores much of the energy lost at the chessboard, even if the effect of the compensatory insert smacks of deliberate inflation. In spite of these efforts, the closing sequences lack smoothness, a difficulty not quite offset by the subtly articulate facial gestures of von Sydow, which give Block's last prayers such authenticity. There remains a dramatic difficulty. At the last crucial moment the expressionistic stage is disturbingly separate from the urgently real world of storm and plague. Faults notwithstanding, Bergman exhibits bold imagination in the cinematic strategy of this film. But uncertainties of style suggest a lingering indebtedness to the theater, an as yet incomplete emancipation from the stage, which opens the way to further experiments in the presentation of spiritual phenomena.

As if unsatisfied with the somewhat contrived character of the symbolic chess match, Bergman sets out in his next film, *Wild Strawberries* (1957), to approximate more closely the exact texture of psychic life through the mode of dream. For this some will never forgive him, and there is no foolproof rejoinder to those who will not tolerate dreams anywhere except in their own beds. But to disparage the somnambulistic action is to miss the distinguishing virtue of the film—its commendably graphic presentation of the cerebral life of Isak Borg. Through a baroque profusion of images, we become active participants in his belated struggle to regain the imaginative vitality he has deliberately shunted aside, and the interest is more than clinical because the desperate compulsion driving the protagonist toward the polyvalent world of childhood is really the measure of his moral integrity. The only fault of the film, ironically (for I have never seen anyone mention it), is the treatment of the daylight world, the public landscape of contemporary Sweden. Here events succeed each other haphazardly, arbitrarily, forming a succession far more loosely arranged than the insubstantial pageant of Borg's mind. Bergman seems willing to tolerate all kinds of improbable incidents provided they help fill the hero's memory with resources for associative fantasy. If *The Seventh Seal* depends too heavily upon theatrical regimentation, *Wild Strawberries* too heavily favors the painterly, achieving its pictorial values at the expense of a strong narrative line. The flaws are not fatal, however, and thus the film reveals a further dimension of Bergman's cinematic creativity.

The most admirable feature of *Wild Strawberries* is Bergman's portrayal of tension and resolution in Borg's interior life. This is first done through skillful counterpointing of sound and scene, later through pictorial composition alone. The overexposed shots which give the opening sequence its hideous whiteness are reminiscent of German cinema, but the use of the sound track achieves an original effect. The poised remarks of the note-taking Professor Borg stand in sharp relief to the terrified groping of his somnambulist double. And though his conscious mind asserts "all I ask

ademic ceremony, full of hothouse Latin and stodgy posturing, is a
umph of realistic comedy which sweeps away the creaking machinery so
ominent earlier. The impressive recovery in the final scenes markedly
creases the persuasiveness of *Wild Strawberries*, though we are still left
ith the sense that this work, for all its undoubted brilliance, takes less
an sufficient account of the intractable data of experience.

After finishing *The Brink of Life* (1957) and *The Magician*, the latter a
olished work in its own right, Bergman completed in 1959 what seems to
ne a genuine masterpiece, *The Virgin Spring*. Delegating the screenplay to
Ulla Isaksson, whose script is adequate if uninspired, the director here
surpasses all his earlier efforts to make the photographic image a vehicle of
thematic import. Expertly foreshadowed, the miracle scene which con-
summates the symbolic pattern is not so theatrical as the chess match in *The
Seventh Seal*. The shots are as fully expressive as those of *Wild Strawberries*, but leave no lingering flavor of preciousness. This latter accomplishment owes much to the promotion of Sven Nykvist to director of photography. "Bergman and I promised each other when we started *The Virgin
Spring*," says the veteran cameraman, "there would be no beauty effects."[2] But Bergman himself is responsible for the timing and rhythm
which gracefully effects the difficult double climax essential to this drama
of crime, vengeance, and regeneration.

*The Virgin Spring* begins with three contrasting scenes, introducing
along with the central characters the basic images to be elaborated in later
sequences. Fire and darkness are immediately associated with the primitive, pagan world of impulsive hatred and suspicion, as Ingeri blows on
glowing embers which flare to illumine her sullen features while she invokes
Odin for redress of supposed injuries. But that her attraction to fire is not
peculiar to servants of the deposed Viking divinity is shown in the next
series of shots which reveals Töre and Märeta at their morning worship.
Töre's wife seems almost to relish the hot wax which sears her arm as it
drips from the sacramental candles burning in honor of Christ. In Märeta,
hatred has been sublimated to quasi-religious masochism, though it retains
its destructiveness. In contrast to the motif of fire, with its suggestions of
malice and pain, the next shift of scene gives us the outdoor world and the
first glimpse of flowing water, faintly anticipatory of the miraculous spring
whose upsurge is the final image of regeneration. A hint of this rebirth
theme is also injected into the dialogue when the servant Frida, amid
sentimental caresses, renews the life of a young chick she "nearly stepped
on . . . out there in the darkness."

2. Sven Nykvist, "Photographing the Films of Ingmar Bergman," *American Cinematographer* (October 1962), p. 628.

of life is to be left alone," Borg's sleep is deeply troub
isolation. Emptiness and silence haunt the dreamer as h
past closed shutters and hasped windows to salute a fa
body crumbles at a single touch. Dream logic continually
of estrangement into new shapes until it receives its ultin
Borg's witnessing his own funeral. Unconsciously, the
already pronounced himself dead, for his embittered emot
clearly a living death. But the doctor, unreceptive to this
dom, awakens determined to purge his demon with the bi
drive.

In further dream sequences, Bergman artfully arrang
tion of his frames to establish the increasing completenes
sorption into the repressed environment of his psychic past.
the dream figure of Sara, his voice dies before reaching her
he still cannot speak the language of impulse. At this momer
between the two characters is underscored in photography
Borg in a separate picture plane, cut off from Sara first by
waving grass, later by portentous shadows. In the scene
however, after Borg has recognized the consequences of h
egoism, a calculatedly slow dissolve telescopes pictorial surfac
late the hero into a barren autumnal landscape. The anguish
self-knowledge entails is also incorporated into the fleeting i
shows his head trapped in the pincerlike clasp of a gnarled tree.
humiliation redeems the doctor as a human agent, qualifying
dream of paradise regained which concludes the film. Her hand
his, Sara now leads Borg to the translucent waters of regener
which the camera hovers until the final cut. Bergman has deftl
the curvature of Borg's perception as he reclaims his power of ir
sympathy.

These carefully wrought images of psychic reality are accom
considerable sacrifice to the dramatized life beyond the mind
Coincidence and manipulation abound. Young Sara, the *anima*
Borg's dreams, seems magically to conjure her double who inha
present and accidentally encounters old Isak during the journey
Her eccentric companions, holding their protracted debate on the c
reason and emotion, are authorial puppets too obviously representi
forces in the hero's personality. Not even the public highway is unc
with Bergman's symbols. A careening automobile overturns as it
conveniently obliging the doctor to take its passengers into his chai
thus adding two essential characters to the gallery of his dream
Contrivance lessens as the film progresses, and the final sequences
perfectly credible. Borg's son Evald is a fully enfleshed character, a

With the introduction of Karin, Bergman initiates movement towards the film's first climax, the brutal rape and murder of this unwary traveler. Foreshadowings of impending disaster are carried in the outdoor imagery. Alternating high and low camera angles play off a backdrop of blooming flowers (with which Karin identifies herself by picking a bouquet) against a darkening sky of billowing thunderheads. Clear running water is muddied by the hooves of horses shortly before Karin, having forded the stream, silhouettes her brightly clad form against the impenetrable darkness of the forest. From the outset of the girl's journey, however, Bergman's long shots have continued to suggest ultimate reconciliation, as the soft focus in which distant landscapes are caught causes patches of light and dark, sun and shadow, to blend with one another.

The tempo of the film quickens from the moment Ingeri abandons Karin, Bergman accentuating the increased number of cuts with rapid changes of place, while the herdsmen entrap the heroine. Individual scenes are full of rapid movement, especially those in which the abrupt gestures and furtive glances of the herdsmen join with other visual details to underline the animalism of Karin's attackers. When the victim and her captors are finally seated together in the clearing, the eruptive restlessness of the herdsmen gains emphasis from Karin's ceremonious behavior, first as the goat seizes the girl's flowers, later in the young boy's ravenous interruption of the food blessing, finally in the obscene gurgling of the mute goatherd. Not only the ferocity of the ensuing attack but the texture of this whole sequence thus helps to characterize the violators of Karin's innocence. The last supporting detail is the rageful leaping of the mute, who crushes the church candles the girl has carried with her. With this ensemble of notes, Bergman reduces the viciousness of the murderers to purely animal proportions, which illumines by contrast both Ingeri's malevolent desertion of Karin and Töre's ritualized revenge of her murder.

After this climactic moment, Bergman gives priority to the fire image in order to develop more fully the character of Töre, who becomes the center of dramatic action upon Karin's death. Fire has already been identified with explosive passion, but the early scenes have also hinted at its association with rite. Its ambivalent application to both instinctive and formal behavior now serves to define the hero's ambiguous response to the herdsmen, who prevail upon him for shelter. Ignorant of their crime, he welcomes them into his home, and the fire built to warm them seems to exemplify his sense of patriarchal duty. "Keep the fire burning tonight," he instructs his guest. "It will be bitterly cold." Later, however, the rights of the patriarch will be used to justify taking the lives of the herdsmen. He will murder them, but the violence will be transacted within the context of ritual. Ironically, of course, the ritual proves inadequate to civilize the act, and the fire image underscores his slipping from civility to barbarism. The fire which warms the strangers becomes the fire which steams Töre's body as he cleanses himself to combat, and finally the fire which absorbs almost the entire screen when he strangles one of his antagonists in wild fury.

The ritualistic aspect of Töre's attack upon the herdsmen is also established by the pace of the film in the moments preceding the killing. Extremely well planned, the sequence reveals how completely Bergman realizes the power of photography to fulfill dramatic objectives. At this point dialogue counts for little, tempo and composition for nearly everything. The movement is slow so that suspense may build, so that we may recover from the emotional stress begotten of earlier violence, but also that we may appreciate Töre's resolve to contain his lust for vengeance in some psychically acceptable frame. As the attack of the herdsmen has been completely visceral, so Töre's revenge is fully rationalized. The effect is to point up his sense of responsibility, later important to the understanding of his guilt.

The effectiveness of the fight scene depends heavily upon Bergman's handling of intercut shots. At the outset these are used sparingly, to create a mood of solemn stillness. Even the preparatory activity (felling the birch tree, taking the sauna bath) has proceeded slowly, but movement virtually ceases for several moments after Töre has entered the herdsmen's quarters. The time element seems infinitely long due to the sparseness of intercuts. The isolated sound of the knife striking wood reverberates ominously in the silence. Nothing allows our attention to stray from the protagonist himself, as he assumes his magisterial stance at the seat of honor, then gradually begins to betray nervousness when the helpless captives fail to awaken, and at last searches uneasily for some means to rouse them. On the verge of the encounter, Töre has lost the godlike composure which the camera has studied from multiple angles. As the battle is joined, all differences vanish between hunter and hunted. Frequent intercutting now heightens the fury of combat as Töre's stylized gestures become spasms of animal desperation in his struggle with the second herdsman. Both are seared by the same fire before the avenger overpowers his victim. Ritual has been utterly dissolved in rage.

The film now takes its final dramatic turn, reintroducing the theme of recovery and renewal, while images of running water assume their earlier centrality. As the family sets out to find Karin's body, the original journey is retraced in detail, providing the time interval necessary for Töre to rethink his actions. The penetration of the forest also permits Bergman to repeat earlier landscape shots, but with important omissions. The troll who seemed to preside over the stream Karin had forded no longer intrudes his hideous presence. The water which had gathered in muddy pools now runs in bright rivulets, already suggesting the regeneration of life which the miracle of the spring confirms. Thus anticipated in this rendering of natural landscape, the miraculous rush of water from dry earth becomes a daring but perfectly legitimate extension of images already operative and invested with metaphoric significance. Its upsurge forms an exactly appropriate analogue to the resurgence of vital energy in Töre. Baffled, bereaved, and guilt-ridden, yet willing to tolerate partial perspectives and endure in the face of catastrophe, Bergman's hero reclaims himself as a man at the same moment the nascent stream begins to lift the turf with the force of its life-giving current. Resisting the impulse to sentimentalize and further assimilating the miraculous event into a natural landscape, Bergman closes the film with shots whose background includes the black recesses into which even the sun-drenched waters of the virgin spring must ultimately flow. By this time action and image have received their full aesthetic shape.

## Conclusion

Looking back from the 1970s, we can now see that these films represent only one phase of Bergman's unfolding career, though—from a formative standpoint—a very important phase. Since about 1960, however, he has been going in a rather different direction. Whereas the films of the fifties were story-centered, Bergman now experiments with more esoteric narrative modes; whereas he used to be genre-conscious (dividing his time between comedies and miracle or morality plays), his films now defy easy categories; and whereas in the fifties he typically made "costume pieces" (almost every film being set at least a generation in the past), his art is now rigorously contemporary and modernist. There has also been a decisive shift of emphasis from masculine to feminine roles. Von Sydow and Björnstrand still figure importantly in Bergman's casting, but they move in what is essentially a woman's world. The allegory of masculine quest in *The Seventh Seal* has been displaced by the introspective feminine explorations of *Persona* (1966); the virile conjuration of *The Magician* has given way to the potent female symbols of divination that control *The Ritual* (1968). Nowhere do we now find the power of von Sydow's Töre from *The Virgin Spring*; maleness seems personified in the helpless dwarfs of *The Silence* (1963) and the floating corpses of *Shame* (1968). The centrality of Liv Ullmann, strong of both body and will, to Bergman's most recent films suitably points up the director's new, and perhaps slightly grudging, homage to the feminine.

As with form and theme, so with style and surface. These too change remarkably as we follow Bergman from the fifties to the sixties. The pace and rhythm of Bergman's pictures has been different since Ulla Ryge took over the cutting room from Rosander and Lennart Wallén in 1961. The transitions are now rougher, deliberately disjunctive, in keeping with the discordant, irresolute tenor of the films themselves. This approach to cutting makes Bergman's films of the sixties look more like early Godard or late Antonioni, less like vintage Dreyer. Composition in the late films differs still more radically, probably reflecting the tastes of Sven Nykvist, who replaced Fischer as head cameraman in 1959. Insisting on "a simplicity which does not disturb,"[3] Nykvist has slowly edged Bergman toward greater naturalism in the handling of light. Gone are the glowering skies of the fifties, made picturesque by heavy filtration. Gone too, for the most part, is the low-key, high-contrast spotlighting of *The Seventh Seal* and *Wild Strawberries,* replete with ominous shadows and unexpected flashes. Bergman's late films depend much more upon the glare of sunshine, highlighted only by glints from glass or polished metal, harsh as the austerity of the director's personal psychology. Even when he moves indoors, his films have less the look of the studio. The lighting is diffuse, with few sharp shadows; the decor is spare, rarely invested with obviously symbolic content. The new look in Bergmanian lighting is already implicit in the outdoor world of *The Virgin Spring* (the first film in which Nykvist had full charge of the photography), but the tendency towards naturalism is much more pronounced in *Winter Light, The Silence,* and *Persona.*

Since 1960 Bergman has also conducted his first experiments with color. He used it badly, or at best unimaginatively, in *All These Women* (1963), overburdening the color scheme with obvious allegorical trappings. But *The Passion of Anna* (1970) represents a more flexible application of color, perhaps foreshadowing the Bergman of the 1970s. More noteworthy, however, is the director's new-found fondness for exceptionally long lenses, which is what gives the flat, disklike appearance to the facial portraiture of his recent films. In the 1950s Bergman did most of his close-ups with standard "portrait-length" lenses (85–105 mm. focal length); now his studies of the human face—increasingly more prominent in his pictures—are typically done with telephoto lenses (135–200 mm. focal length) or zoom lenses at their long focal length settings. This achieves what it is fashionable to call the "planarization" of space, in other words, a shallowness of field and a compression of planes that deprives the image of its depth dimension. More than of merely technical significance, this choice of long lenses is optically analogous to the interest in masks and the apparently depthless surfaces of personality which mark Bergman's work of the sixties. For this director, technique is always dramatically functional.

3. Nykvist, p. 631.

No doubt it is still too soon to speak of Bergman's ultimate stature as a filmmaker. Many complain that he is not a highly original thinker, a charge that to me seems reasonably well grounded. The view that "man lives strictly according to his needs,"[4] which he still advertises as the crux of his philosophy, is hardly a startling new insight. Freud said more as much as half a century ago. But to worry over the quality of Bergman's thinking is to confuse the offices of art and philosophy, for Bergman's profundity is engrained in his aesthetic medium. As his camera plays upon the human scene, the textbook abstractions of his thought receive weight and shape, explored as they are in all their nuances and implications, always with a sure sense of the dramatic engagements they engender. Though perhaps conceived in clinical terms, Bergman's characters nearly always take on moral proportions as they accept their biology and aspire to responsible conduct in spite of inherited drives. His sense of man's persistent struggle toward autonomy usually preserves him from triteness.

Throughout his career, Bergman has said pretty much the same thing: man is limited, vulnerable, defensive—yet hungry to learn, both of himself and his world. In the 1950s, after first finding his own voice, Bergman formulated these feelings according to models of reality inherited from a religious past, the personal religious past of his own theological upbringing and the public religious past of Western culture. The usefulness of these models was eventually depleted, at which point he lost interest in crusades and cathedrals and began to look for new emblems of man's permanent condition. Hence his sacramental confessions have become psychoanalytic soliloquies, and his God-sent plagues are now man-sent air raids. In keeping with this new secularism, he has come to depend more upon the private fantasies of his characters and less upon public myths. But what we have in this transition is not so much a change of mind as a change of metaphor. I know of no very good reason to prefer one Bergmanian mode to another, since both periods of his career are distinguished by major achievements. Perhaps the films of the fifties are a little more intellectually accessible, in spite of their dependence upon costume and fable, though we need not argue these questions. It is sufficient to say that in his first creative flourish Bergman gave us several films which have a continuing claim upon our attention. Among these are surely *The Virgin Spring, Wild Strawberries,* and *The Seventh Seal.*

4. "Bergman Discusses Filmmaking," *Four Screenplays,* p. xxi.

# "The Seventh Seal"

## Andrew Sarris

*And when he had opened the seventh seal, there was silence in heaven about the space of half an hour.*

*Book of Revelation*

*A free mind, like a creative imagination, rejoices at the harmonies it can find or make between man and nature; and where it finds none, it solves the conflict so far as it may and then notes and endures it with a shudder.*

George Santayana, "Art and Happiness"

Although Ingmar Bergman's *The Seventh Seal* is set in medieval Sweden, nothing could be more modern than its author's conception of death as the crucial reality of man's existence. Appearing at a time when the anguished self-consciousness of Kierkegaard and Nietzsche has come back into favor as a statement of the human condition, *The Seventh Seal* is perhaps the first genuinely existential film. The plight of the individual in an indifferent universe would have seemed a fatuous subject for an artist a generation ago when human objectives barely extended to the next bread line, and when, it now seems ages ago, Edmund Wilson could reasonably denounce Thornton Wilder's metaphysical concerns in *The Bridge of San Luis Rey* as socially irresponsible. Liberal reform, Marxist determinism and the Social Gospel of Christianity were variously hailed as the formulas of a blissful world, but something went wrong with these collective panaceas partly because thinking men discovered that endless problem-solving reduced life to its one insoluble problem, death, and partly because population explosions, the hydrogen bomb and the Cold War scuttled the idea of Progress as a cause for rejoicing. Quite obviously, the time has come to talk of other things beside the glories of social reconstruction.

From *Film Culture*, no. 19, 1959. Reprinted by permission of *Film Culture*.

Ingmar Bergman, the son of a clergyman, is aware of the decline of religious faith in the modern world, but unlike Dreyer, he refuses to reconstruct mystic consolations from the dead past. If modern man must live without the faith which makes death meaningful, he can at least endure life with the aid of certain necessary illusions. This is what Bergman seems to be saying in *The Seventh Seal,* a remarkably intricate film with many layers of meaning.

The Biblical context of the Seventh Seal is never fully retold on the screen, but enough excerpts are provided to keynote the theme of the Last Judgment. A hawk suspended in flight opens the film with a striking image of foreboding against a rising chorale of exultant faith. After ten years on a Crusade to the Holy Land, a knight and his squire return disillusioned to Sweden. Riding north to the knight's castle further and further away from Christianity's birthplace where God has died in their hearts, the knight and the squire are cast allegorically into the void of modern disbelief.

They first appear on a lonely beach, the knight seated by his chessboard, the squire flung awkwardly in a lackey's sleep. The two horses prance against the rushing waves as sun, sky and sea converge on the distant horizon. In the midst of a dazzling progression of sun-setting dissolves, the black-hooded figure of Death confronts the blond knight. Bergman's editing is ambiguous here for one cannot be sure that Death has actually materialized out of space. Nor is there any camera trickery involved in Death's subsequent manifestations. Death is presumably too real for magic lantern effects.

The knight challenges Death to a game of chess, the knight's life to be staked on the outcome. As the game begins with Death taking the black pieces, Bergman composes the first of his many tableaux inspired by medieval church murals. Death and the knight resume their match at fixed dramatic intervals later in the film. Bergman's fable is shaped by this chess game, not so much in the symbolism of the moves, most notably Death takes knight, but in the expanding meanings and ambiguities of the two players. While seeking God in the world of men, the knight relentlessly pursues the enigma of his antagonist.

As the knight and the squire continue their homeward journey, towering overhead shots of the two riders alternate with pulsating images of the sun. This cosmic technique would be pretentious for a lesser theme, but here in the beginning, Bergman is suggesting the dimensions of the universe in which his drama will unfold. Once the philosophical size of the film is established, Bergman's camera probes more intimately into his characters.

The fact that the squire does not share the knight's first encounter with Death is consistent with Bergman's conception of the knight's solitude in his quest for God. Since the squire is a confirmed atheist, the knight cannot seek consolation in that quarter. Indeed, the squire's bawdy songs and low comedy grimaces stamp him as the knight's Sancho Panza until a startling incident transforms him into a co-protagonist. Dismounting to ask a hooded stranger the way to the next town, the squire lifts the hood and beholds the death skull of a plague victim. The squire's reaction is that of a forceful intelligence, and he displays an unexpected flair for irony when he tells the unsuspecting knight that the stranger said nothing but was quite eloquent. Bergman achieves his shock effect here with the aid of a dog frisking about its dead master before the squire lifts the man's hood. This is more than a trick, however, and Bergman later develops the flickering idea involved here.

Bergman adds to his chess pieces as the knight and the squire ride past a carnival wagon in which an actor, a juggler, the juggler's wife and their infant son are asleep. Emerging from the wagon into a sunlit world less intensely illuminated than the world of the knight and the squire, the juggler is awed by a vision of the Virgin Mary walking the Christ Child. He calls his wife to describe this latest miracle of his imaginative existence, and as always, she is kind but skeptical. (Bergman has a priceless talent for establishing states of being in quick scenes.) The juggler and his wife are suggestively named Jof and Mia at slight variance from an explicit identification with Christ's parents. They are never quite that, but when Joseph observes wistfully that his son, Michael, will perform the one impossible juggling trick, the screen vibrates with Bergman's first intimations of immortality.

Bergman returns to his central theme as the actor steps out of the wagon to announce that he will play Death in the religious pageant at Elsinore. Donning a death mask, he asks (vanity of vanities!) if the women will still admire him in that disguise. As the pompous director of the troupe, he orders Joseph to portray the Soul of Man, a part Joseph dislikes for theatrical reasons. When the actor returns to the wagon, hanging the death skull on a pole outside, the camera lingers on this symbol long enough for the sound track to record the pleasant laughter of Jof and Mia before cutting back to the couple whose merriment operates both as a conscious reaction to the departing actor and as the director's expression of their irreverent attitude toward death. In all this symbolic by-play, Jof and Mia convey a wondrous innocence, and the scene ends on a note of emotional recollection as Mia's avowal of her love for her husband is underscored by the same musical motif which accompanied Jof's vision of the Madonna.

Bergman shifts from the sunlit innocence of the carnival wagon to the ominous atmosphere of a medieval church. While the knight pursues his quest for God at the altar of Christ, the squire exchanges blasphemies with a morbidly cynical church painter whose fearsome murals of the Dance of Death, the Black Plague and religious flagellations are the visual inspiration of *The Seventh Seal*. This circular recognition of a predecessor typifies Bergman's concern with the role of art in transcending the existential limits of human life.

Unable to find solace at the altar, the knight advances towards a hooded figure in the confessional chamber. The knight's unrecognized confessor is Death, and in an electrifying passage of self-revelation, the knight confesses all the agony of a mortal man seeking God while unwilling to embrace a religion of fear. Death, the confessor, offers no consolation, no guarantees, no answers, and in his tactical role, lures the knight into revealing his chess strategy.

The knight's outrage when he discovers the deception may well be shared by the audience. Why should Death cheat on certainties? It is possible that Bergman is intensifying the horror of life by suggesting ultimate nothingness with intermediate stages of accident and caprice. Since Death's timing follows no logical pattern, he might as well indulge in masquerades and linger over interesting chess games. Bergman suggests also that Death is everywhere—the church, the confessional chamber, perhaps even on the Cross.

The knight achieves heroic stature in his reaction to Death's hoax. Extending his hands before him to feel the blood pulsing in his veins, noting the sun still at its zenith, the suddenly exultant knight proclaims to his hitherto uncertain self the one certainty of an appointment to play chess with Death. Almost any other director would have sustained this great cinematic moment with either an immense close-up or a receding tracking shot to the ceiling of the church looking down upon mortal man in his fullest affirmation. Instead, Bergman truncates his effect with a quick cut to the squire entertaining the church painter with a Rabelaisian account of the Crusade. This abrupt transition from sublimity to ridicule is characteristic of Bergman's balanced treatment of the high-low dualism of human life.

From this point on, the fear-ridden world impinges upon the knight and the squire. The Black Plague is now seen sweeping across Sweden on a trail of hysteria, witch-burnings and religious flagellations. The knight asks a young woman condemned for witchcraft to lead him to the Devil, who might confirm the existence of God. The knight is answered only by a piteous wail which evokes the callous inhumanity of the period. The squire rescues a silent girl from a renegade priest who has degenerated into a robber of the dead. Ironically, this same priest, the closest human equivalent of evil in *The Seventh Seal*, once shamed the knight into embarking on the Crusade.

The various threads of the plot are woven together into the fabric of a town which represents for Bergman many of the evils of society. Art reappears in a musical pantomime of cuckoldry presented by Jof, Mia and the preening actor. The medieval approximation which Bergman attempts in this performance is carried over into the actor's flamboyant affair with a flirtatious blacksmith's wife. With dainty steps and cock-robin flourishes, the seduction in the nearby forest derives its tempo from a bawdy nonsense song rendered in the town by Jof and Mia, their faces gaily painted, their manner joyously abandoned. Their performance is meaningfully interrupted by the wailing of flagellants bearing Christ on the Cross. Bergman cuts with brilliant deliberation back and forth between the painful detail of the incense-shrouded procession and tracking shots of the soldiers and townspeople kneeling reverently in turn as the Cross goes past. The same soldiers who threw fruit at the actors (art) now kneel to their Saviour (fear).

The brutalization of a fear-crazed society reaches its climax in an inn where the patrons suspend their discourses on the End of the World to laugh sadistically at Jof's grotesque dance on a table while the renegade priest brandishes a torch at the juggler's feet. (The ordeal of a performer deprived of his mask and the sanctuary of his stage is more fully explored in Bergman's *The Naked Night*.) Joseph escapes only because of the intervention of the squire, who slashes the priest's face. In a film drenched with death, this is the only instance in which blood is drawn.

Withdrawing from the discord of the town, the knight is moved by the innocent contentment of Jof and Mia to offer them his protection and the sanctuary of his castle. The knight, the squire and the silent girl share with the juggler's family an interlude of resignation. The knight consecrates this moment in his memory with sacramental bowls of milk and wild strawberries, Bergman's personal symbols of the bread and wine of human redemption. The final movement of *The Seventh Seal* is then performed in a forest of unearthly calm and tempest, and a castle of last judgement.

The knight's caravan takes on the spiritual contours of an Ark in a drowning world. Having assumed responsibility of Jof's family, the knight is now engaged in a selfless cause. The squire's instinctive humanism has gained him the loyalty of the silent girl he has rescued and the friendship of the cuckolded blacksmith he has pitied. Yet, the growing intimacy of the characters is itself an ominous portent of Death.

The rising tension is checked momentarily by an encounter with the errant blacksmith's wife and the actor. Here Bergman provides the last bawdy counterpoint to his major theme as the blacksmith is reconciled to his wife while the actor feigns suicide with a stage dagger. This apparently gratuitous scene is a fitting prelude to Death's manifestation in the forest.

When the actor climbs a tree to be safe from the wood animals during the night only to see Death saw down this medieval tree of life, the dark comedy of the incident confirms Bergman's sense of structure. The buffoonery of actor-blacksmith-wife is the film's last semblance of life unconcerned with death, and it is required for Bergman's graded shocks. However, one is suspended between horror and humor as the tree comes down with the actor screaming soundlessly and a squirrel hopping on to the stump chirping loudly. This image of animal life in the presence of human death expands the notion of individual mortality which Bergman touched upon in his earlier conjunction of the dog and the plague victim.

The caravan next encounters the witch, who is to be burned in the forest. Still searching for God, the knight asks her once more for the whereabouts of the Devil. The girl raves that the Devil is in her eyes, but the knight perceives only the reflection of her terror. When he asks an attending monk why the girl's hands have been broken, the monk who turns his face is Death, now cynically inquiring when the knight will stop asking questions. In this stunning moment of recognition, the knight's destiny is revealed. He must continue his quest despite its futility.

Although the knight has given the witch a drug to ease her pain, her last moments on the stake are filled with wild despair as she realizes that the Devil is not going to claim her from the emptiness which lies beyond the flames. The squire confronts the knight for the first time with evidence (?) of the void, but the knight refuses to abandon hope. One would lose all sympathy for Bergman's characters if they treated the witch's ordeal as merely a test of God's existence. Fortunately, Bergman never loses his human perspective on death even when the renegade priest is stricken by the Plague. The silent girl he once menaced rushes toward him until the squire restrains her, virtually pleading that any help would be futile. Dying never becomes a casual process for Bergman. The actor, the witch, the renegade priest all achieve a form of moral purgation in the inescapable self-pity they arouse in their audiences, both real and fictitious.

When Death confronts the knight for the final moves on the chessboard, the once stark tonal contrasts between the two antagonists have merged into relativistic grayness. Gone is the sun and the sea and the sky. Death has enveloped the forest and no longer makes striking entrances with his black cloak. Jof "sees" Death at the chessboard and takes flight with Mia and Michael. Fearing Death's intervention, the knight knocks over the pieces to allow Jof and his family to escape. Inscrutable to the end, Death does not indicate whether he has been taken in by this diversion, or whether he is tolerant or indifferent, or whether, after all, he *is* actually controlled by a Higher Power. Once Death has achieved checkmate and has claimed the knight and his friends at the next meeting, he still denies he possesses any secrets of the after-life, and in a dissolving close-up, his face is slowly and memorably transformed into a hollow mask.

While Jof and Mia are fleeing Death's storm in the forest, the knight leads his remaining companions into his castle where the knight's wife waits alone, a medieval Penelope who seems as weary of life as does her tortured husband. Here Bergman resists the beguiling temptation to sentimentalize the knight's attitude towards death. Having performed a noble service for Jof and Mia and having retained his wife's love for the ten years sacrificed in a futile search for God, the knight might be allowed to meet Death with the lofty grandeur with which most doomed film heroes crash into oblivion. Instead, when Death appears at the long banquet table to claim the knight and his guests, the knight prays hopelessly and, at last, unconditionally, to a God who must exist if life is not to end in senseless terror. The squire remains true to his own colors as he scoffs at the knight's quest for God. Accepting Death under protest, the squire acclaims his life without God, but significantly the last words are spoken by the silent girl: "It is done."

This elliptical declaration of awareness, perhaps miraculously extracted from the text of Revelation, is less meaningful than the glowing expression in her eyes as she awaits the end of her earthly servitude. The silent girl, more than any of the other characters, has been defeated by life, and in her defeat, has embraced the prospect of death. When we first see her, she is about to be raped and murdered. She passively accepts her role as the squire's housekeeper, and is always seen either bearing some burden or accepting the squire's protection. One almost suspects Bergman of a class statement in his conception of this memorable, yet elusive, character.

Yet, all of Death's victims in the forest and the castle have failed in some way. The actor is impaled on his vanity; the witch deluded into a pointless martyrdom by the ignorance of society; the renegade priest stripped of the last vestiges of self-induced consolation; the knight tortured by endless doubt; the squire limited to the easy wisdom and cynicism of the world; the blacksmith and his wife enmeshed in trivialities; the knight's wife deprived of the passion which might once have resisted Death. Strangely, there is little sense of regret. None of Death's victims ever suggest that they would have lived their lives differently if they had another chance. The knight is not even sorry that he embarked on the Crusade. One hesitates to suggest predestination in such an agnostic context, but it is difficult to recall significant opportunities for moral choice in any of Bergman's films released thus far in America.

When Jof and Mia emerge once more into the sunlight, the Black Cloud of Death is safely past. (Some critics have translated this cloud into the H-bomb, but the analogy is both labored and unnecessary. More substantial social parallels can be derived from the scenes of fear and doubt; the squire's description of his outlook as "modern" is deliciously ironic.) Against the distant sky, Jof sees the Dance of Death, Bergman's majestic summation of medieval imagery. As Death leads his six victims, hand to hand, in the fierce merriment of their last revels, *The Seventh Seal* soars to the heights of imaginative cinema.

It is not until Jof describes the Dance of Death that we realize that his vision is inspired by a creative imagination rather than a Divine Revelation. The people he identifies in the Dance of Death—Death, the knight, the squire, the actor, the blacksmith and his wife, and the renegade priest—are not entirely the same people Death confronts in the castle. Jof had never seen the knight's wife, and her absence from his vision is quite logical. The omission of the silent girl is more puzzling. At least two interesting theories suggest themselves. The silent girl's final expression of acceptance slowly dissolves into the watchful expression of Mia. The two women look very much alike, and whatever this means—Jof developing a mental block in imagining death for someone resembling Mia, Jof unconsciously admiring the silent girl, Jof even absent-mindedly overlooking the existence of this girl—a clear link has been established between these two archetypes of woman.

The second theory is almost frighteningly intellectual. Since Jof calls off the names of the Dancers, it is possible that the unnamed silent girl cannot operate in Jof's artistic imagination. Except for the witch, all the other recurring characters are assigned proper names, but the silent girl, like the witch, remains an abstract being beyond Jof's ability to recall in his creations. This theory raises the question of Bergman's immersion in the technical philosophies of logical and linguistic analysis, a question which can be answered ultimately only by Bergman himself. Yet, it is quite clear from his interviews and his past films that he has been influenced by the irrational ideas of illusion and existence expressed in the works of Camus, Sartre, Anouilh, Strindberg and Pirandello.

If Jof and Mia represent the continuity of man, they do so because of certain transcendent illusions—love, art, contentment and the future of their child. These futile distractions from imminent death make life endurable if not justifiable. Yet, the knight and the squire are also aspects of man, the knight as the questing mystic, the squire as the earthbound philosopher. It is possible to identify Bergman in some measure with all three characters since *The Seventh Seal* is a unique amalgam of beauty, mysticism and rational logic. What is most remarkable about Bergman's achievement is that he projects the most pessimistic view of human existence with an extraordinary vitality. Conceding that life is hell and death is nothingness, he still imparts to the screen a sense of joy in the very futility of man's illusions.

For all its intellectual complexity, *The Seventh Seal* is remarkably entertaining. In the high level of acting we have come to expect in Bergman films, Gunnar Björnstrand as the squire, and Bengt Ekerot as Death, provide truly remarkable performances. Björnstrand, previously seen here in *The Naked Night* and *Smiles of a Summer Night,* displays classic range in the sublety and force of his widely dissimilar characterizations. Bengt Ekerot's playing of Death is so uncanny that it is difficult to imagine this unfamiliar actor in any other role. Max von Sydow has the most difficult part as the mystical knight who must communicate from the depths of his soul, but in his dramatic scenes, he fully captures the tortured nobility of his character. Nils Poppe, Sweden's leading comedian, is very moving as Jof through the counterpoint of his comic personality and his cosmic problems. Bibi Andersson as Mia heads a gallery of unaffectedly beautiful women which includes anonymous faces in Bergman's crowd scenes.

Bergman's camera technique is fully equal to his theme. Except for a glaring process shot in the opening scene, his medieval images are clear and solid in the best tradition of realistic cinematography. Bergman is at his best in intimate scenes where his unobtrusively moving camera builds up tensions before his editing exploits them. One is always aware of the meaningful texture of faces as they react to the uncertainties they confront. Bergman indulges in the sun dissolves endemic to Swedish cinema, and the reverse cloak opening of a frame which Hitchcock invented, but which Bergman gives a special flourish in many of his films. In this instance, Death's black cloak must have been irresistible.

Bergman's overall editing maintains a steady flow of images to create visual progressions for each successive plot development. The plastic symbol of the death skull reappears in each shot at a different expressive angle, and Death himself never repeats the choreography of his comings and goings. Bergman's economy of expression actually makes it difficult to absorb all the meanings in each scene. Instead of fully developing his ideas in long, obligatory confrontations of characters, Bergman distributes fragments of what he is saying into every incident. Yet, a great deal that is implied is left unsaid, and it is possible that *The Seventh Seal* will be a source of controversy for years to come, and that like all classics of the mind, its interpretations will vary with the minds and times of its critics.

# *"Persona"*

## Stanley Kauffmann

The word "persona" has several meanings: among them, mask (in the original Latin); person; and a character in a play. *Persona* is the consummate title for Ingmar Bergman's film.

Made in 1965, it is the twenty-seventh film he directed, the twenty-ninth screenplay he wrote or collaborated on. Bergman was born in 1918 near Stockholm, the son of a Lutheran minister, and began his directing career in the theater; in fact, despite his immense film activity, he has spent more than half of his directing career in the theater. But film, of course, is what made his international reputation. By the time he came to *Persona* he was known as one of the cinema's prime explorers of psyche and spirit—strongly influenced by Strindberg—through such works as *The Virgin Spring* and his trilogy, *Through a Glass Darkly, Winter Light,* and *The Silence.* All of these were made with Sven Nykvist, his only cinematographer since 1959, and with a "company" of actors, most of whom he had worked with in the theater for many years. His specific impulse toward *Persona,* Bergman has said, came out of an addition to that company: he saw a film with a new Norwegian actress, Liv Ullmann, and was struck by her resemblance to a long-time colleague, Bibi Andersson.

*Persona* has often been called difficult and abstruse, yet in a poll conducted in 1972 by a British film journal to determine the ten favorite films of eighty-nine critics around the world, *Persona* tied for fifth place. (With Antonioni's *L'Avventura.* Another Bergman film, *Wild Strawberries,* tied for eighth place.) This statistical tally is relevant only in that it substantiates the position of this "difficult" work in the treasury of film art. I am not going to try to show that the picture is not difficult, that its materials are not dark. I want to analyze, if I can, why its difficulty is fruitful.

I propose three separate looks at *Persona*. But I emphasize that these looks are arbitrarily separated: in our experience of the film, all three of these views—and doubtless others as well—occur simultaneously.

First, a map of the story. The picture begins, before the titles and even through the titles, with a series of images, some of which are previsions of matters treated later, some of which only set tonalities for matters treated later. Then we are in a hospital. A nurse, Sister Alma (Bibi Andersson), is assigned by a doctor (Margaretha Krook) to the case of Elisabet Vogler (Liv Ullmann). Elisabet is an actress of about Alma's age, successful, well-known, who has become mute. She is physically well, she is alert and extremely intelligent; but from some psychic imperative, she has simply decided not to speak—not even to her husband and young son.

Although Alma has seen the actress on stage and film and idolizes her, she has inexplicable misgivings about taking the case after she meets Elisabet. But the doctor persuades her to continue. Then the doctor has a talk with Elisabet, the actress keeping absolutely silent as usual, in which the physician shows sharp perception of her patient's condition. She says that Elisabet is in a state of revulsion with the world and herself, and is convinced that every word she might speak would only add to the sum of lies in the world. What can she do? "Suicide?" reflects the doctor. "No, too vulgar." But at least Elisabet can decide to keep silent.

Elisabet's quality of attention indicates that the doctor has diagnosed matters accurately.

The doctor has a cottage by the sea. She says there is no point in keeping Elisabet in the hospital, she is sending the patient and the nurse to her cottage until, as she puts it, the actress is ready to move on to other roles.

Most of the film takes place in this isolated small house on the rocky Swedish coast; and all the rest of the film, except for one episode with one other person, is between these two women, only one of whom speaks. By this very fact that the other woman only and always listens, Alma soon progresses into details of her life at its most intimate and recessed. The cottage becomes a kind of confessional. Alma feels drawn almost entreatingly to Elisabet, her patient; she is stimulated by being here alone with this famous artist, who listens to her; and she tells Elisabet about a long wretched love affair she had with a married man, about the pleasant fiancé she has now, and more.

Then one day Alma drives to town to mail some letters, including one of Elisabet's to the doctor. Elisabet has accidentally left her letter unsealed, and Alma can't resist reading it. In it Elisabet has written patronizingly of Alma, saying that she likes the nurse who has taken to telling her secrets, and that she finds it amusing to study Alma.

The shock is severe for Alma who, though not naive, is straightforward. Her attitude toward Elisabet changes drastically. No longer a nurse and an aspiring friend, she becomes a competitor, an avenger, desperate to avenge the affront to herself in a particular way—by being recognized as a person. Eventually this leads to a physical fight between the two women, during which Alma, in a fury, almost throws a pot of boiling water at Elisabet—her patient—and provokes the one unequivocal, spontaneous utterance the actress makes in the film, a cry of "Don't!"

Later, in a long pleading scene, the tearful Alma follows the outraged Elisabet down the beach, explaining how fond she had become of the actress and how badly the letter had hurt her, saying she knows they must leave this place soon but hopes they can part as friends. But Elisabet keeps walking, as stony as the stony beach.

Now Alma, failed as a nurse, offended as a person, scorned as a suppliant, begins to crack. She begins to have fantasies on the edge of hallucination, including one about Elisabet's husband whom she has never seen. In an effort to reclaim herself, Alma puts off informal country wear and puts on her nurse's uniform; this doesn't help. She is not only no longer her earlier self, she has slipped even closer toward Elisabet, as she imagines her.

She confronts the actress and tells her—twice, once with the camera on the other woman, once with it on herself—why she thinks Elisabet had a child and why she later rejected the boy: that the actress had thought of motherhood as a role but had been frightened by the reality. The account ends with Alma frantically stuttering into gibberish.

These are the last words she speaks in the film, except for some dream utterances. We see the two women packing in silence, closing the house. We see a very quiet Alma leaving. A voice on the sound track tells us that Elisabet returned to the theater "in December" and continued her career (and we get a glimpse of her acting again). Then again we see the quiet Alma getting the bus to take her away from the coast. There is a quick reprise of two images from the very beginning, and the film ends.

Now, a second look at *Persona,* to see how and, principally, why Bergman told this story.

First, the performances by Andersson and Ullmann. They are perfect. Any lesser word would be footling. Andersson, carrying almost all the dialogue, never fluctuates from a complete grip on the truth of the moment and the means of conveying it truly. Ullmann, silent almost throughout, nevertheless creates a complex human being in herself and by the *use* of things that are said to her. To see the film again now is to "hear" Ullmann by virtue of her subsequent appearances in other films: to see *Persona* when it was released was to witness an extraordinary debut, silent but eloquent.

As for the film itself, it begins with a black screen and a thrum of electronic sound. The carbon arcs of a film projector glow into presence, and in a series of disjointed flashes, we see—among other glimpses—a strip of film beginning to roll through a projector, bits of old slapstick comedy, a sheep being dissected, a spike being driven through a hand. Then we are in a morgue, with bodies under sheets. A telephone rings. A dead old woman's eyes blink open. A dead boy sits up, puts on glasses, starts to read. Then he reaches toward the camera and, in a reverse shot, we see that he is reaching toward the immense face of a woman behind glass. It becomes another woman's face. (Later we learn that these are Elisabet and Alma.) The faces blur together. Then the title and credits of the film appear.

The very start emphasizes that what we are going to see is a film: reality is not going to be re-created, it is going to be abstracted. The "meaning" of the various disjointed images is never patly explicated. My feeling when I first saw *Persona,* enforced by subsequent viewings and unchanged by other's views, was that we are being given a quick, jagged tour of Elisabet's mind. This is one of the relatively few sequences in which the film is subjectively hers; usually it is either Alma's or it is objective. It can even be argued that the film-projector and film-strip opening are Elisabet's, since (as the doctor notes) she sees life as a show, a succession of roles.

Through the credits, too, there are flashes of what we have already seen and what we shall see, after which the screen goes absolutely white for a moment. Then, via Nykvist's magic camera, the outlines of a door are sketched in photographically. Alma comes through it and faces us. The "prologue" began with black, into which white penetrated; the body of the film begins with a reversal of this process, as if blackness and whiteness are being established as the visual poles of the work.

The camera holds on the nurse, first from the front, then from behind. The doctor who addresses her is seen only vaguely in the background. Thus Bergman insinuates that Alma is abstracted from the world, a distilled presence, that what we are seeing is only seeming realism. When the doctor says that Elisabet stopped dead in the middle of a stage performance, of *Electra,* we see a flash of this, but we also see a camera filming that performance. Again Bergman seems to be reminding us that everything we see here as reality is itself being observed by at least one other reality. Thus his very method keeps asking the question: Where is truth?

The lighting of that first scene with the doctor and the feeling of a real room floating in space are continued in Elisabet's room, as the nurse and the patient become acquainted. Two moments here are especially important to what follows. First, Alma switches on a bedside radio, for Elisabet's amusement, and a soap-opera actress begins to talk moonily of love. Elisabet giggles, then angrily switches it off. Alma then puts on some music for her—Bach, as it happens—and leaves her. Then comes a minute that is powerful in its simplicity, exquisite in its power. The camera holds on Elisabet's face turned to the radio; listening; her eyes unblinking. (Bergman has said that, to him, film means faces.) The light dims; it is twilight, yet this is a theatrical fading. (Again Bergman leads us subtly over the edge of realism.) In the dusk Elisabet stares intently, held by the music, *feeding* on it. After a long, absolutely motionless moment, she turns her head as if in pain.

This brief scene is crucial to the film. It is no facile exploitation of great music, like the Mozart in *Elvira Madigan*. Bach is not mere sound track accompaniment; he is in this scene, his music is part of the drama. It provides the best statement that Bergman could find of all that is out of Elisabet's reach, so unattainable that she has decided to be silent rather than settle for less. This music, we may infer, is particularly pertinent because of what we know about her. One of the master strokes in the script is that Bergman has made Elisabet an actress, not because she must "lie" every night, pretending to be someone else, but because the truth in that pretense—the truth of art—is greater than any truth she can achieve in her own life. So she is constantly abraded by the difference between the truth of concept and the circumscriptions of self as woman and wife and mother. (Remember, too, that she stopped cold for the first time while playing Electra, the Argive princess whose mission is to cleanse away impurity at whatever cost to herself.) This crystalline moment of Bach is a statement in art to an artist, of a perfection that never existed except in imagination; it is also a reminder of a time in which such imagination was possible but which is now gone.

This is underscored in the second of the two moments. Later Elisabet watches television at night—a filmed report of the Vietnam war. In her nightgown she shrinks into a corner of the hospital room, now lit only by ghostly television light, and watches a Buddhist monk burn himself to death, a man whose protest against imperfection is so strong that it takes the form of permanent silence. Elisabet watches in horror, perhaps with a touch of shame put possibly with some touch of reinforcement for her present "role."

These two moments, one of purity from the past, one of agony in the present, come to her through electronic media of the twentieth century.

The first scene on the island—the two women walking alongside a stone wall, then peeling mushrooms together—is one of the few sequences in sunlight. Most of these island scenes are at night or in rain or in the soft-clear gray light that Bergman and Nykvist have long since established as the climate of the human "interior."

And in this isolated place, with these two physically similar women dressed in similar country clothes, we see a drama of virtually isolated forces, opposed yet melding. One woman of strength and intellect has had a vision of nullity. The other woman, of strength and intelligence, is there to bring Elisabet back (in effect) to her (Alma's) point of view, to a plane of function. Yet the reverse happens: without philosophic process, Alma is drawn more and more to the cavern in which Elisabet is now hiding. What attracts Alma consciously is Elisabet-as-artist; the nurse is happy to be with this gifted and renowned woman. What attracts Alma unconsciously is the sense that Elisabet has found some sort of explanation for the bewilderments of existence, that the actress's so-called abnormality may be a *reasonable* reaction to the confusions and pollutions of life.

This hunger for clarity in Alma is seen most sharply in the sequence where the two women draw closest, a sequence where Alma recounts the story of a sex orgy—a quite spontaneous occasion in which she had found herself participating. As Alma tells the story she feels again the surprise and the dismay that she was able to do these things, to enjoy them, then return to her fiancé and make love with him later that night. She bursts into tears at the end of the story, shocked again at this enlarged knowledge of herself with which she cannot deal. In this sequence Bergman has Elisabet listening as she lies on her bed next to a lamp, with Alma sitting in an armchair in some shadow. The lamp and Elisabet's luminous face seem in themselves to be drawing this secret story out of Alma, almost to be promising her relief and answer.

And that night, apparently because of this closeness and this promise, the film moves for the first time into dream—deliberately difficult to distinguish from reality, perhaps because the reality in this film is itself treated as an abstraction. But it is Alma's dream; in it the breeze moves the gauzy curtains on the doorway to her bedroom and through them Elisabet floats in her nightgown. In one of the most miraculously photographed intimate scenes in all of film, the two women embrace—a communion that is physical without being overtly sexual, a gesture of affinity. This is apparently a symbol of what Alma wishes could happen, a wish that she could join Elisabet wherever, in her inner secretness, she is hiding. (Of course next morning when Alma asks Elisabet whether she came into her bedroom the night before, the actress shakes her head.)

As with this dream scene, the texture of what we see at every moment fulfills what the film is about. Take, for instance, the first scene after Alma has read the unsealed letter. The sun shines, as on the first island day. Alma, on the terrace in a bathing suit and barefoot, breaks a glass and sweeps up the pieces. She discovers one more glass splinter. She picks it up, then she hears Elisabet coming and puts the splinter back. Then she goes inside while Elisabet, also in bathing clothes and barefoot, walks up and down. We wait with Alma. The cry of pain comes, and we see Elisabet glance sharply and suspiciously at the watching Alma inside. Alma stares back stolidly—and then the film itself disintegrates. A hole burns through it and it tears apart. It is as if the tissue of this abstraction—the very film we are watching—has been torn by this sudden savage reversal of feeling.

Then the film fights its way back into being. The next sequence (after a swift reprise of a few flashes from the "prologue") begins quite out of focus, as Elisabet moves around the house, doing some little chores. Slowly, almost painfully, the picture focuses again.

Later, when Alma tells her how hurt she has been by the letter, Elisabet seems only to be startled by the fact that Alma read the letter, and does not yield an inch in apology. Alma gets more and more desperate as she realizes that soon they must leave this place, as she sees that she is getting further and further away from acknowledgment by this woman in whom she has confided so much, as she hates herself for still wanting that acknowledgment, as she feels snared and infuriated by Elisabet's unshakable silence, which now is colored by pride and resentment. That silence seems to have become a kind of victory over everything in Alma: her competence as a nurse, her attempt to draw close as a friend, even her unconscious attempts to hover on the edge of Elisabet's philosophic view.

And interwoven with these scenes of their waking hours, their conflict, Alma's defeat, are her fantasies and dreams: one in which Elisabet's husband makes love to her, thinking her Elisabet, while the actress looks on. In another, the earlier beautiful night embrace is repeated as a kind of glimpse of lost happiness. Another goes back even earlier to Elisabet's hospital room, where Alma finally gets the actress to speak just one word—the word "Nothing."

The climactic scene, in which Alma imagines and tells twice the selfish "role-playing" reasons why the actress had a child, ends with her face and Elisabet's split vertically and joined on the screen. Our first thought is of the two blurred faces that the boy saw in the morgue (especially since the talk here is of a child); but here the joining looks harsh, ugly, schizoid. It is like a danger signal, like the gibberish to which Alma is reduced. Then, in a frenzy of seeming frustration and self-hate, Alma pounds the table, scratches her forearm fiercely, draws blood. Suddenly Elisabet leans forward and sucks that blood. Perhaps she is saying: "You wanted union? I give you a blood bond.'' Or perhaps it is an act of expiation, the only moment when Elisabet literally and figuratively bows to Alma, as if she had implanted a poison that now she wants to draw.

If it is the latter, we never learn positively that it works. Elisabet returns to her career, we know. The shaken Alma returns to her profession and her fiancé—presumably.

The last images are of film running out of the projector and the carbon arcs burning down into darkness; and so the film, to the very end proclaiming itself a film, finishes.

A last look at *Persona*—beneath the action and also beneath the forces of the action. In the year the film was released I saw it two or three times and thought that it was an agon between, to put it crudely, intellectual and biological impulses. The mind of modern man sees the futility of life, the entropy of ideal and hope. But the biological destiny of man is to survive, possibly so that he is able to have such bleak perceptions. The entirely rational disaffection of Elisabet sucks in and almost swamps the extra-rational, vitalist Alma, who pulls herself free to go on living on the other side of this experience, profoundly altered but not by untruth.

Now, after some half dozen further viewings in the intervening years, I think the above is valid enough but incomplete. I think that what Bergman has done here is to try the possibilities for modern tragedy. It is modern because it depends neither on Aristotelian flaw nor on fate nor on vengeance nor on any of the great tragic instruments of the past but on diurnal life. The tragedy lies in the realization of the insuperable distance between truth and possibility. Not death or blindness or suicide is the outcome but *existence,* with increased perception—for both women.

Bernard Shaw once congratulated Chekhov because, as against Ibsen, the Russian understood that the tragedy of the Hedda Gablers in real life is that they do not shoot themselves, they go on living. Elisabet knows (as the doctor indicated) that she will go on living her various roles in the tragedy of *life,* rather than completing an architecturally modeled tragedy in one sequence of her life. Alma's tragedy is that, though primed by experience to be vulnerable to Elisabet's vision, she might not have reached it by herself and must now discover whether she can bear it. Her early misgivings about taking this case may have been a premonition of her vulnerability. Now her premonition is realized: she is not an intellectual "role-player," she now has a new persona she must live with. In an essay on *Persona* Robert Boyers wrote: "The tragic hero is one who loses confidence in reality as he has always known it, and articulated it." The life that Alma will make for herself, he says, "will be tragic, because to be conscious, and to go on living, is to suffer as only our heroes can."

As I understand Bergman, he feels that traditional tragedy is impossible today because, in this god-hungry, probably godless universe, tragedy consists of this very consciousness, this comprehension of the dimensions of imagination and concept as against the dimensions of act and fact. Structurally, however, Bergman has drawn on the ancient sources of the tragic mode. (Surely *Electra* is cited to suggest this.) Some critics have said that *Persona* is related to Strindberg's *The Stronger,* a short two-character play in which a wife confronts her husband's mistress, in which the mistress is silent throughout while the wife speaks, and which leaves us undecided as to which of the two is the stronger. Of course Bergman knows the play, but its domestic gnaw is a long way from the current and thrust of his own much larger work. Particularly in the light of his theater background, I think he may have been strongly influenced by the distilled quality of Greek tragedy—in its earliest form, with only two actors (which essentially are all that *Persona* has) and in one place (which essentially is also true here).

Yet, native of the modern sensibility that Bergman is, he could not rest with archaism. To the above impulse toward classic distillation, he added his understanding of contemporary self-awareness—the literal awareness of self as an entity to be watched, the compulsion or injunction to observe one's own life as a performance, plus the corollary hunger for authenticity in a world where one is now sentenced to observe himself. So, in using the twentieth century's own medium to make a twentieth-century tragedy, Bergman incorporated this modern truth by making the film itself know, so to speak, that it is a film. The work that is watched knows that it is a work made to be watched, not an all-inclusive "real" world; thus in its very being it reflects the self-awareness of its characters and its era.

Ultimately, this difficult, dark, unremitting film is exalting. First, because it shows that a superb artist can still deal with our most terrible knowledges, that high art is still possible in an age that has doubted this possibility. Second, because in the interior action of that art, we see contemporary human beings, in all their feeble self-reliance, still able to experience and survive the very worst, which is one other definition of the heroic. Like Antonioni, like other paramount artists of our time, Bergman has found art to be both a source of moral insight and a means of taking its consequences.

# "Persona"
# The Film in Depth

## Susan Sontag

The difficulty [with *Persona*] is that Bergman withholds the kind of clear
signals for sorting out what's fantasy from what is "real" offered, for
example, by Buñuel in *Belle de jour*. Buñuel has put the clues there; he
wants the viewer to be able to decipher his film. The insufficiency of the
clues Bergman has planted must be taken to indicate that he intends the
film to remain partly encoded. The viewer can only move toward, but
never achieve, certainty about the action. However, so far as the distinction
between fantasy and reality has any use in understanding *Persona,* I should
argue that much more than critics have allowed of what happens in and
around the beach cottage is most plausibly understood as Alma's fantasy.
One prime piece of evidence is a sequence occurring soon after the two
women arrive at the seaside. It's the sequence in which, after we have seen
(i.e., the camera has shown) Elizabeth enter Alma's room and stand beside
her and stroke her hair, we see Alma, pale, troubled, asking Elizabeth the
next morning "Did you come to my room last night?" And Elizabeth,
slightly quizzical, anxious, shaking her head No.

Now, there seems no reason to doubt Elizabeth's answer. The viewer
isn't given any evidence of a malevolent plan on her part to undermine
Alma's confidence in her own sanity, nor for doubting Elizabeth's memory
or sanity in the ordinary sense. But if that is so, two important points may
be taken as established early in the film. One is that Alma is
hallucinating—and, presumably, will continue doing so. The other is that
hallucinations or visions will appear on the screen with the same rhythms,
the same look of objective reality, as something "real." (However, some

This material is excerpted from the essay of the same title, which first appeared in *Sight and
Sound* (1967). With slight revisions it was subsequently included in *Styles of Radical Will*
by Susan Sontag. Copyright © 1966, 1967, 1968, 1969 by Susan Sontag. Reprinted by permission of Farrar, Straus and Giroux, Inc.

clues, too complex to describe here, are given in the lighting of certain scenes.) And once these points are granted, it seems highly plausible to take at least the scene with Elizabeth's husband as Alma's fantasy, as well as several scenes in which there is a charged, trance-like physical contact between the two women.

But even to make any headway sorting out what Alma imagines from what may be taken as really happening is a minor achievement. And it quickly becomes a misleading one, unless subsumed under the larger issue of the form of exposition employed by the film. As I have suggested, *Persona* is constructed according to a form that resists being reduced to a "story"—say, the story about the relation (however ambiguous and abstract) between two women named Elizabeth and Alma, a patient and a nurse, a star and an ingenue, *alma* (soul) and *persona* (mask). The reason is that reduction to a "story" means, in the end, a reduction of Bergman's film to the single dimension of psychology. Not that the psychological dimension isn't there. It is. But a correct understanding of *Persona* must go beyond the psychological point of view.

This seems clear from the fact that Bergman allows the audience to interpret Elizabeth's mute condition in several ways—as involuntary mental breakdown, and as voluntary moral decision leading either towards self-purification or suicide. But whatever the background of her condition, it is much more in the sheer fact of it than in its causes that Bergman wishes to involve the viewer. In *Persona,* muteness is first of all a fact with a certain psychic and moral weight, a fact which initiates its own kind of causality upon an "other."

I am inclined to impute a privileged status to the speech the psychiatrist makes to Elizabeth, before she departs with Alma to the cottage. The psychiatrist tells the silent, stony-faced Elizabeth that she has understood her case. She has grasped that Elizabeth wants to be sincere, not to play a role; to make the inner and the outer come together. And that, having rejected suicide as a solution, she has decided to be mute. She advises Elizabeth to bide her time, to live her experience through; and at the end of that time, she predicts, the actress will return to the world. . . . But even if one treats his speech as setting forth a privileged view, it would be a mistake to assume that it's the key to *Persona;* or even to assume that the psychiatrist's thesis wholly explains Elizabeth's condition. (The doctor could be wrong, or at least be simplifying the matter.) By placing this speech early in the film, and by never referring explicitly to this "explanation" again, Bergman has, in effect, both taken account of psychology and dispensed with it. Without indicating that he regards psychological explanation as unimportant, he clearly consigns to a relatively minor place any consideration of the role the actress's *motives* have in the action.

In a sense, *Persona* takes a position beyond psychology. As it does, in an analogous sense, beyond eroticism. The materials of an erotic subject are certainly present, such as the "visit" of Elizabeth's husband. There is, above all, the connection between the two women themselves which, in its feverish proximity, its caresses, its sheer passionateness (avowed by Alma in word, gesture and fantasy) could hardly fail, it would seem, to suggest a powerful, if largely inhibited, sexual involvement. But in fact, what might be sexual in feeling is largely transposed into something beyond sexuality, beyond eroticism even. The only purely sexual episode is the scene in which Alma, sitting across the room from Elizabeth, tells the story of the beach orgy. Alma speaks, transfixed, reliving the memory and at the same time consciously delivering up this shameful secret to Elizabeth as her greatest gift of love. Entirely through discourse, without any recourse to images (through a flashback), a violent sexual atmosphere is generated. But this sexuality has nothing to do with the "present" of the film, and the relationship between the two women.

In this respect, *Persona* makes a remarkable modification of the structure of *The Silence,* where the love-hate relationship between the sisters had an unmistakable sexual energy. In *Persona,* Bergman has achieved a more interesting situation by delicately excising or transcending the possible sexual implications of the tie between the two women. It is a remarkable feat of moral and psychological poise. While maintaining the indeterminacy of the situation Bergman can't give the impression of evading the issue, and he mustn't present anything that is psychologically improbable. . . .

*Persona* begins with darkness. Then two points of light gradually gain in brightness, until we see that they're the two carbons of the arc lamp; after this, a portion of the leader flashes by. Then follows a suite of rapid images, some barely identifiable—a chase from a slapstick silent film; an erect penis; a nail being hammered into the palm of a hand; a shot from the rear of a stage of a heavily made-up actress declaiming to the footlights and darkness beyond (we see this image soon again and know that it's Elizabeth playing her last role, that of Electra); the immolation of a Buddhist monk in Vietnam; assorted dead bodies in a morgue. All these images go by very rapidly, mostly too fast to see; but gradually they're slowing down, as if consenting to adjust to the time in which the viewer can comfortably perceive them. Then follows a final set of images, run off at normal speed. We see a thin, unhealthy-looking boy around eleven lying under a sheet on a hospital cot against the wall of a bare room; the viewer, at first, is bound to associate to the corpses he's just seen. But the boy stirs, awkwardly kicks off the sheet, puts on a pair of large round glasses, takes out a book and begins to read. Then we see that ahead of him is an indecipherable blur, very faint, but on its way to becoming an image. It's the face of a beautiful woman. As if in a trance, the boy slowly reaches up and begins to caress it. (The surface he touches suggests a movie screen, but also a portrait and a mirror.)

Who is the boy? It seems easy for most people to say he's Elizabeth's son, because we learn later on that she does have a son, and because the face on the screen is the actress's face. But is it? Although the image is far from clear (this is obviously deliberate), I'm almost sure that Bergman is modulating it from Elizabeth's face to Alma's to Elizabeth's again. And if that is the case, does it change anything about the boy's identity? Or is his identity, perhaps, something we shouldn't expect to know?

In any case, the abandoned "son" (if that's who he is) is never seen again until the close of the film, when again, more briefly, there is a complementary montage of fragmented images, ending with the child again reaching tentatively, caressingly, towards the huge blurry blow-up of the woman's face. And then Bergman cuts to the shot of the incandescent arc lamp; the carbons fade; the light slowly goes out. The film dies, as it were, before our eyes. It dies as an object or a thing does, declaring itself to be "used up" and thus virtually outside the volition of the maker.

Any account which leaves out or dismisses as incidental the way *Persona* begins and ends hasn't been talking about the film that Bergman made. Far from being extraneous (or pretentious), as many reviewers found it, this so-called "frame" of *Persona* is, it seems to me, only the most explicit statement of a motif of aesthetic self-reflexiveness that runs through the entire film. This element of self-reflexiveness in the construction of *Persona* is anything but an arbitrary concern, one superadded to the "dramatic" action. For one thing, it states on the formal level the theme of doubling or duplication that is present on a psychological level in the transactions between Alma and Elizabeth. The formal "doublings" are the largest extension of the theme which furnishes the material of the film.

Perhaps the most striking episode, in which the formal and psychological resonances of the double theme are played out most starkly, is the monologue in which Alma describes Elizabeth's relation to her son. This is repeated twice in its entirety, the first time showing Elizabeth's face as she listens, the second time Alma's face as she speaks. The sequence closes spectacularly, terrifyingly, with the appearance of a double or composite face, half Elizabeth's and half Alma's.

Here, in the very strongest terms, Bergman is playing with the paradoxical nature of film—namely, that it always gives us the illusion of having a voyeuristic access to an untampered reality, a neutral view of things as they are. But what contemporary film-makers more and more often propose to show is the process of seeing itself—giving the viewer grounds or evidence for several different ways of seeing the same thing, which he may entertain concurrently or successively.

Bergman's use of this idea here seems to me strikingly original, but the larger intention is certainly a familiar one. In the ways that Bergman made his film self-reflexive, self-regarding, ultimately self-engorging, we should recognize not a private whim but an example of a well-established tendency. For it is precisely the energy for this sort of "formalist" concern with the nature and paradoxes of the medium itself which was unleashed when the 19th century formal structures of "plot" and "characters" were demoted. What is commonly patronized as the over-exquisite self-consciousness in contemporary art, leading to a species of auto-cannibalism, can be seen—less pejoratively—as the liberation of new energies of thought and sensibility.

This, for me, is the promise behind the familiar thesis that locates the difference between traditional and so-called new cinema in the altered status of the camera—"the felt presence of the camera," as Pasolini has said. But Bergman goes beyond Pasolini's criterion, inserting into the viewer's consciousness the felt presence of the film as an object. He does this not only at the beginning and end but in the middle of *Persona*, when the image—it is a shot of Alma's horrified face—cracks like a mirror, then burns. When the next scene immediately begins (again, as if nothing had happened) the viewer has not only an almost indelible after-image of Alma's anguish but an added sense of shock, a formal-magical apprehension of the film—as if it had collapsed under the weight of registering such drastic suffering and then had been, as it were, magically reconstituted.

Bergman's procedure, with the beginning and end of *Persona* and with this terrifying caesura in the middle, is more complex than the Brechtian strategy of alienating the audience by supplying continual reminders that what they are watching is theater (i.e., artifice rather than reality). Rather, it is a statement about the complexity of what can be seen and the way in which, in the end, the deep, unflinching knowledge of anything is destructive. To know (perceive) something intensely is eventually to consume what is known, to use it up, to be forced to move on to other things.

This principle of intensity lies at the heart of Bergman's sensibility, and determines the specific ways in which he uses the new narrative forms. Anything like the vivacity of Godard, the intellectual innocence of *Jules et Jim*, the lyricism of Bertolucci's *Before the Revolution* and Skolimowski's *Le Départ*, is far from Bergman's range. His work is characterised by its slowness, its deliberateness of pacing; something like the heaviness of Flaubert. And this sensibility makes for the excruciatingly unmodulated quality of *Persona* (and of *The Silence* before it), a quality only very superficially described as pessimism.

What is emotionally darkest in Bergman's film is connected particularly with a sub-theme of the main theme of doubling: the contrast between hiding or concealing and showing forth. The Latin word *persona* means the mask worn by an actor. To be a person, then, is to possess a mask; and in *Persona* both women wear masks. Elizabeth's mask is her muteness. Alma's mask is her health, her optimism, her normal life (she is engaged; she likes and is good at her work). But in the course of the film, both masks crack.

One way of putting this is to say that the violence the actress has done to herself is transferred to Alma. But that's too simple. Violence and the sense of horror and impotence are, more truly, the residual experiences of consciousness subjected to an ordeal. It isn't, as I have suggested, that Bergman is pessimistic about the human situation—as if it were a question of certain opinions. It's that the quality of his sensibility has only one true subject: the depths in which consciousness drowns. If the maintenance of personality requires the safeguarding of the integrity of masks, and the truth about a person is always the cracking of the mask, then the truth about life as a whole is the shattering of the total façade behind which lies an absolute cruelty.

It is here, I think, that one must locate the ostensibly political allusions in *Persona*. I do not find Bergman's references to Vietnam and the Six Million genuinely topical, in the manner of seemingly similar references in Godard's films. Unlike Godard, Bergman is not an historically-oriented film-maker. The TV newsreel of a Buddhist immolating himself, and the famous photograph of the little boy from the Warsaw Ghetto, are for Bergman, above all, images of total violence, of unredeemed cruelty. It's as images of what cannot be imaginatively encompassed or digested that they occur in *Persona* and are pondered by Elizabeth—rather than as occasions for right political and moral thoughts. History or politics enters *Persona* only in the form of pure violence. Bergman makes an "aesthetic" use of violence—far from ordinary left-liberal propaganda.

His subject is, if you will, the violence of the spirit. If each of the two women violates the other in the course of *Persona*, they can be said to have at least as profoundly violated themselves. More generally the film itself seems to be violated—to merge out of and descend back into the chaos of "cinema" and film-as-object.

Bergman's film is profoundly upsetting, at moments terrifying. It relates the horror of the dissolution of personality (Alma crying out to Elizabeth at one point, "I'm not you!"). And it depicts the complementary horror of the theft (whether voluntary or involuntary is left unclear) of personality, what is rendered mythically as vampirism: at one point, Alma sucks Elizabeth's blood. But it is worth noting that this theme need not necessarily be treated as a horror story. Think of the very different emotional range in which this material is situated in Henry James's late novel, *The Sacred Fount*. The vampiristic exchanges between the characters in James's book, for all their undeniably disagreeable aura, are represented as partly voluntary and, in some obscure way, just. But the realm of justice (in which characters get what they "deserve") is rigorously excluded by Bergman. The spectator isn't furnished (from some reliable outside point of view) with any idea of the true moral standing of the two women; their enmeshment is a *donnée,* not the result of some prior situation we are allowed to understand. The mood is one of desperation: all we are shown is a set of compulsions or gravitations, in which they founder, exchanging "strength" and "weakness."

But perhaps the main contrast between Bergman and James on this theme derives from their differing positions with respect to language. As long as discourse continues in the James novel, the texture of the person continues. The continuity of language, of discourse, constitutes a bridge over the abyss of loss of personality, the foundering of the personality in absolute despair. But in *Persona* it is precisely language—its continuity—which is in question.

It might really have been anticipated. Cinema is the natural home of those who don't trust language, a natural index of the weight of suspicion lodged in the contemporary sensibility against "the word." As the purification of language has been envisaged as the peculiar task of modernist poetry and of prose writers like Stein and Beckett and Robbe-Grillet, so much of the new cinema has become a forum for those wishing to demonstrate the futility and duplicities of language.

In Bergman's work, the theme had already appeared in *The Silence,* with the incomprehensible language into which the translator sister descends, unable to communicate with the old porter who attends her when she lies ill, perhaps dying, in the empty hotel in the imaginary garrison city. But Bergman did not take the theme beyond the fairly banal range of the "failure of communication" of the soul isolated and in pain, and the "silence" that constitutes abandonment and death. In *Persona,* the notion of the burden and the failure of language is developed in a much more complex way.

*Persona* takes the form of a virtual monologue. Besides Alma, there are only two other speaking characters, the psychiatrist and Elizabeth's husband: they appear very briefly. For most of the film we are with the two women, in isolation at the beach—and only one of them, Alma, is talking, talking shyly but incessantly. Though the verbalization of the world in which she is engaged always has something uncanny about it, it is at the beginning a wholly generous act, conceived for the benefit of her patient who has withdrawn from speech as some sort of contaminating activity. But the situation begins to change rapidly. The actress's silence becomes a provocation, a temptation, a trap. For what Bergman shows us is a situation reminiscent of Strindberg's famous one-act play *The Stronger,* a duel between two people, one of whom is aggressively silent. And, as in the Strindberg play, the one who talks, who spills her soul, turns out to be weaker than the one who keeps silent. (The quality of that silence is changing all the time, becoming more and more potent: the mute woman keeps changing.) As real gestures—like Alma's trustful affection—appear, they are voided by Elizabeth's relentless silence.

Alma is also betrayed by speech itself. Language is presented as an instrument of fraud and cruelty (the blaring newscast; Elizabeth's cruel letter to the psychiatrist which Alma reads); as an instrument of unmasking (Alma's excoriating portrait of the secrets of Elizabeth's motherhood); as an instrument of self-revelation (Alma's confessional narrative of the beach orgy) and as art and artifice (the lines of Electra that Elizabeth is delivering on stage when she suddenly goes silent; the radio drama Alma turns on in her hospital room that makes the actress smile). What *Persona* demonstrates is the lack of an appropriate language, a language that's genuinely full. All that is left is a language of lacunae, befitting a narrative strung along a set of lacunae or gaps in the "explanation." It is these absences of sense or lacunae of speech which become, in *Persona,* more potent than words, while the person who places faith in words is brought down from relative composure and confidence to hysterical anguish.

Here, indeed, is the most powerful instance of the motif of exchange. The actress creates a void by her silence. The nurse, by speaking, falls into it—depleting herself. Sickened almost by the vertigo opened up by the absence of language, Alma at one point begs Elizabeth just to repeat nonsense phrases that she hurls at her. But during all the time at the beach, despite every kind of tact, cajolery and anguished pleading, Elizabeth refuses (obstinately? maliciously? helplessly?) to speak. She has only one lapse. This happens when Alma, in a fury, threatens her with a pot of scalding water. The terrified Elizabeth backs against the wall screaming "No, don't hurt me!" and for the moment Alma is triumphant. But Elizabeth instantly resumes her silence. The only other time the actress speaks is late in the film—here, the time is ambiguous—when, in the bare hospital room (again?), Alma is shown bending over her bed, begging her to say just one word. Impassively, Elizabeth complies. The word is "Noth-ing."

At the end of *Persona,* mask and person, speech and silence, actor and "soul" remain divided—however parasitically, even vampiristically, they are shown to be intertwined.

# Robert Bresson

ROBERT BRESSON was born in France in 1907. After a period of screenwriting in the 1930s, he spent eighteen months as a prisoner of war in 1940 and 1941. His first mature feature film, Les Anges du péché (1943), set in a convent, foreshadows the religious themes of his later work. The better-known Les Dames du bois de Boulogne (1945), a study of passion and revenge, was based closely on a story by Diderot. While the dialogue by Jean Cocteau and a powerful performance by stage actress Maria Casarès remain effective today, they give the film a theatrical quality that Bresson's later films rigorously eschew.

Bresson's quintessential style emerges in three works of the 1950s: Diary of a Country Priest (1951), the masterful A Man Escaped (1956), and the less interesting Pickpocket (1959). Working against the staginess and artificiality of the French cinematic tradition, Bresson, a minimalist and master of spare understatement, developed a highly visual and painterly style. His ascetic manner, with its limited camera movement and stripped-down plot, has been compared to the work of Carl Dreyer, who influenced him, and to the Japanese master Yasujiro Ozu.

Bresson generally uses nonprofessional actors and allows them little dialogue or dramatic expression. His is a director's cinema, which treats performers as ambulatory shapes and images. Though he has frequently been drawn to material from Dostoevsky—perhaps because of its spiritual weight—his style is relentlessly anti-psychological. He trains his camera on blank and empty faces, on parts of the body, or on objects and small gestures in rigidly confined spaces. At times, as in Pickpocket, this rigor seems mechanical, and at its worst, as in The Trial of Joan of Arc (1962), a project already realized brilliantly by Dreyer, it deprives the action of affect and significance and suggests a self-destructive willfulness. Elsewhere, paradoxically, it makes the story exceptionally poignant, transforming the lives of humble individuals into parables of spiritual exaltation and transcendence.

This is especially true in the magnificent Mouchette (1966), which, like Diary of a Country Priest, is based on a novel by the French Catholic writer Georges Bernanos. The central character is a young servant girl, spiritually akin to Dostoevsky's "insulted and injured," who is brutally mistreated and raped and finally kills herself—to the accompaniment to Monteverdi's Magnificat, as though to suggest a triumphant accession to grace that overcomes worldly degradation. Themes of humiliation and grace also dominate Au Hasard, Balthazar (1966), a Christian parable whose protagonist is a donkey. The diminished severity of Bresson's style continues in Une Femme douce (A Gentle Creature, 1969, his first color film) and Four Nights of a Dreamer (1971)—both based on Dostoevsky but set in modern Paris—as well as in Lancelot of the Lake

*(1974), a rich but highly idiosyncratic medieval tableau. In* The Devil Probably *(1977), Bresson even tries to deal with topical material: a world of youthful dropouts, drugs, and ecological disasters. These later films contain images and scenes of profound resonance and suggestiveness, but without the lyrical integration that Bresson achieved in* Mouchette.


*Bresson is as rigorous a theorist as he is a filmmaker. His aphoristic comments on film have been translated in* Notes on Cinematography *(1977), which will be followed by the publication in English of his collected screenplays. For criticism see John Russell Taylor,* Cinema Eye, Cinema Ear *(1964), Susan Sontag,* Against Interpretation *(1966),* The Films of Robert Bresson, *edited by Ian Cameron (1970), and Paul Schrader,* Transcendental Style in Film *(1972).*

# *Robert Bresson*

## Roy Armes

Robert Bresson has made only eight films in twenty-five years as a director, but these have been sufficient to reveal him as one of the great masters of the cinema. It is a tribute to the French film industry that it has allowed this most austere of directors so large a measure of independence. He has had to endure long years of inactivity, but in the films he has made since the war he has not been compelled to make a single concession to commerce and has been able to bring together a team of gifted collaborators, of which the key members have been the veteran photographer Léonce-Henry Burel (who, in the twenties, worked with Abel Gance and Jacques Feyder) and the painter and designer Pierre Charbonnier. Bresson is above all a stylist, perhaps the most rigorous in the history of the European cinema. For him, a style—or in his own phrase *"une écriture"*—is the first essential of a film: "The film is the very type of work which demands a style" and again: "A film is not a spectacle, it is in the first place a style." On all his work he imposes his own vision, but this does not mean that he finds the need to distort the material of his sources. His adaption of Bernanos's novel *Journal d'un curé de campagne* is a model of fidelity, and he has kept completely to the records of Joan of Arc's trial, inventing nothing, in *Procès de Jeanne d'Arc*. His method is to recreate the essence of his material in cinematographic terms, rejecting all that is extraneous and continually refining the work, until it is as bare and intense as a classical French tragedy.

As far as construction is concerned, all of Bresson's postwar films follow the same pattern. He is suspicious of plot in the conventional sense: "I try more and more in my films to suppress what people call plot. Plot is a novelist's trick." Just as one isolated character is the core of every Bresson film, so a single theme runs through each one, and all that is not

From *French Cinema since 1946*, vol. 1, by Roy Armes. © 1966, 1970 by Roy Armes. Reprinted by permission of the publishers, A. S. Barnes & Co., New York, and The Tantivy Press, London.

strictly relevant to this is ruthlessly sacrificed. All the minor dramatic highlights in the action are played down and the director shows a marked liking for ellipsis, moving smoothly from the beginning of one scene to the end of another, or omitting the central portion of a scene.

Bresson is interested only in the spiritual and emotional aftermath of violent and startling events, with the result that these latter invariably occur "off-stage." Everything in the film leads up to the single climax that presages the ending. In *Journal d'un curé de campagne* the death of the Countess marks the turning point in the Curé's relationship with the people around him and foreshadows his own death; in *Un Condamné à mort s'est échappé* the sudden entry of Jost into Fontaine's cell which seems to threaten his escape in fact ensures its success; in *Pickpocket* Michel's meeting with Jeanne after his years abroad leads directly to his submission and salvation; and in *Procès de Jeanne d'Arc,* Joan's withdrawal of her recantation marks martyrdom inevitable. In *Au Hasard, Balthazar* two fates run side by side to a twin climax: the donkey hailed as a saint dies on the mountainside, while Marie runs away from home and ends up naked and humiliated; but in *Mouchette* the pattern is simpler, the girl's rape driving her inevitably to death. In his handling of the final sequences of the films that end in death Bresson shows most forcefully his originality and independence. In the *Journal* the final image which is the culmination of all that has gone before is a long-held shot of the Cross, while in the *Procès* it is the stake, half concealed by smoke at the beginning, clear and empty at the end. The triple attempt at suicide in *Mouchette* with the mood changing imperceptibly from playfulness to determination is perhaps even more audacious.

Bresson's fidelity to his sources is paralleled by his faithfulness to reality in the settings of his films. The places and objects he films are completely authentic and subjected to an intense scrutiny. He films where possible on location—at Fort Montluc for *Un Condamné* or at the Gare de Lyon for *Pickpocket*—and when it was necessary to reconstruct Fontaine's cell in the studios, Bresson insisted on the use of real materials. But mere realism in the sense of adherence to external details is not sufficient for him, as he has said: "I want to and, indeed, do make myself as much of a realist as possible, using only raw material taken from real life. But I end up with a final realism that is not simply 'realism'." He wanted the prison in *Un Condamné* to be as authentic as possible, with all dullness and brutality, monotony and menial actions; but he aimed also at showing the order beneath the surface, what he has called "those extraordinary currents, the presence of something or someone, call it what you wish, which confirms that there is a hand guiding everything." The filming of *Procès de*

*Jeanne d'Arc* set new difficulties for him and since he rejects totally the normal spectacle style of historical films he avoided all the crowd scenes which he thought would destroy the atmosphere he was seeking. His approach to history matches exactly his attitude towards a literary work that he is adapting. He has set out to reveal the universal significance of Joan of Arc's life and to free her from the conventional piety that surrounds a historical figure. He has tried to make Joan as far as possible a contemporary figure: "I wanted Joan of Arc to be a character of today. I wanted to make her up to date; and the inclusion of the few anachronistic details, such as her boots and her bed, was intended to further this impression of contemporaneity."

For Bresson, film and theatre are two completely distinct entities and in his view it is impossible for the film to borrow from the theatre without losing its independence: "As soon as one tries to express oneself through mimicry, through gestures, through vocal effects, what one gets ceases to be cinema and becomes photographed theatre." He has turned almost entirely to using young and inexperienced actors and complete nonprofessionals, for in his eyes a professional actor is a barrier to the portrayal of truth on the screen: "An actor, even (and above all) a talented actor, gives us too simple an image of a human being, and therefore a false image." His main concern with his players is to ensure that they do not try to interpret their parts. He himself establishes the exact tone of each piece of dialogue and then rehearses his actors again and again until they can copy it perfectly. Roland Monod, who played the pastor in *Un Condamné,* has given a fine account of Bresson's attitude to his players. Bresson "would sit there before each new set-up, holding his head in his hands and repeating the lines over to himself, trying to arrive at the quality of directness and simplicity that he would then impose on us."

Bresson's advice on how to speak the dialogue of his films was: "Forget about tone and meaning. Don't think about what you are saying; just speak the words automatically. When someone talks, he isn't thinking about the words he uses, or even what he wants to say. Only concerned with what he is saying, he just lets the words come out, simply and directly. . . . the film actor should content himself with *saying* his lines. He should not allow himself to show that he already understands them. Play nothing, explain nothing." The result of this approach is the remarkable evenness of tone which characterizes all Bresson's films: there is scarcely a single scene containing a real burst of anger or unstifled laughter in the whole of his work.

Bresson disclaims all interest in psychology and refuses to explain his characters: "I dislike psychology and try not to use it." To explain a character in words would be to deny the film as an art and use the methods of the theater or the novel. In the cinema it must be the camera which reveals the personality: "Plastically, one must sculpt the idea into a face by means of light and shade." It becomes clear what Bresson means by this when we consider his explanation of the purpose of the interrogation scenes in *Procès de Jeanne d'Arc:* "The interrogations serve not so much to give information about the events—past or present—as to provoke on Joan's face her profound impressions, to imprint on the film the movements of her soul." It is what goes on in the minds of his characters that is important to him: "It is the interior that commands. I know that it may seem paradoxical in an art where everything is exterior. Only the knots which tie and untie inside the characters give the film its movement, its true movement." The real subject of each of his films is the inner life of the main character: the young priest's progress towards death and near sainthood; Fontaine's intense preparation for his escape and his complete submission to God's will; the struggle within Michel between love and vice; Joan's maintenance of purity and unshakeable steadfastness; Balthazar's passive submission and Marie's wilful search for humiliation; Mouchette's unhappy failure to achieve love.

Bresson originally studied painting and from the very first it was the visual effect that was the basis of his film style: "What I am seeking is not so much expression by means of gesture, speech, mimicry, but expression by means of the rhythm and combination of images, by position, relation and number." Bresson never considers any single image in isolation: the film's effect depends on the combinations and interrelationships of the images. As Bresson has said, the cinema "must express itself not through images but through the relationships of images, which is not at all the same thing." The images must make contact with each other, create a sequence that is more than just the sum of the individual shots, or else the film is not a work of art: "There must, at a certain moment, be a transformation; if not, there is no art." For images to relate fruitfully to one another there are, in Bresson's view, certain basic requirements. The first is that the images themselves are "flat" and seemingly inexpressive: "I have noticed that the flatter an image is, the less it expresses, the more easily it is transformed in contact with other images." This means that the visual style must never have anything, even beauty, that is not strictly functional: "Painting taught me to make not beautiful images but necessary ones." A second requirement is that there must be nothing to destroy the flow from one image to another; the images must share some unity of tone if the flow and transformation is to be maintained. It is for this reason that all the players in a Bresson film are made to adopt a single style of performance: "It is necessary for the images to have something in common, to participate in a sort of union. For this reason I seek to give my characters a relationship and ask my actors (all my actors) to speak in a certain manner and to behave in a certain manner, which is furthermore always the same.''

Whenever Bresson discusses his work it is always in terms of visual effect, but he does nevertheless lavish great care on the soundtrack. Carefully selected natural sounds are used with enormous effect: the creaking cartwheels in *Journal d'un curé de campagne;* the sound of the train at the end of *Un Condamné à mort s'est échappé;* the Parisian street noises in *Pickpocket;* the crackling flames at the end of *Procès de Jeanne d'Arc;* the braying of the ass in *Au Hasard, Balthazar;* the beating wings of the trapped pheasant in *Mouchette.* In the Joan of Arc film the hostile crowds demanding Joan's death are never seen: we only hear their menacing shouts. Music is used sparingly in these films to reinforce the rhythm and to hint at the underlying significance of apparently mundane activity. It is to this end that Bresson employs classical music—the work of Mozart and Lulli—to accompany scenes from *Un Condamné* and *Pickpocket,* while the music of Schubert and Monteverdi adds a new dimension to *Au hasard, Balthazar* and *Mouchette.* Naturally great care is taken too with the film's dialogue. Robert Bresson has always been his own scriptwriter, but during the Occupation he employed Jean Giraudoux and Jean Cocteau respectively to write the dialogues for *Les Anges du péché* and *Les Dames du Bois de Boulogne.* Since the war he has written his own dialogue for all his films and has said that he takes care to ensure that it is always subordinate to the images: "A film dialogue is neither a theatrical dialogue, nor the dialogue of a novel. The words must be extremely compressed so that the image that accompanies them does not become redundant.'' The first three postwar films are built around a balance of image and narrator; while the narrator's words make a major contribution to the creation of the films' rhythm, the images remain the decisive element. In *Procès de Jeanne d'Arc,* however, it is arguable that the dominant aspect is the dialogue of Joan's cross-examination and that the images are in fact subordinate to this, an impression which is strengthened by the increased severity of the visual style.

In his first four postwar films Bresson created a remarkable gallery of heroes. They share the same lean, intellectual and alert appearance and are isolated individuals, set apart from their fellows either by some physical barrier (the prisons of Fontaine and Joan) or by temperament (the Curé, Michel). The richness of their life comes therefore from within and though in outward appearance they may seem weak or timid, their spiritual power is real and is revealed somewhere within the course of the film when we see them in contact with another character: the Curé d'Ambricourt with the Countess, Fontaine with Jost, Michel with Jeanne, Joan of Arc with her judges. As persons they may lack many of the characteristics for which we are accustomed to look, particularly psychological complexity, but they compensate for this by a force and depth which are virtually unique in the cinema, and together they express one man's profoundly felt creative vision of the order underlying the apparent chaos of human life. In his more recent films Bresson has used a wider range of mood and colour to begin an equally impressive gallery of victims. Only the ass can achieve the perfect acceptance akin to sainthood, whereas Marie and Mouchette, led astray by their carnal natures and a stubborn self-assertion, are slowly but remorselessly broken and destroyed by life. Taken as a whole, Bresson's characters show a unique coherence and constitute a profound investigation into the workings of divine grace in a life lived under the shadow of death.

# "Le Journal d'un curé de campagne" and the Stylistics of Robert Bresson

## André Bazin

It has been suggested in criticism of *Les Dames du Bois de Boulogne,* with equal proportions of good sense and misunderstanding, that the psychological make-up of the characters is out of key with the society in which they are shown as living. True, it is the mores of the time that, in the novel of Diderot, justify the choice of the revenge and give it its effectiveness. It is true again that this same revenge seems to the modern spectator to be something out of the blue, something beyond his experience. It is equally useless on the other hand for those who defend the film to look for any sort of social justification for the characters. Prostitution and pandering as shown in the novel are facts with a very clear and solid contemporary social context. In the film of *Les Dames* they are all the more mystifying since they have no basic justification. The revenge of an injured mistress who forces her unfaithful lover to marry a luscious cabaret dancer seems to us to be a ridiculous gesture. Nor can the fact that the characters appear to be abstractions be explained by deliberate cuts made by the director during the filming. They are that way in the script. The reason Bresson does not tell us more about his characters is not because he has no desire to, but because he would be hard put to do so. Racine does not describe the color of the wallpaper in the rooms to which his characters retire. To this one may answer, of course, that classical tragedy has no need of the alibis of realism and that this is one of the basic differences between the theatre and the cinema. That is true enough. It is also precisely why Bresson does not derive his cinematographic abstraction simply from the bare episodes but from the counterpoint that the reality of the situation sets up with itself. In *Les Dames du Bois de Boulogne,* Bresson has taken the risk of transferring one realistic story into the context of another. The result is that these two examples of realism cancel one another out, the passions displayed emerge out of the characters as if from a chrysalis, the action from the twists and turns of the plot, and the tragedy from the trappings of the drama. The sound of a windshield-wiper against a page of Diderot is all it took to turn it into Racinian dialogue. Obviously Bresson is not aiming at absolute realism. On the other hand, his stylized treatment of it does not have the pure abstract quality of a symbol. It is rather a structured presentation of the abstract and concrete, that is to say of the reciprocal interplay of seemingly incompatible elements. The rain, the murmur of a waterfall, the sound of earth pouring from a broken pot, the hooves of a horse on the cobblestones, are not there just as a contrast to the simplification of the sets or the convention of the costumes, still less as a contrast to the literary and anachronistic flavor of the dialogue. They are not needed either for dramatic antithesis or for a contrast in decor. They are there deliberately as neutrals, as foreign bodies, like a grain of sand that gets into and seizes up a piece of machinery. If the arbitrariness of their choice resembles an abstraction, it is the abstraction of the concrete integral. They are like lines drawn across an image to affirm its transparency, as the dust affirms the transparency of a diamond; it is impurity at its purest.

This interaction of sound and decor is repeated in the very midst of elements which seem at first to be completely stylized. For example, the two apartments of the women are almost totally unfurnished, but this calculated bareness has its explanation. That the frames should be on the walls though the paintings have been sold is undoubtedly a deliberate touch of realism. The abstract whiteness of the new apartment is not intended as part of a pattern of theatrical expressionism. The apartment is white because it has just been repainted and the smell of fresh paint still hangs about. Is there any need to add to this list the elevator or the concierge's telephone, or, on the soundtrack, the tumult of male voices that follows the face-slapping of Agnès, the text for which reads totally conventionally while the sound quality of it is absolute perfection.

I have referred to *Les Dames* in discussing *Le Journal* because it is important to point out the profound similarity between the mechanics of their respective adaptations.

The style of *Le Journal* indicates a more systematic searching, a rigour that is almost unbearable. It was made under very different technical conditions. Yet we shall see that the procedure was in each case basically the same. In both it was a matter of getting to the heart of a story or of a drama, of achieving the most rigorous form of aesthetic abstraction while avoiding expressionism by way of an interplay of literature and realism, which added to its cinematic potential while seeming to negate it. In any case, Bresson's faithfulness to his model is the alibi of liberty in chains. If he is faithful to the text this is because it serves his purpose better than taking useless liberties. Furthermore, this respect for the letter is, in the last analysis, far more than an exquisite embarrassment, it is a dialectical moment in the creation of a style.

So it is pointless to complain that paradoxically Bresson is at one and the same time the slave and the master of his text, because it is precisely from this seeming contradiction that he gets his effects. Henri Agel, for example, describes the film as a page of Victor Hugo rewritten in the style of de Nerval. But surely one could imagine poetic results born of this monstrous coupling, of unexpectedly revealing flashes touched off by a translation made not just from one language into another (like Mallarmé's translation of Poe) but from one style and one content into the style of another artist and from the material of one art transposed into the material of another.

Let us look a little more closely now at *Le Journal* and see what in it has not really come off. While not wishing to praise Bresson for all his weak spots, for there are weaknesses, rare ones, which work to his disadvantage, we can say quite definitely that they are all an integral part of his style; they are simply that kind of awkwardness to which a high degree of sensibility may lead, and if Bresson has any reason here for self-congratulation, it is for having had the sense to see in that awkwardness the price he must pay for something more important.

So, even if the acting in general seems poor, except for Laydu all the time and for Nicole Ladmiral some of it, this, provided you like the film, will only appear to be a minor defect. But now we have to explain why Bresson who directed his cast so superbly in *Les Anges du péché* and *Les Dames du Bois de Boulogne* seems to handle them in this film as amateurishly as any tyro with a camera who has roped in his aunt and the family lawyer. Do people really imagine that it was easier to get Maria Casarès to play down her talent than to handle a group of docile amateurs? Certainly some scenes were poorly acted. It is odd however that these were by no means the least moving.

The fact is that this film is not to be measured by ordinary standards of acting. It is important to remember that the cast were all either amateurs or simple beginners. *Le Journal* no more approximates to *Bicycle Thieves* than to *L'Entrée des artistes*. Actually the only film it can be likened to is Carl Dreyer's *Jeanne d'Arc*. The cast is not being asked to act out a text, not even to live it out, just to speak it. It is because of this that the passages spoken off-screen so perfectly match the passages spoken by the characters on-screen. There is no fundamental difference either in tone or style. This plan of attack not only rules out any dramatic interpretation by the actors but also any psychological touches either. What we are asked to look for on their faces is not some fleeting reflection of the words but an uninterrupted condition of soul, the outward revelation of an interior destiny.

Thus this so-called badly acted film leaves us with the feeling of having seen a gallery of portraits whose expressions could not be other than they were. In this respect the most characteristic of all is of Chantal in the confessional. Dressed in black, withdrawn into the shadows, Nicole Ladmiral allows us only a glimpse of a mask, half lit, half in shadow, like a seal stamped on wax, all blurred at the edges.

Naturally Bresson, like Dreyer, is only concerned with the countenance as flesh, which, when not involved in playing a role, is a man's true imprint, the most visible mark of his soul. It is then that the countenance takes on the dignity of a sign. He would have us be concerned here not with the psychology but with the physiology of existence. Hence the hieratic tempo of the acting, the slow ambiguous gestures, the obstinate recurrence of certain behavioral patterns, the unforgettable dream-like slow motion. Nothing purely accidental could happen to these people—confirmed as each is in his own way of life, essentially concerned either against the influence of grace, to continue so, or, responding to grace, to throw off the deadly Nessus-mantle of the old Adam.

There is no development of character. Their inner conflicts, the various phases of their struggle as they wrestle with the Angel of the Lord, are never outwardly revealed. What we see is rather a concentration of suffering, the recurrent spasms of childbirth or of a snake sloughing off its skin. We can truly say that Bresson strips his characters bare.

Eschewing psychological analysis, the film in consequence lies outside the usual dramatic categories. The succession of events is not constructed according to the usual laws of dramaturgy under which the passions work towards a soul-satisfying climax. Events do indeed follow one another according to a necessary order, yet within a framework of accidental happenings. Free acts and coincidences are interwoven. Each moment in the film, each set-up, has its own due measure, alike, of freedom and of necessity. They all move in the same direction, but separately like iron filings drawn to the overall surface of a magnet. If the word tragedy comes to one's pen, it is in an opposite sense since we can only be dealing here with a tragedy freely willed. The transcendence of the Bernanos-Bresson universe is not the transcendence of destiny as the ancients understood it, nor yet the transcendence of Racinian passion, but the transcendence of grace which is something each of us is free to refuse.

If, nevertheless, the concatenation of events and the causal efficiency of the characters involved appear to operate just as rigidly as in a traditional dramatic structure, it is because they are responding to an order, of prophecy (or perhaps one should say of Kirkegaardian "repetition") that is as different from fatality as causality is from analogy.

The pattern of the film's unfolding is not that of tragedy in the usual sense, rather in the sense of the medieval Passion Play, or better still, of the Way of the Cross, each sequence being a station along that road. We are given the key to this by the dialogue in the hut between the two curés, when the one from Ambricourt reveals that he is spiritually attracted to the Mount of Olives. "Is it not enough that Our Lord should have granted me the grace of letting me know today, through the words of my old teacher, that nothing, throughout all eternity, can remove me from the place chosen by me from all eternity, that I was the prisoner of His Sacred Passion?"

Death is not the preordained end of our final agony, only its conclusion and a deliverance. Henceforth we shall know to what divine ordinance, to what spiritual rhythm the sufferings and actions of the curé respond. They are the outward representation of his agony. At which point one should indicate the analogies with Christ that abound towards the end of the film, or they may very well go unnoticed. For example, the two fainting fits during the night; the fall in the mud; the vomitings of wine and blood—a remarkable synthesis of powerful comparisons with the falls of Jesus, the Blood of the Passion, the sponge with vinegar on it, and the defiling spittle. These are not all. For the veil of Veronica we have the cloth of Seraphita; then finally the death in the attic—a Golgotha with even a good and a bad thief.

Now let us immediately put aside these comparisons, the very enumeration of which is necessarily deceptive. Their aesthetic weight derives from their theological value, but both defy explanation. Bresson like Bernanos avoids any sort of symbolic allusion and so none of the situations, despite their obvious parallel to the Gospel, is created precisely because of that parallel. Each carries its own biographical and individual meaning. Its Christ-like resemblance comes second, through being projected on to the higher plane of analogy. In no sense is it true to say that the life of the curé of Ambricourt is an imitation of its divine model; rather it is a repetition and a picturing forth of that life. Each bears his own cross and each cross is different, but all are the Cross of the Passion. The sweat on the brow of the curé is a bloody sweat.

So, probably for the first time, the cinema gives us a film in which the only genuine incidents, the only perceptible movements are those of the life of the spirit. Not only that, it also offers us a new dramatic form that is specifically religious—or better still, specifically theological; a phenomenology of salvation and grace.

It is worth noting that through playing down the psychological elements and keeping the dramatics to a minimum, Bresson is left to face two kinds of pure reality. On the one hand, as we saw, we have the countenance of the actor denuded of all symbolic expression, sheer epidermis, set in a surrounding devoid of any artifice. On the other hand there is what we must call the "written reality." Indeed, Bresson's faithfulness to the text of Bernanos, his refusal, that is, not only to adapt it but also his paradoxical concern to emphasize its literary character, is part of the same predetermined approach to the direction of his actors and the selection of his settings. Bresson treats the novel as he does his characters. The novel is a cold, hard fact, a reality to be accepted as it stands. One must not attempt to adapt it to the situation in hand, or manipulate it to fit some passing need for an explanation; on the contrary it is something to be taken absolutely as it stands. Bresson never condenses the text, he cuts it. Thus what is left over is a part of the original. Like marble from a quarry the words of the film continue to be part of the novel. Of course the deliberate emphasis on their literary character can be interpreted as a search after artistic stylization, which is the very opposite of realism. The fact is, however, that in this case the reality is not the descriptive content, moral or intellectual, of the text—it is the very text itself, or more properly, the style. Clearly the reality at one stage removed of the novel and that which the camera captures directly, cannot fit or grow together or become one. On the contrary the effect of their juxtaposition is to reaffirm their differences. Each plays its part, side by side, using the means at its disposal, in its own setting and after its own style. But it is doubtless by this separating off of elements which because of their resemblance would appear to belong together, that Bresson manages to eliminate what is accident. The ontological conflict between two orders of events, occurring simultaneously, when confronted on the screen reveal their single common measure—the soul.

Each actor says the same things and the very disparity between their expressions, the substance of what they say, their style, the kind of indifference which seems to govern the relation of actor to text, of word and visage, is the surest guarantee of their close complicity. This language which no lips could speak is, of necessity, from the soul.

It is unlikely that there exists anywhere in the whole of French cinema, perhaps even in all French literature, many moments of a more intense beauty than in the medallion scene between the curé and the Countess. Its beauty does not derive from the acting nor from the psychological and dramatic values of the dialogue, nor indeed from its intrinsic meaning. The true dialogue that punctuates the struggle between the inspired priest and a soul in despair is, of its very nature, ineffable. The decisive clashes of their spiritual fencing-match escape us. Their words announce, or prepare the way for, the fiery touch of grace. There is nothing here then of the flow of words that usually goes with a conversion, while the overpowering severity of the dialogue, its rising tension and its final calm leave us with the conviction that we have been the privileged witnesses of a supernatural storm. The words themselves are so much dead weight, the echo of a silence that is the true dialogue between these two souls; a hint at their secret; the opposite side of the coin, if one dare say so, of the Divine Countenance. When later the curé refuses to come to his own defense by producing the Countess' letter, it is not out of humility or love of suffering. It is rather because no tangible evidence is worthy to play a part either in his defence or his indictment. Of its nature the evidence of the Countess is no more acceptable than that of Chantal, and none has the right to ask God to bear witness.

The technique of Bresson's direction cannot adequately be judged except at the level of his aesthetic intention. Inadequately as we may have so far described the latter, it may yet be that the highly astonishing paradox of the film is now a little more evident. Actually the distinction of having set text over against image for the first time goes to Melville in his *Silence de la mer*. It is noteworthy that his reason was likewise a desire for fidelity. However, the structure of Vercors' book was of itself unusual. In his *Journal* Bresson has done more than justify Melville's experiment and shown how well warranted it was. He has carried it to its final conclusions.

Is *Le Journal* just a silent film with spoken titles? The spoken word, as we have seen, does not enter into the image as a realistic component. Even when spoken by one of the characters, it rather resembles the recitative of an opera. At first sight the film seems to be somehow made up on the one hand of the abbreviated text of the novel and illustrated, on the other hand, by images that never pretend to replace it. All that is spoken is not seen, yet nothing is seen that is not also spoken. At worst, critical good sense can reproach Bresson with having substituted an illustrated radiophonic montage, no less, for Bernanos's novel.

So it is from this ostensible corruption of the art of cinema that we begin if we are to grasp fully Bresson's originality and boldness.

In the first place, if Bresson "returns" to the silent film it is certainly not, despite the abundance of close-ups, because he wants to tie in again with theatrical expressionism—that fruit of an infirmity—on the contrary, it is in order to rediscover the dignity of the human countenance as understood by Stroheim and Dreyer. Now if there is one and only one quality of the silent film irreconcilable by its very nature with sound, it is the syntactical subtlety of montage and expression in the playing of the film, that is to say that which proceeds in effect from the weakness of the silent film. But not all silent films want to be such. Nostalgia for a silence that would be the benign procreator of a visual symbolism unduly confuses the so-called primacy of the image with the true vocation of the cinema—which is the primacy of the object. The absence of a soundtrack for *Greed, Nosferatu,* or *La Passion de Jeanne d'Arc* means something quite other than the silence of *Caligari, Die Nibelungen,* or *Eldorado.* It is a frustration, not the foundation of a form of expression. The former films exist in spite of their silence not because of it. In this sense the invention of the soundtrack is just a fortuitous scientific phenomenon and not the aesthetic revolution people always say it is. The language of film, like the language of Æsop, is ambiguous and in spite of appearances to the contrary, the history of cinema before and after 1928 is an unbroken continuity. It is the story of the relations between expressionism and realism. Sound was to destroy expressionism for a while before adopting it in its turn. On the other hand, it became an immediate part of the continued development of realism.

Paradoxically enough, it is to the most theatrical, that is to say to the most talkative, forms of the sound film that we must look today for a resurgence of the old symbolism while the pre-talkie realism of a Stroheim has in fact no following. Yet, it is evident that Bresson's undertaking is somehow related to the work of Stroheim and Renoir. The separating of sound and of the image to which it relates cannot be understood without a searching examination of the aesthetics of realism in sound. It is just as mistaken to see it as an illustration of a text, as a commentary on an image. Their parallelism maintains that division which is present to our senses. It continues the Bressonian dialectic between abstraction and reality thanks to which we are concerned with a single reality—that of human souls. In no sense does Bresson return to the expressionism of the silent film. On the one hand he excludes one of the components of reality in order to reproduce it, deliberately stylized on a sound track, partially independent of the image. In other words, it is as if the final re-recording was composed of sound directly recorded with scrupulous fidelity and a text post-synchronized on a monotone. But, as we have pointed out, this text is itself a second reality, a "cold aesthetic fact". Its realism is its style, while the style of the image is primarily its reality, and the style of the film is precisely the conflict between the two.

Bresson disposes once and for all of that commonplace of criticism according to which image and sound should never duplicate one another. The most moving moments in the film are those in which text and image are saying the same thing, each however in its own way. The sound never serves simply to fill out what we see. It strengthens it and multiplies it just as the echo chamber of a violin echoes and multiplies the vibrations of the strings. Yet this metaphor is dialectically inadequate since it is not so much a resonance that the mind perceives as something that does not match, as when a color is not properly superimposed on a drawing. It is here at the edge that the event reveals its true significance. It is because the film is entirely structured on this relationship that, toward the end, the images take on such emotional power. It would be vain to look for its devastating beauty simply in what is explicit. I doubt if the individual frames in any other film, taken separately, are so deceptive. Their frequent lack of plastic composition, the awkwardness and static quality of the actors completely mislead one as to their value in the overall film. Moreover, this accretion of effectiveness is not due to the editing. The value of an image does not depend on what precedes or follows it. They accumulate, rather, a static energy, like the parallel leaves of a condenser. Between this and the soundtrack differences of aesthetic potential are set up, the tension of which becomes unbearable. Thus the image-text relationship moves toward its climax, the latter having the advantage. Thus it is that, quite naturally, at the command of an imperious logic, there is nothing more that the image has to communicate except by disappearing. The spectator has been led, step by step, toward that night of the senses the only expression of which is a light on a blank screen.

That is where the so-called silent film and its lofty realism is headed, to the disappearance of the image and its replacement simply by the text of the novel. But here we are experimenting with an irrefutable aesthetic, with a sublime achievement of pure cinema. Just as the blank page of Mallarmé and the silence of Rimbaud is language at the highest state, the screen, free of images and handed back to literature, is the triumph of cinematographic realism. The black cross on the white screen, as awkwardly drawn as on the average memorial card, the only trace left by the "assumption" of the image, is a witness to something the reality of which is itself but a sign.

# "Un Condamné à mort s'est échappé": A Review

## Gavin Lambert

The subject is simple. It comes from an escape story by a member of the French secret service called André Devigny. In 1943 he was arrested and interrogated by the Gestapo at Lyons. He made an attempt to escape from a moving car while being taken to prison. It failed. Recaptured and beaten up, he was placed in solitary confinement at the prison called Fort Montluc. He was still determined to escape, only more carefully. After several weeks he managed to dissect three panels from his wooden cell door with an iron spoon that he'd sharpened against the floor. The next stage was to make a rope. The springs of his bed, uncoiled one by one, were a starting point. A parcel of shirts and pyjamas from his family arrived fortunately to be torn into strips and knotted round the springs. Months have passed now. He is ready and yet he does nothing, suddenly overtaken by an inner lethargy. It is only another interview with the Gestapo and the pronouncement of his death sentence that impel him to action. He will escape now. But a sixteen-year-old boy is put in the same cell with him. Is he an informer for the Germans? Ragged and lousy, he tells a story of hiding out and eventual capture, but he wears part of a German uniform. For two days Fontaine, as the hero is called, wonders whether to trust him or kill him. They escape together.

The book is apparently a straightforward personal record of the kind that has served as a basis for many postwar war films, most of them "dignified" and superficial. Robert Bresson uses *Un Condamné à mort s'est échappé* to make a film that is only indirectly about war, directly about a human being in isolation. The result is a work of art that raises inner experience to a very pure, intense, concentrated level. "This is a true story. I show it as it happened, without any embellishment," Bresson says characteristically in a preface. I suppose the important distinction is between "true" and "factual." One can think of many recent war films,

From *Sight and Sound,* vol. 27, no. 1 (Summer 1957). Reprinted by permission of the author.

particularly those made in Britain, which are impeccably factual and utterly untrue, because they have no angle of vision. With Bresson the vision is everything. He has changed many of the facts in Devigny's book. And he himself was taken prisoner by the Germans in 1940. During his stay in prison of more than a year, he met Father Bruckberger, who was to become an important friend and influence in his life and wrote the story for Bresson's first film, *Les Anges du péché*. Bresson has given this one an alternative title: *Le Vent souffle où il veut*.

In *Un Condamné à mort,* war is a presence felt but very little seen. We see, mainly a grey forbidding world enclosed within high medieval walls. Shabby figures move down corridors on their way to a melancholy yard or sit in a stifling cell. Violence happens offscreen, behind a closed door. Sometimes a cry is heard. The Gestapo and even the prison guards are fugitive, momentary figures. As a woman crosses the yard with a slop bucket, the sound of firing is heard. She hesitates for a moment and walks on. Inmates of the fortress, glimpsed in furtive conversation in the washroom or on the stairs, appear and disappear mysteriously. They may have been transferred, tortured, executed. One doesn't know.

The effect of war, though, is always present. It is seen in almost every face and action. It is like a developing tank in which the exposed human negative is laid. The picture comes out, character and personality have taken outline. Fontaine often talks in the washroom to a man with a thin, shifty, haunted face. He learns that he was betrayed to the Germans by his wife. The man is living with this fact in a little cell and each day he looks more desperate and unforgiving. One day he makes a futile, hysterical attempt at escape and that is the end of him. In the cell next to Fontaine's is an old man who always wears a crumpled hat. Morose and aloof, he disparages Fontaine's plans to escape. It will never work. Better to accept imprisonment and hope to escape with your neck. But on his first day in prison Fontaine also looks out from his window at a man walking in the yard. He comes up and offers to smuggle out a letter to his family. Later, he manages to get a safety pin to him which will unlock his handcuffs. Later, he disappears.

All these people come as if from nowhere and encounter each other for the first time. Some feel instinctive solidarities. Other are cautious and mistrustful. So-and-so is reported to be in the confidence of the Gestapo, so-and-so is all right, so-and-so plans to escape but his plan is no good, so-and-so was taken off for questioning today. All this in brief muttered conversations, before returning again to solitude.

So all the real dramas are interior. At the center of the story, Fontaine refuses to despair. He plans and works patiently, minutely for escape. Like the hero of *Journal d'un curé de campagne,* he is a quiet, withdrawn, compassionate man who lives at a distance from his fellows. At first they are uncertain of him, later they recognize his strength. But unlike the priest his end is not in agony but in ecstasy. With Jost, the boy, he has scaled the last wall. Jost looks round with an incredulous grin: "If my mother could see me now!" Fontaine smiles. They walk off together into a cold night, toward smoke from a train passing under a nearby bridge. It is a moment of appropriately strange and muted elation. They are going back into an occupied country and the danger is not over.

Bresson has built up this point with a slow, deliberate concentration. One might think his approach too slow for a story that also contains physical tension, but there is always an inner meaning behind the physical action and the one heightens the other. (Interesting to compare the first part of the film with the first part of Hitchcock's *The Wrong Man*. The Hitchcock is brilliant in its way, which is that of immediate melodramatic effect. He creates no *world* of prison, only a series of surface impressions.) The prison world created by Bresson suggests Kafka in some externals: gray, dreamlike routine, claustrophobia, isolation of the spirit. Yet because of the central character, the effect is never merely passive. The sequences of Fontaine preparing his escape—the iron spoon scraping at crevices in the door, the pajamas torn in strips and plaited round the bedsprings, the telltale shavings whisked out of sight as a guard approaches—are long and detailed and always exist on two levels. Behind the slow, pathetically improvised physical effort one senses the inner dedication. Bresson impregnates each action with faith. And for the first time he finds his most impressive moments in affirmation. The use of the Mass in C Minor by Mozart is a daring example. It accompanies sequences of the most drab routine—emptying of slops, the shuffles down the corridor—and transposes them to a key of pity and exaltation. For throughout this film is sounded a note, faint at first but growing louder, of the release to come.

Most remarkable of all are the closing scenes between Fontaine and Jost. They have an intimacy and implied tenderness that Bresson has never achieved before. With his worried, shifty expression, his hesitant answers and tactless questions, Jost is a wonderfully ambiguous character. Sometimes he has a strange innocence, at others one is sure he is corrupted. He is a test for Fontaine's human instincts. And the escape itself, losing none of its excitement because the film's title predicts the outcome, is also the occasion for a trust and attachment to grow up between them.

The actors are all non-professional, and all perfect. Fontaine is played by François Leterrier, formerly a student of philosophy at the Sorbonne. He has what one might call, after Claude Laydu, the "Bresson face": gentle, strong, with large, deep eyes and a mysterious, sexless authority. A clear mirror, it reflects the loneliness, vision, occasional despair, and ascetic humanity which lies at the heart of this extraordinary film.

# Luis
# Buñuel

LUIS BUÑUEL was born in Spain in 1900, studied first with the Jesuits, and then majored in science at the University of Madrid, where he met Salvador Dali and Federico Garcia Lorca. Inspired by Lang's Destiny, Buñuel went to Paris to study film, worked as an assistant to the experimental filmmaker Jean Epstein, and collaborated with Dali on Un Chien andalou (1928), like his later L'Age d'Or (1930) one of the few masterpieces of surrealist film, and an instant scandal. Breaking with Dali over the anti-Catholicism of L'Age d'Or, Buñuel pursued his interests in anticlericalism and documentary in the harsh Land Without Bread (1932), a study of the contrast between the poverty, disease, and death of the Spanish people and the lush, jewel-filled world of the Spanish Catholic Church.

Between 1932 and 1947 Buñuel directed no films. He dubbed for Paramount in Paris, supervised co-productions for Warner Brothers in Spain, and produced several Spanish films before he left Spain during the Civil War. While then living in the United States, he was director of documentaries at the Museum of Modern Art, supervised Spanish-language versions for M-G-M, made documentaries for the U.S. Army, and once again dubbed for Warners.

In 1946 Buñuel went to Mexico and there, usually in association with producer Oscar Dancigers, made a series of films among which were several that once again brought him to international attention. The greatest strength of these films of Buñuel's Mexican period draws upon a unique combination of surrealist humor, social melancholy, and strict attention to the details of Mexican life. He began to achieve an amalgamation of the factual and surrealist modes of his earlier works, perhaps given new energy by the example of Italian neo-realism and his own return to a kind of native milieu. In this context, less pressured financially and artistically, Buñuel experimented with bringing the often episodic images of surrealism and documentary into the realm of story, creating a more flexible sense of plot and narrative development. His great works of the period are Los olvidados (1950), El (1952), and the whimsically violent Criminal Life of Archibaldo de la Cruz (1955).

Buñuel returned to France in 1955 to begin three co-productions that marked his new presence on the international film scene, although he continued to work in Mexico was well, most notably with Nazarin (1958). Viridiana (1961) was his first opportunity to live and work in Spain itself, where his script was initially approved but his film later banned for its anticlerical images, despite its international recognition. Since then, each of Buñuel's films has been a new step forward, as if he were driven to make up for those lost years between Land Without Bread and his work in Mexico.

Of all the directors whose careers began in the silent period, he now *remains the most innovative and productive. Buñuel's characteristic mock-ing humor, his often discontinuous narrative structures, his preoccupation with themes of faith and belief, and an increasingly subtle and intense use of color appear in many guises through* The Exterminating Angel *(black and white, 1962),* Belle de Jour *(1966),* Tristana *(1970),* The Discreet Charm of the Bourgeoisie *(1972), and* The Phantom of Liberty *(1974). His fascination with religious heresy comes to the fore in* Simon of the Desert *(1965) and* The Milky Way *(1969). His interest in adapting novels, begun with* Robinson Crusoe *(1952) and* Wuthering Heights *(1953), appears again in* The Diary of a Chambermaid *(1964). All his works are preoc-cupied with the varieties of sexuality and repression. They make use of Christian motifs and images to attack Christianity, and they apply an intensely real and concrete treatment to essentially absurd and surreal situations. His most recent work, made in France, is* That Obscure Object of Desire *(1977).*

*An excellent life of Buñuel has been written by Francisco Aranda (1969; in English, 1975); it includes an anthology of his writings. Critical studies include works by Ado Kyrou (1963), Raymond Durgnat (1968), and Freddy Buache (1973). Shorter studies of his career are found in John Russell Taylor,* Cinema Eye, Cinema Ear *(1964), and Peter Harcourt,* Six European Directors *(1974). A collection of essays on Buñuel has been edited by Joan Mellen (1978).*

# The Discreet Charm of Luis Buñuel

## Carlos Fuentes

There exist two tinted photographs of Buñuel as a child. In one of them, dressed in white and holding a beribboned white candle, he prepares for First Communion. In the other, clad in a velvet Lord Fauntleroy suit, he is a charming and discreet little bourgeois gazing with bulging eyes at the surviving ruins of Spain. Buñuel was born in 1900, two years after a most traumatic national experience: the loss of the remnants of empire in the war with the United States, the final collapse of the rigid design of the Counter Reformation. The "critical generation" of 1898 had set about dissecting the national corpse. Ortega y Gasset spoke of an "unvertebrated Spain" and tried to revive her brain with the thick blood of modern German philosophy. Santiago Ramon y Cajal introduced modern scientific methods. And while Europe fought the war that ended the illusion of unlimited peace and progress under liberal bourgeois rule, all these renovating trends met at the students' residence in the University of Madrid.

Federico García Lorca and Rafael Alberti, Salvador Dali and Luis Buñuel: Spain would speak again, Spain would see again. The campus revolutionaries read Marx and Engels, Dostoevski and Freud. And they had a sense of humor: Buñuel and Lorca would shave closely, powder their faces, dress in nun's garb and board tramways, winking at the male passengers, nudging them with hips and elbows as panic crept. Some, like Lorca, had to stay on in Spain and dig into the roots, later to surface with the poetic images buried under the necrophilic tons of granite at the Escorial. Others, like Buñuel, felt that they could only understand the Spanish crisis from the viewpoint of the European crisis. Buñuel packed his Aragonian burro and trotted over the Pyrenees to join the surrealist revolution in Paris.

Excerpted from *The New York Times Magazine*, March 11, 1973. © 1973 by The New York Times Company. Reprinted by permission.

See anew, think anew, mock and scandalize your way through the trembling cardboard facades of the old, positivist, capitalist, academic order; proclaim on Anatole France's death that a corpse has just died; insult the likes of the poet Paul Claudel and the St. Cyr Military Academy; remember your friends stupidly butchered on the Marne and Verdun battlefields; vilify and destroy a society of hypocritical exploiters. All power to dreams, all power to love, all power to the subconscious; spring from false, everyday "reality" to the superreality where the impossible opposites—dream and vigil, art and life, politics and morality, good and evil, saint and demon, man and woman—are once more, as in the origins of being, united, one.

The roster was immense: André Breton and Louis Aragon, Tristan Tzara and Max Ernst, Giorgio de Chirico and Benjaim Péret, Pablo Picasso and Francis Picabia, Marcel Duchamp and Joan Miró, Paul Eluard and Man Ray, Hans Arp and Yves Tanguy. The space was limited: From the Place Blanche in Montmartre to the cafes on the Boulevard Montparnasse. The achievements were extraordinary: The elements of vision and speech were dissembled and associated anew, and poems, paintings, sculptures, plays, magazines, manifestos and mischievous happenings came crashing through the rusty cracks of the *Belle Epoque*.

For a time Buñuel neither painted, wrote nor composed. Apart from being a competent boxer and entomologist, he could dabble in stage direction with Falla's *Puppet Show of Maese Pedro* at the Amsterdam Opera; he could scribble a few movie reviews for the surrealist magazines (but his thematic choices would be significant: Stroheim and Keaton); he could even become Jean Epstein's assistant in the filming of *Mauprat* and *The Fall of the House of Usher*. But in 1928, he obtained a loan from his mother, called in his boyhood friend Dali and made *An Andalusian Dog*. Cyril Connolly was at one of the first showings and said that the effect of excitement and liberation was indescribable. He added that the spectators had been offered the first vision of the fires of disenchantment and madness that smoldered under the complacent postwar world. Nurses were on hand to assist people in the audience who might faint when the eyeball of that impudent flapper gets slashed by a razor as the moon is crossed by a drifting cloud. Pianos are stuffed with dead donkeys and with a ballast of struggling Jesuits strangled by horse's reins; pale hermaphrodites are run down by speeding cars on indifferent boulevards; a man erases his lips, and a woman's pubic hair sprouts on his face, and this in turn liberates the following image, which is a black sea urchin; striped boxes contain mutilated hands; hands are full of swarming ants; fourth floor apartment doors open on wintry beaches where the dummies of lovers will rot this coming spring, buried chest-high in the sand. . . . Free association, said Buñuel and

Dali; no preconceived ideas, pure poetic freedom. But the images *were* inspired by psychoanalysis, and most of them drifted off in the direction of Dali's future paintings.

The first break with Dali came on the first day of shooting *L'Age d'Or,* their second joint venture. They got the money from a Parisian angel called the Comtesse de Noailles, who at the same time was financing Cocteau's *Le Sang d'un poète.* The Castor-and-Pollux relationship between the two Spaniards seems to have been severely damaged when Dali fell in love with Gala, Paul Eluard's wife, and Buñuel tried to strangle the lady on a rock at Cadaqués because he saw in her a diabolical influence. In any case Dali stayed on the set of *L'Age d'Or* for exactly one day. From then on, it was Buñuel on his own, and this, the greatest of the surrealist films and one of the most personal and original works in the history of the cinema, is also a primer of Buñuelian obsessions, procedures, manias and illuminations:

A scientific prologue on the ways of the scorpion gives way to the arrival by launch of a party of bankers, officials and philanthropic dowagers who disembark on a barren beach where the littered skeletons of popes and bishops have become gigantic rock formations, and there they proceed to lay the cornerstone of Western civilization on a pile of excrement—and to murder the original inhabitants, a group of guerilla-fighters. Which leads us to modern-day Rome and what is certainly the first critique of the consumer society ever. The hero (Gaston Modot) who has been dreaming the previous scene, is now actually being led by two policemen; he is accused of making love in a dream, and his eyes wander over advertisements that further entice his erotic appetites: cosmetics, women's stockings and underwear. Excited by the lustful call of the economy, he decides to have his pleasure at once; but the object of his desire, a dreamy-eyed nymph of the upper classses (Lya Lys) is safely ensconced in her father's house, and that worthy gentleman is hosting a concert of Wagnerian music to a packed garden of attentive society leaders.

To get to her, the hero must kick animals, humiliate the maimed, batter down doors and destroy property with the anarchical fury of James Finlayson doing battle against Laurel and Hardy. He is as indifferent as the concert guests to the brutal murder of a child by her gamekeeper father; he slaps a dignified matron on the face; pulls the orchestra leader's white beard and finally rapes the girl (who all this time has been sucking the toe of a marble statue) on the garden gravel as the *Liebestod* surges to its climax and, desire achieved, disillusion sets in. The silken nymph becomes a big cow seated on the connubial bed; old age arrives; the temple of the body is in ruins; the garden of sex withers; snow falls and the scene shifts violently to the snowbound castle of the Marquis de Sade's *One Hundred*

suicide and a debauched parody of Christ's last supper. The Spanish censors were summarily dismissed from their jobs; the film was banned in Spain. And Buñuel had won an international audience.

Two twin parables open and close the most recent period of his work, and both are intimately linked to the theme of survival. The first was *The Exterminating Angel,* or how to escape from an endless supper party: After a night at the opera, a group of upper-class Mexicans meet for dinner and then find that, for some unexplained reason, they cannot leave their host's house or communicate with the outside world—as isolated as shipwrecks, they unlock their true nature, their moral cannibalism, while the social code breaks down. The last was *The Discreet Charm of the Bourgeoisie,* or how to get together for an impossible meal: The six elegant characters constantly plan to get together for a series of gastronomical feasts, but the very act of eating is constantly interrupted by myriad invasions of the rational and irrational facts of their lives—illicit love affairs, drug smuggling, army maneuvers, menaces from Latin American guerrillas, dreams told by total strangers in coffee shops that have run out of coffee, dreams they dream themselves, dreams they dream another one has dreamed.

In between them, he made *Simon of the Desert,* depicting the useless gesture of a man perched on top of his column like a theological Jonathan Seagull, masochistically invoking his own temptations and ending, in the Devil's company, in a New York discothèque. Jeanne Moreau wryly battled her way up from the kitchen and employed her employer's lusts and fantasies in *Diary of a Chambermaid* and Catherine Deneuve dreamily battled her way down to the whorehouse in that marvelous blending of reality and imagination, fate and desire in the mirror of a woman's erotic fantasies that is *Belle de Jour. The Milky Way* portrayed an ambiguous pilgrimage, cutting through times and spaces, in search of lost heresy. Buñeul's most intimate, autobiographical, Spanish, provincial movie was *Tristana,* with its immediate, tangible symbols of fear, deception, mutual damnation and ridiculous social convention.

*Seeing:* In his sixties, Buñuel finally achieved the choice of subject matter, the means, the creative freedom so long denied him. But Buñuel has always proved hardier than the minimal or optimal conditions of production offered him; he constantly remarks that, given a $5-million budget, he would still film a $500,000 movie. An obsessive artist, Buñuel cares about what he wants to say; or rather, what he wants to see. A really important director makes only one film; his work is a sum, a totality of perfectly related parts that illuminate each other. In Buñuel's films, from *An Andalusian Dog* to *The Discreet Charm of the Bourgeoisie,* the essential unifying factor is sight. His first image is that of a woman's eye slit by a razor and throughout the body of his work there is this pervading sense of sight menaced, sight lost as virginity is lost; sight as a wound that will not heal, wounded sight as an interstice through which dreams and desires can flow. Catherine Deneuve's absent regard in *Belle de Jour* is calculated: She is constantly looking outside the confines of the screen, enlarging the space of the screen, looking at something beyond that isn't there, that probably connects the two halves of her life.

But Buñuel's violent aggressions against sight actually force us back to his particular way of seeing. His world is seen first as a grey, hazy, distant jumble of undetermined things; no other director shoots a scene from quite that neutral, passive distance. Then the eye of the camera suddenly picks out an object that has been there all the time, or a revealing gesture, zooms into them, makes them come violently alive before again retiring to the indifferent point of view.

This particular way of seeing, of making the opaque backdrop shine instantly by selecting an object or gesture, assures the freedom and fluid elegance of a Buñuel film. Sight determines montage; what is seen flows into what is unseen. The camera fixes on a woman's ankle or the buzzing box a Korean takes to a brothel; the woman's shoes lead to desire or the Korean's stare to mystery, mystery and desire to dream, dream to a dream within it and the following cut back to everyday normality has already compounded reality with the fabulous; the meanest, most violent or weakest character has achieved a plurality of dimensions that straight realism would never reveal. The brutal gang leader in *Los olvidados* is redeemed by his dream of fright and solitude: A black dog silently races down a rainy street at night. And you cannot altogether hate the stupid, avaricious people in the *The Discreet Charm;* their dreams are too funny; they are endowed with a reluctantly charming dimension: they are doomed, yet they survive.

Cruel and destructive: Such were the adjectives reserved for his early films; now they are elegant and comical. Has the dynamite-flinging miner of Asturias, as Henry Miller called him, mellowed so much? On the contrary: I believe his technique has simply become more finely honed, his sense of inclusiveness through sight wider. More things are seen, understood, laughed at and perhaps forgiven. Besides, the author is debating himself. Is that a Buñuel stand-in who drones in *The Milky Way*: "My hatred towards science and technology will surely drive me back to the despicable belief in God"?

Sight connects. Buñuel has filmed the story of the first capitalist hero, Robinson Crusoe, and Crusoe is saved from loneliness by his slave, but the price he must pay is fraternity, *seeing* Friday as a human being. He has also filmed the story of Robinson's descendants in *The Discreet Charm,* and these greedy, deceptive people can only flee their overpopulated, polluted, promiscuous island into the comic loneliness of their dreams. Sight and survival, desires and dreams, seeing others in order to see oneself. This parabola of sight is essential to Buñuel's art. Nazarin will not see God unless he sees his fellow men; Viridiana will not see herself unless she sees outside herself and accepts the world. The characters in *The Discreet Charm* can never see themselves or others. They may be funny, but they are already in hell. Elegant humor only cloaks despair.

So in Buñuel sight determines content or, rather, content is a way of looking, content is sight at all possible levels. And this multitude of levels—social, political, psychological, historical, esthetic, philosophic— is not predetermined, but flows from vision. His constant tension is between obsessive opposites: pilgrimage and confinement, solitude and fraternity, sight and blindness, social rules and personal cravings, rational conduct and oneiric behavior. His intimate legacies, often conflicting, are always there: Spain, Catholicism, surrealism, left anarchism. But, above all, what is always present is the liberating thrust that could only come from such a blend of heritages. Certainly no other filmmaker could have so gracefully and violently humanized and brought into the fold of freedom, rebellion and understanding so many figures, so many passions, so many desires that the conventional code judges as monstrous, criminal and worthy of persecution and, even, extermination. The poor are not forcibly good and the rich are not forcibly evil; Buñuel incriminates all social orders while liberating our awareness of the outcast, the deformed, the maimed, the necrophiles, the lesbians, the homosexuals, the fetishists, the incestuous, the whorish, the cruel children, the madmen, the poets, the forbidden dreamers. He never exploits this marginality, because he makes it central to his vision. He has set the highest standards for true cinematic freedom.

And finally, this respect for freedom of his characters is translated into respect for the freedom of his audience. As they end, his films remain open, the spectator remains free. A flock of sheep enter the church of *The Exterminating Angel* as civil strife explodes in the streets. An empty carriage rolls down a wooded lane while the horses' bells jingle in *Belle de Jour*. Nazarin accepts a gift of a pineapple from a humble woman as the drums of Calanda start pounding and the whole structure of the priest's mind turns and opens toward the future. Viridiana sits down and plays cards with her cousin and the cook as they listen to rock recordings. A bell with the face of her victim and victimizer telescopes Tristana back to the very beginning of her story. The mad husband in *El* zigzags his way down a monastery garden where he thinks he has achieved peace of mind. The six listless characters in *The Discreet Charm*, driven by an irrational urge, trudge down an unending highway.

If the end in a Buñuel film can mean exactly the contrary, the beginnings of his films can be terrifying. *L'Age d'Or* starts with a scorpion and that scorpion, encircled by fire, is committing suicide with its own poisonous tail. It is the center of a flaming eye. Buñuel has written: "The camera is the eye of the marvelous. When the eye of the cinema really sees, the whole world goes up in flames."

# Buñuel's Mexican Films

## John Russell Taylor

Let us look next at the five highly personal works Buñuel succeeded in making entirely within the framework of the Mexican commercial cinema up to 1955, when he returned briefly to France to make a film and entered a more confused (and confusing) phase of international co-productions. The first of them, *Subida al Cielo* (1951) turned out, surprisingly enough at first glance, to be a light-hearted peasant comedy, written by the poet Manuel Altolaguirre, about a bus journey in which a young innocent learns something of life.* But there is, finally, no reason why we should be surprised at the old surrealist Buñuel turning to this sort of material, for what emerges is not at all the sort of *Bread, Love and . . .* piece it might have been in other hands, but a picaresque tale full of fantastic invention, revelling in the unexpected, the gleeful reversal of an audience's expectations which characterized surrealism even at its most serious, and mixing dream and reality in the bland, unselfconscious way which only Buñuel has achieved in the cinema (by comparison Cocteau seems positively heavy-handed). In this context even the outrageously cardboard rocks through which a very evidently model bus is sometimes seen travelling become quite acceptable and even (though this surely cannot have been part of the original intention) curiously apt to the fantastic world the film creates.

The purpose of the journey for the film's hero, Oliverio, is to bring back a lawyer from a town the other side of the mountains to draw up a new will for his mother which will disinherit his no-good layabout brothers. Called from his own wedding celebrations to carry out his mother's dying wish, he sets out in the local bus with a motley collection of passengers, while his brothers merrily carouse with the Mayor ("Well," says one of

---

*Subida al Cielo*, which literally means "ascent to heaven," was released in the United States under the title *Mexican Bus Ride*. —Eds.

them, "you only have one mother, and she only dies once"). On the bus is a glamorous blonde in an off-the-shoulder blouse who sends Oliverio off immediately into an erotic fantasy in which they make love in a bus overgrown with exotic jungle vegetation. On the way to the town the bus driver makes a detour to visit his old mother on her birthday and all the passengers are welcomed to the celebration; a woman passenger has a baby; Oliverio, driving on apparently by himself from the party to complete his errand, finds the blonde hiding in the bus and they make love there, immobilized in a thunderstorm on "Subida al Cielo," a high pass in the mountains the bus has to traverse. The lawyer, when Oliverio arrives, refuses to come back with him, but sends the necessary papers, which will need only the mother's fingerprint. On the way back a group of peasants get on with a dead child in a coffin, bitten by a viper (accidental or deliberate reference to *Las Hurdes*?). The passengers join in the funeral with as good a will as on the outward journey they joined in the celebration. On his arrival back Oliverio finds his mother already dead, but appends her fingerprint to the papers so that her wishes will be carried out, and then, at long last, a wiser but hardly a sadder man, returns to his waiting bride.

The tone of the film throughout is joyously pagan, full of fresh, physical delights and unashamed acceptance of the way human beings are (Oliverio's infidelity with the girl on the bus is coolly accepted as a perfectly natural occurrence of no particular importance, and no one shows any sign of guilt over it). Birth, marriage and death, celebration and mourning, all just happen because that's the way things are, as natural events on the journey, and even Buñuel's habitual side-swipes at the Church and organized religion (Oliverio seems to be a happy, natural man largely because he comes from a village without a church, and it can hardly be accidental that his infidelity on his wedding night takes place in a location called "The Ascent to Heaven") are light and jovial. *Subida al Cielo*, in fact, gives the impression of being a film made for sheer delight in film-making: Buñuel's technique has never been more simple or unobtrusive; it is almost negligent except that the simplicity is inspired, and the rough edges (evident model-shots and so on) come precisely at the places where they do not matter. When there is something that has to be very precisely managed—you can't, after all, be careless with jokes—it is handled properly: the whole sequence in which the bus gets stuck in the river mud and is finally drawn out by two oxen led by a tiny girl with a piece of string, leaving a passenger with a wooden leg firmly stuck in his turn in the mud, is staged and shot with the exact comic timing of a born humorist—a quality to be usefully in evidence in more than one of Buñuel's subsequent works.

After *Subida al Cielo*, with the evident affinity of its story to an eighteenth-century picaresque novel, there seems a curious rightness in Buñuel's turning to the real thing for the subject of his next major work. Or there would be if the novel selected, Defoe's *Robinson Crusoe,* did not clearly represent at once, neatly combined, a collection of attitudes as violently antipathetic to all Buñuel's ideas as one could off-hand conceive. For Crusoe is, according to his lights and his period, the completely conventional man: Christian, moralistic even, the captive of reason, convinced of the superior mission of "civilization." His whole aim on his desert island is to rebuild his European prison for himself, to reproduce in little the whole system from which his abandonment there has apparently rescued him. Whatever could appear to Buñuel in this? How, even given that he did not choose the subject, could he make a straightforward commercial chore of it without compromising the principles he himself had put forward?

The answer, though hardly anyone seems to have noticed it at the time (perhaps because *Robinson Crusoe* is the sort of book most people vaguely know about rather than actually read) is that in filming it Buñuel neatly reverses practically all the points made in the book. Preserving carefully enough the outline of events, Buñuel has turned their significance inside out, and instead of Defoe's triumphant picture of reason ordering hostile nature he gives us instead a penetrating study of solitude breaking down a "reasonable" man as he tries desperately to bolster his own progressively more shaky beliefs by a hopeless and largely absurd adherence to the external forms of a way of life which has no relevant to his present situation. To do this Buñuel has to add various things to the original narrative, most importantly a sexual element almost entirely lacking—a defect hopefully supplied a few years back with a mildly pornographic Traveller's Companion volume called *The Sexual Life of Robinson Crusoe.* The film might also be called *The Sexual Life of Robinson Crusoe,* for though it is not exclusively devoted to that the theme runs through, coloring everything: Crusoe's dreams, his reactions to Friday's innocent dressing-up in women's clothes, and especially the marvelous scene in which a dress used to shade Crusoe from the sun becomes transfigured in his eyes into something living and desirable. Also, in Buñuel's transformation of Defoe much which appears to be taken over almost literally from the book becomes unexpectedly modified by its context: the irony of Crusoe's attempts to civilize Friday (his first action being to chain him) is unmistakably brought out, and the values attributed to religion in the book are so altered that instead of its being one of the main things to keep Crusoe sane in his trials we appreciate rather that its failure to help him even though he clings desperately to its forms is one of the main factors in driving him mad (or nearly): the words of the psalm, when he shouts them in the valley of the echoes, are not of comfort in themselves, but just meaningless sounds whose echoes from the hills around reassure him that at least he still exists.

*Robinson Crusoe* being (perhaps fortunately) totally misunderstood as a film, it gained wide success and even at one stage presented British filmgoers with the surprising spectacle of a Buñuel film showing the local Rank circuit cinema in a double bill with a new de Sica (*Indiscretion*). But meanwhile Buñuel went on making Mexican films designed, initially and primarily, to satisfy Mexican audiences. And the very next, *El,* proved one of his strangest and most personal works, as well as one of his most popular in Mexico, where it was taken by most people as a conventional melodrama about jealousy. *El* has been described as a realistic remake of *L'Age d'Or,* and the description, though exaggerated, has enough truth in it to be worth investigating more closely. The film is a story of jealousy, based loosely on a popular and apparently fairly conventional novel by Mercedes Pinto. But just as *Robinson Crusoe* took a given story-line and carried it further, explored deeper into things hardly hinted at in the book, so *El* turns little by little into a scathing indictment of Christianity and the social order for turning aside natural passions from their natural course, by perverting them in the cause of conventional morality.

The central character, Francisco, is an obedient son of the Church, a man of the highest moral character. All this is succinctly established in the opening scene, where he is shown assisting in an elaborate and curious church ceremony in which a priest washes and then kisses the feet of a dozen youths; from their feet Francisco's glance travels to a pair of shapely feet in the congregation, then up the legs to take in the face and figure of a beautiful young woman. He is at once obsessed with her, follows her but obtains no response, and takes to haunting the church in the hope of seeing her again. Thus in the space of a few shots Buñuel manages to convey with superb economy Francisco's character and situation as well as the ambiguity of his religious interests: the sensuality of the penitential ritual, with its strong sado-masochistic eroticism, is carefully stressed, and the transition to the overt eroticism of Francisco's sudden interest in the girl is so casually done that its full implications only occur to one later. And ambiguity rapidly becomes direct hypocrisy when Francisco, the perfect churchgoer, begins without apparent qualm to go to church only in hope of making an assignation.

Not that it is as simple as that; Francisco is over forty, and still completely celibate—if the girl who obsesses him so much is to be anything to him she must be his wife. Finding that she is the fiancée of a friend, he carries her off and marries her without a second thought, but passions so long dammed up cannot just flow clear and free. Francisco is too deeply indoctrinated: he does not, like Modot in *L'Age d'Or,* require physical intervention from outside to prevent the proper realization of his desires, since all that is needed is already deeply ingrained in him. Consequently he invents the intervention. He is chronically, insanely jealous. He torments his wife with questions on their wedding night, suspects an innocent bystander, a slight acquaintance of his wife, whom they meet on their honeymoon, of spying on them (he jabs knitting-needles through the keyhole at one point, quite expecting to find an eye impaled on the other end) and of being a past lover of his Gloria. When they get back he throws her into the arms of a lawyer handling a case for him, with instructions that she is to be specially nice to him, and then accuses of her of making him her lover. When she complains, Gloria's mother and the Church both send her back to her husband with elevating but useless instructions. Francisco's behaviour grows madder and madder: sometimes he covers Gloria with passionate affection, at others he threatens to throw her from a high tower, weeps on his valet's shoulder, roams the house at night beating a tattoo with a stair-rod on the bannisters, menaces Gloria with a needle and thread (a direct reference to an episode in de Sade's *La Philosophie dans le boudoir*) and finally suffers a complete mental breakdown in a church to which he has pursued a couple he wrongly believes to be Gloria and her former fiancé. Imagining that the congregation, the choir and the priest are obscenely mocking him (an extraordinary piece of objective-subjective intercutting on Buñuel's part) he tries to strangle the priest, and is carried off to be cared for by the Church. Years later we see him, as Gloria, her new husband and her children come to ask after him; he is supposed to be quite cured, but as he walks away he is still walking in zigzags, as he did at the height of his delusions.

*El* is one of the most bitter, and the most frenziedly intense, of all Buñuel's films. His denunciation of Christianity, both directly and indirectly, through the portrait of the "good Christian" Francisco, has never been so uncompromising, and the transposition of the message of *L'Age d'Or* to a superficially realistic setting if anything increases its power. Incidentally, Buñuel, though he claims to be largely unconscious of what he has put into his films until they are made, would seem to have been aware of the correspondence, since there are things in *El*—the clouds of dust from the neighbouring room during the dinner party at which Francisco entraps Gloria; the party later on, ripe for the tumbrils to grind their way through it—which can hardly be anything but deliberate reminiscences. *El* is also, perhaps necessarily, Buñuel's most elaborate film technically: the overheated mind of Francisco, his inextricable mingling of fantasy and reality, is allowed to work on the spectator in a number of scenes through the use of technical devices usually confined by Buñuel to dream sequences; especially in the church sequence near the end, where we are shown in rapid alternation the priest, choir and congregation as they are and as they appear to Francisco, grimacing and mocking him. But Buñuel's talent for the extremely simple, unobtrusively right has not deserted him either; the sequences of the knitting needles and the midnight sewing are all the more nightmarish and terrifying for being recorded quite calmly and straightforwardly, even remotely, with something of the documentary quality we noticed in *Las Hurdes.*

The last film of this Mexican period, *La vida criminal de Archibaldo de la Cruz* (or *Ensayo de un crimen,* as it is sometimes called), is a sort of comic counterpart to *El,* and one of the most delectable of all Buñuel's films. Of course, it would be possible to see even *El* as a *comédie noire;* there are, in any case, at least moments of ghastly humour in it. But *Archibaldo de la Cruz* is unmistakably a comedy all through, though like *El* it is a study of obsession, and on the face of it an even more sinister one than Francisco's. As the result of a childhood experience Archibaldo finds desire and death indissolubly linked in his life. Told as a little boy that a musical box he has been given can bring death to anyone he wishes dead, he experiments on his governess, who is promptly killed by a stray bullet from a revolution going on in the street (there is an extraordinary image of the child watching the blood run down under her skirts). When by chance he comes across the musical box again—he is now grown up and a famous potter—the link becomes explicit in his consciousness, and the film follows a succession of disastrous attempts on his part to realize his desires by killing their immediate object, without the slightest success, since somehow his plans are always anticipated or frustrated and the police will not accept his confession. First his unsubtle attempt on a nursing sister terrifies her so much she promptly falls down a lift-shaft. Then he marries a girl of good family knowing her to have had a lover and imagining in lushly sadistic detail their wedding-night confrontation and his *crime passionel,* but alas her former lover kills her first. Finally his plot to kill another girl and incinerate her body in his potter's kiln is frustrated when a group of tourists arrive to look round his workroom, and he is reduced to burning a wax mannequin in her place. Realizing at last that it is the spell of the past, represented by the musical box, which is rendering him impotent, he throws it into the river and is cured; about to crush an insect in the park with his cane (a characteristic touch), he refrains, and goes off happily with the girl of the last sequence; for him at least the obsession is disposed of, and after the bad dreams are over he can wake to normal life.

In Archibaldo's case the obsession is seen as a personal matter, the results of an accidental juxtaposition of events in childhood, rather than, as in Francisco's case, as the result of a whole training, a way of life in a

particular religion and a particular social set-up. Hence the relative lightness of the tone; *La vida criminal de Archibaldo de la Cruz* is quite sunny,
the humor residing largely in the classic device (an example offering a
number of parallels which may have influenced Buñuel is to be found in
Preston Sturges's *Unfaithfully Yours*) of showing first of all the way the
plotter thinks things will go and then deflating this ideal picture with the
unforeseeable actuality, in which, of course, everything goes wrong for all
sorts of tiresome, trivial reasons. Buñuel's gifts of fantastic invention have
seldom been so happily (in both senses of the term) employed as in some
sequences here, notably the childhood reminiscence, with the boy dressing
up in his mother's clothes, the wedding reception, and the group of chattering tourists who break into his best-laid scheme.

With *Archibaldo de la Cruz* Buñuel broke the sequence of his Mexican films, but before it he made one more film which deserves brief
comment, a version of *Wuthering Heights* variously called *Cumbres Borrascosas* or *Abismos de pasion* (1953). Buñuel himself tends to reject this
as an anachronism, which in a sense it was, being virtually a literal realization of the script prepared as long before as 1932 in collaboration with
Georges Sadoul and Pierre Unik (with Katharine Hepburn in mind!).
Nevertheless it is remarkable on several counts. For one thing it is, despite
the changes of name and location, a brilliantly clearheaded and faithful
piece of adaptation, far superior to Ben Hecht's and Charles MacArthur's
much-praised script for the Wyler version: it starts with Heathcliff's return
and sweeps the spectator straight into the central conflict in Cathy's soul.
But apart from this it has a number of striking ideas—like Edgar's butterfly
collecting—and several remarkable sequences, notably Heathcliff's brutal
wooing of Isabella before Cathy's eyes on the bare mountainside and the
fantastic finale of *amour fou* (the adaptors' principal liberty with their text)
whereby Heathcliff breaks into Cathy's grave in the family vault and is shot
dead embracing her lifeless body. *Wuthering Heights* was always a favorite
work of the surrealists, and here an old surrealist has paid a surprising
but remarkably effective tribute to it.

# "Viridiana" and "Belle de Jour"

## Andrew Sarris

### "Viridiana"

*Viridiana* has a plot that is almost too lurid to synopsize even in these enlightened times. The heroine is summoned from a convent by her uncle, Don Jaime, an old Spanish *hidalgo* living on a neglected estate (Spain?) in obsessive mourning for his dead wife (the Republic?). The novice arrives on the thirtieth anniversary of Don Jaime's marriage. Viridiana's resemblance to the *hidalgo*'s wife introduces the theme of substitution so dear to Hitchcock, but Buñuel is less concerned with the illusion of the substitution than with the sexual drives aroused by it. Failing to persuade his niece to marry him, Don Jaime orders a compliant maid to drug her. He carries her upstairs to the accompaniment of *The Messiah* while Buñuel intensifies the outrageous eroticism of the situation by photographing the choreography of abduction through the prying eyes of the maid's little girl. Almost inexplicably, Don Jaime desists from the attempted rape. The morning after, in progressive stages of desperation, he tells his outraged niece that she has been violated, then denies the violation, outraging her even more with his mendacity, and after watching her departure, hangs himself. Viridiana returns to atone for her guilt, and the second movement of the film begins with the maid's little girl skipping with the rope that has been the instrument of the *hidalgo*'s deliverance.

The incestuous texture of the film is maintained with the entrance of the novice's virile cousin, Jorge, a pragmatist of the most ruthless kind. He discards his mistress to pursue Viridiana more efficiently, but willingly seduces the adoring maid in the interim. While Jorge is patching up the estate in slapdash Spanish fashion, Viridiana is pursuing the Franciscan ethic by adopting the most revolting beggars in the area. Buñuel intercuts the Angelus recited by Viridiana and her scabrous flock with detail shots of Jorge's rebuilding. Buñuel's despair for Spain leads him to dismiss reform as a possibility; Jorge is moved by humane feelings to purchase a dog that is chained under a cart and forced to trot along at a horse's pace. No sooner is the "liberal" purchase consummated than another dog comes trotting by under another cart going in the opposite direction on the same Spanish road, reversing the pattern of futility. The demolition of Viridiana's principles is reserved for the film's remarkable climax.

The beggar's orgy is set up dramatically by the departure of Viridiana, Jorge, the maid and her little girl on business in the town. For the first time the beggars move into the house itself, and they assault every sacred feeling of property that any audience could be presumed to possess. Wine and food smear fancy tapestries, antique furniture is smashed, ornate dishes and glasses are broken. But unlike their colleagues in depravity from *La dolce vita,* the beggars enjoy themselves, and suddenly, with *The Messiah* blaring on the phonograph, the screen reverberates with a hymn to liberation. These vile creatures (and Buñuel leaves no doubt of their vileness, their cruelty, even their mean hypocrisy), these blind, halt, leprous, syphilitic dregs become gloriously human.

When Viridiana and Jorge return, they are assaulted, and Viridiana's slowly vanishing purity is saved only when her cousin bribes one of the beggars to murder the would-be rapist. Deciding that two lives are too high a price to pay for her chastity, Viridiana casts her cross and her crown of thorns into the flames and prepares to surrender to Jorge. The production's government supervisor, who must have been dozing until this point, finally intervened. Viridiana and Jorge must not be left alone in a room after this, he ordered. Buñuel dutifully complied with a *ménage-à-trois* ending in which Jorge, Viridiana, and the maid play cards together in the long Spanish evening while the camera recedes on the hellish tableau to the accompaniment of some appropriate American jukebox slop.

How Buñuel managed to realize *Viridiana* at all under the Spanish censor may never be fully explained. The intangibles of national prestige may have played a part. Also, the myopic vision of the bureaucratic mind may not have fully grasped the almost magical transformation of images into ideas between shooting and screening. It would be naïve to think that Buñuel was without guile in this undertaking. The deviousness of his subsequent interviews was worthy of Hitchcock, and there is enough ambiguity in the film itself to confound the most perverse critics. For example, there seems to be some controversy about the fate of the beleaguered heroine. To put it bluntly, is Viridiana, the chaste novice in the film, actually raped by the syphilitic beggar who murders her first attacker? If so, does she then renounce her vows of chastity as result of a D. H. Lawrence awakening? The argument for this interpretation depends upon the time gap assumed in the editing of the action. The fact that Buñuel compels normally fastidious critics to ponder such lurid questions reflects the dark humor that rescues him from the absurdities of Ichikawa.

Whether or not Buñuel has circumvented the censor with suggestive elisions, the plot of *Viridiana* gives one pause. The modern cinema, such as it is presumed to be, is supposed to have supplanted plot with mood. Then suddenly Buñuel bursts in like a resurrected Victorian novelist steeped in violent depravity and unashamedly flourishing the most obvious symbols. The spectacle of a contemporary director cutting away metaphorically from a brutal seduction to a cat pouncing on a mouse jolts the critic who has finally adjusted to the languorous introspection of an Antonioni. Then, too, the flagrant display of eroticism, sadism, and fetishism reveals the director's personality with the embarrassing Krafft-Ebing frankness one recalls in the films of Stroheim and Lang. Bruñuel may have been more shocking in the past, but never before have his shock effects seemed so much the warp and woof of his philosophy. *Un Chien andalou* and *L'Age d'Or* have their moments, of course, but audiences are usually cushioned for "avant-garde" cinema, where anything goes. *Las Hurdes* (*Land Without Bread*) and *Los olvidados* (*The Young and the Damned*) mask details of horror with a socially conscious narration. Even though it is hard to imagine any other director conceiving of a mountain goat falling off a mountain or a legless beggar being rolled down a hill, the spectator can console himself with the thought that this is not the best of all possible worlds and the next election or the next revolution may improve conditions. There is no such consolation in *Viridiana,* Buñuel's despairing allegory of the Spanish condition. For the first time in his career Buñuel ends his action in an existential enclosure in which hell, in Sartre's phrase, is other people.

If every director must be assigned a political station, Buñuel is unmistakably a man of the left. He actively supported the Spanish Republic against Franco's insurgents, and he has been highly critical of the Establishments in Mexico, America, and France. A story is told about Buñuel, perhaps apocryphal but still relevant. It seems that Jean Epstein, with whom Buñuel began his career in 1926, once offered his Spanish assistant an opportunity to work with Abel Gance. Buñuel reportedly refused because of what he considered Gance's fascist leanings. Epstein, a Gallic product of apolitical *amitié,* was outraged, but Buñuel stood his ground. Later Buñuel had a falling out with Salvador Dali over the sacrilegious treatment of *L'Age d'Or.*

The point is that Buñuel has been more intransigent over the years than most of his colleagues, and he has had more than his share of problems, but whereas one sometimes suspects the temptation of martyrdom in a Stroheim or a Welles, one is struck mainly by Buñuel's tenacity. During the long drought between 1932 and 1947, without any directorial opportunities, he remained on the fringes of the industry in New York and Hollywood. Despite several canceled projects in Mexico and France since 1947, he has managed to direct twenty films, about half of which are meaningful projections of his ideas and personality. Even in a potboiler like *Susana,* released in 1950, the year of *The Young and the Damned,* there are one or two passages that foreshadow *Viridiana.*

There is a danger in attaching an explicitly political moral to Buñuel's carrer. For a director of the left, Buñuel has evidenced almost no interest in the mechanics of reform or revolution. The superimposed narrations in *Land Without Bread* and *The Young and the Damned* suggest amelioration, but the images of the films operate autonomously in terms of a fatalistic Spanish temperament. Even in his Mexican films there is no trace of the theory of progress through technology, and one could never imagine his making a tractor film behind the Iron Curtain. He has never concerned himself with the mystiques of peasant and worker; nor has he dramatized the injustices of economic exploitation in any detail. As the late André Bazin observed, Buñuel lacks the Manichean tendencies of a propagandist. As cruel as his world may be, its characters are never divided into villains and victims. His obsession with mental and physical deformities generally deprives his plots of any sociological plausibility. Even his handling of the racial issue in *Robinson Crusoe* and *The Young One* is too perverse to serve as a respectably liberal blueprint.

Ado Kyrou's recently published book on Buñuel sheds some new light on the paradoxes of the director's personality. Particularly interesting is some of the director's own film criticism in the late twenties, when, like many critics today, he tried to establish polar relationships. Whereas Truffaut has invented the Lumière-Delluc and Sagan-Queneau games, Buñuel pioneered in the Keaton-Jannings game. Buñuel preferred Keaton, with all the hostility to German expressionism such a preference implies. He frankly admired the American cinema for its empty-headed grace and rhythm, qualities that he attributed to a Jungian sense of racial instinct. Conversely, he understood his own limitations, and his perceptive humility is still one of his greatest virtues. Buñuel is not and never has been a stylist of the first rank. He would have been lost in the Hollywood shuffle on commissioned projects, even though he functioned creditably and efficiently on impossible Mexican assignments. To Buñuel the cinema is simply a vehicle for his ideas. Once these ideas have taken the appropriately plastic form, he shoots very quickly, and any additional values are either incidental or accidental. One of his Mexican producers has reported that Buñuel seems bored by the actual shooting of a film.

Even though one may treat Dali's accusations of atheism as malicious slander designed to get Buñuel fired from the Museum of Modern Art in New York, Buñuel's films are clearly not intended to win friends and influence people for the Church. As a director who began his career by throwing live priests and dead jackasses out the window, and then compounded his sacrilege by confusing Christ with the Marquis de Sade, he has been almost exclusively identified in terms of these and subsequent impieties. Because he titillates anticlerical audiences with glimpses of forbidden frankness, Buñuel has found it difficult to convey the full dimensions of his metaphysical rebellion. As soon as he introduces the theme of sexual liberation into the argument, the latent puritanism of the organized left reacts against the degeneration of protest into anarchy. Yet even Buñuel's anarchy is unusually individualistic. Whereas Vigo is concerned with the disavowal and destruction of social institutions, Buñuel invokes the biological anarchy of nature to reconstruct humanity. Buñuel finds it quite natural for the protagonist of *El* to notice the legs of a pretty girl while he is washing a priest's feet for a Catholic ceremony. Buñuel's defiance of the Church for excluding nature from the altar thus takes on a mystical quality. The pleasure Buñuel takes in the beggar's orgy in *Viridiana* is almost indistinguishable from the religious ecstasy of self-denial one finds in Bresson. It is perhaps appropriate that Buñuel lacks Bresson's sensibility while Bresson lacks Buñuel's force.

The odd circumstances of Buñuel's career preclude an analysis of periods and stylistic progression. More than most other directors of comparable stature, the man is inseparable from his art. His camera has always viewed his characters from a middle distance, too close for cosmic groupings and too far away for self-identification. Normally this would make his films cold and his point of view detached, but by focusing on the abnormality of life, Buñuel forces his audience to accept man unconditionally. When we look at the monstrous long enough and hard enough, we realize, in Truffaut's phrase, that there are no monsters. The drawback to Buñuel's choice of distance is that he creates horror without terror, and pity without catharsis. In short, he lacks the sense of tragedy his ideas demand.

How a director who seems so disconcertingly obvious can turn out to be so complex is one of the mysteries of the cinema. For example, it seems too symmetrically ironic to synchronize a beggar's orgy with Handel's *Messiah*. However, Buñuel has never been a champion of background music. He simply does not care enough about his score to seek something more subtle. Yet his indifference to details that more clever directors have mastered only reminds us that ingenuity is no substitute for genius. Buñuel's blend of the real and the surreal, the grotesque and the erotic, the scabrous and the sublime never quite fits into any critical theory. The triumph of *Viridiana* leaves us just about where we were before, but henceforth we shall have to allow Buñuel to tailor his own straitjacket.

### *"Belle de Jour"*

Luis Buñuel's *Belle de Jour* has evoked in many critiques that all-purpose adjective "beautiful." Catherine Deneuve is undeniably beautiful, never more so than in this context of Buñuelian perversity, and almost any meaningfully designed color film seems beautiful, if only because the vast subconscious sea of the cinema is safely gelatinized within the frames of an academic painting. Describing a film as beautiful is unfortunately too often a device to end discussion, particularly nowadays when irrationality and hysteria have become institutionalized as life styles. *Elvira Madigan* is beautiful in the way flowery poems are poetical, not through functional expressiveness but through lyrical excessiveness. *Bonnie and Clyde* is beautiful when its concluding slow-motion ballet of death and transfiguration takes the audience off the hook by distancing the characters back into legend and fantasy. The fact that the close-ups contradict the distancing is immaterial to the film's admirers. *Bonnie and Clyde* is beautiful, and consistency is the hobgoblin of little minds.

I would argue that *Belle de Jour* is indeed a beautiful film, but not because of any anesthetizing aesthetic of benevolently mindless lyricism. Nor is the film beautiful because its director's visual style transcends its sordid subject. The beauty of *Belle de Jour* is the beauty of artistic rigor and adaptable intelligence. Given what Buñuel is at sixty-seven, and what he has done in forty years and twenty-seven projects of film-making, and what and whom he had to work with and for, *Belle de Jour* reverberates with the cruel logic of formal necessity. From the opening shot of an open carriage approaching the camera at an oblique ground-level angle to the closing shot of an open carriage passing the camera at an oblique overhead angle, the film progresses inexorably upward, an ascent of assent, from the reverie of suppressed desires to the revelation of fulfilled fantasies. But whose desires and whose fantasies? Buñuel's? His heroine's? Actually, a bit of both. The exact proportion of subjective contemplation to objective correlative can best be calculated by comparing Joseph Kessel's basic anecdotal material with what appears on the screen.

In his preface to *Belle de Jour* Kessel writes: "The subject of *Belle de Jour* is not Séverine's sensual aberration; it is her love for Pierre independent of that aberration, and it is the tragedy of that love." Kessel concludes his preface with a reprovingly rhetorical question for those critics who dismissed *Belle de Jour* as a piece of pathological observation: "Shall I be the only one to pity Severine, and to love her?"

The "sensual aberration" of which Kessel writes undoubtedly seemed more shocking in 1929, when the first French edition was published, than it would seem in the current period of erotic escalation. Severine Serizy, happily married to a handsome young surgeon, goes to work in a house of ill repute, actually less a house than an intimate apartment. The money involved is less the motivation than the pretext for her action. Pierre, her husband, provides for her material needs handsomely, but his respectfully temporizing caresses fail to satisfy her psychic need for brutal degradation, a need first awakened by a malodorous molester when she was a child of eight. To preserve a façade of marital respectability, Severine works at her obsessive profession only afternoons from two to five, the mystery of her matinee schedule causing her to be christened Belle de Jour. Kessel's novel, like his heroine, is fatally divided between clinical observations on sexual psychology and novelistic contrivances to overcome the innate lethargy of a woman of leisure. Husson, a weary sensualist in her husband's circle of friends, is a particularly intricate contrivance in that he triggers much of the novel's intrigue. It is Husson who first alerts Severine to her own frustrations by his unwelcome advances. It is he who inadvertently supplies her with the address of her sensual destiny, and who, discovering her double life, poses such a threat to her non-Belle de Jour existence that he precipitates, almost innocently, the final catastrophe.

Marcel, a gold-toothed gangster infatuated with Belle de Jour, provides a violently melodramatic climax to the novel by agreeing to murder Husson to preserve Severine's secret and Belle de Jour's respect. Irony is piled upon irony as Marcel's assault on Husson is deflected by Pierre, who is so grievously wounded that he is confined for life to helpless paralysis in a wheelchair. Marcel and Husson remain silent about Belle de Jour, thus enabling Severine to escape a public scandal and even prosecution. But perverse to the end, she confesses everything to Pierre, and is rewarded not with his forgiveness but with his stern silence.

Buñuel and his coscenarist, Jean-Claude Carrière, have retained most of the characters of the novel. Severine goes to work for Madame Anaïs in both novel and film, and Belle de Jour's colleagues are Charlotte and Mathilde in both versions. The most striking variation between novel and film is in the elaborately structured dream apparatus of the film. Kessel's Severine never dreams the concrete images of Buñuel's surreal reveries of feminine masochism. There are no floggings in the book, as there are in the film, no binding of hands with ropes, no sealing of mouths, no splattering with mud. Kessel's Severine never really dreams at all; she merely recollects the past and anticipates the future. If the novel had been filmed in the

thirties or forties by a French director trained in the Tradition of Quality, a
Marcel Carné or Claude Autant-Lara perhaps, Severine would probably
have been played with many shimmering close-ups to dramatize the desperate conflict between her feelings and her senses. The background music
would have been exquisitely sentimental. Except for the bells that signal
the movement of the horse-drawn carriage, Buñuel uses no music whatsoever. No Simon and Garfunkel, no Beatles, no Donovan, not even the
realistically based music of radios and record players. There is no radio or
television in the modern world of Belle de Jour, but there is a Geisha Club
credit card. Buñuel has stripped modernity of its specificity. Thus we are
not bothered so much by the suspicion that horse-drawn carriages are not as
likely to figure in the reveries of Severine's (or Catherine Deneuve's)
generation as in the memories of Buñuel's. The fact that Buñuel does not
employ music in *Belle de Jour* is not significant as a matter of general
aesthetic policy. Buñuel himself has derived ironic counterpoint from the
musical backgrounds of such recent films as *Viridiana* and *Simon of the
Desert*. He must have felt that he didn't need music to underscore the
fundamental irony implicit in a woman with the face of an angel and the
lusts of a devil. Still, *Belle de Jour* overcomes an awesome handicap of
affect by disdaining the facile frissons of music.

   Many of the script changes were dictated by the differences in the
media. Pierre emerges through Jean Sorel as a much duller character than
in the book, but it is difficult to see what any director could do with the
character of the Noble Husband in such a grotesque context. The changes
in Husson's character are more meaningful. Kessel's Husson was more
mannered in his ennui, but he takes advantage of Severine's degraded
status as Belle de Jour to possess her body. Buñuel's Husson (Michel
Piccoli) is more fastidious; he loses interest in Severine at precisely the
instant she becomes available to him as Belle de Jour. But it is Buñuel's
Husson who tells Pierre of Belle de Jour after the accident; Kessel's
Husson never seriously contemplated such a course of action before or
after.

   Kessel wants us to love Severine by identifying with her; Buñuel
wants us to understand Severine by contemplating the nature of her obsession. Instead of indulging in Kessel's sentimental psychology by staring
into Catherine Deneuve's eyes, Buñuel fragments Deneuve's body into its
erotic constituents. His shots of feet, hands, legs, shoes, stockings, under-
garments as the shots not only of a fetishist but of a cubist, a director
concerned simultaneously with the parts and their effect on the whole.
Buñuel's graceful camera movements convey Deneuve to her sensual destiny through her black patent-leather shoes, and to her final reverie through
her ringed fingers feeling their way along the furniture with the tactile

tenderness of a mystical sensuality—Severine's, Deneuve's, or Buñuel's, it makes little difference.

The beauty of the filmed version of *Belle de Jour* arises from its implication of Buñuel in its vision of the world. It is Buñuel himself who is the most devoted patron of Chez Madame Anaïs and the most pathetic admirer of Catherine Deneuve's Severine-Belle de Jour. Never before has Buñuel's view of the spectacle seemed so obliquely Ophulsian in its shy gaze from behind curtains, windows, and even peepholes. Buñuel's love of Severine is greater than Kessel's, simply because Buñuel sees Belle de Jour as Severine's liberator. The sensuality of *Belle de Jour* is not metaphorical, like Genet's in *The Balcony* or Albee's in *Everything in the Garden*. Most writers, even the most radical, treat prostitution as a symptom of a social malaise and not as a concrete manifestation of a universal impulse. Buñuel reminds us once again in *Belle de Jour* that he is one of the few men of the Left not afflicted by puritanism and bourgeois notions of chastity and fidelity.

The difference between Buñuel and, say, Genet is not entirely a difference of ideology. It is more a difference between a man of images and a man of words. What distinguishes *Belle de Jour* from most movies is the impression it gives of having been seen in its director's mind long before it was shot. There is a preconceived exactness to its images that will inevitably disconcert middlebrow film critics, especially those who are highbrows in other cultural sectors. It is only the specialist in film who can fully appreciate the directness of Buñuel's images above and beyond the novelistic nuances he sacrifices on the altars of shock and laughter.

# The Fierce Imagination of Luis Buñuel

## Michael Wood

*Dear imagination, what I love most about you, is that you do not forgive.*

—André Breton

*Film-making is easy and has no secrets.*

—Luis Buñuel

A razor blade slicing into a living eye; a well-dressed man kicking a violin down a street; a severed hand crawling across a table; a severed head serving as the clapper of a huge bell; a dinner party which turns into a play where you don't know your lines. These dream-images from five films by Luis Buñuel (*Un Chien andalou*, 1928, *L'Age d'Or*, 1930, *El angel exterminador*, 1962, *Tristana*, 1970, *Le Charme discret de la bourgeoisie*, 1972, in that order) are the marks of an unforgiving imagination, an imagination which exacerbates the sudden cruelties of reality. But of course the same imagination can forgive all too easily, and can offer merely whimsical surprises and discontinuities: a cow in a bed, a dead donkey draped across a piano, bears and sheep in an upper-class Mexican kitchen. It is customary to attribute the unforgiving vision to Buñuel, and the cheaper desire to shock and amuse an audience to Salvador Dali, who collaborated with Buñuel on the screenplays for *Un Chien andalou* and *L'Age d'Or*. Buñuel himself, disappointed that so many people should have *enjoyed* the first of those two films, insisted that it was not intended as entertainment, but was a "desperate, passionate call for murder," and made sure that the second was more seriously upsetting. Successfully enough, since the cinema where it was showing was smashed up by a crowd of young

This essay was written especially for the present volume.

defenders of church and state, and the film was banned a few days later. Dali had in fact contributed very little to *L'Age d'Or.*

But the truth is that Breton was only half right about the imagination, even an imagination as fierce as Buñuel's, which forgives when it has to, when the continuities of culture and history absorb its interruptions. The crucial thing about the astonishing acts and images of the surrealists was not whether they were slick or authentic, light-hearted or destructive, but whether they were genuinely arbitrary or not. The least flicker of motivation or meaning could ruin them. And of course no piece of human discourse can remain arbitrary for long. Surrealism insisted on a vital incoherence beneath all the false coherences of reason, morality and dogma, but it was always a fragile, short-term enterprise, since an incoherence which remained incoherent would simply be chaos, and an incoherence which yielded a meaning of its own would simply have given in to the coercions of reason: Freud reclaiming dreams from the darkness in the way the Dutch reclaimed land from the sea. The great, bright, frightening moments of surrealism—and Buñuel in this sense has been a lifelong surrealist—offer neither insights nor assertions, but brief seasons of escape, holidays from the all-encompassing activity of interpretation.

In Buñuel's *Viridiana* (1961) a crucifix turns, at the touch of a finger, into an ugly little knife, and the many obvious meanings of this image are not long delayed, come flooding in on us whether we like it or not: Christ's blood and Christ's cross, Christianity and suffering, and perhaps foremost, the violence of Christianity, the instrument of pain hidden in the emblem of sorrow. But *before* these meanings come, there is a moment of pure, uninterpreted surprise, a surrealist epiphany. Similarly, in *El angel exterminador,* we hear a hostess say to her butler, "And they'll have to go in the garden too," and Buñuel cuts to a group of three sheep huddled together under a kitchen table. The dialogue later suggests that they are part of a practical joke the hostess is cooking up, and the film uses the sheep further on to reinforce its main message, which is roughly that those who behave like sheep (socially and religiously) will be treated like sheep (politically). But again, the meaning of the sheep, and the reason for their presence, come late enough to leave intact in our minds the sheer nonsense of their first appearance, the joy of their random intervention in the movie.

There are two other kinds of image in Buñuel; and what I am saying about images goes largely for twists of plots and aspects of character too. One is the clearly, instantly moralized image. This is a form of straight *montage* borrowed from Eisenstein. A young man, in *Viridiana,* makes a move toward a woman, and Buñuel cuts to a cat pouncing on a mouse. A conversation in the same film concerns the neglect of an illegitimate child, and the screen shows us an all too meaningful bee rescued from a barrel of water. *Viridiana,* in my view, is horribly overloaded with meaning in this sense, and visually represents something like the reverse of the liberation the surrealists were after. Even the beggars, whose orgy in another Buñuel movie would no doubt have looked like a promise of revolution, manage only shabby and nasty pleasures, and the style of the film thus corresponds to an oppressed view of human chances, a sense that escape from spectacular falsehood seems less of a possibility than ever.

The other kind of image presents a meticulously observed piece of material reality, and Peter Harcourt is right to say (in *Six European Directors,* 1974) that Buñuel is the most *realistic* of moviemakers. Surrealism, after all, was a way of seeing the given world, not a way of running from it or substituting something else for it. "I saw reality differently from the way I would have seen it before surrealism," Buñuel told André Bazin and Jacques Doniol-Valcroze. I'm thinking of a closely watched spider in Buñuel's *Cumbres Borrascosas* (1953), a version of *Wuthering Heights,* and of a slaughtered pig in the same film; of a battle between scorpions in *L'Age d'Or.* But the effect of these images, curiously, is similar to that of the wilder surrealist figures: in both cases a comfortable, nominal reality is stripped away and we are left with a naked, unexplained piece of life—dream, joke, or daily fact, it doesn't matter which, since it strikes us with the force of a first-time vision, as a sight of something never seen before. Buñuel has said that he likes only those films which *discover* something, and in *Los olvidados* (1950) he wanted (but was not allowed) to combine a realistic murder with a glimpse of a hundred-piece orchestra playing in an unfinished building.

With this in mind, we can bridge the apparent gap between Buñuel's first two surrealist films and his next work, a documentary called *Las Hurdes,* 1932, a bleak, sobering report on a starved and disease-ridden Spanish community. But *Las Hurdes* will also teach us something else. The community has no bread and no proper means of farming; and it has no culture, no folkore, no songs or stories or paintings. It is thus a society which in one sense represents what *L'Age d'Or,* and many later Buñuel films, seem to long for: a life purified of the deceptions of civilisation. And the horror of that life will serve to remind us of the ambivalence which haunts Buñuel's whole work. Buñuel is not, except in isolated early pronouncements, a romantic anarchist, a man who thinks the world will be improved by our tearing it down. And he is not, as far as I can see, a man who has matured into a wise acceptance of the necessary limitations on human desire. He is the most anxious of moviemakers, early and late; and he urges us to wreck the false structures of our social and religious life, not because bliss and salvation lie that way but because our dignity and integrity demand the attempt from us, require an onslaught on all visible untruth. The fact that the life we escape to may well be much worse than the life we are escaping from is a measure of the risk that people who care about freedom ought to be ready to take.

The same complication of feeling governs Buñuel's responses to the other major article of surrealist faith: passionate, all-obliterating love. We find Stendhal's heroes, Breton wrote, where Stendhal has lost them—that is, in their romantic, seemingly unmotivated crimes. And the surrealists cherished *Wuthering Heights* for similar reasons, because it portrayed a love which simply dwarfed all social and moral constraints. The alternative title for Buñuel's film of *Wuthering Heights* was *Abismos de pasion* (*Abysses of Passion*), and this whole line of thought and belief is saved from sentimentality only by the violence of the emotions involved. Yet again, Buñuel's view of a love which breaks all barriers is not a hopeful one, indeed it is if anything dimmer than Buñuel's view of politics. In politics, he seems to suggest, we can change the world but we may not be any better off. In love, he implies, we can't really throw off the repressions of self and society, we can only make the indispensable attempt. The damage we do and suffer will merely reflect the depth and the extent of the original repressions. Cyril Connolly said the same thing in more old-fashioned terms when he spoke of *Un Chien andalou* as bringing out "the grandeur of the conflict inherent in romantic love, the truth that the heart is made to be broken, and after it has mended, to be broken again." "For romantic love," Connolly added, "is more than an intensifying of life; it is a defiance of it."

In sadder, less heroic terms, this is precisely the suggestion of both *Viridiana* and *Tristana,* films which comment ironically on each other, and all the more strikingly because Fernando Rey plays a similar character in both of them. In *Viridiana,* a girl is shocked by her uncle's desire for her and outraged by his (false) claim that he has raped her while she was drugged. This shock and outrage might seem fairly legitimate responses, but Buñuel manages to make them seem the reactions of a starchy prude, hopelessly contaminated by religion. The girl leaves, and the uncle, a weird, beneficent smile on his face, makes his will, and shortly after hangs himself. The implication, clearly, is that repression, personal and social, is the source of much of life's unhappiness—even if we don't have to go quite as far in this direction as Raymond Durgnat, who thinks that Viridiana's later rape by a couple of beggars has "very promising . . . spiritual potentialities." (Actually, it's not clear that she is raped at all. The print I saw most recently cuts away at the crucial moment, but does suggest, to me at least, that a rape takes place. The published screenplay hints that she is saved in the nick of time, and a number of critics read the scene this way too). In *Tristana,* however, in the equivalent situation, the young girl simply gives herself to the old man, and nothing is improved. The man becomes jealous and possessive, and the girl becomes his prisoner for life, since in spite of her love for a younger man and her escape with him to another city, she still returns to her uncle-lover, to drag out her days in an intimate hatred which she can't do without. Love perhaps, unlike the imagination, really does not forgive.

But the perspective here is still social, these are still hearts riddled with the requirements and contrarieties of life in society, and this may be the one concern which holds all Buñuel's very different films together. He is interested in psychology only as it reflects the deformations a culture may impose upon character, interested in the individual only as he may represent a chance for transcendence in a world which no one seriously expects to transcend. Closed, complacent social groups recur again and again in his films, from *L'Age d'Or* to *Le Charme discret de la bourgeoisie,* and even *Robinson Crusoe,* with its shipwrecked hero on a desert island, merely shows how civilization pursues a man even into the utmost isolation. Crusoe on his island is as cluttered as he ever was by the moral and intellectual baggage of the England he has lost, and the smugness of his smile as he returns to Europe at the end is one of the finer touches in this otherwise rather undistinguished movie. Perhaps more than any other director Buñuel depicts the weight of culture and civilization as they press on particular lives, and the wit and verve and courage with which he contemplates this burden make idle all attempts to separate Buñuel's "serious" films from his frivolous ones. Dark and light, they bury us, as Buñuel buries his characters in the final shot of *Un Chien andalou,* in the deep sands of our accumulated past.

# Frank
# Capra

FRANK CAPRA was born in Sicily in 1897 and came to Los Angeles with his family at the age of six. His films exude the earthy vitality of his peasant background, as well as the poor immigrant's boundless faith in American opportunity and American values. He earned a college degree in chemical engineering, but later went to work as a gag writer for Hal Roach and then for Mack Sennett. It was at the Sennett studio that he helped develop the screen character of comedian Harry Langdon; and when Langdon left to make feature films, Capra soon joined him. He helped write and direct Tramp, Tramp, Tramp (1926) and directed The Strong Man (1926) and Long Pants (1927), which are among the few comedies of the period on a par with those of Chaplin and Keaton. In retrospect, the lucky simpleton of the Langdon films, with his childlike innocence, anticipates the common-man hero who emerges in Capra's later work.

He went to work at Columbia in 1928 and helped turn it from a cheap back-street operation into a major studio. After a series of increasingly ambitious bread-and-butter films, which taught him his craft, he achieved spectacular success with Clark Gable and Claudette Colbert in a "screwball" comedy, It Happened One Night (1934). But Capra's best period did not begin until 1936 with Mr. Deeds Goes to Town. Capra had long since become a smooth professional; his films were lively, punchy, and fluent; he had an intuitive feeling for American speech and behavior, and he knew how to tell a story with bounce and economy. But in Mr. Deeds, with the help of his favorite scenarist, Robert Riskin, Capra also became a man with a message, one that he was never to abandon.

In his autobiography, The Name above the Title, Capra paraphrases his favorite theme in the following terms:

> A simple honest man, driven into a corner by predatory sophisticates, can, if he will, reach down into his God-given resources and come up with the necessary handfuls of courage, wit, and love to triumph over his environment.

A true auteur whoever his screenwriter, Capra developed this theme with increasing complexity and sophistication in three later masterworks, Mr. Smith Goes to Washington (1940), Meet John Doe (1941), and It's a Wonderful Life (1946), without losing the entertainer's gift that had made him an audience and industry favorite.

Capra's career declined after State of the Union (1948), and two of his last four films were remakes of earlier efforts. But recently his best films, all of them social and political fables, have come in for renewed appreciation from serious film scholars, some of them under the influence of the individualist politics of the New Left, who show how Capra used fairy-tale comic plots as vehicles for serious social criticism.

Capra's films have always had detractors who find them corny and shallow. Andrew Sarris even finds them vaguely fascist, despite their direct satire on fascists, industrial magnates, and scheming undemocratic politicians, usually personified by Edward Arnold, the classic Wall Street heavy of the 1930s. "In Meet John Doe," Sarris argues, "Frank Capra crossed the thin line between populist sentimentality and populist demagoguery." Yet in that very film, the most complex of his political fables, Capra not only makes Arnold an overt fascist, with dictatorial ambitions and his own pack of storm troopers, but is also most ambiguous in his treatment of the common people and their anonymous hero, John Doe (played to perfection by Gary Cooper, who had also played Mr. Deeds). While exhibiting their virtues, Capra also stresses their gullibility, their naiveté, their fickleness, and their weakness for being manipulated; and he gives John Doe a hobo sidekick, the Colonel, whose pungent comments make short shrift of "the People" and of society in general. John Doe himself, their epitome, is much more beleaguered and less shrewd and heroic than Mr. Deeds or Mr. Smith. As his made-up name indicates, he has even less identity than they do, and is easily manipulated by everyone around him. As the film's somber ending shows, Capra's faith in the people had given way by 1941 to an anxiety for their future.

This dark side of Capra's vision is even more marked in It's a Wonderful Life, in which Jimmy Stewart, who had also been Mr. Smith, plays a man who is so virtuous and self-abnegating that he almost forgets to live his own life. Finally, despondent, he contemplates suicide, and in the film's most remarkable sequence he's shown what his world would have been like if he had never lived. The overall message is uplifting—yes, each man does make a difference—but the sequence itself is nightmarish and terrifying. To be purged of his suicidal wishes, the character is robbed of all identity, so that even his nearest and dearest fail to know him. In this dark fantasy Capra's heroes confront the hideous underside of their own blank anonymity. Yet to many people the film remains heartening enough for an annual television screening on Christmas eve.

Besides Capra's engaging autobiography, The Name Above the Title (1971), we can recommend Frank Capra: The Man and His Films, edited by Richard Glatzer and John Raeburn (1974), which collects some first-rate criticism and signals the revival of serious interest in Capra's best work. For further discussion of Capra's films in a social context, see Robert Sklar's Movie-Made America (1975).

# A Director of Genius: Four Reviews

## Graham Greene

### "Mr. Deeds Goes to Town"

*Mr. Deeds* is Capra's finest film (it is on quite a different intellectual level from the spirited and delightful *It Happened One Night*), and that means it is a comedy quite unmatched on the screen. For Capra has what Lubitsch, the witty playboy, has not: a sense of responsibility, and what Clair, whimsical, poetic, a little precious and à la mode, has not, a kinship with his audience, a sense of common life, a morality; he has what even Chaplin has not, complete mastery of his medium, and that medium the sound-film, not the film with sound attached to it. Like Lang, he hears all the time just as clearly as he sees and just as selectively. I do not think anyone can watch *Mr. Deeds* for long without being aware of a technician as great as Lang employed on a theme which profoundly moves him: the theme of goodness and simplicity manhandled in a deeply selfish and brutal world. That was the theme of *Fury,* too, but Capra is more fortunate than Lang. Lang expresses the theme in terms of terror, and terror on the screen has always, alas! to be tempered to the shorn lamb; Capra expresses it in terms of pity and ironic tenderness, and no magnate feels the need to cramp his style or alter his conclusion.

Mr. Deeds is a young provincial who inherits twenty million dollars from an uncle he has never seen. An ardent tuba player in the local band, he makes his living by writing verses which are printed on postcards on such occasions as Mothers' Day. The uncle's solicitors, who have absorbed, with the help of a Power of Attorney, half a million dollars of his

These reviews appeared originally in *The Spectator* in August 1936, April 1937, November 1938, and January 1940, respectively. The material is reprinted from *The Pleasure Dome* by Graham Greene (Martin Secker & Warburg Ltd.), by permission of Laurence Pollinger Limited, and from *Graham Greene on Film,* by permission of Simon & Schuster, a Division of Gulf & Western Corporation. The latter book copyright © 1973 by Graham Greene.

money, hope to continue the process with his unsophisticated nephew who is quite unexcited by his fortune and only wants to do good with it. They bring Deeds up to town. Wealth educates Deeds, he learns the shabby side not only of business, but of art, with the help of the opera directors and the fashionable poets; he learns, too, the deceit which may exist in ordinary human affection (the girl he loves, and who loves him, is all the time writing newspaper articles which make front-page fun of the activities of the Cinderella Man). A revolver and a would-be assassin's nerveless hand educate him socially, and he is arranging to use the whole of his fortune in providing ruined farmers with free land and free seed when society— controlled by racketeers—strikes its last blow at the elements it cannot absorb, goodness, simplicity, disinterestedness. Claimants are found to dispute his sanity and to try to remove the management of the estate from his hands.

It sounds as grim a theme as *Fury;* innocence lynched as effectively at a judicial inquiry as in a burning courthouse, but there is this difference between Lang and Capra; Lang's happy ending was imposed on him, we did not believe in it; Capra's is natural and unforced. He *believes* in the possibility of happiness; he believes, in spite of the controlling racketeers, in human nature. Goodness, simplicity, disinterestedness: these in his hands become fighting qualities. Deeds sees through opera directors, fashionable intellectuals, solicitors, psychologists who prove that he is insane merely because he likes playing the tuba and isn't greedy for money. Only for a few minutes in the courtroom does he lose heart and refuse to defend himself: he is never a helpless victim, like the garage man behind the bars watching the woman lift her baby up to see the fun, and he comes back into the ring with folk humour and folk shrewdness to rout his enemies for the sake of the men they have ruined. The picture glows with that humour and shrewdness, just as Lang's curdles with his horror and disgust; it is as funny, most of the time, as *Fury* was terrifying. It is not a question of truth or falsehood: two directors of genius have made pictures with curiously similar themes which present a conviction, a settled attitude towards life as it is lived. The pessimist makes a tragedy, the optimist (but how far from sweetness and complacency is Capra's optimism) makes a comedy. And Capra, as well as Lang, is supported by a perfect cast. Every minor part, however few the lines, is completely rendered, and Mr. Gary Cooper's subtle and pliable performance must be something of which other directors have only dreamed.

## *"Lost Horizon"*

Nothing reveals men's characters more than their Utopias: the scientific sentimentality of Mr. Wells, the art-and-craftiness of William Morris,

Mr. Shaw's eternal sewing machine, Samuel Butler's dusty alpaca. Shangri-La must be counted among the less fortunate flights of the imagination, the lamaserai in Thibet ruled by a Grand Llama, a Belgian priest who discovered the rich valley among the mountains in the eighteenth century and who was still alive when Robert Conway, explorer, diplomat and—rather improbably—Foreign Secretary elect was kidnapped from a Chinese town and brought there by aeroplane. This Utopia closely resembles a film star's luxurious estate on Beverly Hills; flirtatious pursuits through grape arbours, splashings and divings in blossomy pools under improbable waterfalls, and rich and enormous meals. "Every man carries in his heart a Shangri-La": but I prefer myself the harps and golden crowns and glassy seas of an older mythology. Shangri-La is intended to represent a haven of moderation, beauty, and peace in the middle of an uncompromising and greedy world, but what Conway finds there, what he loses in a weak moment of disbelief, and struggles across the Himalayas to find again, is something incurably American; a kind of aerated idealism ("We have one simple rule, Kindness") and, of course, a girl (Miss Jane Wyatt, one of the dumber stars), who has read all the best books (his own included) and has the coy, comradely manner of a not too advanced schoolmistress.

It is a very long picture, this disappointing successor to *Mr. Deeds,* and a very dull one as soon as the opening scenes are over. These are brilliantly written and directed, and show Conway (Mr. Ronald Colman) organizing the aerial evacuation of the white inhabitants from a Chinese town in the middle of a revolution before he takes the last plane himself in company with a crooked financier wanted by the police, a prostitute (sentimental variety), a scientist (comic), and a younger brother. Here the Capra-Riskin partnership is at its best, and we are unprepared for the disappointments which follow: the flavourless uplifting dialogue, the crude humour, the pedestrian direction, and the slack makeshift construction. "You shouldn't look at the bottom of the mountains. Try looking at the top." So Chang, the suave philosophical second-in-command of Shangri-La, addresses the prostitute who believes that she is dying of consumption (one of the virtues of this mysterious valley is health, the body beautiful, and a life which goes on and on and on ). It might be Wilhelmina Stitch translated into American prose, and one can hardly believe that this script is from the same hands as *Mr. Deeds,* though perhaps Mr. James Hilton, the author of the novel and of *Goodbye, Mr. Chips,* may be responsible for the sentimentality of these sequences.

Of course, the picture isn't quite as bad as that. It does attempt, however clumsily and sentimentally, more than the average film; a social conscience is obscurely at work, but at work far less effectively than in *Mr. Deeds,* and as for the humour—it consists only of Mr. Edward Everett

Horton wearing Eastern clothes. The conscious humour that is to say, for the glimpses of English political life give a little much needed relief. "The Far Eastern Conference must be postponed. We cannot meet these nations without Conway": the Prime Minister's measured utterances to his Cabinet gathered Gladstonianly round him fall with an odd sound on ears accustomed to more dispensable foreign secretaries. But it is in the last sequence that the Capra-Riskin collaboration fails most disastrously. Conway, persuaded by his younger brother that the Grand Lama has lied to him, that there is misery and injustice in this seeming Utopia, makes his way back to China across the mountains. A few newspaper headlines tell us that Conway has reached safety, and it is only at secondhand in a long uncinematic scene in a London club that we learn what we should have seen with our own eyes: Conway's reaction to "civilization." If the long dull ethical sequences had been cut to the bone there would have been plenty of room for the real story: the shock of Western crudity and injustice on a man returned from a more gentle and beautiful way of life.

## *"You Can't Take It with You"*

It is really what we should have expected from Frank Capra, whose portrait hangs outside the cinema; bushy eyebrows, big nose, and the kind of battered face which looks barnacled with life, encrusted with ready sympathies and unexacting friendships, a good mixer. It is always dangerous, of course, to generalize about a director's subjects—he hasn't invented his own stories; but the Capra-Riskin combination is strong enough by now to dictate, and we can assume Capra is doing what he wants to do. What he wants is increasingly what the public wants. It will adore the new picture which contains what it treasures most—a good laugh and a good cry.

As for the reviewer, he can only raise his hands in a kind of despair. The new picture is the *Christmas Carol* over again—with its sentimentality and its gusto and its touches of genius: no technical mistakes this time as there were in *Lost Horizon*. The director emerges as a rather muddled and sentimental idealist who feels—vaguely—that something is wrong with the social system. Mr. Deeds started distributing his money, and the hero of *Lost Horizon* settled down in a Thibetan monastery—equipped with all the luxury devices of the best American hotels—and Grandpa Vanderhof persuades, in this new picture, the Wall Street magnate who has made the *coup* of his career and cornered the armaments industry to throw everything up and play the harmonica. This presumably means a crash in Wall Street and the ruin of thousands of small investors, but it is useless trying to analyze the idea behind the Capra films: there *is* no idea that you'd notice, only a sense of dissatisfaction, an urge to escape—on to the open road with the daughter of a millionaire, back to small town simplicity on a safe

income, away to remote, secure Shangri-La, into the basement where Mr.
Vanderhof's son-in-law makes fireworks with the iceman who came seven
years ago with a delivery van and stayed on. A belief, too, in bad rich men
and good poor men—though Mr. Vanderhof doesn't, when you come to
think of it, seem to lack money. Like the British Empire, he has retired
from competition with a full purse.

That is really all there is to the film—a contrast between life on Wall
Street and life in the Vanderhof home, where everybody is supposed to
lead the life he likes and like the life the others lead. A granddaughter
practices ballet-dancing while she lays the table, a boy friend plays on the
marimba, a daughter writes novels which will never be published, just for
fun—what an extraordinary idea of fun! It is very noisy with the fireworks
going off, and good-hearted and Christian in the *Christmas Carol* tradition.
The most embarrassing moments in a film which is frequently embarrassing occur at meal-times when Grandpa Vanderhof (Mr. Lionel Barrymore) talks to God in a man-to-man way instead of saying Grace. "Well,
sir, here we are again. We been getting on pretty well for a long time
now. . . ." This whimsical household is meant, I think, to be symbolic of
life as it should be lived (one prefers Wall Street), and mixed up in the
whole thing is the routine love story of Vanderhof's granddaughter and the
magnate's son, played sensitively by Miss Jean Arthur and Mr. James
Stewart.

It sounds awful, but it isn't as awful as all that, for Capra has a touch
of genius with a camera: his screen always seems twice as big as other
people's, and he cuts as brilliantly as Eisenstein (the climax when the big
bad magnate takes up his harmonica is so exhilarating in its movement that
you forget its absurdity). Humour and not wit is his line, a humour which
shades off into whimsicality, and a kind of popular poetry which is apt to
turn wistful. We may groan and blush as he cuts his way remorselessly
through all finer values to the fallible human heart, but infallibly he makes
his appeal—by that great soft organ with its unreliable goodness and easy
melancholy and baseless optimism. The cinema, a popular craft, can
hardly be expected to do more.

## *"Mr. Smith Goes to Washington"*

Here is Capra, without the help of Riskin, back to his finest form—the
form of *Mr. Deeds*. It has always been an interesting question, how much
Capra owed to his faithful scenario writer. Now it is difficult to believe that
Riskin's part was ever very important, for all the familiar qualities are
here—the exciting close-ups, the sudden, irrelevant humour, the delight—
equal to that of the great Russians—in the ordinary human face. (Claude
Rains has not got an ordinary human face, and for that reason he seems out
of place and histrionic, great actor though he is, in a Capra film.)

The story is regulation Capra in praise of simplicity and virtue and acting naturally. As a fairy tale it is a little Victorian: it is not that we are less moved by virtue in these days, but we are more aware of how the author cheats—virtue is not bound to win, and the easy moral of a Capra tale comes dangerously close to a Benthamite apothegm about honesty being the best policy. Young Jefferson Smith, acted with a kind of ideal awkwardness by James Stewart, is appointed a senator to fill an unexpired term: he is a leader whose guilelessness is considered useful by the other State Senator, Joseph Paine, and his business boss, Jim Taylor. They are putting over a tricky piece of graft and they don't want a new senator who can see his way. So Smith goes up to Washington with his naïve ideals and his patriotism (he knows Lincoln's speeches off by heart) and his sense of responsibility: he feels rapture at the sight of the Capitol dome, stands like a worshipper below the bony marble fingers of the Lincoln statue, and Paine entertains him and sidetracks him.

Then suddenly Smith's secretary, with all the harsh, don't-give-a-twopenny-curse charm of Miss Jean Arthur, opens his eyes to the real Washington, where you can't look round a monument without starting a grafter. He refuses to be a party to fraud and Jim Taylor (Edward Arnold) proceeds to break him—papers are forged, witnesses perjure themselves, he is declared by a Committee of the Senate unworthy to hold his seat. "Beautiful," says a reporter at the framed inquiry, "that Taylor machine." But Smith won't surrender: when the Senators refuse to listen to him, he takes advantage of the Constitution and holds the floor for twenty-three hours, hoping that his State will support him—in vain because the newspapers have been bought by Taylor. This constitutional battle of one man against the Senate is among the most exciting sequences the screen has given us. But it is a fairy tale, so Smith wins: Joseph Paine, like a Dickensian Scrooge, is caught by conscience, and I imagine it is easier for us, than for an American who knows his country's politics, to suspend disbelief.

It is a great film, even though it is not a great story, acted by a magnificent cast, so that Capra can afford to fling away on tiny parts men like Eugene Pallette, Guy Kibbee, Thomas Mitchell, and Harry Carey. A week later one remembers vividly the big body of Pallette stuck in a telephone box, the family dinner of the weak crooked Governor (Kibbee) whom even his children pester over the nomination, the whole authentic atmosphere of big bland crookery between boss and politician—the "Joes" and the "Jims," the Christian names and comradeship, the wide unspoken references, and one remembers too the faces chosen and shot with Capra care—worried political faces, Grub Street faces, acquisitive social faces and faces that won't give themselves away.

# American Madness

## William S. Pechter

In an enterprise as vast and impersonal as the making of a film, it is rare enough that a director creates his own style; if, then, he also creates his own genre, it is indeed a signal accomplishment. That Frank Capra did both, and then abruptly climaxed his spectacularly successful career by a self-imposed premature retirement, would serve to make him an absolute conundrum. For Hollywood directors are notoriously like old soldiers in the way in which they just fade out and away.

The unique Capra genre has been defined by Richard Griffith, the film historian, as the "fantasy of goodwill," and he has also described its archetypical pattern. "In each film, a messianic innocent, not unlike the classic simpletons of literature ... pits himself against the forces of entrenched greed. His inexperience defeats him strategically, but his gallant integrity in the face of temptation calls forth the goodwill of the 'little people,' and through their combined protest, he triumphs." This ritual of innocence triumphant did little to ingratiate Capra to an intellectual audience to whom he represented only the triumph of the *Saturday Evening Post*. But though the apparent vein of cheery optimism which informs this ritual's re-enactment *is,* of course, precisely that quality which both endears Capra to his popular audience and alienates an intellectual one, yet, in seeing the films again, this quality seems strangely elusive, forever asserting itself on set occasions, but always dissipating itself finally in a kind of shrill excitement. There are even intimations of something like melancholy constantly lurking beneath the surface glare of happy affirmation.

The sense of this becomes particularly emphatic if one views the films—and I restrict myself to his most famous and characteristic comedies—in chronological sequence. From this perspective, although the pattern is already set in such early work as *The Strong Man,* a 1926 Harry

Langdon seven-reeler, *Mr. Deeds Goes to Town* is its first major exposition, at once the prototype and the exception. Compared to Capra's subsequent films, it is the most unreservedly "positive" in tone, Longfellow Deeds does, indeed, win out, and innocence triumphs. The rustic poet *cum* tuba confronts the powerful presence of metropolitan venality, and not only effects a personal victory, but manages to impress the cynical—a reminder of their own lost innocence—with his exemplary goodness as well.

The memory of innocence lost is a crucially disturbing one in Capra's films, and central to any understanding of them. While the progress from small-town purity to big-city corruption may not, in fact, be part of the audience's personal history, it remains a fact of its acquired cultural legacy. That is, it is part of the inherited myth of an American past—of quiet, shady, tree-lined streets of white wood homes—which is so concretely a part of an American childhood that it persists into adulthood as a psychological fact, with the force of memory. And while the audience is asked to, and indeed must, identify with the innocent hero, it cannot fail to recognize itself, if not quite consciously, more nearly depicted in the images of his antagonists—the cynics, smart guys, hustlers, chiselers, opportunists, exploiters, hypocrites: all the corrupt; all our failed selves; what we have become. We respond finally to the classic Capra hero, whether Mr. Smith or John Doe, the uniquely American Everyman, with a kind of reluctant longing. He is our conscience *manqué*, the image of our childhood selves, reminding us, as we do not wish to be reminded, of the ways and degrees to which we have failed this image; all reaching some comic apotheosis in the figure of Jimmy Stewart, as Mr. Smith, in Washington, quite literally, a big Boy Scout.

What moderates the merely Sunday school piety of the Capra hero, what keeps his meaning just short of the moralizing "essay" on the page before the murder case in our Sunday supplements, is always some specifically foolish, specifically human trait which becomes the comic correlative of virtue: Mr. Deeds plays his tuba, John Doe plays his baseball, and Mr. Smith is not simply a patriot, but an absurdly fanatical one, who cannot pass the Washington Monument, however casually, without adopting some posture of ridiculously extravagant reverence. The virtue of the characters seems inseparable from their absurdity, and, bound up as it is with this absurdity, passes from the ideality of the Sunday moral to the reality of a concrete human embodiment. It becomes a human possibility; that is to say, the peculiar impact of the Capra hero is as an assertion that it is possible to be that good . . . and human, too.

It is the formularized happy ending which has always seemed the fatal weakness of Capra's films; the apparent belief that everything will turn out all right in the end serves, finally, only to nullify any serious moral concern. Yet this convention of the happy ending seems, on closer look, to be curiously quarantined in Capra's films, and the observance of it has often been strangely perfunctory. Only *Mr. Deeds Goes to Town* appears comfortably to adopt a happy ending, and, while this film remains the prototype of the others, much of their interest derives from the variations they work on the original pattern. In *Mr. Smith Goes to Washington,* the dramatic climax is brought off with such astonishing abruptness as to be over before we can consciously comprehend it. The filibuster has dragged on interminably. Mr. Smith seems defeated, and with the arrival of the hostile letters he suddenly becomes aware of his defeat. More suddenly still, the corrupt Senator leaps to the railing—admits the truth of Smith's accusation—Smith collapses in exhaustion and disbelief—wild commotion—Jean Arthur smiles—The End. The entire dramatic reversal takes place in less than a minute.

The finale of *Meet John Doe* is almost the reverse in quality. With John Doe's suicide an apparent inevitability, the film closes on an episode of almost dreamlike tranquility. It is Christmas Eve; there is an all but unendurably slow elevator ride to the top of a deserted skyscraper; the snow is falling, thick and silent; John Doe appears and moves to the edge of the roof; Edward Arnold appears with his henchmen; the Girl appears with specimen types of little folk who have regained faith in the idea of John Doe, and Doe allows himself to be persuaded to return to life. Distant church bells. In both cases, the tone and tenor of the final sequence are seriously at odds with the rest of the work: in *Meet John Doe,* it seems to take place in a vacuum; in *Mr. Smith Goes to Washington,* on a roller coaster. I am not at all sure that Capra rejects the validity of the happy ending, but what one detects, in the abrupt changes of style, is some knowledge, if less than conscious, of the discrepancy between the complex nature of his film's recurring antitheses and the evasive facility of their reconciliation.

To understand this is to come to a film such as *It's a Wonderful Life* with a fresh eye. For it is in this film that Capra effects the perfect equipoise between the antitheses he poses and the apparatus by which he reconciles them; there being, in fact, no recourse in "real life," the end is served by the intervention of a literal *deus ex machina.* And, as George Bailey, the film's hero, jumps into the river to commit suicide as the culmination of his progress of disastrous failures, he is saved . . . by an angel! This is, of course, the perfect, and, in fact, only, alternative for Capra; and the *deus ex machina* serves its classic purpose, from *Iphigenia in Tauris* to *The Threepenny Opera;* namely, to satisfy an understanding of the work on every level. It creates, for those who wish it, the happy ending par excellence, since it had already become apparent, in the previous Capra movies, that the climaxes, by the very extremity of the situations which gave rise to them, were derived *de force majeure*. Yet, for those who can accept the realities of George Bailey's situation—the continual frustration of his ambitions, his envy of those who have done what he has only wanted to do, the collapse of his business, a sense of utter isolation, final despair—and do not believe in angels (and Capra no more says *we* must believe in slightly absurd angels, although *he* possibly does, than Euripides says we may not believe in slightly absurd gods, although he surely doesn't), the film ends, in effect, with the hero's suicide.[1]

*It's a Wonderful Life* is the kind of work which defies criticism; almost, one might say, defies art. It is one of the funniest and one of the bleakest, as well as being one of the most technically adroit, films ever made; it is a masterpiece, yet rather of that kind peculiar to the film: unconscious masterpieces. Consciously, except in the matter of his certainly conscious concern with the mastery of his medium's technique, I don't imagine Capra conceives of himself as much different from Clarence Budington Kelland, from whose story *Mr. Deeds Goes to Town* was adapted. *It's a Wonderful Life* is a truly subversive work, the *Huckleberry Finn* which gives the lie to the *Tom Sawyers;* yet I am certain Capra would not think of it in this way, nor boast of pacts made with the devil. I mention Twain and allude to Melville not haphazardly; Capra's films seem to me related in a direct way to the mainstream of our literature; and the kind of case Leslie Fiedler makes with regard to the American novel, leaving aside questions of its truth or falsity, might equally have been derived from the American film. Just as *Pull My Daisy* is clearly out of *Huckleberry Finn*, so *A Place in the Sun* (once one forgets Dreiser, as the film itself was quite ready to do) is pure *Gatsby;* and Capra seems to me, in many ways, the analogue of Twain, always, but once, flawing his genius. I would not wish to press this analogy, for, as artists, Twain and Capra are vastly dissimilar; yet they seem to me comparable in their situation with respect to art and consciousness. And, like Twain also, Capra is a "natural"; a folk artist in the sense of drawing imaginatively for his substance on some of the most characteristic matter of our national folklore.

Capra (whose life, in actuality, was in imitation of that most classic American cliché: poor Italian immigrant makes good) has made our clichés the stuff of his art; compounding his most significant films of the ritual elements of the peculiarly American mythos of innocence. The image of metropolitan corruption, the hatred of the city slicker, the suspicion of

1. I don't mean to give the impression here that Capra employs his *deus ex machina* with any Euripidean irony (all the film's irony is contained in its title). The agonizing pathos of the film's climax derives precisely from the tension one senses between Capra's deeply felt desire to save his protagonist and his terrible knowledge that he cannot.

sophistication, the distrust of politics and the fear of government, the virtue of the rural: what is this if not a compendium of the beliefs of Populism and of Progressivism, which, in turn, are Jeffersonianism, grown ossified and anachronistic. Even the agrarian quality of Jeffersonianism has been curiously preserved; Mr. Deeds wants to use his twenty-million-dollar inheritance to aid homeless farmers with free land and seed, and Mr. Smith wants the disputed tract of land to be used as an outdoor camp for boys. And there is, in addition, in Capra's work, a preoccupation with still another aspect of our national subconscious. All of his heroes are made to undergo some extraordinarily harrowing ordeal before their final triumph: Mr. Deeds is placed on trial; Mr. Smith is forced to filibuster; John Doe is hissed, jeered, and ridiculed before an assemblage of his followers; George Bailey is humiliatingly bankrupt. There is, as Dwight Macdonald has observed, something very American in the idea of an uncrucified Christ.

But Capra's genius is a comic one, and there remains that quality of irreducible foolishness in the Capra heroes, a foolishness that is the emblem of their humanity: Mr. Deeds' tuba and awful poetry, Mr. Smith's patriotic mania, John Doe's hobo language and legends, George Bailey's consummate awkwardness. And their innocence, their virtue, their beauty is inextricable from this. In a world of cleverness and corruption, they have allowed themselves to be "fools for Christ's sake"; and it hardly seems a flaw in this scheme that George Bailey's antagonist in *It's a Wonderful Life* is made a Dickensian caricature of villainy, embodying his single trait; rather, he becomes an abstracted converse of the George Baileys, the incarnation of pure, natural malignity. He exists not so much as a human being as an operative force in this world; and, by the suicide of George Bailey, the triumphant one; in the end, the cross will not be cheated of its suffering.

I have mentioned the breaches of Capra's style, but it remains to mention the style as such. It is a style—although one might never guess it from the most part of his recent work—of almost classic purity; and it seems somehow appropriate to the American ethos of casual abundance that the director of quite probably the greatest technical genius in the Hollywood film, post-Griffith, pre-Hitchcock—a genius, as Richard Griffith has suggested, on the order of those of the silent Russian cinema at its zenith—should have placed his great gifts at the service of an apparently frivolous kind of comedy. It is a style, one is tempted to say, based solely on editing, since it depends for its effect on a sustained sequence of rhythmic motion. There is very little about Capra's style which may be ascertained from a still, as, say, each still from Eisenstein has the carefully composed quality of an Old Master. A Capra still is unbeautiful; if anything, a characteristic still from Capra will strike one as a little too busy, even chaotic. But whereas Eisenstein's complex and intricate editing seems, finally, the attempt to impose movement on material which is essentially static, Capra's has the effect of imposing order on images constantly in motion, imposing order on chaos. The end of all this is indeed a kind of beauty, a beauty of controlled motion, more like dancing than like painting, but more like the movies than like anything else.

A comic genius is fundamentally a realistic one, and, in his films, his various conclusions notwithstanding, Capra has created for us an anthology of indelible images of predatory greed, political corruption, the cynical manipulation of public opinion, the murderous nature of private enterprise, and the frustration and aridity of small-town American life. There is always a gulf between what Capra wishes to say and what he actually succeeds in saying. He seems obsessed with certain American social myths, but he observes that society itself as a realist. The most succinct statement of this discrepancy between intention and accomplishment is put by Richard Griffith, in his monograph on Capra, simply by juxtaposing a commonplace phrase of Capra criticism—"engrossing affection for small American types"—against a still of the witnesses at the trial of Mr. Deeds. Their faces remain more expressive than any comment one could make upon them: mean, stupid, vain, petty, ridiculous; they form an imposing catalogue of human viciousness.

And Capra seems always to realize this. His films move at a breathtaking clip: dynamic, driving, taut, at their extreme even hysterical; the unrelenting, frantic acceleration of pace seems to spring from the release of some tremendous accumulation of pressure. The sheer speed and energy seem, finally, less calculated than desperate, as though Capra were aware, on some level, of the tension established between his material and what he attempts to make of it. Desperation—in this quality of Capra's films one sees again the fundamental nature of style as moral action: Capra's desperation is his final honesty. It ruthlessly exposes his own affirmation as pretense, and reveals, recklessly and without defense, dilemma.

Perhaps mention should be made, in passing, of what was, in effect—the rest being only a few remakes, a few frank time-killers, and eight years of silence—Capra's last film, *State of the Union;* despite its prodigal talent and virtuoso style, an acknowledgment of defeat. With *It's a Wonderful Life,* the ideal form for the Capra comedy had been established, but it was a form which could be employed only once. Despite the fact that, in *State of the Union,* such actual names as Vandenberg and Stassen (*O tempora! O mores!*) are mentioned with considerable irreverence, these ostensible signs of daring only serve to emphasize a more fundamental lack of it. Unlike any of Capra's other films, *State of the*

*Union* seems anxious to retreat into its subplot, one of romantic misalliance. And all the hoopla of its finale, as frenetic and noisy as anything Capra has put on the screen, cannot disguise the fact that the hero resigns from politics with the implication being that he is, in fact, *too good* to be involved. In one sense, this is Capra at his most realistic, but also at his least engaged. For the artist, withdrawal from the world—the world as he perceives it—is never achieved without some radical diminution of his art.

Perhaps, having made *It's a Wonderful Life,* there was nothing more Capra had to say. His only fruitful alternative, having achieved a kind of perfection within his own terms, had to be to question the very nature of those terms themselves. Without a realization that the dilemma existed inherently in the terms in which he articulated it, he could, in effect, go no further. It remains only to note that he went no further.

# Under Capracorn

## Stephen Handzo

Optimism is critically suspect. Too often it implies insulation from the evidence of experience, or yeasaying to the status quo—the Norman Vincent Peale, Bruce Barton brand of sales-seminar boosterism that promises individual liberation while leaving the rules of the game unchanged. For Frank Capra, especially in the film-making decade beginning with *Mr. Deeds Goes to Town* and climaxing with *It's a Wonderful Life,* optimism was a dynamic force making possible what was thought impossible. His espousal of this philosophy has made him an easy, even willing target for those socially-conscious critics who despise happy endings as the opiate of the masses. And yet, as has often been mentioned, Capra's own life is a success story more preposterous than any in his films.

Contemporary American attitudes oscillate between the poles of Capra (society can be redeemed) and, say, Samuel Fuller (society is so corrupt that the individual can survive only through guerrilla warfare). But it should be recalled that the films of the *early* thirties were often as derisively cynical as those of today. It wasn't until the Depression's psychic shocks had been absorbed, and confidence was slowly being rebuilt, that Capra's optimism caught the public fancy. The director has always defended his "platitudes" by saying, "They're all true, aren't they?" If at this point he can still believe in the goodness of man . . . well, blasphemous old Harry Cohn surrounded himself on his deathbed with a priest, a rabbi, and a Christian Scientist, on the theory that "maybe one of them knows something I don't." Maybe Capra knows something the rest of us don't know, or have forgotten. I hope so.

*Mr. Deeds Goes to Town* (1936) continues to dominate discussion of the films synonymous with Capra's name. The facility with which the film can be attacked—by Raymond Durgnat, among others—indicates its

From *Film Comment,* vol. 8, no. 4 (November–December 1972). Copyright © 1972 by Film Comment Publishing Corporation. Reprinted by permission of The Film Society of Lincoln Center.

weaknesses: obviousness and too many cheap shots at targets already exhausted by Warner Brothers (e.g., shyster lawyers, greedy heirs, culture parasites).

Interestingly, the theme of country-boy virtue versus city-slicker snobbishness (as well as its underlying anti-intellectualism) is more pronounced in ex-Broadway-playwright Robert Riskin's script than in cracker-barrel-storyteller C. B. Kelland's original "Opera Hat," an "up-to-date" murder mystery from which only the character Longfellow Deeds and some vestiges of the opera background survived. Rooting the film in such traditional American mythology strategically countered its departures: fusing romantic comedy and social urgency, and casting doubt on the hero's sanity. Subsequently, Capra would draw his "little people" from an urban polyglot neighborhood for *You Can't Take It with You,* and attack *rural* political machines in *Mr. Smith Goes to Washington.* The anti-intellectualism charge may be overdrawn, too; the greedy, power-hungry Capra villain—typically Edward ("Business-is-my-hobby") Arnold—is hardly intellectual, but Deeds can quote Thoreau.

Politically, Capra films have something for everybody. His villains are stock characters from the demonology of the Left—an interlocking directorate of industry/press/government that is militarist and incipiently fascist (*Meet John Doe*)—while his heroes counter with 110 percent Americanism: voluntary association, self-reliance, Lincoln, the Boy Scouts. (Marxists found this especially vexing.) Capra films uphold the non-ideological nature of American politics (the most powerful American ideology of all), but the off-screen activities of his characteristic interpreters, James Stewart and Gary Cooper, indicate the practical impact of these values. Of course, the iconography of popular stars transcends ideology. Theoretically, Ayn Rand's ideas are diametrically opposed to Capra's—and yet Cooper's trial in *The Fountainhead* suggests nothing so much as Deeds all over again, with even the same silver-haired Establishmentarian character actors as antagonists.

The politics of these films need not concern us further. The failure of the Durgnat approach is that it gives no sense of what watching *Deeds* is actually like. Surely, the face of Gary Cooper and *voice* of Jean Arthur are the film's real "content." In their first appearances in a Capra film, Arthur and Cooper join the list of stars (Clark Gable, James Stewart, Ronald Colman) whose screen personalities were forever cast or recast under his direction. He, in turn, would hold up production for months to get the "right" cast, knowing that nothing flaws a film more completely than inappropriate or inadequate performances.

For all the tumultuous precision of Capra's mass scenes, the best moments in *Deeds* are the oases of feeling far from the madding crowd.

Arthur and Cooper in Central Park (she playing "Swanee River" on a garbage can) foretell the equivalent Arthur-Stewart scene in *You Can't Take It with You* played in one five-minute unbroken shot, perhaps the longest to that time, that intuitively anticipates Bazin's single-take aesthetic of psychological integrity through space/time unity. The nocturnal love scenes in *Deeds,* played in the semi-darkness of Joseph Walker's backlighting, are some of the loveliest romantic evocations this side of Borzage—something for which Capra is never credited.

While the acting in his films has been a source of wonder, Capra demagicalizes it, saying he doesn't believe in "acting" at all. While critics attacked stars for playing themselves, Capra encouraged them to be hyper-typically themselves. With no stage experience, but lots of life experience, Capra pioneered Stanislavsky acting without knowing it, giving every extra an emotional history, cajoling grizzled Harry Carey into believing he really *was* Vice-President of the United States. Always "leery of the Method," Capra found in Peter Falk's total absorption during the filming of *Pocketful of Miracles*—wearing his costume overcoat everywhere—the kind of affinity he always sought to inspire. By *Deeds,* Capra had come so far from the embarrassingly flat line readings in, say, *Dirigible* that the social clash of the film and the psychological "set" of the characters is conveyed in the rhythm of speech. One never doubts the absolute honesty of Cooper's laconic lines, while lawyer Douglas Dumbrille's rapidity and polish seem mentally prerehearsed, a product of too many business lunches with words used as the currency of self-advancement.

Capra's characters are always *doing* something. Arthur plays with a yo-yo; Deeds' trial becomes a fugue of finger-drumming, doodling, and "O-filling." His films are *very* stingy with close-ups, which are used mainly for crucial reactions. Scenes are constructed within the middle distance, where characters can relate to the objects around them and to each other with their whole bodies. Watching Capra, who talks with his hands, makes it easy to see where such previously inert actors as Gable and Glenn Ford suddenly acquired those animated Sicilian gestures.

Capra's reputed pacing isn't just speed; his thirties films are not particularly fast by either today's standards of those of the time. Rather, Capra—a great storyteller on screen, in print, and in person—knows the value of a logical, well-developed narrative that nevertheless allows for digressions. Robert Riskin, who took over as regular script collaborator with his original story and screenplay for *American Madness,* brought to Capra films a craft in story construction and an ear for dialogue previously absent. The earlier *Dirigible* and *Miracle Woman* had been rickety structures whose only function was to frame the novelty elements (polar exploration, evangelical quackery) that absorbed the director's interest. Capra and Riskin eliminated outdated genre elements by creating their own genre.

From his non-Capra scripts—*The Whole Town's Talking* (with a proto-*Deeds* Jean Arthur), *Magic Town,* and *Mr. 880*—it seems probable that Riskin introduced the subject of the little people who march to their own drum and become prey for the cynical. But the undisciplined moralistic mawkishness of *Magic Town* and the low quality of his directed film *When You're in Love* prove him dependent on a strong director. Ironically, Capra's most effective and visually sophisticated films—*It's a Wonderful Life, Mr. Smith Goes to Washington, The Bitter Tea of General Yen*—are all non-Riskin, suggesting that Riskin's virtue and limitation is his conception of film narrative in playwrighting and novelistic terms. (He once said he introduced "invisible act curtains.") Riskin's script for *Deeds,* with its metrical alternation between Deeds and his antagonists, exemplifies Eisenstein's observation in his essay on Griffith: the application to film of Dickensian parallel action.

The "reactive character" is a key to Capra's cinema. It's hardly an original device—Lubitsch played whole scenes through the medium of keyhole snoopers—but Capra perfected it to serve the TV laugh-track function of cueing audience response. More importantly, for a director who walks a slack tightrope between the ridiculous and the sublime, the reactive character anticipates audience skepticism and enables Capra to undercut his own sentimentality (and perhaps express his own qualms). Whenever things get too marshmallowy, there is always an insert of an abrasive Lionel Stander or Peter Falk to object. As Capra puts it: "The *world* objects."

What William S. Pechter calls the quality of "irreducible foolishness" in Capra's heroes necessitates someone else with whom the audience can identify—like experienced, common-sensical Jean Arthur, the hero's simultaneous confidante and betrayer. If a sophisticated newspaperwoman can be "converted," the audience must succumb to the suspension of disbelief. To a great degree, thirties films, especially Capra's, are a "people's theater": the reaction shot is a kind of Shakespearean aside, and the on-screen crowd in *Deeds* (shifting its allegiance as Cooper gains the initiative) is a continuation of the nineteenth-century melodramatic tradition of audience participation.

Only three years older than *Mr. Smith, Deeds* looks and sounds much more archaic and is often technically ramshackle: the opening shot of a boxy sedan hurtling off a cliff looks like the "sock" opening of one of Harry Cohn's deadly "B"'s, and the routine montages of newspaper headlines superimposed on crowds are only a pale hint of effects to come.

"Good will" triumphs a little too easily; as "populist" values lose out to the New Deal, Capra films develop internal tensions that make them more interestingly ambiguous.

But *Deeds* still has some of the freshness that made it one of Hollywood's true originals, because the roles and situations are not yet hardened formulae. Longfellow Deeds is a genuine character, the greatest in the Capra gallery, and not a dour "archetype" like John Doe. Also remarkable is the Sicilian-born, slum-raised Capra's talent for evoking the hopes and dreams of Middle America, creating in Cooper the WASP's idealized image of himself. Perhaps the greatest tribute to *Deeds* was paid by the Nazis, who made the film required viewing for officers in their prospective army of occupation for the United States.

That *Deeds* became the basis of Capra's later films was probably the audience's choice rather than the director's. *Lost Horizon* (1937) was a complete departure in setting and plot, and proved one thing: that an urbane Colman was as much a Capra hero as a folksy Cooper.

One of Western man's great delusions, said H. L. Mencken, is that there is a great store of wisdom in the East. With the spell the photography, sets, and music can still cast, "Love They Neighbor" admittedly sounds more exotic from marmoset-like Sam Jeffe in a cardboard lamasery, but the great ironic truth of *Lost Horizon* is that Shangri-la is a bore. The power of *Lost Horizon* is in its early images: the hysterical mobs of refugees, the escape in an airplane mysteriously diverted and crashing, the treacherous trek to the hidden city. The dramatic momentum isn't regained until Colman and his brother brave the elements to leave. The implication is clear: without conflict, like stagnates. And so does film. "Utopia," after all, means "nowhere."

"Shangri-la in a frame house" was one critic's view of *You Can't Take It with You* (1938), a huge hit that today seems badly slowed by too many reaction shots, and by ponderous Lionel Barrymore's self-conscious, head-scratching impishness. When few had it, the film's anti-money philosophy was welcome, though today it smacks of sour grapes, since the Depression effectively froze social mobility. Actually, the Vanderhof clan's income is ambiguously adequate to support (Negro) servants; and massive socio-psychological evidence suggests that the least happy are the very rich and the very poor.

*You Can't Take It with You* was praised for making the play's madcap ménage of cartoon cutouts into plausible people, for bringing warmth and balance to a "screwball" genre already out of public favor. Hawks' contemporaneous *Bringing Up Baby,* in making everybody crazy, left the audience no one to identify with—and paid for it. Today, diametrically reversed audience preferences have released the anarchic Id uncensured by the social Superego. But the short-lived "screwball" genre produced fewer important films than the serio-comic viewpoint: Sturges's Capraesque *Sullivan's Travels* and *Christmas in July,* Stevens's last stand of literate populism, *The Talk of the Town,* and the Cukor-Kanin *The Marrying Kind,* which deftly wedded thirties sociology with fifties sitcom.

With three Oscars in five years for best direction under his belt, Capra combined the stars of *You Can't Take It with You,* the general plot line of *Deeds,* and the symbols of popular sovereignty into the archetypal Capra political drama, *Mr. Smith Goes to Washington* (1939). The pitting of Claude Rains, with his noblest-Roman profile demanding perpetuation on the face of coins, against James Stewart, the younger and more emotional and counterpart of Gary Cooper, helped produce Capra's best pre-war film, and a significant escalation in aspiration and achievement.

As in *Deeds,* sudden death catapults a good-hearted nonentity into a lonely ordeal on the national stage; but in *Smith* every scene, every shot exudes new assurance. From the opening profile close-up of a hawk-nosed, rat-faced reporter callously spewing the news of a Senator's death in office into the mouthpiece of an old-fashioned pay phone, a swish-pan/wipe sets in motion rapidly successive scenes leading to James Stewart's "honorary stooge" appointment, the expository pace driven relentlessly by wipes to establish the premises and power relationships in one minute flat.

Capra's accidental entry into film inspired a conviction that the neophyte who breaks all the rules, unaware that there are any, can triumph over seasoned mediocrity. Stewart's elevation by the toss of a coin that lands on its edge is even more whimsical. His selection is heralded in a "star-spangled banquet" allowing montage-expert Slavko Vorkapich to gently satirize democracy's rites in a shower of stars, stripes, popping corks, and dutifully clapping hands. During an "Auld Lang Syne" send off *à la* Deeds, Stewart receives his first briefcase in a triptych frame uniting the film's three main protagonists: Jefferson Smith (whose very name symbolizes agrarian democracy and the American Everyman) and, via portraits, Washington (the institutional symbol of America's founding) and Lincoln (martyred hero of its greatest crisis—the original Mr. Smith and Christ-figure of U.S. politics).

The scenes in the Senate rise above the rest, with the Chamber meticulously recreated and every word of the ritualistic procedure authentic, except for party and state affiliations. Though he is today regarded as a sentimental fabulist, Capra's main impact in the thirties was as a realistic director; the veracity in *Smith* is still astonishing, and Jean Arthur's explanation of how Congress works, or doesn't, should be in civics texts. A thousand details are woven into a tapestry: Smith's upheld hand unobtrusively framed against the flag during his swearing in; the microphone feedback adding hollowness to Rains's fraudulent testimony in hearings framing Smith in a land deal after his proposed Boy Ranger camp runs afoul of his mentors' graft schemes; the way Claude Rains's glasses, glinting wildly during his perjury, equate him with Boss Edward Arnold— whose rimless spectacles glare all the time, and whose tool Rains has totally become.

*Smith* flags a bit at mid-point—with some hollow scenes between Arthur and Thomas Mitchell, and exposition-laden sequences of political machinations given visual interest only by Walker's use of table lamps for sinister low-angle source light—but reawakens with an amazing scene played in semi-silhouette at the feet of the statue of Lincoln (a continuous presence), in which Arthur finds Stewart, in tears, seething with the bitterness of the wounded idealist, and conceives the idea of the one-man filibuster. The last quarter of the film spirals to the most dizzying surge of dialectical frenzy since silent Eisenstein, with Capra orchestrating hundreds of vignettes and reactions into a virtuoso whirlwind.

But unlike Eisenstein's analytic fragmentation, Capra's editing never loses the main character. The central image established early as a visual plot-correlative starts to pay off: Stewart standing behind his desk on the Senate floor, a slightly depressed angle suggesting heroic potential; the walls of the chamber converging behind him so that he is, figuratively and literally, cornered; fuzzily-focused spectators—The People omnipresent— looking down from the galleries, passing judgment. The classical repetition of this core image makes Stewart an immobile bastion as the Senate Chamber becomes both the eye of a cyclone and a gladiatorial arena. (Such imagery makes *Smith* a *film,* rather than a good script well-directed, like *Deeds.*)

In place of Eisenstein's mass-hero, Capra gives us the mass "reactive character," the technical equivalent of a main tenet: individuals lead, masses huddle. The shortest vignettes are staged with remarkable density: as a youthful protester is carried kicking and screaming from a meeting, the camera pans a row of oblivious spectators and catches on one the fatuous expression of all the yes-men of history. With flawless timing, as Smith announces his filibuster will continue with a reading of "The Constitution of the United States," already-exhausted Senators groan in unison; one spins in his chair and throws up his hands.

Some of the cutting is almost subliminal. Into Harry Carey's hesitation on "The chair recognizes . . . Senator Smith," Capra cuts in flashes of Stewart and Rains vying for attention. And after Grant Mitchell deftly deflates Stewart's "Either I'm dead right or I'm crazy" ("You wouldn't care to put that to a vote, would you, Senator?"), Capra undercuts *him* with a quick glimpse of Jean Arthur curling her lip—using a character of established sophistication and intelligence to reinforce the audience's pain.

Stewart's anguished expression and limp torso during his one-man filibuster suggest for a moment "Ecce Homo" as he faints and is buried in an avalanche of "Taylor-made" hostile telegrams. It would be hard to top that but Capra does, as Rains attempts suicide and rushes to the floor screaming "I'm not fit to be a Senator!" The film ends ambiguously, with the Senate in turmoil and the fate of the political machine unresolved.

Often hollow in its moralism and rhetoric, for example the disproportionate cheering by Legionnaires at some belligerent homily of Stewart's, *Mr. Smith* is probably a failure by the highest critical standards. But the whole thing is put across with such verve that it hardly matters.

If *Mr. Smith* is archetypal Capra, *Meet John Doe* (1941) is Capracorn Kabuki, with the earlier film's formal richness solidifying into formula and ritual. Despite Edward Arnold's strong performance as the evil newspaper magnate, his character has all the depth of a Herblock cartoon, with neither the inner conflicts of *You Can't Take It with You*'s Kirby nor a morally ambiguous Claude Rains to front for him. But the Arnold character does at least understand that reaction in America cannot present itself undisguised; it needs the trappings of populism. Thus the choice of ex-baseball-player Gary Cooper as the plain-talkin' mouthpiece for a fascistic Corporate State. And thus the mass scenes in *Doe,* which combine the Spirit of Woodstock with the Substance of Spiro.

At the "John Doe Rally," the camera tracks through row upon row of singing, rain-soaked conventioneers, and provides a "set piece" of political spectacle equaling *Potemkin* or *Triumph of the Will.* As the convention turns into a riot, a wet newspaper thrown at Cooper streaks the headline "John Doe a Fake" across his face, so timed to climax his humiliation. One wonders if Capra isn't *too* perfect and deliberate for modern taste.

The basis of the *Deeds-Smith-Doe* trilogy is its modern recasting of the Gospels. (No wonder they have such strong plots.) It is implicit in *Deeds*—"People have been crucified before"—and quite explicit in *Doe*—"the first John Doe . . . two thousand years ago." But Barbara Stanwyck's hysterical histrionics intervene, in a last-minute Calvary cavalry charge; neither Capra nor his audience was prepared to carry this hypothetically plausible Second Coming *that* far. As Dwight Macdonald has observed, there is something very American in the idea of an uncrucified Christ.

*Meet John Doe* is self-defeating for reasons other than the publicized confusion over its ending; Capra is appealing when extolling vagabondage and eccentricity, less so when glorifying plebeian averageness in terms akin to a George Wallace rally—all the more ironically since his own film shows the ulterior exploitability of "typical" Americanism. Not until con-

temporary TV commercials has such concentrated technical virtuosity
served such aggressively banal content.

In retrospect, Capra's slippage can be dated from *Doe,* his first film in
years failing either to make the National Board of Review Ten Best or
figure importantly in the Academy Award nominations. There were signs
too that audiences were starting to rebel against "messages." The solitary
dissent of Alistair Cooke on *Deeds*—that Capra had begun making films
"about themes instead of people"—became a chorus. The "little people"
in his films were sounding more and more like ventriloquist dummies
speaking with one voice: the director's. Preston Sturges, unconstrained by
having to fit his human "found objects" into a social theory, was stealing
Capra's thunder in satirical Americana—*Sullivan's Travels* tweaking
show-biz social-consciousness *à la* John Doe—while Orson Welles seemed
to make Capra a stylistic anachronism.

*It's a Wonderful Life* (1946) is best described as *A Christmas Carol*
from Bob Crachit's point of view. Capra's first post-World War II
production—and the maiden effort of Capra's independent Liberty
Films—is, surprisingly, not forward-looking but reflective. Perhaps lack of
confidence accounts for Capra's taking refuge in a reprise of characteristic
themes and situations and surrounding himself with familiar faces, both in
the cast and behind the camera.

Whatever the reason, *Wonderful Life* thus became Capra's contribution to what Andrew Sarris has called the forties "cinema of memory." It
is his *Ambersons,* his *How Green Was My Valley*—one man's life and the
collective autobiography of a small town (the archetypal American microcosm) in the era spanning the two world wars. Abandoning his customarily
linear narrative, Capra makes the entire film an extended flashback. Instead of the usual time-span of weeks or months culminating in a decisive
act, the film chronicles decades through the character George Bailey—a
Deeds who never got rich, a Smith who never got appointed to the Senate,
a Doe who remained obscure—who just got old. Bailey is less a character
than a container into which James Stewart pours every nuance of his own
being, exposing his whole emotional range in a two-hour *tour de force*.
Surpassing even *Mr. Smith,* it remains Stewart's own favorite performance, as *Wonderful Life* is Capra's favorite of his films. It is also Capra's
most Ford-like film, dealing with themes of community and continuity,
and taking place in the generation just past.

Capra draws upon the common experiences of those years, including
the shared movie experience of which his own films were a preeminent
part. Consequently, as the decades pass, the style of the film is modulated
to match the evolution of Capra's work. The high-school prom that writes
*finis* to the twenties is done in the style of late silent slapstick comedy with

an elaborate sight gag—pranksters part a dance floor to reveal a swimming pool as the dance becomes an aquacade. The coming of the Depression, with Stewart and bride Donna Reed sacrificing their honeymoon money to salvage the building-and-loan, is handled with the click-clack pacing of early thirties films, specifically *American Madness*. Stewart's collisions with tycoon Lionel Barrymore (erstwhile Grandpa Vanderhof, now in the Edward Arnold part) obviously recall *You Can't Take It with You, Mr. Smith,* and *John Doe*, while World War II is depicted with "Why We Fight"-style documentary clips and the actors ingeniously and unobstrusively integrated via a new blue-screen process.

George Bailey's adult life is picked up in 1928 when he assumes charge of the building-and-loan; 1928 was the year Capra joined Columbia and his career, after two false starts, began in earnest: Stewart weds Donna Reed in 1932, the year of Capra's marriage to his wife of forty years. Bailey has four children, as Capra would have but for the death of his little son. *Wonderful Life* is, then, a personal and professional autobiography, though usually less specific. One can find the wild oscillations of euphoria and despair of Capra's films in his own life: an over-achieving childhood and adolescence followed by a long drought of unemployability and emotional paralysis, a film career launched by accident leading to temporary success (with Harry Langdon) followed by despair again, success (with Harry Langdon) followed by despair again, success again. Violent shifts of mood gives his films the sense of life being lived. In *Wonderful Life*, with the audience not yet recovered from the swimming pool scene, Stewart's playfully erotic pursuit of Reed through the bushes is chilled by news of his father's death. (From the triumphant press preview of his biggest hit, *You Can't Take It with You,* Capra was called to the hospital where his son had just died.)

Stewart, facing ruin, snarls viciously at his family, exposing the streak of paranoia and self-pity always implicit in a Capra hero (Deeds punching a poet; Smith beating up reporters). Stewart here is remarkably like Capra's account of his own actions during the year of enforced inactivity because of a contract dispute with Harry Cohn. It is supposed that Capra's theme is that people are basically good; instead it seems to be that people are good under the right circumstances. Careless critics think Capra sentimentalizes poverty, but real need in his films appears as desperation close to madness (the crazed farmer who tries to shoot Deeds; Stewart's sadism). Perhaps Capra, whose book begins, "I hated being poor, hated the ghetto," has created a portrait of The Man I Might Have Been.

The crisis of values has shifted from the millionaire in *You Can't Take It with You* to the character who upholds the Capra ethos. The perpetually falling "Home Sweet Home" sign in the earlier film is replaced by a less convivial anthropomorphic prop—the loose bannister knob constantly reminding Stewart of his shabby surroundings. Amid the *Mildred Pierce*-ish acquisitiveness of the middle forties, Stewart's adherence to the *Our Town* virtues seems an anachronism. And his planned suicide is not an act of principle like Doe's, but an admission of defeat. When a folk-hero like Stewart contemplates suicide, it is indirectly as clear an indication of post-war confusion as *The Best Years of Our Lives*—and a mirror, perhaps, of Capra's own self-doubts.

If forties Hollywood was a cinema of memory, it was also a cinema of imagination abundant in fantasy and dream sequences. Sidney Buchman's *Here Comes Mr. Jordan* was just one of many films depicting Heaven as a super-efficient air-traffic control tower. Mercifully, Capra deleted a similar opening scene in the *Wonderful Life* script (Scene: Interior. Ben Franklin's Workshop in Heaven) in favor of Christmas-card views of small-town streets, a sound montage of praying voices *à la* Norman Corwin's radio plays, and animated stars twinkling in conversation.

Guardian angel Henry Travers—the original Grandpa Vanderhof on stage—lets Stewart see the world from the outside looking in, as if he had never been born. This harrowing film-within-the-film, a nocturnal parody of the sunlit main narrative, is enacted over a four-acre small-town set deep in highly realistic snow, and is punctuated with anguished close-ups of Stewart's baggy-eyed face.

One's ultimate critical estimate of *It's a Wonderful Life* depends on whether divine intervention is viewed as a *deus ex machina* cop-out or as a legitimate recourse to the classical tradition of metaphor. That other Italian, Dante, pioneered the didactic guided tour; and what is *Wonderful Life* but an inverted *Faust* in which life is taken, not given?

Instead of the editorial virtuosity and "set pieces" of earlier films, Capra gives individual scenes a new emotional density: a Bailey family dinner in which a whole meal is consumed in one take; an erotic telephone scene between Stewart and Reed in which a Capra hero actually evidences sexuality; Stewart's isolation in the frame when his brother's marriage insures that he (Stewart) will stay chained to the building-and-loan— anticipating the thematic-spatial unity of the last shot in *The Searchers*.

*It's a Wonderful Life* certainly has faults. Apart from his rescue by a guardian angel, Stewart's suicidal intentions aren't particularly consistent with his character as established; the scenes with Barrymore (imitating his annual Scrooge performance on radio) are too rhetorical and dully shot. Indeed, the whole Barrymore character is oddly nineteenth-century—and extraneous—as the real conflict is no longer between good and bad characters but has shifted to the affirmative and suicidal/nihilistic traits warring within the protagonist. Nevertheless, *Wonderful Life* is one of the most personal visions ever realized in commercial cinema. Rich in performance, unflinching in its confrontation of the "permanent things" of human existence, it is probably the film for which Capra will ultimately be remembered. Capra has said he tried for no less.

It is tempting to connect Spencer Tracy's fall from grace in *State of the Union* (1948) with Capra's sell-out of his figurative and literal Liberty to a major studio, giving an ironic dimension to what Andrew Sarris has called the obligatory scene in Capra: "the confession of folly in the most public manner possible." Tracy in *State:* "I lost faith in you, faith in myself... was afraid I wouldn't be elected. That's why I'm withdrawing... because I'm dishonest." Capra in his autobiography: "I fell never to rise to be the same man again either as a person or a talent.... I lost my nerve... for fear of losing a few bucks."

To a remarkable extent, Capra's films caught the mood of America in the thirties and forties. When sufficiently little was happening in the world for the masses to be bemused for weeks by the deserved misfortunes of the rich, Capra rebuilt the Depression-bruised male ego with reassurance that, despite unemployment, he was still virile and the master of any situation: "Twenty million dollars and you don't know how to dunk." *Deeds* and *You Can't Take It with You* combined the folk experience of the Depression (bankruptcy, eviction), with an optimism born equally of the renewed confidence inspired by the New Deal and the need to dispel the lingering malaise. *Mr. Smith* tempered the muckraking of the earlier thirties with the vindication of a flawed democracy that was threatened with extinction abroad. *Doe* (visually darker than earlier Capra, and not just because of a different cameraman) caught that moment when, in Roosevelt's phrase, Dr. New Deal gave way to Dr. Win-the-War. *State,* released by Louis B. Mayer's M-G-M, had Tracy advocating immediate world government and mass public housing—a poignant reminder of the hopes cherished for the "post-war world" before the Cold War and the long night of McCarthyism froze the New Deal-Fair Deal reform impulse at its root.

Internally, the Capra films became more pessimistic, though this was not immediately apparent. Only in *Deeds* does the hero win a clear victory by his own efforts. In *Smith,* the popular protests are all beaten down and the end is more absurdist than triumphal. (Even in these two films, the arbitrariness of the "happy" endings was underscored when the Russians circulated throughout Europe captured prints of *Deeds* and *Smith,* respectively retitled *Grip of the Dollar* and *The Senator.*) In *Doe* the people's movement is completely discredited, and it is unlikely that Cooper's few remaining adherents can rebuild it. In Capra's later films, the hero is often saved by a directorial decree as dictatorial as it is delirious.

The acquisition of awareness, simultaneously social and sexual, is the subject of *Mr. Deeds, Mr. Smith,* and *John Doe.* In *State of the Union,* awareness includes the hero's own culpability. After 1948, Capra made only four more features. Ironically—for a director who had accused his colleagues of learning about life from each other's movies—two of the four were remakes of his own films; auteurism had become autocannibalism. Various explanations, some plausible, have been advanced. Most probably, Capra put all he had and all he was into *It's a Wonderful Life.* And, after the confession of *State of the Union,* there was no place left to go.

# Charles Chaplin

*CHARLES CHAPLIN was born in 1889 in London, the son of music hall entertainers. He never forgot the poverty of his early years in the East End, which he described in vivid Dickensian detail in* My Autobiography *(1964). He first went on the stage at the age of five, and at seventeen he joined a famous vaudeville troupe run by Fred Karno. There he developed many of the comedy routines he later used in his films. On the Karno company's visit to America in 1913 he was signed by Mack Sennett to make movies for Keystone, which had pioneered the kind of madcap slapstick comedy at which Chaplin soon excelled. Chaplin soon began to direct as well as to star in these films, and eventually he settled on the tramp character he was to continue playing for the next twenty-five years.*

*In 1915 Chaplin signed with Essanay, in 1916 he moved on to the Mutual Company, in 1918 he went to the First National Company, and finally in the 1920s he began to make and control his own feature films. Chaplin was a shrewd business man as well as an increasingly ambitious and careful craftsman. Each of these moves signifies another chapter not only in his growing fame and wealth but also in his artistic aims. As he achieved worldwide success he also improved as an artist. The French film historian Georges Sadoul calls him "the greatest genius the cinema has ever produced."*

*Chaplin's genius is founded on what he himself calls "the noble art of pantomime." There seems to be nothing human that Chaplin cannot physically mime, and his sense of comic tact and timing is unmatched. Chaplin's development carried him from brilliant but random slapstick skits toward larger dramatic situations, which increasingly mingle pathos with comedy, and constantly deepen the significance of the tramp character without abandoning his childlike comic appeal. The tramp evolves from a roguish, amoral runt to a poignant but still scrappy idealization of the underdog.*

*From the beginning, class distinctions and social situations enlarge the range of the tramp's meaning. He is often set off against people who are larger, more powerful, more respectable, more pompous and rigid, more innocent, or more malevolent. His ability to win out—or at least to survive—in the face of these imposing tormentors is close to the heart of all comedy. It reassures us that, despite rigid social hierarchies, despite inequities of power, even the least of us, by dint of sheer agility, pluck, and resourcefulness, can learn to make his way in a callous and brutal world.*

*Moreover, Chaplin performs his feats with unique grace and style. The precision and elegance of his movements have been compared, sometimes derisively, to those of a ballet dancer. But Chaplin's elaborate elegance and energy are more than physical. When he sits down to dine on shoe leather in* The Gold Rush *(1925), his splendid table manners, hurried only by starvation, become an exquisite act of the imagination, unavailable to his coarse companion. Such rituals not only show us, as he often does elsewhere, that the starving tramp is a true gentleman; they also turn a desperate repast into a hilarious mental banquet, which feeds the spirit even though it can hardly nourish the body. Chaplin's themes frequently border on sentimentality, especially in his treatment of women in his longer films. But at its best this sentimental idealization of waif-like women is consistent with the genuine pathos of the tramp's character and his point of view.*

*The dramatic development of the tramp figure culminates in* The Gold Rush *and* City Lights *(1931).* Modern Times *(1936) and the less successful* The Great Dictator *(1940) shift directly to social and political themes, in which the central character becomes secondary to the farcical portrayal of such matters as the industrial assembly line and the grotesqueries of Hitlerism. On this last subject both the technique of farce and Chaplin's dramatic vision proved inadequate, as he himself recognized in concluding the film with a direct harangue at the audience.*

*Despite his success and wealth, Chaplin, like many in Hollywood, flirted with left-wing politics in the 1930s, perhaps a natural consequence of the tramp point of view; along with his scandalous marital history, his politics would make him a controversial figure in the anti-Communist atmosphere that followed World War II. Chaplin's vague anti-capitalism is best expressed in the one unquestionable masterpiece among his late films, the savage black comedy* Monsieur Verdoux *(1947). He abandons the tramp character to play a suave, embittered, fortune-hunting Bluebeard, a wife-killer and an unusually pointed embodiment of the entrepreneurial spirit. Though his theme is serious, Chaplin manages to infuse some uproarious humor into the grisly plot and sit-com mise en scène, especially in Verdoux's attempts upon his only unkillable victim, played superbly by Martha Raye.*

*Chaplin was less successful in the more sentimental* Limelight *(1952), a personal and autobiographical film set in the old music-hall days in London, in which he deals movingly with growing old, his fear of losing his touch, and his diminishing rapport with his audience. Chaplin, who had never become an American citizen, exiled himself to Switzerland in 1952, in the face of growing McCarthyite attacks. In Europe he made* A King in New York *(1957), a very uneven satire on America and McCarthyism, and* The Countess from Hong Kong *(1966), a feeble and witless romantic comedy in which he himself makes only a brief appearance. But Chaplin returned to New York and Hollywood in 1972 to receive a triumphal accolade as a living legend. He died in Switzerland on Christmas Day, 1977.*

*Books on Chaplin include Parker Tyler's* Chaplin: Last of the Clowns *(1947), Theodore Huff's* Charlie Chaplin *(1951), Jean Mitry's* Charlot et la fabulation chaplinesque *(in French, 1957), and Roger Manvell's* Chaplin *(1974). Chaplin told his own life story in* My Autobiography *(1964).*

# Chaplin:
# Charles and Charlie

## Michael Roemer

A year after Chaplin was born, his parents separated. At the age of five, he appeared on stage in place of his mother, a vaudeville singer who was losing her voice. He sang, danced, and picked up the coins that the audience threw at him.

When Hanna Chaplin could no longer support her children, she moved into the Lambeth workhouse. Chaplin and his half-brother, Sidney, were sent to a Dickensian orphanage, where children were flogged. A brief family reunion did occur, but then Hanna Chaplin went mad and had to be confined to an asylum. Her sons were sent to another orphanage, even more frightful than the first.

When Chaplin was seven, a court forced his father to take care of the boys. For several months they lived with him and a woman called Louise. Both adults drank heavily and fought constantly. Louise, who had a child of her own, resented the boys, and frequently locked them out of the house. As soon as their mother was better, they rejoined her. Chaplin found a job with a troupe of clog dancers and performed in London and the provinces for a year. Then he developed asthma and had to be sent home. With his mother, he spent a strange summer at the fashionable house of a friend, who had left the stage to become the mistress of a wealthy old colonel.

In 1899, Chaplin's father died of dropsy and alcoholism. His friends had had to get him drunk so they could take him to the hospital. Sidney went off to sea, and Chaplin—now nine—talked his way into a series of odd jobs. He worked for a chandler, in a printing shop, as a glassblower, old-clothes salesman, and as a page boy in the home of a rich doctor. He taught dancing and tried making toy boats. Often he was fired the day he was hired. One evening he came home and found that his mother was mad

From *The Yale Review*, vol. 64, no. 2 (December 1974). Copyright Yale University. Reprinted by permission of *The Yale Review* and Michael Roemer.

again. She was returned to the asylum. Terrified of being sent back to the orphanage, Chaplin spent his days roaming the street.

He tried finding work as an actor. In 1901, at the age of twelve, he landed his first part in a play. During the next four years, he played drama and comedy in London and the provinces. While his life with a theatrical company was far from sheltered or secure, the days of sheer physical want were over. When he was seventeen, Sidney—himself an actor now—found him a job with Fred Karno, the most successful impresario of music hall in England. Chaplin quickly established himself as a gifted and popular comedian. On a company tour of the United States he was spotted by Mack Sennett, who hired him for the movies.

If his early life resembles the dark trial that begins so many fairy tales, his good fortune from this point forward seems like a magic reversal. In the years 1914–1917, he turned out sixty-two short films, writing and directing all but the first few. His work was so phenomenally successful that in 1916 he signed a contract for $670,000 a year, plus a bonus of $150,000. By the time he was twenty-six, he had become the most popular entertainer in the world.

Most people are emotionally destroyed by a childhood like Chaplin's, even if they survive it physically. They are permanently robbed of a whole range of feelings, and their existence seems to depend on locking their early experience into a walled-off chamber of the heart. Providentially for Chaplin and for us, he had early access to the theatre, which thrives on extremes and in which the excesses of his childhood could find expression. By virtue of his extraordinary gifts and the happy circumstance that brought him to the silent cinema, his childhood—instead of being forever buried—became instead the source material of his work.

Chaplin has said, "All my pictures depend on the idea of getting me into trouble." In the first films Chaplin made for Mack Sennett, Charlie's troubles are still minor and mostly of his own making. But soon the pressures take on a palpable, physical urgency and the situations confronting him take an ominous turn. By the time of the Mutual and Essanay shorts—*Easy Street, The Adventurer, The Immigrant, A Dog's Life,* and *Shoulder Arms*—Charlie is in constant danger, forever on the run from cops, prison guards, enemy soldiers, or some huge bully. The wellspring of his farce is violence, hunger, fear, greed, need, desolation, mistrust, despair, suicide, and drugs. A catastrophic imagination is at work. "Almost everyone frightens me," Chaplin once told Lita Grey. Everyone and everything—for Charlie lives in perpetual jeopardy of being beaten, imprisoned, wiped out. Nothing less than his survival is at stake.

The basic comic situations in *The Gold Rush* are built on hunger and cannibalism. Charlie is threatened with death by starvation or cold, with getting eaten or shot. The comic here is deeply rooted in the terrifying. The shoe-eating sequence was inspired by a documentary account of the Donner Pass crossing: some of the settlers ate their dead and others their moccasins. Chaplin's version of the great Yukon gold rush is a story of dire need. Greed for gold may motivate Big Jim and Black Larsen, but Charlie himself is simply trying to survive. He has stumbled into the white wilderness without design or ambition; *his* needs are far more primary than gold: he is looking for food, shelter, warmth, and human affection.

Chaplin's films thrive on physical tension. The cabin in *The Gold Rush* teeters on the edge of an abyss; Charlie and Jim cling by their fingernails to the steeply slanted, ice-covered floor, and every time Charlie coughs they drop closer to diaster. In *The Circus,* he is caged with a sleeping lion who threatens to wake up at the slightest noise, and besieged by a troupe of monkeys when he tries to balance on a high wire. In *Modern Times,* he skirts destruction by roller-skating blindfold along a sheer drop. And in *The Great Dictator* an enormous artillery shell keeps pointing itself at the little barber and a live grenade gets lost inside his bulky uniform.

Many scenes are structured by mounting tension, with disaster threatening till the very end. In the restaurant of *The Immigrant,* a starved Charlie orders food that he plans to pay for with a found coin. When another customer is brutally beaten and kicked because he is ten cents short, Charlie anxiously feels for the coin in his pocket; it's gone. Panicked, he spies another coin on the floor and manages to get hold of it, but the villainous-looking waiter twists it in his teeth and tosses it back onto the table: counterfeit! Charlie desperately plays for time but muffs an opportunity to extricate himself and doesn't escape until the last moment.

Even when the issue isn't survival, things are touch-and-go. In *The Circus,* Charlie unwittingly takes away the chair of the evil ringmaster and lands him on the floor. A moment later, he removes the chair a second time—and just barely manages to slip it back under the ringmaster's bottom. A continuous sequence of kinetic effects like this keeps us in a state of physical tension that explodes into laughter whenever the danger is averted.

Chaplin steers much closer to the dark and dangerous edge of existence than most comedians. There are people who respond so strongly to the tension and danger in his work that they can't laugh. But though his comedies are fed by dark waters, Charlie's survival is assured from the start; his annihilation is constantly threatened but never—in the silent films—carried out. Survival is guaranteed by his very continuity as a character from one picture to the next. He is as indestructible as the heroic creatures of our animated cartoons, who reconstitute themselves miraculously after orgies of destruction. Charlie may not get the girl at the end and the last shot often finds him walking alone into the horizon. But he *is* walking or running—and not so much into the horizon as into the next film. In Charlie's world, to survive is to win. Cast perpetually into jobs for which he is unfit—as a boxer, a singing waiter, a policeman, or a trapeze artist—he inevitably finds some ingenious and unorthodox way out. Even in his romances there are occasional victories—in *Easy Street, The Pawnshop, The Immigrant, The Gold Rush,* and *Modern Times.*

One of the chief pleasures of watching him lies in the extraordinary skill with which he extricates himself from every predicament. His physical agility borders on the magical. He is infinitely resourceful, and can transform an ordinary object into a weapon or means of escape. He is forever surprising us: we think he is going to throw a punch but he delivers a kick instead—or sits suddenly in his opponent's lap. Energized by fear, he never stops moving. His physical agility is supported by stupendous energy and other unique gifts. Like a great dancer, athlete, or magician, he seems to defy man's physical limits. Watching him is exhilarating: he appears to defy the physical laws that the universe has imposed on the rest of us. In his greatest moments, action resolves into dance, and movement is so harmonized that it comes close to music. As he threads his way through disaster after disaster, Charlie is graceful in the oldest and deepest sense of the word: full of grace, blessed, a darling of the gods.

With notable critical consistency, Charlie has been called a representative of the common man. Chaplin himself has described him as the Little Fellow, beset by misfortunes and dreaming of some simple happiness that is forever out of reach. But as we watch these films—or, rather, live through them—something more is at work than our identification with Charlie as a universal underdog. The secret of his appeal and power is that he draws, in a most direct way, on our deep and universal experience of childhood. For this little fellow is just that—a child—and what we so continually recognize in his films are the feelings and experiences we had as children.

Charlie is frail and small—most often the smallest figure on the set. He has trouble walking, keeps falling down and tripping over his own feet. His clothes don't fit: his trousers and shoes are too large. Like a child, he is forever trying to make friends with those who are bigger and stronger. He pats Big Jim in his fur coat as though he were a large, tamable beast. He will jump into someone's lap to ingratiate himself, stop him from hitting, or to express his affectionate delight. He plays dead. He holds Limburger cheese with one hand and his nose with the other. He is perpetually playful and quick to turn any situation into a game. Even when he kisses another man, we're not shocked or surprised, for we respond to him as to a child. His reactions are those of a child. In *The Gold Rush,* Georgia accepts his invitation for New Year's eve; as soon as she leaves the cabin, he goes berserk with joy, jumps up onto the bed, swings on the rafters, punches open a bag of flour, rips up his pillow, and sits on the floor in a cabin afloat with feathers.

Food, a central concern of childhood, is surely the most common ingredient in Chaplin's gags: Charlie at the dinner table of the rich; Charlie eating watermelon; Charlie eating soup on a rolling ship; the Kid cooking for Charlie; Charlie eating a candle or a child's hot dog; Charlie the baker, and countless variations on Charlie the waiter. Few films are without their food scene, and most of them—including the food-fight between Hynkel and Napoloni at the buffet table—have a primary, elemental intensity that takes us right back to childhood. In contrast, Chaplin's drunk acts, though extraordinary in their inventiveness and grace, seem like variations on a music-hall routine. Alcohol never achieves the compulsive reality of food.

Of course, Charlie isn't the only child. Big Jim in his peaked cap that makes him look like an out-sized goblin, the huge round clown in *The Circus,* even the millionaire in *City Lights,* all act and think like children. "You're my best friend! . . . Come on, we'll have a party!" They squabble and fight like children. In *The Pawnshop,* Charlie and his fellow clerk pounce on each other the moment the storekeeper leaves, and go into an elaborate charade of work as soon as he returns. When Edna surprises them in the midst of battle, Charlie flings himself on the floor and goes into a heart-breaking crying act to arouse her maternal pity.

They treat each other like children. When Charlie has cooked the shoe, in *The Gold Rush,* he helps himself to the uppers and serves Jim the ugly-looking sole, spiked with long nails. But Jim simply switches plates, and since he is stronger that settles the issue.

Other comedians also draw in some measure on the reality of child-hood. Laurel and Hardy behave like overage boys: Ollie looks like a baby, Stan has a crying act, and when there is no outsider to unite them, they invariably turn on each other. The Marx Brothers, like naughty boys, reject all order and authority and thrive on anarchy and destruction; they don't just deflate the pompous and fraudulent but gleefully attack everything and anything. As Groucho puts it: "Whatever it is, I'm against it."

But in Chaplin's work the experience of childhood is evoked on the broadest and deepest level. Most children are spared the extremes of Chaplin's early years, yet they too are familiar with danger and fear. Like Charlie, they often find themselves in situations over which they have no control. Like Charlie, they're at the mercy of those who are bigger and stronger, and their days are full of dramatic physical confrontations. Haunted by a fear of failure, they dream of sudden power and glory, a dream that for Charlie often becomes fictive reality. Such dreams are not idle wish-fulfillment, for they touch on our secret strength and resilience: they help us to balance and survive. Like the novels of Dickens, the films of Chaplin transmute extreme hardship into laughter and fictively redeem a threatened and anguished childhood in which many of us recognize our own.

Nowhere is Charlie more explicitly a child than with women. In the early Keystone shorts, he was still a distinctly sexual creature, enmeshed in plots of classical farce—mixed-up bedrooms, philandering husbands, and cheating wives. As late as *The Count,* there is a magnificent scene in which he is brought to the verge of ecstasy by a curvaceous vamp: he works out his sexual frenzy on a buffet table instead of her—plunging his cane into a fried chicken, chopping up a huge cream cake, and finally wrecking every dish in sight.

But, as his work developed, Chaplin turned away from traditional farce and Charlie loses his sexuality. He becomes younger and more innocent—a shy and gallant figure, who races to the rescue whenever the villain makes his indecent advances. This Charlie is capable at most of a chaste and embarrassed kiss on the cheek. The women, too, lose their sexuality. Mabel Normand, in the Keystone films, still has an air of naughtiness. But her place is soon taken by Edna, Georgia, Merna, Virginia, and Paulette, who are children at heart if not in body and play with Charlie in utter innocence. In *The Circus,* Merna is sent to bed without supper by her cruel father; Charlie sneaks food to her and, when she stuffs herself greedily, he gives her a lesson in table manners. In *Modern Times,* he shares a shack with the Waif but sleeps in the doghouse; and in *The Great Dictator* the little barber is so unaware of Paulette as a woman that he lathers her face with shaving cream instead of doing her hair.

Charlie's approach to women is utterly consistent and predictable, but in everything else he displays a protean inconsistency. He is infinitely changeable and can accommodate every kind of contradiction: he scraps like a street urchin one moment and displays perfect drawing-room manners in the next; he waddles like a toddler yet possesses uncanny physical skill; he can shift from rank stupidity to suavest sophistication. In *The Adventurer,* he tries to make a woman more comfortable by shoving a pillow under her wooden stretcher, then brilliantly outwits a whole pack of pursuers. In *Modern Times,* he can't serve a meal without spilling the food but performs an enchanting love song in a mixture of fake Romance languages.

Because he is a child at heart, Charlie has no self-limiting consistency or "integrity," and is still wide open to the polarities of human nature. His behavior veers mercurially. Like Punch, he can play any number of roles without rupturing his elastic identity; he is equally real as a vagabond, sophisticated drunk, innocent lover, or rich swell. In several films he takes two parts: he can even play a woman without ceasing to be Charlie. Beside him, Keaton, Lloyd, Fields, and even the Marx Brothers are models of consistency.

Like the Karamazovs, Charlie has a broad soul. Mack Sennett first cast him as a villain and, though he soon became purer and more innocent, he retained much of his original craftiness. He even remained capable, until much later, of deliberate and unwarranted cruelty. Walt Disney is said to have detested the character, and surely Mickey Mouse is Charlie's antithesis—a child without darkness and impurity, without breadth or depth.

Protean inconsistency is fascinating in fiction, but makes for anarchy in life. Real children are obliged to grow up—define and limit themselves, become integrated, specialized, and predictable. They learn to suppress their contradictions and try to become reliable citizens who won't spring too many surprises on their fellow men. But Charlie is fiction and can remain a child. He continues to act out the impulses the rest of us have learned to repress. His films, like so much of the theatre, live out the hidden and forbidden, the spontaneous and violent. Everyone in the film can respond directly and immediately; no one stays neutral or cool, and action leads to liberating reaction without inhibition or delay. Theatre has always thrived on characters who react strongly and express themselves openly. Oedipus, Lear, and Mother Courage don't hide what they feel; like Charlie, they are caught in situations that won't permit them to stay neutral. In tragedy, as in slapstick farce, feelings are translated into direct action.

All slapstick is inherently violent, but the violence is seldom personal. Mack Sennett's films are packed with pratfalls, chases, and wrecks, but the characters don't often attack each other except with pies. When Laurel and Hardy have a score to settle with someone, they turn on his home or car, and even the Marx Brothers don't often resort to bodily aggression.

In Chaplin's shorts, however, violence is emphatically personal. Blows, beatings, and kicks govern most relationships. Charlie himself is no kindlier than the rest: he treats people the way they treat him—brutally. His cane is primarily a slap-stick, a weapon more lethal than Punch's, for it has a sharp point at one end and a useful hook at the other. In *The Kid,* he bashes a bully on the head with a brick till he has him staggering, then administers a few lighter blows to finish him off. No one is safe from violence in Charlie's world.

In the films of Keaton, the hero is often alone. There is a sense of space around him, and his problem may be a runaway train, an abandoned ocean liner, or a rushing river. But Charlie moves through a crowded social scene. Like Keaton and Lloyd, he has trouble with objects, but his real problem is other people. Personal violence in his films is developed to the highest level of sophistication, for without that defense he would perish.

Of course we get the satisfaction of hitting without the painful consequences. Even the most ferocious blows fail to injure, let alone kill. Though the big bully in *East Street* is struck on the head by a cast-iron stove which Charlie drops from an upstairs window, he turns up in the following scene in the best of health. Aggression and violence may be deeply rooted in Chaplin's past, but his films transmute them into farce.

The constant movement in Chaplin's work produces a strong kinetic effect in us—a muscular empathy that may well be the most direct response film can elicit. His work, moreover, is rich in sensory detail that arouses our physical participation.

In *The Adventurer,* a scoop of ice cream slips into Charlie's pants, slides down his trouser leg, drops through the balcony grating to the floor below, lands on the bare back of a stately dowager, and disappears inside her dress. In *The Count,* Charlie and Eric Campbell engage in a kicking duel on the dance floor and maneuver their unsuspecting partners around like shields; the soft, billowing posteriors of the women are in constant danger of being kicked and create a very palpable, fleshy sense of participation.

When Keaton, in *The Navigator,* is trapped under water, the effect is largely graphic. But the water in the dugout of *Shoulder Arms* is sensory and wet; everything is soggy and submerged in it: Charlie lies down on his flooded bunk, fluffs out his soaked pillow, rests his head on it, and covers himself with a dripping blanket.

There is, of course, something primary and even primitive at work here. When we grow up, most of us lose touch with our senses; we no longer use our skin but cover and neutralize it. The pristine experience of what things feel like is lost to us; we increasingly use our eyes and ears— abstracted and aphysical senses—and surrender our concrete, tactile relationship to the world; in effect, we give up one kind of experience for another. But Charlie continues to live in the sensory world that we have, for the most part, forgotten. Significantly, the one area in which adults develop some capacity for tactile sensation and response—their sexuality— is the one area in which Charlie remains aloof and aphysical.

In Chaplin's work we never feel the absence of speech, as we so often do in silent films. Charlie's silence is not imposed on him by a limited technology; it is his natural state. Unlike the pantomime of most silent screen actors, who were forced to render complex adult responses in gestures that were often reductive and oversimplified, Charlie's mime is perfectly suited to express his true nature and experience. It constitutes an original, preverbal language.

Chaplin's encounter with the silent cinema was a happy coincidence that fostered and developed his extraordinary gifts. On the vaudeville circuit he had performed largely in sketches that depended on the spoken word, and had he continued on stage he would never have confined himself to pantomime though it was his forte. But in front of the camera, speech was useless, and everything had to be transformed into gesture and movement—a limitation that may well have pushed him into exploring and mining the rich resources of his own childhood.

Much has been made of Charlie's pathos and deep feeling. Perhaps too much. The shorts are existential farces without a moment's pause for feeling or thought. They are packed with violent action, but the emotions of violence—anger, rage, hurt, and anguish—are never rendered. All scenes involving sentiment are passed over very quickly. In *The Immigrant,* the death of Edna's mother is accorded only the briefest mention while every gag is given loving and extended attention. Occasionally, there is a trace of feeling: Charlie loses the girl in *The Bank* and *The Tramp,* and a torrential downpour lends the end of *The Immigrant* a faintly melancholy air. But by and large the characters are no more vulnerable to feeling than the wooden figures in a puppet show.

Chaplin himself says of the early Charlie: "His brain was seldom active then—only his instincts, which were concerned with the basic essentials: food, warmth and shelter. But with each succeeding comedy the tramp was growing more complex. Sentiment was beginning to percolate through the character." In the shorts, Charlie's survival is so insistently at stake that there is room only for his immediate, physical reactions. But in the features the physical pressure on him lets up and he can, for the first time, afford the luxury of feeling.

Chaplin was clearly interested in letting Charlie develop into a more complex figure, capable of feeling. But he was well aware that sentiment presents a serious threat to comedy, especially to slapstick farce. The problem is apparent in his first long film, *The Kid.* Here he is working with a highly charged, emotional subject, the relationship between Charlie and an abandoned child. But though the story has poignant reference to Chaplin's own childhood, the situations are almost entirely transformed by laughter.

When Charlie first finds himself stuck with the unwanted infant, he tries to get rid of it. No sentiment here: he even considers dropping it down a sewer. Though he grows fond of the Kid, their relationship continues to unfold in a sequence of gags. Throughout the film, the awful threats of separation and loss are undercut by passages of brilliant comedy. Feelings serve as the subsoil of the farce—its point of departure. They inspire the comic situations much as the threat of physical annihilation inspired the shorts. They create tension by posing a threat of suffering—a threat that is never fulfilled, just as Charlie in *The Gold Rush* teeters on the abyss without ever falling into it. Suffering is consistently short-circuited for, like danger and disaster, it is funny only as long as it is averted. We are spared the hurt and find ourselves laughing with relief.

In *The Kid,* as in so many of the films, even the corrosive anguish of poverty is sublimated into farce. A graphically rendered flophouse becomes a scene of such deft comic invention, we quite forget that fear and desperation are the source of our laughter. Even poverty can be funny as long as we're not emotionally involved.

Chaplin observed that his mixture of "raw slapstick and sentiment . . . was something of an innovation"—an innovation that works only when sentiment is contradicted by laughter. Wherever pure feelings appear in the films, they threaten the very reality and texture of farce.

Most comedy denies the reality of feeling, for feelings open us to empathy and suffering. Comedy is often unfeeling to the point of derision and cruelty. It holds nothing sacred and takes an unempathetic, alienated view of the world. Nietzsche says: "A joke is an epigram on the death of a feeling." And Parker Tyler quotes Chaplin's comment that "comedy is life viewed from a distance." For distance—in time or space—has a distinctly cooling effect: the closer we are to an event, the more it involves us; the further we are away, the less we feel it. Significantly, there are few close-ups in Chaplin's films—and surely the most memorable is the last shot of *City Lights,* in which the mask of Charlie's face is broken apart by deep and uncontradicted feeling.

In Charlie's world, pure feeling is focused almost entirely on women. In the shorts, women had been part of the comic scene and occupied no special, elevated position; they could even be villains, a monstrous wife stalks Charlie throughout *Pay Day,* and in the alternate end to *The Vagabond* he is saved from drowning by a woman so ugly, he takes one look at her and jumps right back into the water. But starting with *The Kid,* Chaplin's heroines are no longer part of the comedy. Once they become the object of Charlie's feelings, they stop being funny.

The women he worships don't often take Charlie seriously, for he is childlike, naive, and far too romantic. They feel protective about him at best and naturally reject him for men who are more adult. Their rejection crushes Charlie; it is the one experience he can't seem to handle, for he opens his heart to them as he does to no one else. When his best friend, the millionaire in *City Lights,* refuses to recognize him and throws him out of the house, Charlie bounces right back into action. Men have no power to wound him, but women can sap his energy and reduce him to helpless hurt.

The word "tragic" has been used extensively and rather too easily in descriptions of Chaplin's work. We are certainly touched by Charlie, by his loneliness and disappointment. But to speak of tragedy here is careless and sentimental, for Charlie's pathos springs almost entirely from his blighted romances, and his feelings for women are too much like puppy love to evoke our deepest response. Chaplin mined his dark childhood for some of the most beautiful comedies of our time, and this in itself may have denied him access to tragedy. For surely the tragic is found in the very realm of feeling and suffering, of disaster and death, that his films so skillfully avoid and subvert. Disaster and suffering may be the springboard of Chaplin's farce, but Charlie himself is no tragic figure. He has the dark eyes and the quick, uncertain smile of our common diaspora, but his genius is that of the eternal survivor.

From the start, Chaplin's style was intensely theatrical. His silent films, particularly the shorts, are surreal pirouettes in which everything is pushed to the limit. There are no normal people or ordinary events: every moment is heightened and intensified, every action accelerated. Nothing happens at a natural pace; the end of one motion is already the beginning of another, and incident follows incident without break or pause. The screen is a whirl of activity in which a great deal happens at once: Charlie courts Edna even as he is engaged in a kicking context with Eric Campbell.

The acting is as pushed and unrealistic as the action. Chaplin's performance is a rapid sequence of shifts and transformations that violate every rule of naturalistic acting. To evade the huge masseur in *The Cure,* Charlie becomes in rapid succession a ballet dancer, wrestler, and bullfighter. In *The Pawnshop,* he examines a defunct alarm clock as if he were a doctor listening to its heart, opens it with a can-opener, shakes it as though it were a cocktail, extracts a spring as if it were a bad tooth, peers at it through a jeweler's glass, and finally squirts the whole sorry mess with oil. Allusions, quotations, and metaphors follow each other in free, playful association; the style has the range and flexibility of Elizabethan blank verse.

The theatricality of the films easily accommodates dreams and fantasies. When, in *The Kid,* Charlie has his vision of Paradise, the ghetto street is simply decorated with flowers and the slum-dwellers—dressed in nightgowns and white wings—swoop around the set on wires. When hunger drives Big Jim to hallucination, Charlie turns into a chicken right in front of us. There is no attempt at a realistic illusion, for his disguise is a moth-eaten costume—a theatrical effect that beautifully points up Charlie's dilemma: Jim sees him as a huge chicken but he is clearly human to the rest of us.

The staging and camera work are derived from the theater. Space is treated two-dimensionally: sets and action are photographed from a single vantage-point—most often from the center of the missing fourth wall; there are few reverse shots and we never see one character from the point of view of another. The camera seldom moves. In *The Gold Rush* there is just one dolly shot—with Charlie and Jim strolling down the ship's deck like royalty, attended by their retinue of flunkies. But the very limitations of the camera-work—its flat, restricted point of view—are perfectly expressive of Charlie's experience. Like a child, he is preoccupied with *what* is happening—with effects, not causes. He deals with things as they come upon the stage of his awareness and doesn't look into the wings for their origin. Esthetically, his restricted vision is not simply a limitation: it permits Chaplin to leave out what he doesn't want us to see. Most filmmakers, even those who are suspicious of montage, depend on editing to condense their action and to eliminate whatever is obvious or time-consuming. But Chaplin, working in a theatrical tradition, can edit the *action* instead of the film—just as he would on stage.

All of the great comedians of the American screen—Chaplin, the Marx Brothers, Fields, Laurel and Hardy, Lloyd, and even Keaton—worked in a flagrantly theatrical style. Their films thrive on the very stylization, excess, and exaggeration that we tend to think of as uncinematic.

In a persuasively "real" medium like film, comedy may well have to stress its own unreality more emphatically than it does on stage. For once we *believe* in something, we're apt to lend it our feelings; if we were to believe in the aggression and cruelty of American comedy, they would horrify us instead of making us laugh. Since film, with its persuasive reality, has immediate access to our feelings, comedy may well have to disrupt our emotional involvement by insisting on its own unreality.

But Chaplin's work, unlike most screen comedies, confronts us with an apparent contradiction. For though his style is patently theatrical, he continually uses the persuasive reality of the medium to anchor his stories firmly in the physical world. Indeed, much of his comedy *depends* on the physical credibility of his scenes. The teetering cabin in *The Gold Rush* might well have been built on stage—but the abyss under the cabin could only have been suggested and would never have had the urgent immediacy it has on the screen. In the theater, the antics of the men would have been charming and funny, but there would have been none of the danger, tension, or kinetic involvement that are so essential to Chaplin's work.

Unlike the farce of Mack Sennett or the Marx Brothers, Chaplin's farce has a startling authenticity that seems to belie his theatrical style. In part this no doubt derives from the way in which Charlie's world coincides perfectly with the visible, physical realm that the medium renders so persuasively. He is in constant motion and expresses himself wholly in physical terms. Moreover, his films are a mosaic of precisely observed detail that the camera reports with stunning fidelity.

The most preposterous farcical events occur in utterly realistic settings and are substantiated with painstaking detail. In *One A.M.*, while Charlie wrestles with the Murphy bed, one of its legs comes down inside his top hat. A few moments earlier, if we're very watchful, we can just barely catch Chaplin placing the hat in the required position on the floor; it is done so casually in the course of a drunken stumble that, unless we're actually looking for it, we remain unaware of it till the moment it is spiked by the bed.

Some of these preposterous moments are authenticated by Chaplin's mimetic genius. When Charlie eats the shoe, we feel the grease on his fingers; when he swallows a penny-whistle, his hand moves to his chest in a gesture so frail and pained, we respond to every burp; and when his uncanny gift for observation and mimicry turn Charlie's face and two dinner rolls into a ballerina, we seem to share in the transformative magic of art itself: we're enchanted and persuaded by the reality of the unreal.

Though Chaplin said that "comedy is life viewed from a distance," he continually pulls us into the action. This effort to *involve* us is crucial to his work, for his comedy thrives on tension—building on our involvement till it erupts in laughter. Yet surely his concern with authenticity was no mere attempt to snare us into theatrical participation. Surely the source of his work was so central to his existence and the stories it thrust upon him so utterly "real" that he was compelled to report them with utmost "reality." The films may be entertainment for us, but for Chaplin they were the transformation of a central existential experience.

Perhaps Charlie's world seems real to us in spite of its theatricality because childhood authenticates even the most extreme moments. To a child, life is intensely theatrical, full of surprises, excesses, and dramatic confrontations. Moreover, Chaplin used the imaginative freedom of the theater to render the *subjective* component of our experience—which the naturalistic cinema has so largely had to neglect and ignore. When Charlie turns into a thinly disguised chicken, the very theatricality of the moment gives us a sense of how he feels: he is trapped inside the clumsy costume just as he is in Jim's hallucination, and flaps his wings in a futile effort to escape. Far from undermining reality, the theatrical here gives us access to Charlie's subjective experience and so endows the scene with palpable reality.

Proust said: "We must never be afraid to go too far, for truth lies beyond." Perhaps even the camera must find an essential part of its truth "beyond"—in the subjective experience of reality that has ever been the source and province of art. This poses a serious problem for a medium so committed to the visible and material world. But surely no esthetic reality is long viable that cannot accommodate the invisible and subjective along with the visible and objective world. Carl Dreyer spoke regretfully of "the fence with which naturalism has surrounded the medium." It isn't a fence that ever contained Chaplin, for he drew his work from the reality of childhood, which is far too inclusive to be rendered by a narrow naturalism.

Childhood authenticates his films from within and validates the broad range of his style. Perhaps his use of the medium is ultimately so rich and effective because he could give—as only childhood can—to the invisible and subjective the concrete imminence of fact. In childhood, as in Charlie's world, there is no hard, defining line between inner and outer experience; to children and Charlie, both are equally real—the imagined and the actual, the tangible and the fantastic, the visible and invisible, "fiction" and "fact."

# The New Chaplin Comedy

## Edmund Wilson

The fundamental device of American moving-picture humor is what is technically known as the "gag." A gag is a comic trick, the equivalent in cinema action of the spoken gag of the stage. When Buster Keaton on a runaway motorcycle knocks the ladder out from under a house painter and goes off with the bucket of paint on his head, or when a clothesline, strung between two houses, on which Harold Lloyd is escaping, it cut at one end by an enemy and Harold, still clinging to it, swings into a room below where a séance of spiritualists are awaiting a materialization, this is a movie gag. Inventing such tricks is today one of the principal professions of the film industry. In Hollywood, the gag writers of the comic stars are among the most influential and the most envied members of the community; for without them the stars would be nothing. There are moments when Buster Keaton gives evidence of a skill at pantomime which his producers do nothing to cultivate; but one may say of these comics in general that they hardly need to be actors any more than Baby Peggy, Rin-Tin-Tin, Strongheart, or Silver King.

The one performer of Hollywood who has succeeded in doing anything distinguished with this primitive machinery of gags is, of course, Charlie Chaplin. In the first place, he is, I believe, the only comic star in the movies who does not employ a gag writer: he makes everything up himself; so that, instead of the stereotyped humor of even the best of his competitors, most of whose tricks would be interchanged among them without anyone's knowing the difference, he gives us jokes that, however crude, have an unmistakable quality of personal fancy. Furthermore, he has made it a practice to use his gags as points of departure for genuine comic situations. Thus in his latest picture, *The Gold Rush,* there is a cabin—with Charlie and his partner in it—which is blown to the edge of a cliff while the occupants are asleep. This in itself is a gag like another: for

From *The American Earthquake* by Edmund Wilson. Copyright © 1958 by Edmund Wilson. Reprinted by permission of Farrar, Straus and Giroux, Inc. This material was revised from an article which first appeared in *The New Republic* (September 2, 1925).

any other screen comedian it would have been enough to startle the audience by showing them the little shack rocking on the dangerous brink and then, by acrobatics and trick photography, to follow this with similar shudders. But Chaplin, given his gag, the same kind of thing as Lloyd's clothesline, proceeds to transport his audience in a way of which Lloyd would be incapable, by developing it with steady logic and vivid imagination. Charlie and his companion wake up: the panes of the shack are frosted; they do not realize what has happened.

Charlie sets out to get breakfast, but whenever he moves to the side of the room where his heavy companion is lying—the side hanging over the abyss—the house begins to tip. He puts this down, however, to dizziness—he has been drunk the night before—and goes resolutely about his business. But when his companion—the gigantic Mack Swain—gets up and begins to move around, the phenomenon is aggravated: "Do you have an illusion that the floor is tipping?"—"Ah, you notice that, too, do you?" They jump on it to see if it is standing solid; but as Charlie is jumping on the overhanging side while Swain is holding it down on the other, they do not at once find out what is wrong, and it is some time before the fatal combination—both men on the projecting side—almost sends them over the cliff. They rush back to the safe side of the room, and Charlie goes to the door—which has been frozen tight in the night—to see what is going on: after a struggle, it suddenly flies open, and he falls out into the void, only saving himself by a clutch at the sill. His companion rushes down to save him, but by the time he has pulled him in, their double weight has set the cabin sliding: it is anchored now only by a rope which has caught fast to something not far from the cliff. Charlie and his companion, abject on their bellies, try to crawl up the terrible floor, now at an angle of sixty degrees. At first, though the eyes of his companion are popping, Charlie remains cool and sensible. "Just go easy! A little at a time." But no matter how little they attempt, every movement makes the cabin slip. And so on, through a long passage of pantomime.

Conversely, however, the gag is sometimes resorted to by Chaplin to break up the non-farcical sequences—ironic or even pathetic—that are becoming more frequent in his comedies. Thus the love story in *The Gold Rush* is, on the whole, treated seriously, but from time to time enlivened by such low comedy incidents as that in which Charlie accidentally saturates his bandaged foot with kerosene and then has it set on fire by a match dropped by one of the ladies. In these sequences, it sometimes happens—as in parts of *The Pilgrim,* his previous film—that such gags in the straight situations produce a jarring effect. They seem to be introduced in order to hold Chaplin's old public, who expects their full allowance of "belly laughs." He has never dared desert this public, who first saw him in the

Mack Sennett comedies and who still go to him for the same sort of entertainment that they find in Fox and Christie comedies. Yet in proportion as his reputation has grown with the sophisticated audience and the critics, his popularity has hardly gained—it has not even, perhaps, held its own—with this original popular audience, who do not seem to feel any difference between Chaplin himself, on the one hand, and his imitators and rivals, on the other. They seem, in fact, to be coming to prefer the latter. Buster Keaton and Harold Lloyd have, in a sense, carried gagging far beyond Charlie Chaplin. Their films have more smartness and speed; they cultivate more frightening mechanical devices. With their motorcars, their motorcycles, their motorboats, their airplanes, their railroad trains, their vertiginous scaling of skycrapers and their shattering cataclysmic collisions, they have progressed a long way beyond Chaplin, who has made no attempt to keep up with them, but continues with the cheap trappings and the relatively simple tricks of the old custard-pie comedy. For Chaplin is even more old-fashioned than the old-fashioned Mack Sennett movies; he is as old-fashioned as Karno's Early Birds, the unusual music-hall turn in which he originally appeared and which was at least a school for actors, not for athletes.

What turn Charlie Chaplin's career will take is, therefore, still a curious problem. He is himself, I believe, acutely aware of the anomaly of his position. In the films, he seems hardly likely to play an important role in the artistic development of the movies, which is at present making such remarkable advances, seems not to interest Chaplin. His pictures are still in this respect nearly as raw as *Tillie's Punctured Romance* or any other primitive comedy, and it is only when the subject is sordid—as in *Pay Day*, with its crowded city streetcars taking people home after work and its suffocating slatternly city flat—that the *mise en scène* in Chaplin's comedies contributes in any way to their effectiveness.

The much-praised *A Woman of Paris* was handicapped particularly, it seemed to me—since it did not have Chaplin as the central figure—by this visual lack of taste. It was intended as an attractive, a serious picture, yet, for all the intelligence he brought to directing it, he allowed it to go out as if naked in its flat light and putty make-up. He is jealous of his independence in this as in other matters. He is very unlikely to allow himself to be written for, directed or even advised. If he is not carrying along his old public, he will unquestionably in time have to give it up; but whether he will then simply retire from the screen or try something altogether different, it is impossible to predict. In the meantime, it may be that his present series of pictures—*The Kid, The Pilgrim,* and *The Gold Rush*—with their gags and their overtones of tragedy, their adventures half-absurd, half-realistic, their mythical hero, now a figure of poetry, now a type out of the comic strips, represents the height of Chaplin's achievement. He could scarcely, in any field, surpass the best moments of these pictures. The opening of *The Gold Rush* is such a moment. Charlie is a lone adventurer, straggling along after a party of prospectors among the frozen hills: he twirls his cane a little to keep his spirits up. On his way through a narrow mountain pass, a bear emerges and follows him. Any ordinary movie comedian, given the opportunity of using a bear, would, of course, have had it chasing him about for as long as he could work up gags for it. But Charlie does not know that the bear is there: he keeps on, twirling his cane. Presently the beast withdraws, and only then does Charlie think he hears something: he turns around, but there is nothing there. And he sets off again, still fearless, toward the dreadful ordeals that await him.

1957. Years later, on visits to London, I went to the Christmas pantomime and realized that the bear of *The Gold Rush* was one of the many things that Charlie Chaplin had borrowed from the British popular theater. There is always, in the pantomime, a scene in which the comedians are lost in a forest, and there used to be always a bear—though in the winter of '53–'54 a space man was substituted—which is following them but hides when they look around. Eventually, however, they must face the bear: it was Chaplin's original touch never to allow the traveler to see the bear at all. In the meantime, the pantomimist Chaplin—contrary to my expectations of 1925—had quite sloughed off the old vagabond and emerged on the speaking screen in characterizations wholly new: the contemporary Bluebeard of *Monsieur Verdoux* and the old music-hall comedian of *Limelight*. Though the last of these takes us back to the music hall, it is no longer to the music-hall devices as material for Hollywood comedy. Chaplin has outgrown these, and he now recreates the music hall, makes it one of the subjects of a work of art. The sequences in which Chaplin's hero is seen in his professional act, have something poetic, daemonic. They are among the high points of Chaplin's career. As funny as any of his earlier scenes, they are also intensely emotional. The clown with a breaking heart is as ancient as any of the stock situations which Chaplin has never hesitated to exploit; but the result is, as usual, astonishing: the nightmare of the deadpan accompanist, whose music keeps slipping off the stand while the comedian diverts the audience by primitive clowning tricks that are at once unashamed and embarrassing; the sudden and mad climax in which the aging comic produces a small violin and fiddles feverishly till he falls into the orchestra.

The accompanist here is Buster Keaton, who had passed into eclipse in Hollywood but was invited by Chaplin to take part in this film and is perfect in the uncanny atmosphere of this music hall of Hell. Not long afterward—in February, 1954—I saw Buster Keaton perform at the Cirque Médrano in Paris, and was confirmed in my opinion of twenty-eight years before that Hollywood had not made the best of him. He is a pantomime clown of the first order, and his act at the Cirque Médrano—a presser's boy, morose and detached, attempting to deliver a dress suit while the circus is going on—seemed to me the best thing I had seen him do. His loss of reputation in the United States and his appearance in an engagement abroad is only another example of the perversion and waste of talent for which Hollywood has been responsible. Who could ever, in 1925, have believed that Charlie Chaplin would escape from it—having always been his own manager—and take his place among his age's first artists?

# "Monsieur Verdoux"

## Robert Warshow

Chaplin's Tramp, taken in his most direct significance, represented the good-hearted and personally cultivated individual in a heartless and vulgar society. The society was concerned only with the pursuit of profit, and often not even with that so much as with the mere preservation of the ugly and impersonal machinery by which the profit was gained; the Tramp was concerned with the practice of personal relations and the social graces. Most of all the Tramp was like an aristocrat fallen on hard times, for what he attempted in all his behavior was to maintain certain standards of refinement and humanity, to keep life dignified and make it emotionally and aesthetically satisfying.

The relationship between the Tramp and his society never solidified. Sometimes the Tramp was able to make use of the society of his own peculiar ends. Sometimes the society in its mysterious processes seized upon the Tramp and endowed him with wealth and honor. The constant difficulties between the two never developed to the point where the Tramp could begin to think of himself as opposed to the society; indeed, it was essential to his character that he should take the society as given and make his own life on its margin. And the society, for its part, had nothing against the Tramp; even when it knocked him down, it did so not because he was a threat—the society was too impersonal even to conceive of such a possibility—but simply because his behavior was preposterous; the blow was always delivered in a fit of abstraction, so to speak, without serious intent. The satiric point of the relationship lay precisely in this element of fortuitousness and innocence: it *happened* that the Tramp and the society were in constant collision, but neither side was impelled to draw any conclusions from this. The absurdity of the Tramp's behavior consisted in its irrelevance to the preoccupations of the society; the viciousness of the

From *The Immediate Experience* by Robert Warshow (New York: Doubleday Publishing Co., 1962). Reprinted by permission of Paul Warshow. This material appeared originally in *Partisan Review*, July–August 1947.

society consisted in its failure to make any provision for the Tramp, in its complete indifference to his fate.

After 1933, it became increasingly more difficult to maintain such a picture of the relationship between the individual and his society. Now the two were compelled to become conscious of each other, openly and continuously, and the quality of innocence—could no longer be preserved between them; from this point on, there would always be on each side a clear *intent* in regard to the other. The society, seeing in the individual both an indispensable instrument and a constant danger, would find it necessary to take a more and more active and organized interest in all his concerns. And the individual would be forced thereby to assume a position: he would have to be for or against the society, and his decision in this regard would immediately become the determining factor in his life and the defining element of his character. The margin in which the Tramp had managed to survive and carry on his life, on however small a scale, was becoming narrower; at length it would disappear.

This had an immediate effect on Chaplin. The impact of his art, its comic point, has always come in large measure from his insistence on pushing everything to its extreme. He creates his movie world by a process of logical extension (this is of course true of most satire), and he has an unfailing instinct in the selection of precisely those leading elements that will bear extension. (In this he is helped rather than hindered by a certain simplicity in his conception of political and social problems.) From the moment that he could no longer define society (in its logical extreme) by its indifference to the individual, then, for his purposes, the position of the Tramp became questionable, for the Tramp and his society, despite the instability and tenuousness of their relations, were aesthetically inseparable.

The change begins to appear in *Modern Times,* made during the Depression. In the factory's treatment of the Tramp there is neither accident nor innocence; the factory is a living, malevolent organism bent on putting the Tramp to certain specific uses. An atmosphere of personal and intended viciousness appears—in the inescapable, nagging voice of authority over the public-address system, or in the terrible experiment with the feeding machine—and this viciousness is a new thing in Chaplin's movies, residing as it does neither in individual human beings nor in the mechanical imperviousness of mere organization, but in a system that has acquired personality. The Tramp can still keep his innocence—he is put in jail because of a political demonstration that takes place *around* him, while he himself is not involved and does not understand what is happening—and in the end he can still escape from the system and disappear down the road. But he cannot circumvent the system or turn it to his own account, and there are ominous signs that the situation will soon be beyond his power of adjustment. In this movie more than ever before, one is kept aware of his ultimate helplessness; certainly he never seems so *little* a man as when he finds his arms still twitching after the hours of tightening an endless series of the same two bolts.

The end comes in *The Great Dictator,* where the whole mechanism of society is brought to bear against the Tramp in a deliberate effort to make him suffer and, ultimately, to kill him. This direct threat demands a direct response. Merely to escape is not enough, for the final meaning of such a society must be that there is no escape; what is required of the Tramp is that he should attempt to destroy the society. But the Tramp is simply not adequate to the attempt, and in the end Chaplin feels compelled to speak out in his own voice—what could the Tramp have to say about politics? (The quality of Chaplin's own politics is of course not in question here.) Thus the failure of *The Great Dictator* results primarily from Chaplin's reliance on an instrument that was no longer suitable. This becomes quite plain, I think, when one considers how successfully he handles the figures of Hitler and Mussolini; if it were simply a matter of his having chosen "the wrong theme," then one would expect this "wrongness" to be most apparent in just those scenes where the Tramp does not appear. The fact is that the theme was almost the only possible one for Chaplin; it was wrong only for the Tramp.

The Tramp has the proportions of a legendary figure. Though he is among the least "real" of artistic constructs, yet by the very disproportion of his personality, by his deep and unshakable eccentricity, he can carry everything before him, like Falstaff or Micawber, achieving a kind of independent existence apart from the particular movies in which he has appeared. The Tramp creates his world, and everything else must take its color from his presence.

Verdoux is not so tremendous a creation. He exists for one movie, and his whole meaning is contained in the movie. He has made his point, once and for all.

Verdoux does not create the world, he is only an element of the world. At bottom, it is his own consciousness of this limitation that drives him. He is a man with needs and responsibilities, he must make his way. What are the mechanisms of society? Where are the opportunities? These questions are vitally important to him he is therefore a busy and enterprising man, full of plans. For the Tramp, it was enough simply to exist; Verdoux must analyze his situation and find ways to meet it. He is like the Tramp in many ways: he has the same social charm and physical gracefulness, above all the same civilized feeling for the possibilities of personal intercourse and good living; but he must put all these qualities to use—he becomes like a cultured jewelry salesman, or the manager of a high-class restaurant, making a profit out of his refinement.

He is only an element of the world, but he carries the world inside him. With Verdoux, the opposition between the individual and society has lost its old simplicity. The society has flowed into the individual, and the two have in a sense become co-extensive; the struggle is now an internal struggle, full of ambiguities and contradictions; it is man himself who is corrupt, both as individual and as society, and Verdoux's problem is to make some working order out of the conflicting needs of his own personality. When he makes his decision, it is as much a decision about his own nature as about the nature of society.

Indeed, we do not see the society at all, except in Verdoux and through Verdoux's eyes. There is no background. There is only Verdoux and his family and his victims, and a few supernumeraries—a friend, a girl in a flower shop, a detective, some reporters (the detective and the reporters are not society, they are only making a living in *their* way), a court of justice, a priest (these are not society either, but only the necessary instruments for Verdoux's triumphal progress to the guillotine; he makes use of them). There is also, at one point, some political documentation—shots of Hitler and Mussolini, marching soldiers, newspaper headlines, ruined businessmen committing suicide, etc.—but this is really Verdoux's own documentation, the evidence in his defense. Verdoux remains an isolated figure without a context—or, rather, the context is a projection of his mind, and all we are told of it is what he tells us.

Thus there is no solid point of reference; everything is open to question. The meanings shift and turn and spread until the whole movie, and ultimately the whole world, is enveloped in ambiguity and irony, and it is no longer certain whom the joke is on. Not only is Verdoux caught in his own irony; sometimes it is we in the audience who are caught, and sometimes Chaplin himself—it is significant of the character of this movie, and to some extent, perhaps, of Chaplin's personal character, that one should feel that he does not always understand the implications of his work.

Complex and sustained irony is a rare thing in literature and rarer still in the movies, if indeed it has ever before appeared in the movies at all. Probably the closest analogy to *Monsieur Verdoux* is Swift's *Modest Proposal,* where, despite the simplicity of the basic idea, one can never quite get to the bottom of the irony. Just as there have been people who could see nothing funny about eating babies, so there are people who can see nothing funny about the mass murder of women. And there is in both cases a certain difficulty in critical discussion. I can do best here by paraphrasing what George Saintsbury wrote of the *Modest Proposal:* "That Chaplin does not really mean to recommend mass murder, though perfectly true, could hardly be urged by anybody capable of enjoying *Monsieur Verdoux,* and would not be listened to by anyone whom it horrifies." But even this is too simple. While it *is* perfectly true that Chaplin does not mean to recommend mass murder, it is also true that he makes out the best possible case for it: the spectator is likely to find himself following Verdoux's activities with eagerness and sharing Verdoux's irritation when his plans are frustrated.

Verdoux's original point is clear enough: business is like murder and therefore murder is only a kind of business. Obviously this is not the strict truth; just as obviously, it is more valuable than the strict truth: no satirist could do much with the proposition that business is *sometimes* like murder. And, of course, the final product of the totality of the world's business usually does turn out to be murder. Verdoux is on firm ground, theoretically.

In practice, however, the matter immediately becomes more complicated, as Verdoux himself is to some extent forced to recognize. Crime does not pay, after all—not in a small way, that is. "Numbers sanctify," Verdoux says, trying to prove that his death on the guillotine is no more than a business failure. But he is wrong to minimize the guillotine. What could be worse than a business failure? Perhaps there is more justice in his death than he is prepared to admit.

The complications go further than this. Despite the clarity of his original perceptions, Verdoux becomes corrupt, and with the corruption not so much of a murderer as of a businessman. It is a hard struggle, he tells us; I go into the jungle only because I must fight for my wife and my child, all that I love in the world. When he says this he is not to be trusted. The jungle is everything to him and his home is only his convenient excuse—characterless blond child and colorless dull wife (how useful that she is crippled!), existing only so that he may have a symbol to justify his ambition. This is not my doing, he says; I found myself unwanted and I was forced to go into business for myself. But is it not best of all to be in business for oneself? He betrays himself as we watch: only in the jungle world of his calling does he display animation and charm, competence as a social being and a man of affairs, a sense of his own powers and his own position. At home he is only the suburbanite, momentarily relaxed and safe, indeed, but impatient to get back to the real world of business. Even a great domestic event—when Verdoux on his wedding anniversary brings his wife the deed to their home, a pledge of security and the happy fruit of his labors—is made flat and insignificant. "What is that?" the child asks, and the mother replies, "It is the deed to this beautiful house and garden"—the blessings of the bourgeois home must be counted to be seen.

Much later—after Verdoux has been ruined in a financial crash, and after the shots of newspaper headlines and marching men—there is one sentence to tell us what became of this home: "Soon after the crash, I lost my wife and child," Verdoux says, explaining why he has no more heart for business. And he adds, insisting on his point: "However, they are happier where they are." Thus with a word the crippled wife and the blond child are gone, and as their existence seemed not enough to account for his activity, so their disappearance seems not enough to account for his decline. One feels again that Verdoux is deceiving himself—is not self-deception the great bourgeois sin? Perhaps it was the crash itself that broke his spirit; perhaps it is simply that the aging and unsuccessful murderer, like the aging and unsuccessful businessman, comes to feel that his time has been wasted.

The peculiarly mechanical and almost unconcerned treatment of Verdoux's family is one of the elements that seem to get Chaplin himself involved in the movie's ambiguities. There has often been an obvious morbidity in Chaplin's sentiment: he has been really tender only with the maimed and the helpless, as if he required some palpable sign of misfortune and innocence before he could feel sympathy. This sentimentality is in one aspect simply the reverse of his humor, for the helpless cripple is also a kind of logical extension. But where the satiric extension has the effect of broadening the satiric view of society, bringing more and more objects into the field of the ridiculous, the sentimental extension does not broaden sentiment. On the contrary, by concentrating all sympathy upon the obviously helpless, it becomes a means of narrowing the field of sentiment (if you are not crippled, then you are not innocent), and it thus reinforces the satire instead of counterbalancing it.

In *Monsieur Verdoux,* where Chaplin's view of society has taken on a new savagery, it would appear that he has correspondingly narrowed the field of his sympathies even further. The crippled wife and the helpless child are here, but they have become formal symbols without content, expressing only an abstract belief in the moral importance of helplessness. Chaplin still feels these figures to be necessary, but he seems unable to take a direct interest in them. The true object of his tenderness is another figure, the homeless girl on whom Verdoux plans to test his new poison. This girl personifies the gallant and lonely individual bearing up confidently against the cruelties of life. She is alone, but she is not helpless at all—except before Verdoux, and everyone is helpless before Verdoux: even when he is caught at last, it must be by his own choice. She is like Verdoux in many ways: she, too, is trying to make her way; she, too, has suffered the world's blows; he can feel that she understands the problem of life in his terms (she carries a volume of Schopenhauer), and if her conclusions are in opposition to his, this is all to the good, for it permits him to regard her as a child and to feel his own wisdom. (But in the end it will be she who "succeeds"—as the mistress of a munitions manufacturer—and she will sit weeping at Verdoux's trial.) Most important, she has loved an invalid—it is this that makes him decide to spare her life. Thus it is no longer the cripple who embodies virtue; it is only the person who loves the cripple. In short, it is Chaplin himself, and the projections of himself that he puts upon the screen.

The film's quality of ambiguity—its tendency to make its statements incompletely, or to take them back after they have been made, or to modify and complicate them—is perhaps most apparent in the talk. There is a great deal of talk, and a number of critics have found it objectionable, either because it bored them or because they saw it as a violation of the rather artificial principle that a movie must rely only on the camera. I do not wish to claim that Verdoux's expositions of his ideas are among the best things in the movie, but I found them full of interest in themselves and extremely important in developing the total effect of the movie's involved irony.

It may take some freshness of mind to reach the conclusion that business is like murder, but there is also a certain puerility in laboring the point. When Verdoux enunciates his ideas, they quickly become platitudes, so that in attacking capitalist society, however sharply, he simultaneously betrays the corruption of his own mind. But then the irony takes one more turn, for, as I have said, the corruption of Verdoux's mind is precisely the corruption of the bourgeois mind, and in exposing himself he again exposes his society. When he says, "This is a ruthless world," or "Violence begets violence," what is that but the self-satisfied voice of the practical man of business who takes a certain pride in his "philosophy"?

In the final scenes before Verdoux's execution, the irony of his speech and behavior reaches a climax of intensity and complication. "I go to meet my destiny," he says, half seriously, as he prepares to deliver himself to the police. And he maintains this ironic grandeur to the end. He scores off everybody, for he has his clear-sighted "philosophy" and the others have only their miserable falsehoods. "As a mass killer, I am an amateur," he says in the court room, and then, his last little dig before he is sentenced: "I shall see you all very soon . . . very soon." In the death cell during his last minutes, he is still eloquent: good and evil—"too much of either will destroy us all"; sin—"who knows what ultimate purpose it serves?" Graciously, he dismisses a reporter: "I hope you will pardon me; my time is limited." He greets the priest, bowing: "Ah, Father! And what can I do for you?" He is, you might say, magnificent. Is this not how we should all wish to go to our executions—smiling, dignified, witty, waving aside the last cigarette, accepting the last drink ("Rum? I've never tasted rum . . ."), quietly laughing at the whole world? At the same time, this dream is after all a little childish (it is a curious fact that Chaplin actually looks like the elder Douglas Fairbanks in this last scene), and Verdoux's triumph is really not much: they *will* cut his head off, and the one thing he has failed to do with all his talk is to establish a single reason why they should not.

So everything goes down together, all caught in the same complex absurdity: the capitalist world; then, in a heap, Verdoux the murderer and man of business, Verdoux the cracker-barrel philosopher, Verdoux the lonely romantic; then Chaplin himself, who believes in Verdoux even if he also believes in the irony that denies him; then we in the audience, who sit watching Chaplin and somehow believing everything at once; finally, the capitalist world again, which produced Verdoux, murderer, philosopher, and all. The final word, canceling all others, is in the movie's last shot: Verdoux is a very small figure as he walks to the guillotine, limping, overshadowed by his guards.

The nearest approach to solidity and directness is in the treatment of Verdoux's victims and intended victims. These women are not simple characters, but they are simpler than Verdoux, if only because he manipulates them, and the important facts about them are clear and unambiguous: they are stupid and unhappy, in varying degrees, and they want glamour and love. Since their dramatic function does not require them to be active, their qualities remain constant; they are not touched by the irony that envelops everything else—indeed, in the case of the Martha Raye character, Annabella, one cannot even conceive of the possibility of irony: she is too uncompromising a statement of the value of life. The women are stationary points, and the argument, so to speak, rages around them: they naturally have no idea of what is at stake; it is only for Verdoux that the situation is complicated.

Chaplin does wonderful things with these women. Even Thelma, whom we never see except as a billow of black smoke pouring from an incinerator, is made clear to us: when we have seen her family, we know all we need to know. In the scenes with Lydia, the only woman actually murdered during the time covered by the movie, the menace of Verdoux's character, his immense coldness, is at its height. Lydia is an old and bitter woman, and we can see in her face and her posture the whole long unhappiness of her life, while Verdoux thinks only of her money, moving around like a cat as he makes his soft and gentlemanly speeches ("Life can so easily degenerate into something sordid and vulgar. Let us try to keep it beautiful and dignified") and glancing occasionally at the clock to see whether there is still time to win her over before the bank closes. Later, when it is time to go to bed, Verdoux flexes his fingers a little as he gets up to follow her, and they walk upstairs, Lydia nagging at him—did you lock the door? did you close the window?—and Verdoux answering softly, patiently: yes, dear, yes dear; then she goes into the bedroom and he stops for a moment in the hall, looking out at the moon and quietly speaking some lines of poetry that occur to him; and then he follows her, to carry out his necessary and melancholy task.

With Madame Grosnay, the wealthy widow whom he pursues at various times throughout the movie, Verdoux is at his most charming—in this case, the question of murder is still in the future. And it is here that Verdoux is most like the Tramp—a man of taste and sensibility (how gracefully he handles the roses!), but awkward, impetuous, rather boyish. What finally wins Madame Grosnay's heart is most of all his delightful lack of sophistication, the seeming transparency of his intentions. In the midst of one speech, Verdoux suddenly falls out the window—how could she distrust him after that? And later, when Madame Grosnay has at last suggested that Verdoux need not hope in vain, there is one of Chaplin's great moments: overcome by this encouragement, the happy lover lunges at his lady on the sofa, overshoots the mark, recovers himself, and throws himself upon her again—all without spilling the cup of tea in his hand; it is the perfect symbol of the two sides of Verdoux's character.

But the most interesting of the women is Annabella. Any attempt to disentangle Chaplin's own values from the movie, or to identify him absolutely with Verdoux, must take her into account. Annabella is the full antithesis of Verdoux; she is loud and vulgar and stupid, and she is as far removed as possible from the world of practical business enterprise: her money has been won in a lottery, and she invests it in harebrained enterprises exclusively—for instance, a project for generating electric power by harnessing the rocking motion of the sea ("If it works, we'll just own the ocean, that's all!"). She is even in some degree resistant to Verdoux's charm, and she regards him with a moronic suspicion that is not to be overcome by the most disarming behavior. It is this creature who defeats Verdoux, and she defeats him not by opposing a superior reason or a superior morality to his, but simply by a kind of blind fatality, as if she were a force of nature. Not only does she defeat him: she overshadows him at every moment. With Annabella, Verdoux is a subdued man; intelligence is on his side, but in this case intelligence does not count—Annabella has the vitality. There is a kind of desperation in his painstaking and elaborate attempts to kill her: he is like a patient and conscientious man who tries to accomplish some perfectly reasonable and simple act and finds himself unaccountably blocked. In the end, when the lonely lake and the rope with a rock tied to it have failed, even he as he picks up the oars seems to sense that he is up against a force greater than his own.

Verdoux's society cannot completely destroy him, even on the guillotine, for he *is* the society, and his complete destruction would be the society's death. But the existence of Annabella means that a different answer is possible: the one thing that Verdoux cannot destroy, and thus the one thing that the society cannot destroy, is the simple and unrefined fact of mere vitality.

A great deal could be said of the many other elements that help to give the movie its moment-to-moment qualities of imagination and dramatic force: the peculiar involutions and profundities of Chaplin's feelings for women, the complete confidence of his technique (he always does whatever is needed in the most direct way possible), the variety of his invention, above all his unfailing awareness of *all* the emotional and dramatic possibilities of every situation. (This last quality is shown perhaps most brilliantly in the treatment of Annabella's maid. Few things in the movie are at once so completely funny and so completely terrible as the scene in which this miserable creature begins to lose her hair.) But what I have primarily tried to demonstrate here is that the movie must be approached with a willingness to understand and enjoy it as a shifting pattern of ambiguity and irony, made up of all the complexities and contradictions not only of our society but of Chaplin's own mind and the mind of the spectator. Much of the hostility to the movie seems to come from reluctance to accept its shifting point of view, its remarkable quality of being at once uncompromising and uncommitted. We are used to flat and simple statements, especially in the movies; as a consequence, some who have seen *Monsieur Verdoux* have found it unpleasantly disturbing, and some have simply refused to recognize its complexity at all, condemning Chaplin because they disagree with *Verdoux*—though Verdoux certainly does not ask for agreement, and, if he did, it would still not be clear what he wanted us to agree to.

Chaplin is surely one of the few great comic geniuses who have appeared so far in history. It seems to me relatively unimportant to decide whether or not *Monsieur Verdoux* is his best movie; we do not have all his movies before us, and at any rate, as I have tried to show, *Monsieur Verdoux* is the product of a radical change in his vision of the world. Taken by itself, it is a great work of irony; and it is unique among movies, for it requires of the spectator that he should constantly reflect upon what he sees on the screen and what he discovers in his own mind.

# Carl Theodor Dreyer

CARL DREYER *was born in Copenhagen in 1889 and died there in 1968. He began his career as a journalist and theater critic and, after 1912, a screenwriter.* He directed eight films in Denmark and Germany in the early 1920s, but they have rarely been seen in the United States. Instead, his reputation rests on five of the six films he directed between 1928 and 1964, beginning with The Passion of Joan of Arc *(made in France), one of the most revered and famous films of all time.* It was followed by Vampyr *(1931),* Day of Wrath *(1943),* Ordet *(The Word, 1955), and, finally,* Gertrud *(1964). A cherished project on the life of Jesus never came to fruition, but Dreyer's script has been published in English, as have his occasional writings on film.*

*Dreyer's style and his subjects vary in his later films, which have invited comparison to Bresson and Ozu in their rigor and minimalism, and especially in their sparing use of camera movement. Religious themes recur from film to film, culminating in the almost inhuman mysticism of* Ordet; *yet Dreyer's final film,* Gertrud, *though austere and rigid in style, is a eulogy of romantic love, and the title character, who has lived for love, may be compared to Truffaut's Catherine in* Jules and Jim. *Both* The Passion of Joan of Arc *and* Day of Wrath *deal with witchcraft, intolerance, and religious persecution, but visually the films are dissimilar. The carefully reconstructed world of* Day of Wrath *recalls the seventeenth-century Dutch genre painters, such as Vermeer and de Hooch, but* Joan *is an album of searing and wrenching close-ups and an unforgettable emotional experience.*

*Dreyer, a tyrant and perfectionist in production, subjected his cast, especially Marie Falconetti, who played Joan, to an ordeal that paralleled that of the original victims. When her hair is shorn, Falconetti does not simply act, she suffers, and Dreyer's unrelenting camera draws us inexorably into the vortex of her pain. The result, however, is strangely impersonal, for the director—perhaps under the influence of Eisenstein's* Potemkin—*tends to isolate and aestheticize separate shots, and this diminishes the flow and continuity. (Eisenstein himself was one of the first to lodge this objection.)*

*In* Day of Wrath, *on the other hand, as in Eisenstein's late films of the same period, Dreyer strives for visual opulence, and fashions a meticulous decor modeled on painting. Robert Warshow has argued that the film is flawed by the break between the pageant and ritual of the first part and the more personal drama which follows, but both are impressive in their slow and stately formality. Dreyer's rigorous, detached manner is not for the many, but no one would gainsay its distinctiveness and stubborn integrity.*

*Dreyer's writings on film have been translated in* Dreyer in Double Reflection *(New York, 1973). Studies include Tom Milne's* The Cinema of Carl Dreyer *(1971),* *Ken Kelman's essay in* The Film Culture Reader, *edited by P. Adams Sitney,* *Paul Schrader's* Transcendental Style in Film *(1972), and David Bordwell's* Film *Guide to La Passion de Jeanne d'Arc (1973). See also Dreyer,* Four Screenplays *(1970) and* Jesus *(1972), which includes tributes by Renoir, Fellini, and Truffaut.*

# Carl Dreyer's Jeanne d'Arc

## Luis Buñuel

Certainly the most original and interesting film of the new cinema season. Based on an original scenario by Delteil, it begins at the moment when Jeanne appears before her tribunal, and ends with the stake.

Based on extreme close-ups, the director very rarely if at all uses two-shots or even medium close-ups. Each of them is composed with such attention and art that often it remains a "frame" without being a "shot." Unusual angles with violent foreshortening, and frequent tilting of the camera.

None of the actors wears make-up; in the pitiful geography of their faces—pores like wells—the life of flesh and blood is the more evident. At times the whole screen is the naked white of a cell, and in a corner the malicious visage of a friar. Its storms can be anticipated with meteorological exactitude. Nerves, eyes, lips which explode like bombs, tonsures, forefingers launched against the innocent breast of the maid. She replies or weeps, or, weeping, is distracted like a child, by her fingers, by a button, by the fly that settles on the nose of the friar.

The actors had to shave their heads and let their beards grow, because crêpe hair was definitively relegated to the theater, and the genius of Dreyer lies in his direction of his players. In this respect the cinema has given us nothing comparable. The humanity of the people overflows the screen and fills the cinema. We all feel such truth in our throats and the marrow of our bones. Antidote against snake bite and against histrionism! The playing of Jannings compared with that of the least of the friars of Jeanne d'Arc appears as flabby as lard and as theatrical—though not as great—as that of Ludmila Pitoëff.

And the humanity of the Maid in Dreyer's work transcends that of any other interpretation we know. We all feel the urge to prescribe her a whipping so that we can give her a sweet afterwards. To take away her

From *Luis Buñuel: A Critical Biography* by Francisco Aranda, translated and edited by David Robinson (New York: Da Capo Press, 1976). Reprinted by permission of the publisher.

dessert from her, to punish her childlike integrity, her transparent obstinacy, yes; but, why burn her? Lit by tears, purified by flames, head shaved, grubby as a little girl, yet for a moment she stops crying to watch some pigeons settle on the spire of the church. Then, she dies.

We have kept one of her little tears, which wandered our way, in a little celluloid box. An odorless, tasteless, transparent tear, a droplet from the purest fountain.

# The World Beyond

## Tom Milne

*La Passion de Jeanne d'Arc* is probably the Dreyer film that separates the sheep from the goats where his admirers are concerned. Or, to put it another way, the film that divides those who believe that Dreyer was a Christian for churchgoers, from those who, like myself, see him as a pagan or a pantheist, living, like Gertrud, by one credo alone: *Amor Omnia*. Perhaps this is simply another way of saying that since Dreyer spent fourteen films denouncing the cruelties, prejudices, superstitions, hypocrisies, and dogmatic assertions that make up so great a part of the history of so many established churches, it is difficult to imagine him being seriously involved in any debate as to whether Joan of Arc was or was not a witch, was or was not a saint. This, of course, is the stumbling block in any film or play about Joan: it is virtually impossible to engage the mind in any discussion about the whys and wherefores, rights or wrongs, of her trial, since the dice are so completely loaded from the very start. All one can do is wait for the outcome, harrowed to a greater or lesser degree by the portrayal of her suffering. Even Bernard Shaw, the great debater, couldn't find much to say of any conviction, though he said it wittily enough and padded out the gaps with petty squabblings and much byplay between Joan and her male friends and enemies. Even Bresson couldn't really engage one's passions, except pity for the sufferings and terror at the bleak final image of the charred, empty stake. Ultimately, Joan is an impossible heroine, at least for Dreyer's kind of cinema, since she stands alone, her fears and hopes communicated by and to those mysterious invisible voices, which even he couldn't quite seize through her eyes, her expressions, her gestures.

After the enormous success in France of *Master of the House,* Dreyer was approached by a French company, the Société Générale de Films, to make a film for them. Dreyer proposed three historical heroines—Catherine

Excerpted from the chapter "The World Beyond" in *The Cinema of Carl Dreyer* by Tom Milne (1971). Reprinted by permission of A. S. Barnes & Company, Inc.

de' Médici, Marie-Antoinette and Joan of Arc—and the last was selected, with a script to be based partly on a novel by Joseph Delteil and
partly (rather more than partly, as it would seem to have turned out) on the
original transcripts of the trial. As usual, Dreyer approached the project by
making extensive preparations, so that the film took a year and a half to
complete from conception to final cut: the costumes were exhaustively
researched, details of everyday life in the Middle Ages were copied from
the illuminations in a medieval manuscript, as were the vast, incredibly
solid sets: ''The sets were all built into one complete construction: a great
septagonal or octagonal castle with a very tall tower in each of the corners
and a high wall running between the towers. Inside there were little houses
built very simply, but with crooked angles and windows set out of line, like
those in the miniatures. In the centre of the courtyard, opposite the
drawbridge, was the church or chapel, and at the side the entrance to the
churchyard where the burning took place. The walls consisted of a cement
shell ten centimetres thick, enough to carry the weight of the actors and
technicians during the shooting. The whole construction was painted pink
to give it a grey effect against the sky, which stood out white in the film.''

The whole set was never seen, of course, only small segments of it,
since the action was very fragmented and shot largely in close-up, but it
helped Dreyer not only to inspire a sense of authenticity in his actors, but to
reduce the story of Joan of Arc's trial (which in reality dragged out over
some eighteen months) to *Kammerspiel* proportions. To this end, the
twenty-nine examinations she underwent are telescoped into one, and the
film starts with Joan at the end of her drama, so that the action takes place
in a single day; all pre-history and picturesque detail, such as one finds in
Shaw's *Saint Joan* or Anouilh's *L'Alouette,* is ruthlessly expunged so that
the entire action takes place within the Palais de Justice at Rouen and its
surrounds; and the action itself is reduced to what is virtually a symphony
of faces. The last essential ingredient was a Joan *pre-existing* enough not to
have to build a performance: ''I went to see her [Falconetti] one afternoon
and we talked for an hour or two. I had seen her in a play in a little
boulevard theatre whose name I have forgotten. She was playing a light
modern comedy and she was very elegant in it, a little flighty, but charming. She didn't win me over right away, and I didn't have immediate
confidence in her. I simply asked if I could come to see her the following
day, and during that visit we talked. It was then I felt that there was
something in her which could be brought out; something she could give,
and something, therefore, that I could take. For behind the make-up,
behind the pose and that ravishing modern appearance, there was something. There was a soul behind that façade. So I told her I would like to do
some tests with her the next day. 'But without make-up,' I added, 'with

your face completely naked.' The next day she came, ready and willing. She had removed her make-up, we did the tests, and I found in her face exactly what I wanted for Joan: a country girl, very sincere, but also a woman of suffering.''

Falconetti's performance is unarguably superb, no matter how it was achieved (rumour said that Dreyer made her kneel on stone floors until she was suffering enough, or played rushes back over and over again in an exhausting attempt to refine the tiniest detail of an expression, and she certainly submitted to having her head shaved for the cause), and the rest of the cast is beautifully chosen, even if inclined to resort to the heavy grimacing which disfigured *The President, Leaves from Satan's Book,* and *Love One Another.* Yet somehow the style Dreyer found for the film seems irremediably false. Instead of flowing naturally from his chosen materials, as it does in *The Parson's Widow, Mikaël,* and *Master of the House,* here it seems imposed upon them. The opening track, for instance, which takes one slowly right through the court, past soldiers and ecclesiastics, to close-ups first of Cauchon, then of Joan and Massieu, irresistibly recalls the long, slow pans in *Day of Wrath* which become a terrible sign of doom attending the victims of justice; here, although the slow track (or pan) becomes associated with Joan's movements, dogging her footsteps as she is led from place to place, this opening shot seems simply an introductory flourish in a film that is to be articulated so precisely on a balanced exchange of close-ups. Throughout the film there is a constant stylistic uncertainty, an impurity, which jars heavily today: in the zoom effects, for instance, when the camera darts in to over-stress a cruel or sardonic point made by one of Joan's persecutors; in the overhead shots of the crowds rushing about which seem totally arbitrary; in the irritating cross-cutting which ruins the beautiful scene where Joan smiles at seeing a cross on the floor of her cell made by the shadow of her barred window, fragmenting it unnecessarily in order to show the preparation of a supposed letter from the King of France. One might even query the validity of the mannerism whereby the camera is almost invariably looking up at the characters, giving them a sense of dominating majesty. Ebbe Neergaard justifies this *motif* by suggesting that it implies Dreyer's ''humility in the presence of great human emotion.'' This may be true, but it still *feels* like an attempt to impose reverence.

Again, it is difficult to avoid making comparisons between the judges in *La Passion de Jeanne d'Arc* and those of *Day of Wrath.* In the later film, the camera moves slowly over serene, impassive faces with all the calm, withdrawn dignity of impartial justice. The outcome is the same—a summary condemnation of the witch—yet somehow their presence, reasoned and almost indifferent, is twice as effective as the vindictiveness etched in every nook, pock-mark, and cranny of Cauchon and his colleagues. Of course Dreyer was right to want to get down to the truth in the naked human face; but with Joan exuding simple grace and Massieu (Antonin Artaud at his most handsome) glowing like an angel, all the wrinkles and the warts, the gross pouches of fat and the sadistic sneers, begin to look like an attempt to have one's cake and eat it. One thinks of Godard's remark that there isn't much point in making a film about concentration camps nowadays because the emotion is too automatic—unless one changed perspective to make a film about a typist working at Auschwitz, the day-to-day problems, the calculations necessary for the disposal of bodies, the inventories she was required to make, and so on. In *Day of Wrath* Dreyer does change those perspectives, making ordinary human beings of his judges, and giving an edge of real malevolence to both the poor helpless women accused of witchcraft.

Finally, there is the problem of the "dynamic" editing style of the film, which goes back via Eisenstein to Griffith and Dreyer's own clumsy beginnings in the cinema. Without getting into aesthetic deep waters about the validity of the montage principle which underlies the (over-rated) excitements of the ice-floe sequence in *Way Down East* or the Odessa Steps sequence in *Battleship Potemkin,* one can say that it is inimical to Dreyer's nature as a director who loves to savour the feel and texture of people, places, objects. In theory, since the central *motif* of the film is the rhythm of question and answer, the alternation or parallel editing of very brief shots is right; in practice, the constant cutting away to take in a sneering face, a baby at its mother's breast, the shots of the doves that punctuate the march to the stake and the burning, is not only distracting, but tends to dissipate the film's emotional charge.

And yet. . . and yet. Like Gance's *Napoléon,* like *Intolerance,* like *Battleship Potemkin* even, *La Passion de Jeanne d'Arc* has a majestic power which steamrollers its way through all its faults and excesses, a power mostly stemming from Falconetti's performance, but partly at least created by the sheer weight of Dreyer's conception. Many critics have claimed that, with its constant stream of titles quoting question and answer as Joan's agony proceeds to its remorseless conclusion, *La Passion de Jeanne d'Arc,* was a silent film crying out for sound. Comparison with Bresson's *Procès de Jeanne d'Arc,* made in 1962, suggests that they are wrong on purely aesthetic grounds, since Bresson's film proceeds like an actual trial, Dreyer's like an agonized commentary on it, with the divorcement between words and image acting as the equivalent of a Brechtian distantiation device. Sound would have been absolutely incompatible with Dreyer's conception, in which the titles and the huge close-ups of Joan and her judges are intercut as the two separate dramas—the farce of a trial which is being manipulated to a desired end, and the tragedy of Joan alone with herself and her fear—evolve only tangentially to each other. Ultimately, in other words, it is perfectly possible to forget all the mannerisms which remind one that the film was made in France in 1927–1928 at the height of the avant-garde movement and its technical excesses—or at least relegate them to the background of one's mind—and concentrate on Joan's interior, rather than exterior, experience.

So one comes back to Falconetti's performance, and the almost Brechtian manner in which Dreyer used artifice to strip it of artifice. Ebbe Neergaard has described the way in which he insisted on absolute truth from his actress: "When Dreyer was about to shoot an important scene with Falconetti, everyone not directly concerned was banished from the set, and absolute silence was demanded. . . . When he was describing what he wanted, he would stammer and go red in the face, not from shyness or any hesitation as to what he meant, but simply from eagerness to make his feelings and intentions completely understood. The blotchy red face and the disjoined speech were evidence of his unswerving belief that there is only one expression that is right, that can and must be found. But just because it seemed so difficult for him to express himself clearly, the actress was fired to work in with him with all her power. She was, as it were, activated into expressing what Dreyer could not show her, for it was something that could only be expressed in action, not speech, and she alone could do it, so she had to help him. And she realized that this could only be done if she dropped all intellectual inhibitions and let her feelings have free access from her subconscious to her facial expression. 'When a child,' says Dreyer, 'suddenly sees an onrushing train in front of him, the expression on his face is spontaneous. By this I don't mean the feeling in it (which in this case is sudden fear), but the fact that the face is completely uninhibited.' In a big scene the face must be relaxed to the point of emptiness, then the expression will appear of itself."

All this is good Stanislavsky system* or Actors' Studio Method, and unlike the rest of the cast, Falconetti's feelings never seem manufactured: her agony simply exists, naked, unromantic and real in its ugly, sweat-soaked torment. But of course Dreyer's *use* of this emotion is artificial in the extreme. One notices, for instance, that while Joan's lips move during the trial scenes, they rarely frame more than a word or at most a phrase, so that she seems to be suffering her judges rather than answering them.

---

*In his lecture to the Danish Students League, delivered in Copenhagen on December 1, 1943, Dreyer stated that he was an adherent of the Stanislavsky system, adding: "No actor is able to create real and true feelings to order, because you cannot *extort* feelings, they must appear from within."

Similarly, his use of panchromatic film to photograph the faces in close-up against white walls or backgrounds gives them an extraordinary quality of etched relief, in which the lighting ensures that high contrasts shadow Joan's tormentors with lines of malice while she herself is seen in the neutral tones of passive despair. Inexorably, Dreyer highlights his heroine's isolation, her helplessness to counter the weight massed against her, so that the dry, chapped lips, the face streaked with sweat and tears, the eyes shadowed with intolerable pain, the head thrown back in supplication, can still move an audience to tears today as they do Nana in *Vivre sa vie* with their marvelous soundings of the wellsprings of the human will.

Yet there is something more to the film than Joan's suffering, something that Dreyer would probably have described as that abstract spiritual quality he never tired of defining: "Where is the possibility of artistic renewal in the cinema? I can only answer for myself, and I can see only one way: *abstraction*. In order not to be misunderstood, I must at once define abstraction as something that demands of the artist to abstract himself from reality in order to strengthen the spiritual content of his work. More concisely: the artist must describe inner, not outer life. The capacity to abstract is essential to all artistic creation. Abstraction allows the director to get outside the fence with which naturalism has surrounded his medium. It allows his films to be not merely visual, but spiritual. The director must share his own artistic and spiritual experiences with the audience. Abstraction will give him a chance of doing it, of replacing objective reality with his own subjective interpretation." There are, however, abstractions and abstractions, and although Dreyer and Bresson both approached Joan from the same orthodox view of her sanctity, their interpretations of her spirituality, as Robert Vas has pointed out very neatly, are very different as seen through the texture of the films. Noting that Joan's tragedy lies in her agony between faith and doubt, Vas observes: "With a peasant stubbornness, Dreyer's Joan wanted to live; Bresson's Joan doesn't mind dying. When Joan sees the pigeons in Dreyer's film, you feel that she *must* leave something behind, something that would have been worth living for. But Bresson's pigeons flutter their wings above a world not worthy of such a sacrifice. Dreyer's heroine is left painfully alone; Bresson's is made lonely by Bresson."

Dreyer's film, in other words, is not so much concerned with the eternity of peace and salvation that awaits Joan after her brief martyrdom, as with the life she is losing for ever, and so she is constantly surrounded by intimations of mortality, by the presence of the natural world, by the purely material malice of her trial. Not merely the fluttering pigeons which accompany her to the stake, the sunlight filtering through to the floor of her cell, or the child at its mother's breast; there is also the sudden spurt of blood as Joan is bled, the skull thrown up by a gravedigger in the cemetery where she is taken to be questioned, the pathetic remnants of hair being swept up after her head has been shaved. Appropriately enough, her journey to the stake is accompanied by a *danse macabre* of contortionists and jugglers, since this is a film in which life is made a mockery of by a travestied spiritual ideal which can only impose itself through pain and torture. And as inescapably present as anything in the film are the weapons with which life is threatened: the fire and the stake, of course, and the monstrous instruments of torture, but also the spears between which Joan walks to her martyrdom, the huge clubs thrown down from a tower to waiting soldiers as the crowd beings to murmur, the chains knobbed with whirling iron balls with which the soldiers quell the impending riot.

In a curious way, therefore, one can see the whole film as a primordial struggle between life and death, in which the opposing forces are personified almost as literally as those in a medieval mystery play, with Joan and Massieu as the angels of light, and the gross, sneering judges as the demons of darkness. Antonin Artaud was perhaps thinking along these lines when he said, in the course of an interview about his work in the cinema, that Dreyer's purpose was to ''reveal Joan as the victim of one of the most terrible of all perversions: the perversion of a divine principle in its passage through the minds of men, whether they be Church, Government, or what you will.'' Ultimately, the conception does not quite come off, since the material is too intractably rooted in its historical and religious contexts; but it was a theme—the dissolution of life by death as humanity struggles to keep its tenuous foothold on earth—to which Dreyer was to return and realise to perfection three years later in *Vampyr*.

# "Day of Wrath":
# The Enclosed Image

## Robert Warshow

Carl Dreyer's basic problem as an artist is one that seems almost inevitably to confront the self-conscious creator of "art" films: the conflict between a love for the purely visual and the tendencies of a medium that is not only visual but also dramatic. The principle that the film is a medium based on movement has often been used to justify a complete preoccupation with visual patterns, as if the ideal film would be one that succeeded in divorcing movement from content, but it is this principle itself that raises the problem, for the presentation of human beings in movement necessarily leads to the creation of drama; thus the maker of "art" films, unless he limits himself to complete abstraction or to generalized poetic symbolism, tends to raise aesthetic demands that he cannot satisfy within the framework he has set. Only in the earlier parts of *Day of Wrath* can Dreyer be said to have solved this problem. And the solution, though brilliant, is essentially unstable; the weaknesses of the film's later parts grow out of the virtues of its beginning.

The film opens with the playing of *Dies Irae*, a dreadful, insistent hymn prolonged to the point where it comes to seem a kind of outrage; it is music that does not aim at the listener's pleasure or require his consent. In effect, this music establishes the existence of a world whose graces pretend to no connection with the needs of human beings, a world that may find it proper in the realization of its designs to burn a woman alive for being a witch.

There is only the most unemphatic indication that such a world is supposed to have existed in Denmark early in the seventeenth century. It is not a historical world—though it exemplifies certain historical ideas—and

From *The Immediate Experience* by Robert Warshow (New York: Doubleday Publishing Co., 1962). Reprinted by permission of Paul Warshow. This material appeared originally in *Partisan Review*, December 1948.

the primary tendency of Dreyer's direction is to keep it from becoming historical, to preserve it self-enclosed and static. Everything leading up to the execution of the witch Marthe is presented like a pageant: each movement is graceful and dignified, each figure in some particular fashion beautiful, each shot "composed"; and the camera focuses always on the leading figures of the pageant itself, following their slow and predetermined movement with an entranced solemnity that permits no glance at the actuality which has brought them into being. Not a single shot is spent on documentation, and though the whole "issue" is between good and evil, these concepts, too, exist only as parts of the spectacle: "evil" is the figure of an old woman whose function is to be thrown upon a fire after completing certain movements of flight, suffering, struggle, and despair; "good" is the process by which this ceremony is carried out.

No dramatic conflict surrounds the witch herself—her one mistaken effort to bargain for life remains no more than an expected stage in her destruction—and there is only the barest beginning of the drama that is to take place after her death. Her very sufferings are given an explicit quality of formality: three screams mark the three decisive moments—capture, confession, death; when she lies bound to the ladder and impotently shaking her fist, one's attention is drawn to a pattern of leaf-shadows that moves across her face. And all problematical aspects of the subject— questions of justice and authority, the reality of witchcraft, the existence of God and the Devil—are avoided or postponed: it is shown, for example, that the pastor Absalon, who is the leading figure in the witch's condemnation, is himself in an ambiguous situation, but this is not permitted to become a dramatic problem until after her death; and the activities that constitute the witch's crime, though formally indicated, remain vague— only later on is it shown that she might have been regarded as actually dangerous.

Yet this formalized and narrow spectacle creates a degree of excitement beyond anything one experiences during the later, more dramatic portions of the film; by the time the witch falls screaming upon the fire, the tension has come close to a point at which it might be reasonable to leave the theater. The chief source of this tension seems to be in the interplay between Dreyer's general approach to art and certain of the specific tendencies of his medium.

Dreyer's initial impulse, in his deliberate exclusion of the historical and dramatic, is to deprive events of the quality of reality; it is this, indeed, which accounts for his concern with the past: since the past can be contemplated but not changed, it exists from one point of view as an aesthetic object ready-made—one can experience it "pure." But he practices his aestheticism on events that possess *a priori* an unusual emotional importance, and in one of the most realistic of all mediums. In the screen's absolute clarity, where all objects are brought close and defined unambiguously, the "reality" of an event can be made to inhere simply in its visible presence; so long as the internal structure of a film remains consistent, all its elements are in these terms equally "real"—that is, completely visible. Thus at his best—which means, in this film, when he is creating his own images and not imitating the creations of seventeenth-century painting—Dreyer is able to give his aestheticized vision of the past all the force of reality without impairing its aesthetic autonomy; in the absence of a historical-dramatic reality, the purely visible dominates and is sufficient: the witch is an object of art, but she is also—and just as fully—a human being (she is *there*), and she is burnt; the burning is so to speak accomplished by the camera, which can see the witch without having to "interpret" her.

The effect is something like a direct experience of the tension between art and life. In a sense, the image *as* image becomes a dramatic force: the issue is not, after all, good against evil or God against Satan, but flesh against form; stripped as it is of all historical or social reference, the spectacle is of a woman burnt to serve beauty. It is a spectacle not to be understood—the image itself is all the meaning—but to be endured; and the enormous excitement that surrounds it, the sense almost of a prolonged assault on one's feelings, results largely from the exclusion of all that might be used to create an appearance of understanding. Even to see the witch as a victim of injustice would provide a certain relief by placing the events on the screen within some "normal" frame of response. But no such opportunity appears, nothing *in* the film is allowed to speak for the audience or to the audience (two of the characters cannot bear to watch the burning, but this is not what is wanted: it is merely a sign of their weakness). It is as if the director, in his refusal to acknowledge that physical movement implies dramatic movement, were denying the relevance of the spectator's feelings; one is left with no secure means of connecting the witch with reality, and yet she is real in herself and must be responded to; as responses are blocked, the tension increases.

In this blocking of responses, it is again important that Dreyer's aestheticism leads him to the past. The historical past, being real, embodies a multitude of possibilities; the aesthetic past is created by eliminating all possibilities but one, and that is the accomplished one. Thus time becomes fate: the image is distant and untouchable because its form was fixed long before we come to see it; the witch *will* be burnt because witches *were* burnt. The feelings of the spectator really are in a way irrelevant: he is watching what has ceased to exist, and thre is no one to "care" what he feels. He has his feelings nevertheless.

In the later parts of the film, in order to relieve the tension that has been established, it became necessary to permit a reassertion of those historical-dramatic elements which have been so rigidly suppressed. But the basic style of the film is already fixed, and this need to introduce new elements results in incongruities, passages of boredom, and dramatic incoherence.

The dramatic plot which begins to work itself out after the witch's death concerns the adultery of the pastor's young wife Anne and his son Martin; Anne becomes a witch, ensnaring her lover and later killing her husband by the power of evil. The ambiguity of the pastor's position, too, is involved with witchcraft: his sin was to conceal the fact that Anne's mother was a witch. Thus witchcraft is no longer pure image, it is a way of behaving, and the question of its reality is no longer to be avoided. A psychological answer is impossible: Dreyer is already committed to keeping the past *in* the past. But the supernatural answer, which is the one he chooses (and with a hesitation that only makes matters worse), is just as bad: once the question of witchcraft is raised, no one can be expected to believe in its reality.

The attempt to impose belief by purely aesthetic means is inevitably a failure, both dramatically and visually. There is a scene in which the pastor walks home at night through an "evil" storm that is the height of visual banality; then his wife, at home with her lover, is shown saying, "If he were dead—"; then back to the pastor, who suddenly straightens up in the howling wind and says to his companion, "I felt as if Death had brushed me by." And there is a continual effort to use the camera for symbolic comment that eventually becomes clear enough but is never convincing: when Anne first tries her "power" in order to call Martin to her side, Dreyer repeats on her face the shifting pattern of leaves that appeared on the face of the old witch before she was burnt; when the lovers walk in the fields, the camera keeps turning upward to the trees above their heads. In general, there is an attempt to equate the outdoors, the world of nature, with evil (the pastor's mother, who is the one firm moral pillar, is never seen outside the rigidly ordered household she controls); but the camera cannot create a religious system.

The purely dramatic failure is most obvious in the film's conclusion, when Martin turns against Anne and thus leads her to confess her witchcraft. Martin's defection is not made to seem an adequate reason for Anne's confession, and Martin's action itself is entirely without motivation: the very skill with which the director now tries to transmute visual patterns into drama (as earlier he had tried to make dramatic patterns purely visual) becomes a kind of irrelevancy. But even in this later section of the film there is still much that is successful. When Anne resolves to kill her husband, a virtual transformation of character is accomplished by the manipulation of lighting. And whenever the aesthetic image does not come into direct conflict with the dramatic structure, it can still take on some of the purity and completeness of the earlier scenes—for example, in the procession of choir boys at the pastor's funeral—except that now the image is felt as an interruption of the action.

At bottom, the film is an aesthetic paradox: out of the pure and enclosed image Dreyer creates a sort of "pure drama," in which the point of conflict is precisely the exclusion of drama; but this in turn creates a tension that the image alone cannot resolve; the dramatic nature of the medium must reassert itself in the later portions of the film, and Dreyer is involved again in the initial contradiction.

# "Vampyr" and "Gertrud"

## Ken Kelman

### "Vampyr"

*Vampyr* transpires in no *earthly* world at all; but clearly in the realm of absolute vision. *Vampyr* is a veritable initiation into the mysteries of death. It fits the form of what Parker Tyler has called trance-film, the prototype of which is *Caligari:* in which an essentially passive hero experiences events which function primarily as manifestations of the unconscious. Dreyer goes so far as to exaggerate the unearthliness of landscape and characters, "spiritualizing" all in twilight and mystic air, so all perception is as through a glass darkly; as if there were a distance greater than space between this region and our mortal eyes. Moreover, the characters' movements are automatic and fated, as though the real actors were invisble forces; and their voices float so hollow and distant on the sound-track as to hardly belong to the speakers, rather suggesting disembodied spirits.

The shading of *Vampyr* is awfully fine, since the action itself is treated matter-of-factly even when bizarre, and the point of view is never fantastical but literal and realistic. Indeed, there appears to be a more or less traditional and coherent story, with the implicit promise that all may be explained. But it never is. Causal connections between events are deviously lacking, and stranger powers rush into the vacuum. Logic is undermined, and the "plot" can be followed at best with the aid of our most hidden resources. This subversion of "reality" reaches its climax toward the end, when the scene of David Gray finding the bound heroine is repeated exactly, a visual echo and more, the very ghost of event.

By such ellipsis and abstraction, Dreyer relates crucial *emotional* images without adequate *reason;* creating an apparent reality as immediately convincing as dream, but as ultimately elusive. Thus, the viewer

Excerpted from "Dreyer" by Ken Kelman in *Film Culture*, no. 35, Winter 1964–65. This material is taken from the revised version appearing in *The Film Culture Reader*, edited by P. Adams Sitney (New York: Praeger Publishers, 1970). Reprinted by permission of *Film Culture*.

is truly taken in. And not only are we involved in the structure of dream which is the film; the characters are entranced within the trance. So we experience "the strange adventures of David Gray" the way *he* does; and the crucial vision of evil and death which he suffers, his own funeral, we see right along with him, through his eyes, staring up out of the coffin.

The whole film becomes ultimately the kind of dream-vision had in "primitive" cultures, whether induced by solitude, hunger, or drugs; a revelation of the terrible secrets of existence, often in the form of a journey, an adventure of the dreamer's spirit in other worlds or underworlds. In this case, the matter of life and death is epitomized in the figure of the vampire. Through experience of this *tremendem*, David Gray is shocked to awareness and pressured to pass from innocence and ignorance to consciousness of forces that must be confronted. First he—or his spirit—shrinks from the horror, then investigates it, and finally resists it. And, as I mentioned, Dreyer subtly brings us right along on this rite of passage into the dark world and back.

An early image, of a reaper and his scythe in silhouette, graphically establishes *Vampyr*'s preoccupations. The death-scented smoke from *Joan of Arc* seeps into this film as a thick mist pervading the whole landscape. There is not a sunny frame in the whole movie. Even when the hero and heroine get across the Stygian waters, the picture does not appreciably brighten, as they walk through tall trees arranged in disquieting symmetry, straight row after row. But youth and love do survive and escape age and death, the land of the old, the old Count, the old servants, the old doctor and old vampire who drain the life-blood of the young (as the old doctor bled and weakened Joan).

And death again, as it did for Joan, has its salubrious side. It is a deliverance for the Count and the bedridden girl, animated as they are by evil spirits. On the other bony hand, it is unnatural and horrible for the hero, David Gray, as he is borne, alive and healthy, but trancefixed, in a coffin toward his grave.

So Dreyer's old themes operate in a very new way in *Vampyr*. And other changes accompany those in plot and character conception. Camera movement is less insistent and consistent than in *Joan,* and the image is a blend of that film's abstraction with the picturesque qualities of earlier work. Most notable as technical departure is Dreyer's only use ever of superimposition, to create shadows which leave bodies and return, as well as transparent spirits; supernatural effects to reinforce the other strangeness. The soundtrack is quite successful in this too, with its precisely eerie music; and the strange noises which serve as characters' voices, from the canine growls the old villain intermittently emits, to the weirdly distant, unearthly tones of David Gray's love. A poignant touch occurs when the

hoarse voice of the possessed girl alters, at the moment of her final liberation, to the pure high pitch of the ethereal heroine.

A very special film, obscure enough in origin, though a little is lit up
by tracking traces of its literary basis. Dreyer took, it looks like, whatever
appealed to him, I mean, struck his fan(ta)cy, out of a collection five
stories wide by Sheridan Le Fanu, titled *In a Glass Darkly*. Thus, from *The
Familiar,* comes the concept of a malevolent being that materializes as a
bird; from *Mr. Justice Harbottle,* a procession emerging from a closet (the
peg-legged henchman comes out of the clock in *Vampyr*); from *The Room
in the Dragon Volant,* the hero, fully conscious, lying helpless and immobile in a coffin gazing upward; and, from *Carmilla* (the basis of Va-
dim's *Blood and Roses*), the vehement passion of the girl vampire for her
female victim. The apparent randomness of selection does indicate how
much *Vampyr* is imagined rather than thought-wrought.

Other influence, specifically Griffith's, may be discerned in the film's
finale. The situation of a villain meeting his death in a granary, buried
under heaps of cascading flour, is the same as the conclusion of *A Corner
in Wheat*. The machinery which grinds out doom here is much like the
torture apparatus in *Joan of Arc,* with its inexorable wheels, and the wheel
again turns, less elaborate and abstract, in the inquisition of the witch in
*Day of Wrath*.

The conclusion, with good triumphant and evil destroyed, would be
more comforting were it the integral function of a complete process; and
not the fluke of a fanciful providence and literal *deus ex machina*. But the
happy end is just a fragment of a figment of fantasy, and the afterimage of
the whole is disturbing, a dark taste in the eye. . . .

## *Disillusion—Senses of "Gertrud"*

*Gertrud* is like one of those old, slow, gloomy Scandinavian sex
movies before they discovered flesh; like a theater melodrama eternalized
on film; like a Bergman picture minus chic; except, as a dear friend of mine
remarked, it takes forever—a scale on which all love becomes a movement
toward salvation.

All the formalities are religiously observed in *Gertrud*—so rigorously
that it becomes clear they are the mere tense surface of life. The time of the
film swallows all words, and runs strong between, deep beneath all gestures. These are not merely the petty social formalities, but art, marriage,
rank, morality, fame, and, indeed, the accustomed ideas and ideals of man.
Success in these is shown to have no power against the ultimate failure.

The characters talk to each other, according to the conventions of
speech, only a bit more so. They speak a little too deliberately, and looking
past each other. Their isolation is clear. And it is clear that they are never

talking about the real issues, but using speech as a habitual indirection, a way of brushing things they cannot come to grips with; and, finally, their speech possesses a ritual opacity: It is the series of symbols and expressions with which man clothes himself to take on personality and to live (act a life) on the way to his definitive death. This is not so much a film on the difficulty of communication, as on the difficulty of existence.

All the people of *Gertrud* have the same sense, manifest in various ways, that they are not living the real life. They have intimations of what a mere show it is that passes for reality, that nothing they do is any less vain than the procession of students and the speeches honoring the poet—ostentation, acting, the merest illusion.

All are profoundly, precisely disillusioned. The process of *Gertrud* is the baring of painful partial truth after truth, with no prospect of full revelation. Gertrud's husband is continually disillusioned by her, though it is obvious how he creates over and over the illusions she must destroy, from her first hint of leaving to her final admission that she loved him "in a way." Her old lover, the poet, is disillusioned by what he discovers of the past, but mainly because of the hopes of her he maintains, which are plainly doomed to failure. Her young lover, the musician, the object of her own illusion, is ironically enough quite disillusioned from the start and, indeed, goes on to show that the absence of illusion means defeat—at least when it is not founded in truth and consciousness, but only in muddled despair. Gertrud herself is most thoroughly and systematically disillusioned. The poet disillusioned her once, and for all time, so it seemed; so, she was able to enter into a conventional, good, realistic marriage with no nonsense, no illusions; and yet the composer revived love in her, that love that must mean (dis)illusion, being an absolute passion directed toward a mutable creature.

Dreyer is most pointedly revealing in *Gertrud* why love on this earth must fail. It is always partial, always conditional, of a particular place and time. Yet the characters grasp at it as their redemption from what they stare at past each other—nothing, eternity. Sometimes the sense of reality's unreality, of nothing, seizes them. Gertrud's husband muses on it all seeming like a dream, as he rides back from the opera. She herself disquiets her young lover, toward the crowning of his desire, by murmuring of life as "a dream, a long dream"; and, just after this, she undresses as he plays his nocturne, and only her shadow can be seen—an ironical image of life as dream indeed.

We create our own worlds, Dreyer shows, in *Day of Wrath,* where human belief creates life in its images, and in *Ordet,* where human faith overcomes the "natural," the "real." The people of *Gertrud* exist in a godless, rational world, where they are still driven to seek solace and hope and grace, irrationally, in love. But the stark reality of illusion, of the emptiness of the worldly show, stares them in the face, stares from their faces, all the time. They tremble with doubt and mortality, and only Gertrud has the strength to face it all directly. She who will not compromise, who will settle for no less than the absolute in love, must find the absolute elsewhere.

At the end we find her, at home in aloneness, cherishing memories (not so much with regret or nostalgia for past lost reality, as with aesthetic or philosophic appreciation for beautiful illusions), having found no belief, no greater love, no final truth; resigned and even serene in her disillusion, meditative and almost saintlike in her austere isolation. Gertrud practices a religious discipline, but she has no faith. The world is as nothing, but there is nothing to fill that vacuum. Gertrud has achieved her absolute, a relative, but no more, of absolution. The last shot of *Gertrud,* held interminably, is of an empty room, a closed door.

# Sergei Eisenstein

SERGEI EISENSTEIN was born in Riga, Latvia, in 1898, and died in Moscow in 1948. His reputation has gone through drastic shifts both in the U. S. S. R. and abroad. His second film, Battleship Potemkin *(1925)*, was a worldwide success, and for several decades his films and writings were almost venerated by film students and artists around the world. In recent decades a reaction has set in, in particular against his theories of montage and the supposed intellectuality of his films, few of which, after Potemkin, were completed precisely according to his plans.

In Russia during Stalin's rule he frequently ran afoul of the political line and was forced to perform self-criticism and alter his style, especially after socialist realism was enshrined as the prevailing artistic doctrine. He himself was more an aesthete than a Marxist, despite his ardent faith in the Revolution, and he was never truly a realist, whatever his lip service to the official line. The bloated cartoon capitalists in his first film, Strike *(1924)*, are as stylized as the costumed operatic figures in his last works, Alexander Nevsky *(1938)* and Ivan the Terrible *(Part I, 1944; Part II, 1946)*.

Though Potemkin may have given some thrust to realism within the prevailing artificial conventions of the silent film, Eisenstein has little concern for individuals and the minute particulars of their lives. His gift is for visual poetry, so that his films become increasingly painterly in the latter part of his career. Though he came to films from work in the avant-garde theater, Eisenstein was trained as an engineer and architect. He was a gifted draughtsman and for his later films he made intricate sketches of many of the shots in advance. Though his literary style is bare and ungainly, he became a prolific writer and had a wide range of theoretical interests in every aspect of cinematic creation, especially in problems of montage and in technical innovations such as sound and color. He was active also as a teacher and lecturer, especially in later years when the political climate kept him from filmmaking. (He completed only seven films in twenty-five years.)

Eisenstein's two masterpieces come at opposite ends of his career. Potemkin is the only complete demonstration of the methods of montage that he had developed under the influence of D. W. Griffith, but its most striking images and sequences, especially the famous Odessa Steps scene, transcend any single theory of filmmaking. Eisenstein invented the whole episode of the massacre on the Odessa steps, and he creates an almost musical rhythm of counterpointed images—the marching soldiers, the shadow of their guns, the woman with the pince-nez, the woman whose son is shot, the seemingly endless cascade of steps, the plummeting baby carriage—which build up visually and emotionally in a powerful crescendo. If Eisenstein had done nothing else of value, he would still be one of the cinema's great masters on the strength of this sequence alone.

233

*Eisenstein later masterpiece was* Ivan the Terrible, *notably Part II, with its brilliant color sequence. These two films have been compared to the ritualized movements and elemental passions of the Kabuki theatre. They are strikingly opulent and visual, "like frescoes come to life" (as Marie Seton puts it). The rarefied human motives and movements are subsumed in a larger ritual pattern, which includes Prokofiev's music, the remarkable indoor sets with their Byzantine murals, right down to the rhythm of the folds of the nobles' heavy robes as they proceed to the chamber of the dying Tsar. Because of Stalin's disapproval, however, Part II was not released until ten years after Eisenstein's death; a projected third part was planned but never filmed.*

*There are two comprehensive biographies: by Marie Seton,* Sergei M. Eisenstein *(1952), and by Yon Barna,* Eisenstein *(1973). Some of Eisenstein's voluminous writings have been translated in* The Film Sense *(1942),* Film Form *(1949),* Notes of a Film Director *(1959), and* Film Essays *(1968). A standard history of the Soviet film industry is Jay Leyda's* Kino *(1960). Two valuable studies in French are by Jean Mitry,* S. M. Eisenstein *(1961), and Barthélémy Amengual's* Premier Plan *volume (no. 25, 1962). See also Ivor Montagu,* With Eisenstein in Hollywood *(1969), Léon Moussinac,* Sergei Eisenstein *(1970), and Annette Michelson's essay "Reading Eisenstein, Reading Capital" in* October *(1976, 1977). On the spectacular disaster of* Que Viva Mexico!, *Eisenstein's most ambitious unfinished film, see Wilson,* The American Earthquake (1958), *and Harry M. Geduld and Ronald Gottesman, eds.,* The Making and Unmaking of Que Viva Mexico! *(1970).*

# *"Potemkin"*

## Stanley Kauffmann

Sometimes one imagines that there is a small but constant supply of genius throughout the world and that a particular juncture of circumstances in any one place touches the local supply to life. Otherwise, how explain the sudden flowering of Athenian architecture or Elizabethan drama or Italian Renaissance painting? Can one believe that there had been no previous talent and that geniuses were born on cue? It almost seems that the right confluence of events brings dormant omnipresent genius awake; without those events, nothing. Possibly the man with the greatest potential genius for symphonic composition lived in New Guinea five hundred years ago, but there was nothing in his world to make him know it.

This theory, admittedly fanciful, gets some support from what happened in Soviet Russia in the 1920s. A new revolutionary state was born as a new revolutionary art emerged, and that combination brought forth at least three superb creators in the new art: Vsevolod Pudovkin, Alexander Dovzhenko, and—the most important because the most influential—Sergei M. Eisenstein. Conjecturally, all of them might have had outstanding careers in other fields, but the Soviet Revolution and its need for film, one may say, made geniuses of them.

For all the joy and ebullience that attended the birth of Soviet film and Eisenstein's entrance into it, his career as a whole is a sad story, and it puts my comments on *Potemkin* in true, cruelly ironic light to have some of the biographical facts first. Sergei Mikhailovich Eisenstein was born in Riga in 1898, studied engineering in St. Petersburg, and entered the Red Army in 1918 to fight in the civil war. While in the army, says Yon Barna in his recent biography, Eisenstein became involved in amateur theatricals, which intensified an interest in the theater he had felt since he was a boy. He decided to abandon an engineering future for a theatrical career. In 1920 he was demobilized, got himself to Moscow, and found a job at one of the new workers' theaters as a scene designer. He went on to do some designing for the renowned theater director Vsevolod Meyerhold, whose anti-psychological, anti-"internalizing" views influenced him greatly; then in 1922–1924 Eisenstein himself directed plays, including one called *Gas Masks*. But his impulse toward direction, as he later wrote himself, was much more cinematic than theatrical: he staged *Gas Masks* in a gas-works!

From there he moved quickly into film. He had already done a short film interlude for a theatrical production, and in 1924 he made his first feature, *Strike*. In 1925 he made *Potemkin,* which is sometimes known as *Battleship Potemkin* or *Armored Cruiser Potemkin.*

Absolutely congruent with his bursting film energies was his fervor for the Communist Revolution and the establishment of the Soviet state. These factors are integral in any talk of Eisenstein. To think of him as a director who just happened to be Russian or who (in those early days) was subservient to a state-controlled industry and managed to slip some good art into his films despite this subservience, is to miss the core of Eisenstein. His works in those days were cinematic exponents of his beliefs.

With his next completed film, *October,* released in 1928, the complications begin. Originally the film had sequences showing Trotsky's part in the revolution of 1917, but while Eisenstein was finishing it, Trotsky went into disrepute and then into exile as Stalin ascended. Eisenstein had to revise his film to take account of this rewriting of history.

His troubles increased as time went on. The Stalin era was not exactly a continuation of the high, shining Bolshevik days. To sum it up: the rest of his career, until his death in 1948, is a story of frustration and frequent abortion. Out of numerous projects he completed only four more films. Even an expedition he made to the West ended abortively. He was allowed to go to America in 1930, discussed several projects with a Hollywood studio, made none, and then shot a lot of footage in Mexico for a film he never edited, although others have arranged versions of it.

He spent much of his time in his later years teaching at the Institute of Cinematography in Moscow, writing (most of these writings are not yet in English), and not complaining about the state. Still the facts speak for themselves: this furiously imaginative and energetic man left a total of only six completed films. One virtually completed film, *Bezhin Meadow,* was apparently destroyed by the Soviet government in 1938, although the official line is that it was destroyed by German bombs in World War II. (Isaac Babel worked on the final script of *Bezhin Meadow,* which was based on a Turgenev story that echoes the ideological difference between Eisenstein and his conservative father.) The U.S.S.R.'s waste of Eisenstein, melancholy in any view, is especially grim when seen in the light that blazes off the screen from *Potemkin*.

When it was first shown abroad in 1926, it was hailed by many, including such disparate figures as Max Reinhardt and Douglas Fairbanks, as the best film that had yet been made anywhere. Agree with that opinion or not; few can see this relatively short picture—five reels, eighty-six minutes—without being catapulted into an experience that is stunning in itself and illuminating of much that followed in film history.

During the mid-1920s the Soviets were busy trying to consolidate ideologically their political and military victories, and they called on the arts to help. Eisenstein was assigned to make a huge film called *The Year 1905*, dealing with the events of the earlier, failed, but momentous outbreak against Czarism. He and his script collaborator Nina Agadzhanova-Shutko wrote a scenario in which, says Barna, "the *Potemkin* mutiny took up a relatively tiny part." When Eisenstein went to Odessa to shoot that part, he decided to limit the film to that single *Potemkin* episode.

Here is the episode, as he presents it. While the warship is anchored in the Black Sea near Odessa in June 1905, the restive crew protest against the maggoty meat that they are served. The captain orders the execution of the dissenters. Instead of obeying orders, the firing squad joins the crew in mutiny, and they take over the ship. One of the leaders is killed; his body is taken ashore so that it may lie "in state." The sympathetic citizens of Odessa pay homage to him and support the sailors on the anchored vessel with gifts of food. When a mass of these citizens gathers on a huge flight of steps overlooking the harbor to cheer the *Potemkin*, the Czar's troops appear and march down the steps, scattering the crowd and killing some of them. The government sends a naval squadron to retake the *Potemkin*, which sails to meet them in battle. At the moment of encounter, the fleet allows the mutineers to pass through. In fact, the ship sailed to Constanta in Rumania, where the crew opened her seacocks, then sought refuge inland; however, Eisenstein leaves the story open-ended, with the *Potemkin* sailing onward through the friendly squadron, bearing the seed of revolution that was to bloom twelve years later.

Now, irrespective of the viewer's political beliefs, this story is a natural thriller. Nothing has more wide or direct theatrical appeal than resistance to tyranny, whether it is Spartacus or William Tell or the Boston Tea Party. Any competent Soviet director could have made the *Potemkin* story into an exciting film. But Eisenstein—and, to repeat, this is the core of his importance—was an *artist of revolution,* not merely a good director, not merely a gifted propagandist. That revolution was as central and generative for his art as, to cite a lofty precedent, Christianity was for

Giotto. There are acres and acres of fourteenth-century Italian frescoes and canvases that present Christian ideas more or less affectingly, but the Arena Chapel in Padua is the work of a Christian genius and a genius that was Christian. In proportion, the same relation exists between Eisenstein's genius and Soviet communism.

The dynamics behind the particularity of his art can be traced to Marxist concepts and, I think, to none more clearly than to some in the *Communist Manifesto* of 1848 by Marx and Engels. I do not maintain that Eisenstein used the *Manifesto* as an explicit text, but he certainly knew it well and its ideas were certainly part of his intellectual resources. One idea in the *Manifesto* seems outstandingly relevant. In the second section, where the authors anticipate objections to their arguments, they write:

> Does it require deep intuition to comprehend that man's ideas, views, and conceptions—in one word, man's consciousness— changes with every change in the conditions of his material existence, in his social relations and in his social life?

Straight to this profound concept, that a changed world means a changed awareness of the world, Eisenstein struck in his filmmaking, and never more deeply than in *Potemkin.* That he was following Marx preceptively I cannot say, but clearly he felt that a new society meant a new kind of *vision;* that the way people saw things must be altered; that it was insufficient to put new material before, so to speak, old eyes. Anyone anywhere could tell a story of heroic resistance in traditional style; it was his duty as a revolutionary artist, Eisenstein felt (and later wrote), to find an esthetically revolutionary way to tell a politically revolutionary story.

The prime decision was in the visual texture. He wanted to avoid historical drama; he wanted to make a drama of history. He and his lifelong cameraman, Edouard Tissé, aimed at a kind of newsreel look: not coarse graininess (there is, indeed, a good deal of subtle black-and-white gradation), but not painterly chiaroscuro either, no imitation museum-look. He wanted the feeling, essentially, of extraordinary eavesdropping.

A recent scion of this approach was Pontecorvo's *The Battle of Algiers,* except for the difference that, in these earlier days, Eisenstein relied very much less than Pontecorvo on individual performances. That was Eisenstein's second decision; he used very few actors. Mostly, he used ordinary people whose faces and bodies he liked for particular roles—a furnace man as the ship's doctor, a gardener as the ship's priest—and each one was used for a relatively short performance that the director could control easily and heighten with camera angles and editing, in a kind of mosaic process. Eisenstein called this approach "typage," the casting of parts with such striking faces—often introduced in close-up, sometimes intense close-up—that our very first glimpse tells us most of what we need to know about him or her as an element in the mosaic. In his subsequent films *Alexander Nevsky* and both parts of *Ivan the Terrible,* Eisenstein blended the use of "typage" with large roles for professional actors, but in *Potemkin* human depths come from the combination of pieces rather than the exploration of any one piece.

The "typage" idea leads directly to the cinematic technique most closely associated with Eisenstein: montage. Basically, montage is editing: the selection and arrangement of bits of film to produce certain effects. Every film ever made, from *Potemkin* to TV commercials, literally contains montage. But Eisenstein's use of montage was different from any use of it before him, including the work of his acknowledged master D. W. Griffith, is immediately recognizable as Eisenstein's, and is the source of much that followed after him.

He wrote often on the subject, which for him was the heart of cinema. For him, there were five kinds of montage. Briefly put, these are: metric montage, which is simply a relation between the lengths of the various pieces; rhythmic montage, which is based on the contents, in movement and composition, of the various pieces; tonal montage, based on the emotional colors of the pieces; overtonal montage, which is the conflict between the principal tone of the piece and its overtonal implications; and intellectual montage, a conflict that arises when similar actions are seen in conjunction but have been performed for different reasons (e.g., a hammer blow by a blacksmith, a hammer blow by a murderer).

These were not academic formulations. These five kinds of montage were, for Eisenstein, organs of a vibrant, live art. With them, and combinations of them, he fashioned *Potemkin* into a kind of bomb that penetrates our customary "entertainment" apperceptions to burst below the surface and shake us from within.

The story itself he phrased into five movements: Part One, Men and Maggots; Part Two, Drama on the Quarterdeck; Part Three, An Appeal from the Dead; Part Four, The Odessa Steps; Part Five, Meeting the Squadron. Each of these parts, like an act in a good drama, is a structure in itself, with its own cantilevered stress and tensions, that contributes to the structure of the whole.

Commentators have pointed out that both the montage in *Potemkin* and its five-part structure had their origins at least partly in practical considerations. Raw film stock was in very short supply in the early Soviet days. Most of what was available was in relatively short snippets, so directors had to work in short takes. Eisenstein developed the esthetics of montage out of an exigency. Also, most Soviet film theaters at the time had only one projector; there was a pause when one reel ended and another reel had to be put on the machine. The five parts of *Potemkin* are on five reels, so the pauses come at reasonably appropriate moments. But, as is so often true in the history of art, the practical needs were not constrictive but stimulating. Another great precedent: the *David* in Florence is huge because the city had a huge block of marble on its hands, left over from an unfulfilled commission, and asked Michelangelo to make use of it.

With the very opening moments of *Potemkin,* we know we are in the presence of something new, and the miracle is that we know it every time we see the film. The waves beat at the shore, the lookouts converse, the ship steams across the sea, and all this is modeled with an energy, controlled yet urgent, that bursts at us. Then, when we cut to the crew's quarters and we move among the slung hammocks, we know we are in the hands of an artist who sees the difference between naturalism and realism. The scene of the sleeping sailors is accurate enough, yet Eisenstein sees the arabesques that the hammocks form, and he uses these graceful, intersecting curves as a contrast to the turbulence of the waves earlier and the mutiny that is to come. Shortly thereafter, he uses the swinging of the suspended tables in the mess hall in the same way—another moment of irrepressible grace in iron surroundings.

Fiercely, electrically, the film charges forward into the confrontation between officers and men, the action caught in flashes that simultaneously anatomize and unify it—in Eisenstein's double aim to show things as they are yet make us see them as never before. One of his methods, which has been likened to cubism and is a forerunner of a technique used in *Last Year at Marienbad,* is to show an action and then repeat it immediately from a slightly changed point of view. A celebrated instance of this is the moment when a young sailor smashes a plate on which is inscribed "Give us this day our daily bread." We see his action twice in rapid succession, from two angles, and the effect is intensification, italicized rage.

Eisenstein shot the quarterdeck sequence on board *The Twelve Apostles,* the surviving sister ship of the *Potemkin,* which had to be altered somewhat but which nevertheless gives the sequence a steely verisimilitude. (Remember *Gas Masks!*) When the obdurate sailors are herded together and a tarpaulin thrown over them before they are to be shot—itself a simple, dehumanizing image—the firing squad prepares, and the film cuts away: to a close-up of two cannon, to a view of the ship at anchor, as if to implicate the environment. Of course it is D. W. Griffith's old technique of intercutting to distend a moment of climax, but it is used here for thematic as well as visceral effect.

At the last moment the firing squad goes over to the sailors' side, and in the fight that follows Eisenstein uses another of his favorite devices, which he himself called synecdoche. After the corrupt ship's doctor is thrown overboard, we see a close-up of his pince-nez dangling from the rigging—the same pince-nez with which he had inspected the maggoty meat and pronounced it edible. The man's corruption and what followed it are caught in that shot. And there is another such moment. Before the fight, we have seen the ship's priest, one of the clerics whom Eisenstein was constantly caricaturing in his films, lifting his crucifix and bidding the men obey. During the fight, after the priest has been knocked down a flight of steps, we see a close-up of the crucifix, an edge of its lateral bar stuck in the deck where it has fallen, like an axe plunged into wood—an axe (Eisenstein implies) that has missed the necks for which it was intended.

The most noted sequence in the film, without question the most noted sequence in film history, is the Odessa Steps. It is oceanic. With some hundreds of people, Eisenstein creates the sense of an immense, limitless upheaval. With the quick etching of a few killings, he creates more savagery than thousands of commonplace gory films. With crosscurrents of perspective and tempo, he evokes the collision of status quo and inevitable protest.

Here are two examples of Eisenstein's montage in this sequence that is a treasury of montage aesthetics. First, as he himself noted, the recurring shots of the soldiers' boots coming down the steps toward the frightened and angry citizens are always in a different rhythm from the rest of the sequence, ideationally establishing a different political impulse, aesthetically creating an exciting counterbeat. Second, he establishes, by typage, a woman with glasses protesting the soldiers' butchery. Shortly afterward, we see an officer swinging a saber at the camera; then we cut to her face, one lens of her glasses shattered, her eye streaming blood, her features frozen in shock. (The bank teller in *Bonnie and Clyde* who was shot through the car window is her direct descendant.) The suggestion of the blow's force by ellipsis is masterly enough; but in the brief moment in which we see the officer swinging his saber at us, totaling less than two seconds, there are *four different shots* of him, exploding his fury into a horrifying prism.

This episode raises one more point to be made about the whole sequence, the whole film. Even when one sees *Potemkin* without musical accompaniment, which is preferable to most of the scores that have been tacked on to it, when it is seen absolutely silent, the effect is of roaring tumult. One strong impulse to the development of montage in the days of silent film was the attempt to create visually the effect of sound: shots of train whistles or church bells or door knockers so that you could see what you couldn't hear. But in this film, by the way he counterpoises rhythms and faces, marching boots and guns and moving masses, Eisenstein draws from that silent screen a mounting and immense "roar" that has rarely been surpassed in sound films.

The double vision of *Potemkin*, subjectivized and also cosmic, is paralleled in its double effect throughout the world. Subjectively, it was made as a celebration for those already fervent in communism; but it was simultaneously intended as propaganda for the unconverted world. Emotionally and aesthetically, if not politically, it unquestionably has had a great effect; but those who control the film have much less faith in it than its maker had. No important picture has been more seriously tampered with. Political messages have been tacked on fore and aft on some prints; some prints have been snipped internally; thirty-five years ago in New York the picture was given a filmed prologue and epilogue spoken by American actors. The only music that Eisenstein approved was written by an Austrian, Edmund Meisel, for the Berlin premiere, and this score has only recently been rediscovered. Most prints of *Potemkin* have some other music ladled on.

Eisenstein's carrer, in terms of its free growth, describes a curve that coincides with the rise and fall of worldwide radical hope for Soviet communism. But at the height of his faith, he created a film that both proclaimed his faith and transcended it, a work of political fire that lives because it is a work of art.

# Eisenstein and Constructivism

## Standish D. Lawder

### Eisenstein as a Constructivist Artist

Sergei Mikhailovich Eisenstein (1898–1948) was born in Riga, Latvia, and spent most of his childhood in St. Petersburg. As a child he showed great precociousness in drawing. Ivor Montagu has called him an "almost Picasso-level infant prodigy," and several youthful sketches in the Eisenstein Collection of the Museum of Modern Art prove this is no exaggeration. While still living at Riga, he attended the School of Fine Arts for a brief period. His parents became separated, and in 1914 the young Eisenstein went to St. Petersburg to live with his father, who discouraged his career in art and enrolled him in the Institute of Civil Engineering at the university to study engineering and architecture.

Eisenstein's earlier interests had been in art, philosophy, and literature. Now immersed in a new discipline so distant from his beloved humanities, he developed a fascination with the scientific reasoning involved in engineering problems. In a later autobiographical note he realized the significance of this scientific training:

> . . .armed with technical-engineering method, I eagerly delved deeper and deeper into the fundamentals of creative art, instinctively seeking the same sphere of exact knowledge that has succeeded in captivating me during my short experience in engineering.[1]

Not only with Eisenstein did the study of engineering shape the form of his art. The work of other Constructivists as well bears the mark of this influence, whether or not they formally studied engineering. Gabo's

1. From *International Literature,* no. 4 (Moscow, 1933); reprinted in Marie Seton, *Eisenstein* (New York, 1952), p. 479.

From *The Essential Cinema,* ed. P. Adams Sitney (New York: Anthology Film Archives in cooperation with New York University Press, 1976). Reprinted by permission of Anthology Film Archives.

studies in engineering were, by his own admission, a decisive influence in his becoming a sculptor. El Lissitzky, too, had studied engineering in Darmstadt before realizing himself as an artist. Tatlin must have absorbed similar lessons at home from his father, an engineer by profession. Later Tatlin actually entered a metallurgical factory near St. Petersburg in his attempt to become an artist-engineer; he, above all others, believed passionately that the forms and the methods of engineering must replace the pre-revolutionary bourgeois art. Even Malevich, whose mystical philosophy of art was far removed from the scientific reasoning of Constructivism, knew that the realization of his idea of a Suprematist architecture lay in the hands of the engineers. The writings of the Constructivists speak glowingly of a future formed by Soviet engineering and technology, and their actual artistic accomplishments reveal this faith even more clearly. The work of Constructivist plastic art which most clearly typifies their program for the future was Tatlin's famous project for a *Monument to the Third International*. It was equally a monument to their faith in engineering.

This 1300-foot glass and iron structure was to house the headquarters of the Communist Party in the very center of Moscow. Only a sixty-five-foot model in wood and wire was actually completed. An iron spiral, symbolic of the growing force of the Revolution, was to wind upwards around a central core containing, one on top of the other, a glass cone, cylinder, and sphere. Like an enormous kinetic symbol of the Soviet cosmology, various parts of the structure were to be set in motion according to their symbolic function within the building. Thus the cylinder containing annual congress halls and the like would rotate yearly, the cone containing executive activities would rotate once a month, and the uppermost sphere containing an information center would rotate daily as it transmitted a continual stream of messages throughout the Soviet Union.

The theory and practice of engineering was, therefore, very much a part of Russian Constructivist art. Its forms and materials, as with Tatlin and Rodchenko, were taken from industry. Moreover, engineering provided a model for the very means of constructing a work of art. As stated by Alexei Gan, a leading Constructivist theorist: "Nothing by chance, uncalculated, nothing from blind taste and aesthetic arbitrariness. Everything must be technically and functionally directed." A few years later, a statement by Eisenstein revealed how strongly he regarded himself as an "artist-engineer." At the height of his fame as director of *Strike* and *Potemkin,* he said:

> I am a civil engineer and mathematician by training. I approach the making of a motion picture in much the same way as I would the equipment of a poultry farm or the installation of a

water system. My point of view is thoroughly utilitarian, rational, materialistic.[2]

The ultimate goals of Constructivism, like those of engineering, were essentially to serve the people of the new Soviet society. This is particularly true after 1921 when the ideology of the "production group" of Inkhuk (The Institute of Artistic Culture) dominated the "laboratory art" group. The former was represented by Rodchenko, Tatlin, Popova, and others who held that the artist must "become a technician, that he must learn to use the tools and materials of modern production in order to offer his energies directly for the benefit of the Proletariat," while the "laboratory art" group, represented by Malevich, Kandinsky, Gabo, and Pevsner, maintained that art was essentially a spiritual activity, its value absolute and nonutilitarian.

"Laboratory art" was neither more nor less abstract than "production art." The debate which raged between these two factions at Inkhuk was not concerned with the *style* of revolutionary art, but rather its function, and, too, the function of the artist as a member of the new Communist society. Those who insisted art was a spiritual activity soon realized their views were unacceptable to Inkhuk and, by 1921, had withdrawn from the scene. Malevich moved to Vitebsk and ceased to have a following in Moscow. Gabo, Pevsner, and Kandinsky left Russia to develop their versions of Constructivism in the West.

In Russia, the victorious supporters of the "production art" ideology soon began to put into practice their favorite slogan: "Art into Life!" All agreed that easel painting was dead, and exhibitions of paintings became infrequent and unimportant after 1921. Many of these artists—Rodchenko, Lissitzky, Popova, Stepanova—turned to typography and industrial design. A more important activity was the application of Constructivist principles to theatrical set design. While working in the Meyerhold Theater, many of these Constructivist artists must have met a bright young man who also joined Meyerhold in 1922 as a set designer. His name was Sergei Eisenstein.

During the first winter of the Bolshevik Revolution (1917–1918), Eisenstein had continued his studies of engineering without interruption. By this time he intended to become an architect, to combine his old love of art with his new one for engineering. While he went to and from his classes at the university in St. Petersburg, the Revolution surged about him. Politically he remained indifferent—at first. Then suddenly one day the decision

2. In an interview with Louis Fischer, originally in *Die Weltbühne* (Berlin, Dec. 6, 1927), and reprinted in "Mass Movies," *The Nation*, 75, no. 3253 (Nov. 9, 1927), p. 507.

was forced upon him: his entire class at the university united with the Red Army. Eisenstein, despite his cosmopolitan and cultured background, joined the Bolsheviks without hesitation. Now in the Red Army, he was first utilized as an engineer to build defenses, then as an artist to decorate troop trains and to design pictorial propaganda for the front.

After the civil war, in the fall of 1920, Eisenstein arrived in Moscow and almost immediately joined the avant-garde Proletkult Theater as a designer. For the next three years he experimented with the theater as a set designer and, more importantly, as a director. This period was of fundamental importance to the future filmmaker. The steps which led Eisenstein through the theater into cinema are well known through his writings and from subsequent studies, and consequently only a few points need be mentioned here before we turn to an examination of his first film, *Strike*.

Eisenstein worked in the theater for four years, from 1920 to 1924. In 1922, which he later called the "decisive year," he became director of the Proletkult Theater, and also joined Meyerhold's theater workshop as a designer. Despite appalling shortages of food, shelter, and money in these immediate post-war years, the young artists of these theater groups flung themselves into an ecstasy of creative activity. The wildest imaginable experiments in the arts were made possible only by generous support from a tolerant government. The focus of this feverish activity was in the theater, which attracted every species of artist—painter, poet, writer, stage director, architect, and actor—all of whom believed the traditional form of their respective arts was obsolete. The Revolution had killed the past. They stood on the threshold of the future, searching for the most radical means of creative expression. The most imaginative Constructivist designers in Moscow worked at Meyerhold's revolutionary work shop: Vesnin, Stepanova, and Popova. Rodchenko, in the meantime, was busy working with the experimental documentary filmmaker, Dziga Vertov, and his *Kino-Pravda*, a new and highly dynamic type of newsreel. By this time also, most of the artists in Inkhuk with Constructivist tendencies had already joined the Proletkult, of which Eisenstein's theater was an active branch.

Yet another link between Eisenstein and the Constructivists can be seen in his collaboration with Esther Schub, the wife of Alexei Gan. This remarkable couple should be introduced more fully, for their activities in this crucial year of 1922 are revealing. Gan was the major spokesman, polemicist, and theorist for Constructivism; his book *Constructivism*, already quoted from, was written in Moscow in 1920, but not published until 1922. His wife, Esther Schub, was a gifted film editor who almost singlehandedly created a new film-form, that of the compilation film. In addition, she edited foreign films for distribution in Russia; Eisenstein was her assistant in one such chore, that of condensing Fritz Lang's lengthy two-part *Dr. Mabuse* (1922) to conventional size. This was his first film work, and it was, as Jay Leyda neatly puts it, an ideal exercise to teach him the power of scissors and cement in relation to meaning. Esther Schub, together with Lev Kuleshov, whose classes Eisenstein attended briefly, must be regarded as Eisenstein's principal teacher in film. He later came to her with his plans for *Strike* and they worked together on the shooting script for two months. These sessions were at her home and it is not hard to imagine that her husband, Alexei Gan, must have had his say in the creation of this first Constructivist film.

But still, it was primarily at the theater that Eisenstein absorbed Constructivist ideology and the Constructivist style of graphic design. This is hardly surprising for the focus of the movement, as we have seen, was at the theater. Although Eisenstein's earliest artistic activity was in painting and drawing, he never really became an easel painter—and by 1922 this kind of painting was a dead issue in modern Russian art. It was too small in scale, too intensely self-expressive of the individual artist, and too close to the despised nineteenth-century patterns of private patronage for an elite few. By this time, in 1922, Constructivism *was* modern Russian art and Eisenstein, in addition to his other creative activities, was a Constructivist artist working in the theater before he became a film director. That this is so can be demonstrated by an examination of the two major elements of Eisenstein's theater work: first, the graphic style of his set design, and, second, his use of kinetic movement on stage in accordance with the Constructivist credo. Let us first consider Eisenstein's work as a set designer.

Constructivism in the Meyerhold Theater reached its highest point in 1922 with Popova's setting for *The Magnificent Cuckold*. This was the year Eisenstein joined Meyerhold as a designer for his projected production of G. B. Shaw's *Heartbreak House*. Eisenstein's drawing for the stage setting is very close to other Constructivist designs at the Meyerhold Theater, for instance, to Popova's poster for Meyerhold's 1922 production of *The Earth Rebellious* (rewritten from Martinet's *La Nuit* by Eisenstein's friend, the playwright and scientific journalist Tretyakov). Both are constructed of geometric and linear forms that recall industrial images of scaffoldings, cables, wheels, and other mechanical elements. In both, objects are suspended from above the stage or from the scaffolding, and, too, both employ printed signs or billboards whose function was to quicken visual interest and to stimulate the spectator with messages through yet another channel of communication, that of the written word. In fact, Popova's messages in *The Earth Rebellious* were not only static printed ones, but also included changing slogans and pictures projected onto white screens built into the scaffolding of action. Quite possibly this idea inspired Eisenstein to go one step further when, following his work for Meyerhold on *Heartbreak House,* he returned to the Proletkult Theater as its director in the fall of 1922, and for his production of *The Sage* (1923) enlivened the happenings on stage with an actual cinema insert.

Another sketch by Eisenstein for the design of *Heartbreak House* is known. Shaw's play called for a stage setting in which an old ship was represented, but instead, Eisenstein took the forms of a modern ship and transformed them according to the Constructivist aesthetic. The result was an angular tangle of spiraling ramps, tilting masts, cables, ladders, open staircases, and suspended spheres. Many elements of this design he later discovered on board the battleship where Potemkin was filmed.

Eisenstein's sketches for *Heartbreak House* made prominent use of aerial cables from which objects are suspended or by which tall and tilting spars are anchored to the ground. The structural device of the tensile cable was used frequently by the Constructivists and particularly by Vesnin, as in his *Red Dawn,* or later in his designs for an open elevator system in a projected Pravda building, 1924, or in his remarkable designs (with Liubov Popova) for the mass pageant *Battle and Victory* in commemoration of the October Revolution. The best known piece of Constructivist design for the theater was Popova's setting for Meyerhold's production of *The Magnificent Cuckold* in 1922. This remarkable stage construction resembled nothing so much as a rickety assemblage of jungle-gyms and windmill skeletons. Like Tatlin's *Monument to the Third International,* it was a kinetic work of art; the pulse of dramatic action was continuously signaled by the changing speed of the revolving wheels, slow for moments of calm and whirling furiously about at the climax. A similar device was employed by Varvara Stepanova, another Constructivist designer for Meyerhold, whose wooden slatted cages and constructions were set in motion during the performances of *The Death of Tarelkin* (1922).

Eisenstein was assistant director for this production, and carried these ideas into his own stage designs for *Heartbreak House.* Whether Eisenstein intended the large segment of a wheel in his drawing to move with a see-saw or rotary motion is difficult to judge from this drawing alone. Certainly movement on stage is indicated by the trapeze and the acrobats' rings, and quite possibly the black and white rectangles (representing platforms for actors?) moved up and down on cables like little elevators.

Eisenstein's first total production at the Proletkult Theater was *The Sage,* complete with clowns and performing acrobats. Eisenstein's version of the classic comedy quite literally turned the Proletkult Theater into a circus. His actors danced on ropes above the audience, vaulted, threw somersaults, and stood on their heads. At the end of the performance, firecrackers were exploded under the seats of the spectators. Hardly a trace of Ostrovsky's original plot remained. While Eisenstein's method had little to do with traditional theatrical form, it was not sheer madness. As in Hugo Ball's Dada *soirées* at the Cabaret Voltaire in war-time Zürich, such buffoonery swept away the bourgeois notion of theater as a means of presenting "real life." An acrobat—or, as Eisenstein soon discovered, a filmed person—strikes an audience as far truer to life than a stage actor. The cry of the Constructivists is again heard: "Art into Life!" In his passion to generate in the audience an intense involvement with the happenings on stage, Eisenstein turned to various dramatic devices that foretold his life's work, for in *The Sage* his awareness of film technique was born. In his later words: "In the midst of the flood of eccentricity in *The Sage,* including a short film comedy,[3] we can find the first hints of a sharply expressed montage." By staging two or more scenes simultaneously, by the cross-cutting of dialogue, and the rapid "cutting" between scenes, he brought himself to the brink of a truly cinematic means of expression.

Even before Eisenstein had joined Meyerhold in 1922, he was fascinated with the idea of creating an art of movement. When he fell in with the Proletkult Theater in 1920, he had had no previous experience with the stage. All the more astonishing therefore were his plans (never realized) for the second stage production he had ever designed. The play was *The Precipice;* its theme, the helplessness of the individual in the big city; Eisenstein's solution, far more radical than the paintings by Picasso, and possibly Boccioni, which inspired it. He later recalled:

> An amusing combination occurred to me, not only to use running scenery—pieces of buildings and details... but also, possibly under the demands of shifting scenery, to connect these moving decorations with people. The actors on roller skates carried not only themselves about the stage, but also their "piece of city." Our solution of the problem—the intersection of man and milieu—was undoubtedly influenced by the principles of the Cubists. But the "urbanistic" paintings of Picasso were of less importance here than the need to express the dynamics of the

3. *Strike* is usually called Eisenstein's first film, and it is little known that this "short (120 metres) film comedy" preceded it by two years. One incident from Ostrovsky's play, the theft of Glumov's diary, was filmed and shown in the middle of his stage production as part of the "montage plan of the spectacle." This was typical of Eisenstein's desire to overwhelm the spectator with a bewildering variety of images and events. A print of the film is in the Belgrade archive. Peter Kubelka, co-founder-director of the Oesterreiches Filmmuseum, Vienna, informs me that this archive possesses a short film showing Eisenstein during the staging of *The Stage* although apparently this is not the film actually used in the play.

city—glimpses of façades, hands, legs, pillars, heads, domes. . . . I still remember the four legs of two bankers, supporting the façade of the stock-exchange, with two tophats crowning the whole. There was also a policeman, sliced and quartered with traffic.

Costumes blazing with perspectives of twirling lights, with only great rouged lips visible above. These all remained on paper—and now that even the paper has gone, we may become quite pathetically lyrical in our reminiscences.[4]

The point must be stressed that Eisenstein's passion for creating an art of movement, which led him ultimately to the film, was based on convictions held by all the Constructivists, namely that a static art was outmoded and hence fundamentally unrealistic, that only art in motion was expressive of their youthful and revolutionary states of mind, and, perhaps most important, that only by creating a truly kinetic art could they bring art closer to life itself. Their kinetic art, particularly in theater and certainly in film, was not developed as an aesthetic experiment, but sprang from their passionate desire to incite the spectator to action. To charge their art with the intensity of immediate reality—this was their goal, and one that seemed far more important than mere exercises in formal design. At the very core of this reality was movement, and to make their art come alive, it must possess movement itself. This is what Malevich meant when he said, "Suprematism has revealed that from the idea of movement grows the fundamental origin of all origins [of art]." Gabo, too, announced movement as a new element of art in his "Realist Manifesto" (Gabo's italics): "We renounce *the thousand-year-old delusion in art that holds the static rhythms as the only elements of the plastic and pictorial arts. We affirm in those arts a new element, the kinetic rhythms, as the basic forms of our perception of real time.*" These statements are known today only because Gabo and Malevich managed to leave Russia, but nonetheless they speak for the inner circle of Constructivists working in Moscow during these years. Hopefully in the future, access to the frozen vaults of Constructivist documents and art will reveal in greater detail their early efforts to create a truly kinetic art.

Still, there are other indications of the tendency toward movement and dynamism in the Constructivist art of the early twenties. As we have seen, these were major expressive elements in theater set design. Even outside this most important arena of Constructivist art, examples of kinetic art are known, many of them pre-dating the theater work by several years. Gabo,

4. Sergei M. Eisenstein, "Through Theater to Cinema," in *Film Form—Essays in Film Theory*, edited and translated by Jay Leyda. New York (Meridian edition, 1957), p. 14.

for instance, created a kinetic sculpture, 1920, in which a small electric motor rotated a tall semi-flexible metal rod at great speed so that its undulating trajectory carved a shaft of reflected light from the space circumscribed by its movement. This tangible motion sculpture by Gabo prefigured similar work by Len Lye by more than two decades. Motion was also used by Rodchenko as a prime element of design, as in his suspended sculptures of about 1920, a system of concentric circular orbits, somewhat like the free-floating mobiles of Calder.

There is one astonishing Constructivist project, little known since its initial formulation in Moscow, 1920–21, which represents an apotheosis of this urge to construct with movement and light. This is El Lissitzky's design for an *Electrical-Mechanical Spectacle*. Typically, it was never realized, yet in Lissitzky's description of the project, we can recognize that Constructivist tendency toward the creation of a dynamic *Gesamtkunstwerk* simultaneously assaulting all the senses. Typically also, it was a spectacle for mass audiences, a public display, an expanded cinema event. Lissitzky's fantastic machinery was never built but his words describe the intended result:

> We are constructing a scaffolding in a public square, open and accessible on all sides. It is the SPECTACLE MACHINERY. This scaffolding provides every possibility of movement for objects in play. The individual forms of the scaffolding must therefore, be capable of movement into various positions, rotations, extensions and so forth. The different levels must quickly interpenetrate. All is of open ribbed construction, in order not to hide from view the play of objects running through it. Each of the objects themselves is formed according to requirements and intentions. They glide, roll, float in the air, above and inside the scaffolding. All parts of the scaffolding system and all the play objects are activated by means of electrical-mechanical forces and devices, controlled from a central station by one man. He is the SHAPER OF SPECTACLES. His place is in the middle point in the scaffolding, in control of all the energies at the switchboard capsule. He directs the movements, the capsule and the lights. He switches on the radio speaker, and over the public square is heard the deafening clamor of a railroad station, the thunder of Niagara Falls, the hammering of a boiler factory. When the play objects are in proper position, the SHAPER OF SPECTACLES speaks into a telephone connected to an arc-lamp, or into some other apparatus, which transforms his voice according to the character of his figures of speech. Electrical sentences glow and fade away. Beads of light follow objects, fractured by prisms and mirrors. In this way, the SHAPER OF

SPECTACLES brings the elementary prelude to its highest pitch of intensity.[5]

This section has dealt with two principal elements of Constructivist art: (1) its attempt to penetrate into the immediate reality of life itself; and (2) its kinetic dynamism. In Eisenstein's work as a Constructivist designer, he not only shared these goals, but carried them further than perhaps anyone else of his group. In 1924, he carried them to their obvious conclusion, film. . . .

## The Aerial Construction

Eisenstein's tendency to use diagonal or boldly direct images, shared by Constructivists in other media as well, grew from the desire to incite the spectator to action. They were meant to be dynamic images. Not so for this third category, for these images of aerial construction bespeak a love of modernism, and not necessarily of dynamism. By this term is described Eisenstein's fondness for images of objects suspended high above the normal viewing point. The forms of these aerial constructions were taken directly from industry—which, as we know, was a Constructivist idol. Let us look again at his films.

In an early shot of *Strike* we see factory workers and machine elements silhouetted against a translucent glass factory wall. The forms have no density and no weight; like elements of a Suprematist painting by Malevich, they seem to hover weightlessly in space. And too, in its flat patterning of form and rectilinear grid, the image recalls Eisenstein's own Constructivist design for the stage setting of *Heartbreak House*. The real factory setting of *Strike* was rich in images that must have delighted this Constructivist-turned-filmmaker. For no thematically justified reason, he

5. From El Lissitzky's introduction to a folio of his lithographs, *Figurinen—Die plastische Gestaltung der elektro-mechanischen Schau—Sieg über die Sonne,* Hannover, 1923, English translation by Standish D. Lawder, in *Form* (Cambridge, England), no. 3 (December 15, 1966), pp. 12–14. "*Sieg über die Sonne*" refers to the famous Futurist opera—with libretto by Aleksei Kruchonykh and settings by Malevich—which Lissitzky somehow wished to perform with his "Spectacle Machinery." The original, and presumably only, performance of *Sieg über die Sonne* at the Luna Park Theater in St. Petersburg, December, 1913, was an event of considerable importance Malevich has traced the beginnings of his Suprematism from his set designs for the opera (Malewitsch, *Suprematismus—Die Gegenstandlose Welt,* Cologne, 1962, p. 273), and indeed one of his sketches for a backdrop represents perhaps the earliest instance in the history of modern art of such extreme geometric purity of design. Kruchonykh's memoirs have yielded some interesting details about the event: "The choral song of the grave-diggers which was composed with unexpected intervals and dissonances was performed to a completely furious public." (From Camilla Gray, *The Great Experiment: Russian Art—1863–1922,* London, 1962, p. 308, n. 6).

included such shots as the one of workers perched high up on a scaffolding. Presumably they are plotting the strike up there, but of course the real reason for its inclusion was Eisenstein's love for the open angular aerial construction of this image which he had discovered in the factory during shooting. On the other hand, his shot of the factory steam whistle, again typically Constructivistic in design, was put to brilliant use as a shrill echo to the scream of a rebellious worker. It was precisely this dual exactitude of form and meaning that makes *Potemkin* such a finely crafted work of art. Such touches are less the stuff of *Strike,* but they nonetheless point the way to Eisenstein's first real masterpiece, *Potemkin.*

Many of the typically Constructivist shots in *Potemkin* must have been conceived like Eisenstein's idea for the Odessa steps sequence, in "the instant of immediate contact." Shooting of the film took place on board a battleship of 1905 vintage, "The Twelve Apostles," a sister ship of the actual "Potemkin," and on the ship Eisenstein discovered countless images similar to those he had designed and staged in the theater: the bold geometry of the ship's flanks and cannons, its multi-leveled decks, its complex web of rigging, and its profusion of open metal ladders, gratings, and the like. For instance, the very first shot on board the "Potemkin," that of the crew's sleeping quarters, reveals Eisenstein's Constructivist aesthetic through the taut and linear angularity of objects in suspension. The motif is again utilized in the shot of the ship's galley, in which bowls of maggoty soup are lined up on tables suspended by long thin cables. In syncopated rhythm, they sway back and forth in response to the gentle pitching of the ship at sea.

Many of these aerially suspended compositions, like those of other types previously examined, were overlaid with meanings only comprehensible within the context of the film. For example, a life-saver bearing the name "Potemkin" appears immediately after the order is given to execute the sailors under the tarpaulin. Thus it seems to ask, will they be saved? It appears again when the sailors throw the ship's doctor into the sea, and this time, like an enormous round eye, it seems to watch his death by drowning, impassive and immobile. Another example of Eisenstein's ability to draw mute objects into the participation of drama is seen when the leader Vakulinchuk has been shot by an officer, and his body has fallen into the ropes used to lower lifeboats. As his comrades attempt to retrieve him, Eisenstein interrupts the rescue operation to give us a quick glimpse, five frames, or less than a third of a second, of the mechanism of this crane which literally holds Vakulinchuk's life in balance.

Such shipboard images awakened Eisenstein's old love for the cables and ropes he so frequently used in Constructivist designs for stage settings. Sailors and officers chase each other through the black linear forms of suspended ropes, and elsewhere Eisenstein's camera recorded glimpses of the mutiny seen through the tangle of shipboard rigging. Similarly, the citizens assembled on the Odessa pier are seen through a curtain of taut cables. And for the interlude of calm after the mutiny but before the slaughter on the Odessa steps, Eisenstein inserted a waterfront image of spars and ropes seen in ghostly silhouette through the fog.

A few more aerial constructions in *Potemkin* merit brief mention. While the citizens on the Odessa steps wave to the battleship anchored in the harbor, Eisenstein isolates the sailors from their sympathizers by lifting them high in the air. From their crowded perch in the ship's "crow's-nest" they wave back at the citizens on the steps.

In the final reel of *Potemkin* can also be found weightless images of aerial construction. As the rebellious battleship advances toward the other ships of her fleet, the suspense is heightened by the intercutting of shots of the engine pumping under full steam and images of sailors on deck watching for a signal from the other ships. Etched in black against a glowing night sky, the forms of sailors amidst battleship fittings fill the screen with designs of considerable beauty. These final shots in which the anonymous heroes of *Potemkin* are seen only in silhouette recall the first glimpses of the heroes of *Strike,* the workers seen in silhouette through the translucent glass wall of their factory.

## The Scaffolding and the Ramp

It was altogether natural that Meyerhold and Eisenstein should have replaced the conventional naturalistic stage settings with constructions of various levels. They rejected the traditional stage with its flat floor and cube-like space. Even Alexander Tairoff, a theater director with only mildly Constructivist leanings, was in agreement on this point: "a level floor is notoriously expressionless. It permits no articulation of the performance." Hence they turned to a multi-leveled stage space, a scaffolding of platforms and interconnecting ramps.

These stage settings by Eisenstein, Popova, Stepanova, Vesnin, and the other Constructivist designers should be understood not as plastic constructions, but as space-articulating devices. First of all, this was their function during the theatrical performances. More importantly, this concept reveals them to be an organic continuation of a fundamental and traditional Russian aesthetic.

Constructivist multi-level stage settings were a direct and obvious solution to the demands of the theatrical performance in accordance with the traditional nature of Russian art. That is, the Constructivist stage settings were: (1) abstract in form; (2) utilitarian in their function by articulating spaces for the performance of the drama staged in them and on them; and (3) they fulfilled a social function by serving a public art of widespread appeal, the theater.

While still working in the theater, Eisenstein used ramps, scaffoldings, platforms, ladders, and other aerial constructions to give appropriate scenic form to the montage methods of his stage productions. This, of course, was common practice in the avant-garde Soviet theaters, particularly Meyerhold's and Tairoff's—and yet this tendency to shatter a theatrical performance into tiny pieces and throw the fragments up in the air reached perhaps its most extreme form in Eisenstein's staging of *The Sage* (1923). Glumov, a character in Ostrovsky's play, ran up and down a platform across the stage "taking a fragment of dialogue from one scene, interrupting it with a fragment from the other scene—the dialogue thus colliding, creating new meanings and sometimes word-plays." For his exits from the stage, Glumov mounted a circus tightrope and walked out over the spectators' heads, they holding their breath while he held his balance.

His last theatrical production, *Gas Masks,* written by Sergei Tretyakov, takes place in a gas factory. And so Eisenstein took this play about real workers in a real gas factory, and staged it in the middle of the Moscow Gas Works. Again, art into life. By Eisenstein's own admission, the production was a failure, for "theatrical accessories in the midst of real factory plastics appeared ridiculous. The element of 'play' was incompatible with the acrid smell of gas. . . . The cart dropped to pieces, and its driver dropped into the cinema." Only on film are actors and non-actors indistinguishable, only here does everything on the screen appear equally "real" to the unsuspecting eye whether photographed in the studio or in "reality."

Thus Eisenstein escaped the illusionism inherent in the theater. He transfered his theories of montage from the stage to the most realistic of the arts, the cinema. In this new medium, his artistic eye sought out the same formal patterns that were used in his theatrical staging. Some of these formal patterns have already been separated out and analyzed. In *Strike* and *Potemkin* can be seen a continuation of those Constructivist devices for elevating the actor into the air and breaking up the space in which they perform. This development grew from Eisenstein's desire, while working in the theater, to break down the barriers between spectators and performers, and may be briefly summarized: in *Heartbreak House* (1922), a typical Constructivist construction of ramps, ladders, platforms, in the manner of Popova or Stepanova; in *The Sage* (1925), an almost total elimination of stage sets altogether, and the use of catwalks and elevated platforms within the factory itself. In *Strike* (1924–25), called by its maker a reverse mirror image of *Gas Masks,* the setting is again an actual factory, explored now by the mobile eye of a camera.

The shadowy pattern of a factory scaffolding in the opening passages of *Strike* has already been noted, and elsewhere in the factory scenes of this film similar images are caught by Eisenstein's camera. It is in the violent last reel of *Strike,* however, that Eisenstein surpasses any production of Meyerhold's theater in filling such multi-leveled constructions with action. The ramps, balconies, and bridges of the workers' tenements overflow with activity. In a typical shot for example, workers and mounted Cossacks move through this construction on four different levels, and on each level is a different *type* of movement. On the uppermost balcony, workers race away from the camera, below them a stream of workers run toward it. On the next lowest level, workers and police are fighting on a connecting bridge, while below them two Cossacks charge forward on horseback. The screen explodes in a pattern of movement whose variety and speed is almost beyond visual comprehension.

In Eisenstein's next film, *Potemkin,* there is an increased use in multi-leveled settings for dramatic action. He was instinctively drawn to such devices, not only because of his background as a Constructivist designer in the theater, but also because they served essentially the same purpose as certain passages, of filmic montage. That is, by simultaneously showing several movements of an incident in different areas of the screen, he achieved an effect similar to the intercutting of various details of an incident through montage. In one case a scene is expanded spatially, in the other, temporally. The innovations in editing (or montage), we must remember, are chiefly responsible for the fame of *Potemkin,* and for its maker. "The most important part of our work," he wrote, is the "interlacing of close-ups, of side-views, top-views, bottom views." But this interlacing of views was also achieved in single shots—through the Constructivist device of multiple-leveled settings. *Potemkin* is full of them.

For example, in the opening reel, a number of shots show the sailors going about their morning chores. Rather than weave a number of isolated details of this activity together through montage, Eisenstein positions his camera to reveal it in a single shot in which we are shown sailors crowding together and moving about on various levels of the ship's decks. Such shots are more or less informational: "the ship is alive with activity."

When the mutiny occurs, the chase along the many passages and levels of the ship recalls the shots previously studied in *Strike* in which mounted Cossacks invaded the workers' tenements. As in *Strike,* an oblique camera angle records movements in contrasting directions. On an upper deck sailors run away from the camera, below them run sailors in the opposite direction. Such a shot also echoes Meyerhold's stage production. Popova's interconnecting ramps for *The Magnificent Cuckold* were redis-covered by Eisenstein on board the battleship "Potemkin."

Further examples of these multiple ramps have been previously noted under the heading of "diagonal movements," as in the mass scenes on the magnificent staircases of the Odessa bridges. And here, too, these con-structions are used as a scaffolding for movement; the crowds move down the staircases on either side of the bridge and then flow forward underneath it. In a later shot the movement of the figures above and below the huge barrel-vaulted bridge achieves an even greater contrast; atop the bridge a single file of moving figures is seen in finely silhouetted profile, below a mass of people swarms forward down to the Odessa pier.

And then the Odessa steps. Here is a Constructivist ramp of colossal scale. In this single scene were realized a dynamism, a monumentality, and a glorification of the cause of the Revolution which only Tatlin's *Monu-ment to the Third International* had attempted to embody. The Odessa steps were discovered by Eisenstein as a setting for action, and certainly not as a "work of art" in their own right. In his words,

> it was the very *movement* of the steps that gave birth to the idea of the scene . . . the panicky *rush* of the crowd, "flying" down the steps—is no more than a materialization of those first feelings on seeing this staircase.
>
> And, too, it is possible that this was helped by some looming from the womb of memory, some illustration in a magazine of 1905—a horseman on a staircase veiled in smoke, slashing someone with a sabre . . .
>
> Be that as it may, the Odessa steps become the decisive scene at the very spine of the film.[6]

The foregoing analysis has dealt with specific types of formal imagery predominant in Eisenstein's first two films. Similarities with formal imag-ery in works of Constructivist plastic art have also been pointed out. There are, however, other important elements of these films which shed light on the nature of Constructivism in the visual arts, elements which are not specifically formal, but rather thematic in nature. Three of these thematic elements a quest for raw reality, a glorification of the masses as a collective

6. Eisenstein, "The Birth of a Film," *Hudson Review*, 4, no. 1 (Spring 1951), p. 217.
    In connection with the Odessa steps sequence, Jay Leyda has written me (August 14, 1967), "Have you ever seen a stylized film by Granovsky, *Jewish Luck?* Tissé worked on it between *Strike* and *Potemkin*, and re-seeing it the other day I was struck by a dramatic use (in a dream sequence) of those same steps! So that even if it was all new to Eisenstein, it was not to Tissé—he was on familiar and recently used ground."

hero, and a distinctly anti-aesthetic approach—are typical of Constructivism in general and *Strike* and *Potemkin* in particular.

## 1.  *Eisenstein as a Realist*

In both his theater and film work, Eisenstein attempted to extend his art into the very arena of life itself. In a general sense, this attitude flows as a mainstream through all of modern art, its source a reaction against the nineteenth century concept of art as a contemplative activity. Van Gogh, Kirchner, Boccioni and other modern painters all sought to express basic realities of modern life. They sought not to illustrate life, but rather to embody its essence, to strike at the core of reality lying below surface appearances. Likewise, Russian Constructivism, seemingly so abstract and formalistic, was in fact deeply concerned with expressing its view of raw reality. Its formalism was only a discipline, never an end in itself. Even Gabo, who believed art to be essentially a spiritual activity, understood Constructivism as a kind of realism, hence his *Realist Manifesto*. As he later explained, "the word realism was used by all of us constantly, because we were convinced that what we were doing represented a new reality and it is, therefore, that I used the word realistic as the title for our manifesto." But Gabo's art, like that of Kandinsky and Malevich, represented a search for an inner reality, that of the human spirit. Such spiritual speculation was denounced by the "Production Art" group of Inkhuk, and it was their industrialized version of Constructivism that Eisenstein embraced.

For each group of artists who profess to be realists, there is, of course, a different "reality." What exactly was the realism of Constructivism, and specifically of Eisenstein?

Eisenstein, as he would, put the answer in a nutshell: "I get away from realism by going to reality." Viewed against his artistic achievements, we can understand this statement in a dual sense.

One has already been touched on: to forge a work as intensely real as life itself, to create an artistic reality charged with a sense of immediate actuality—this was their burning desire, and to this end they would employ any device. Almost immediately, easel painting was ruled out. Its voice was too thin, its audience too limited in those clamorous years after the Revolution. Instead, Mayakovsky's call was heeded:

> Forget your old whining for truth
> Slice the old from your heart:
> The streets are our brushes,
> Our palettes—the city squares!

This is exactly what the Constructivists did. They took their art into the streets. Designs for mass pageants, public commemorative monuments, and other government structures now absorbed the interests of Tatlin, Lissitsky, Gabo, Vesnin, and others of their circle. Of the mass pageants, one of the grandest was the first anniversary celebration of the Revolution in Petrograd, for which Nathan Altman erected enormous abstract decorations in a Cubo-Futurist style. The most grandiose of such projects, like Tatlin's *Monument to the Third International* or Vesnin's designs for the pageant *Battle and Victory,* were, of course, never realized.

As we have seen, it was in the theater under Meyerhold and Eisenstein that the Constructivist urge to break down the barriers between art and life reached its highest point. Curtain and proscenium arch were removed. Traditional theatrical realism, which in fact was not real at all but merely superillusionistic, gave way to a kind of staged actuality. Even the stage was frequently abandoned in these productions, as in *The World at an End* (Meyerhold, 1922) when motorcycles raced over the footlights and around the auditorium, or in *The Mexican* (Eisenstein, 1920) when the climactic boxing match was to take place amongst the spectators, or in *The Sage* (Eisenstein, 1923/24) when, as we have seen, an actor took his exits over the audience on a circus tightrope. Eisenstein's production of *Gas Masks,* staged in a real gas factory, was their most extreme experiment in this search to imbue theater with a heightened sense of reality. Its failure was a fortunate one, for otherwise Eisenstein might never have turned to film. Asked why he left the theater, he replied, "because all theaters depend on illusion and I want to get to realities." Together with Valeri Pletnyou, Chairman of the Proletkult Theater, Eisenstein planned a series of films to celebrate pre-Revolutionary history through the depiction of incidents leading up to the October Revolution. Only one film was realized, *Strike,* chosen by Eisenstein as the first of the projected series, for in his opinion it presented the "greatest reality."

The same urge that drove him to stage *Gas Masks* in a real factory now opened his eyes to seek out other real locales in which to film *Strike.* His passion for reality led him to use the camera in a totally new way. He ignored the lessons of the Germans, whose most recent films he had certainly studied in Russia, and whose studio techniques were developed to a sophistication unheard of even in Hollywood. Entire streets, villages, landscapes of majestic forest or rocky gorges were all fabricated in the film studios outside Berlin. Eisenstein rejected this technique of pre-styling reality before the camera; his method in *Strike* and *Potemkin* was precisely the reverse of that used on the studio lots of Hollywood or Neu-Babelsberg. The Americans and Germans first planned on paper every detail of a film, built the sets, and then photographed the actors performing in them. Eisenstein, once the theme of his film was selected, went out in search of real settings suitable for its filmic depiction. As might be expected, this led to considerable improvisation. It is a fairly safe conjecture that, in *Strike,* such scenes as the meeting among the discarded railroad wheels, the spying by the wall of rope at the waterfront, the wine-vats as hiding-places were never part of his original scenario; like the scene on the Odessa steps, they were undoubtedly born in "the instant of immediate contact." Thus the designs for *Strike* and *Potemkin* underwent an amoeba-like transformation, expanding and contracting as new fragments of reality were worked into the film and old ones were discarded.

Eisenstein's criterion for the selection of each shot, each fragment of photographed reality, was its power to impress the spectator—in a calculated and predetermined manner—with strong emotional or psychological impact, or, to use his term, "its power of attraction." Eisenstein's reasoning here derives from Pavlov's theory of conditioned reflexes; the underlying influence of Pavlov, one should not forget, was as important to Marxist art as Freud has been to Western art. Thus, the spectator was to react as if in the presence of reality itself. Jay Leyda's comment that, "*Strike* is a deluge of real things and surroundings," echoes the words of Ernst Kállai when he wrote in 1924 that, "The Russians [i.e., the Constructivists] revel in objects and realities." Eisenstein's first film sharpened his eyes and his control of this new medium, and, in *Potemkin,* the recreation of reality is so intense that still today it is frequently and wrongly called a documentary film.

In *Potemkin,* Eisenstein aimed at a film recreation of history. Not only must the spectacle on the screen appear to be intensely real, as if taking place before our very eyes, not only must it be forged from real elements of physical actuality—these two aspects of reality in *Potemkin* have already been discussed—but, moreover, Eisenstein strove to create a work of such highly realistic force that the film would be experienced as a revelation of bald historical fact, a precisely accurate playback, as it were, from the historical past. *Potemkin* was intended to recreate the 1905 uprising in Odessa as it really happened.

And indeed, *Potemkin* is remarkably close to the historical fact. There is some question whether the tarpaulin incident actually occurred, and of course Eisenstein's victorious ending gives no hint that the revolt was quickly crushed by Czarist forces. His greatest liberty with historical truth was taken with the scene of the massacre which, although brutal enough— several thousands were killed—did not, for the most part, take place on the great staircase of Odessa.

But on the whole, such dramatic inventions were few, and Eisenstein's later recollection of his working method is essentially true: "We tried to take the historical events just as they were and not to interfere in any shape, manner or form, with the process as it was actually taking place." In preparing the film, he sought out the facts from recently uncovered Czarist records and from popular press accounts of 1905, and attempted to bring them to life in his film. For example, in the scene on the Odessa pier where citizen sympathizers and impromptu orators gather about the tent containing the body of the martyred sailor, Eisenstein must have been guided by a sketch made in 1905 and published in *L'Illustration*. This was probably one of the "series of sketches by a French artist who had witnessed the massacre on the Odessa stairway" mentioned by Marie Seton, although of course she is mistaken about the location of the massacre. Or perhaps Eisenstein's memory, the probable source of Miss Seton's information, has been altered by his filmic recreation of the event. His recollection that the Odessa steps sequence was possibly "helped by some looming from the womb of memory, some illustration in a magazine of 1905—a horseman on a staircase veiled in smoke, slashing someone with a sabre—" sounds like Géricault's sketch for his painting in the Louvre, *Officer of the Imperial Guard,* published in *L'Illustration* in 1909.

There is further evidence that Eisenstein had studied back issues of *L'Illustration* from 1905, probably initially to obtain factual details about the Odessa uprising that naturally could not be found in the Russian press of Czarist times, and then as a kind of source book of pictorial imagery. An issue of April 22, 1905, contains a photograph of a Japanese battleship that is almost identical with a recurring shot in *Potemkin*. In both images the deck is experienced as a kind of stage space. In both, two great cannons loom out over the deck, stabilizing the image almost like a ship's rudder. In both, too, the uptilted plane of the deck, photographed from above and framed by the parabolic curve of the bow, lacks geometric perspective and transforms the photographs from an illusion of space extending forward into a flatly patterned Constructivist design reaching upward, a vertical-weightless plane, an abstract and empty stage setting used by Eisenstein to introduce the violent second reel, "Drama on the Quarterdeck."

## 2. *Eisenstein's Anti-Aesthetic*

Overnight, the Revolution separated the old from the new. Since most of the older academic painters and filmmakers fled with the White army, the young avant garde of both arts were quite literally justified in believing they had suddenly inherited the world. In reaction against the despised art of the past, they not only rejected its forms, they also rejected the notion of art altogether.

In painting, this idea sprang from two roots: from Malevich's view of art as a development towards pure spirituality and from Tatlin's view of art as industrial process. Thus Malevich believed art to be "moving towards its self-appointed end of creation, to the domination of the forms of nature," and Tatlin believed it to be merging with the goals and accomplishments of industry. Despite the obvious differences, both Malevich and Tatlin fundamentally agreed that the creative activity traditionally understood as "art" was becoming obsolete, one way or another.

As long as the Constructivists continued with their painting, the influence of Malevich's Suprematism exerted the dominant influence. At their 1921 group exhibition in Moscow, for example, Rodchenko announced: "The last painting in the world has been painted"—and exhibited a uniformly red canvas. This "zero paint" in the art of painting is a conscious echo of Malevich's famous *White on White* paintings of 1918. Stepanova, Vesnin, Popova, and Exter also joined in this exhibition to signal the "end of easel painting." But once their painting activity had ceased, as it apparently soon did for most of them, it was Tatlin's concept of an industrialized art they embraced, while Malevich's philosophical speculations and his type of painting were scorned as an idle and useless activity.

The 1917 Revolution did not precipitate this anti-aesthetic attitude. It existed before, embodied in the art of Malevich and Tatlin and made explicit in their writing and teaching. But the Revolution crystalized this attitude, provoked its widespread acceptance and, above all, gave it a sociological justification through Marxist theory. Constructivism, we must remember, cannot be divorced from Communism. Most of these artists were only vaguely acquainted with the complexities of Marxism, but they knew enough to believe in its prophecy of the ideal Communist state where all men would be free. In this utopian world, the need for art would naturally disappear along with other "opiates for the masses" such as religion and the desire for private ownership of material possessions. The new god was industry, and the acolytes of this religion were the workers. Aesthetic theorizing was heresy. The production of works of art, still necessary until the ideal Communist state was attained, was now the responsibility of a new member of society: the artist-engineer.

These two aspects of the Constructivist anti-aesthetic attitude—its distrust of artistic theorizing and its faith in technology—were constantly stressed in their own statements. Thus Gabo's assertion that "we construct our work . . . as the engineer constructs his bridges, as the mathematician his formula of the orbits," is repeated by Eisenstein in his insistence that filmmaking was "purely a mathematical matter." A number of similar statements supporting this Constructivist belief in the artist-as-engineer have been cited earlier. They were equally vociferous in their dislike of aesthetic theory. Alexei Gan's first slogan of Constructivism stated their position: "Down with speculative activity in artistic work! We declare unconditional war on art." Tatlin expressed his views on art and technology with a truly Constructivist precision and economy:

> Down with art.
> Long live technic.

Eisenstein joined in this debunking of aesthetic speculation with a slogan of his own: "Down with intuitive creation." His point of view towards filmmaking, as he explained, was "thoroughly utilitarian, rational, materialistic." When foreign visitors came to visit Eisenstein in Moscow, nothing seemed to delight him more than ridiculing their notions about his creative genius. Artistic inspiration was for Eisenstein an old-fashioned romantic myth. Instead, he insisted that his films were simply the product of what he called "artistic engineering." Scientific reasoning determined the entire process. His studies in Freudian and Pavlovian psychology formed Eisenstein's method of evaluating the "power of attraction" within each shot. And the structure of their presentation, that is, the editing or montage of the film, was the natural result of his training in mathematics and engineering. "They see poetry in what I have done. No, I apply my method and that is all there is to it."—Seurat's famous words could as well have been uttered by Eisenstein.

# "Ivan the Terrible, Part II"

## Dwight Macdonald

*Ivan the Terrible, Part II,* is the last work of the greatest talent the cinema has yet known. Griffith was the instinctive genius, creating a whole new art form *ex nihilo;* Eisenstein was the talented—and conscious—theorist who developed the filmic vocabulary Griffith had invented without quite knowing what he had done. *Ivan II* is the late, final decadence of this talent and this consciousness. But the dying lion is still a lion.

Part I of *Ivan* was shown in 1945, but Part II was suppressed. Its current release is part of the post-Stalin "thaw." I applaud the decision of Khrushchev's bureaucrats but I think Stalin's were smarter. For *Ivan II* is ambiguous, if not worse, as propaganda; and as art it is clearly Formalistic. Blocked since the early thirties by State decree from montage, Eisenstein smuggles formal beauty into his film by fantastic sets and costumes and by directing the acting in the most heavily stylized mode of grand opera. As Premier Khrushchev might, and perhaps has, put it: The Devil Creeps in by the Back Door.

The film shows the disintegration of Eisenstein's personality under the frustrations and pressures he had endured for fifteen years. His homosexuality, for instance, now has free play. Of the eleven leading roles, only one is female—the witchlike Efrosinia. There are an extraordinary number of young, febrile and—there's no other word—pretty males, whose medieval bobbed hair makes them look startlingly like girls. Ivan has a favorite, a flirtatious, bold-eyed young police agent, and many excuses are found for having Ivan put his hands on the handsome young face. But Eisenstein was ashamed of his homosexual tendencies and their liberation meant despair, not joy. Has any orgy been less pleasurable than the womanless banquet scene at which Ivan soberly plots Vladimir's death? There is a wild (all

From *Dwight Macdonald on Movies* by Dwight Macdonald (New York: Prentice-Hall, 1969). Reprinted by permission of the author. This article appeared originally in *Esquire.*

male) dance, true, but the dancers fling themselves about not in sensuous abandon but in desperate frenzy. Everything in the film emphasizes this mephitic, airless, neurotic atmosphere. The Caligari-like sets are claustrophobic—the doorways so low that people have to stoop to go through them. There are almost no outdoor scenes; we are trapped in the oppressive gloom of Ivan's palace. The leading characters are men become beasts: Ivan is a lean, tired old wolf; the boyars are great fat bears billowing in furs; the two leaders of Ivan's Oprichina police are bulls with curls low on their brutal foreheads; the wicked Efrosinia is a beaked hawk.

Taken on the surface, *Ivan II* is a parable justifying Stalin's policies. Ivan is the determined leader of the Russian people against their foreign and domestic enemies; his Oprichina is the GPU; the boyar nobles are the kulaks and other bourgeois elements, and they join with the Church in working against Ivan-Stalin. Efrosinia, Ivan's aunt, who has poisoned his wife in *Ivan I* and who now plots to kill him and put her son, Vladimir, on the throne—these treacherous kinsfolk are the Old Bolsheviks. Ivan-Stalin is reluctant to believe in Efrosinia's guilt—"Touch not the kinsmen of the Czar!" he orders the Oprichina-GPU—which is a bit of court flattery, since Stalin showed no such hesitation about condemning the Old Bolsheviks. Finally he acts when Efrosinia proclaims her jubilation over what she thinks is Ivan's murdered body. (It is actually that of her son, whom Ivan, in a Stalinesque bit of double-crossing, has persuaded to wear his robes, so that Vladimir receives the dagger meant for Ivan.) The film ends with Ivan on his throne proclaiming: "Now that we have put down internal treachery, our sword will be used only against foreign invaders."

But this surface reading is—superficial. Ivan is shown becoming a bloodthirty beast, of course from the highest motives. "A monarch should follow the right if possible, but he should follow the evil path if necessary," says one of his advisers.

The crucial scene comes after Ivan has appealed for friendship to Philip, head of the Moscow Church, saying pathetically, "I am alone." Philip—who alone of the leading characters looks like a man and not like a beast—agrees on condition he will be consulted before Ivan executes any more of Philip's boyar friends and kinsmen. Ivan accepts this not unreasonable condition for friendship. But Malyuta, the chief of his Oprichina, has overheard the promise and there follows a curious scene in which Malyuta's great shaggy head is fondled by Ivan as he calls himself Ivan's hunting dog. "Trust nobody," he says. "You have power, use force!" He insists that Philip merely wants to gain time for his plots and he suggests that the thing to do is to execute Philip's kinsmen, the Volynetski. The next scene shows Malyuta beheading the three leading Volynetski. Ivan appears, views the bodies, and says, "That's not enough." Philip is then arrested and executed. It seems impossible that this rapid transition from vows of friendship to betrayal to butchery is not meant to suggest certain aspects of Stalin's statecraft.

There are two open homosexuals in the film, both villains. The minor one is the King of Poland, who is shown in his effete court camping around in a fantastically huge ruff—and, of course, plotting to lead a crusade of civilized Europe against barbarous Muscovy. The major one is the very odd character of Efrosinia's son, Vladimir, who is presented as drunken, cowardly, and effeminate. He keeps telling his mother—a woman who makes Disney's witches look positively benevolent—that he doesn't *want* to replace Ivan, that he can't *stand* bloodshed, and that his only desire is to live in peace. These humane sentiments are accompanied by pouts and girlish eye-play. It is very confusing. But I think Vladimir is the key. He gets drunk at the banquet—the only one who showed that much spontaneity at that dreary carousal—and when Ivan craftily uses his old gambit, "I am alone and friendless," Vladimir is moved to say: "You have one friend—me." He shows his sincerity—a drunken one, true, but in *Ivan II* any sincerity is welcome—by confiding that his mother is always after him to take away the throne from Ivan but that (pout) he doesn't *want* to. Ivan-Stalin at once begins to persuade Vladimir to dress up in his clothes, with the fatal results noted above.

Is it too much to speculate that Eisenstein identified himself with homosexual Vladimir, the helpless victim of palace intrigues who just wanted to live in peace (*read:* to make his films in peace) and thought all this political intrigue was nonsense? The late James Agee used to insist to me that in *Nevsky* and *Ivan I* Eisenstein was satirizing Stalinism, on the principle of Swift's *Modest Proposal:* exaggeration that covertly suggests the opposite conclusion to the one overtly put forward. I didn't agree then but after *Ivan II* I think Jim may have been right. Vladimir, for example, keeps falling asleep at crucial moments. This shows his frivolous nature, of course. But considered a little more deeply—or obliquely—may it not be intended to present him as the only sensible, decent person in that nightmare ambiance where the fight for power—or mere survival—makes men snarl and bite like animals? In Ivan's court, as in Stalin's, only the sleeping can be wise—or human.

# Federico Fellini

*FEDERICO FELLINI was born in Rimini, Italy, in 1920. As a young man he became a newspaper caricaturist, first in Florence, then Rome, wrote comic radio scripts, and began to collaborate on film scripts. After meeting Rossellini toward the end of World War II, he worked on* Open City, Paisan, The Miracle, *and* The Little Flowers of St. Francis, *making his acting debut as "St. Joseph" in* The Miracle.

*But Fellini's natural bent was less toward acting than toward conjuring up films remarkable for the energy of their autobiographical metamorphoses, either through characters representing Fellini himself or those played by his actress wife Giulietta Masina, whom he had married in 1943. With Alberto Lattuada he co-directed* Variety Lights *(1950), a first exploration of the world of popular entertainment that came to animate many of his later films. Fellini's first film as sole director was* The White Sheik *(1952), which drew upon his experiences as a cartoonist, while the second,* I vitelloni *(1953), dealt with the lives of aimless postwar youths in a town like Fellini's own.*

*Fellini's interest in the groups outside Italian life, especially the entertainers and conmen, was elaborated still further in* La strada *(1954),* Il bidone *(1955), and* The Nights of Cabiria *(1956), the first and third centering on Giulietta Masina. In these films the autobiographical element was strengthened by his own variation on the "objective" observation of lower-class settings that had characterized early neo-realism. But unlike neo-realist films, they are built increasingly around dreams, fantasies, and an often episodic story line, usually focused by a central character who is part observer and part actor, such as the melancholic prostitute of* The Nights of Cabiria.

*Fellini's success with these films led to his first film with a comparatively high budget and his first international success,* La dolce vita *(1960), a picaresque, satiric journey through modern Italian culture from the point of view of a jaded journalist, played by Marcello Mastroianni.* 8½ *(1963) cast Mastroianni as an even more autobiographically conceived character, a film director who is simultaneously having difficulty with his personal life and with a new film project. The title* 8½ *refers to the number of films Fellini had made to that point, and its free mingling of fantasy, memory, and reality helped—along with similar films by Bergman, Truffaut, and Godard—to fashion a new rhetoric of subjectivity. More and more, character was becoming the heart of Fellini's plot. The smooth movement in* 8½ *between what Guido, the director-hero, sees, used to see, thinks he sees, or wishes to see makes an assertion of the personal character of filmmaking, the overlap between the life lived and the world imagined. This is partly a reaction to the more objective and episodic narrative of* La dolce vita, *with its detached and finally irresponsible journalist-hero.* Juliet of the Spirits *(1965) also seems to respond to 8½ in its turn, here with a neglected wife, played by Masina, who is the fantasizing observer of a world of infidelity and self-consciousness—completing a his-and-hers, husband-wife diptych with 8½.*

*The two stable elements in Fellini's world seem to be the point of observation and the geographic setting—the director and his city.* Fellini Satyricon *(1969) delves into the classical Roman past through the eyes of Petronius Arbiter;* Roma *(1972) observes the present through Fellini's own perceptions;* Amarcord *(1974) returns Fellini to the Rimini of his youth. In these later films Fellini's sense of narrative construction has become even more flexible, playing between an elaborate sense of observation, often intricate and decorated, and a commitment to the solidity of place.*

*There have often been plans (as yet unrealized) for a joint directorial project involving Fellini and Bergman. At first the two—the lavish Italian and the austere Swede—seem worlds apart. Yet both Fellini and Bergman have developed unique yet related methods of using film as a canvas for personal themes and obsessions, and both have experimented extensively with the possibility of structuring a film according to character rather than plot. Fellini takes neo-realism out of its documentary preoccupation with the everyday and transforms it into a preoccupation with the other everyday world, of fantasy—as in* The Clowns *(1970), his television tribute to the popular entertainers from whom he draws so much strength.*

*Scripts of Fellini's films available in book form include* La dolce vita *(1961);* Juliet of the Spirits *(1965);* Il bidone, Satyricon, La strada, The Temptations of Dr. Antonio, *and* I vitelloni *(1970);* Variety Lights *and* The White Shiek *(1971); and* Amarcord *(1973). Fellini's career has been surveyed by Gilbert Salachas (1963; in English, 1969), and a comprehensive anthology of material has been collected by Peter Bondanella in* Federico Fellini: Essays in Criticism *(1978).*

# The Ambiguity of Satire

## Gilbert Salachas

Paradoxically, the complexity of a Fellini character can be reduced to a few simple lines. Let us not forget that before Fellini began sculpting bodies, consciences, and souls in film, he worked in line. In a certain sense Fellini remains a caricaturist to this day, even in his richest inventions on celluloid. I don't mean to imply he is limited. Daumier engraved unforgettable portraits all the more eloquent for being simple. The same is true for Fellini. Some of his gargoyles spring from a satirical imagination inherited across the ages; the zoomorphic character of certain Fellini people could, as already mentioned, serve as the point of departure for fascinating studies. The bestiary awaits, trembling and restless, ready to be deciphered. (But don't try to get me to say it reveals the filmmaker's Franciscan spirit.) According to the pleasure of one's imagination, a character may metamorphose into a familiar or rare animal. A world of fable shines through the transparent screen of cinematographic realism. Gelsomina is a titmouse, Il Matto a hare, Zampano an alligator, and the *vitelloni* are penguins. As we continue exploring the Ark we find the beetle Augusto, the puppy Picasso, the jellyfish Emma, and Sylvia, the filly, surrounded by so many termites, the *paparazzi*.[1]

Those who like this game of associations will make their own. As for myself, I would block in the following: pelicans, glowworms, larks, snakes, panthers, chameleons, owls, ladybirds, wolves, grasshoppers, and of course entire processions of caterpillars.

Fellini's frescoes reveal an obvious flair for medieval imagery. Happily, he exploits neither the corresponding symbolism nor quaintness.

---

1. The *paparazzi* are a special, peculiarly obnoxious, species of free-lance photographer that flowers in Italy. They make their living by selling pictures of the famous or of sensational events to tabloid papers, movie magazines, and so on, and in their (often ingenious) persistence for a picture, they make life a misery for their subjects.

From *Federico Fellini* by Gilbert Salachas, translated by Rosalie Siegel. © 1963 by Edition Seghers, Paris. Reprinted by permission of Crown Publishers, Inc.

What I wish to emphasize with this digression is Fellini's natural and doubtless subconscious inclination for satiric metaphor. First he fashions his characters in drypoint (the actual sketches that precede the production of each film); then he selects costumes and make-up for his actors to correspond to his already established plastic conception. Those who hold to the orthodox tenets of neo-realism have never forgiven Fellini this mortal sin.

But this constitutes only the most summary, most external aspect of Fellini's satire. By remodeling shapes or exaggerating a line, Fellini takes the first step toward the demystification of certain habits. The grotesque appearance of the characters who are the most cynical or ridiculous representatives of our mores carries an implicit condemnation of these mores.

Thus all the luxury and show, the artificial *joie de vivre,* paid cheer, and systematic optimism of vaudeville are ridiculed and exposed in *Variety Lights* and *I vitelloni.* The magicians in their shimmering costumes, the ballerinas kicking their legs in unison, the spellbinding exoticism of these performances that are supposed to serve as escape—all this is savagely derided by Fellini's pitiless camera. With their soft flesh and shabby costumes, these itinerant dispensers of fantasy are simply mediocre drudges who work hard to be amusing and take pleasure in the delusion that they belong to the world of the artist. While he relentlessly destroys the glory behind this type of theatrical life, Fellini laughs, but sickly. Because beyond ridicule or derision lies a certain anguish that is not really very funny.

We constantly discover this dual approach in Fellini. On the one hand, a hostility born from lucidity, and on the other, sympathy. One might say that Fellini makes a universal condemnation of our mores, but that individually he ''saves'' the people who are either the victims, agents, or creators of these mores.

Fellini castigates the provincial bourgeoisie (the class into which he was born) with an affectionate compassion that is no way attenuates his ruthless powers of observation. The synthesis between the extremes of Fellini's duality is sadness. The pusillanimous husband and wife in *The White Sheik* move us with their unfailing stupidity. The complicated tangle of their adventures makes us laugh, for it reveals the most futile reactions of the mediocre provincial in such situations: the idea that respectability must be preserved at the price of perilous lies, naïveté, affectation, and incurable conformity. In *I vitelloni* the depiction of bourgeois morality is more ambiguous, and its defender is a resolute but rather pathetic figure. The dealer in religious objects, lecturing an employee guilty of trying to seduce his wife, intones a hymn vibrating with traditional virtues. Fellini, rather jeeringly, it seems to me, records a moral credo (a credo both wise and narrow) with serene impassivity.

However, let us make no mistake, workers are not scorned for surrendering their freedom—the freedom that free-lancers or adventurers use as their favorite alibi for not working. One might even claim that certain "irregulars" could be vaguely tempted by the restful security of the salaried state. Moraldo perceives (and almost envies) the youthful railroad worker's confidence in his uneventful future. Marcello receives a refreshing lesson from Paola's simple profession—a fleeting temptation, but, like all resolutions born in the mind of the lazy dreamer, it is quickly forgotten "under the pressure of circumstances." Only the cheerful Picasso in *Il bidone* manages to combine, without effort, the joys of family life with the call of adventure.

In any event, a sane and ordered existence appears more as a menace than as a liberation (the fate of Marcello's father is another example). Fellini's characters are sarcastic, and prudently avoid the straight and narrow path, which they see as a trap. All things considered, they prefer a type of existence that ends in the same hardening of the arteries, but that seems to offer more exalting charms—the high life. See how the night people of *8¹/₂* amuse themselves; consider the wild *mise en scène* that rules the Witches' sabbath of the imperial and carnal neighbor of Juliet!

What is their program? It is offered either by a magnate from some old family or by a newcomer, an expert, or by a simple promoter of the new religion. Temples are erected. Little vestals officiate, as well as great priests responsible for the maintenance of the altar and the correct profession of the liturgy. The ceremony is grandiose; the places of worship are marvelous, the traditions, picturesque. An actor sinks deep into the lush sofas in his personal fortress (*The Nights of Cabiria*), and a star emerges from an airplane with the triumphant stance of a goddess (*La dolce vita*). The performance continues unabated; it is a performance reserved for the kind of intellectual who frequents press conferences, for the gaping spectator, the excited or weary nouveau riche, or for those who were once rich and now breathlessly follow the saraband while dreaming of the snows of yesteryear.

In taking apart the elements of a contemporary world, itself in the process of falling apart, Fellini remembers that he too is part of this world. He is determined to share his intimate knowledge of such a world with his audience. We must clarify, however, that this is in no way a question of spitefully settling old accounts. Although Fellini made many enemies by revealing simultaneously in *La dolce vita* both the polish and squalor of a certain milieu, he did not seek to humiliate anybody in particular. His is a broad accusation. His satire has nothing in common with the country-fair game of throwing objects against Kewpie dolls with the aim of satiating the aggressiveness of the gaping onlookers.

It is by the individual depiction of an avaricious peasant, or mean pair, bragging comedian, debauched aristocrat, proud swindler that Fellini points the trigger at greed, meanness of spirit, aimlessness, and vice.

Religion is treated in the same way, and Fellini's anticlericalism discloses a fundamental ambiguity. At the beginning one may readily discern the persistent obsessions that haunt the former pupil of a religious school. Many of the biting details that have clearly been transposed from memory expose a derisory, hypocritical piety that Fellini never loses a chance to stigmatize. The store full of rosaries, tapers, crucifixes, tasteless religious statues is, ironically enough, the setting of the first job of the spiritual leader of the *vitelloni*. It is in the back room of this quasi-surrealist warehouse, stocked with effigies of the saints, that the incorrigible young man (O blasphemy) attempts to seduce the wife of his benefactor, herself a stern Penelope.

The favorite trick of the swindlers in *Il bidone* was to disguise themselves as priests in order to inspire confidence. It is an ingenious stratagem. Everyone knows that in the traditionally Christian countries a priest's robe is a substitute for a pass card. Besides, Fellini visibly enjoys playing this game of derisive comparisons. Just to see these swindlers disguised in ecclesiastic garb is amusing enough in itself. But when we listen to these fake priests talk we realize that we are up against deliberate satire. The subtle blackmail of emotions, the greedy nature of the swindler's victims expose in barely disguised terms the disturbing dialectic of certain transactions.

The satire is virulent. The pious who find it so shocking have most probably forgotten the reaction of an angry young man who did not refrain from employing his whip on the steps of the temple.

A much more innocent kind of blasphemy enlivens the sequence in *La dolce vita* in which the famous star Anita Ekberg runs up the steps within St. Peter's dome. To fit into the landscape, this attractive creature had the bad taste to clothe herself in an adaptation of the clerical garment that sculpts her generous curves. And the cineast Guido, haunted by the memory of mental torturers (the educators of his youth), asks for an audience with a dotard of a prelate, more laughable than impressive.

When the spirit has abandoned the letter to such a degree, the external features of religion become decorative, picturesque curiosities one is allowed to smile at but which one is also recommended to distrust. But even more serious, the pathetic outbursts of faith, with their naïve sincerity, yield to dangerous deviations. A kind of barbaric superstition grips the maddened crowd; the sacred litany is degraded into tribal incantations.

I have already mentioned the procession in *La strada* that joins the faithful massed behind holy banners together with the circus people. It is not by accident that these two groups meet. But the atmosphere of pseudomystical delirium is even more intense in *The Nights of Cabiria*. The pilgrimage of "divine love" is a savage outburst of a long collective cry, freed of all human dignity, of all restraint. A disturbing phenomenon, the call of a people who have given themselves up to their most primitive instincts. *La dolce vita* contains an even crueler description of this phenomenon in the lengthy sequence of the fake miracle. Because two children who obviously are shamming say they have seen the Madonna, because the press and television have exaggerated the event out of all proportion, because the parents of these self-appointed "chosen" ones hope to extract some material advantage from such a windfall, an enormous crowd of the curious and of the naïve gathers together. Over-excited, the onlookers wish to witness another miracle and hurl themselves upon what might well become precious relics. The wait is intolerable; the crowd grows wild. A sudden torrential downpour disperses the frenzied believers as well as the organizers of the show. It is a fiasco—a sick child, instead of undergoing a miraculous cure, dies at dawn.

Fellini grows absolutely ruthless when depicting the rash observance of certain rites. Exaggerated religiosity, naïve superstition as exploited by cynical profiteers, the puerility of a social form of Christianity, the insignificance of the flock, and the impotence of the shepherds are all signs of religious decay that Fellini takes pleasure in revealing. Thus an ironic detail or a long frenzied scene can be so intense as to be somewhat monstrous. Carried away by his own enthusiasm, Fellini can abandon all discretion, and embark upon the dangerous course of the fable-farce. For example, his sketch in *Boccaccio 70*, "The Temptations of Dr. Antonio." The fierce puritanism of its pitiful hero becomes madness, literal madness, thus giving us the first truly "unreal" scenes in Fellini's opus. The satire of the narrow, petty-bourgeois morality of a repressed bigot explodes into burlesque, and its effect, to say the least, is debatable.

All the same, whether working with realism or fantasy, Fellini's satire discloses certain ambiguities. Clearly he asks us to share his censure of the vice he depicts. Yet he grows so attached to what we might call "individual" victims, or to the accomplices of crime, that the public prosecutor imperceptibly metamorphoses into a lawyer for the defense. Thus, in each successive film, he never fails to plead extenuating circumstances. Aimlessness, vice, debauchery, futility, superstition, the shame of an individual or a group sprout like arborescent tumors, and encourage the germination of fascinating *"fleurs du mal."* As poisonous as such flowers may be, they exude a powerfully seductive perfume. And as we follow Fellini's creative development, he obliges use to inhale this odor to the point of nausea.

But might the moral or mental perversions not be a device, a way for Fellini to conjure up, to liberate inavowable fantasies? The harem of $8^1/_2$, Guido's entourage, the temptations of Juliet call attention as much to self-indulgent delectation as to self-defense. Still, the erotic dream descends at once into nightmare.

# "I vitelloni" and "La strada"

## John Russell Taylor

*Vitelloni,* it should be explained, are drifters, wastrels, not necessarily bad but aimless, restless and bored. Fellini himself and his two invariable script collaborators from this film on, Ennio Flaiano and Tullio Pinelli, had all shared such a condition in their time, and the film arose from an evening laughing over old times, old escapades, and the melancholy which descended afterwards. So the film is in a vital sense autobiographical: not necessarily that the details of any single incident actually happened to Fellini or Pinelli or Flaiano, but that the depiction of a way of life—a very unsatisfactory way of life as it turns out—is very much from the inside.

But what is Fellini's attitude to his film *vitelloni?* There has been much argument, and in the abstract, judging solely from the script, a number of solutions are possible. The film might, for instance, be a light social satire about wild boys with a happy ending when the two principals reform and opt respectively for happy fatherhood and a new constructive life somewhere else. It might be a grim picture of a lost generation, cut adrift in the modern world from their roots in a settled faith and a stable social order. It might be a denunciation of the decadent petty bourgeoisie. A case, of sorts, could be made out for any of these views from the script, but the film itself rejects them all. To begin with, it is clear at once from the way the actors are directed that though none of the characters is exactly a shining hero, they are certainly not either double-dyed villians, but merely contradictory, likeable, insufficient human beings. Nor can the "happy ending" of the ringleader, Fausto, with his wife and their child be taken at its face value: his last appearance, playing childishly with his new son under the troubled gaze of his wife, makes it clear that the child is just

another new toy, and that nothing has really changed. And as for the view
of the film as a moralistic tract for the times, one can set against it scene
after scene in which the camera is very much with the characters, involving
us willy-nilly on their side, inviting us irresistibly to sympathize with them
instead of shake our heads.

The first way that this is done is by a very flexible, subjective attitude
to time. The time of the film is the vitelloni's time, not ours. It can expand
suddenly for an improvised dance in the street, an impromptu game with
the stones or, stretched out beyond endurance, it can crucify its victims in
an aching void before the aimless, endless fury of an icy, windswept sea.
Equally it can contract as the camera weaves and dodges and turns in an
ecstasy of swift motion at the climactic ball sequence which swallows them
all and then at length spews them out into the empty, unwelcoming streets.
We are with them; this is the way not so much that it was as that it felt. And
as the film progresses it becomes heavier, as the characters become heavier
with the weight of ills unremedied and chances missed, so that when the
elusively idyllic interludes of Moraldo, the quietest and most sensitive of
them, with a mysterious boy railway worker (a smiling embodiment of
innocence) lead finally to Moraldo's secret departure for the city, the sense
of escape brought by the smooth, purposeful acceleration of the train is
almost palpable.

Moraldo's crisis, though—the confrontation with the unspoilt boy
which finally decides him to break away completely—is only the last of
several. Nearly all the vitelloni meet themselves face to face at some point,
and all except Moraldo turn back from this crucial encounter. For Fausto it
is the marriage he is pushed into and slips out of at the side door, the rules
of the job he is finally edged into which require a decision of him that he
shirks, and fatherhood, which will soon bore him. Alberto is shattered by
the departure of the sister he dearly loves with her lover in the dawn after
the ball, but even in his utmost grief continues to act, to pose (significantly,
at this juncture he is heavily disguised for the ball in cloche hat and
twenties dress); the affectation and the real thing are no longer distinguishable. Leopoldo, a budding poet, is disillusioned when an old actor performing in the town who seems interested in his work proves merely to be
sexually interested in him. But though they all have to face some sort of
unpalatable truth about themselves and the world they live in, only
Moraldo assimilates it and makes use of it to move on: the rest avoid,
smother it, and go on as if nothing had happened. They are Peter Pans,
eternal boys who will never grow up.

Or, as Geneviève Agel perceptively remarks in *Les Chemins de Fellini, I vitelloni* could be a sort of modern *Grand Meaulnes:* and the comparison suggests precisely the magical tenderness which irradiates Fellini's

evocation of this life no longer wholly innocent but yet rejecting the fruits of experience and the adult responsibilities that come with them. It is an intensely romantic view, of course, and the physical appearance of the film is similarly romanticized: the real streets taking on the aspect of deserted baroque stage sets; the delicate, diffused greys of the railway and Moraldo's morning departure; the harshly etched scene on the shore; the almost expressionist lighting of the theatre sequences; the hysterical, nearly indecipherable eddies of movement which rip and swirl over the screen during the showily impressionistic ball scene. Indeed the *vitelloni,* whose real background one half appreciates to be drab and ordinary, live through Fellini's eyes in a world full of unexpected, inexplicable beauties almost as visionary as Alain-Fournier's own distant land of lost content.

The technical means by which Fellini achieves his effects, here as elsewhere in his work, are in principle very simple, though the application of the simple principles is often extremely complex. Fellini's films are built round a number of long, sustained scenes worked out in the characters' own good time: not only are we encouraged to adjust our time-tense to that of the characters, but we are forcibly compelled to, since there is no escape in constant changes of locale, artful intercutting of separate sequences or anything like that: once we embark on a key sequence we are with it obsessively through to the end. Fellini loves to begin his scene with a long shot establishing at once the place, the number of people involved and their spatial (and generally by implication emotional) relationship with each other and their surroundings. This done (as in the scene on the seashore, or the aftermath of the ball) he can move in to a closer examination of his actors. Faces fascinate him—well, to a certain extent I suppose they must fascinate all directors, but few go so far as Fellini in casting by lining his office walls from top to bottom with photographs and then eliminating day by day until he is left with faces which still have some mystery intact, faces he can live with. He casts, then, with a most meticulous attention to physical type—the face, one sometimes suspects, is for him the ultimate in symbolic landscape, the object which is at once a thing-in-itself and a token of something more.

In *I vitelloni* the face that everyone remembers is Alberto Sordi's, puffy, melancholy, self-indulgent, and irresistibly comic, and in the scene in which he weeps for his lost sister still terrifyingly all these things and heart-rending as well. It is a combination of qualities which has served many artists well—and for the moment inevitably gets them branded "Chaplinesque." This, indeed, was the almost invariable word applied to the character of Gelsomina, the waif in Fellini's next feature film, *La strada,* played, of course, by his wife Giulietta Masina, possessor of the most memorable face in all Fellini's *oeuvre.* It was the face and the character, a perpetual underdog brutalized by her "husband," Zampano, ignored by almost everyone else, and yet preserving throughout a Franciscan (the word is Fellini's) cheerfulness and simplicity, which won the world's affections, for all sorts of reasons only marginally filmic; it was the face which first and foremost enabled Fellini to win through to a mass audience. For *La strada*, made very rapidly on a relatively tiny budget, was an enormous success commercially, and has perhaps susbsequently fallen rather into critical disrepute for this very reason.

But there is far more to *La strada* than a wonderfully expressive face and a sentimentally appealing character—and that far more we are now probably in a better position to appreciate than we were at the time. Again the parallel with *Le Grand Meaulnes* is illuminating: the inspiration of the story we know dates back to the earliest memories of which Fellini has told us: those of childhood holidays spent at his grandmother's in Gambettola, where gipsies still wandered and traveling showmen were the principal diversion of a poor and remote countryside. And where in *I vitelloni*, which harked back to Fellini's young manhood in Rimini, the material never loses touch with recognizable actuality despite the nostalgic aura which surrounds it, as we move farther back in Fellini's life the link with actuality grows thinner. In *I vitelloni* the landscapes may represent "states of soul," but they are also acceptable on the realistic plane; in *La strada*, though they are still "real" in the sense that the film was made in real places, not constructed in a studio like Visconti's snowbound Italian town in *Le notti bianche*, they are so selected and so photographed that their "soul-state" aspect predominates and their actuality is minimized (*La strada*, as a matter of fact, represents Fellini's farthest swing in this direction). Similarly in *La strada* the characters themselves become even more patently projections of different sides of Fellini's own character, as he himself has explicitly recognized, though defending nevertheless his claims to be a realist ("There are more Zampanos than bicycle thieves in the world").

*La strada*, in fact, is, more overtly than any other of Fellini's films, a parable, and for that reason perhaps more liable to provoke violent partisanship or violent hostility. I had better own up, I suppose. to a high regard for the film in spite of the gravest doubts about its premises, and so *La strada* for me is the key demonstration in Fellini's works of his sovereign quality as a thinker in film, whose script is merely a sketch of the complete film in his mind, as against the scriptwriter who writes first and then sets laboriously about translating a finished article into film terms. I am prepared to believe that any competent director could make something interesting out of the script of *I vitelloni*, possibly even in a different way something almost as effective; but I doubt whether anyone else, given the script of *La strada*, could have made it seem anything but tiresome and pretentious. But the script—the story-line and the words said—is only a single strand in the intricate pattern existing in Fellini's mind and now put on the screen: it is story seen in a certain way—a symphony of muted greys, beautifully caught by Martelli's camera; a pattern of sounds and music—and not only the Gelsomina theme by Nino Rota which sold millions of copies round the world; a journey through, conditioning and conditioned by a series of bleak, ghostly winter landscapes which hardly seem to belong to this world at all. Because it is all these things simultaneously and indissolubly, and has the unmistakable feel of springing fully armed from one man's brain, it is a great film whatever one thinks of the ideas behind it; with films, after all, it is not where they start from but where they get to that counts.

The story has been described by G. B. Cavallaro in a famous phrase as "the fantastic history of a sad honeymoon with a posthumous declaration of love," which is all right as far as it goes. Like *I vitelloni,* it is built round a series of key sequences which bring characters face to face with the truth, but this time there are only two characters involved, Gelsomina and Zampano, and the crises, not being shunned, bring progressive revelation, first to her and then, after a long evasion, to him. The principal progress in the film is that of Gelsomina from innocence to active goodness, goodness tested by an intuitive encounter with religion during the procession early on; a confrontation with suffering (the sick child at the wedding party); a realization of the woman's role as a wife (at the convent); and a first experience of violent death when Zampano kills Il Matto, the well-disposed, mercurial but to him slightly demonic acrobat who keeps crossing their path. Zampano's realization of himself and his role comes more slowly and with a greater struggle: the crucial moments of his life are the first almost involuntary act of taking on Gelsomina, his decisive abandonment of her after several twists and turns on the hook of his unacknowledged love for her, and his final facing of the truth after she is dead and he is left alone, weeping on the shore of a dark and desolate sea.

The symbolic pattern of the story, it will be seen, is very precisely laid out and schematic: in fairy-tale terms it could be described as the Beast melted and transformed—too late, of course—by his feelings for Beauty; in terms of the novelette it would be the strong bad man touched at the last by the love of a good woman; in religious terms it would be the way of two souls to redemption, one through understanding and sacrifice, the other finally through the effects of that sacrifice. In severely realistic terms, however, what is it? A mildly incredible fantasy about the relations of two people bizarrely atypical in themselves and divorced by their situation and occupation from any recognizable pattern of social behavior. At best, the neo-realistic purist could take comfort only from the sharply observed peasant wedding (which even then would be rather too formally handled for his comfort) and a few hints of satire at the expense of the clergy. In short, while proclaiming himself a realist and indeed making the film, save for the employment of professional actors, in a way of which even the earliest, most doctrinaire theorists of neo-realism would have to approve, Fellini has produced something which has more genuine validity on practically any level one can think of than that of straightforward realistic observation of things as they are. And in doing so, of course, he has shown up the fallacy of doctrinaire neo-realism very clearly: its failure to accept that film realism is entirely in the eye of the beholder. We may say that Rossellini's early films are more objective—and therefore more "realistic"—than Fellini's, and mean something by it; but what we mean is that when his camera is turned on a scene it is likely to be recorded with the emphases falling where they would normally fall for most of us, and with the ordinary and typical receiving more attention than the atypical and extraordinary. When Fellini looks at the same scene, though, with equally "realistic" intentions, it is precisely the extraordinary, unexpected, and unpredictable which catches his eye.

When, for example, at one point in *La strada* Gelsomina is sitting alone and dejected by the side of the road a solitary, riderless horse suddenly traverses the screen the effect is positively surrealistic: totally arbitrary, yet giving an instant visual reinforcement to the mood of the scene. The lost horse might well be a figment of Gelsomina's imagination, an image of her own state. But it is also a real horse, and its appearance here at this time is not impossible, only mildly peculiar. There may, for all we know, have actually been a stray horse there at the time of shooting which was seized on and pressed into service, in the same way that the three musicians whom elsewhere she falls in behind as they march along playing cheerfully to the empty countryside were, in fact, itinerant musicians who turned up in just this way. But what has struck Fellini about the horse and the musicians is their peculiarity and oddity, their—terrible word to the neo-realist—picturesqueness, their ability to embody the mental states of the protagonist, rather than their value as documents of any sort. All Fellini's films filter and select—and therefore color and distort—external realities in this way, but the process is so much clearer, so stripped of ambiguity in *La strada* that it can at once be recognized and accepted for what it is.

Up to *I vitelloni*, or even *Un' agenzia matrimoniale*, Fellini's subsequent contribution to *Amore in citta*, a portmanteau film of documentary reconstructions (of which more anon), it would have been quite possible, if increasingly odd, to continue regarding Fellini as a realist with a special gift for social satire, but *La strada* makes it clear (or should have made it clear, though by *La dolce vita* many seemed to have forgotten the lesson) that he is nothing of the sort and never has been: his forte, even when his films have nearly all the trappings of external reality in their expected places, is symbolic fantasy of almost baroque elaboration and artificiality (the word, in this context, had no hint of denigration). Looking back from the viewpoint of *La strada* at the earlier films we have been considering, indeed, we are likely to find that the perspective changes everything, and that brilliant though the touches of observation are (whatever else one may say about Fellini's films, every frame of them is undeniably bursting with life) it is the non-realistic side which now comes uppermost in the mind, so that even the most obviously comic and "social" in its outlook, *Lo sciecco bianco*, comes in retrospect to look like a variation on the plot of *La strada*, played for laughs and with the male and female roles reversed.

This is all worth spelling out at this juncture—though most of it has been at least implicit in my comments on the other films—because from *La strada* on the purity and directness of the style, which enable us at once to discern its precise nature in this film (inevitable consequence of its being the farthest stage of Fellini's voyage into his own past?) become overlaid and transformed: the later films, while not deserting Fellini's basic source of inspiration in his own experience, become increasingly complex in their handling of their resources, the interplay between "real" reality and imaginative reality becomes increasingly involved and elusive.

# "Cabiria"

## Andrew Sarris

*Cabiria (Le notti di Cabiria),* with its titular evocation of D'Annunzio and
the epic tradition of early Italian films, is the name of a shabby prostitute in
Federico Fellini's parable on the human condition. Attired in a sleeveless,
zebra-striped blouse, a moth-eaten fur stole, and grotesquely inappropriate
bobby socks, Giulietta Masina's Cabiria impishly burlesques her ancient
calling and the poignantly transcends it in a burst of tragic irony. The film
ends on a note of high pathos, comparable to the finest moments of Chaplin, as Miss Masina's final close-up sums up one of the most resourceful
performances in screen history.

The plot of *Cabiria* consists of five events in the heroine's life, each
event logically related to the development of her character. The film opens
with Cabiria running across a lonely field with her lover. The camera
remains distant from the apparently carefree couple. The two figures are
framed against a bleak, gray-lit landscape, its pastoral simplicity marred by
telephone poles and distant housing developments. The absence of mood
music and expository dialogue creates some of the sinister tension of the
first sequences in *Great Expectations*. The suspense heightens as Cabiria
stops at the edge of a stream and gaily swings her handbag in an ever-
widening arc while her lover furtively glances about. Suddenly Cabiria's
escort seizes her handbag, shoves her into the stream, and runs off, never
to be seen again.

This one episode establishes the pattern of Cabiria's life from illusion
to disillusion. In the early scenes the loud, vulgar, ungainly aspects of
Cabiria's personality are emphasized. She is literally dragged from the
stream and absurdly handled like a sack of soggy potatoes. Her rescue and
the inept artificial respiration that follows deny her even the dignity of a

From *Film Culture,* no. 16 (January 1958). The material appears also in *Confessions of a
Cultist* by Andrew Sarris. Copyright © 1961, 1962, 1963, 1964, 1965, 1966, 1967, 1968,
1969, 1970 by Andrew Sarris. Reprinted by permission of Simon & Schuster, a Division of
Gulf & Western Corporation.

disaster. The audience is almost invited to laugh at her plight, but the physical discomfort of the situation—her young rescuers shivering in their bathing suits, Cabiria almost collapsing as she calls her lover and tries to escape from her nightmarish predicament—kills the laughter her appearance would normally arouse. At this point in the film it is not clear what mood Fellini is trying to achieve. His manner is cold and impersonal.

Cabiria soon resumes the nightly routine of her existence with her circle of prostitutes, dope peddlers, and procurers on the Via Borghese. Here Fellini does not glamorize Cabiria's profession. Actually, prostitutes are merely another tribe in the confederation of wanderers and outcasts, wastrels and opportunists, with whose irregular patterns of living Fellini has been concerned throughout his distinguished career. In his first film, *The White Sheik,* Fellini satirized the bumbling artisans of the Italian comic strips. (Giulietta Masina appeared briefly here as a whimsical lady of the evening.) *Vitelloni* dramatized the aimless existence of young loafers in a resort town; *Il bidone* examined the machinations of confidence men; *La strada* was an odyssey of itinerant circus performers. In each instance Fellini approached his untidy characters on a plane of universal meaning.

By casting the diminutive, clown-visaged, essentially sexless Giulietta Masina as his prostitute, Fellini has automatically divorced himself from the currently fashionable exploitation of lurid themes. His treatment is neither sensual or sentimental. By depicting Cabiria's spirited recovery from her ludicrous betrayal, Fellini indicates his concern with the indestructibility of his heroine, and by implication, of the human spirit generally. We sense that Cabiria's dunking in the stream is not her first setback, and Fellini quickly insures that it shall not be her last.

Cabiria jauntily plies her wares in a more fashionable part of Rome, where she witnesses a violent argument between a famous actor (Amedeo Nazzari) and his glamorous mistress (Dorian Gray). After the mistress stalks away, the actor curtly summons Cabiria to his car. They drive to a nightclub, and from there to his palatial villa. Cabiria stands up in the actor's convertible and waves to more elegant prostitutes in the neighborhood to display her good fortune.

When they arrive at the villa, Cabiria is overwhelmed by the splendor around her. The actor solemnly plays Beethoven's Fifth Symphony on his phonograph and confides to Cabiria that he is fond of this music. The actor and Cabiria are at emotional cross-purposes in this situation, but both are equally silly in their poses. There is something unpleasant in the actor's condescension to Cabiria; he seems to have no desire to make love to her, and his reluctance to do so curiously reaffirms Cabiria's stylized, somewhat unreal personality.

The actor's disaffected mistress returns unexpectedly; the actor hastily conceals Cabiria in his sumptuous bathroom, where she spends the night while the actor and his first desire renew their relationship. Cabiria is surreptitiously released the next morning. As the actor quietly leads her through the bedroom, Cabiria looks wistfully over her shoulder at the girl sleeping contentedly. The pathos of the situation is intensified when Cabiria attempts to return the money the actor gives her. Her gesture is clearly intended to make the actor recognize her as a human being, and like every other such gesture in her life, it fails.

As it turns out, this is the funniest episode in the film. The pace is leisurely as Miss Masina runs through her bag of low-comedy tricks. She collides with glass doors, grapples with endless curtains, scales heavily carpeted stairs with the hunched-forward determination of an Alpine skier, and grimaces at every new situation with the knowingly pursed lips of a fishwife at an art gallery. Her defeat here is less of a downfall than a pratfall, and the entire sequence seems gratuitous until the total symmetry of the film is perceived.

Suddenly God enters Cabiria's life in the guise of a miracle-seeking procession to a shrine of the Virgin Mary. Here Fellini divides his attention between Cabiria, who prays for the intangible miracle of a new life, and a crippled procurer and dope peddler, who has come to have his limbs healed. In a brilliantly composed and edited passage, Cabiria and the procurer alternately struggle through a milling, hysterical crowd of penitents to reach the altar. At the edge of one overhead shot, an elaborate loudspeaker subtly mocks the spontaneity of the occasion. The forward motion of the scene accelerates until the procurer throws away his crutches and collapses, writhing and threshing briefly on the floor before Fellini tastefully fades out the scene.

Fellini's treatment of this episode is crucial to an understanding of his general position. Although he does not believe in the more obvious manifestations of the miraculous (he was the author of Rossellini's controversial work, *The Miracle*), Fellini does not indulge in De Sica's sly anticlericalism. The problem for Fellini is one of individual faith rather than social responsibility. The emotional power of the religious spectacle he creates suggests that God is sanctioned by man's need for faith, possibly even that God was created by man to supply hope for a better life. Fellini never spells out his personal commitments, but he seems to accept the Church as part of the furniture of his environment. There are indications in *Cabiria* as well as in *La strada* that Fellini is more kindly disposed to the humanistic influences within the Church than to its authoritarian dogmas. A mendicant friar whom Cabiria meets on a lonely road has a greater impact on her soul than all the elaborate machinery of the miracle festival. However, like Cabiria and Gelsomina, and the nun in *La strada*, who shares Gelsomina's sense of rootlessness, the friar is something of an outcast in the eyes of the Church. To accept the universality of these people as Fellini apparently does, it is necessary to consider the notion that in some sense we are all outcasts in our moments of loneliness and in the individual paths we follow to our salvation. In any event, by stressing the pugnacity and indestructibility of Cabiria, Fellini comes closer to creating a viable symbol of humanity than does De Sica with his whining protagonist in *The Bicycle Thief.*

Although Fellini has a limited degree of compassion for his band of stragglers, he never ignores the probabilities of their existence. When Cabiria attempts to regenerate herself, Fellini rewards her efforts with the most disastrous experience of her life. After denouncing her companions for remaining unchanged after their pious invocations to the Madonna, Cabiria temporarily abandons her profession and visits a tawdry music hall, where a hypnotist recruits her for his act. Cabiria is quickly thrust into a romantic fantasy before a boorish audience. She gracefully dances with an imaginary lover whom the hypnotist calls Oscar as the orchestra plays a tinny version of "The Merry Widow Waltz." After picking some imaginary flowers, Cabiria relives her youthful innocence, which is symbolically evoked by her memory of her long black hair. In a breathtaking scene of dramatic recall, Cabiria worriedly asks Oscar if he really loves her and is not just deceiving her. She is then snapped out of her trance to find herself an object of derision and ridicule.

Outside, a shy young man (François Périer) tells her that he was moved by the purity of her memories, and the final movement of the film starts slowly toward its preordained conclusion. After a series of meetings, Cabiria's suspicions are lulled by the apparent guilelessness of her admirer, whose name, by what he claims to be a fateful coincidence, is Oscar. Even after Cabiria reveals her profession, he asks her to marry him. On the day they are to leave for the country to be married, he lures her to the edge of a cliff overlooking the sea. Lacking the courage to push Cabiria to her death, he leaves her clawing the ground in grief-stricken revulsion against her fate while he ignobly picks up the handbag she has dropped at his feet and runs and stumbles through the forest.

Cabiria rises eventually and slowly makes her way to the road, Fellini's perennial symbol of life. There a group of adolescents lightheartedly serenading each other include Cabiria in their merry circle. A young girl smilingly greets Cabiria, whose tears are suddenly illuminated by her smile as the camera closes in on her face, slightly turned, slowly moving forward toward an unconditional acceptance of life. At that final moment Cabiria is in a state of secular grace, innocent and inviolate despite all the deceptions that have been practiced upon her.

In *Cabiria* one sees the familiar landmarks of the anarchic sub-world of Fellini's imagination. Empty fields, roads, and streets set off by solitary travelers and distant buildings convey an image of the world as a lonely desert peopled by insubstantial De Chirico figures vainly striding toward mathematically improbable intersections of humanity. In such a world, social theories are meaningless, since society itself seems to exist beyond the horizon of any given individual. Personal relationships, however tenuous, achieve an exaggerated intensity, and the mystiques of romantic illusion and religious faith become the indispensable components of existence. This would be a forbiddingly dismal view of life if Fellini did not provide compensations with a rich sense of humor and a perceptive eye for colorful detail. Fellini does not merely assert that life is worth living under the worst circumstances, he demonstrates the strange joys that flourish in the midst of loneliness and suffering. Without this demonstration *Cabiria* would be an unbearably sadistic experience.

Fellini's work since *The White Sheik* has been a continuous adventure in symbolism within the framework of unusually complex plots. Yet Fellini's technique does not lend itself to what we are accustomed to in the way of symbolic imagery. He does not give surfaces or objects any special gloss or lighting to emphasize their significance. There are never any meaningful shadows in a Fellini film, or any unusual contrasts between sunlight and darkness. His shots, day or night, fall into a neutral zone of grayness.

It might be argued that Fellini does not need to construct bizarre images, since such oddities abound in the Italian landscape. Italian religious festivals, for example, outdo Orson Welles in their addiction to grotesque shock effects. However, no matter how colorful the paraphernalia of Italian Catholicism may be, prop symbolism is only a small part of Fellini's achievement. It is in the symbolism and dreamlike quality of experience itself that Fellini excels. Here the lonely streets and fields serve their main function. What are Fellini's unforgettable images? The young men walking slowly on a deserted beach in *Vitelloni;* Gelsomina marching behind three musicians in *La strada;* Cabiria dancing on a stage suddenly detached from the audience—these are his magical moments.

It is odd to think of Fellini following in the footsteps of the neorealists, but it would be an error to consider his work completely apart from their influence. Indeed, it is the realism in Fellini's technique that enriches his symbols. He does not prettify reality although he tends to control it somewhat more than his predecessors. He does not shrink from dirt or grime or the garish ugliness of stage make-up. Indeed, like most neorealists, Fellini seems more at ease with settings of poverty and moderate means than with citadels of luxury. His cheap, noisy music hall in

*Cabiria* seems more authentic than the plush, unusually quiet nightclub. Cabiria's drab house seems less of a caricature than the actor's incredibly palatial villa. It is not a question of visual reality but one of camera treatment. Fellini looks at the poorer settings objectively, picking out their most characteristic elements. However, the luxurious settings are viewed satirically and only their most ridiculous features are emphasized.

Similarly, in *Cabiria* at least, the upper-class people—the actor and his mistress—are seen mechanically from the viewpoint of a lowly wide-eyed prostitute. Fellini's unwillingess to study a wider range of social strata does not imply an inability to do so. Still, with all its merits, *Cabiria* may represent the point at which Fellini's concern with the stragglers of society begins to yield diminishing returns. Somehow *Cabiria* does not have the feel of greatness that *Vitelloni* communicates. In *Vitelloni* every character counts for something and every incident advances toward a common truth. *Cabiria* is too much of a one-woman show, with Giulietta Masina's heroine achieving a sublime illumination while all the other characters linger in the darkness of deception and irresolution. Like *La strada,* Fellini's other near-masterpiece, *Cabiria* has some of the limitations of an acting vehicle that sometimes loses its way on the road of life and forks out into the bypaths of a virtuoso performance.

# On "8½"

## Ted Perry

8½ *is the film of* 8½ *being made;* the "film in the film" is, in this
case, the film itself.

*Christian Metz*

*In 8½ Fellini clearly shows himself to be what we have always at
least half suspected him of being, a baroque fantasist whose private world
has nothing more than a few accidents of time and place in common with
any "real" world.*

*John Russell Taylor*

*It seems to me that this must be my* mythos: *to try and throw off my
back the upbringing I have had; that is, to try and uneducate myself in
order to recapture a virginal availability and a new type of personal,
individual education.*

*Federico Fellini*

Regardless of their form, Fellini's films have been intimately concerned
with mental processes, with human subjectivity, the felt response of
the individual *persona* to itself and the world. That is why writers discussing Fellini's world have so often resorted to words like dream, document of
a dream, science fiction, nightmare, surreal, and fantasy. *8½,* with *Last
Year at Marienbad,* was among the first commercial feature-length films to
abandon the relations between the film experience and ordinary expectations of time, place, and sequence.

One of the chief ways in *8½* that Fellini lifts viewers away from
their usual concern with plot and meanings is to show the filmmaking
process and to entwine it with the film being seen to the point that the two
become inseparable. During many scenes of the film, the sound stage
buzzer intrudes; there are bright set lights in Guido's bathroom; the rear of

the set is exposed in the hotel lobby; lights, cameras, and technical crew are present in the final scene; in the piazza scene, Claudia comments on Guido's costume and makeup. Such things make it impossible to separate the film being planned, being shot, or being shown—"8¹/₂ is the film of 8¹/₂ being made." Thus are viewers led away from issues of subject matter and into direct experience with the form of the film, an experience in which the sensuous material celebrates the processes of the mind.

The crux of subjectivity in Fellini's films often concerns escaping the fate of the world. There are the strange structures in *Cabiria* and *8¹/₂*, the recurring disguises in the films, the frequent allusions to flying, the repeated acts of unexplained grace and unexplained miracles which seem to resolve the problems of living. There are recurring angels and other creatures that fly—even as Guido does in the opening of *8¹/₂*.

In its subjectivity, *8¹/₂* goes beyond the use of such obvious dream images to use basic dream modes of narrative. It leaps from event to event according to internal principle and not external narrative convention, and it confounds the world of the dreamer with the dream he is dreaming. In its interaction of memory and fantasy and present tense, *8¹/₂* seems to be a rendering of a mind trying to see, know, and reflect upon itself, to utter (or "other") itself into some palpable form.

The film continually displays Fellini's affection for the extraordinary visual statement, preferably in motion. *8¹/₂* relies heavily on movement in all its variant forms—camera, people, cutting, music, eye attention. In some scenes the camera moves incessantly, to pick up a minute detail, to enjoy a face that has never been seen before but which absolutely expresses a certain personality, to reveal a new perspective, to displace foreground with background. There is no way to describe Fellini's visual sense verbally: the similarity is perhaps to music. It is almost as if the lack of flow of notes in a piece of serial music were somehow translated into a visual flow evoking as powerful an emotional response. Surprising notes and disquieting chords find equivalents in the unusual and resonating details that Fellini juxtaposes to create his unique, exciting *mise-en-scène*. He undoubtedly has one of the most extensive visual palettes in the cinema.

The sense of movement in *8¹/₂* is also created by the rapid displacement of one space by another, not only through camera movement but also by the continual changing of scenery and locale. Few spaces are used more than once, and then in different contexts and lighting. The shifting locales are used to stress different feelings, and many transitions involve changes in mode of experience. Viewers may be confused as to where they are at the beginning of a scene; the point, of course, is not to pose a puzzle to unravel but to confound the levels of experience and to involve the viewer in the process.

Throughout the film, viewers are made to feel the situation as Guido experiences it. At times the camera movement traps Guido in the frame and, no matter where he goes, he is transfixed in its attention while other people are allowed freely to enter and exit frame, to be revealed and then disappear. At other times the camera may lose Guido, assuming its own personality and moving gratuitously. In the press conference, for instance, it often moves freely through the chaotic scene. More typically, the camera will assume Guido's point of view so that people can stare into it, harass it, accost it. This identification of Guido and the camera point of view, the self-referential ("mirror construction") nature of the film's form, and the camera movement that continually suggests something fearful off-screen, are the dominant strategies of the film.

*Satyricon* is the pinnacle of Fellini's progression into something more and more like documents of dreams and even science fiction. After it, the celebration of individual subjectivity takes more complex and subtle forms. The exposure of the camera, Fellini, and the business of filmmaking in *The Clowns* and *Roma* are variations of the same purpose.

Although *8½* is a transitional film in Fellini's work, revealing its process of taking form as content more readily than the others, it is unique and merits study for its own qualities. The man pinned in its view is in the midst of a middle-age crisis in which his creativity is paralyzed. In the course of trying to work out of his entrapment, he undergoes a primary process in which he regresses deeper and deeper into a desire for the liberation, spontaneity, comfort, and freedom from decisions that child-hood and certain mother figures represent. The process takes the form of dreams, fantasies, and memories. He dreams to redeem himself. His relations to women are crucial to the evolution of the narrative—to simplify perhaps too neatly, Luisa (the wife) and the mother are distant and critical; Carla, La Saraghina, the nurse, and the early Claudia are there unequivocally to love, envelop, and care for him.

The film ends in a celebration which is not necessarily a solution to the problems it has posed. Guido's final conversation with Luisa is tentative, but whatever the words, the tone of the last scene is one of involvement and action. As always, Fellini indicates his preference for action over intellectualization. The strengths of *8½* are the fecundity of invention, the extraordinary visual sense, and its creator's unique imagination. . . . Parenthetically, a critic is tempted to discuss at length the use of glasses, sunglasses, and water throughout *8½*. Sometimes, for instance, taking off or putting on or moving glasses on the nose seems to be an obvious cue to some change in the character's insight. Certainly there is a very strong thread throughout the film which often deals with Guido's propensity for lying: when Guido touches his nose, one thinks of Pinocchio and his revealing nose. By the same token, a great deal of emphasis is given to various aspects of water: Claudia and Guido drive near running waters, Guido pours water on his head in the bathroom, he has come to "healing waters," La Saraghina's place and the tower are beside the sea. But as in so much of Fellini's work, the use of glasses or the meaning of water or white dresses or whatever is not consistent. Fellini jokes with us and with himself. Sometimes, in a very specific context, the critic can point to some particular meaning being evoked, but it is dangerous to make generalizations. What can be said is that the film is deeply concerned with truth and falsehood, with the relationship of water and healing (salvation).

Claudia's appearance is a case in point. The meaning of the scene is the overall effect created by the simplicity of her dress, her smile, the floating quality created by her movement and the camera movement, and Guido's reaction. He sees, or remembers, or imagines, someone who offers him water. He takes great pleasure in her, in the way she moves, in the way she looks, in what she offers him. It is a moment of day-dreamt ecstasy, visualized in the form of a woman, something abstract and perhaps idealized, something he needs and wants, or so he seems to think at that moment.

Just the reverse is true of Carini, the writer whose criticism is resumed shortly after Guido has been awakened from his vision of Claudia. Guido is again being prodded about his proposed film and its philosophic premise. For Guido that way of working seems impossible, however much of his present paralysis may lead him to be influenced by Carini. He would like to listen to Carini, or so he tells himself, but actually he prefers spontaneous, intuitive action.

The appearance of Mario Mezzabotta, an old friend of Guido's, comes at that propitious moment when Guido is unsuccessfully trying to answer Carini. Indeed, there are a number of moments in the film when Guido, for one reason or another, fails to answer some direct questions put to him—about his script, about a person's role, about the film rushes. There is a pattern of Guido avoiding direct encounters or of fate luckily intervening to help him avoid them. That is his plight, of course; he is unwilling or unable, as Rossella will say later, to choose—which persons to cast, how to use the tower, when to start the film, what the film is, whether or not he has lost his inspiration.

Mezzabotta, on the other hand, has made a very decisive choice. He has left his wife of thirty-one years and is at the spa with a young girl, Gloria. She seems part wood nymph and part sorceress. As she approaches the camera, beginning to speak about the bee and the flower, a section from "Dance of the Mirlitons" accentuates the appearance of her face from under her hat. When Gloria sits down and presents her shapely legs for viewing, that is the moment she ironically selects to reveal the title of her university thesis: "The Plight of Modern Man As Reflected in the Contemporary Theater." Everything about her is just a little too obvious. But Mario and Gloria reflect Guido's problems. Mario has made a decision, and his decision involves dealing with his middle-age crisis in and through a younger woman. Guido, too, finds that his crisis involves women—his mistress, his wife, his remembered mother, La Saraghina, Claudia, several actresses. If he is to be a whole man, he must be so sexually as well as physically.

During all this, the camera has not been still. First, until Carini and Guido sit down, the camera is relentlessly moving—long trucking shots, dolly movements, up and down boom movements. The camera speeds across the grounds, catching the faces of the people, their movements. Certain camera movements play with foreground and background by pulling a foreground action into the frame, sometimes even from the off-screen space below, and then pushing the foreground activity out of the frame to reveal and emphasize action in the background. The effect is to call attention emphatically to the off-screen world.

The camera movement is closely choreographed with the movement of people. As a man turns and moves in a certain direction, the camera follows him as if his movement determined the movement of the camera. Indeed, most of the camera movement here is so motivated. (In some other scenes the camera moves of its own accord, not following any movement on the screen.)

Rare and therefore the more disquieting are those camera movements which are gratuitous, especially when such movement suddenly pulls into the frame from off-screen an unexpected sight, such as the conductor of the orchestra. As in the scene in the tunnel, this unexpected thrust into the frame throws the viewer off-guard and reminds him again that even in such a simple scene, the frame line is not sacred and the off-screen space is always to be reckoned with. Like the ringing of the telephone in Guido's bathroom, the outside world beyond the frame can and does intrude itself at any time.

This continual camera movement provokes other resonances, too. First, the choreography of people and the camera movement, coupled with the music, accentuates the inexorable movement of time itself. There is a feeling that nothing can stop the rapid acceleration of time passing. The lively camera is ironically juxtaposed with the images of so many aging people, moving slowly and decrepitly around the grounds, marching one slow foot at a time to obtain their doses of mineral water. The presence of these aging people suggests that one of the themes of the film is aging; Guido would at times like to return to some of the things and states he enjoyed as a child. "You would like to live another hundred years" is the thought of the aging lady as revealed by Maya. "They're not old enough," Guido says, referring to the men his assistant has brought to play the part of the father. "You're not the man you used to be," Conocchia says to Guido.

The most dramatic aspect of the use of the camera in this particular scene is that the shots seem to be taken from Guido's point of view. People look directly into the camera (even more than they did in the tunnel): they giggle at it and turn away; one person even waves at the camera.

The camera-as-Guido occurs not only in the long opening shot of the scene, where the camera trucks by several people who look at Guido (directly into the camera) but also in numerous other places in the scene. In the conversation where Mario introduces Gloria and the group moves as they talk, the moving camera is closely identified with Guido's direct point of view. The long exchange between Carini and Guido, in which Carini walks beside the moving camera (Guido) and talks toward it, is another example. Having identified the camera point of view and Guido, the viewer is surprised to see, as the camera stops and pans screen right, that Guido is seated down in the frame. Through use of the subjective camera, with people staring and making demands directly into it, the pressure mounts upon the director and all those who have identified with him.

The setting and the people can hardly be characterized as anything other than comic. It is not burlesque, but comedy which celebrates life—in all its curious, disproportionate, humorous, unusual details. What could be more pathetically comic than a man in a state of spiritual crisis taking himself among aging, sick, dying people, queuing up like them to receive "healing waters?" The frequent discrepancy in dress and music helps to accentuate both the comic and the pathetic aspects of Guido's crisis. He finds himself surrounded not only by older people but also by music and costumes that belong to an earlier era. These discrepancies are particularly apparent in the nightclub sequence and when the people are standing in line for their dosage of water.

The hero's personal crisis is being reflected in and through his occupation as film director. Few hints are offered as to the cause of Guido's crisis. Perhaps he has become aware of his age; perhaps he fears he has lost his creative ability; perhaps he dislikes the film that he has begun making; but nothing is made specific.

As Fellini has said in several interviews it was only after giving his protagonist other occupations that he decided to make him a film director. I suspect that it was difficult to make such a decision. Fellini had to expect that many film viewers would read *8¹/₂* as explicit autobiography and never push past the glib observation to understand the film's deeper concern with the spiritual, emotional, physical, and intellectual crisis of a character—an Everyman perhaps—who finds himself paralyzed, moving vertically among various levels of experience without progressing forward; man regressing into childhood, at times seeking to escape responsibility, questioning who he is and what he can do well; man surrounded by people busy about their own concerns and indifferent to his needs and difficulties; man forced to make decisions immediately over matters that are not easily decided.

I can only presume that Fellini chose a film director as the hero because that occupation so perfectly mirrors and focuses such crises. Few occupations force a person to make such decisions, dictate such immediate action, require such a high degree of preplanning and improvization. There is surely no other occupation that requires so much play between a personal vision and requirements of technology, time, and business. It is also the one profession Fellini knows in the greatest detail and at the deepest levels. At the same time, it should be noted that there is an entire tradition in the independent film (Mekas, Brakhage, Deren) and the commercial film (Truffaut's *Day for Night,* for instance) in which autobiography and the film-making process are central concerns.

Guido's crisis is not tragic, of course. It seems integrative and not disintegrative, and its form is therefore comic. When the French actress is introduced (perhaps she has come to play Carla in the film that Guido hopes to make), the soundtrack plays the Tchaikovsky section of the "Concertino alle terme," and this in turn is followed by "To Love Again," a tune based on Chopin's "E-flat Nocturne." Guido is worried by his own aging and yet the prospective fathers are not old enough. A mysterious woman floats by the background and Guido is stunned by her appearance. The lobby of the hotel is a harsh juxtaposition of *art nouveau* and signs of construction. Perhaps the construction is meant to reveal that it is a movie set, much like the buzzer sound which is here repeated when the Cardinal is moving from the elevator toward the door. The dramatic appearance of the producer, from the sky as it were in an open-cage elevator, and Guido's homage also are comic. The godlike producer brings a watch, reminds Guido of the pressure of time, and asks if the director's ideas have matured. Comic though they are, the demands beating at Guido from every side compound his crisis and the scene increases the tension that he must deal with.

The last two scenes of the film can best be understood as an experience which begins in paranoid frenzy and ends with celebration, the simple flute-playing of a child. There are definite ellipses in this process, but it does occur. At the beginning of the two scenes Guido was trying to escape and by the end of the two scenes he has taken command, using a megaphone to direct the players and crew and then joining the people in the dance. That is the overall experience which the scenes impress upon the viewer.

The change in Guido is presented in the form of a spectacle, one in which director, actors, viewers, crew, and film equipment (lights, megaphone) are seen simultaneously. The experience has no tenses but the present; it is immediate. For Guido the confusion of life and spectacle has momentarily ended. Life has become spectacle. The appearance of the clowns and the circus ring support this impression. The film about a film has become the film. The last scene brings together, in one spectacle, what was previously incoherent, disparate, and confused, and does so in a purely filmic way—the only way possible for Guido.

As life becomes spectacle, it is interesting to note that the close-up emphasis on Guido becomes a long-shot de-emphasis. The camera frees him, pulling back to more distant wider views which see him within a community of people. The scale is readjusted and he becomes part of a world. The off-screen space has been incorporated into the on-screen space. Claustrophobia gives way to panorama; the jail of self opens to a world of spatial horizons and human community.

On a very "realistic," factual level, the viewer does not know precisely what happened at the press conference (regarding the experience of the film; of course, what happens is what is shown) and what decision Guido might have made to lead to the dismantling of the tower. That earlier dismantling did not preclude the presence of motion picture lights and cameras on the tower for the final scene. The viewer does not know the relationship between the aborted film and the one Guido is directing at the end of the film. All of these explanations are deliberately left ambiguous to focus attention on the central structure, which is Guido's movement from paralysis, fear, and frustration, on the one hand, to involvement, action, and direction on the other hand. The film presents Guido trying to escape at the press conference and it then presents him taking control of a situation.

What the viewer knows through experience is that what has been at times disparate, separated in space and time, gratuitous and fragmented, is now somehow woven together. The filmic space is now filled with the separate elements and they are unified by their simultaneous existence within the frame and their context. A filmic space which was formerly subject to internal impolsions and external manipulations has now been given wholeness. This union, this celebration, this affirmation is articulated not only through spatial unity but also by the similarity of dress, the dance around the ring, the presence of the child Guido, and by "La passerella di addio," a version of the *8¹/₂* theme which includes almost every musical motif in the film. The epiphany is then an affirmation and

celebration, however simple, of unity, of spontaneity, of freedom, of innocence.

And how did this dramatic change occur? How did it happen that the
film moved from a reluctant, estranged Guido to an active film director?
On one level, of course, and the more rational one, there is some indication
that something Guido did during or after the press conference helped to
initiate the sequence of events. The link between such an action and the
finale are tenuous, however. What is directly shown to the viewer is
Maurice, the magician who earlier aided Maya. Waving his wand, he
appears in front of the car and tells Guido that they are ready to begin. It is
only after Maurice appears and speaks that Guido is led to a state of
understanding and action. What really happens is that a transformation
takes place, its beginning visualized through a magician, and that the
transformation has very little to do with rational explanation. The transformation cannot be accounted for as the logical and necessary result of any
actions and processes that have been developing in the film, at least not in
the acceptable manner that dramatic action leads to a probable and necessary conclusion. One moment Guido has given up on his film and the next
he is overcome with certain feelings that lead him to pick up the
megaphone and direct the action. Nothing attempts to explain logically that
change, except for Guido's verbal rationalizations of what he has experienced. The change in Guido (and no one should assume that it is permanent) comes as magically and mysteriously as any muse. He has not
"earned" his salvation in any conventional sense. There has been a descent into Hell (the producer says, "We've been waiting for you three
days") and now the dead person has arisen. The man who was once
lifeless, fearful, and paranoid, threatened continually by unknown forces
off-screen and trapped by a relentless camera, is now filled with energy,
action, affirmation. It is an act of grace rather than of will.

All of Fellini's films have celebrated, in some form, such mystical
and magical moments. In *La strada,* when Gelsomina's sense of life's
meaning and purpose was most threatened, three clowns appeared out of
nowhere in a field and she joined them as they played and marched. The
references in *8½* to magic and mysticism help to prepare the viewer for
such a transformation. This gift of grace is visualized primarily through the
unity and movement in space of the major characters in the film, their
joining in a circle to dance together, the camera's pulling back for lengthy
shots of the entire scene, and also by Guido's willingness to pick up the
megaphone, direct, and join in the dance. Once salvation has been given to
him, however tentative, he suddenly becomes capable of spontaneous and
vigorous action. The boy inside the man has been freed and restored, not
by design, deliberation, or development, but by an act of grace.

# Mirror Construction in Fellini's "8½"

## Christian Metz

Like those paintings that show a second painting within, or those novels written about a novel, *8½* with its "film within the film" belongs to the category of works of art that are divided and doubled, thus reflecting on themselves. To define the structure peculiar to this type of work the term *"construction en abŷme"* (literally "inescutcheon construction"), borrowed from the language of heraldic science,[1] has been proposed, and indeed it lends itself quite well to that structure permitting all the effects of a mirror. [At the risk of losing some of the accuracy of the original term, the translator has preferred to substitute the term "mirror construction," which is less unfamiliar, certainly less awkward-sounding, and therefore perhaps more suggestive than "inescutcheon construction." The image is that of a double mirror, reflecting itself.]

In a very interesting study devoted to Fellini's film, Alain Virmaux has shown that, although mirror construction in the cinematographic domain is not an invention of Fellini's, since it is found already in various earlier films—*La Fête à Henriette,* by Jeanson and Duvivier, René Clair's *Le Silence est d'or,* Bergman's *The Devil's Wanton*[2]—the author of *8½* is nevertheless the first to construct his *whole* film, and to order *all* his elements, according to the repeating mirror image. In fact the precursors of *8½* only partially deserve to be called "mirror-construction" works, because in them the "film within the film" was only a marginal or pic-

1. In heraldry the term "inescutcheon" refers to a smaller shield placed at the center of a larger shield, and reproducing it in every detail, but on a smaller scale.—TRANS.
2. One might add Roger Leenhardt's *Le Rendez-vous de minuit,* in which the "film within the film" already played a more central and complex role. [*The Devil's Wanton* is also known in English as *Prison.*—EDS.]

turesque device (*Le Silence est d'or*), at times a simple "trick" of the script-writer's (*La Fête à Henriette*), at best a fragmentary construction (*The Devil's Wanton*) lending perspective to only part of the film's substance, the rest being presented directly, and not through reflection.

Moreover, Alain Virmaux, Raymond Bellour, Christian Jacotey, and Pierre Kast have all emphasized the fact that the content of the entire film, and its deepest thematic structure, are inseparable from its relfecting construction: The character of the director, Guido, Fellini's representative in the film, resembles his creator like a twin, with his narcissistic complacency, his immense sincerity, his disorderly existence, his inability to make a choice, his persistent hope in some kind of "salvation" that will suddenly resolve all his problems, his erotic and religious obsessions, his open desire to "put everything" into the film (just as Fellini puts all of himself into his films, and especially into *8½*, which is like a pause in his career, a general viewing of the past, an aesthetic and effective summing up).[3] As Pierre Kast observes, the criticisms one might address to the style of the film, or to the style of Fellini's work in general (that it is confused, disparate, complacent, has no real conclusion) are already present in the film, whether they are expressed by Guido himself or by his scenario-writer, Daumier, his inseparable companion, a companion Guido curses but whom he needs as he needs his bad conscience; thus, again it is the mirror construction alone that has allowed Fellini to integrate into his film a whole series of ambiguous reflections on whatever his own film might be accused of.

There is however a point that, I believe, has never been emphasized as much as it deserves to be: For, if *8½* differs from other films that are doubled in on themselves, it is not only because this "doubling in" is more systematic or more central, but also and above all because it functions differently. For *8½*, one should be careful to realize, is a film that is *doubly doubled*—and, when one speaks of it as having a mirror construction, it is really a double mirror construction one should be talking about.[4]

3. As Alain Virmaux observes, the title *8½* designates the film less in terms of its own characteristics than in terms of a sort of retrospective reference to all of Fellini's previous work. [Since it was, literally, his eighth-and-a-half film.—TRANS.]

4. One might also say—it is essentially a question of vocabulary—that the expression "mirror construction" refers *only* to those works defined here as "doubly self-reflecting," and not to the majority of cases where a film appears within a film or a book within a book or a play within a play. A shield is not said to be "inescutcheon" everytime it contains some other shield, but only when the other shield is, except in size, identical to the first. [Metz is, of course, referring to the heraldic term "construction en abýme," which I have changed to "mirror construction." A double mirror reflects itself into infinity—and this captures something of the suggestiveness of "en abime," "abime" meaning "abyss" or "chasm"—each reflection being identical to, though one degree smaller, than what it reflects.—TRANS.] If

It is not only a film about the cinema, it is a film about a film that is presumably itself about the cinema; it is not only a film about a director, but a film about a director who is reflecting himself onto his film. It is one thing in a film to show us a second film whose subject has no relationship, or very little relationship, to the subject of the first film (*Le Silence est d'or*); it is entirely another matter to tell us in a film about *that very film* being made. It is one thing to present us with a character who is a director and who recalls only slightly, and only in some parts of the film, the maker of the real film (*The Devil's Wanton*); it is another matter for the director to make his hero into a director who is thinking of making a very similar film. And, if it is true that the autobiographical and "Fellinian" richness of *8½* is inseparable from its mirror construction, it is nevertheless only explained in its opulent, baroque entirety by the self-reflecting of that construction.

Guido's problems, it has been said, are those of Fellini reflecting on his art: Was it enough, then, for Guido to be a filmmaker, like Fellini? The similarity would have remained very general. But Guido is a director reflecting on his art, and by a curious irony these two successive reflections end by canceling each other out to a certain extent, so that *8½* is finally a film of perfect coincidence; extremely complex, its structure nonetheless attains a lucid simplicity, an immediate legibility. It is because Guido is thinking of his film, and reflecting on himself, that he merges—at least temporarily[5]—with Fellini; it is because the film that Guido wanted to make would have been a study of himself, a film-maker's summing up, that it becomes confused with the film that Fellini has made.[6] The ordinary interplay of reflection would never have yielded such a wealth of echoes and relationships between Fellini and his character had it not been reflected by the reflecting of that character himself; filmmaker and reflecting filmmaker, Guido is doubly close to the man who brought him to life, doubly his creator's double.

It is even in the concrete details of its handling that the device of "the

---

one agrees to this acceptation, one will have to say that *La Silence est d'or* contains nothing resembling mirror construction and that in *The Devil's Wanton* or in *Le Rendez-vous de minuit,* mirror construction remains partial and fragmentary.

5. Taken as a whole, the relationships between Guido and Fellini are obviously more complex; among other things, Guido's character is not entirely identical to Fellini's. However, I am not concerned with psychology here, but simply with identity (in the sense that one speaks of identity cards). *For the duration of the film,* Guido fully represents the person of Fellini.

6. Must I point out that I am speaking here of the film Guido dreamed of making, not the film that outside pressures (his producer, etc.) might perhaps have imposed on him had he finally decided to start filming? For Fellini's film, although it tells us only very little about the exact state of his working plans, or the intentions of his producers, is on the other hand extremely precise about Guido's deepest wishes concerning his film.

film within a film'' diverges here from its more common use. For *we never see* the film that Guido is to make; we do not even see extracts from it, and thus any distance between the film Guido dreamt of making and the film Fellini made is abolished: Fellini's film is composed of all that Guido would have liked to have put into his film—and that is precisely why Guido's film is never shown separately. The reader can judge for himself the extent of the difference between this structure and the structure in *Le Rendez-vous de minuit,* for example, where large extracts of the ''film within the film'' are explicitly shown at several specific points in the first film, which suffices to create a distance between the two films. In *8 ¹/₂* we do not *even* see Guido shooting his film or working on it—and here it differs from *The Devil's Wanton,* for example; we see him, simply, in the period when the film is being prepared, living or dreaming, accumulating in the very stream of his own chaotic existence all the material that, without ever succeeding, he would like to place in his film and that Fellini is able to put into *his* film. It is, therefore, because the ''film within the film'' never appears separately within the first film that it can coincide with it so completely.

All that we see of this film Guido is dreaming about are the screen tests of the actresses; but it is here that the *tripling* of the film most clearly manifests itself. Guido has an actress to play the role of his wife in the film; the latter is played, in *8¹/₂,* by Anouk Aimée; and she in turn can only be an incarnation—very much interpreted, it goes without saying—of the problems Fellini encounters in his own life.[7] It is during the sequence of the screen tests that a character in *8¹/₂,* watching the private screening and thinking of Guido, whispers, ''Why, that's his own life,'' making a reflection that one can only reflect on by applying it to Fellini himself.

It is therefore not enough to speak of a ''film within the film'': *8¹/₂* is the film of *8¹/₂* being made; *the ''film in the film'' is, in this case, the film itself.* And of all the literary or cinematographic antecedents that have been mentioned in connection with Fellini's work, by far the most convincing— as critics have often pointed out, but perhaps without ever entirely explaining why—is André Gide's *Paludes,* since it is about a novelist writing *Paludes*.[8]

7. If one reflects that the actress in the screen test was herself played, in Fellini's film, by another actress—and that, at the other end of the chain, Fellini's wife (Giulietta Masina) is also an actress—one will become positively dizzy. More seriously, one can observe that, following *8¹/₂* Fellini shot *Juliet of the Spirits,* which is, as we know, a sort of feminine version of the preceding film; the woman's role is played by Giulietta Masina. This confirms the tripling process that appears in the screen-test sequence in *8¹/₂.*

8. One thinks of course also of *Les Caves du Vatican* and *Les Faux-monnayeurs.* Alain Virmaux, Raymond Bellour, Pierre Kast, and Max Milner (articles already quoted) have all

This triple-action construction gives the ending of the film, which has been variously interpreted, its true meaning. The version Fellini finally retained[9] contains not one but three successive dénouements. In a first resolution, Guido abandons his film because it would have been confused, disorderly, too close to his life to become a work; because it would have been reduced to a disparate series of echoes and resonances; because it would have carried no central message capable of unifying it; and finally, and above all, because it would not have changed his life. That is the meaning of Guido's symbolic suicide at the end of his stormy press conference, as well as of the last words of Daumier. In a second movement—the allegory of the fantastic rondo—the abandonment of the film returns Guido to his life, as he sees all those who have peopled it parading in front of him; he asks his wife to accept things as they are; he has given up, at the same time he has given up his film, that rather messianic hope of a "salvation" that would suddenly bring order to all the elements of his chaos and thus modify their profound meaning and lend them the perspective of the future. But it is at this moment that Guido—who is no longer a director but is again a man like other men—once more takes up his director's megaphone to direct the audience of his memories. Therefore the film will be made; it will have no central message, and it will not alter life, since it will be made out of the very confusion of life; but out of that very confusion *it will be made*.

Notice that this second phase of the film's resolution heralds not only the existence of *8½* itself, but also the principle of its creation: It will be a film woven from the life of its author and possessing the disorder of his life. Things, however, do not stop there: Having organized his fantastic dance, Guido, holding his wife by her hand, *himself now enters the circle*. Is this merely the symbol of that complacent tenderness—Fellini's as well—that ties Guido to his own memories and to his own dreams, and of which he has accused himself (not without some complacency and some tenderness) in earlier sequences? Are we not at last witnessing the final casting off of this great vehicle of a film, which, like a rocket freed from its

---

emphasized the Gidian aspects of Fellini's work. Alain Virmaux quotes this sentence from Gide's *Journal* (1899–1939): "J'aime assez qu'en une oeuvre d'art on retrouve ainsi transposé à l'échelle des personnages, *le sujet même* de cette oeuvre." ("I rather like the idea that in a work of art one finds, transposed in this way to the scale of the characters, *the very subject* of the work.") I have underlined *"le sujet même"* (*"the very subject"*): Gide, one sees, was thinking less of ordinary "doubling in" than of the peculiar variety of "doubling in" I am discussing in these few pages. Similarly, one should remember that Gide was one of those who have used the term *"construction en abŷme."*

9. Fellini had first planned another resolution. See Camilla Cederna, 8½ *de Fellini: Histoire d'un film* (Paris: Julliard, 1963).

various supports, will be able to soar on its true flight? Having entered the circle, Guido has also come to order; this author who dreamed of making *8¹/₂* is now one of the characters of *8¹/₂;* he can give his hand to the maid, the producer, the cardinal, his mistress; he no longer needs his megaphone, for it is now Fellini's film that will commence. No longer is Guido at the center of the magic circle; now it is only the small child dressed in white, and blowing his pipe, the ultimate, and first, inspirer of the whole fantasy—Guido as a child has become the symbol of Fellini as a child, since, in any case, *the place of the director, which is now empty,* can only be occupied by a character external to the action of the film: by Fellini himself.

And so Fellini's film begins. And though one is right to underline the paradoxical and startling thing about *8¹/₂*—that it is a powerfully creative meditation on the inability to create—the fact remains that this theme takes us back, beyond any possible affectation on Fellini's part, to a situation more fundamental and less paradoxical than it is occasionally said to be. Out of all the confusion we have witnessed in the film, an admirably constructed film and one that is as little confused as possible will, it is true, be born; but is this not simply because the last stage of creation—that voluntary awakening that *stops* the undefined course of things in order to *establish* the work—can never be described in the created work, which owes its creation only to that ultimate step back, to that infinitesimal yet gigantic instant that is all that separates Guido from Fellini?

# Robert Flaherty

ROBERT FLAHERTY *was born in Michigan in 1884 and died in Vermont in 1951. Often called the father of documentary, Flaherty came into filmmaking only by chance. As a young man, he explored and trapped in Canada with his father, then studied mining and from 1910 to 1916 served as a guide for the mapping expeditions of Sir William Mackenzie to Hudson Bay. On one of these trips he took along film equipment and photographed the land and the people he knew so well. Although this film was accidentally destroyed, it became the inspiration for Flaherty's first film,* Nanook of the North *(1922), which after early troubles with distribution quickly gained worldwide acclaim.*

*Flaherty was almost always his own cameraman and at least co-scriptwriter. The number of feature films he completed on his own was small—*Moana *(1926),* Man of Aran *(1934),* Elephant Boy *(1936),* The Land *(1941), and* Louisiana Story *(1948)—but his influence was immense. John Grierson and the British documentary filmmakers of the 1930s considered him a master, and Flaherty worked with them on* Industrial Britain *(1931), lending what one young documentarian called "his wonderful eyes." Almost thirty years later, young French documentarians like Jean Rouch would found their theories of* cinéma vérité *on Flaherty's practice.*

*Flaherty's best work contains a unique mixture of clear observation and poetic perspective that has been the basis of continuous argument among theorists of documentary film—the need to balance the debt to the nature of what is perceived with the debt to the nature of the perceiver—what one critic called the characteristic documentary process of having an idea of a place, visiting the place and discovering the idea wasn't true, and then making a film that combined how it was with how it should be.*

*Flaherty's career embodied also another paradox of filmmaking, one that stretched beyond the realm of the documentary: the conflict between the artistic and the commercial, between the pressures of making a film and the pressures of selling it. Each of his projects had a separate financing arrangement:* Nanook *supported by the fur-trading company Revillon* Frères, Moana *by Paramount,* Man of Aran *by the British production firm* Gainsborough, Elephant Boy *by Alexander Korda,* The Land *by the United States Film Service and the Department of Agriculture, and* Louisiana Story *by Standard Oil of New Jersey. Besides frequent conflicts with his producers on these productions, Flaherty also participated in many intriguing projects that either were never completed or from which he withdrew. He left work on films with W. S. Van Dyke (*White Shadows in the South Seas, *1928) and F. W. Murnau (*Tabu, *1931), had a similarly abortive collaboration with Orson Welles, and became a casualty of the friction between Frank Capra and the Army during the World War II period of the War Department Film Division, which Capra headed.*

*Flaherty's special integrity as a filmmaker, however it may have disrupted his own career, was very attractive and even symbolic to many of his own generation and to many who came later. The paradoxes of his personal aesthetic, his refusal to use documentary as a tool of social and political conditioning, and his effort to convey what Arthur Calder-Marshall has called "that wonderfully humble exploration of human skills," have left their traces in descendants as different as Jean Rouch's* Lion Chase *(1965), D. A. Pennebaker's* Don't Look Back *(1967), and Albert and David Maysles's* Salesman *(1969).*

Flaherty's life has been written by his widow, Frances Hubbard Flaherty (The Odyssey of a Film-maker, *1960*), and by Arthur Calder-Marshall (The Innocent Eye, *1963*). Discussion of Flaherty's work can be found in any book dealing with documentary film, such as the histories by Richard Barsam (*1973*) and Erik Barnouw (*1974*); a fuller account is contained in Richard Griffith's The World of Robert Flaherty (*1953*).

# Flaherty

## John Grierson

A happy fortune has at last brought Robert Flaherty to England. Flaherty was the director of *Nanook* and *Moana,* the originator of *White Shadows of the South Seas,* the co-director, with Murnau, of *Tabu.* He was the initiator of the naturalist tradition in cinema, and is still the high priest of the spontaneities. The happy fortune lies in the fact that of all distinguished foreign directors he is the one whose sympathies are most nearly English. Technically, he is American, but the major part of his life has been spent exploring or filming within the British Empire.

This long association, together with his explorer's hatred of Hollywood artificialities, makes him the one director whose cinematic persuasion is most likely to benefit our present England. He comes to London for the first time with an eye for its authority in the world, which adds fantasy to the most familiar. He has seen Eskimos travel a thousand miles to buy an English blanket which would last them a lifetime, when the shoddy article of more recent commercial tradition was at their igloo doors. He has eaten out an Arctic winter on the superior construction of English bully-beef tins, which refused to rust with foreign competitors. He has blessed the name of England ten thousand miles away for the one glue in the world which the tropics could not melt.

I knew Flaherty in New York, and he was the only man I knew there whom Babel did not enthrall. This seemed to me a most perverse feat of the mind at the time, but in these later days I would more sensibly describe it as a feat of most necessary simplicity. It is only now apparent how the Blazonry of American ballyhoo was selling a generation into slavery. Flaherty used to say: "They are a tribe of sharks preying on the weakness of their neighbors. This is their way of being ferocious." He contrasted the public decency of Polynesians. Economics, of which he professes nothing, have most strangely found him right. I know not how many millions the

From *Grierson on Documentary,* compiled and edited by Forsyth Hardy (Praeger, 1972). Reprinted by permission of Faber & Faber Limited.

American people will have to pay their irresponsible exploiters when prosperity comes again; for goods consumed.

Now in London I find Flaherty's eye for things as fascinating as before. He tells me that wholesomeness went out of American humor when Mark Twain died, and that behind all the flashing wit of American cross-talk is an essential unkindliness. He tells me that England is dirty and scrambled, that its humor is simple, but that this original human wholesomeness remains to it. He tells me that English faces retain an individuality which stands up to the buildings as American faces cannot. He contrasts the manicured landscape of the Continent with the informality and intimacy of the Chilterns. He praises, most unfashionably, craftsmanship.

These hints and emphases are very close to the problem we have to solve in our English cinema, for we are more than ever in search of the national certainties we are to proclaim. We have not yet evolved a *style*. We imitate Hollywood, and occasionally we imitate Neubabelsburg and Moscow. There is some original lack of affection for our own English worth, a lack of knowledge of it, a lack of bravery in it which prevents our bringing beauty, and convincing beauty, out of the films we make.

It is, I know only too well, difficult to be sure of one's attitudes in a decade like this. Can we heroicize our men when we know them to be exploited? Can we romanticize our industrial scene when we know that our men work brutally and starve ignobly in it? Can we praise it—and in art there must be praise—when the most blatant fact of our time is the bankruptcy of our national management? Our confidence is sapped, our beliefs are troubled, our eye for beauty is most plainly disturbed: and the more so in cinema than in any other art. For we have to build on the actual. Our capital comes from those whose only interest is in the actual. The medium itself insists on the actual. There we must build or be damned.

Flaherty's most considerable contribution to the problem is, as always, his insistence on the beauty of the natural. It is not everything, for it does not in the last resort isolate and define the purposes which must, consciously or unconsciously, inform our craftsmanship. But it does ensure that the raw material from which we work is the raw material most proper to the screen. The camera-eye is in effect a magical instrument. It can see a thousand things in a thousand places at different times, and the cunning cutter can string them together for a review of the world. Or he can piece them together—a more difficult task—for a review of a subject or situation more intricate and more intimate than any mortal eye can hope to match. But its magic is even more than this. It lies also in the manner of its observation, in the strange innocence with which, in a mind-tangled world, it sees things for what they are. This is not simply to say that the camera, in its single observations, is free from the trammels of the subjective, for it is patent that it will not follow the director in his enthusiasms any more than it will follow him in the wide-angled vision of his eyes. The magical fact of the camera is that it picks out what the director does not see at all that it gives emphasis where he did not think emphasis existed.

The camera is in a measure both the discoverer of an unknown world and the re-discoverer of a lost one. There are, as everyone knows, strange moments of beauty that leap out of most ordinary news reels. It may be some accidental pose of character or some spontaneous gesture which radiates simply because it is spontaneous. It may be some high angle of a ship, or a crane, or a chimney stack, or a statue, adding some element of the heroic by a new-found emphasis. It may be some mere foreshortening of a bollard and a rope that ties a ship to a quay in spirit as well as in fact. It may be the flap of a hatch cover which translates a gale. It may be the bright revelation of rhythms that time has worn smooth: the hand movement of a potter, the wrist movement of a native priest, or the muscle play of a dancer or a boxer or a runner. All of them seem to achieve a special virtue in the oblong of the screen.

So much Flaherty has taught us all. If we add to it such instruction as we have taken from Griffith and the Russians, of how to mass movement and create suspense, of how to keep an eye open for attendant circumstance and subconscious effect, we have in sum a most formidable equipment as craftsmen. But the major problem remains, the problem I have mentioned, the problem the critics do not worry their heads over, though creators must: what final honors and final dishonors we shall reveal in this English life of ours: what heroism we shall set against what villainy. The field of cinema is not only a field for creators but also for prophets.

The method followed by Flaherty in his own filmmaking might give us a most valuable lead. He took a year to make his study of the Eskimos and this after ten years' exploration in the Eskimo country of Labrador and Baffin Land. He took two years to make his study of Samoan life, and only now, after three more years in the South Seas, feels he could do justice to it. He soaked himself in his material, lived with it to the point of intimacy and beyond that to the point of belief, before he gave it form. This is a long method, and may be an expensive one; and it is altogether alien in a cinema world which insists on forcing a preconceived shape (one of half a dozen rubber-stamped dramatic shapes) on all material together. Its chief claim to our regard, however, is that it is necessary, and particularly necessary in England. We know our England glibly as an industrial country, as a beautiful country of this epic quality and that; we know it by rote as a maker of Empire and as a manipulator of worldwide services. But we do not know it in our everyday observation as such. Our literature is divorced from the actual: it is written as often as not in the south of France. Our culture is divorced from the actual: it is practiced almost exclusively in the rarefied atmosphere of country colleges and country retreats. Our gentlemen explore the native haunts and investigate the native customs of Tanganyika and Timbuctoo, but do not travel dangerously into the jungles of Middlesbrough and the Clyde. Their hunger for English reality is satisfied briefly and sentimentally over a country hedge.

We might make an English cinema, as we might make English art again, if we could only send our creators back to fact. Not only to the old fact of the countryside which our poets have already honored, but to the new fact of industry and commerce and plenty and poverty which no poet has honored at all. Every week I hear men ask for films of industry. They want it praised and proclaimed to the world, and I would like to see their money used and their purposes fulfilled. But what advice can I give them? We can produce them the usual slick rubbish, some slicker, some less slick; but who of us knows an industry well enough to bring it alive for what it is? And what statescraft is willing to send a creator into an industry, so to know it: for a year, for two years perhaps, for the length of a hundred thousand feet of film and possibly more. Our businessmen expect a work of art to schedule, as the housewife expects her daily groceries. They expect it of a new medium. They expect it from raw material which they in their own hearts despise.

Flaherty, as an individual artist, cannot answer the whole problem. He knows his primitives and will do a job for them out of the strength of his affection. He could do a job for English craftsmanship and for the tradition of quality in English work, and for the native solidity in English institutions, and English criticism and character; but he is of a persuasion that does not easily come to grips with the more modern factors of civilization. In his heart he prefers a sailing barge to a snub-nosed funnel-after, and a scythe to a mechanical reaper. He will say that there is well-being associated with the first and none with the second, and in a manner he is right: right in his emphasis on well-being. But how otherwise than by coming to industry, even as it is, and forcing beauty from it, and bringing people to see beauty in it, can one, in turn, inspire man to create and find well-being? For this surely is the secret of our particular well-being, that men must accept the environment in which they live, with its smoke and its steel and its mechanical aids, even with its rain. It may not be so easily pleasant as the halcyon enironment of Tahiti, but this is beside the point.

I think in this other matter one may turn to the Russians for guidance rather than to Flaherty. Their problem, of course, is different from ours. The industrial backwardness of the country, the illiteracy of their people, and the special factors of Russian psychology make for a rhetoric in their cinema which we cannot blindly imitate. Apart from this national difference, which is in effect their *style,* there is an ardour of experiment in their treatment of industrial and social material. They have built up rhythms from their machinery; they have made their work exciting and noble. They have made society on the move the subject-matter of art. Their sense of rhythm is not necessarily our sense of rhythm. Their sense of nobility and sense of social direction need not be identical with ours. The essential point, however, is that they have built up this rhythm and nobility and purpose of theirs by facing up to the new material. They have done it out of the necessity of their social situation. No one will say that our own necessity is less than theirs.

When I spoke with Flaherty on the Aran Islands he was full of the possibilities of the British documentary cinema. If on these islands—only so many hours from London—there was this story of romantic life ready to the camera, how many more must there be! He mentioned the Hebrides and the Highlands, and sketched out a film of Indian village life. He spoke of the tales of fine craftsmanship which must be tucked away in the Black Country. But first, he emphasized, there must be the process of discovery and freedom in discovery: to live with the people long enough to know them. He talked with a certain rising fury of the mental attitude of the studio-bred producer who hangs a slicked-out story of triangles against a background of countryside or industry. Rather must the approach be to take the story from out the location, finding it essentially there: with patience and intimacy of knowledge at the first virtues always in a director. He referred to a quotation I once wrote for him in New York, when his seemingly tardy method of production was first an issue in the studios. It was Plato's description of his metaphysics where he says that no fire can leap up or light kindle till there is "long intercourse with the thing itself, and it has been lived with." No doubt the studios, with their slick ten- or fifteen-day productions of nothing-in-particular, still disagree with Flaherty and Plato profoundly. His idea of production is to reconnoiter for months without turning a foot, and then, in months more perhaps, slowly to shape the film on the screen: using his camera first to sketch his material and find his people, then using his screen, as Chaplin uses it, to tell him at every turn where the path of drama lies.

No director has the same respect as Flaherty for the camera; indeed very few of them even trouble to look through the camera while it is shooting their scenes. Flaherty, in contrast, is always his own "first cameraman." He spoke almost mystically of the camera's capacity for seeing beyond mortal eye to the inner qualities of things. With Fairbanks he agrees that children and animals are the finest of all movie actors, because they are spontaneous, but talks also of the movements in peasants and craftsmen and hunters and priests as having a special magic on the screen because time or tradition has worn them smooth. He might also add—though he would not—that his own capacity for moving the camera in appreciation of these movements is an essential part of the magic. No man of cameras, to my knowledge, can pan so curiously, or so bewilderingly anticipate a fine gesture or expression.

Flaherty's ideal in the new medium is a selective documentation of sound similar at all points to his selective documentation of movement and expression in the silent film. He would use the microphone, like the camera, as an intimate attendant on the action: recording the accompanying sounds and whispers and cries most expressive of it. He says the language does not matter at all, not even the words, if the spirit of the thing is plain. In this point as in others, Flaherty's cinema is as far removed from the theatrical tradition as it can possibly be. His screen is not a stage to which the action of a story is brought, but rather a magical opening in the theater wall, through which one may look out to the wide world: overseeing and overhearing the intimate things of common life which only the camera and microphone of the film artist can reveal.

# Robert Flaherty:
# The Man in the Iron Myth

## Richard Corliss

If, alone among the gods in Andrew Sarris's "pantheon," Robert Flaherty is today scorned or ignored, it may be because of the sanctimonious reverence he was granted while alive and the premature deification that immediately followed his death in 1951. Now, when the profane "Hollywood hacks" of the 1930s and 1940s have become auteurist divinities, Flaherty can just barely be noticed in a remote niche: the Brattleboro reliquary. Ironically, the icons erected in his name have fudged our perspective and obscured his stature. For Flaherty is not so completely *other* that we cannot approach his career with the same unawed respect we (should) bring to a Hitchcock or a McCarey. Otherwise, critical filmographies can turn into gaga hagiographies, in which neither the film maker nor the art of criticism is served. Movies were not meant to be seen from a kneeling position.

Flaherty once said, "First I was an explorer; then I was an artist." For him, the journey was at least as important as reaching the destination. And, in one sense, his films are so many flags marking the ends of expeditions into Hudson Bay, Samoa, the Aran Islands, India, the American heartland, the billabong bayous of Louisiana. In another sense, of course, these films—*Nanook of the North* (1922), *Moana* (1926), *Man of Aran* (1934), *Elephant Boy* (1937), *The Land* (1941), and *Louisiana Story* (1948)—mark Flaherty's excursions into various regions of the human soul, to discover elemental truths and to project them onto the mind screens of the rest of us, who may have forgotten them in our century-long rush toward catatonic computerism. But, though these truths may not have been self-evident, Flaherty was hardly the only filmmaker to hold them. Indeed, there are enough similarities between him and Ford, Chaplin, Borzage, even Disney, to place him in a tradition of the romantic-visionary American.

From an article in *A Critical Dictionary of the Cinema,* edited by Richard Roud, to be published by Martin Secker & Warburg Ltd (London) and The Viking Press (New York) in 1978.

Flaherty has been accused, in his film explorations, of finding only what he was looking for: the Innocent Eye as Cyclops. As he grew older, this may have been truer, for *Moana* and *Man of Aran* can be seen as spin-offs from the *Nanook* story line. But in his finest films, *Nanook* and *The Land,* he simply saw the truth and brought it home. These films stand at opposite ends of Flaherty's psychical spectrum. *Nanook* was his response to a subject with which his nature was in complete harmony; *The Land* was an atonal wail of compassionate horror. Standing alone among his works, they also stand tallest.


Seen today, Flaherty's first film is something of a revelation as both artwork and artifact. Though it was released in 1922, *Nanook* seems like an afterimage of the cinema's prehistory and man's preconscious. The sharp whites and grays produced by Flaherty's orthochromatic stock suggest a tonal morality play between Good and—not Evil—the Unknown. His uncanny knack for capturing on film the swirl patterns of soil and sea (the innocent eye was also a painterly one, worthy of Monet) can be traced to the palpable landscapes of *Nanook.* And here, the ability of his camera to record texture but not temperature helps universalize his setting: the Arctic snowstorm. Nanook is a Bedouin, and we are all Eskimos.

Without Nanook himself, however, Flaherty's film might have been a turning point in world cinema, but it would not have been a popular success. From the moment *Nanook of the North* opened at New York's Capitol Theatre (on a double bill with *Grandma's Boy*), Nanook was a star. He was also a remarkable natural actor. It's easy to imagine that at first Flaherty led Nanook and his family through showmanlike bits of business (as in our introduction to the six, when they emerge from their kayak, one by one, like so many midget clowns from a circus auto) and gradually learned to anticipate and trust his star, his subject, his collaborator, his friend, until the two became one—became the film.

Nanook's austere exoticism presents a danger for the contemporary viewer. Because it seems hatched from some Ice Age time capsule, the film—as well as its protagonist *and* its director—can too easily be classified as a "noble primitive" deserving of a civilized man's awe and condescension. What's missing from this overview is the respect for a craftsman that Nanook earns from Flaherty, and Flaherty from us. The sequence in which Nanook fits an ice window for his igloo stands as the collaborative fusion between two men who respected craftsmanship as both a tool for survival and a fine art. And the film as a whole stands alone—not as a mausoleum of textbook cinema but as a memorial proclaiming the immortality of a noble, atavistic way of life.

Before *Nanook,* in the words of Arthur Calder-Marshall, Flaherty was "the son of a mining prospector," who "because he loved the North so much went back there to make a film." But from the moment he accepted Jesse Lasky's offer of employment at Paramount, "Flaherty was a film director, an explorer in search of film subjects and the money to make them." Lasky's telegram, as quoted by Flaherty, exhorted him to "go off somewhere and make me another *Nanook.*" But in most respects, *Moana* is *Nanook's* polar opposite: from the frozen subarctic to the South Seas; from a family fighting the elements to stay alive, to a society so lacking in hardship that it must invent a ritual of pain as the conduit to manhood; from Flaherty as explorer-collaborator to Flaherty as filmmaker-observer; from *Nanook* the film to *Moana* the production.

For anyone who has seen both films, the temptation to make moral judgments—about both Flaherty and his subject—is strong. Nanook is an emblem of primitive man at his courageous, pacific best; Moana, the nice-looking young Samoan, is an icon of the childman at play, a prophecy of man in the automated future. There's also a temptation to blame the Samoans for an accident of geography that makes of their lives an eventless idyll, as opposed to Nanook's epic struggle. What can be said is that, without the bone-chilling conflict that a situation like Nanook's offers Flaherty—and without Flaherty's comradely commitment to a man rather than his contractual commitment to a studio—his films run the risk of degenerating into pretty pictures.

Certainly *Moana* is very pretty. Flaherty's camera (making exquisite use of the new panchromatic stock) catches light glistening off the water, or off the Samoans' mocha-colored skin, with all the dappled silkiness of a William Daniels portrait of Garbo. But to say this is already to note a transition in Flaherty from artist to technician and to suggest that, after making a masterpiece, Flaherty composed an étude. Though he films the native craft of tattooing with the same care he had shown toward Nanook's ice-cutting, Flaherty's respect seems trivialized here: The craftsmanship is not elemental but ornamental—as is the film. Only at the end of *Moana* does he come to grips with the static, undramatic quality of Samoan life, as the camera stoops and stops to contemplate a lovely young boy, in a gaily colored bedspread, watched over by a loving mother—peace. But peace is not box office. Nor, more importantly, is it part of Flaherty's obsessive concern to hear his own voice above the ta-pocketapocketa of the Industrial Age. Ironically, Flaherty was now discovering that, to express this viewpoint on film, he must teach himself the mechanisms of the movie camera—and try to ingratiate himself with the motion-picture industry. The story of *Moana* is the record of Flaherty's attempt to learn these hard lessons.

One mechanism Flaherty never could fathom was the movie mogul's mind. As the film maker's career progressed, his clout with the major distributors diminished to the vanishing point; and, after *Nanook* (a Pathé release) and *Moana* (Paramount), the films he'd hoped would have universal appeal were seen largely by bureaucrats and buffs. The history of his 1926 experimental short *The Twenty-Four Dollar Island* is instructive. Subtitled "a camera impression of New York," the film presents Manhattan as a skyscraper ghost town, with the spectral movements of tugboats on the East River recalling the entrance into Bremen of Nosferatu's charnel cargo—a sort of Styx and stone. Its temperament and technique are hardly mainstream Flaherty, and its importance to him would seem to have been as a celluloid sketch pad for some unspecified future project. But in light of his career's subsequent turn, the final disposition of *The Twenty-Four Dollar Island* is poignant and ominous; it was cut from two reels to one and used as the backdrop for a stage show at the Roxy Theatre.

In 1926 John Grierson saw *Moana* and called it a "documentary" film, thus baptizing a genre and investing Flaherty with its spiritual paternity. But it's really Grierson who deserves to be called "Father of the Documentary Film"; Flaherty was more precisely its godfather (in the pre-Puzo sense). You can see the difference between these two giants in a sequence from *Industrial Britain,* a film Flaherty began in 1931 and left for Grierson to complete. Five years earlier, Flaherty had shot a crude fourteen-minute study, called *The Pottery Maker* for The Metropolitan Museum. Now, in *Industrial Britain,* his camera homes in on the beautiful, clay-caked hands of a strapping young potter at work at the wheel. It is an image (like many from Flaherty's later films) of great formal and tonal beauty, and Flaherty would certainly have let it speak, by itself, its admiration for yet another obsolescent skill. But Grierson's narrator must exclaim—and exhort—"Look at those hands!" If Flaherty would have us understand (in his own way, and in our own good time), Grierson would have us learn (and *now,* because tomorrow may be too late). And if the wild Irishman was both anthropologist and artist, the wily Scot was both sociologist and socialist. In its final form, therefore, *Industrial Britain* celebrates individual craftsmanship only to the extent that it can be bent toward communal consumption, if not mass production.

Given this dialectic, it's odd that Flaherty's next film, *Man of Aran,* should be criticized by Griersonians as dramatically sensational and socially irrelevant. Flaherty had gone off to the Aran Islands and, instead of returning with a fulsome indictment of the absentee landlordism responsible for Aran's poverty, he brought back a tale of dewy-eyed urchins and anachronistic sea monsters. Grierson himself, in a "defense" of the film, put the argument gently but pointedly: "I like my braveries to emerge otherwise than from the sea, and stand otherwise than against the sky. I imagine they shine as bravely in the pursuit of Irish landlords as in the pursuit of Irish sharks."

Here Grierson is skillfully indulging in a mode of attack he calls foolish earlier in his remarks: "to complain of a pear that it lacks the virtue of a pomegranate." The pear is the Flaherty documentary, which he created and which remained uniquely his own; the pomegranate is the Grierson documentary, the film of social realism, which *Man of Aran* never pretended to be. Flaherty's films were epic, not episodic; they were built around a hero, not around a cast of faceless proletarian thousands. (*The Land* proves the great exception to both these rules.) As for the anachronism of the Aran Islanders hunting basking sharks—which they had not done for fifty years—this was not a new device for Flaherty. He had dressed Nanook in more "genuine" Eskimo costumes, and taught him a more picturesque method of catching seals. He had subjected Moana to the painful and unnecessary ordeal of tattooing, and indeed painted as a primitive paradise a Samoan island that had for years been wallowing in British Imperial corruption. But Flaherty's concern was always for the truth, not facts: "One often has to distort a thing to catch its true spirit."

Still, if *Man of Aran* should not be condemned for what it is not, it can be criticized for what it is. For the first time, we can see the lyrical naïveté of *Nanook* solidifying into an attitude. We can follow Flaherty's eye as it wanders away from the people and toward the sea, away from individuals and toward archetypes. We can sense a conscious attempt on Flaherty's part to create a pictorial style; and here, the chiaroscuro compositions (charcoal rock, black-clad figures against a gray sky) are light-years removed from the natural grandeur of *Nanook,* the easy elegance of *Moana.* We suspect that Flaherty's spiritual kinship with nature is in danger of degenerating into either adoration or exploitation; the spectacular shark-hunting and sea-fury scenes smack of (very) special effects. And for the first time, we dare to put impertinent questions to the characters in a Flaherty film: If life is so tough, why don't they move? It's a measure of *Man of Aran's* failure, by Flaherty standards, that the appropriate analogues are not other Flaherty films; for *Aran* suggests nothing so much as a harpoon-gun wedding between the abstract immersion of Steiner's $H_2O$ and the narrative bathos of *Ryan's Daughter.*

By the late 1930s, Flaherty was in trouble. Jobless, broke, and angry, he had just failed in his third try at collaborating with the commercial-film enemy (M-G-M and W. S. Van Dyke on *White Shadows of the South Seas,* F. W. Murnau on *Tabu,* and finally Alexander Korda on *Elephant Boy*).

Career ironies were becoming unpleasant, and inevitable. Within two years of *Nanook,* Flaherty had gone to Hollywood, and Nanook had gone back north to die of starvation; within a year of *Elephant Boy,* Sabu had gone to Hollywood, and Flaherty was left in London, where he might have succumbed to the artistic death of stagnation if Pare Lorentz hadn't invited him back home, to make a movie for the U.S. Film Service.

America was one country Flaherty had never really explored. Geographically and metaphysically, his life's itinerary had led him to primitive lands in search of timeless truths. On four continents, he had found patches of land—of sub-zero solemnity (*Nanook*), tropical torpor (*Moana*), oceanic ferocity (*Man of Aran*), jungle impenetrability (*Elephant Boy*)—that Nature, in its setting of climate and character, seemed to be offering to Flaherty as a ready-made metaphor. And each film had been a safari into the darkest memories of the race, an expedition to capture on film the endangered species of living legends before they receded irrevocably into myth. But now, in the America of 1939, his government sponsors had assigned him the task of resolving on film a horrifyingly tangled mass of contradictions and complexities. Why, at the tail end of the Great Depression, were so many migrant workers out of work? How could they be (in Calder-Marshall's words) "near to starving in a land where farmers were being paid by the government not to raise hogs?" Where had the government failed its people?

Flaherty's refusal to absolve the New Deal with a fast shuffle made *The Land* a failure as propaganda (the film was effectively suppressed, and to some degree remains so today), but his willingness to explore the faces of America's dispossessed, without flinching or equivocating, helped make it a great document. The film's very lack of cohesion reflects, in the splinters of a broken economic mirror, a human catastrophe too overwhelming to be shoehorned into the microcosm of a narrative scenario. Instead of a single, simple vision, *The Land* projects a series of eloquent images. A dozen men crowd around a foreman; one stays outside the group, sitting hopelessly. A dying cow, a dead house, dead-eyed children—all are still standing. Unemployed scarecrows of men stare into the camera; it seems they have all the time in the world to pose for film portraits that echo Dorothea Lange even as they prefigure Diane Arbus. An old Negro, oblivious to the camera, emerges from a rat-infested, death-corroded house, looks around, sees nothing, polishes and rings an old carillon, surveys the land again, says, "Where they all gone?" and returns to his home, closing the door on his unseen voyeurs to converse at peace with his demons. A boy sleeps, his hands moving; his mother says, "He thinks he's picking peas"; she strokes his hair and the hands stop; as the scene fades out, the hands start moving again.

*The Land* is a film without heroes or villains—only victims. The closest Flaherty comes to an *éminence grise* is the abstract shadow of mechanized farming, which turned farmers into foremen and "farm hands" into exactly that: factory workers on an endless belt. And the closest he comes to an optimistic conclusion—if we discount, as we should, the apocalyptical prose announcing the advent of "the ever-normal granary"—is his camera's infatuation with contour farming. Flaherty had always delighted in swirls and eddies of snow (*Nanook*), sea (*Moana, Man of Aran*), and smoke (*The Twenty-Four Dollar Island*). Here it's the soil. In long, graceful helicopter shots, you can see his eye take in the rolling, man-made designs of earth, and feel his hands caress this huge, gorgeous, *functional* sculpture.

It's appropriate that Flaherty should proclaim his independence from the state-sponsored documentary by finding this particular aesthetic solution to their pressing political problem. Certainly this is the only "solution" *The Land* offers. After limning the beauty of this "pattern that will hold the soil," this "new design" (which, as Flaherty has shown in other films and other lands, is as old as the earth), he asks, "But what about the people?" It is an unanswered question. *The Land* is Flaherty's belated attempt to come to terms with the twentieth century: a fragmented work on an insoluble puzzle. Typical of its maker, a man with a magnetic sense for unpopular truths, the film dared to ask the one question no machine man could answer.

At the end of the war, Flaherty recalled Helen van Dongen—the editorial mind behind his camera eye on *The Land,* a collaborator who was really a coauthor—into his service, and enlisted the young Rickey Leacock as cameraman, for a project commissioned by Standard Oil. This time, there was a story: of a half-wild boy whose exploration of the bayou fauna intersects with his discovery of Civilization in the guise of a Humble drilling team. At first suspicious of the men and their machines, the boy soon becomes friendly, and the film ends, suitably, with mutual economic and spiritual blessings. However naïve or dissembling this scenario may sound in a time of controversy over oil spills, pipelines, and tax shelters, there's no doubting Flaherty's emotional and artistic commitment to this, his last film. For *Louisiana Story* we can read the artist's autobiography: The bayou boy is an icon of Young Bob, the adventurer and fantast; and the man who plays his father is a Flaherty look-alike and talk-alike. (At the punch line of one of his stories, you can hear the film crew cracking up with laughter—and perhaps a sense of *déjà vu*.)

*Louisiana Story* marks the signing of Flaherty's détente with the machine. And his sympathetic treatment of the great oil derrick is a triumph of humanist anthropomorphism. Gliding through the luminous backwater, the derrick has the silent mystery and ponderous grace of some prehistoric monarch, an aristocratic relative of the area's alligators and water snakes; but once anchored, it willingly becomes man's servant, honored to have been domesticated in a worthy cause. (And when it leaves, the film tells us, it even cleans up after itself.) In the climactic explosion of the gusher, nature is tamed but not enslaved. As with *Man of Aran* and *The Land*, Flaherty spotlights lone figures standing by impotently as nature whips itself across the screen; but here the force is benign, productive— and all because of man's ingenuity and craftsmanship. As nocturnal meditations on the machine, *The Land* is a nightmare symphony, and *Louisiana Story* is a dream play.

Flaherty's features trace a line from actuality (*Nanook*) to ideal (*Moana*) to possibility (*Man of Aran*) to miracle (*Louisiana Story*). With each succeeding film the narrative becomes fuller and more clearly defined until, at last, Flaherty made a fiction film with real people. In its relaxed pace, rural *genius loci,* and subjective use of a child's viewpoint, *Louisiana Story* recalls some of Clarence Brown's 1940s work (*National Velvet, The Yearling, Intruder in the Dust*). Indeed, Flaherty even indulges in a bit of Hollywood Darwinism, with his film's survival of the nicest. One reason for the generally ecstatic response of Flaherty's long-time admirers to *Louisiana Story* may have been their hope that its relative accessibility might suggest to the moguls that finally the old renegade could make a personal but salable film for them. If this was so, their hope was futile. Flaherty had no sustaining work between the completion of *Louisiana Story* and his death three years later.

There were really three Robert Flahertys: man, myth, and moviemaker. To judge the third, it would be helpful if we had never heard of the first two—if we could bring to the criticism of his films the same innocent eye that he brought to his film subjects. The enshrinement of the Flaherty myth, which has become a minor industry, clouds that vision. As a result, Flaherty's reputation is in danger of drowning in a swamp of hype and half-truths, when it could keep afloat, easily and gracefully, on its own. The man is dead. The myth must die. The films will live.

# John Ford

JOHN FORD was born Sean O'Feeny in Maine in 1894, the youngest child of a large Irish immigrant family, and died in California in 1973. He grew up speaking both English and Gaelic, and later made some of his best-known films in Irish settings. He came to Hollywood in 1913 and did small acting parts in a number of films, among them Griffith's The Birth of a Nation (1915). He was hired mainly to direct Westerns starring Harry Carey in 1917, and had made some thirty films by 1921, nearly all of them lost. Only a dozen of his silent films survive today, including one that made him famous, The Iron Horse (1924), which shows the influence of Griffith.

Ford became established as an all-around director in the 1930s. In Men Without Women (1930) he began a successful collaboration with the scriptwriter Dudley Nichols, who worked on thirteen more of his films, including The Lost Patrol (1934), The Informer (1935), Steamboat Round the Bend (1935), Stagecoach (1939), and The Long Voyage Home (1940). Ford became particularly recognized during this period for his high-toned but robust literary adaptations, including The Informer and The Grapes of Wrath (1940), but these films have worn less well than the series of Westerns he initiated with Stagecoach and resumed after World War II with My Darling Clementine (1946) and the so-called Cavalry trilogy (Ford Apache, 1948; She Wore a Yellow Ribbon, 1949; and Rio Grande, 1950). The stark lighting, garish acting, and overall visual stylization of The Informer show the influence of F. W. Murnau and German expressionism, which can still be seen in the town shoot-out scenes in Stagecoach, My Darling Clementine, and later films. In the postwar Westerns, however, Ford also evolved a fluid, naturalistic style with a strong sense of milieu and locale. With Stagecoach he discovered both Monument Valley in Arizona, where many of his later Westerns were shot, and John Wayne, who until then had been relegated to a series of undistinguished films. After World War II, with the help of a stock company of talented actors (especially Wayne) and a new scenarist (Frank S. Nugent), Ford would give these settings an increasing resonance of myth and memory. His films became reflections on the American past and meditations on timeless themes of courage, honor, justice, and community.

During the war, Ford had been on active duty with the Navy as head of the Field Photography Branch, and many of his later films emphasize naval settings and the problems of men at war, infused with the sense of the past and the delicacies of personal conflict that so mark his Westerns. Like Hawks, to whom he is often compared, Ford is intrigued by professionalism and the professional, usually male, group. Yet, with his meditative weight and rollicking Irish good humor, Ford is also more attuned to the abrasive individuality and eccentricity of the members of

*the group than to their submersion in camaraderie and courage. It is diffi-
cult to generalize about a career that includes more than one hundred
films. But Ford does seem drawn to stories of pioneers and immigrants,
people on the edge of civilization who somehow manage to keep and
nurture their humanity even while they face unprecedented challenges.
Again unlike Hawks, Ford makes women and family centers of value within
his celebration of community and historical tradition. Yet he also remains
fascinated by the individual, the men and women in the process of creating
themselves, or the hero whose cynicism is the measure of a buried idealism,
like Wayne in* The Man Who Shot Liberty Valance *(1962) or Anne Bancroft
in Ford's last film,* Seven Women *(1966).*

*By 1941 Ford had won three Academy Awards for direction (the
fourth would come in 1952 for* The Quiet Man*). But his critical reputation
after the war sank to that of a genre director, even though it was just in
these years that Ford was doing his deepest and most personal work, which
culminated in the major statement of* Liberty Valance. *There Wayne and
Jimmy Stewart (like Wayne and Henry Fonda in* Fort Apache*) represent
two conflicting approaches to life as well as two successive phases of
American history. One is that of the Man with the Gun, the Westerner, the
old-style frontier individualist; the other, that of the Easterner, the dude
(or, in Fonda's case, the rigid West Point martinet), who belongs to the
new political order of impersonal justice and governmental authority that
has superseded the old West. As usual, Ford's sympathies are divided,
for his epic sense of American history—whether in the West, in the South,
or in New England, whether among the Irish, the Yankees, or the Indians—
demands not only that the future be seen and accepted but also that the past
be understood and mourned.*

*Much information can be gleaned from Peter Bogdanovich's* John Ford *(1967).
Critical studies include John Baxter's* The Cinema of John Ford *(1971),* Warren
French's *Filmguide to "The Grapes of Wrath" (1973),* John Ford *by Joseph
McBride and Michael Wilmington (1975), and* The John Ford Movie Mystery *by
Andrew Sarris (1976).*

# The Noble Outlaw

## Joseph McBride and Michael Wilmington

### "Straight Shooting"

From guesswork and from Ford's descriptions, it had been possible to formulate a mental composite of his early Westerns which went like this: Carey, rugged, candid and unaffected, plays a "saddle tramp" akin to William S. Hart's "good bad man," but more volatile, more human, the precursor of the John Wayne-James Stewart line rather than the laconic Gary Cooper-Randolph Scott model. His picaresque ramblings bring him in contact with an increasingly interesting gallery of Ford character actors, the villains probably less flamboyant than their descendants, the girls probably more a plot necessity than the individualized, strong-willed ladies of Ford's maturity. But as Ford told Peter Bogdanovich: "They weren't shoot-'em-ups, they were character stories. Carey was a great actor, and we didn't dress him up like the cowboys you see on TV—all dolled up . . . Carey was sort of a bum, a saddle tramp, instead of a great, bold, gun-fighting hero. All this was fifty per cent Carey and fifty per cent me. He always wore a dirty blue shirt and an old vest, patched overalls, very seldom carried a gun—and he didn't own a hat." Plot synopses indicate that these early Westerns clung doggedly to the theme of moral reformation—Harry is repeatedly brought out of his aimless frontier solitude into conflict with social injustice, and forced to opt for the homesteaders against the outlaws. Later Ford Westerns, such as *My Darling Clementine* and *Wagon Master,* also fit this pattern, and it was only in his 1950s and 1960s Westerns, like *The Searchers* and *Liberty Valance,* that Ford settled firmly on an entirely unidealized view of the civilized order. There, both the wilderness *and* civilization are seen as dead-ends, and the hero's dilemma becomes tragically insoluble.

From the hindsight of fifty-seven years and 137 films, the most interesting section of *Straight Shooting* (1917) is the long dénouement in which Cheyenne Harry, after marshalling his outlaw friends to save the

From *John Ford* by Joseph McBride and Michael Wilmington (New York: Da Capo Press, 1975). Reprinted by permission of the publisher.

homesteaders from the ranchers, is forced to choose between civilization and the wilderness. The entire film foreshadows *The Searchers:* the obsessive framing of characters through doorways (the introductory shot of Danny Morgan is identical to that of Martin Pawley in *The Searchers*— jumping off his horse, seen through the doorway of the home), the attack on the isolated family, the girl's vacillation between the rootless Harry and the tame, domesticated Danny (a very young Hoot Gibson). And John Wayne revealed recently that the moving gesture he makes at the end of *The Searchers*, grasping his arm protectively as Olive Carey and her family vanish into the home, was a conscious echo of a Harry Carey gesture which occurs near the end of *Straight Shooting.* (Wayne said he imitated Carey because he thought the gesture made him seem lonely and also because "his widow was on the other side of that door, and he was the man Pappy said taught him his trade.") Ethan rides away from the homestead into the desert at the end of *The Searchers;* Harry stays with the girl at the end of *Straight Shooting.* But it would be misleading to see this as a simple affirmation of the civilized order Ford would later come to reject. . . .

## *"Stagecoach"*

*Stagecoach* was Ford's triumphant return to the Western after a thirteen-year hiatus. Since *Three Bad Men* in 1926, he had been working in a variety of genres, honing his style, developing a greater facility with actors, and proving his credentials as a versatile and "hard-nosed" craftsman. In the 1920s at Fox, Ford was often forced to do films in which he had little interest. When he branched out to other studios in the 1930s, he began to win back some of the creative freedom he had enjoyed in the early silent days at Universal. With this went a growing desire for critical recognition, a desire evidently springing more from a need to keep his new-found freedom than from simple pride, because after World War II, when his status in the industry was secure, he again began making films primarily for his own amusement.

But in 1939, when he returned to the genre which had preoccupied him at the beginning of his career, it was with a story of Balzacian scope and gusto. *Stagecoach* revolutionized the Western. Nowadays it is fashionable to speak of it as "the Western which created the clichés," but *Stagecoach* did not create clichés nor even sustain them. It defined Western archetypes and created a new frame of reference rich in irony and sophistication. It was not a new realism which Ford introduced to the genre, as reviewers of the day claimed (one could argue that the Western is innately fantastic), but a new sense of tradition and a new dramatic flexibility.

The effect of the film has been mixed. On the one hand, the self-consciousness is brought to the form has enabled the Western to continually transform itself, chameleon-like, to pressures in the society which produces it. Before *Stagecoach,* the Western seemed to be dying; after *Stagecoach,* it became the one permanently popular film genre. Fritz Lang was not exaggerating when he said that the Western is to America what the Niebelungen Saga is to Germany, for the traditions to which Ford gave definitive shape have proved capable of sustaining the most extreme inflections. On the other hand, Dudley Nichols's schematic and overtly allegorical screenplay has encouraged the misconception that the Western form is worthy of discussion only when it is used to teach a moral lesson. Making it possible for "prestige" directors to make Westerns without having it seem that they were slumming, *Stagecoach* has left a long trail of bastard children, "Westerns for people who don't like Westerns," of which *High Noon* is the most typical. Ford has not helped matters by claiming that *Stagecoach* "sort of blazed a trail for the adult Western," as if his early classics and those of William S. Hart were insignificant.

What makes *Stagecoach* so durable, however, is not its historical significance but the vividness with which it creates a dream landscape from the American past and peoples it with simple and striking characters who, despite their reincarnation in countless "A" and "B" Westerns, still retain a believable ambivalence and depth. *Stagecoach* bears a family resemblance to the popular omnibus films of the 1930s (*Grand Hotel, Shanghai Express, Lost Horizon, The Lady Vanishes,* and the Ford-Nichols collaboration of 1934, *The Lost Patrol*) in which a colorful collection of characters from different social strata are thrown together in dangerous or exotic circumstances. The "chance" society of these films is typically treated as a microcosm, with the characters acting out among themselves the social tensions which interest the writer and director; what seemed to delight Ford most in *Stagecoach* was the possibility of glorifying disrepute by plunging a group of pariahs into danger and having the most apparently abject of them emerge as heroes. (If Ford had not suffered from the critical neglect of his later Westerns, he might be able to savor a delicious irony. A film which exalts outcasts over the members of "respectable" society made the Western respectable.)

The passengers on the stage are not so much a social microcosm as a counter-society, like the Irish revolutionaries in *The Informer.* They include a drunken doctor, a former Confederate officer turned cardsharp, a timid whisky drummer who is constantly mistaken for a clergyman, a prostitute, an escaped convict, a bank embezzler and the pregnant wife of a Calvary lieutenant, whose child is born during the journey. Just before he made the film, Ford gleefully announced, "There isn't a single respectable character in the cast." He would seem to have overlooked the young mother, but an Army wife has little social currency back East and, besides, she guards her respectability so starchily (refusing to sit with the prostitute) that she makes it a mockery of decency. The other characters have all been thrown out of or are fleeing from the straightlaced town of Tonto, ruled by the dour Ladies' Law and Order League, who march to Ford's favorite hymn, "Shall We Gather at the River?" (Critics who complain of Ford's "orthodoxy" should be required to account for moments like this.)

Although Ford and Nichols adapted the movie from an Ernest Haycox story, *Stage to Lordsburg,* Ford has speculated that Haycox actually took his idea from Guy de Maupassant's *Boule de Suif,* the story of a prostitute and prominent members of the bourgeoisie traveling in a carriage through war-torn France. It would be fairly easy to work out a symbolic reading of the plot and characters of *Stagecoach.* The coach is America, a nation of exiles, riven with warring and contradictory factions; the Indians are the wild forces of nature; the pregnant woman is Liberty; the banker is the corrupt Republican Establishment, the spokesman for selfish individualism; the benevolent sheriff riding shotgun is Roosevelt; the Plummer Gang are the Axis powers; Buck, the driver, and his Mexican wife "Hoolietta" are the ethnic mixtures which give the country its democratic character.

But like all good fables, *Stagecoach* has a universal application. It is the idea of the noble outlaw, the "good bad man" represented most concretely by John Wayne as the Ringo Kid, which provides the film's centre. Outlaws (and outcasts in general) have always fascinated Ford not so much for their rebellion as for the subtle ways they are linked to the society which scorns them. They act *for* society in ways society cannot see, and they understand society better than society understands itself. Their rebellion (even at its most complex level, that of Ethan in *The Searchers*) is as much a matter of circumstance as of temperament. As Ringo puts it, "I guess you can't break out of jail and into society in the same week." His vendetta is a family matter—he is trying to avenge the murder of his father and brother. In the process, he symbolically ensures the continuance of the forces of order, by saving the Cavalryman's wife and child, and the destruction of the forces of anarchy, by outlasting the Indians and killing the corrupt Plummer family. At the end, with the sheriff's acquiescence, he rides towards the Mexican border to start his own family with Dallas, the prostitute (Claire Trevor).

The ending is a paean to primitivism, but it is important to realize that the film is endorsing primitivism as an *ideal* rather than as a viable reality. Ringo, the Rousseau noble savage, takes the law into his own hands, but he ultimately brings about the very Law and Order which the film attacks in its caricature of the overcivilized ladies of Tonto, described by Dallas as "worse than Apaches." *Stagecoach* leaves the question of American imperialism, the Cavalry vs. the Indians, tantalizingly unresolved. The Indians are totally one-dimensional here, but Ford's attitude to the role of the Cavalry, which will undergo complex metamorphoses in his later work as his interest in the Indians grows, is strangely ambiguous: he has the corrupt, hypocritical banker continually abuse the Cavalry, and the priggish young mother defend it. Ringo, the prime mover in the tale, more or less ignores the threat of the Indians and the authority of the Cavalry, relying purely on his own resources. The gambler views the Indian threat with a Griffith-like Aryan rectitude. The barrel of his pistol protrudes into the close-up of the mother praying frantically in the last moments of the attack, and he is saved from firing his last bullet into her head (a copy of a scene in Griffith's 1913 Western *The Battle at Elderbush Gulch,* with Lillian Gish) only by being shot himself seconds before we hear the Cavalry bugle.

Ringo's showdown with the Plummers has been regarded by some critics as an anticlimax, coming as it does after the legendary chase across the Monument Valley salt flats and the Cavalry rescue. But it is only through his heroic action in the chase that Ringo wins the sheriff's respect and with it the right to bypass civilized law and carry out primitive justice. And the attack, which significantly occurs just before the stage reaches its destination, is the final test of the group's ability to survive. In the end their salvation depends on the appearance of a *deus ex machina*. But the Indians are just as much a part of the machinery of chance as the Cavalry, and as Ford has pointed out, if the chase had been staged realistically, with the Indians shooting the lead horses of the coach instead of firing madly into the air, "it would have been the end of the picture." Both the challenge and the salvation are metaphorical. What was it, after all, that threw the outcasts together but the rupture of order in their own lives? The war-ravaged desert through which the stage passes (the curtains on the windows for ever whipping in the wind) becomes a metaphor for the instability of this archetypal primitive community, thrown together of necessity and chance and forced to rediscover the meaning of society. The passengers' vindication or condemnation is sealed by the time they enter anarchic, wide-open Lordsburg (a puckishly American diminution of "Heaven"). Their real destination is within themselves.

Since the group in *Stagecoach* is an inversion of a stable community, it is poetically logical that the most disreputable characters—the drunken doctor, the prostitute, and the convict—perform best in the two major crises (the childbirth and the Indian attack, life and death). As Jean Renoir (who has called this his favorite Ford film) did in *La Règle du jeu* the same year, Ford develops his social thesis by minutely examining the tensions which threaten to shatter the group's order. The rules of Ford's game are simplicity and direct attack. At one extreme, there are the community's rhetoricians: the gambler Hatfield (John Carradine) and the banker Gatewood (Berton Churchill). Hatfield, glacial and stiff, is decked out impeccably. The rote nature of his chivalry is emphasized by his corpse-like attenuation and his deep, over-cultivated voice; his is the nobility of the suicide, the passing-on of dead forms and lifeless ideals. Gatewood, who spends most of the journey fulminating against big government and taxes, clutches the briefcase containing his embezzlement. Against these two figures, the simple, instinctual gallantry of Ringo and Dallas takes on great eloquence. It is an eloquence expressed not in rhetoric but in action: when the pregnant woman sits piously aloof from Dallas at the dinner table, Ringo nonchalantly helps Dallas with her chair and sits next to her; when the woman enters labor, Dallas acts as midwife and then sits up all night holding the baby.

Somewhere in between these extremes of fraud and candor is Doc Boone (Thomas Mitchell), whose flushed, unruly features and comic versifying mask an intense privacy of emotion. The poet of the community, he alone is able to see the situation from the outside and articulate its meaning. His is a natural nobility which accepts its own limitations and absurdity, and he often acts as Ford's spokesman, both verbally and through reaction shots in the moments of crisis. When a vote is taken on whether the journey should continue in the face of imminent attack, Boone comments, "I am not only a philosopher, I am also a fatalist. Somewhere, some time, there may be the right bullet or the wrong bottle waiting for Josiah Boone. Why worry when or where?" Simultaneously Hatfield cuts a deck of cards and comes up with the ace of spades. But he casts his "aye" with the doctor. This note of fatalism is picked up at the end, when the brutish Luke Plummer, waiting in the El Dorado saloon for the showdown with Ringo, is dealt the "dead man's hand" of aces and eights. The idea is not quite predestination, but rather a stoic, almost comic awareness of individual responsibility. What happens to a man, no matter what the extenuating circumstances, is finally determined by what he *is*—by what he demonstrates of himself in the face of circumstances.

Boone does not let his alcoholism destroy his ability to function. Religious and military men in Ford's films are often frustrated in their pursuit of transient or illusory goals, but doctors have a simple and concrete function, the preservation and transmission of life, and their alcoholism is often a result of this awful responsibility. It is no accident that the whisky drummer who keeps Boone supplied is thought to be a minister: the bag from which he produces his bottles resembles a doctor's instrument kit or the valise in which a priest carries his wine for the sacrament of Communion. The physical agony which Boone undergoes in sobering up for the delivery of the child is a metaphor for the mental and moral agony of the doctor's role. Like the noble outlaw, he is both the savior and the cynosure of society.

As Dallas and Ringo disappear from the dark, boisterous streets of Lordsburg, Boone comments, "Well, they're saved from the blessings of civilization." The sheriff, removing his badge, offers him a drink, and the doctor replies, after a grand moment of protraction, "Just one." This exchange (not in the script, which ended on a last bit of exposition about the murder plot) adds the perfect note of irony to the film's portrait of society. The primitive couple's flight into the freedom of the wilderness is seen through the eyes of society's watchdogs, the lawman and the doctor-poet. It is as if they are watching their own dream being realized at a distance—a dream whose beauty lies in its contrivance and improbability. This is Ford's vision of primitivism and the American past. We can feel it, watch it and cherish it, but we cannot quite touch or recapture it.

# Mirage of the Sunken Bathtub

## Parker Tyler

Not long ago, at a New York repertory theater specializing in Russian films and those of a proletarian nature, there appeared a most illuminating double bill consisting of Hollywood's most generous contribution to the propaganda cause of the underprivileged classes. The more important item was the version of John Steinbeck's novel about Okies, *The Grapes of Wrath,* and the lesser was a straightforward propaganda offering, which took for its title a casual phrase from one of President Roosevelt's speeches—*One Third of a Nation,* denoting the percentage of the inadequately housed in the United States.

*The Grapes of Wrath* was directed by Hollywood's best director, John Ford, and thus was supplied not only with the latest style gadgets for speaking cinematically—the year was 1940—but with those effective emphases in dramatic and pictorial speech for which Mr. Ford's work is noted. The feeling for the flattish, desolated landscape from which the Joad family is unwillingly uprooted by circumstance is beautifully rendered by the camera, especially when the truck, overloaded with all the family possesses, including too many of themselves, starts out on its cross-country trek and in each successive shot seems to lose some of its visual detail, so that when it hits the main highway, it is no more than, like some dark ship at sea, an untethered entity of abstract design, moving small under the huge sky. In these shots the lens is not too fine. There is a sort of newsreel coarseness about the blacks and whites and their contiguous edges that makes one feel the frayed margins of everything—the boards of the ramshackle house that the Joads leave, exactly like that in the less serious *Tobacco Road,* the weeds, the clothes and belongings of the Joad family, and their very lives. These first scenes, just after Tommy Joad is released from prison on parole, are almost flawless in their feeling for the quality of the Joads and the spot of nature where they have existed.

As the truck of fortune approaches the land of milk and honey where the Okies expect to find work and happiness, California, the gradual transformation of the quality of the natural scene, the figures of the Joads, and the pattern of the story create an odd logic. That history provides a striking parallel to the Joad migration was doubtless present in Mr. Steinbeck's mind when he devised his original highly wordy fable. Despite its evident merits the novel is no better than second-rate literature, but the poetic and ironic analogy of the Okies' saga with that of the families who settled pioneer America and also of those who abandoned their homes and traveled to California during the Gold Rush is quite valid and, protracted as it is, imparts to the film a simple, eloquent arabesque, unhappily weakened at its climax.

Some families fattened in the ambiguously golden land of California; many did not. As the capitalistic structure gained in significance and strength, those who had struck gold and knew how to capitalize on it became the sons of heaven; the many and the less clever remained definitely sons of earth. The Okies of course are the sons of the earth inherited from those who may have deliberately abandoned their share of it generations before in the flight for the pot at the end of the rainbow. Yet in our time the poor whites, unable to make enough grow from the land in order to exist themselves and frowned on even by nature, have been lured to California by what might better be termed the will-o'-the-wisp of the promise of jobs, and there have become itinerant workers whose only subsequent blessing was the war industry. At the time of which the novel speaks, fruit-growers and other industrialists in California distributed thousands of leaflets offering work when only hundreds of jobs were available. The trick of the ranchers was to lessen the wages for fruit picking through the plethora of labor. The Joads learn this ruse only when it is too late for them to turn back. Hence they eventually run into a strike at a big peach farm and innocently are led to the slaughter as strikebreakers.

*The Grapes of Wrath*, like novels of Zola with a similar intention, falls automatically into the naturalistic pattern, and Mr. Ford's direction has borne this admirably in mind. As *The Informer* originally proved, he is the best casting director in Hollywood, and in casting the Joads he was phenomenally successful. Although a bit too pretty of feature, Henry Fonda's big-boned face and tall, spare limbs make him an excellent Tommy, and Jane Darwell's massive face with its finely expressive eyes is striking enough in its homeliness to make Ma Joad an apt and memorable image, comparable to what we think of at the words "Mother Earth." In particular

336 JOHN FORD

Grandpa Joad, who stages a sit-down strike at the last moment before leaving home, is marvelously acted, and the subsequent scenes of his death and that of Grandma Joad, at different stages of the journey, are very well handled. The elderly Joads prove too frail to withstand the violence of the uprooting. Along with their deaths goes some of the film's naturalistic feeling. Not that incident and episode in this part of the story are not well realized. The incident of the two spic-and-span gas-station attendants who wonder that human beings can live, as the Okies do, like animals . . . the awkward and self-conscious charity of the roadside diner's proprietor, his waitress, and the lunching truck drivers toward the foodless plight of the Joads—so typical of hard-boiled American sentiment and here not in the least exaggerated . . . the scenes in the unbearably sordid workers' camps . . . all this is depicted with unusual artistry, but these isolated scenes seem smartly efficient somehow, a part of the gathering narrative art of the cinema, which gains ground with the truck as it speeds toward California, the land of Goldwyn and colleagues. We may note here that this state is the site of the biggest industry in American art, the very material of the present book; thus a symbolic appropriateness attaches to the fact that as streets, roads, and countryside become neater and cleaner as the wheels of the Joad truck turn, the movie craft shows its stuff and reveals a surface increasingly city-planned. After all, fruit and movies have made California what it is today. I am not precisely complaining about the course of Mr. Steinbeck's story; rather I am showing that it can boast of more than a simple truthfulness.

As the fortunes of the Joads, once in California, continue black despite the sun-drenched scenery, and as Tommy, backed by his friend, the "red" ex-preacher, gets mixed up in a ruckus with the private guards on the peach farm and kills one of them, the miseries of this family and of the other workers are almost too bitter for the spectator to bear. One feels like leaving the theater, obliterating such rock-bottom suffering from the sight. Of course one stays, for, as expected, the pressure is eventually relieved, and suddenly one is shown the Joad truck lumbering underneath a decorative wooden arch whose sign reads, in smaller letters below the camp name, "Department of Agriculture." Like magic a pleasant white-trousered man appears before the truck and informs the Joads that premises within are available to them at a dollar a week; his description of sanitation facilities makes the new ground the family has struck seem like a golden fairyland indeed and hence hard to believe. One's impulse is to think, "Only a camouflaged trap—another blow!" But it is all bona fide, true, for the simple reason that the government, with one of the various national agencies that were created during the depression period, has manifested itself to salvage the apparently hopeless cause of the Joads.

The little man in white pants is a *deus ex machina,* and at this point we are faced squarely with the true definition of the Joad burden. It is an affliction of the spirit proceeding from a specifically material foundation; that is, its remedy logically lies entirely in the material realm. True, the government does not provide work for the Joads, whose name is all that makes them individuals, for they number, of course, hundreds of thousands and actually, if we accept the phrase quoted above, compose one-third of the nation. Yet the fact is that the Okie class is on the lowest of the economic levels, and their spiritual unhappiness originates from lacking a great part of the time even the minimum for proper subsistence. It happens therefore that the chief focus in both pictures, *The Grapes of Wrath* and *One Third of a Nation,* is on the housing problem, the former applying to the country and the latter to the city, where old-law tenements make firetraps. The latter film is amateurishly done and somewhat naïve, but the artistic factor in no way alters the common economic physiognomy underlying both fables.

In *One Third of a Nation* the landlord class, whose economic interests are responsible for the maintenance of outmoded and dilapidated buildings, is proved to have its humane and class-conscious members by the example of the hero, who, coincidentally enough, falls in love with a young dweller in one of his unsound tenements. The plot in which he moves is as much a claptrap as his building a firetrap. There is no comparison in regard to seriousness of conception between Mr. Steinbeck's book and the bromidic fable of the other piece, but the correspondence of their patterns is not to be overlooked.

Doubtless the solution of an important part of human unhappiness on earth is the proper housing and feeding of its fulsome populations. But in the portrayals of art we not only view the human spirit in the sort of travail occasioned by inadequate solution of this vital problem but are privileged to discern the nature of what brings about the lessening of the anxiety as to mere animal existence and to note, moreover, the opinion of artistic creations as to the mechanism of this lessening, which permits human beings rest and peaceful blossoming of spirit as well as of body. At a moment when we were still engulfed in hideous war, the strategies of peacetime toward this special solution could not seem of paramount eloquence. But since it is a permanent problem, which the appearance of war only complicates and which at this postwar moment looms in international proportions, its structure may be regarded as highly fundamental.

If we turn for a moment to an illustration in movie art of a somewhat different kind of poverty and its attendant joylessness I think that a certain sharp illumination will delineate the features of the Joad misfortunes. In the French filmic version [by Jean Renoir] of Gorki's *The Lower Depths* pov-

erty coexists with a direct equivalent of *spiritual hopelessness;* in other
words the old, outused, and criminal outcast take refuge in obscure dor-
mitories at the mercy of a hard landlord, whose figure to them is that of
implacable fate. Eventually in the French film the landlord is mobbed to
death by his tenants, enraged by his personal abuse of a girl rather than by
any conception of his economic crime. The characters here, who range
from actors and philosophers to thieves, are all possessed with a feeling of
fatal resignation to their lot, a kind of stupor from which only the younger
and more active emerge to make a gesture toward reinstatement in normally comfortable and respectable society.

Despair is the spiritual keynote of these unfortunates—despair and the
outlet of lunacy. But in the American film the Okies as represented by the
Joads are an optimistic, energetic lot—they are honest workers, whereas
Gorki's characters are ex-workers, past professionals, and petty criminals;
in fact in having among them poet, philosopher, and actor they are a group
testifying to the frustrated ideals of humankind, not only to the frustrated
ideal of jobs for all but to every aborted ideal of culture, art, and humane
society. They are the dregs of a society that has ultimately failed on all
levels, whereas the Joads in essence are merely *economic* dregs, although
we cannot overlook that, realistically as they are portrayed, they can
hardly, considering the level of culture in the American rural working class
as a whole, be considered average, for they are in spiritual tone slightly
above the average. Still their economic identity is the determining factor,
and they visualize work as a means of obtaining their highest objective in
life, a certain standard of animal comfort; that is, all the gadgets of the
modern home, chiefly the sanitary ones. Their humanity, one might even
say their human culture, is made directly equivalent to this economic
aspiration, whereas, if the Joads of the world should grow so prosperous
that each family owned that celestial object, a radio, the question of what in
all their materialistic bliss they listened to would be, to put it succinctly, a
peach of an entirely different color.

When Ma Joad reaches the Department of Agriculture's camp and its
sanitary delights, her pleasure is given a status corresponding to the emotion of an embrace or, in the higher brackets of human culture, that of
poetic love; and one receives consequently a sense of her spiritual elevation. But as an ideal, viewed from a broader perspective than that of this
film, a decent home with all its modern appointments and conveniences
cannot evoke any emotional trace, however contingent, of sublimity. If we
wish to appreciate this sublimity, we have to descend to the cultural level
of the Joads, whose human animal dignity at this moment is presumed to
have the muted roseate colors of something like a religious experience . . .
as though conceivably Ma Joad had discovered in the spiritual atmosphere

of the camp a vision of one of those sunken bathtubs seen in the movies. In the case of *The Lower Depths* there is no question of the perspective, no necessity to reorientate one's culture. Here the human spirit is being tried in an isolation area that has the unalterable stigma of fate; most tenants of the dormitory have reached the end of the line and have faced a kind of self-evaluation that could never occur to a genuine Joad, who measures himself by his animal well-being—a well-being relative only, here today and gone tomorrow, but always nevertheless just beyond the horizon.

It is difficult not to detect in the pathetic fate metaphysic of the Joad family a viable element of the same cheap optimism, the same tawdry conception of happiness and fate, that dominates fifth-rate art in all its multiplicity as well as the majority of Hollywood products. True enough, if we look at the real Joads, which means looking at all the underprivileged, we applaud their courage and what in great part is their basic human decency. *The Lower Depths* has its rural equivalent in the spiritual malaise of the Jeeter Lesters and their families, who are ground into the dirt and never rise. But we must note that *Tobacco Road* is comedy, not tragicomedy; the latently lively animalism of the Lester family is an antic that provided endless fascination for audiences economically more fortunate than they. This play and movie formed that grotesque thing, an economic circus in which poverty was clown. But at least *Tobacco Road* had more mood than does *The Grapes of Wrath,* which rather naturally is less spiritually a tragedy on the screen than in the novel.

I am only vaguely familiar with Mr. Steinbeck's original treatment, but, as I said, plot and truck in the movie take their synchronous progress toward the end of the story while things in general become neater, more efficient, and artier. For one thing, whereas the effective scenes in the first workers' camp and then on the peach farm are supposedly in the open and, with one or two exceptions, photographed in actual daylight, the scenes in the sanitary government camp, while some are in the open and in daylight, have a studio sort of air. As a matter of fact, this is inevitable for the good reason that the camp itself has precisely that sort of air, being a relatively makeshift arrangement, containing homes neither permanent nor quite real, since each family throws up its tent on a flat wooden foundation for an indefinite time. New jobs may soon take the tenants elsewhere, not adjacent to such a camp; and indeed this is the way the picture ends, after Tommy has abandoned his family to join the organized effort of workers to improve their living conditions.

The plot, too, in the last quarter of the picture, takes on an increasingly conventional air, its final important scene being the highly arranged interview between Tommy and his mother. One night Tommy in his tent is awakened to see two police officers taking down the license number of his truck, signifying that the authorities are hot on his trail as a man-killer. He cannot be arrested on suspicion because it is the legal regulation of the camp that no arrests can take place without a warrant. A flaw in the plot's strength is that Tommy's flight is more or less compelled and not, as he rationalizes the fact to his mother during their interview, the direct result of his desire to join the fight for better labor conditions. He is abandoning her in her struggle to keep her family together because, he says, he believes it vitally important that help be given those who are called "reds" whenever they attempt to organize workers.

This is a conversion of the familiar situation in which the young stalwart leaves the farm in order to make his fortune, sometimes for a selfish reason, sometimes to save the farmstead. From the broad, historic arc of the pioneer trek the movie is now, willy-nilly, reduced to the more particular conventions of a more recent art. Truly this is a relatively signifi- cant and realistic version of a familiar situation, but the mellow sentiment, the display of emotion between mother and son, centered squarely as it is in the dramatic and camera focus, has a quality of banality despite the modernity and realism of the fable. Moreover, the commission of crime as an unforeseen contingency of fighting for a just cause, which commission has befallen Tommy, has a patina that testifies to a rather too honorable old age as well as too old an honorableness. A weakness in logic rather than in artistic invention is that, although Tommy's rough and rapid proletarian education brings him to the conclusion that he must regard a police badge as the sign of an enemy, the government-sponsored camp is deemed sacred ground on which no one with a badge may enter without permission or a full-blown warrant. But, according to the actual experience of the working class, there are no such charmed areas—as it has perpetual cause to re- member. The makers of the film, and possibly Mr. Steinbeck, chose to forget, in giving an incidental impression, that a warrant is simply some- thing that exists at the will of a judge of law, and a judge is arbitrary interpreter of the legal letter. This myth character of the camp corresponds to the historic legend of California as a land of golden opportunity as well as to the democratic myth of free expression in art, of which Hollywood takes peculiar advantage in this film.

Cops truly enough are made out an ornery and vicious lot in *The Grapes of Wrath,* but the point is that the worst of these officers of the law are deputies engaged by private interests, in other words only a little removed from being in substance uniformed gangsters or domestic storm troopers. Not only this fact conveys that these cops are not quite American. We are also given occasion to remember that whereas America may be a land of democracy, one must be realistic enough to understand that all individuals in it are not equally democratic. Hence grounds of political reasoning appear, and on these we recall the late President's attack on the economic royalists, those among the big capitalists who opposed his economic reforms. Suddenly the economic pattern of the film can be orientated to the propaganda viewpoint of liberal, reformist democracy as conceived by the historic New Deal government of the United States. Whence did the taxes come that enabled the government to build such camps for workers as the Joads found in California? Largely, and whether they liked it or not, from those very fruitgrowers who most viciously tried to break the strikes of fruit pickers.

The camp to which finally the Joads come as the first realization of their ideal goal is therefore merely a modest and tentative version of a housing project and a literal extension of the ideology of home relief. Quite unlike their comrades in morality, those of *Tobacco Road* as well as of *The Lower Depths,* the Joads have cleanliness for an ideal, with all that ideal implies with respect to material means. Earth is naturally dirty, and without considerable means nothing in our modern and especially our urban civilization can be properly clean. A similar discontentment afflicts the heroine of the other film, *One Third of a Nation,* which grapples forthrightly though clumsily with the housing situation in big cities. This young woman complains not only of the messiness of her domestic surroundings but especially of the fact that she has to undress before her father. . . .

Taking the longer view of the Joads' worldly ambition to be comfortably clean and well fed and housed, we must go beyond the formal conclusion of the film, with its note of grim hope for the struggle of the working classes, and speculate that perhaps a whole vulgar morality dangles at the end of the Joads' ideal, beyond their own limited sight but prevalent in modern society—I mean the primitive conception of moral cleanliness that originated in the scene of this country in the puritan moral code. For there is no trace of tragic catharsis in the experience of the Joads, nothing of transcendent beauty or power, unless it be that fugitive mirage of the sunken bathtub; they intuit nothing fatal in their misfortunes, which are just bad luck. Only Tommy, fortuitously tutored by the radical-minded ex-preacher, sees the ominous silhouette of the system overhanging them and finally seeks on principle to oppose it. In this movie an ambiguous morality, requiring stern justification of itself, is again identified with crime. *Ideological* compulsion here supplants *psychological* compulsion. But the film, like the novel, leaves off where more imaginative and serious fiction sagas of militant action in behalf of labor begin.

Perhaps it may seem gratuitous or exaggerated to say that the Joads can do no better, at best, than develop the vulgar, materialistic complacency of the middle class. But, as Ma Joad pathetically replies to Tommy's metaphors about how the many can exist in the one and the one in the many, she doesn't understand, because for all her solid virtues Ma can understand nothing but the most modest fundamentals of instinctive human decency. Well, perhaps the Joads *should* be taken more symbolically than their naturalistic mold seems to warrant; after all, they are proletarian symbols, not just people. But perhaps our two perspectives on them can be reconciled if we return to the point that as time and truck advance in the movie, cinema technique becomes more efficient.

The fact is, we are under no obligation to conceive the idea of moral cleanliness as limited to the narrowly puritanical. Modern psychology, through the technique of psychoanalysis, has given us a conception of moral cleanliness dominated not by vulgar material issues and a primitive notion of sexual decency but by a conception that relates to the modern scientific ideal of efficiency, of maintaining the normal working order of the personality in its subjective existence and its social relations—the same ideal that may have haunted the young woman who could not make up her mind if she really loved her soldier husband and who was assisted, when she did make up her mind, by a modern instrument of efficiency, the telephone. The psychic knot of psychoanalysis, which sometimes is an obstacle to the spiritual and material happiness of an individual, is nothing but an obdurate piece of dirt whose exculpation must be effected by a precise analysis of its structure—just as certain spots on clothing can be removed only by specific chemical antidotes or as dust in a watch can be located only through microscopic cleaning. By parallel logic the ideally normal life of the Joads can be achieved only by dislodging the handicaps of their economic existence, by curing the economic disease of unemployment.

The apocalyptically sanitary camp thus becomes a wayside station in this social variety of psychoanalysis, a clean home being the basis for animal contentment: in the movie's scheme the camp symbolizes such a cure, since the life of the Joads dramatically changes its spiritual complexion once they are settled in it; it receives there, so to speak, a Hollywood make-up. On California ground the lives of the Okies become photogenic, and the fresh optimism attached to their saga illustrates the release of the popular spirit toward those horizons that ornate movie interiors in their super-Sears-Roebuck reality offer to the American public as every man's dream and every man's possible privilege. Perhaps the sophisticated reader will sigh lightly here and say to himself, "Yes... yes... just another popular delusion that Hollywood is here ritually, if more subtly than usual, insinuating as its routine moral propaganda."

But, as I have said, *The Grapes of Wrath* does more than just this; it makes deliberate feints at taking the economico-political dilemma by its horns. With this in mind we must deny the possible implication that economic unhappiness, of which the Okies are so convincing and eloquent a symbol, can be psychoanalyzed out of existence by devices of a type like the New Deal reform program of lending a helping hand in major crises. Yes, Tommy Joad goes out to fight the workers' fight, but we have no guarantee in this fable that he can understand the true principles in this fight any better than his mother can understand the nature of his poetic metaphors. In these very metaphors one gets a whiff of the most unfortunate sort of mass metaphysics, a metaphysics that can exist so easily on paper—for instance, in our own Constitution or in Lincoln's Gettysburg Address—and with so much difficulty in material fact. The movie holds its own refutation as to Tom's idealistic capacity for real labor education. The fallacy of his essentially verbal logic in telling his mother that he will be with her always, since he will always be in the fight to determine their common destiny as workers—this very fallacy lay in the fatal handbill the Joads had found, stating that three hundred workers were wanted and inducing every one of ten thousand who found the same bill to imagine himself as one of the three hundred. Indeed, does the outdated legend that four hundred people rule New York society limit the entries in the Social Register any more than it limits the aspirations of thousands of social climbers to enter the sacred realm of high society or be entertained by Elsa Maxwell? So long as material definitions do not limit mind, any Okie outhouse may, in terms of pure expectation, equal the sanitary quarters of a movie star.

The "we the people" slogan raised by Ma Joad in the very last moments of the film is pure Hollywood, pure metaphysics, for it represents only the snobbery for the lower classes that upper-class interests seek to popularize. The only sense in which it has any *effectiveness*, any significant application, is that in which we can conceive Ma Joad climbing down from the truck when the camera stops turning and getting her pay envelope from the studio cashier. As a result of Steinbeck's book the lot of some of the real Joads was eased by legislation. It is therefore to be deemed fortunate that the freedom of the press still exists to some practical end, however qualified. Moreover, with the opening up of war industries in California the resident Okies came to have enough extra cash, no doubt, to take in the movies. Perhaps *The Grapes of Wrath* is being kept well under cover in California now, but if any of the Joads were ever privileged to see themselves, how pitifully far and plain those days must have seemed to them when their war-time salaries brought them hot and cold running water and a bathtub, even if not the latest model.

# John Ford:
# A Persistence of Vision

## William S. Pechter

*The frontier is the outer edge of the wave—the meeting point between savagery and civilization.*

Frederick Jackson Turner

*The Man Who Shot Liberty Valance* is a fascinating film, but a film whose fascination lies less in what it is in itself than in what it reveals about the art of its maker, John Ford. In itself, it is a sporadically imagined work; passages which are fully realized artistically alternating with others which merely point sketchily to what they might have been, with another cast, perhaps, or another budget, or in another time. And yet, in a curious way, the sight of a barrel-bellied, fifty-five-year-old John Wayne heaving himself onto a horse, hopelessly destructive as it is of any suspension of disbelief, does nevertheless evoke feelings which no then thirty-five-year-old actor could summon. At moments such as these and others played out in obvious sets and against painted backdrops, the film as an artistic creation is scarcely even pretended at; rather, the effect is of a lecture-demonstration, or an essay on the Western; a summing up. And it is as this—as a self-exegetical essay—that the film takes on its peculiar but real excitement—even those sets and backdrops charged with their special significance. Despite its bearing on his films before, nothing in John Ford's previous work could have quite prepared one for it, and, faced with the fact of its existence, the stock figure of John Ford, nortoriously taciturn interviewee and putative "folk artist," will hardly stand up to further perpetuation.

The film opens on an image of a nineteenth-century railway train, whistling and steaming its way round a bend through a pastoral landscape;

an image which, in the serene self-sufficiency of its curves and perspectives, seems somehow to contain a world. The train pulls into a small Western town where an old man is waiting to greet two of the passengers, who, it transpires in the flurry of activity which follows their arrival, are Ransom Stoddard, a United States senator, and Hallie, his wife. Questioned by a reporter on the reason for his surprise visit, the senator replies with a smooth politician's blend of orotundity and evasiveness, but he finally consents to visit the newspaper office to give an interview. His wife and the old man are left in the latter's buckboard wagon, where they sit awkwardly and exchange guarded reminiscences without looking at one another; the moment, as indeed the entirety of the opening and closing sequences which frame the action of the film, photographed in a just sufficiently higher key than the body of the film to impart a slightly bleached or faded quality to the image. The man, Link, tells her that the cactus rose is blooming, and, at her request, they drive out to the site of an old, burned-down house near whose ruins he picks a cactus rose for her.

At the interview, the senator refuses to divulge more than that he has come to attend the funeral of Tom Doniphon, whose name is unknown to the reporters. He is rejoined by his wife and the old man, and together they enter the undertaker's establishment; the three walking stiffly to view the plain wooden box provided for county burials. An old black man sits beside it; slowly, he and the newcomers recognize each other; the black man crying, the woman going consolingly to him. The senator looks inside the coffin, and is angered to see the body is without boots, spurs, and gun; he orders the undertaker to put them on. "He didn't carry no hand gun, Ranse," Link tells him. "He didn't for years." The four sit silently, absorbed in their mourning of the past, when the present breaks rudely in on them in the form of the newspaper editor pursuing his story in the name of the public's right to know—contemporary cant. The wife nods her consent and the senator goes out, leaving the other three to their private griefs. Repairing to a place nearby, the senator discovers the cobwebbed wreck of a stagecoach, and is led by memory into his story.

At once, in a flashback, we are met with a burst of vigorous action in a world seen more vividly than the "present" in its low-key, high-contrast photography. A stagecoach—in a "landscape" that, to strange effect, is recognizably a set—is ambushed and robbed with brutal viciousness by a band of men in long white coats. One of the passengers, the young Ransom Stoddard, protests, as a lawyer, in the name of the law; the gang's leader, thrown by this into a paroxysmal rage, sets upon Stoddard, rips up his lawbooks and takes him off to beat him savagely, shouting: "I'll teach you law—Western law!" Ironically, the bandit's name is "Liberty." Later, the beaten man is found and brought to a house in town by Tom Doniphon and his black "boy," Pompey; Tom treating Stoddard with an odd mixture of roughness and gentleness, a mixture which he manages to impart even to the name by which he addresses him: "Pilgrim." Revived, Stoddard discovers that the robbery has been committed outside the jurisdiction of the town's timorous sheriff, and he declares his intention to bring his assailant to justice—to jail, not kill, him. "Out here a man settles his own accounts," Tom tells him. "You're saying what he said! What kind of community have I come to?" Stoddard exclaims incredulously. But his only answer is Tom's exit line, an admonition, classic Western-hero-style, to remember that: "Liberty Valance is the toughest man west of the picket wire—next to me."

The house to which Tom has brought Stoddard is that of his girl, Hallie, and there, robbed and without his lawbooks, Stoddard is forced to remain, working as a kitchen helper in the restaurant run by Hallie's parents. Soon he has become a competitor with Tom for Hallie's affections, offering her, as Tom cannot, the refinements of "civilization"; among them, teaching her to read and write. When Tom brings her a cactus rose (a symbol, through the film, of his peculiar gentleness in toughness), she shows it to Ranse and asks, "Isn't it beautiful?" "Hallie, did you ever see a real rose?" he asks her in reply. Yet Tom's kind of toughness remains indispensable, and, when Liberty Valance makes a sudden appearance at the restaurant and humiliates Ranse, it is Tom and his (and Pompey's) recourse to a gun which causes Valance to back down. "Now I wonder what scared him off. The spectacle of law and order?" Tom derides Ranse. But "I'm staying, and I'm not buying a gun!" Ranse stubbornly reaffirms.

And he stays, setting up practice not only as the town's lawyer but as its schoolteacher; becoming, in fact, the Promethean bringer of all that is civilization in the frontier community; the sense of this effectively conveyed even in such lapsed form as the naïve lesson in racial equality which Pompey's presence in the schoolroom at one point occasions. But civilization burgeons under the threat of Liberty Valance's return, and, when that return suddenly impends, the classroom is abandoned; Pompey fetched by an irate Tom; and Ranse left alone in it to erase the blackboard motto, "Education is the basis of law and order." Surrendering to his situation, Ranse rides out for a shooting lesson to Tom's place; a ranch (an addition to the house being built in the expectation of Tom's marriage to Hallie) where, alone in the film, we experience a movement out into natural landscape and a sense of expansive space.

Liberty Valance's return is for the purpose of taking by intimidation the town's votes as delegate to a statehood convention—to cast his vote against the encroachment of civilization on the frontier wilderness. Yet, despite his fiercest efforts (and he is played by Lee Marvin, in the film's best performance, as constituting virtually a sustained explosion of pure, natural malignity), he is frustrated by Tom, who, declining the nomination himself, secures it instead of Stoddard. But the victory only precipitates the final confrontation, a classic Western showdown between Ranse and Valance, in which, despite Ranse's incompetence with a gun and his being first wounded, he manages to kill his antagonist. Tom arrives to find Hallie lovingly tending Ranse, and tersely steps aside in the contest for her: "Sorry I got here too late. . . . I'll be around." But, once away from them, his emotions erupt violently in a fight with two of Valance's former lackeys and a bout of drinking (during which he is watched over by Pompey, acting—see Leslie Fiedler—the devoted wife); the outburst ending with Tom returning home in desperate agitation and setting fire to the house he has built for Hallie, where he sits insensibly until carried out by Pompey. The unfinished addition bursts into flame as the entire house and stable are enveloped by the spreading conflagration. At Tom's command, Pompey frees the horses. The sense, unmistakably, is of not simply a place but an entire style of life being consumed by the fire.

The scene shifts abruptly to the circus-like, recognizably contemporary atmosphere of the statehood convention, in the midst of electing a man to represent the territory in Washington; one of the nominees is Ranse, described in the nominating speech as a "lawyer, teacher, but more important . . . a champion of law and order." During the course of the oratory, Tom appears at the back of the assembly hall, looking haggard. Another speaker attacks Ranse as a man whose "only claim" is "that he killed a man" (someone shouts: "Do you call Liberty Valance a man!"). Ranse leaves the auditorium, under attack; Tom follows him, calling: "Pilgrim!" The two seclude themselves to speak to one another, and Ranse demands: "Isn't it enough to kill a man without trying to build a life on it?" Then, in a flashback within the flashback, Tom tells Ranse (while we re-see the event from his perspective) that the shooting of Liberty Valance was actually done by him as he stood in the shadows while Ranse and Valance fought; declaring, in conclusion, that it was "cold-blooded murder . . . but I can live with it." Tom urges Ranse to go back and take the nomination, and take Hallie, too; "You taught her to read and write." Ranse returns to a gala welcome, the band playing; Tom leaves alone; and the flashback which is Ranse's story to the editor comes to an end. But the editor declines to publish the story. "This is the West, sir. When the legend becomes fact, print the legend."

Ranse rejoins the others still gathered around the coffin, upon which a cactus rose has been placed. Later, back on the train which is about to depart, Ranse sits stiffly next to Hallie and asks her if she'd like to return home to the town to live. "If you knew how often I dreamed of it," Hallie replies. "My roots are here. I guess my heart is here. . . . Look at it. It was once a wilderness. Now it's a garden."

He asks her who put the cactus rose on Tom's coffin. She tells him that she did.

But the conversation is suddenly interrupted by the intrusion of the train's conductor, fawning ostentatiously on the senator, who responds by resuming his public face and unctuous politician's manner. The conductor leaves them, declaring, "Nothing's too good for the man who shot Liberty Valance!" and they sink again into silence resonant with a sense of loss and sadness. The train pulls away from the station. The film's last image is the same as its first but for the reverse of the train's direction as it traverses the landscape, winding through the garden that once was a wilderness: a world.

The world that *The Man Who Shot Liberty Valance* makes manifest is, in fact, that contained by all of John Ford's most personal and deeply imagined films, and the uniqueness of *The Man Who Shot Liberty Valance* consists in its bringing into explicitness what has for so long lain covertly beneath the surface. It is a world not our own but parallel to our own; existing in a relation to our world not that of a mirror but of an analogy; and, though couched most appositely in an historical past we may think we recognize, finally independent of any historical reality and wholly self-contained. That world's archetypal drama is the winning of the West, and the Western the most natural form for its embodiment. Yet, as one watches this archetype being fleshed out imaginatively throughout Ford's work, one gradually comes to see that the winning of the West is ultimately a metaphor for something else, and that the vision which informs Ford's most personal work persists undiminished in films outwardly as diverse as *Young Mr. Lincoln, They Were Expendable,* and *The Quiet Man.*

What the winning of the West means in the context of Ford's films is the conquest of wildness by civilization; the remaking of wilderness into garden; the progress toward union and community. Yet, while it is a relatively simple matter to identify the elements of this drama in such early works as *Drums Along the Mohawk* or even others as late as *Wagonmaster,* it is not quite so easy to get one's bearings toward the more complex distribution of conceptual values in *The Man Who Shot Liberty Valance.* I don't mean to suggest that these earlier films are slighter works than *The Man Who Shot Liberty Valance;* they are both far greater. And already in the earlier films there is that complex network of cross-reference, of variation and elaboration, which so distinguishes Ford's work and enriches it: the Indian friend of *Drums Along the Mohawk* reappearing to say a last farewell to Nathan Brittles in *She Wore a Yellow Ribbon;* the Indian's handing of a switch to Gil for him to beat his wife in the earlier film and Mary Kate's handing her husband a stick with which to beat her in *The Quiet Man* sounding echoes of each other across a distance of thirteen years; while the Clegg family in *Wagonmaster* seem both the unmistakable heirs of the Clantons in *My Darling Clementine* and the progenitors of Liberty Valance as personifications of an elemental savagery. Nor is it yet that the earlier films are any more conventional than the later; on the contrary, *Wagonmaster* is the film which, in its dispensing with an individual hero for a communal one and with a dramatic structure for the more open, epic form of narrative, spectacle, dance and song, has been characterized by Lindsay Anderson as an avant-garde Western.

Yet in both *Drums Along the Mohawk* and *Wagonmaster* the archetypal drama of the progress toward community is played out with a confident balance and a tranquil acceptance of the values that the polarities of wildness and civilization are assumed to possess. Artistically, these works are complex creations; in their meaning, they are whole and beautifully simple. But, by the time of *Liberty Valance,* the scheme of values within which the film's meaning is contained has become so fragmented and ambiguous that one may wonder if it is not that very complexity which accounts for Ford's unwillingness or inability to make of it a wholly satisfying artistic creation. In any event, were a satisfying artistic creation to be made of so ambiguous a clash of values, it would, one feels, be of necessity a drastically different kind of work than those serene and harmonious creations his greatest films have always been.

What is wildness and what civilization in *The Man Who Shot Liberty Valance?* At first, the answers may seem easily come by. Liberty Valance, his name one letter away from the nomenclature of allegory, is the incarnation of the frontier's savage wildness, and he is conquered by Ransom Stoddard as the agent of civilization. Yet it isn't Stoddard but Tom who is the man who shoots Liberty Valance; and Tom, too, represents wildness— the expansive liberty of the frontier; indeed, he alone in the film is associated with a sense of unconfined space. (Though, for all I know, the film's use of sets as its use of black and white may have been dictated by budgetary considerations, the effect obtained by both is of a stricter measure of control by the director over the work's formal and conceptual scheme. This control to some extent represents a failure of imagination; it would have been possible and certainly well within Ford's powers to have linked Tom's presence with spaciousness in a less abstract and artificial way. Nevertheless, what I wish to stress here is the intention, both clearly conscious and unmistakable.)

Nor is the film's vision of civilization any less divided. It is, to be sure, embodied in Ransom Stoddard, the pilgrim, who comes in the name of the law and nurtures a community in the wilderness; but again it is Tom whose power and sacrifice make the civilizing process possible; who is able not only to confront and use violence but to accept the moral responsibility for this: to "live with it." Yet in what balance is his sacrifice weighed? At the end, he lies, without guns, stripped of his power, his way of life vanished into extinction. And Hallie, whom he has given over to civilization, seems to look back longingly, with no evidence of her having found happiness, on what she has left behind. Only Ranse, or the public person he has become, seems to have flourished in the garden he has cultivated, and even he shows visible signs of an awareness that it is not Eden.

If Liberty Valance incarnates the furthest extreme of the frontier's wildness, a wildness taken by its extremity to the borders of abstraction ("Do you call Liberty Valance a man?"), it is also true that there is an element of this wildness in Tom, and that, in killing Valance, he kills also something of himself. This element—the appropriation to the individual of the sole power to determine the content and contours of his life; the claim, as it were, to an unbounded moral space—cannot coexist with civilization; nor is it something we, the civilized audience, find congenial to our own sense of moral style. Probably, apart from Ford, there is no other filmmaker fundamentally within the community of liberal sentiment (excepting, that is to say, such cryptofascists as Samuel Fuller) who is able to draw a character so offensive to the liberal sensibility as Tom Doniphon with so great a responsiveness to the heroism and even beauty of his nature. I think there can be no doubt where Ford's sympathies lie in the tendentiously egalitarian sequence of Pompey in Ranse's schoolroom, and yet Stoddard's relation to Pompey smacks unmistakably of paternalism while between Tom and his "boy" one senses a bond of something like love.

It would be wrong to suggest, as I may have, that Tom is the sole hero of the film, although he alone is indisputably at its center. The heroism is divided between the two men, and, at least in the earlier sections, one is kept keenly aware of both the gentleness and decency of Ranse and of the moral crudity of Tom's world, across the precarious terrain of which a Liberty Valance can maraud unchecked but for Tom's individual authority. In that world, whatever survives must be able to grow wild; there are no roses but the cactus rose; it is a wilderness. Yet, if Ranse's values are admitted to be both necessary and inevitable, *The Man Who Shot Liberty Valance* is still an elegy to the cactus rose. The future, which is to say the present, belongs to Ranse; yet, for all the gain in stability, a certain grandeur has gone out of it, and even the pilgrim has given way to the politicians. And, though the present may legitimize itself with edifying legends, the film remains a dissenting tribute to the stature of the man who "really" shot Liberty Valance.

John Ford has been making films since 1917, and his work has come, in its entirety, to resemble one vast fiction of such breadth and limpidity as virtually to make it seem a creation of the art of another age. (In speaking of Ford's work, I exclude of necessity his silent films, only one of which I have seen, and have in mind chiefly those of his films dating from the mid-thirties.) More specifically, I think that period of Ford's activity extending roughly from *Stagecoach, Young Mr. Lincoln,* and *Drums Along the Mohawk* in 1939 through *The Sun Shines Bright* in 1953 comprises a body of work constituting an efflorescence of artistic creativity unparalleled in the American film but for the work of Chaplin and Keaton. Moreover, it seems to me that, again but for Chaplin and Keaton, Ford is the only American director of films whose body of work has the formal beauty, richness of imagination, thematic unity, and wholeness of vision which we associate with artistic greatness as it is commonly understood with respect to the traditional arts. In order to see this, I believe one has to accept and reject several things; to accept, for instance, the Hollywood system in which Ford has had to function and which has required his continually having to buy again the freedom to make a film of his own choosing with others that were commercial successes (a system, however, in which Ford, like Chaplin, could thrive because of having by nature the gifts of a truly popular artist); and accept also Ford's imperfections of nature—his penchant for low comedy and his occasional inclinations toward sentimentality (good Shakespearean and Dickensian faults, respectively). I believe one has to reject, or at least have serious reservations about, such a textbook classic as *The Informer,* which bogs down in a middle-brow artistic pretentiousness that—Ford's characteristic flaws being of another kind (as witness *Three Godfathers*)—seems in retrospect to be more the contribution of Dudley Nichols than of Ford. And one must reject as well the cult of Ford; whether taking the form of Andrew Sarris and *Sight and Sound* hailing a potboiler such as *Seven Women* as a masterwork, or of thirty years of "Fordoltary" restricted to gauzily impressionistic tributes to his masterly visual style; both, in their insularity, confining to the dimensions of a ghetto an art whose reach encompasses a world.

The great theme which runs like a current through Ford's major work is that of the civilizing of wildness; on the largest scale, in the settlement of the West; on the most intimate, in the domestication of his heroes by his heroines through their union. Thematically, the two are twin manifestations of the same process. Through their experience of love, Ford's heroes become civilized; the personal love story becomes a kind of microcosm of the myth of winning the West; the individual instance of the coming of civilization; the entrance into the community of human feeling. Yet, ultimately, the macrocosm is also reciprocative, and the myth of winning the West an external symbolic representation of the individual's initiation into that state of communion. In both instances, there is the same dramatic clash of values natural values versus civilized ones, to oversimplify—because Ford's women, the agents of civilizing values, certainly possess a natural force as well. And, in both, the process is envisioned as always entailing a loss with the gain: a loss in power and freedom, a gain in insight and humanity.

It has been said that the degree of one's responsiveness to Ford may be measured by whether or not one prefers *Stagecoach* or his subsequent Westerns, and I suppose it is true that, if, like Manny Farber or Robert Warshow, one conceives of the genre as essentially unvaried ritual, *My Darling Clementine* can seem, in Farber's phrase, "a dazzling example of how to ruin" a Western. I think *Stagecoach* is a fine film, and virtually a model of narrative cinema; yet, if it is also a model and perfection of the genre of the action Western, it seems to me still a species of dogmatic rigidity to fail to appreciate the extent to which Ford was able subsequently to create variations on the genre and increasingly to imbue it with a personal content. *Stagecoach,* Ford's first Western in sound, is, of course, already rich with details of sentiment and portraiture that mark it as his own, and, technically, it is a splendid achievement and an announcement of the consolidation of Ford's control over the formal resources of his medium. Yet, in *Drums Along the Mohawk,* made later the same year (and a Western in all but the literal sense, its frontier being New York's Mohawk Valley during the time of the Revolutionary War), one is aware, as one is not in *Stagecoach,* of an imaginative thrust born of the artist's discovery in his materials of the theme which is his own.

*Drums Along the Mohawk* is a simple film; a narrative of the settlement of a wilderness, with a married couple, the partners relatively undifferentiated in their thematic roles, as its foreground; the two seen against a developing community in which they come to take their place; and the struggle waged between the settlers and their hostile environment (of which Indians, inflamed by a mysterious British agitator, are a virtually abstracted expression) providing its action. It is also a beautiful film; tender in its depiction of new marriage and burgeoning community, heroic in its description of the settlers' determination, and fierce in its portrayal of pioneer suffering and sacrifice. But, by the time of Ford's next Western, *My Darling Clementine,* seven years later, the simple elements of *Drums Along the Mohawk* have been elaborated into a vision as wholly charged with meaning and as distinctively personal as any in films; a vision refined throughout a seven-year period of intense and prolific creativity.

Between *Stagecoach* and *Drums Along the Mohawk,* Ford, in fact, made one other film, *Young Mr. Lincoln,* and, before *My Darling Clementine,* two others, *How Green Was My Valley* and *They Were Expendable,* that are all among his finest achievements. *Young Mr. Lincoln* relates an incident from Lincoln's early life imagined as a legend of his bringing justice to a frontier town, and manages, with lyricism and humor, to evoke both the Lincoln of folklore and the shrewdly practical, inexhaustibly interesting person that the folklore usually obscures; the two Lincolns merging in the astonishingly austere, climactic image of Lincoln, following his first courtroom triumph, framed in the doorway of the courthouse, stiff and awkward against a flat background in a shaft of blinding sunlight, as he steps out into the world to accept the crowd's acclaim. *How Green Was My Valley* is a loving remembrance of a child's coming of age set against the dissolution of a family and community in a Welsh mining village; a sweet and poignant work marred slightly by a tendency toward prettification. *They Were Expendable,* with Wellman's *The Story of G.I. Joe,* one of the two great films of World War II, is Ford's tribute to the gallant last stand of MacArthur's troops in the Philippines in 1941; an epic of valor in defeat realized in a majestic succession of images of PT boats cutting through the sea and straggling lines of men on beaches whose heroic poetry seems to me to justify an attempt to rescue "Homeric" as an adjective with a meaning; and a work, as much as *Young Mr. Lincoln,* having as its imaginative center the establishment of a community at the edge of civilization.

It was also in this period between *Stagecoach* and *My Darling Clementine* that Ford made *The Long Voyage Home,* a vividly atmospheric adaptation (photographed by Gregg Toland) of four short sea plays by O'Neill, and *Tobacco Road* from a stage adaptation of the novel whose grossness would defeat any attempt at reclamation, as well as *The Grapes of Wrath,* which, however one may now regard it as a work of social conscience, remains alive in the extraordinary expressiveness of Ford's (and Gregg Toland's) great figures in landscapes.

*My Darling Clementine* marks the resumption of Ford's work as a maker of Westerns, five others following between it and *The Quiet Man* in 1952. Of these, *My Darling Clementine, Wagonmaster,* and *Rio Grande* seem to me Ford at his best, and the rougher *She Wore a Yellow Ribbon* (in which John Wayne quite movingly plays an old man twenty years before *True Grit*) for long stretches not far below this; all of them, with the exception of the bathetic *Three Godfathers,* engaging with greater or lesser directness the thematic materials made explicit by *The Man Who Shot*

*Liberty Valance*. Though *She Wore a Yellow Ribbon* and *Rio Grande* are often grouped with *Fort Apache* as Ford's "cavalry trilogy," their combined effect is less that of companion pieces than of a progressive reworking and revision of common materials, the crudeness of the last named (and first made) eventuating in the refinement of the third; such elements as the soldiers' serenade passing from the awkwardness of *Fort Apache* to the off-screen song of *She Wore a Yellow Ribbon* to be rewoven into the texture of *Rio Grande,* whose whole fabric is rich with a sense of ceremony and tradition.

Rio Grande seems equally, in the relation between its principals, a preparation for Ford's last great film, *The Quiet Man,* and, almost as much as that work, tremulous with a pervasive sexuality. Ironically, Ford spoke of *The Quiet Man* at the time of his making it as his first love story; it is his last. It was followed by a nostalgic and charming return to the desexualized pastoral of *Judge Priest* and *Steamboat Round the Bend* in *The Sun Shines Bright* and by a lightweight erotic entertainment in *Mogambo.* Apart from one occasionally grand and inconsistent work in *The Searchers,* it is not until *The Man Who Shot Liberty Valance,* ten years after *The Quiet Man,* that one encounters another Ford film with a thematic charge comparable to that his work from *Young Mr. Lincoln* to *The Quiet Man* almost invariably bore; and, by the time one does, it is the differences as much as the similarities of which one is aware.

Earlier, I mentioned the special qualities which John Wayne brings to *The Man Who Shot Liberty Valance,* his association with Ford as long and as fertile as any between actor and director in films. I think there is no need to exaggerate Wayne's capabilities as an actor to appreciate how wonderfully right he is for Ford's films, with that suggestion of both physical bravery and moral crudity his presence now almost iconographically conveys—the icon very much of Ford's creation. Ford's films with Henry Fonda, a much finer actor than Wayne but also a more gentle kind of presence (and, in the context in which Ford tends thematically to see the encounter between male and female, a more androgynous presence), tend to be less dramatic, more lyrical than those with Wayne, and, when they fail, somewhat static. As realized by Fonda, the Ford hero suggests the self-sufficient embodiment of both masculine and feminine grace; in the terms of the Platonic myth of love, needing no complement; an essentially lyrical figure remaining outside the action which he affects but by which he remains largely unaltered. Even in Ford's two masterpieces with Fonda, *Young Mr. Lincoln* and *My Darling Clementine,* the hero remains essentially a figure of undifferentiated sexuality, responding fraternally to the devotion of the young girl in the former and extending his love alike to Clementine and Doc Holliday in the latter.

In *My Darling Clementine,* Victor Mature's is really the dramatic role, and his more nearly than Fonda's the figure which, in Wayne's performances, the Ford hero was to become. But it is not really until the succession of films after *My Darling Clementine* through *The Quiet Man* that the Ford hero is consistently imagined as a dramatic one, and Ford's major theme finds its place decisively at his work's center. Yet the effect of these films, revolving so steadily about their thematic polarities, remains not one of repetition but rather of incessant variation and diversity; though the thematic elements remain constant, their imaginative embodiment embracing both the communal hero of *Wagonmaster* and the role reversal of *The Quiet Man,* in which it is the hero who presses the claims of civilization and the heroine who is brought from wildness into domesticity; the idea of the frontier itself proving capable of exerting its figurative power despite a removal to rural Ireland.

Given the unusual degree to which Ford's films have required certain "natural" qualities of the performers in them, the decline in their thematic intensity soon after *The Quiet Man* surely owes in part to their lack of apposite casts due to the loss of some of Ford's favorites through death or aging. A Richard Widmark or Carroll Baker may be a better actor than a John Wayne or Maureen O'Hara, but they are unable to suggest those special thematic attributes which the screen presences of Wayne and Maureen O'Hara in Ford's work project so perfectly; which may explain, in part, why *Cheyenne Autumn,* one of Ford's few attempts to come to grips with actual Western history (the history of injustice to the Indians) remains so static a pageant. But, if most of Ford's films since *The Quiet Man* seem almost deliberately to step aside from the kind of material which might engage his major theme (though it insistently reasserts itself, if only peripherally, even in such minor works as *The Wings of Eagles* and *Donovan's Reef*), the appearance of *The Man Who Shot Liberty Valance* ten years after *The Quiet Man* is testimony to the hold which that theme continues to have on him, and the extent to which his work's excitement is bound up with the centrality of his theme's place in it. But it is testimony also to the extent to which that theme's elements have been reconceived in a new relationship. For no longer is the Western conquest imagined in the instance of the individual's progress toward community. Already, in *The Searchers,* one could see the beginning of a withdrawal of the hero from the center of the personal drama. In *The Man Who Shot Liberty Valance,* the love story is gone, and the "woman's" role (Hallie being merely a passive trophy in the contest for predominance) taken by Stoddard; he acting as the agent of civilization, and seen as the custodian of the future. And, with this shift of emphasis in the values whose tension is sustained through Ford's major work of more than a decade, the balance of that work is drastically altered. The finest of Ford's films remain among the few great Apollonian creations in the art of this century. *The Man Who Shot Liberty Valance* is a sad and bitter postlude to them: an old man's reverie on the glory of a vanished wildness.

I have stressed, in this piece, the thematic unity of Ford's work; the presence throughout it of a persistent imaginative vision; and have concentrated so much attention on *The Man Who Shot Liberty Valance* because of the way it retrospectively throws that vision into a sharper focus. Yet I would be unfaithful to what is best and what I value most in Ford were I to pretend that *The Man Who Shot Liberty Valance* is more than a half-created epilogue to his finest achievements; or to seem to say that his best work's greatness is experienced through an apprehension of its thematic unity. That Ford's work, like the work of all great literary and dramatic artists, has a thematic unity has been insufficiently stressed,[1] so I have stressed it here. But the experience of that work's greatness remains largely of its sweep and color, its narrative vigor and visual beauty. Ford's films are easy to enjoy; the difficulty to which I have addressed myself is that of properly appreciating them. Above all, however, they are not texts to be explicated but sensuous creations in which to take pleasure. And yet even that immediate pleasure which Ford's work offers so accessibly seems increasingly to lie beyond the pale of the cultivated modern sensibility. At a time when all sentiment has become suspect, is there any basis left to us for appreciating or understanding the work of an artist capable in his greatest films of responding with so unambiguous a strong, simple feeling, such wholeness of spirit and normality of temperament, to the fundamental human virtues of manly gallantry, womanly grace, love, heroism, gentleness? It may be that there is none, in which case the loss is ours.

1. Peter Wollen's section on Ford in his mainly jargon-clogged *Signs and Meaning in the Cinema* (Bloomington: Indiana University Press, 1969) is a worthy exception to this, and particularly good in analyzing the range of antinomies that Ford's theme may contain, but a case in which the author's assumption that the continuity of theme in Ford's work is in itself the measure of the work's artistic achievement renders him seemingly incapable of distinguishing Ford's failures from his successes.

# Jean-Luc Godard

*JEAN-LUC GODARD was born in Paris in 1930, to a Protestant family which, unlike Truffaut's, was well-to-do and middle-class. His father was a successful doctor; his mother came from an influential family of bankers. He became a Swiss citizen during World War II, but returned to Paris to study ethnology at the Sorbonne in the late 1940s. He began writing film criticism in 1950, developing special interests in montage and editing, in expressionist atmosphere, and in genre stories. Eventually he became an important member of the* Cahiers du Cinéma *circle, which was presided over by André Bazin and included François Truffaut, Eric Rohmer, Jacques Rivette, and Claude Chabrol, the same men who later, as directors, became the nucleus of the* nouvelle vague *or New Wave.*

*Godard directed several short films in the late 1950s, and his first feature film,* Breathless, *in 1959. Dedicated to Monogram Pictures, which produced a large number of low-budget "B" films in the forties and fifties, Godard's film, like Truffaut's later* Shoot the Piano Player *(1960), was in part a self-conscious tribute to American genre movies. Jean-Paul Belmondo plays an aimless young hood, and Jean Seberg is the shallow American girl who finally betrays him. The story is slight, in reaction to the traditional French "cinema of quality," with its elaborate scenarios and artificial studio décor. Godard's technique—which relies on hand-held cameras, jagged jump-cuts, location-shooting in streets, cafés, and apartments, and a loose and casual script (said to be based on an idea by Truffaut)—gives the film a startling air of improvisation that perfectly suits the lifestyle of its characters.*

*Drenched in earlier movies, with a hero who models himself on Bogart and a style that distances us from the characters, the film remains a moving story, especially at the end when the police close in on Belmondo and shoot him in the back as he runs away, though he has nowhere to run to. Godard's later films move away from even this modest interest in plot and character. In the early 1960s he made several highly personal imitations of genre films, including a spy thriller (*Le Petit soldat, *1960), a musical (*Une Femme est une femme, *1961), an absurdist war movie (*Les Carabiniers, *1963), a gangster movie (*Band of Outsiders, *1964), and a science-fiction film (*Alphaville, *1965). Increasingly these films detach themselves from narrative cinema and use plot as the ground for an associative collage of scenes and images. Like Bresson, Godard pares away the psychological concerns that films have inherited from novels and plays. Like Antonioni, he gives relentless attention to the glossy surfaces of modern life in a way that heightens the solitude of his characters, letting them dangle in an environment that lacks the consolations of intimacy and personal affect.*

*Godard's use of Brechtian alienation effects, including direct political harangues and interviews with real people, re-introduces modernism into* the cinema for the first time since the surrealists of the 1920s. It was this self-consciousness about the film process that had the most dramatic impact on younger filmmakers in the sixties. By the time of Made in USA and Two or Three Things I Know about Her (both 1966), his sound track had become as much a collage of disparate materials as his imagery.

Godard is especially daring in his direct treatment of ideas. Instead of integrating them dramatically, he offers us chunks of abstraction in the form of monologues, propagandistic speeches, interviews, or philosophical arguments—the cinematic equivalent of a politics of direct action. In his episode in Far from Vietnam (1967) Godard contributed a film essay, a lucid and brilliant personal meditation with only the barest visual accompaniment, mainly Godard himself behind his camera. In La Chinoise (1967), a prescient anticipation of the French student upheaval of May 1968, Godard orchestrated an astonishing cacophony of talk, talk, talk. In many other films, however, his intellectuality proved more elusive, disjointed, and ungainly.

After the political events of 1968, which heightened and transformed his commitment to radicalism, Godard completed few feature films, devoting himself instead to collective and political projects of an agitational nature. But between 1959 and 1968 he was a true filmmaker, however tedious and infuriating his experiments sometimes became. His eye for apt images never deserted him, even in the most puzzling contexts, and his ear for lucid texts and ingenious, intuitive juxtapositions can always startle us. His originality lay in his disjunctive style, which stood as a major challenge to the whole tradition of narrative cinema. As with Bresson, however, his best films were those that made concessions to personal experience and became affecting stories almost in spite of themselves. These include Breathless, My Life to Live (1962), Contempt (1963), Band of Outsiders, Pierrot le fou (1965), Masculine-Feminine (1966), and Weekend (1967), as well as his brief return to commercial filmmaking in Tout va bien (1972).

Godard's writings on film have been collected in Godard on Godard, edited by Tom Milne (1972). Essays about him have been collected by Toby Mussman (1968), Ian Cameron (1969), and Royal S. Brown (Focus on Godard, 1972). Several chapters are devoted to Godard's films in James Roy MacBean's Film and Revolution (1975). See also James Monaco, The New Wave (1976).

# "Breathless" Revisited

## Jonathan Baumbach

*Art and theory of art, at one and the same time; beauty and the secret of beauty; cinema and apologia for cinema.*

*Godard on* Elena et les hommes

*Breathless* has aged well. Seventeen years later, Godard's least overtly political film remains his most radical work of art, one of the half dozen signal events in the short history of film. Its imitators—and its influence has been pervasive even among directors who clearly despise its esthetic—have in no way compromised the originality of Godard's first feature. As with most deeply instinctive works, visions not so much of a world as of the art form itself, *Breathless* is essentially inimitable. Audacity is the work's defining impulse. "I wanted," says Godard in an interview, "to give the impression of just finding or experiencing the processes of cinema for the first time." It is not only its freshness and sense of discovery, its breakneck energy and wit that make *Breathless* so exhilarating to watch, but in addition its moment-by-moment defiance of aesthetic injunctions, its thumb of the nose at conventional tyrannies. *Breathless* translates discontinuity into coherence, revises our idea of the possibilities of cinema.

Chance informs the movement of Godard's world (chance and a certain anti-psychology) as instinct seems to be at the heart of his method. The plot, which serves as both parody and metaphoric occasion, is derived from a mélange of American gangster film conventions. In the opening shots, Michel (Belmondo) steals a car, is followed by the police, and, finding himself trapped, takes a gun from the glove compartment and kills the policeman. (We see Michel fire the gun and in a separate shot we see the policeman fall, making it seem as if the firing of the gun and the death of the policeman were only cinematically connected.)

This essay was written especially for the present volume.

This series of chance conjunctions dooms Michel. Godard assumes the Hollywood code of the thirties and forties in which if a character commits murder, the filmmaker is obliged to murder him in return as a form of symbolic deterrence. The unintentional effect of this code was to predicate the outcome of certain films in advance and to create in the consciousness of the filmgoer a race of doomed anti-heroes and a vision of a mechanically moralistic universe. *Breathless* is the reconstituted fantasy of Godard's filmgoing, and is at once homage to and parody of the American action film and poetic transformation of it.

*Breathless,* then, is the secret life of the *film noir* (a self-subverting genre itself at its best) made manifest, the film of our filmgoing fantasies. In the American gangster film, we tended to root, despite ourselves, for the survival of the doomed anti-hero, lamenting the mischance that set him wrong. In *Breathless,* the anti-hero, Michel, becomes the rebel we imagine ourselves, a man living his idea of freedom without the compromise of civilized constraint, a figure of ultimate romantic integrity. Humphrey Bogart is his icon. In one of the film's characteristically self-conscious moments, Michel stops to admire a poster of Bogart in *The Harder They Fall* and imagines himself as Bogart, rubbing his thumb across his lips in identification. Michel's self-willed audacity parallels the film's method so that we experience Michel/Belmondo as an agency of Godard, the filmmaker as outlaw, the outlaw as artist. Although romanticized, Michel is never treated sentimentally. He is a character in a fiction, Godard is at pains to keep us aware, and not a real person. His death at the end is exhilarating rather than sad or, perhaps, something of both. Godard is a dialectician, moving between abstraction at one pole and realism at the other. It is the energy and vision of *Breathless* and not the outcome of its narrative that moves us.

Before *Breathless,* cutting had been used in films for the most part as an invisible seam, a smoothing over of transitions so as to spare us the bumps. The jump-cutting of *Breathless* creates disruption, calls attention to shifts in time and place, to the film as film. By showing us his iconoclastic craft, Godard humanizes the technology of filmmaking. *Breathless* asserts the personality of the filmmaker, who appears in it himself in the ironic role of an informer, betraying his own hero. I can think of no other serious film that lets us get as close to process. Paradoxically, while *Breathless* is an exceptionally naked work, or seemingly naked, it is at the same time mysterious and opaque. Godard gives away the trick of his tricks without undermining the magic of his art.

The film's main disguise is in its narrative which may cause some problems for those viewers (and reviewers) who believe that serious art needs to deal with demonstrably significant themes. Clearly, the hero of

*Breathless* is a disaffected punk who breaks the law (who kills) as an emblem of his freedom. Yet we experience him in the context of the film as a vital force, a man inventing his life moment by moment as if he were improvising a movie. The key to Michel's survival is his unequivocal self-interest—integrity is sanity in Godard's world—his seemingly pathological cool.

Love, as the convention goes, undoes him. He moves in with an American girl (Grade B, I am tempted to add), the schizzy Patricia Franchini (Jean Seberg), who sells *Herald Tribunes* on the Champs-Elysées and aspires to be a reporter. Patricia is the self-deceived American bitch-goddess *manquée*. It is the *manquée* that redeems her for us. When she seems most in love with Michel she betrays him to the police—a way, she reports, of testing whether she loves him or not, although more likely it is a repudiation of the demands of love. Michel's death is circumstantial or offers us that appearance. He is tired of running, Michel says, when Patricia tells him that the police are coming. A friend comes by and offers Michel a gun, which he refuses. Nevertheless, as chance has it (or is it that character is fate?), he is shot down, running away, carrying the very gun he refused. Patricia's betrayal, within the film's borrowed conventions, is the killing blow. It is also a fulfillment of character, an act of integrity: a killer kills; a bitch betrays. After his death, in the last shot of the film, Patricia imitates Michel's ritual gesture, rubbing the side of her thumb across her lips, an act of identification. Michel is dead; the rebellious spirit survives. Earlier in the film, Patricia reads the last line of Faulkner's *The Wild Palms* to Michel, "Between grief and nothing I will take grief." Michel is unimpressed. "Grief's a waste of time," he says. "I'd choose nothing. Grief's only a compromise. And you have to have all or nothing." (There are texts in all of Godard's films, literary fragments that coexist with the visual, that parallel and illuminate the action and sometimes merely decorate it.) Throughout *Breathless*, Michel seems to speak as much for Godard as for himself. The character (the icon of Belmondo playing him) embodies the liberating spirit of the film. Godard as critic deplored the impersonality of the well-made French film (what Truffaut called "The Tradition of Quality," the Masterpiece Theater of its day), choosing after a point to refuse discussion of it altogether. *Breathless* is an extension of Godard's criticism, a vision of uncompromising personal cinema, a demonstration of what is possible when a radical idea is carried through to its conclusion.

There are certain unexpected pleasures in *Breathless* that are not often noted in discussions of that work. In contrast to the romance of the gangster plot, the relationship between Michel and Patricia is precisely and realistically observed. Godard takes characters, or prototypes of characters, from Grade B movies and presents them to us with the attention to detail of a realistic novelist. The love story between Michel and Patricia, both self-involved to the point of alienation, is so exactingly perceived that it becomes moving and true within the ironic distance of the film's mode.

In almost all of his films—some, of course, more stylized than others—Godard mixes metaphoric action and realistic behavior, creating a world that accommodates both without obvious disparity. The tension in *Breathless* comes out of the attempted synthesis of opposites: cool and hot, intellection and action, documentary and fiction, truth and beauty. There are a number of flawed masterpieces in Godard's prodigious career—*Weekend, Two or Three Things I Know about Her, Pierrot le Fou, Band of Outsiders, Alphaville, Masculine-Feminine, A Married Woman, My Life to Live*—but *Breathless* is his most original and fortuitous achievement, a film in which every miscalculated risk transforms itself into grace gesture.

# Godard

## David Thomson

Just as Rouch's *Lion Hunt* impresses as an epic adventure and as a factual account, so all Godard's films are not only the events of their plots and characters but documentaries on the making of a film. Godard's interest in the cinema is such that his work can have no other subject. He is at the same time the last great artistic director—because of the prestige he has— and the first great new filmmaker in that he synthesizes the two categories of cinema, the film director and the scientist, the artist and the layman. With synthesis there comes dissolution of previous terminology. Every person rediscovers his infinite capacity. In *Bande à part* two of the central characters are traveling in the Metro. They look at a man and imagine two reasons for his presence: he is transporting a bomb; he is visiting his child in hospital. Benovolence and malevolence are supported equally by the man's bland face. There is no meaning in the world, only supposition and its food, fact.

If one tries to discuss Godard's characters, in the way one talks of Hitchcock's or Renoir's, one notices immediately how they straddle the worlds of the film and the filmmakers, not in the idyllic sense of Renoir, but because of an insecurity of identity deriving from a contemporary inability to discern reality from fantasy. People are isolated and their attempts at communication are only the sending of conflicting signals. The audio-visual society is such that words are no longer the perfect Jamesian instrument of intention. *Vivre sa vie* opens with Nana in a café, about to end an affair with Paul:

PAUL: Ce type, il t'intéresse vraiment?
NANA: Tu sais . . . je ne sais pas, je me demande á quoi je pense.
PAUL: Il a plus d'argent que moi?
NANA: Qu'est-ce que ça peut te faire? Qu'est-ce que ça peut te faire? . . . Qu'est-ce que ça peut te faire? Qu'est-ce que ça peut te faire?

PAUL: Ca ne va pas . . . non?
NANA: Non . . . rien . . . je voulais dire cette phrase avec une idée pré-
cise . . . et je savais pas quelle était la meilleure façon d'exprimer cette
idée, ou plutôt, je le savais, mais maintenant je ne le sais plus . . . alors que
justement je devrais le savoir.[1]

Nana can be no more confident of social criteria than she can of
understanding between people. Godard shoots the scene with such disregard for cinematic convention that Nana and Paul sit with their backs to the
camera. The absence of an attempt to make a connection of understanding
with the audience predicts the course of the rest of the film in which Nana
becomes a prostitute, falls in love with a young man, but is killed as one
pimp double-crosses another. These events are not experienced as narrative
because Nana encounters them without purpose. In all of Godard's films
there exists a state of spiritual boredom which is the complement of an awe
of discovery. Macha Meril in *Une Femme mariée* is shocked by nothing
because she knows anything can happen. Like Anna Karina in *Vivre sa vie*
she measures her reactions and attempts to define her position. The social
obstacles to being a prostitute or to loving two men at the same time are
irrelevant. Attempts to understand life, to finalize its complexities are
useless but they cannot be avoided because the human intelligence has
reached the stage of evolution when every event is interrogatory.

In a conversation with Nana, the philosopher, Brice Parain, tells a
story about Porthos from *The Three Musketeers*. Porthos has planted a
bomb. As he walks away he looks at his feet and wonders how they move.
He stops. The bomb explodes, and as Parain says, "La première fois qu'il
a pensé, il en est mort." This tragic joke forebodes the frailty of intellect,
and when Nana finds someone to love they read Edgar Allan Poe's story,
"The Oval Portrait," in which a young man paints (or renders into Art) the
woman he loves.

Et, pendant un moment, le peintre se tint en extase devant
le travail qu'il avait travaillé . . . mais une minute après, comme il
contemplait encore, il tremblait et il fut frappé d'effroi. Il criait
d'une voix éclatante: "En vérité, c'est la vie elle-même!" Il se
retourna brusquement pour regarder sa bien-aimée . . . elle était
morte.[2]

The literary allusiveness is typical of Godard's work because his men
in particular are representatives of a literary culture having landed on a new

1. *Vivre Sa Vie, L'Avant-Scène*, no. 19.
2. Ibid.

planet seeing the situations of literature occur haphazardly instead of purposefully. In *Le Petit Soldat* the end of Cocteau's *Thomas l'imposteur* is quoted: "Une balle, se dit-il, je suis perdu si je ne fais pas semblant d'être mort. Mais, en lui, la fiction et la réalité ne formaient qu'un. Guillaume Thomas était mort." The sort of consciousness that witnesses its own death is exactly that of the actress watching herself die on the screen, and Godard's usual actress is Anna Karina, his wife and ex-wife. This personal association is of great importance in Godard's movies in that there exists a tension between the cinematic enjoyment of Karina and the literary understanding of her. This tension is strongest in *Pierrot le fou* in which Belmondo plays a writer who runs away from a political maelstrom with Karina. Their love is constantly threatened by his intellectuality and the contrast it makes with her intuitiveness. Thus Godard associates the woman, either Karina or Macha Meril, most closely with the nature of film, while the man has the greater difficulty in conforming with the novel conditions of the visual society. All moral and authoritative criteria have vanished and in their place there exist equivalents of the camera's rules: life must move on; from one instant to another anything can happen; one cannot judge by appearances.

The logical consequence of these new rules is a society towards which Godard's films have been gradually evolving. It embodies the view that people are so effectively isolated by loneliness and subjectivity that they are like machines and that the only possible way to continue to live without breaking down is as a machine. Godard has thus turned Cocteau's romantic flourish at the end of *Thomas* to an image of a machine recording its own cessation. The ending of *Pierrot le fou* in which Belmondo wraps his head round with dynamite, lights the fuse and is unable to extinguish it in time, is an experiment and an accident because life has reached a stage when every action is an experiment and when every consequence can be experienced as an accident.

It is the complete dissolution of the humanist tradition. The conscience of the computer rather than that of the most sensitive artist is required to measure events. A perfect example of this is the return of the two soldiers, Ulysse and Michel-Ange, from the war in *Les Carabiniers*. They bring back postcards as symbols of their plunder. In a long, monotonous shot they put one after another on the table, their dull voices itemizing their titles. Cities, art treasures, beautiful women, wonders of the world. The fantastic contained by the commonplace. Godard's style is utterly photographic and non-interpretative. There is no question of how accurately the camera is recording an event. No more distinction exists between the two than between Rouch's tribesmen and their lion.

People cannot understand each other but neither can they avoid each other. The spatial relationship is the only language of human relationships. The hands that come together across a sheet at the beginning and part at the end of *Une Femme mariée* are attempts at a relationship. They are very personal emblems of sexuality representing the nakedness of the rest of the body. The images of hands, thighs, knees, shoulders and faces are cut together, creating an effect of serene eroticism. But this serenity is not romantic; it is the response of detachment. The hands are not only the private means of touch and caress but signs of identity—the rings indicating married status, smoothness female and hair male. They are at the same time intimate and impersonal. Their actions are independent to the point of being mechanical and consequently their intentions are interchangeable. The emotion in these sequences is by necessity generalized because Macha Meril senses the fallibility of depending upon personalization.

This reflective automatization of private behavior is very typical of Godard and it constitutes what one might call a bathroom apprehension of life. Allowing that in the bathroom the most personal acts are carried out with the least self-consciousness, the torture scene in *Le Petit Soldat* and the analysis of prostitution in *Vivre sa vie* provide further examples of the way in which emotional involvement to the extent of degradation is absolved by a cold, factual account. Anna Karina lying with customer after customer and washing her hands between sessions—like the couples in *Une Femme mariée*—paradoxically discovers her soul through a consciousness of her precarious withdrawal. She might say like Meril: "Je sais pas c'qui arrive . . . Ca m'empêche de devenir folle."

The face of Macha Meril is a sign of human existence and human mortality: its elements are its own means of observation—eyes, ears, nose and mouth. Almost as if we were looking at the face of an insect we reject attributions of our own meaning and ideas that we might apply to it. We realize the anthropomorphism of such ideas. Looking at her face is like looking at a camera.

The means by which the apparatus of the film observes the characters is equally mechanical. No attempt is made to make them items in a construct or to make incidents pregnant with the evidence they contribute towards a construct. The sequence of events is perfectly compatible with the camera, rather than with the intellect. Godard's characters are in a position of affluence that is typical of the Western potential. They are cut off from the simple pastoral reality that supports life and from the possibility of finite relationships; they face the capacity of a mechanized society. The "social" and "economic" pressures on character of the novel have been removed and no profounder sequence is looked for than that of time. The variations of outer form in the different films are all random, even in *Vivre sa vie* which is divided into chapters, but where there is such a contrast between the literary structure and the inconsequent, unmotivated events that we realize that the idea of Karina's life that the chapters convey does not exclude all others from her consciousness. Her discovery of her own soul is not a religious experience or the artistic climax of self-knowledge like Lear's ''I am a very foolish, fond old man,'' but her description for herself of a consciousness, a method of treating chaos without being overcome by it.

Godard's people move and act, often, as if by random selection, pleased to be free from choice. In *Pierrot le fou* Belmondo runs away with Karina on impulse without questioning the corpse in her room. He is a writer and he has recollections of a literary culture—when he falls in love with her he cries. They move south into an image of the primeval forest, living alone on an island with a fox and a parrot. In this unaccompanied existence man is not a social being but a species characterizing his surroundings with his imaginative projections. The removal of the signs of society fulfills the consciousness they have already reached. For the idea of society has existed long enough in the abstract without a practical example and now must be given up. Like language it is not absolute but is effective only for as long as people respect it, like the rules of a game. The actions are private, their immediacy of execution overcoming doubts about explanation just as their physical contiguity obliterates the idea of emotional communication. The great actions in Godard's films—Karina dancing and writing a letter in *Vivre sa vie;* the moment's silence in *Bande à part;* Macha Meril being chased by her husband through their house in *Une Femme mariée,* and Belmondo and Karina crossing a river in *Pierrot*—are not indications of character and meaning, but revelations of total cinema in the sense that the cinematic method is providing a complete replica of human experience. The equality Godard's work realizes is a chilling one: that every person, every event is equally worth watching, that choice and selection, the distinctions of the artist, are tyrannous and deluding. *Pierrot le fou* is perhaps the first film that does not aspire to or need to be a masterpiece. It is a freedom won with more difficulty than its flawless autonomy suggests, for *Alphaville* does need to be a great work. In consequence it is Godard's dullest film. The primitive adoption of forces of good and evil has reverted to a tension of narrative and philosophical banality even though some of the particularization—Caution's arrival at the hotel, for instance—are brilliant metaphors of our present degradation. *Alphaville*'s intellectual pessimism makes it the sort of film Belmondo in *Pierrot* might have made. In it the savagery of life is focused sharply on its contemporary examples. The feminine imperturbability of *Pierrot* absolves the savagery and observes the events. Godard's greatest admission is his humility before Karina, who was his wife when they made *Vivre sa vie,* but who had left him when they made *Pierrot le fou.*

# Godard

## Susan Sontag

The relation to models offered by literature illuminates a major part of the history of cinema. Film, both protected and patronized by virtue of its dual status as mass entertainment and as art form, remains the last bastion of the values of the nineteenth-century novel and theater—even to many of the same people who have found accessible and pleasurable such post-novels as *Ulysses*, *Between the Acts*, *The Unnamable*, *Naked Lunch*, and *Pale Fire*, and the corrosively de-dramatized dramas of Beckett, Pinter and the Happenings. Thus, the standard criticism leveled against Godard is that his plots are undramatic, arbitrary, often simply incoherent; and that his films generally are emotionally cold, static except for a busy surface of senseless movements, top-heavy with undramatized ideas, unecessarily obscure. What his detractors don't grasp, of course, is that Godard doesn't want to do what they reproach him for not doing. Thus, audiences at first took the jump-cuts in *Breathless* to be a sign of amateurishness, or a perverse flouting of self-evident rules of cinematic technique; actually, what looks as though the camera had stopped inadvertently for a few seconds in the course of a shot and then started up again was an effect Godard deliberately obtained in the cutting room, by snipping pieces out of perfectly smooth takes. (If one sees *Breathless* today, however, the once obtrusive cutting and the oddities of the hand-held camera are almost invisible, so widely imitated are these techniques now.)

No less deliberate is Godard's disregard for the formal conventions of film narration based on the nineteenth-century novel—cause-and-effect sequences of events, climactic scenes, logical dénouements. At the Cannes Film Festival several years ago, Godard entered into debate with Georges Franju, one of France's most talented and idiosyncratic senior directors. "But surely, Monsieur Godard," the exasperated Franju is reported to have said at one point, "you do at least acknowledge the necessity of having a beginning, middle and end in your films." "Certainly," Godard replied, "But not necessarily in that order."

Still, unsatisfactory as the plots of his films may be to many people, it would hardly be correct to describe Godard's films as plotless—like, say, Djiga Vertov's *The Man With the Camera,* the two silent films of Buñuel (*L'Age d'Or, Un Chien andalou*) or Kenneth Anger's *Scorpio Rising,* films in which a story-line has been completely discarded as the narrative framework. As in many conventional feature films, Godard proposes an interrelated group of fictional characters located in a recognizable, contemporary, usually urban landscape (Paris), but the sequence of events suggests a fully articulated story without adding up to one. The audience is presented with a narrative line that is partly erased or effaced (the structural equivalent of the jump-cut). Disregarding the traditional novelist's rule of explaining things as fully as they seem in need of explanation, Godard provides simplistic motives or frequently leaves motives unexplained; actions are often opaque, and fail to issue into consequences; occasionally the dialogue itself is not entirely audible. (Of course, there are other films, like Rossellini's *Journey to Italy* and Resnais' *Muriel,* employing a comparably "unrealistic" system of narration, in which the story is decomposed into disjunct objectified elements; but Godard, the only director with a whole body of work along these lines, has suggested more of the diverse routes for "abstracting" from an ostensibly realistic narrative than any other director. It is important, too, to distinguish various structures of abstracting—as, for instance, between the systematically "indeterminate" plot of Bergman's *Persona* and the "intermittent" plots of Godard's films.)

Thus, it is precisely the presence, not the absence, of story in Godard's films that gives rise to the standard criticism made of them. Godard's modifying, rather than making a complete rupture with, the conventions of prose fiction underlying the main tradition of cinema seems to have made more difficulties for audiences than the forthright "poetic" or "abstract" narration practiced by the official cinematic avant-garde. Another difficulty is the sources from which Godard draws some of the plots he will modify but not altogether obliterate. Like many directors, he prefers mediocre, even subliterary material, finding it easier to dominate and transform by the *mise-en-scène.* "I don't really like telling a story," Godard has written, somewhat simplifying the matter. "I prefer to use a kind of tapestry, a background on which I can embroider my own ideas. But I generally do need a story. A conventional one serves as well, perhaps even best." Thus, Godard has ruthlessly described the novel on which his brilliant *Contempt* was based, Moravia's *Ghost at Noon,* as "a nice novel for a train journey, full of old-fashioned sentiments. But it is with this kind of novel that one can make the best films." Although *Contempt* stays close to Moravia's story, Godard's films usually show few traces of their literary origins. At the other extreme but more typical is *Masculine-Feminine*, which bears no recognizable relation to the stories by Maupassant, "La Femme de Paul" and "La Signe," from which Godard drew his original inspiration.

But whether used as text or pretext, it hasn't ordinarily been a novel of old-fashioned sentiments that Godard has chosen as his point of departure, but heavily-plotted action stories. He has a particular fondness for American *kitsch*. *Made in U.S.A.* was based on *The Jugger* by Richard Stark, *Pierrot le fou* on *Obsession* by Lionel White and *Band of Outsiders* on Dolores Hitchens' *Fool's Gold*. Godard resorts to popular American narrative conventions as a fertile, solid basis for his own antinarrative inclinations. "The Americans know how to tell stories very well; the French not at all. Flaubert and Proust don't know how to narrate; they do something else." Though that something else is plainly what Godard is after too, he has discerned the utility of starting from crude narrative. One allusion to this strategy is the memorable dedication of *Breathless:* "To Monogram Pictures." (In its original version, *Breathless* had no credit titles whatever, and the first image of the film was preceded only by this terse salute to Hollywood's most prolific purveyors of low-budget quickie action pictures during the nineteen thirties and early nineteen forties.) Godard wasn't being impudent or flippant here—or only a little bit. Melodrama is one of the integral resources of his plotting. Think of the comic-strip quest of *Alphaville;* the gangster-movies romanticism of *Breathless, Band of Outsiders* and *Made in U.S.A.;* the spy-thriller ambiance of *Le Petit Soldat* and *Pierrot le fou.* For, precisely melodrama—which is characterized by the exaggeration, the frontality, the opaqueness of "action"—provides a framework for both intensifying and transcending traditional realistic procedures of serious film narrative, but in a way which isn't necessarily condemned (as the Surrealist films were) to seeming esoteric. By adapting familiar, second-hand, vulgar materials—popular myths of action and sexual glamor—Godard gains a considerable freedom to "abstract" without losing the possibility of a commercial theater audience.

These materials being what they are, Godard's films retain some of the vivacity of their simplistic literary and cinematic models. Even as he employs the narrative conventions of the *série noire* novels and the Hollywood thrillers, transposing them into abstract elements, Godard has responded to their casual, sensuous energy and been able to introduce some of that into his own work. One result is that most of his films give the impression of speed, verging sometimes on haste. In some respects,

Godard seems to be applying the same assumptions about material as the great silent director, Louis Feuillade, who worked in the debased form of the crime serial. Feuillade's temperament, though, seems more dogged. On a few essentially limited themes (like ingenuity, ruthlessness, physical grace), Feuillade's films present a seemingly inexhaustible number of formal variations. His choice of the open-ended serial form is thus entirely appropriate. After the twenty episodes of *Les Vampires*, nearly seven hours of projection time, it's clear there was no necessary end to the exploits of the stupendous Musidora and her gang of masked criminals, any more than the exquisitely matched struggle between archcriminal and archdetective in *Judex* need ever end. The rhythm of incident Feuillade establishes is subject to indefinitely prolonged repetition and embellishment, like a sexual fantasy elaborated in secret over a long period of time. Godard's films move to a quite different rhythm; they lack the unity of fantasy, along with its obsessional gravity, and its tireless, somewhat mechanistic repetitiveness.

The difference is accounted for by realizing that, while the hallucinatory, absurd, abstracted action tale is a central resource for Godard, it doesn't control the form of his films as it did for Feuillade. Although melodrama remains one term of Godard's sensibility, what has increasingly emerged as the opposing term is the resources of fact—the impulsive, dissociated tone of melodrama contrasting with the gravity and controlled indignation of the sociological exposé (note the recurrent theme of prostitution in *Une Femme coquette, My Life to Live, A Married Woman, Deux ou trois choses,* and *Anticipation*), or the even cooler tones of straight documentary and quasi-sociology (in *Masculine-Feminine, La Chinoise*).

Though Godard has toyed with the idea of the serial form, as in the end of *Band of Outsiders* (which promises a sequel, never made, relating further adventures of its hero and heroine in Latin America) and in the general conception of *Alphaville* (proposed as the latest adventure of a French serial hero, Lemmy Caution), Godard's films don't relate unequivocally to any single genre. The open-endedness of Godard's films doesn't mean the hyperexploitation of some particular genre, as in Feuillade, but a successive devouring of genres. The countertheme to the restless activity of the characters in Godard's films is an expressed dissatisfaction with the limits or stereotyping of "actions." Thus, in *Pierrot le fou,* Marianne's being bored or fed up moves what there is of a plot; at one point she says directly to the camera: "Let's leave the Jules Verne novel, and go back to the *roman policier* with guns and so on."

The organizing principle of Godard's films is not serial repetitiveness and obsessional elaboration, but the juxtaposition of contrary elements of unpredictable length and explicitness. If Feuillade's work implicitly conceives art as the gratification and prolongation of fantasy, Godard's work implies a quite different function for art: sensory and conceptual dislocation. Each of Godard's films is a totality that undermines itself, what Sartre calls a de-totalized totality.

Instead of a narration unified by the coherence of events (a "plot") and a consistent tone (comic, serious, oneiric, affectless or whatever), the narrative of Godard's films is regularly broken or segmented by the incoherence of events and by abrupt shifts in tone and level of discourse. Events appear to the spectator partly as converging toward a story, partly as a succession of independent tableaux.

The most obvious way Godard segments the forward-moving sequence of narration into tableaux is by explicitly theatricalizing some of his material, once more laying to rest the lively prejudice that there is an essential incompatibility between the means of theater and those of film. The conventions of the Hollywood musical, with songs and stage performances interrupting the story, supply one precedent for Godard—inspiring the general conception of *A Woman Is a Woman*, the dance trio in the café in *Band of Outsiders*, the song sequences and Vietnam protest skit performed on the street in *Pierrot le fou*. His other model is, of course, the nonrealistic and didactic theater expounded by Brecht. An aspect of Godard's Brechtianizing is his distinctive style of constructing political micro-entertainments: in *La Chinoise*, the home political theater-piece acting out the American aggression in Vietnam; or the Feiffer dialogue of the two ham radio operators that opens *Deux ou trois choses*. But the more profound influence of Brecht resides in those formal devices Godard uses to counteract ordinary plot development and complicate the emotional involvement of the audience. One technique is the direct-to-camera declarations by the characters in many films, notably *Deux ou trois choses*, *Made in U.S.A.* and *La Chinoise*. ("One should speak as if one were quoting the truth," says Marina Vlady at the beginning of *Deux ou trois choses*, quoting Brecht. "The actors must quote.") Another frequently used technique derived from Brecht is the dissection of the film narrative into short sequences: in *My Life to Live*, not only is this done, but Godard puts on the screen prefatory synopses to each scene which describe the action to follow. Another, simpler device is the relatively arbitrary subdivision of action into numbered sequences, as when the credits of *Masculine-Feminine* announce a film consisting of "fifteen precise actions" (*quinze faits précis*). A minimal device is the ironic, pseudoquantitative statement of something, as in the brief monologue of Charlotte's little son explaining how to do an unspecified something in exactly ten steps in *A Married Woman*.

Apart from the general strategy of "theater," perhaps the most striking application of the dissociative principle in Godard's narrative technique is his treatment of ideas. Certainly ideas are not developed in Godard's films systematically, as they might be in a book. They aren't meant to be. In contrast to their role in Brechtian theater, ideas are chiefly formal elements in Godard's films, units of sensory and emotional stimulation. They function at least as much to dissociate and fragment as they do to indicate or illuminate the "meaning" of the action. Often the ideas, rendered in blocks of words, lie at a tangent to the action. Nana's reflections on sincerity and language in *My Life to Live,* Bruno's observations about truth and action in *Le Petit Soldat,* the intellectually articulate self-consciousness of Charlotte in *A Married Woman* and of Juliette in *Deux ou Trois Choses,* Lemmy Caution's startling aptitude for cultivated literary allusions in *Alphaville* are not functions of the realistic psychology of these characters. (Perhaps the only one of Godard's intellectually reflective protagonists who still seems "in character" when ruminating is Ferdinand in *Pierrot le fou.*) Although Godard proposes film discourse as one constantly open to ideas, ideas are only one element in a narrative form in which there is an intentionally ambiguous, open, playful relation of *all* the parts to the total scheme.

A variant on the presence of ideas in Godard's films is the introduction of literary "texts." Among the many instances: the Mayakovsky poem recited by the girl about to be executed by a firing squad in *Les Carabiniers;* the excerpt from the Poe story read aloud in the next-to-last episode in *My Life to Live;* the lines from Dante, Hölderlin, and Brecht that Lang quotes in *Contempt;* the passage from Elie Fauré's *History of Art* read aloud by Ferdinand to his young daughter in *Pierrot le fou;* the lines from *Romeo and Juliet* in French translation dictated by the English teacher in *Band of Outsiders;* the scene from Racine's *Bérénice* rehearsed by Charlotte and her lover in *A Married Woman;* the quote from Fritz Lang read aloud by Camille in *Contempt;* the passages from Mao declaimed by the FLN agent in *Le Petit Soldat;* the antiphonal recitations from the little red book in *La Chinoise.* Usually someone makes an announcement before beginning to declaim, or can be seen taking up a book and reading from it. These texts introduce psychologically dissonant elements into the action; they supply rhythmical variety (temporarily slowing down the action); they interrupt the action and offer ambiguous comment on it; and they also vary and extend the point of view represented in the film.

Alien to movies as this kind of material may seem, at least in such profusion, Godard would no doubt argue that books and other vehicles of cultural consciousness are part of the world; therefore they belong in films. Indeed, by putting on the same plane the fact that people read and think and go seriously to the movies as the fact that they feel and act, Godard has disclosed a new vein of lyricism and pathos for cinema: in bookishness, in genuine cultural passion, in intellectual callowness, in the misery of someone strangling in his own thoughts. (An instance of Godard's original way with a vein hardly neglected in movies, the poetry of loutish illiteracy, is the twelve-minute sequence in *Les Carabiniers* in which the soldiers unpack their picture-postcard trophies.) His point is that no material is inherently unassimilable. But what's required is that literature indeed undergo its tranformation into material, just like anything else. All that can be given are literary extracts, shards of literature. In order to be absorbed by cinema, literature must be dismantled or broken into wayward units; then Godard can appropriate a portion of the intellectual "content" of any book (fiction or nonfiction), borrow from the public domain of culture any contrasting tone of voice (noble or vulgar), invoke in an instant any diagnosis of contemporary malaise that is tactically relevant to his narrative, no matter how inconsistent with the psychological scope or mental competence of the characters as already established it may be. The spectator is almost bound to be misled if he regards these texts simply, either as opinons of characters in the film or as samples of some unified point of view advocated by the film which presumably is clear to the director. More likely, just the opposite is or comes to be the case. Aided by "ideas" and "texts," Godard's film narratives tend to consume the points of view presented in them.

Like the ideas, which function partly as divisive elements, the fragments of cultural lore embedded in Godard's films serve in part as a form of mystification and a means for refracting emotional energy. Inevitably, Godard broaches the menace of the bastardization of culture, a theme most broadly stated in *Contempt* in the figure of the American producer with his booklet of proverbs. And, laden as his films are with furnishings of high culture, it's perhaps equally inevitable that Godard should also treat the project of laying down the burden of culture, as Ferdinand in *Pierrot le fou* does when he abandons his life in Paris for the romantic journey southward carrying only a book of old comics. The theme of cultural disburdenment is treated most fully and ironically in *La Chinoise*. One sequence shows the young cultural revolutionaries purging their shelves of all their books but the little red one. Another brief sequence shows just a blackboard at first, filled with the neatly listed names of several dozen stars of Western culture from Plato to Shakespeare to Sartre; these are then erased one by one, thoughtfully, with Brecht the last to go. The five pro-Chinese students who live together want to have only one point of view, that of Chairman Mao; but Godard shows, without insulting anyone's intelligence, how chimerical and inadequate to reality (and yet how appealing) this hope actually is. For all his native tendency to sympathize with the most radical view, Godard himself still appears a partisan of that other cultural revolution, ours, which enjoins the artist-thinker to maintain a multiplicity of points of view on any material.

All the devices he uses to keep shifting the point of view within a film themselves contribute to a larger strategy of overlaying a number of narrative voices, whereby Godard appears to bridge the difference between first-person and third-person narration. Thus *Alphaville* opens with three samples of first-person discourse: first, a prefatory statement spoken off-camera by Godard; then a declaration by the computer-ruler Alpha 60; and only then the usual soliloquizing voice, that of the secret-agent hero, shown grimly driving his big car into the city of the future. Instead of, or in addition to, using "titles" between scenes as narrative signals (for example, *My Life to Live, A Married Woman*) Godard seems now more likely to install a narrating voice in the film. This voice may belong to the main character: Bruno's musings in *Le Petit Soldat,* Charlotte's free-associating subtext in *A Married Woman,* Paul's commentary in *Masculine Feminine.* It may be the director's, as in *Band of Outsiders* and "Le Grand Escroc," the sketch from *Les Plus Belles Escroqueries du monde.* What's most interesting is when there are two voices: as in *Deux ou trois choses,* throughout which both Godard (whispering) and the heroine comment on the action. *Band of Outsiders* introduces the notion of a narrative intelligence which can "open a parenthesis" in the action and directly address the audience, explaining what Franz, Odile and Arthur are really feeling at that moment; the narrator can intervene or comment ironically on the action or on the very fact of seeing a movie. (Fifteen minutes into the film, Godard off-camera says, "For the latecomers, what's happened so far is. . . .") Thereby two different but concurrent times are established in the film—the time of the action shown, and time of the narrator's reflection on what's shown—in a way which allows free passage back and forth between the first-person narration and the third-person presentation of the action.

Although the narrating voice already has a major role in some of his earliest work (for instance, the virtuoso comic monologue of the last of the pre-*Breathless* shorts, *Une Histoire d'eau*), Godard continues to extend and complicate the task of oral narration, arriving at such recent refinements as the beginning of *Deux ou Trois Choses,* when Godard off-camera first introduces his leading actress, Marina Vlady, by name and then describes her as the character she will play. Such procedures tend, of course, to reinforce the self-reflexive and self-referring aspect of Godard's films, for the ultimate narrative presence is simply the fact of cinema itself; from which it follows that, for the sake of truth, the cinematic medium must be made to manifest itself before the spectator. Godard's methods for doing this range from the simple ploy of having an actor make rapid playful asides to the camera (i.e., to the audience) in mid-action, which happens in many of his films, to the aggressive devices in *La Chinoise* such as flashing the claque on the screen from time to time, or briefly cutting to Raoul Coutard, the cameraman on this as on most of Godard's films, seated behind his apparatus. But then one immediately thinks of some underling holding another claque while that scene was shot, of someone else who had to be there behind another camera to photograph Coutard. It's impossible ever to penetrate behind the final veil and experience cinema unmediated by cinema.

But perhaps it would be more accurate to say that Godard proposes a new conception of point of view, thereby staking out the possibility of making films in the first person. By this, I don't mean simply that his films are subjective or personal, like those of many other directors, particularly in the cinematic avant-garde and underground, but something stricter and more original—namely, the way in which Godard, especially in his recent films, has built up a narrative presence, that of the film-maker, who is the central *structural* element in the cinemaic narrative. This first-person film-maker isn't an actual character within the film. That is, he isn't to be seen on the screen (except in the episode in *Far from Vietnam*, which shows only Godard at a camera talking), though he is to be heard from time to time and one is increasingly aware of his presence just off-camera. But neither is this off-screen persona a lucid, authorial intelligence, like the detached observer-figure of many novels cast in the first person. The ultimate first person in Godard's movies, his particular version of the filmmaker, is the person responsible for the film who yet stands outside it as a mind beset by more complex, fluctuating concerns than any single film can represent or incarnate. The most profound drama of a Godard film arises from the clash between this restless, wider consciousness of the director and the determinate, limited argument of the particular film he's engaged in making. Therefore each film is, simultaneously, a creative activity and a destructive one. The director virtually uses up his models, his sources, his themes, his ideas, his latest moral and artistic enthusiasms— and the shape of the film consists of various means for letting the audience know that's what is happening. This dialectic has reached its furthest development so far in *Deux ou trois choses,* which is more ambitiously a "first-person film" than any Godard has made.

The advantage of the first-person mode for cinema is presumably that it vastly augments the liberty of the film-maker while at the same time providing incentives for greater formal rigor—the same pair of goals espoused by all the serious post-novelists of this century. Thus Gide has Edouard, the author-protagonist of *The Counterfeiters,* condemn all previous novels because their contours are "defined," so that, however perfect, what they must contain is "captive and lifeless." He wanted to write a novel that would "run freely" because he had chosen "not to foresee its windings." But the liberation of the novel turned out to consist in writing a novel about writing a novel: presenting "literature" within literature. In a different context, Brecht discovered "theater" within theater. Godard has discovered "cinema" within cinema. However loose or spontaneous-looking or personally self-expressive his films may appear, what must be appreciated is that Godard has subscribed to a severely alienated conception of his art: a cinema that eats cinema. Each film is an ambiguous event that must be simultaneously promulgated and destroyed. Godard's most explicit statement of this theme is the painful monologue of self-interrogation which was his contribution to *Far from Vietnam*. Perhaps his wittiest statement of this theme is a scene in *Les Carabiniers* (similar to the end of an early Mack Sennett two-reeler, *Mabel's Dramatic Career*) in which Michelangelo takes time off from the war to visit a movie theater, apparently for the first time, since his reaction resembles that of audiences sixty years ago when movies first began to be shown. He follows the movements of the actors on the screen with his whole body, ducks under the seat when a train appears, and at last, driven wild by the sight of a girl taking a bath in the film within a film, bolts from his seat and rushes up to the stage. After first standing on tiptoe to try to look into the tub, then feeling tentatively for the girl along the surface of the screen, he finally tries to grab her—ripping away part of the screen within the screen, and revealing the girl and the bathroom to be a projection on a filthy wall.

Though all of Godard's distinctive devices serve the fundamental aim of breaking up the narrative or varying the perspective, he doesn't aim at a systematic variation of points of view. Sometimes, to be sure, Godard does elaborate a strong plastic conception—like the intricate visual patterns of the couplings of Charlotte with her lover and her husband in *A Married Woman;* and the brilliant formal metaphor of the monochromatic photography in three "political colors" in *Anticipation*. Still, Godard's work characteristically lacks formal rigor. The jump-cuts in *Breathless,* for instance, are not of any strict rhythmic scheme, an observation that's confirmed by Godard's account of their rationale. "I discovered in *Breathless* that when a discussion between two people became boring and tedious one could just as well cut between the speeches. I tried it once, and it went very well, so I did the same thing right through the film." Godard may be exaggerating the casualness of his attitude in the cutting room, but his reliance upon intuition on the set is well-known. For no film has a full shooting script been prepared in advance, and many films have been improvised day by day throughout large parts of the shooting; in the recent films shot with direct sound, Godard has the actors wear tiny earphones so that while they are on camera he can speak to each of them privately, feeding them lines or posing questions which they're to answer (direct-to-camera interviews).

From Godard's penchant for improvisation, for incorporating accidents and for location shooting, one might infer a lineage from the neorealist aesthetic made famous by Italian films of the last twenty-five years, starting with Visconti's *Ossessione* and *La terra trema* and reaching its apogee in the postwar films of Rossellini and the recent debut of Olmi. But Godard, although a fervent admirer of Rossellini, is not even a neo-neorealist, and is far from aiming to expel the artifice from art. What he seeks is to conflate the traditional polarities of spontaneous mobile thinking and finished work, of the casual jotting and the fully premediated statement. Spontaneity, casualness, lifelikeness are not values in themselves for Godard, who is interested rather in the *convergence* of spontaneity with the emotional discipline of abstraction (the dissolution of ''subject matter''). The results are, needless to say, far from tidy. Although Godard achieved the basis of his distinctive style very quickly (by 1958), the restlessness of his temperament and his evident intellectual voracity impel him to adopt an essentially exploratory posture in relation to film-making, in which he may answer a problem raised but not resolved in one film by starting on another. Still, viewed as a whole, Godard's work is much closer in problems and scope to a radical purist and formalist in film like Bresson than to the neorealists—even though the relation with Bresson must be drawn largely in terms of contrasts.

Bresson also achieved his mature style very quickly, but his career has throughout consisted of thoroughly premeditated, independent works conceived within the limits of his personal aesthetic of concision and intensity. (Born in 1910, Bresson has made eight feature films, the first in 1943 and the most recent in 1967.) Bresson's art is characterized by a pure, lyric quality, by a naturally elevated tone and by a carefully constructed unity. He has said, in an interview conducted by Godard (*Cahiers du Cinéma,* no. 178, May 1966), that for him ''improvisation is at the base of creation in the cinema.'' But the look of a Bresson film is surely the antithesis of improvisation. In the finished film, a shot must be both autonomous and necessary; which means that there's only one ideally correct way of composing each shot (though it may be arrived at quite intuitively) and of editing the shots into a narrative. For all their great energy, Bresson's films project an air of formal deliberateness, of having been organized according to a relentless, subtly calculated rhythm which required their having had everything inessential cut from them. Given his austere aesthetic, it seems apt that Bresson's characteristic subject is a person either literally imprisoned or locked within an excruciating dilemma. Indeed, if one does accept narrative and tonal unity as a primary standard for film, Bresson's asceticism—his maximal use of minimal materials, the meditative "closed" quality of his films—seems to be the only truly rigorous procedure.

Godard's work exemplifies an aesthetic (and, no doubt, a temperament and sensibility) the opposite of Bresson's. The moral energy informing Godard's film-making, while no less powerful than Bresson's, leads to a quite different asceticism: the labor of endless self-questioning, which becomes a constitutive element in the art work. "More and more with each film," he said in 1965, "it seems to me the greatest problem in filming is to decide where and why to begin a shot and why to end it." The point is that Godard cannot envisage anything but arbitrary solutions to his problem. While each shot is autonomous, no amount of thinking can make it necessary. Since film for Godard is preeminently an open structure, the distinction between what's essential and inessential in any given film becomes senseless. Just as no absolute, immanent standards can be discovered for determining the composition, duration and place of a shot, there can be no truly sound reason for excluding anything from a film. This view of film as an assemblage rather than a unity lies behind the seemingly facile characterizations Godard has made of many of his recent films. "*Pierrot le fou* isn't really a film, it's an attempt at cinema." About *Deux ou trois choses:* "In sum, it's not a film, it's an attempt at a film and is presented as such." *A Married Woman* is described in the main titles: "Fragments of a Film Shot in 1964" and *La Chinoise* is subtitled "A Film in the Process of Being Made." In claiming to be offering no more than "efforts" or "attempts," Godard acknowledges the structural openness or arbitrariness of his work. Each film remains a fragment in the sense that its possibilities of elaboration can never be used up. For granted the acceptability, even desirability, of the method of juxtaposition ("I prefer simply putting things side by side") which assembles contrary elements without reconciling them, there can indeed be no internally necessary end to a Godard film, as there is to a film of Bresson. Every film must either seem broken off abruptly or else ended arbitrarily—often by the violent death in the last reel of one or more of the main characters, as in *Breathless, Le Petit Soldat, My Life to Live, Les Carabiniers, Contempt, Masculine-Feminine,* and *Pierrot le fou.*

Predictably, Godard has supported his views by pressing the relationship (rather than the disjunction) between "art" and "life." Godard claims never to have had the feeling as he worked, which he thinks a novelist must have, "that I am differentiating between life and creation." Or the familiar mythical terrain is claimed once again: "the cinema is somewhere between

art and life.'' Of *Pierrot le fou,* Godard has written: ''Life is the subject,
with Scope and color as its attributes. . . . Life on its own as I would like to
capture it, using pan shots on nature, *plans fixes* on death, brief shots, long
takes, soft and loud sounds, the movements of Anna and Jean-Paul. In
short, life filling the screen as a tap fills a bathtub that is simultaneously
emptying at the same rate.'' This, Godard claims, is how he differs from
Bresson, who, when shooting a film, has ''an idea of the world'' that he is
''trying to put on the screen or, which comes to the same thing, an idea of
the cinema'' he's trying ''to apply to the world.'' For a director like
Bresson, ''cinema and the world are moulds to be filled, while in *Pierrot*
there is neither mould nor matter.''

Of course Godard's films aren't bathtubs; and Godard harbors his
complex sentiments about the world and his art to the same extent and in
pretty much the same way as Bresson does. But despite Godard's lapse into
a disingenuous rhetoric, the contrast with Bresson stands. For Bresson,
who was originally a painter, it is the austerity and rigor of cinematic
means which make this art (though very vew movies) valuable to him. For
Godard, it's the fact that cinema is so loose, promiscuous and accom-
modating a medium which gives movies, even many inferior ones, their
authority and promise. Specifically, this fact is what gives film the decisive
advantage over literature in the quest for a truly spontaneous or discovered
form such as Edouard envisages for the novel in *The Counterfeiters*. Film
can mix forms, techniques, points of view; it can't be identified with any
single leading ingredient. Indeed, precisely what the film-maker must
show is that nothing is excluded. ''One can put everything in a film,'' says
Godard. ''One must put everything in a film.''

A film is conceived of as a living organism: not so much an object as a
presence or an encounter—a fully historical or contemporary event, whose
destiny is to be transcended by future events. Seeking to create a cinema
which inhabits the real present, Godard regularly puts in his films references to current political crises: Algeria, de Gaulle's domestic politics,
Angola, the Vietnam war. (Each of his last four features includes a scene in
which the main characters denounce American aggression in Vietnam, and
Godard has declared that until that war ends he'll put such a sequence into
every film he makes.) The films may include even more casual references
and off-the-cuff sentiments—a dig at André Malraux; a compliment to
Henri Langlois, director of the Cinemathèque Française; an attack on irresponsible projectionists who show 1:66 films in CinemaScope ratio; or a
plug for the unreleased movie of a fellow-director and friend. Godard
welcomes the opportunity to use the cinema topically, ''journalistically.''
As photography, cinema has always been an art which recorded temporality; but up to now this has been an inadvertent aspect of feature fiction

films. Godard is the first major director who deliberately incorporates certain contingent aspects of the particular social moment at which he's making a film—sometimes making these the frame of the film.

Unworried by the issue of impurity—there are no materials unusable for film—Godard is, nevertheless, involved in an extremely purist venture: the attempt to devise a structure for films which speaks in a purer present tense. His effort is to make movies which live in the actual present, and not to tell something from the past, relate something that's already taken place. In this project, of course, Godard is following a direction already taken in literature. Fiction, until recently, was the art of the past. Events told in an epic or novel are, when the reader starts the book, already (as it were) in the past. But in much of the new fiction, events pass before us as if in a present coexisting with the time of the narrative voice (more accurately, with the time in which the reader is being addressed by the narrative voice). Events exist, therefore, in the present—at least as much of the present that reader himself inhabits. It is for this reason that such writers as Beckett, Stein, Burroughs, and Robbe-Grillet prefer to use an actual present tense, or its equivalent. (Another strategy: to make the distinction between past, present and future time within the narration an explicit conundrum, and an insoluble one—as, for example, in some of the tales of Borges and Landolfi and in *Pale Fire*.) But if the development is feasible for literature, it would seem even more apt for film to make a comparable move since, in a way, film narration knows *only* the present tense. (Everything shown is equally present, no matter when it is "said" to have taken place.) What was necessary for film to exploit its natural liberty was to have a much looser, less literal attachment to telling a "story." A story in the traditional sense—something that's already taken place—is replaced by a segmented situation in which the suppression of certain explicative connections between scenes creates the impression of an action continually beginning anew, unfolding in the present tense.

And, of necessity, I should argue, this present tense must appear as a somewhat behaviorist, external, antipsychological view of the human situation. For psychological understanding depends on holding in mind simultaneously the dimensions of past, present and future. To see someone psychologically is to lay out temporal coordinates in which he is situated. An art which aims at the present tense cannot aspire to this kind of "depth" or innerness in the portrayal of human beings. The lesson is already clear from the work of Stein and Beckett; Godard demonstrates it for film.

Godard explicitly alludes to this choice only once, in connection with *My Life to Live* which, he says, he "built . . . in tableaux to accentuate the theatrical side of the film. Besides, this division corresponded to the external view of things which best allowed me to give a feeling of what was going on inside. In other words, a contrary procedure to that used by Bresson in *Pickpocket,* in which the drama is seen from within. How can one render the 'inside'? I think, by staying prudently outside." But though there are obvious advantages to staying "outside"—flexibility of form, freedom from superimposed limiting solutions—the choice is not as clear-cut as Godard suggests. Perhaps one never goes "inside" in the sense Godard attributes to Bresson—a procedure already considerably different from the reading-off of motives and summing-up of a character's interior life promoted by nineteenth-century novelistic realism. Indeed, by those standards, Bresson is himself considerably "outside" his characters; for instance, more involved in their somatic presence, the rhythm of their movements, the heavy weight of inexpressible feeling which they bear.

Still, Godard is right in saying that, compared with Bresson, he is "outside." One way he stays outside is by constantly shifting the point of view from which the film is told, by the juxtaposition of contrasting narrative elements: realistic alongside implausible aspects of the story, written signs interposed between images, anecdotes or "texts" recited aloud interrupting dialogue, static interviews as against rapid actions, interpolation of a narrator's voice explaining or commenting on the action and so forth. A second way is by his rendering of "things" in a strenuously neutralized fashion, in contrast with Bresson's thoroughly intimate vision of things as objects used, disputed, loved, ignored and worn out by people. Things in Bresson's films, whether a spoon, a chair, a piece of bread, a pair of shoes, are always marked by their human use. The point is *how* they are used— whether skillfully (as the prisoner uses his spoon in *Un Condamné à mort* and the heroine of *Mouchette* uses the saucepan and bowls to make breakfast coffee) or clumsily. In Godard's films, things display a wholly alienated character. Characteristically, they are used with indifference, neither skillfully nor clumsily; they are simply there. Godard has written: "Objects exist, and if one pays more attention to them than to people, it is precisely because they exist more than these people. Dead objects are still alive. Living people are often already dead." Whether things are the occasion for visual gags (like the suspended egg in *A Woman Is a Woman,* and the movie billboards in the warehouse in *Made in U.S.A.*) or introduce an element of great plastic beauty (as do the Pongeist studies in *Deux ou Trois Choses* of the burning end of a cigarette and of bubbles separating and coming together on the surface of a hot cup of coffee), they always occur in a context of, and serve to reinforce, emotional dissociation. The most noticeable form of Godard's dissociated rendering of things is his ambivalent immersion in the allure of pop imagery and only partly ironic display of the symbolic currency of urban capitalism—pinball machines, boxes of detergent, fast cars, neon signs, billboards, fashion magazines. By extension, this fascination with alienated things dictates the settings of most of Godard's films: highways, airports, anonymous hotel rooms or soulless modern apartments, brightly-lit modernized cafes, movie theaters. The furniture and settings of Godard's films is the landscape of alienation— whether he is displaying the pathos in the mundane facticity of the actual life of dislocated, urban persons such as petty hoodlums, discontented housewives, left-wing students, prostitutes (the everyday present) or presenting antiutopian fantasies about the cruel future.

A universe experienced as fundamentally dehumanized or dissociated is also one conducive to rapid "associating" from one ingredient in it to another. Again, the contrast can be made with Bresson's attitude, which is rigorously nonassociative, and therefore concerned with the depth in any situation; in a Bresson film there are certain organically derived and mutually relevant exchanges of personal energy that flourish or exhaust themselves (either way, unifying the narrative and supplying it with an organic terminus). For Godard, there are no genuinely organic connections. In the universe of pain, only three strictly unrelated responses of real interest are possible: violent action, the probe of "ideas" and the transcendence of sudden, arbitrary, romantic love. But each of these possibilities is understood to be revocable, or artificial. They are not acts of personal fulfillment; not so much solutions as dissolutions of a problem. It has been noted that many of Godard's films project a masochistic view of women, verging on misogyny, and an indefatigable romanticism about "the couple." It's an odd but rather familiar combination of attitudes. Such contradictions are psychological or ethical analogues to Godard's fundamental formal presuppositions. In work conceived of as open-ended, associative, composed of "fragments," constructed by the (partly aleatoric) juxtaposition of contrary elements, any principle of action or any decisive emotional resolution is bound to be an artifice (from an ethical point of view) or ambivalent (from a psychological point of view).

Each film is a provisional network of emotional and intellectual impasses. With the probable exception of his view on Vietnam, there is no attitude Godard incorporates in his films that is not simultaneously being bracketed, and therefore criticized, by a dramatization of the gap between the elegance and seductiveness of ideas and the brutish or lyrical opaqueness of the human condition. The same sense of impasse characterizes Godard's moral judgments. For all the use made of the metaphor and fact of prostitution to sum up contemporary miseries, Godard's films are not "against" prostitution and "for" pleasure and liberty in the unequivocal sense that Bresson's films directly extol love, honesty, courage and dignity and deplore cruelty and cowardice.

From Godard's perspective, Bresson's work is bound to appear "rhetorical," whereas Godard is bent on destroying rhetoric by a lavish use of irony—the familiar outcome when a restless, somewhat dissociated intelligence struggles to cancel an irrepressible romanticism and tendency to moralize. In many of his films Godard deliberately seeks the framework of parody, of irony as contradiction. For instance, *A Woman Is a Woman* proceeds by putting an ostensibly serious theme (a woman frustrated both as wife and as would-be mother) in an ironically sentimental framework. "The subject of *A Woman Is a Woman*," Godard has said, "is a character who succeeds in resolving a certain situation, but I conceived this subject within the framework of a neo-realistic muscial: an *absolute contradiction,* but that was precisely why I wanted to make the film." Another example is the lyrical treatment of a rather nasty scheme of amateur gangsterism in *Band of Outsiders,* complete with the high irony of the "happy ending" in which Odile sails away with Franz to Latin America for further, romantic adventures. Another example: the nomenclature of *Alphaville,* a film in which Godard takes up some of his most serious themes, is a collection of comic strip identities (characters have names like Lemmy Caution, the hero of a famous series of French thrillers; Harry Dickson; Professor Leonard Nosferatu, alias Von Braun; Professor Jeckyll) and the lead is played by Eddie Constantine, the expatriate American actor whose mug has been a cliché of "B" French detective films for two decades; indeed, Godard's original title for the film was *Tarzan versus IBM*. Still another example: the film Godard decided to make on the double theme of the Ben Barka and Kennedy murders, *Made in U.S.A.,* was conceived as a parodic remake of *The Big Sleep* (which had been revived at an art house in Paris in the summer of 1966), with Bogart's role of the trench-coated detective embroiled in an insoluble mystery now played by Anna Karina. The danger of such lavish use of irony is that ideas will be expressed at their point of self-caricature, and emotions only when they are mutilated. Irony intensifies what is already a considerable limitation on the emotions in the films that results from the insistence on the pure presentness of cinema narration, in which situations with less deep affect will be disproportionately represented—the expense of vividly depicted states of grief, rage, profound erotic longing and fulfillment, and physical pain. Thus, while Bresson, at his almost unvarying best, is able to convey deep emotions without ever being sentimental, Godard, at his less effective, devises turns of plot that appear either hardhearted or sentimental (at the same time seeming emotionally flat).

Godard "straight" seems to me more successful—whether in the rare pathos he has allowed in *Masculine-Feminine,* or in the hard coolness of such directly passionate films as *Les Carabiniers, Contempt* and *Pierrot le fou*. This coolness is a pervasive quality of Godard's work. Strikingly, for all their violence of incident and sexual matter-of-factness, the films have a rather muted, detached relation to the grotesque and painful as well as to the seriously erotic. People are sometimes tortured and often die in Godard's films, but almost casually. (He has a particular predilection for automobile accidents: the end of *Contempt,* the wreck in *Pierrot le fou,* the landscape of affectless highway carnage in *Weekend.*) And people are rarely shown making love, though if they are, what interests Godard isn't the sensual communion but what sex reveals "about the spaces between people." The orgiastic moments come when young people dance together or sing or play games or run—people run beautifully in Godard movies—not when they make love.

"Cinema is emotion," says Samuel Fuller in *Pierrot le fou,* and one surmises that Godard shares that thought. But emotion, for Godard, never comes unaccompanied by some decoration of wit, some transmuting of feeling that he clearly puts at the center of the art-making process. This accounts in part for Godard's preoccupation with language—with words both heard and seen on the screen. Language functions as a means of emotional distancing from the action. The pictorial element is emotional, immediate; but words (including signs, texts, stories, sayings, recitations, interviews) have a lower temperature. While images invite the spectator to identify with what is seen, the presence of words makes the spectator into a critic.

But Godard's Brechtian use of language is only one aspect of the phenomenon. Much as Godard owes to Brecht, his treatment of language is far more complex and equivocal; and relates rather to the efforts of certain painters, who use words actively to undermine the image, to refute it, to render it opaque and unintelligible. It's not simply that Godard gives language a place that no other film director has before him. (Compare the verbosity of Godard's films with Bresson's verbal severity and austerity of dialogue.) He sees nothing in the film medium that prevents one of the subjects of cinema from being language itself—as language has become the very subject of much contemporary poetry and, in a metaphoric sense, of some important painting, such as that of Jasper Johns. But it seems likely that language will become the subject of cinema only at that point when a film-maker is obsessed by the problematic character of language—as Godard so evidently is. What other directors have regarded mainly as an adjunct of greater "realism" (the advantage of sound films as compared with silents) becomes in Godard's hands a virtually autonomous, sometimes subversive instrument.

Not only does Godard not regard cinema as essentially moving photographs; on the contrary, precisely the fact that movies, which purport to be a pictorial medium, admit of language being added in is what gives cinema its superior range and freedom compared with other art forms. Pictorial or photographic elements are in a sense only the raw materials of Godard's cinema; the transformative ingredient is the presence of language. Thus, to cavil at Godard for the talkiness of his films is to misunderstand his materials and his intentions. It is almost as if the pictorial image had a static quality, too close to "art," that Godard wants to infect with the blight of words. In *La Chinoise,* a sign on the wall of the student Maoist commune reads: "One must replace vague ideas with clear images." But that's only one side of the matter, as Godard knows. Sometimes images are too clear, too simple. (*La Chinoise* is Godard's sympathetic, witty treatment of the arch-Romantic wish to make oneself entirely simple, altogether clear.) The highly permutated dialectic between image and language is far from stable. As he declares in his own voice at the beginning of *Alphaville:* "Some things in life are too complex for oral transmission. So we make fiction out of them, to make them universal." But again, it's clear that making things universal can bring oversimplification, which must be combated by the concreteness and ambiguity of words.

Godard has always been fascinated by the opaqueness and coerciveness of language, and a recurrent feature of the film narratives is some sort of deformation of speech. Complementing these mutilations of speech and language are the many explicit discussions of language as a problem in Godard's films. The puzzle about how it's possible to make moral or intellectual sense by speaking, owing to the betrayal of consciousness by language, is debated in *My Life to Live* and *A Married Woman;* the ambiguities of language, in the mystery of "translating" from one language to another, is a theme in *Contempt* and *Band of Outsiders;* the language of the future is a subject of speculation by Guillaume and Veronique (it is to be altogether different; each word or phrase will be separate) in *La Chinoise;* the nonsensical underside of language is demonstrated in the exchange in the café between Marianne, the laborer and the bartender in *Made in U.S.A.;* and the effort to purify language of philosophical and cultural dissociation is the explicit, main theme of *Alphaville* and *Anticipation,* the success of an individual's efforts to do this providing the dramatic resolution of both films.

At this moment in Godard's work, the problem of language appears to have become his leading motif. Behind their obtrusive verbosity, Godard's films are haunted by the duplicity and banality of language. Insofar as there is a "voice" speaking in all his films, it is one that questions all voices. Language is the widest context in which Godard's recurrent theme of prostitution must be located. Beyond its direct sociological interest for Godard, prostitution is his extended metaphor for the fate of language, that is, of consciousness itself. The coalescing of the two themes is clearest in the science-fiction nightmare of *Anticipation:* in an airport hotel some time in the future (that is, now), travelers have the choice of two kinds of temporary sexual companions, someone who makes bodily love without speaking or someone who can recite the words of love but can't take part in any physical embrace. This schizophrenia of the flesh and the soul is the menace that inspires Godard's preoccupation with language, and confers on him the painful, self-interrogatory terms of his restless art. As Natasha declares at the end of *Alphaville:* "There are words I don't know." But it's that painful knowledge, according to Godard's controlling narrative myth, that marks the beginning of her redemption and—by an extension of the same project—the redemption of art itself.

# D. W. Griffith

DAVID WARK GRIFFITH was born in Kentucky in 1875 and died in Hollywood in 1948. He started out as a playwright and entered films as an actor, in 1907. He began directing one-reel and then two-reel films for the Biograph Company the following year, turning out several hundred by the time he left Biograph in 1913. These films were like sketches or short stories; they ransacked a wide range of literary sources, including Victorian poems, and gave Griffith abundant opportunity for the technical innovations by which he made his mark. Eventually, with the help of his cameraman, Billy Bitzer, Griffith perfected the visual language of film narrative. His contributions, which influenced all subsequent filmmakers, included explorations of montage (breaking down an action into a sequence of shots), the cross-cutting of different strands of action, and an extraordinarily poetic use of close-ups, for emphasis and emotional intimacy.

By 1913 Griffith had outgrown the narrow scope of the one- and two-reeler. His last Biograph film, Judith of Bethulia, an ambitious, expensive Biblical reconstruction, marked his transition to the feature film and foreshadowed the far more grandiose Intolerance (1916). Griffith's first masterpiece and greatest popular success was The Birth of a Nation (1915), an epic account of the Civil War and the rise of the Ku Klux Klan, seen through the eyes of two families caught on opposite sides. Griffith at heart was a nineteenth-century Southern gentleman, and many were offended by the film's Negro stereotypes and its glorification of the Klan and the Confederacy. Still, Griffith had a genius for sentimental melodrama and a gift for exciting, suspenseful narrative. In all his films his touching treatment of his heroines, played with delicacy and force by such actresses as Lillian and Dorothy Gish, Mae Marsh, and Blanche Sweet, offers us many remarkably poignant moments.

Griffith's next film, Intolerance, was far more expensive and ambitious; its failure with the public damaged Griffith's career. The film interweaves four separate stories which take place in different periods of history and are only loosely linked by the title theme. The most opulent and famous is the Babylonian story, for which Griffith constructed a monumental set that completely dwarfs the rather ridiculous action, especially in the outdoor scenes; the best is the affecting modern story, which develops a vein of low-life realism Griffith had already revealed in his short films; it concludes with a last-minute rescue for which Griffith's montage technique was ideally suited. Along with the thrilling rescue on the icy river at the end of Way Down East (1920), it had an important influence on world cinema, particularly on Soviet filmmakers of the 1920s such as Eisenstein and Pudovkin.

After the fiasco of Intolerance Griffith made several effective films on *a smaller scale, including two love stories,* Broken Blossoms *(1919) and* Way Down East; Orphans of the Storm, *a melodrama set in the period of the French Revolution (1922), with the Gish sisters; a historical tableau,* America *(1924); and a film shot partly on location in postwar Germany,* Isn't Life Wonderful *(1924), a further development in the direction of realism. His films of the late 1920s showed a sharp decline, since he no longer had full control over their production; even so, he ended his career with two interesting talking pictures,* Abraham Lincoln *(1930) and* The Struggle *(1931), a melodrama about a drunkard, withdrawn from circulation soon after it was released.*

*Robert M. Henderson has written a thorough biography,* D. W. Griffith: His Life and Work *(1972). Memoirs published by Griffith's co-workers include Lillian Gish,* The Movies, Mr. Griffith, and Me *(1969), and Karl Brown (Bitzer's assistant),* Adventures with D. W. Griffith *(1973). A classic essay on Griffith is Sergei Eisenstein's "Dickens, Griffith, and the Film Today," which can be found in* Film Form *(1949). See also the collections of essays edited by Harry M. Geduld and by Fred Silva (both 1971) and the detailed discussion by Edward Wagenknecht and Anthony Slide in* The Films of D. W. Griffith *(1976).*

# D. W. Griffith, or Genius American Style

*DWIGHT MACDONALD*

David Wark Griffith is the great pioneer of the cinema who, years before any other director, realized the possibilities of his medium. Intuitively, he grasped those essentials of cinematography which the Russians developed systematically a decade later. The typical finale he developed for his pictures, so invariable that it is called "the Griffith ending," is a crude but effective use of montage: the camera shuttling back and forth between the whites besieged in the cabin and the galloping Klansmen (*The Birth of a Nation*) or between the girl drifting toward the falls and her lover coming to her rescue (*Way Down East*) creates a rhythm that is purely cinematic. Griffith was also the first to make extensive use of the close-up, another basic element in modern technique, as well as of many lesser devices such as fade-outs and fade-ins. These devices are today such commonplaces that one notes chiefly the crudity with which Griffith employs them, but in his time they represented an advance into unexplored territory. Marlowe's development of blank verse was no more revolutionary.

If Griffith foreshadows the Russians in technique, he anticipates them even more strikingly in the subject matter he chooses and the way he treats it. His *Birth of a Nation* (1915) and *Intolerance* (1916) are the first movies to make use of the *extensive* powers of the cinema. They are the first movies conceived on such a scale that the individuals are less important than the vast background of time and space against which they move. Griffith treats his epic subjects as Eisenstein does, not as historical narratives running through time but as cinematizations in space of abstract themes. He shapes them primarily to express an *idea* ("War is terrible." "Through the ages love and intolerance have been at strife") to which the

From *Dwight Macdonald on Movies* by Dwight Macdonald. (New York: Prentice-Hall, 1969). Reprinted by permission of the author. The first section appeared in *The Miscellany* (March 1931), and the second in *Encounter* (January 1957).

story is subordinated as a mere allegory. Hence the point of view of *The Birth of a Nation* is as one-sided as is that of *Ten Days that Shook the World*. Both films are propaganda, with Negroes as the villains and southerners as the heroes in one as against the same relationship between bourgeois and workers in the other. This agreement between Griffith and the Russians on the essentials of cinematography is all the more impressive when one considers the difference in environment as well as in time, between the U.S.A. of 1915 and the U.S.S.R. of 1925.[1] Griffith would seem to have hit upon a universally valid approach to the cinema. The phrase ''hit upon'' is accurate.

Temperamentally Griffith is of the theater. His is the lantern jaw, the aquiline nose, the gleaming eye of the old-style Shakespearean actor. He began life as a stage actor (he must have been a good one) and he has most of the actor's traits of character. When he is making a picture, he is said to have no sense of money and little concern for what is ''practical.'' Like von Stroheim he will go to any lengths to get the effect he wants. Like all able directors, he insists on dominating his productions and treating his actors merely as so much cinematic material. The better to do this he sometimes intentionally misleads his players about the plot, telling them only what he wants them to express in each scene and taking on himself the entire responsibility for fitting their performances into the whole structure. His theatrical temperament gives him a sense of the dramatic whether in acting or in montage and shot-composition.

An even more important gift is a certain emotional facility. The censoring of *Intolerance* moved him to write and publish ''The Rise and Fall of Free Speech in America,'' a pamphlet which describes the late Mayor Gaynor of New York as ''that great jurist who stood out from the ordinary, gallery-playing, hypocritical type of politician as a white rose stands out from a field of sewer-fed weeds.'' Strong language, but the Mayor was on Griffith's side of the argument. The moral earnestness of this is repeated in the subtitles of *The Birth of a Nation*, which equal the loftiest flights of Daniel Webster. An emotional conviction of the importance and rightness

---

1. Griffith's influence on the modern Russian cinema was probably small compared to that of the Constructivist Theatre, Pavlov's theories of reflex action, and, above all, the experiments of Kuleshov in cinematic theory. Though Pudovkin cites many examples from Griffith films in his book *On Film Technique* and though he says that Griffith's *Intolerance* opened his eyes to the possibilities of the cinema, his association with Kuleshov must have been the prime formative influence on his art. Pudovkin's turning from epics like *Storm over Asia* to the domestic drama of *Life Is Good* is curiously parallel to Griffith's progression from the epical *Intolerance* to the intimate human drama of *Broken Blossoms* and *Isn't Life Wonderful?* Let us hope Pudovkin's artistry suffers as little by the change as Griffith's did. (As of 1968, or 1938, we are disappointed.—D.M.)

of whatever idea possesses him at the moment is the driving force of his movies. It sweeps them to triumph or dashes them to disaster according to the artistry with which Griffith handles it. I doubt if Griffith knows when he succeeds; I am sure he does not know *how* he succeeds. His genius seems to be purely instinctive. The work of no other director presents such violent contrasts between emotional power and bathetic sentimentality. His people act according to the conventions of the popular novel—yet what superb cinema he gets out of their actions. From any point of view except a cinematic one, his pictures are absurdities.

Griffith is a typically American product. He is to the cinema what Edison is to science: a practical genius who can make things work but who is not interested in "theory," i.e., the general laws that govern his achievements. Although his intuitive sense of cinema grasped the essentials of movie technique long before the Russians, he never really understood what he had discovered—which accounts for his not developing montage beyond the see-saw stage used in his finales, and for the fact that his latest picture, *Lincoln,* is less interesting technically than the *Birth of a Nation.* A few years of analysis, of comparing notes, of thinking about cinematic theory, and the Russians carried Griffith's discoveries far beyond anything he himself has done. During the past ten years Griffith has gone to seed with a thoroughness possible only to the American artist. The process has been all the more complete because Griffith, as seems inevitable for the man of talent in this country, has always been an isolated figure, one who grew up in no school and who leaves none behind him, a self-made genius. Unaware of his own powers, without the intelligent communication with his fellow directors that gives Eisenstein and Pudovkin perspective on their work, guided only by his extraordinary flair for the cinema, Griffith pioneered into virgin lands whose richness he only half suspected.

Goethe said of Byron that as a poet he was a genius, "but when he thinks he is a child." I would put it the other way round: the "poetic" side of Byron seems dated and stagey now, while *Don Juan* and the letters reveal a surprisingly mature mind, tough, humorous, masculine. But Goethe's epigram applies very well to the three great masters of the American silent film—Griffith, Stroheim, and Chaplin—each of whom combined an instinctive mastery of cinematic effects with a naive unconsciousness of the meaning of their films. I once spent an evening with Griffith; it was in the thirties, years after he had made any films; he looked and behaved like an old-style ham actor of the Walter Hampden school, hawk-nosed, dramatic in gesture and voice. He was quite drunk and kept putting in long-distance calls to Hollywood stars who always seemed to be "on the lot"; this didn't discourage him—"Just tell her it's Mr. Griffith calling;

she'll come." But she never did. Later he had a print of *Intolerance* run off
for us. As we followed the monumental architectonics of the film, the most
ambitious use of montage ever attempted, with its four stories in different
historical epochs counterpointed one against the other, with the fantastic
Babylonian scenes and the stark gray newsreel realism of the modern strike
and prison scenes—as we decided cineasts followed, or tried to, his
masterpiece, Griffith kept up a running stream of comment. "That's Jack
Barrymore," he would say as a super emerged briefly from the mob around
Christ (H. B. Warren) on the cross. "His first screen appearance." "See
that girl with the plate of grapes? That's Joan Crawford [or some such]; I
gave her her first part." We couldn't get him talking on the magnificent
technique; what evidently impressed him, and what he thought would
impress us, was his prowess as a "star-maker." What we thought his
badge of honor—that Hollywood couldn't use him—he was ashamed of;
his comments, like his long-distance calls, were to show he wasn't a
back-number, a has-been. Griffith was the inventor, and to this day remains, except for Eisenstein, the most creative user of the two basic elements in cinematic technique, montage and the close-up; but when he
thought, he was a child. It was a comically frustrating evening—like meeting Titian and getting from him only gossip about the dukes he had painted.

# Griffith and the Technical Innovations

## Paul Goodman

A season of typical blanks gives the usual opportunity to talk in a genetic way about why American films of 1940–41 don't hang together. Restricting myself to merely formal considerations, I'd like to make two points: 1) Especially after Griffith, the technique has developed ahead of the art; 2) the atmosphere and style have a meaning apart from the action and thought. These failings have, of course, been obvious for twenty years, but perhaps I can enliven the discussion of them by reporting some current events in New York.

### I.

An important difference between the history of cinema and all the other arts is that in other arts the technical innovations were mostly invented one at a time and as part of the total expression that the artist was to achieve; in an incorrect teleological formula we could almost say: "To express something new he invented a new means." In cinema, on the contrary, it seems *as if* a unique technique was available all at once but with nothing unique to express. (The falseness of this "as if" in the case of D. W. Griffith is what I here want to demonstrate.) The only similar outstripping of total expression by technical means that comes ready to my mind is the introduction of steel-construction and, again, of mass-production into modern architecture; and this is an important reason, surely, why most skyscrapers and most Hollywood movies vie with each other in aesthetic blankness. (I do not mean in aesthetic "badness," as, e.g., a painting by Benton is bad because it is inflated, etc.; but rather that you cannot approach these things formally, their parts have so little formal relation.)

From *Partisan Review,* vol. 8, no. 3 (May–June 1941). Copyright April 1941 by Partisan Review. Reprinted by permission of the publisher and Sally Goodman for the Estate of Paul Goodman.

Recently (Fall 1940) the Film Library of the Museum of Modern Art gave a Griffith Festival, accompanied by a little volume by Iris Barry: *D. W. Griffith: American Film Master*. The relation between these films and this book is most interesting. On the one hand we have a series of art works, ranging from 1909 short filmed-dramas like *Edgar Allan Poe*, through such a remarkable combination of cinema and drama as *The Musketeers of Pig Alley* (1912), up to such fine, almost great cinema as *Broken Blossoms* (1919) and *Isn't Life Wonderful* (1924); in all of these, under whatever conditions of story or manner, we have integrated works concentrated to a total effect, often to a single effect; indeed, Griffith is so insistent on this unity, whether of mood, climax, or idea, that the film often seems schematic. On the other hand we have the description of an artist's work as if it were a series of introductions of novel technical means, such as moving the camera, trick-lighting, vignetting, plunging *in medias res*, and cross-cutting; or of novel categories of content, such as realism, psychology, social significance, or the Civil War. But to see these films in this light is to see them all wrong. Let me illustrate.

"Early in 1909 they"—Griffith and Bitzer his cameraman— "together contrived a strikingly novel effect of light and shade in *Edgar Allan Poe*, and a firelight effect which was widely remarked in the otherwise primitive and stilted *A Drunkard's Reformation*" (p. 16). But this "novel effect of light and shade" is the *whole* of *Poe*, which is nothing but the fusion into this chiaroscuro of the misunderstood poet, his suddenly appearing Raven, his wife dying of starvation, as against the callous publishers in their ordinary light; in fact this sad little picture is almost comic because it concentrates so powerful an expression into such a tiny magnitude. Again, that "widely remarked firelight effect" happens to be the *summation* of the drunkard's reformation: his home rather than his vice, etc. To conceive of these expressions as "technical innovations" or, to use another of the author's phrases, as "the development of screen syntax" is to make of D. W. Griffith a tramp like, say, Mark Sandrich, who is also a great innovator. For before illustrating further, let me draw the moral: How can Miss Barry make such a silly error? *It is precisely because she is thinking, when she thinks of cinema, of all the Hollywood output which employs such a warehouse of technical devices—yes, "introduced" by Griffith and others—with nothing whatever to say.*

Let me cite one or two of her favorite phrases: "Here he hit upon a new way of handling a tried device—the last-minute rescue—which was to serve him well for the rest of his career." (16) "It was a device which had seldom failed Griffith in the past and stood him in good stead now." (30) "Whether as a study in realism, as an ancestor of the gangster films of later decades, or as an exercise [*sic!*] in motion-picture composition *The*

*Musketeers of Pig Alley* is a remarkable piece. The photography is extraordinary and the whole film predicts what was to come in the modern section of *Intolerance.*'' (19) As if, that is, the documentary photography, the carefully contrived chaos of the slum-alley, the gangster subject, and the wonderful montage of the man-hunt sequence (= ''an exercise in composition'') had no intrinsic connection, but were a congeries of ''beauties''; but if you imagine you are to hear of the intrinsic connection in the remarks on *Intolerance* of which this was a ''forecast,'' you are sadly deceived. In general, that is the mode of criticism here is like those books which tell of The Legacy of Egypt, as if the Egyptian culture consisted in the invention of the sundial for English country gardens.

   *Broken Blossoms* is almost great; to my taste it is Griffith's most complete work. Miss Barry's remarks on it are in her usual vein and of no account, but let me indicate a few isolated appreciations of the picture itself in order to bring out my main point, which is *the difference between a film where every technical means is in intimate relation with the whole expression, and our films where a bit of technique is a distracting short-cut to convey indirectly some picayune information by the way.* Consider, for instance, Griffith's persistent vertical masking of half of the screen in this film; this is not a ''special effect'' but *comes to be expected;* thus our attention is centered on each character in his separateness and loneliness; when several come together on the whole screen, it is these isolated persons who come together. Recall, on the other hand, the numerous vignettes and arc-masks in *Birth of a Nation,* which generate the sentiment of being an onlooker at a panoramic spectacle, first distant (telescope), then filling the scene (arc). Such masking and vignetting has been called a mannerism of Griffith's! Yes, used as Ford would use it, it would be a mannerism. Again, consider the employment of color in *Broken Blossoms;* Griffith uses three or four tints (not Technicolor, of course); these are introduced from the very outset to express dominant mood, and they come to be expected; then what a triumph, by what simple means, when the awakening of the Chinese boy to the beauty in his chamber is fortified by the change from a darker hue to the strange pink-violet which had appeared (if my memory serves) in the earlier scene of his peaceful homeland. And the green fog at the climax. But a 1941 director has all the rainbow of Technicolor at hand and says nothing. Again, when a character, e.g. the pugilist, is introduced, it is with the following action: he is restrained from pleasure by his manager and does not dare revolt, *therefore* he tyrannizes over the girl; the psychology is schematic (though sufficient for the story), but it *is* a psychology, it gives depth and pity to the action, and humanity to the catastrophe;—whereas the characters in so ''psychological'' a film as *The Long Voyage Home* are in the end nothing but faces, without human interest. Again, since so much has been said against Griffith's colorful subtitles, what of the remarkable rhapsodic titles in this film? The characters are again and again shown at their most meaningful moments, no footage is spent on merely expository matters: the poetic, often imagistic title fixes this moment as if in a different dimension; indeed, no higher praise can be given to *Broken Blossoms* than to say that the scene of the catharsis, where the Chinaman brings home the dead girl, is great enough and sufficiently well prepared to carry the famous title "All the tears of the world washed over his heart." Lastly, in the face of the trivial bits of hectic synthetic montage that ornament current movies (for instance, the Extras rolling off the presses to loud music), I would point to those strokes of lightning cunningly withheld by Griffith till the climax, where the wildly bowing young Chinaman suddenly bows at infinite speed and where rushing through the fog he rushes into the camera at infinite speed.

## II.

These are random examples of "technical innovations" as part of the art. In an appendix on photography to *American Film Master,* however, Beaumont Newhall concludes: "During the last 25 years the scope of cinematography has broadened enormously. Bitzer's experiments have been universally adopted and refined. Yet, looking back at the photographic beauty of the epic Griffith-Bitzer films, one is amazed that the quality of cinematography has not kept pace with its technical growth." I should think that there is nothing amazing about it, considering the institutionalizing of cinema as a business, the kind of success aimed at, and the kind of talent attracted. Further, where a medium has an important mechanical part, non-aesthetic laboratory researches will produce innovations beyond the contemporary requirements of either expression or communication—e.g., Technicolor. Then further, the commercial appeal of sensational innovations will introduce them into the expression anyway. But it is not these causes I am here discussing, but rather the formal effect: What is the formal effect of such an independent development of technique?

The answer is simple: it is the streamlined professional "Style" in which all stories are indirectly communicated—one can hardly say "cinematically presented." By professional I mean such an attitude toward the technique as makes it impossible to overhaul it afresh for each problem. But this uniform "Style" is not a chaos of effects, but a unified complex of: brightly reflected lighting; photogenic make-up; spacious interiors obviously without four walls; the ritual series of facial close-up—cut from face to face—*pan* of the interior (nothing is still for a moment)—and the follow-shot of the angelic person moving down halls and thru walls, freed from the laws of matter; the music that sounds from nowhere; the continuity of fades; the scrambling montage in which all dissolves into kaleidoscopy. Etc., etc., for it is worked out in all details. And make no mistake, this Style is itself a realized work of art with an unmistakable total expression: here is freedom, ease, domination of obstacles, evaporation of solidity, speed, super-humanity, day-dream (surely not night-dream!), and the pleasant destruction of the universe.

Well! what objection can even a critic have to so admittedly successful an expression of the abundant life? I confess that my bother is again a merely formal one. It is that the actions, thoughts, and virtues, the conversation, acting, and even beauty of the persons in these films is incommensurate with the prodigious lighting, scenery, camera-work, and cutting. Even the happiest ending (a skip of *two* grades up the economic scale) is not so liberating as the follow-shot through the solid walls; the most brilliant beauties cannot people this clear space; and the wit and insight of the best Californian poets is not so clever as the montage. To put it another way, we have already seen these plots, this wit and philosophy, in literary romances of even an earlier day; but this world of the cinema style we have never seen on land or sea or in books. Therefore, it seems to me, the aesthetic problem of Hollywood is as follows: *To find an action and a system of philosophy and ethics, and to construct out of aluminum a cast of characters, that will fit into an integrated pattern with the professional style of the cameraman and scene designer.*

# David Wark Griffith

## James Agee

He achieved what no other known man has ever achieved. To watch his
work is like being witness to the beginning of melody, or the first conscious use of the lever or the wheel; the emergence, coordination, and first
eloquence of language; the birth of an art: and to realize that this is all the
work of one man.

We will never realize how good he really was until we have the
chance to see his work as often as it deserves to be seen, to examine and
enjoy it in detail as exact as his achievement. But even relying, as we
mainly have to, on years-old memories, a good deal becomes clear.

One crude but unquestionable indication of his greatness was his
power to create permanent images. All through his work there are images
which are as impossible to forget, once you have seen them, as some of the
grandest and simplest passages in music or poetry.

The most beautiful single shot I have seen in any movie is the battle
charge in *The Birth of a Nation*. I have heard it praised for its realism, and
that is deserved; but it is also far beyond realism. It seems to me to be a
perfect realization of a collective dream of what the Civil War was like, as
veterans might remember it fifty years later, or as children, fifty years later,
might imagine it. I have had several clear mental images of that war, from
almost as early as I can remember, and I didn't have the luck to see *The
Birth of a Nation* until I was in my early twenties; but when I saw that
charge, it was merely the clarification, and corroboration, of one of those
visions, and took its place among them immediately without seeming to be
of a different kind or order. It is the perfection that I know of, of the tragic
glory that is possible, or used to be possible, in war; or in war as the best in
the spirit imagines or remembers it.

This is, I realize, mainly subjective; but it suggests to me the clearest
and deepest aspect of Griffith's genius: he was a great primitive poet, a

man capable, as only great and primitive artists can be, of intuitively
perceiving and perfecting the tremendous magical images that underlie the
memory and imagination of entire peoples. If he had achieved this only
once, and only for me, I could not feel that he was what I believe he is; but
he created many such images, and I suspect that many people besides me
have recognized them, on that deepest level that art can draw on, reach,
and serve. There are many others in that one film: the homecoming of the
defeated hero; the ride of the Clansmen; the rapist and his victim among the
dark leaves; a glimpse of a war hospital; dead young soldiers after battle;
the dark, slow movement of the Union Army away from the camera, along
a valley which is quartered strongly between hill-shadow and sunlight; all
these and still others have a dreamlike absoluteness which, indeed, cradles
and suffuses the whole film.

This was the one time in movie history that a man of great ability
worked freely, in an unspoiled medium, for an unspoiled audience, on a
majestic theme which involved all that he was; and brought to it, besides
his abilities as an inventor and artist, absolute passion, pity, courage, and
honesty. *The Birth of a Nation* is equal with Brady's photographs, Lincoln's speeches, Whitman's war poems; for all its imperfections and absurdities it is equal, in fact, to the best work that has been done in this
country. And among moving pictures it is alone, not necessarily as "the
greatest"—whatever that means—but as the one great epic, tragic film.

(Today, *The Birth of a Nation* is boycotted or shown piecemeal; too
many more or less well-meaning people still accuse Griffith of having
made it an anti-Negro movie. At best, this is nonsense, and at worst, it is
vicious nonsense. Even if it were an anti-Negro movie, a work of such
quality should be shown, and shown whole. But the accusation is unjust.
Griffith went to almost preposterous lengths to be fair to the Negroes as he
understood them, and he understood them as a good type of Southerner
does. I don't entirely agree with him; nor can I be sure that the film
wouldn't cause trouble and misunderstanding, especially as advertised and
exacerbated by contemporary abolitionists; but Griffith's absolute desire to
be fair, and understandable, is written all over the picture; so are degrees of
understanding, honesty, and compassion far beyond the capacity of his
accusers. So, of course, are the salient facts of the so-called Reconstruction
years.)

Griffith never managed to equal *The Birth of a Nation* again, nor was
he ever to strike off, in any other film, so many of those final images.
Nevertheless, he found many: the strikers in *Intolerance*—the realism of
those short scenes has never been surpassed, nor their shock and restive-
ness as an image of near-revolution; the intercutting, at the climax of that

picture, between the climaxes of four parallel stories, like the swinging together of tremendous gongs; the paralyzing excitement of the melodrama near the waterfall, in *Way Down East;* Paul Revere's ride and the battle of Bunker Hill, in *America;* Danton's ride, in *Orphans of the Storm;* most subtle and remarkable of all, the early morning scene in his German film, *Isn't Life Wonderful?,* in which the ape-like Dick Sutherland pursues Carol Dempster through a grove of slender trees. All these images, and so many others of Griffith's, have a sort of crude sublimity which nobody else in movies has managed to achieve; this last one, like his images of our Civil War, seems to come out of the deep subconscious: it is an absolute and prophetic image of a nation and a people. I will always regret having missed *Abraham Lincoln,* his last film to be released: a friend has told me of its wonderful opening in stormy mid-winter night woods, the camera bearing along toward the natal cabin; and that surely must have been one of Griffith's finest images.

Even in Griffith's best work there is enough that is poor, or foolish, or merely old-fashioned, so that one has to understand, if by no means forgive, those who laugh indiscriminately at his good work and his bad. (With all that "understanding," I look forward to killing, some day, some specially happy giggler at the exquisite scene in which the veteran comes home, in *The Birth of a Nation.*) But even his poorest work was never just bad. Whatever may be wrong with it, there is in every instant, so well as I can remember, the unique purity and vitality of birth or of a creature just born and first exerting its unprecedented, incredible strength; and there are, besides, Griffith's overwhelming innocence and magnanimity of spirit; his moral and poetic earnestness; his joy in his work; and his splendid intuitiveness, directness, common sense, daring, and skill as an inventor and as an artist. Aside from his talent or genius as an inventor and artist, he was all heart; and ruinous as his excesses sometimes were in that respect, they were inseparable from his virtues, and small beside them. He was remarkably good, as a rule, in the whole middle range of feeling, but he was at his best just short of his excesses, and he tended in general to work out toward the dangerous edge. He was capable of realism that has never been beaten and he might, if he had been able to appreciate his powers as a realist, have found therein his growth and salvation. But he seems to have been a realist only by accident, hit-and-run; essentially, he was a poet. He doesn't appear ever to have realized one of the richest promises that movies hold, as the perfect medium for realism raised to the level of high poetry; nor, oddly enough, was he much of a dramatic poet. But in epic and lyrical and narrative visual poetry, I can think of nobody who has surpassed him, and of few to compare with him. And as a primitive tribal poet, combining something of the bard and the seer, he is beyond even Dovzhenko, and no others of their kind have worked in movies.

What he had above all, his ability as a craftsman and artist, would be hard enough—and quite unnecessary—to write of, if we had typical scenes before us, or within recent memory; since we have seen so little of his work in so many years, it is virtually impossible. I can remember very vividly his general spirit and manner—heroic, impetuous, tender, magniloquent, naive, beyond the endowment or daring of anybody since; just as vividly, I can remember the total impression of various major sequences. By my remembrance, his images were nearly always a little larger and wilder than life. The frame was always full, spontaneous, and lively. He knew wonderfully well how to contrast and combine different intensities throughout an immense range of emotion, movement, shadow, and light. 'Much of the liveliness was not intrinsic to the characters on the screen or their predicament, but was his own vitality and emotion; and much of it—notably in the amazing flickering and vivacity of his women—came of his almost maniacal realization of the importance of expressive movement.

It seems to me entirely reasonable to infer, from the extraordinary power and endurance in the memory of certain scenes in their total effect, that he was as brilliant a master of design and cutting and form as he was a composer of frames and a director of feeling and motion. But I cannot clearly remember one sequence or scene, shot by shot and rhythm by rhythm. I suspect, for instance, that analysis would show that the climactic sequence on the icy river, in *Way Down East,* is as finely constructed a piece of melodramatic story-telling as any in movies. But I can only venture to bet on this and to suggest that that sequence, like a hundred others of Griffith's, is eminently worth analysis.

My veneration for Griffith's achievements is all the deeper when I realize what handicaps he worked against, how limited a man he was. He had no remarkable power of intellect, or delicateness of soul; no subtlety; little restraint; little if any "taste," whether to help his work or harm it; Lord knows (and be thanked) no cleverness; no fundamental capacity, once he had achieved his first astonishing development, for change or growth. He wasn't particularly observant of people; nor do his movies suggest that he understood them at all deeply. He had noble powers of imagination, but little of the *intricacy* of imagination that most good poets also have. His sense of comedy was pathetically crude and numb. He had an exorbitant appetite for violence, for cruelty, and for the Siamese twin of cruelty, a kind of obsessive tenderness which at its worst was all but nauseating. Much as he invented, his work was saturated in the style, the mannerisms, and the underlying assumptions and attitudes of the nineteenth century provincial theater; and although much of that was much better than most of us realize, and any amount better than most of the styles and non-styles we accept and praise, much of it was cheap and false, and all of it, good and bad, was dying when Griffith gave it a new lease on life, and in spite of that new lease, died soon after, and took him down with it. I doubt that Griffith ever clearly knew the good from the bad in this theatricality; or, for that matter, clearly understood what was original in his work, and capable of almost unimaginably great development; and what was over-derivative, essentially non-cinematic, and dying. In any case, he did not manage to outgrow, or sufficiently to tranform, enough in his style that was bad, or merely obsolescent.

If what I hear is right about the opening scene in *Abraham Lincoln,* this incapacity for radical change may have slowed him up but never killed him as an artist; in his no longer fashionable way, he remained capable, and inspired. He was merely unadaptable and unemployable, like an old, sore, ardent individualist among contemporary progressives. Hollywood and, to a great extent, movies in general, grew down from him rather than up past him; audiences, and the whole eye and feeling of the world, have suffered the same degeneration; he didn't have it in him to be amenable, even if he'd tried; and that was the end of him. Or quite possibly he was finished, as smaller men are not, as soon as he had reached the limit of his own powers of innovation, and began to realize he was only repeating himself. Certainly, anyhow, he was natural-born for the years of adventure and discovery, not for the inevitable following era of safe-playing and of fat consolidation of others' gains.

His last movie, which was never even released, was made fourteen or fifteen years ago; and for years before that, most people had thought of him as a has-been. Nobody would hire him; he had nothing to do. He lived too long, and that is one of few things that are sadder than dying too soon.

There is not a man working in movies, or a man who cares for them, who does not owe Griffith more than he owes anybody else.

# A Great Folly

## Pauline Kael

"She is madonna in an art as wild and young as her sweet eyes," Vachel Lindsay wrote of Mae Marsh, who died on Tuesday of last week. She is the heroine of D. W. Griffith's *Intolerance,* which came out in 1916 and which will soon have its annual showing at the Museum of Modern Art. "Intolerance" is one of the two or three most influential movies ever made, and I think it is also the greatest. Yet many of those who are interested in movies have never seen it. *The Birth of a Nation* which Griffith brought out in 1915 (with Mae Marsh as the little sister who throws herself off a cliff through "the opal gates of death"), still draws audiences, because of its scandalous success. But those who see it projected at the wrong speed, so that it becomes a "flick," and in mutilated form—cut and in black-and-white or faded color—are not likely to develop enough interest in Griffith's art to go see his other films. *Intolerance* was a commercial failure in 1916, and it has never had much popular reputation. After the reactions to *The Birth of a Nation,* Griffith was so shocked that people could think he was anti-Negro that he decided to expand some material he had been working on and make it an attack on bigotry throughout the ages. *Intolerance* was intended to be virtuous and uplifting. It turned out to be a great, desperate, innovative, ruinous film—perhaps the classic example of what later came to be known as *cinéma maudit.* Griffith had already, in the over four hundred movies he had made—from the one-reelers on up to *The Birth of a Nation*—founded the art of screen narrative; now he wanted to try something more than simply telling the story of bigotry in historical sequence. He had developed cross-cutting in his earlier films, using discontinuity as Dickens did in his novels. In *Intolerance,* he attempted to tell four stories taking place in different historical periods, crosscutting back

This material appeared under the title "A Great Folly, and a Small One" in *Going Steady* by Pauline Kael. Copyright © 1968 by Pauline Kael. The essay appeared originally in *The New Yorker,* February 24, 1968. Reprinted by permission of Little, Brown and Co. in association with the Atlantic Monthly Press.

and forth to ancient Babylon, sixteenth-century France, the modern American slums, and Calvary. He was living in an era of experiments with time in the other arts, and although he worked in a popular medium, the old dramatic concepts of time and unity seemed too limiting; in his own way he attempted what Pound and Eliot, Proust and Virginia Woolf and Joyce were also attempting, and what he did in movies may have influenced literary form as much as they did. He certainly influenced them. The events of *Intolerance* were, he said, set forth ''as they might flash across a mind seeking to parallel the life of the different ages.'' It doesn't work. *Intolerance* almost becomes a film symphony, but four stories intercut and rushing toward simultaneous climaxes is, at a basic level, too naïve a conception to be anything more than four melodramas told at once. The titles of *Intolerance* state the theme more than the actions shows it, and the four parallel stories were probably just too much and too bewildering for audiences. Also, the idealistic attack on hypocrisy, cruelty, and persecution may have seemed uncomfortably pacifistic in 1916.

No simple framework could contain the richness of what Griffith tried to do in this movie. He tried to force his stories together, and pushed them into ridiculous patterns to illustrate his theme. But his excitement—his madness—binds together what his arbitrarily imposed theme does not. *Intolerance* is like an enormous, extravagantly printed collection of fairy tales. The book is too thick to handle, too richly imaginative to take in, yet a child who loves stories will know that this is the treasure of treasures. The movie is the greatest extravaganza and the greatest folly in movie history, an epic celebration of the potentialities of the new medium—lyrical, passionate, and grandiose. No one will ever again be able to make last-minute rescues so suspenseful, so beautiful, or so absurd. In movies, a masterpiece is of course a folly. *Intolerance* is charged with visionary excitement about the power of movies to combine music, dance, narrative, drama, painting, and photography—to do alone what all the other arts together had done. And to do what they had failed to. Griffith's dream was not only to reach the vast audience but to express it, to make of the young movie art a true democratic art.

Griffith's movies are great not because he developed the whole range of film techniques—the editing, the moving camera, the closeup, the flexible use of the frame so that it becomes a pinpoint of light or a CinemaScope shape at will—but because he invented or pioneered those techniques out of an expressive need for them. When Griffith is at his best, you are hardly aware of how short the shots are, how brilliantly they are edited, how varied the camera angles are. Reaching for color, he not only had the prints of his movies dyed in different hues selected to convey the mood of the sequences but had crews of girls adding extra color by hand, frame by frame. Still dissatisfied, he had the projectionists throw beams of red or blue light to intensify the effects. Reaching for sound, he had scores specially prepared and orchestras playing in the pit. In *Intolerance,* he overstretched. There is hardly anything that has been attempted in movies since (except for sound effects, of course) that was not tried in *Intolerance.* *The Birth of a Nation,* the longest American film up to that date, was rehearsed for six weeks, shot in nine weeks, and edited in three months; it cost a hundred thousand dollars—a record-breaking budget in those days. *Intolerance* cost several times as much. The huge statue-cluttered Babylonian set, which is the most famous of all movie sets, is big in the way DeMille's sets were to be big later on—a picture-postcard set—and neither the camera nor any of the players seems to know what to do with it. The steps on this set undoubtedly inspired Eisenstein's Odessa Steps sequence, but the action that Griffith staged on them looks mechanical and confused. The movie had got too big, and even Griffith was crushed by the weight of it. Yet the enormous project released his imagination, and there are incomparable images—for example, the death of the young mountain girl, with the toy chariot drawn by doves at her feet—and miraculously successful sequences: the prison scenes, later imitated in the Warner Brothers social-protest films of the thirties, and almost reproduced in *I Am a Fugitive from a Chain Gang;* the strike scenes, which influenced the Russians; the great night-fighting scenes, originally in red, which are imitated in practically every spectacle.

One can trace almost every major tradition and most of the genres, and even many of the metaphors, in movies to their sources of Griffith. The Ku Klux Klan rides of *The Birth of a Nation* became the knights of Eisenstein's *Alexander Nevsky;* the battle scenes, derived from Matthew Brady, influenced almost all subsequent war films, and especially *Gone with the Wind.* A history of Russian movies could be based on the ice breaking up in Griffith's *Way Down East,* taking that ice through Pudovkin's epic *Mother* up to the Chukhrai's *Clear Skies,* where the thaw after Stalin's death is represented literally by the breaking up of ice. One can also trace the acting styles. Mae Marsh returned to us via the young Garbo and other Scandinavian actresses, and Lillian Gish returned to us via Brigitte Helm of *Metropolis,* Dorothea Wieck of *Mädchen in Uniform,* and *most* of the European actresses of the twenties. Griffith's stylized lyric tragedy *Broken Blossoms* (which will also be shown at the Museum of Modern Art), though smaller in scope than "The Birth" or *Intolerance,* is, I think, the third of a trio of great works. It is the source of much of the poignancy of Fellini's *La strada.* Donald Crisp's brutal prizefighter became Anthony

Quinn's Zampano, and Lillian Gish's childish waif must have strongly influenced the conception of Giulietta Masina's role as well as her performance.

Griffith used Lillian Gish and Mae Marsh contrastingly. In his films, Lillian Gish is a frail, floating heroine from romantic novels and poems—a maiden. She is the least coarse of American screen actresses; her grace is pure and fluid and lilylike. She is idealized femininity, and her purity can seem rather neurotic and frightening. Mae Marsh is less ethereal, somehow less actressy, more solid and "normal," and yet, in her own way, as exquisite and intuitive. She is our dream not of heavenly beauty, like Gish, but of earthly beauty, and sunlight makes her youth more entrancing. She looks as if she could be a happy, sensual, ordinary woman. The tragedies that befall her are accidents that could happen to any of us, for she has never wanted more than common pleasures. There is a passage in *Intolerance* in which Mae Marsh, as a young mother who has had her baby taken away from her, grows so distraught that she becomes a voyeur, peeping in at windows to simper and smile at other people's babies. It's horrible to watch, because she has always seemed such a sane sort of girl. When Lillian Gish, trapped in the closet in *Broken Blossoms,* spins around in terror, we feel terror for all helpless, delicate beauty, but when Mae Marsh is buffeted by fate every ordinary person is in danger. Mae Marsh died at seventy-two, but the girl who twists her hands in the courtroom scene of *Intolerance* is the image of youth-in-trouble forever.

It took Griffith years to pay off the disaster of *Intolerance,* and though he later made box-office successes, like *Way Down East,* he wasn't financially strong enough to keep his independence. By 1925, he was forced to go to work for Paramount as a contract director, which meant doing the scripts they handed him, and doing them *their* way. By the thirties, he had sunk even further; he was called in to fix films that other directors had messed up, and he didn't receive screen credits anymore. There was so much emphasis in Hollywood on the newest product that it was feared his name would make people think a picture old-fashioned. Eventually, alcoholic and embittered, he could get no work at all. Until his death, in 1948, Griffith lived in a hotel room in near obscurity in the Hollywood he had created—which was filled with famous directors he had trained and famous stars he had discovered. They could not really help him. Motion pictures had become too big a business for sentiment, or for art.

# The Films of David Wark Griffith:
## The Development of Themes and Techniques in Forty-two of His Films

### Richard J. Meyer

Every creative artist in the history of mankind has been influenced by his environment. Whether his work demonstrates rebellion, reflection, or anti-art, it nevertheless is a product of that particular age which gave birth to its creator. Art is the sum total of all human experience and as such does not discover new thematic material down through the ages; yet in each century there are a few individuals who are given the rare opportunity to express themselves in a new medium. These geniuses have at their disposal a free art form; they are tied to the boundless stream of man's total consciousness in the development of art, but they are also linked to their contemporary surroundings, from which they never break away. Such a man was D. W. Griffith.

There is no disagreement among film historians and critics anywhere in the world that David Wark Griffith was the first giant of the new film art and that he paved the way for contemporary cinema. But some argument concentrates on whether he actually invented certain innovations or whether he was merely the first director to use them in a meaningful filmic manner. Such conjecture aside, what is paramount is that Griffith was the first man to create undeniable film masterpieces.

This study traces the development of Griffith's narrative themes and film techniques, using as primary source material forty-two of his films screened at the Museum of Modern Art in the spring and summer of 1965. Biographical material will be used only if pertinent, because of disagreements among biographers. Similarly, criticism by dozens of writers will be kept relevant.

From *Film Comment*, vol. 4, no. 2/3 (Fall/Winter 1967). Copyright © 1967 by Film Comment Publishing Corporation. Reprinted by permission of The Film Society of Lincoln Center. This article is reprinted as it appears in *Focus on D. W. Griffith*, Prentice-Hall, 1971.

Griffith initially attempted, unsuccessfully, to sell film stories. He entered the film business as an actor for Edwin S. Porter at the Edison studio in 1907. *Rescued from an Eagle's Nest* tells the story of a woodsman (Griffith) who rescues a baby from the nest after an eagle has captured it. At that time, film technique and acting had not changed much since Porter's *The Great Train Robbery* of 1903. The contrast between a painted backdrop and the real outdoor scenery in *Rescued from an Eagle's Nest* is still great, and the major improvement by Porter in *Rescued* is the use of overlapping action when Griffith goes down the cliff, with a cut to a reverse angle shot.

In 1908, Griffith succeeded in selling stories to the Biograph Company as well as acting in some. Actors were paid five dollars a day, but writers received fifteen dollars for a "scenario." He was given an opportunity to direct. *The Adventures of Dollie* released July 14, 1908, was an immediate success and revitalized the insecure Biograph. Most of the films released by the company from then until December 1909 were made by Griffith and all of the major ones thereafter until 1913.[1] His output between 1908 and 1915 was about 440 films.[2] He averaged one film per week, working fourteen hours a day.

Readers will recall in *The Great Train Robbery* how Porter created parallel action by cross-cutting the bandits with shots of the gathering of the posse. Griffith commenced to improve Porter's technique of parallel action by tightening up his editing of these early Biographs. Almost immediately, he discovered other methods. His cameraman, Billy Bitzer, collaborated in these many innovations, but it was Griffith who served as the spark in this creative relationship.

By the time *A Drunkard's Reformation* was released (April 1, 1909), Griffith had brought financial success to Biograph as well as to himself. Linda Arvidson, secretly Mrs. Griffith, played the drunkard's wife in this one-reeler. The film uses the play within a play device. A heavy-drinking father with his child views a stage presentation about the evils of alcohol and resolves to reform. Besides the much-improved interior scenery, the firelight effect during the last shot was an innovation.

*The Lonely Villa* with Mary Pickford (June 10, 1909) was shot out of the studio, in New Jersey. The film gave a clear indication that this director would be developing not only realistic settings and new styles in screen acting, but suspenseful climaxes that eventually would be labeled "the Griffith ending." Cross-cutting from the wife and daughters trapped by the

---

1. Iris Barry, D. W. *Griffith: American Film Master* (New York: Museum of Modern Art, 1965), p. 11.
2. Seymour Stern, "Griffith: Pioneer of the Film Art," *Introduction to the Art of the Movies,* ed. Lewis Jacobs (New York: Noonday Press, 1960), p. 158.

villain to the father who comes to the rescue with the police was the finest example of editing to that time. The "last minute rescue" was to remain with Griffith throughout his career.

A social commentary, *A Corner in Wheat* (December 13, 1909), begins with farmers under great hardship planting wheat. A tycoon corners the market, causing privation to the populace, but he dies when he slips into one of his own grain elevators and is buried by the grain. The early films delighted in such irony. For the first time, there is a fade to black at the end of the film. Griffith and Bitzer closed the iris diaphragm of the camera for a fade-out originally to solve the problem of the screen kiss, according to Homer Croy.[3] However, Seymour Stern, self-styled Griffith "Boswell," disputes Croy's account vigorously.[4]

*A Corner in Wheat* has an effect of special interest. From a scene of business crooks at a gala party celebrating their financial coup, Griffith cuts to a "freeze" frame effect (using actors in a tableau) of poor people waiting in a breadline.

The players hold still for over twelve seconds to create the effect. The technique was devised by Griffith to point out the social implications by comparing wealthy revelers with the poor who are "frozen" as they wait in line for bread which cannot be purchased because of the doubling in price. From this "freeze" frame effect, Griffith cuts back again to the scene at the festivities.

The weakest Griffith film screened was *The Last Deal* (January 27, 1910). Except that the camera moves closer for a card game, the film shows lackluster technique. A man gambles away his money and his wife's jewels and embezzles from the bank. The wife's brother saves the loser by winning at cards and giving the money to his brother-in-law just in time to prevent his suicide. At the close, the errant husband tears up the deck of cards. The stall for time between the card game and the contemplated suicide is particularly dull.

Another social commentary with a violent death at the end, similar to *A Corner in Wheat,* was released on August 15, 1910. In *The Usurer* a man forecloses the mortgages of sick girls and old mothers, then revels with his ill-gotten wealth. Later he is locked in a vault while counting his coupons and dies of suffocation. The evicted families get back their furniture and their apartments. Cross-cutting is used extensively.

On March 23, 1911, the most advanced one-reeler of its time was released by Biograph. *The Lonedale Operator,* with Blanche Sweet, was

3. Homer Croy, *Star Maker* (New York: Duell, Sloan and Pearce, 1959), p. 39.
4. Seymour Stern, "Biographical Hogwash," *Films in Review,* May 1959, pp. 284-96 and June-July 1959, pp. 336-43.

shot in California on location. The camera was mounted on the locomotive and on many other placements that change frequently. The medium shot replaces the long shot while the tight close-up of the wrench, with which the telegraph girl holds evildoers at bay, achieves an unparalleled excitement. Griffith improved his cross-cutting by inter-cutting among three separate scenes. He also had actors walk toward the camera to give a feeling of screen depth. Each shot is short. The story concerns the last-minute rescue of a girl by her railwayman friend as she prevents thugs from stealing money.

*Enoch Arden* was an attempt by Griffith to make a two-reeler. Biograph did not permit its release as such and separated it into Part I (June 12, 1911) and Part II (June 15, 1911). It was thought that audiences would accept only twelve-minute film plots. Based on a poem, *Enoch Arden* did not adapt well. It tells the story of two men who vie for a girl. She marries Arden, who later departs on a voyage, leaving behind her and their children. He is shipwrecked and presumed lost, and after twenty years the widow marries the old rival. But Arden is rescued and comes home to discover secretly what has transpired. He dies without interfering with the new happy family. Abrupt cuts from medium shot to close-up are awkward, but the use of children at various stages of their growth to denote passage of time is quite effective.

A long shot with action in both the background and foreground is a feature of *Man's Genesis* (July 11, 1911). Realistic interiors are a vast improvement over the interior painted scenery of a few years earlier, and composition is better. *Man's Genesis* begins with a preacher telling two children a story about cavemen days. The scene fades to black, then fades in a scene where a strong caveman takes away the girl of a weaker caveman. He regains the girl by making a stone weapon. Befitting a film made on the eve of World War I, Griffith's concluding moral states that as man develops new and better weapons, he will have to develop more wisdom. The picture returns to the preacher and the children. Flashback is accomplished by the fade to black and the fade-in.

Violence and action continued to dominate the Griffith one-reelers. In *The Miser's Heart* (November 20, 1911), a poor girl befriends a miser. Crooks threaten to kill her if he does not give them the combination to his safe. The miser finally tells, but the rascals are caught after a hobo summons the police. Two typical Griffith elements emerge from this film: the poor hero or heroine; and the use of children as sentimental devices. The camera moves still closer to the action in *The Miser's Heart*.

A jump cut to indicate the passage of time—while a killer changes from a disguise to his own clothes—is a highlight of *A Terrible Discovery* (December 21, 1911). The killer, dressed as a woman, sneaks into the house in order to kill the boy's father (who has an artificial arm). The father lowers the boy out of a window to summon help as the killer breaks into the room. In a typical Griffith ending, the police race to rescue the dad, who is saved just as he is about to be shot.

One criticism of Griffith has been that his humor was crude. In *The Goddess of Sagebrush Gulch* and other films, he used humor to relieve the tension of his melodramatic Victorian plots and to add an artistic touch. Broad laughter, within limits, is in the American tradition of humor and is not "crude" within that context. *The Goddess of Sagebrush Gulch* (March 25, 1912) depicts a Western girl who loses her boyfriend, the sheriff, to a female visitor from the East. The latter asks the sheriff for his money, then villians take the cash, tie her up, and set fire to the house. She is rescued after the rejected heroine runs for the sheriff. The crooks are killed in a gun battle, and the Western girl walks off with a successful prospector. Realistic mountain scenery, beautifully photographed, makes the film technically good, but the story is below Griffith's standards.

Apparently Griffith realized that *The Lonedale Operator* was one of his most successful films, because he remade it a year later as *The Girl and Her Trust* and improved on the original. It was released March 28, 1912. The tracking shot was achieved by placing the camera on a train while photographing another train. Griffith also had the camera pan during the moving shot. Through cross-cutting, he heightened suspense as the boyfriend rescues the telegraph girl.

The best Griffith one-reeler is *The Musketeers of Pig Alley*. The story and action of this film, released October 31, 1912, are exciting even by today's standards. Griffith incorporated not only violence and death, but also the social problems of his time. Shot in the back alleys of New York, the film had the look of the Ash Can School of art. If one looks for the predecessor of *Open City* and Italian neorealism, he may find it in *The Musketeers of Pig Alley*. The story, set in the slums, opens with a poor musician leaving his wife and mother to find work. He returns with money, but it is stolen by thieves. In a gang fight, he gets back his money. When the police ask him to identify the chief hoodlum, he protects him because the hood had protected his wife in an earlier bar incident. The final scene shows a cop winking at the hood and a hand reaching into the frame with money for him. The closing title announces—"Links in the system."

Six weeks later, another Griffith early masterpiece was released on December 15, 1912. *The New York Hat* possessed a good story as well as fine acting for the period. Lionel Barrymore and Mary Pickford starred, and Mae Marsh, Mabel Normand, and Lillian and Dorothy Gish rounded out the cast. The minister (Barrymore) buys a girl an expensive hat with money left secretly to her by her deceased mother. Small-town gossips wag tongues about the minister until the mother's letter, which explains the situation, is revealed.

*The God Within,* released eleven days later, uses an interesting device for dialogue scenes—trees and bushes serve as foreground during these medium shots. The plot is typically Victorian. A bad girl loses her baby at birth while a saintly girl dies giving birth. The doctor arranges for the live baby to live with the surviving mother. She is forced to choose between her old lover and the good widower. She chooses the latter "for the child's sake."

Using California scenery, *Olaf—An Atom* (May 19, 1913) starred Harry Carey. This one-reeler uses a moving camera and a great variety of camera placements, including one on top of a mountain looking down into a valley and another from inside a building looking through a doorway to action outside. A drifter helps a family in need and then silently goes on his way.

The end of one era and the beginning of another was signified by *Judith of Bethulia,* filmed in 1913 and released by Biograph March 8, 1914 as its last Griffith film. *Judith of Bethulia* was the first American four-reeler. Its style incorporated all of Griffith's previous techniques, refined them, and created new ones. The iris-out and the iris-in were used. Many shots had background movement with a still foreground. Excellent spatial depth was achieved by long shots with action both near and far. A gobo is created when branches part to expose a view of the Assyrian Army. Flashbacks are achieved by quick cuts. An "S" curve is used when the Israelites chase the Assyrians and fill the screen with hordes of soldiers stretching from one side of the frame to the other. Spectacular crowd and battle scenes are used for the first time in Griffith. He also masked off portions of the frame to achieve pictorial and psychological effects, in one case to block out a view that Holofernes does not want to see.

The story from the Old Testament relates how Judith saves Bethulia from the Assyrians by taking the head of their general. The tale is intercut with a subplot about Naomi and Nathan. She is captured by the Assyrians and is rescued by him after Judith's heroic deed.

Biograph and Griffith parted company in 1913 because he wanted to make longer, more spectacular films. He joined Reliance-Majestic, which distributed through the Mutual Film Corporation. Griffith took with him from Biograph his stock company of actors and cameraman Billy Bitzer. The days of the one-reeler were over.

At Biograph, it had been Griffith's practice to take advantage of natural surroundings and weather. He was to exploit these elements in many of his later films. Linda Arvidson, his first wife, remembered: "A beautiful sleet had covered the trees in Central Park, and we hurried out to photograph it, making up the scenario on the way.''[5]

An era had passed. The skills that Griffith had acquired from the one-reelers would now provide a foundation for longer films, films that would demonstrate to the world that this new medium could be much more than mere entertainment.

Griffith produced, directed, and wrote four films for Mutual. *Home, Sweet Home* and *The Avenging Conscience* foreshadow both in technique and acting *The Birth of a Nation* and *Intolerance. Home, Sweet Home,* six reels, opened in New York May 17, 1914. It is made up of four separate stories linked in an epilogue. A common theme underlying the song, ''Home, Sweet Home'' binds the plots together. Part I tells about the writing of the ballad and of composer John Howard Payne's downfall. Part II takes place in the West with an Easterner bonded to a girl by the song. Part III shows hate between brothers who finally kill each other. The mother lives in order to bring up her remaining dull son. Part IV tells about a wife who remains faithful to her husband although tempted to have an affair with another man. Just as she is about to yield, she hears strains of ''Home, Sweet Home'' and is saved. In the epilogue Payne is in hell trying to get to his sweetheart in heaven who has died waiting for him. She flies around in heaven and finally—because of the contribution of Payne's song to the world—he is united with her.

This last allegorical section clearly foreshadows the one in *Intolerance,* while the sets, costumes, and cast are almost identical to those in *The Birth of a Nation.* Besides incorporating key lighting and many iris effects, Griffith introduced the tilt or pan down of the camera to start a scene and the tilt or pan up to end a scene. He again used the growth of children to denote the passage of time and the double exposure for a dramatic effect in heaven.

As Ingmar Bergman does today, Griffith had his own repertory company. Through various roles, large and small, Blanche Sweet, Lillian Gish, Mae Marsh, Henry Walthall, Robert Harron, Spottiswoode Aitken, Donald Crisp, and many others acquired depth and range. Similarly, as many of the Swedish director's films reflect the current *Zeitgeist,* so Griffith mirrored the Victorian concepts still prevalent as World War I began.

*The Avenging Conscience,* which opened in New York August 2, 1914, a month after shooting for *The Birth of a Nation* had begun, polished further Griffith's many techniques. He shifted the iris from character to

5. Linda Arvidson Griffith, ''Early Struggles of Motion Picture Stars,'' *Film Flashes* (New York: Leslie-Judge Company, 1916), p. 5.

character. The long shot is used for a picture-postcard effect. Close-ups are used as sound effects and to heighten tension—e.g., a shoe kicking a door, and cuts from a pencil tapping to a clock pendulum to nervous hands. The double exposure is used effectively for the ghost scenes, the moon and cloud shots, and the religious sequences with Christ, Moses, and ghouls. The last action may have been achieved by masking portions of the lens rather than by double exposure. A precursor of the impressionistic montage occurs at the end of the film. From a shot of the lovers, Griffith cuts away to Pan and a nineteenth-century dance of children and animals.

The plot of *The Avenging Conscience* is weak. An uncle brings up his nephew to follow in his footsteps as a scholar. The boy wants to marry, but the uncle disapproves. The lad bids his sweetheart goodbye and then kills the uncle. He is discovered by a detective in a direct steal from Poe's "The Tell-Tale Heart." The boy hangs himself and his girl throws herself off a cliff. Suddenly a *deus ex machina* occurs—it was only a dream. The nephew wakes up and sees the uncle alive. The lovers are reunited and the old man permits marriage. "They all live happily ever after."

Griffith's next film was to have a most profound effect upon the future of motion pictures. Siegfried Kracauer wrote that the battle scenes in *The Birth of a Nation* have never been surpassed despite newer technical innovations.[6] Even Sergei Eisenstein, while calling the film "a celluloid monument to the Ku Klux Klan," recognized its director as the greatest master of parallel montage.[7] Terry Ramsaye does not blame the film for the subsequent rise of the Klan, but he credits Thomas Dixon's novel, *The Clansman,* for the success of both.[8] Whether, as some claim, Griffith contributed to the resurgence of the Klan or whether his film merely mirrored U.S. social attitudes, all critics agree that *The Birth of a Nation* raised the screen to the level of an art form.[9]

The major contribution of this film was not its financial success ($50-million overall gross)[10] but its demonstration to the world that film was the greatest medium for propaganda yet devised. Emotions evoked by audiences brought riots, praise, prejudice, and criticism. The original version opened as *The Clansman* in Los Angeles February 8, 1915. It appeared in New York March 3, 1915, as *The Birth of a Nation.* Five weeks

6. Siegfried Kracauer, *Theory of Film* (New York: Oxford University Press, 1965), p. viii.
7. Sergei Eisenstein, "Dickens, Griffith, and the Film Today," *Film Form,* edited and translated by Jay Leyda (New York: Meridian Books, 1958), p. 234.
8. Terry Ramsaye, *A Million and One Nights* (New York: Simon and Schuster, 1964), pp. 635–44.
9. Bosley Crowther, "D. W. Griffith: The Most," *The New York Times,* April 25, 1965.
10. Seymour Stern, "Griffith—*The Birth of a Nation,*" Part 1, *Film Culture* (Spring–Summer, 1965), p. 72.

later 170 shots were removed because of pressure from Black groups and Major John Mitchel. According to Stern and Croy, those portions of the film deleted were the most violently anti-Negro.[11] The story lends itself to propaganda because it deals with history. A vast tale of the Civil War and Reconstruction, *The Birth of a Nation* uses the device of tracing one Southern and one Northern family throughout the period. The families are intertwined as was the nation in the 1860s. The heroic treatment given the rise of the Klan graphically illustrated that the motion picture was a dynamic force in the dissemination of pseudo-fact. In the fifty years since its release this film has been shown as true history to millions of schoolchildren. The writer recalls its use as a good example of the Reconstruction by a history professor in a large Midwestern university a few years ago.

The film technique of *The Birth of a Nation* was, for the most part, not new. Griffith had been developing his cinematic style for eight years. What was fantastic, however, was the total integration of all his major innovations. The use of the iris to highlight emotion was magnificent, such as in love scenes and in the pan from the iris shot of a mother with her children to the slow opening up on Sherman's troops. Split screens and masking the camera to create spatial and depth effects created a new language of film. Bitzer's camera was constantly moving—on a dolly as the Confederates danced at the farewell ball; elevated as troops marched below, under the hooves of Klan horses as they headed to the rescue; and high above the battlefields as soldiers fought. Composition and contrasts were as seen by Matthew Brady photographs. Silhouette shots of the Klan and the many "historical facsimiles" of real events captured the spirit of mid-nineteenth-century America. Griffith's use of double exposure to show the seating of the Black legislators was copied many times by early Soviet filmmakers—indeed, so was his sophisticated parallel editing. The freeze frame effect that Griffith had developed in *A Corner in Wheat* was used to show dead soldiers on the field after battle. He used overlapping action during the famous homecoming scene and provided relief to break tension by comic bits, such as the forlorn sentry. An impressionistic ending again displayed Jesus Christ with the carnage of war.

*The Birth of a Nation* was too big to be financed by Mutual. A separate company, the Epoch Producing Corporation, was created in 1915 to finance and distribute the film. Harry Aitken, president of Epoch and the man who hired Griffith away from Biograph, was instrumental in the formation of Triangle Film Corporation. The new enterprise consisted of Griffith, Thomas Ince, and Mack Sennett, each a successful producer. Griffith supposedly supervised many films for Triangle, but did not direct.

11. Ibid., p. 66, and Croy, op. cit., pp. 105–9.

He did, however, write eight original scenarios under the pseudonym "Grandville Warwick" in 1915 and 1916. Griffith spent most of his time planning for *Intolerance*, which was to "out-spectacular" *The Birth of a Nation*.

The actors and directors at Triangle were all Griffith-trained, so it was no surprise to discover that *Hoodoo Ann*, directed by Lloyd Ingraham, possessed touches of the master. The film, released in 1916, starred Mae Marsh and Robert Harron and served as a prelude to their screen love affair in *Intolerance*. Griffith directed part of *Hoodoo Ann*,[12] which concerns an abused girl in an orphanage who saves another girl during a fire. Adopted by a wealthy couple, she is later courted by the neighbor boy who wants to be a cartoonist. In an incident, the girl thinks that she has killed the man next door, but he returns as she is about to confess to police. The orphan marries the cartoonist, who embarks upon a successful career.

The stars of *Hoodoo Ann* are introduced at the beginning with cuts to each, with an appropriate title. The iris was used to go into the girl's imagination. Cross-cutting between a film within this film and its two separate stories is effective and serves the same purpose as the cutting between a stage-play and the characters in the earlier *A Drunkard's Reformation*. Masking of the camera for a look into the closet and a tricky mirror shot demonstrated that Ingraham had captured his mentor's techniques. A tender bit of business transpires when the hero leaves the frame to kiss the girl and returns right afterward.

Profits from *The Birth of a Nation* were enormous. Griffith had no trouble in attracting investors, most of whom had financed Epoch, to back the Wark Producing Corporation. This separate organization was created to finance and distribute *Intolerance*, which opened at the Liberty Theater in New York September 5, 1916. Although the film received vast publicity and came on the heels of the successful *The Birth of a Nation*, it was a commercial failure. But as an artistic and creative venture, *Intolerance* may have been the most influential film ever made.

In his earlier achievements, Griffith hinted at the techniques he was to use in *Intolerance*. One sees the language of cinema used as few have ever employed it. The photography and its composition as well as all of the camera effects had been executed in *The Birth of a Nation; Intolerance* became a masterpiece at the editing table.

Griffith inter-cut four separate stories, linked only by a shot of Lillian Gish rocking a cradle and a quote from Whitman's *Leaves of Grass*—". . . endlessly rocks the cradle, Uniter of here and Hereafter."[13]

12. Eileen Bowser, "An Annotated List of the Films of D. W. Griffith," in Barry, op. cit., p. 49.
13. Ramsaye, op. cit., p. 756.

A modern story, "Christ in Judea," a pseudo-historical Huguenot tale, and a Babylonian saga are presented side by side, with a fantastic climax featuring shorter and shorter cuts from each story. All but the modern one end in tragedy. *Intolerance* closes with a pacifist montage— prison walls become fields of flowers and battle scenes change into strolling family groups.

Filmmakers in later years not only copied *Intolerance*'s editing style but lifted many scenes. Eisenstein copied the factory workers' strike and the baby-spearing scenes; Pudovkin took the courtroom scenes. The tempo and rhythm of Griffith's instinctive use of short shots laid the foundation for the entire crop of Soviet directors while his impressionistic montages influenced the German school. Hollywood utilized Griffith's new concept of spectaculars interjected with sex in the films of Cecil B. De Mille.

Griffith used blue, red and yellow tinting for subliminal effects; for example, the cradle scene is blue and the society dance red. His characterizations of people and events in *Intolerance* can scarcely be described, and has been likened to plastically created photographed objects being dramatized by the camera "as though it were an individual spectator noting them in ensemble and then in detail, or vice versa."[14]

Early in 1917, before America's entry into World War I, Griffith reached the zenith of his fame. He was invited to England to make a propaganda film for the British government. *Hearts of the World* was made for Artcraft after his severance from Triangle. Starring Lillian and Dorothy Gish and Robert Harron, the film exploited anti-German feeling in the United States. It opened in New York on April 1, 1918, and was a commercial and propagandistic success.

*Hearts of the World* was shot in France, England, and California. It combined newsreel pictures, stock war footage, and recreated incidents. This eclecticism was used extensively a little over a decade later by the Nazi masters of propaganda. *Hearts of the World* opened with a newsreel shot of Griffith at the front, followed by a scene of him with Lloyd George at 10 Downing Street. Historical facsimiles developed in *The Birth of a Nation,* depicted "The Shadow" (the Kaiser in a sinister portrait), Churchill and Lloyd George waiting for news, the House of Commons, and the French Chamber of Deputies.

The story concerns two American families living in France in 1914. They are caught up in the German invasion. The boy goes to fight with the French to defend their common homeland, while the girl remains in a village subsequently occupied by German troops, who commit many atroc-

14. Parker Tyler, "The Film Sense and the Painting Sense," *The Three Faces of the Film* (New York: Thomas Yoseloff, 1960), pp. 44–45.

ities. The French regain the town with the aid of the English and Americans. The Germans flee as the Americans parade in the village with the stars and stripes. The film closes on Woodrow Wilson's photograph draped with American flags.

Some of the more blatant propaganda scenes include children ravaged by war, the Huns whipping a French girl who cannot perform slave labor, and the obvious Wilson-American flag finish. One scene contrasts a bacchanal of German officers with the death of a French mother, victim of the war, and her burial by her sons. Another scene shows a girl walking alone on the battlefield after the fight, a scene that Eisenstein may have adapted consciously for *Alexander Nevsky*. *Hearts of the World* was considered highly effective propaganda in 1918.[15] Dorothy Gish as the quasi-streetwalker dubbed "The Little Disturber," was the highlight of the film, and her performance led to a brilliant career as star of a comedy series.

Another Griffith war film was *The Girl Who Stayed at Home* (March 23, 1919). Begun during the war and completed after, the film had no propaganda value. Pro- and anti-German elements mix ambivalently. One title describes a pro-Kaiser character—"Turnverein, half-drunk and half-German." The story deals with the granddaughter of a Confederate who had refused to surrender and now resides in France. Her fiancé, a French nobleman, is killed in the war, and she falls in love with an American fighting in France. A Hun attempts to rape her but a good German intervenes. The American has a young brother who returns to the U.S. to marry a Broadway showgirl loyal to him during the war. Griffith used limbo lighting for close-ups of the female stars. He employed some footage shot for *Hearts of the World*.

American movie-goers wanted to forget World War I. Griffith produced and directed several pastoral films for Artcraft in 1919. *True Heart Susie* featured a marvelous performance by Lillian Gish. Susie has put William through college secretly by selling her cow. He becomes a minister but marries a "bad" girl. She dies, but he cannot marry Susie because of a mistaken vow. In time, he learns the truth and proposes. The plot sounds clichéd, but the acting and unassuming camera work combine to produce a delightful cameo of innocence. *True Heart Susie* opened in New York June 1, 1919, and included two touches that Hollywood would later make hackneyed: gauze in front of the camera lens for a daydream sequence, and the shadow of the boy at the window during a love scene, talking to the girl who is not in shadow.

While at Artcraft after World War I, Griffith commenced one of his "specials," *Broken Blossoms*. It was released May 13, 1919, by United

15. Eileen Bowser, op. cit., p. 54.

Artists, a company Griffith had formed with Douglas Fairbanks, Mary Pickford, and Charles Chaplin. *Broken Blossoms* was an artistic and commercial success. Its narrative reflected the "Yellow Peril" fears prevalent at the turn of the century and even today. Griffith appeared to be trying to combat intolerance again, but with a "white man's burden" attitude. The alternate title of *Broken Blossoms* was *The Yellow Man and the Girl.* The illegitimate daughter of a villainous boxer is abused by him. A Chinese storekeeper treats her wounds and nurses her back to health. A spy tells her father, who smashes up the store and beats his daughter to death, whereupon the Chinese shoots the father and commits suicide. Lillian Gish and Richard Barthelmess starred.

Griffith, under controlled studio conditions of setting, lighting, and special effects, created a poetic image of Limehouse. His use of tinting for titles as well as different colorings for interior and exterior sequences, together with man-made fog, influenced the German studio films of the 1920s. The yellow tint for the Chinese-temple scene was striking. When Griffith showed the anger of Donald Crisp as the father, he cut from close-up to tight close-up to extreme close-up shots of the face. A scene of policemen reading a newspaper and exclaiming: "Better than last week, only 40,000 casualties," may have been a pacifist comment about World War I. In 1922, a "poor-man's" version of *Broken Blossoms* appeared with Lon Chaney starring in *Shadows.*[16] It proved that Griffith had already achieved what this film attempted.

In order to finance films for UA and to build himself a studio at Mamaroneck, New York, Griffith agreed to make three films for the First National Company. They were done hurriedly and lacked depth. First was a melodramatic potboiler, *The Greatest Question,* which opened in New York December 28, 1919. There are glimpses of primitive poetic symbolism, a technique that Dovzhenko was to bring to maturity a decade later,[17] e.g., Griffith cut from a shot of a dying mother to rushing water and back to the dying mother. Another example of such editing lyricism was a cut to the river from the lover's embrace and back again. Griffith inserted poetic titles among these shots but Dovzhenko let his images stand alone. *The Greatest Question* opens with a 180-degree pan to establish a rural locale. Defocusing of the camera was used for the revelation scene, as the girl remembered her past glimpse of a murder.

With these "quick and dirty" money-makers, Griffith introduced humor based upon stereotypes which he was to repeat in most of his

---

16. *Broken Blossoms* was remade also as a sound film, in England, in 1935. Emlyn Williams took the role originally played by Richard Barthelmess.
17. Arthur Knight, *The Liveliest Art* (New York: New American Library, 1959), pp. 83–86.

speedily made films. When Griffith had time to create characterizations, he seldom resorted to the one-dimensional sterotype. Zeke, the Negro servant in *The Greatest Question*, played by Tom Wilson in blackface, is portrayed as a liar and a thief. He eats at a separate table and possesses all of the "Uncle Tom" characteristics. As the picture ends and the poor family for whom Zeke works strikes it rich in oil, he enters in top hat and tails, with his dog bedecked in jewels.

Stereotypes of cannibals and natives appear in the second of Griffith's First National productions. *The Idol Dancer* (March 21, 1922) deals with a white trader and his half-breed daughter on a South Sea island. The savages are led by a renegade white "Blackbirder" in an attack upon the good Anglo-Saxons. Love scenes are extremely unsubtle. Aside from a typical last-minute rescue using cross-cutting, the film is distinguished only for its use of cutaways from the primitive island to civilized New York, a contrast effected without expository titles. Richard Barthelmess is telling the savage girl about the city, and there are cuts to the Third Avenue El and the Flatiron Building.

"No pushee-me good boy," is a line from Griffith's third First National film, *The Love Flower* (August 22, 1920). His conception of a South Sea native who is half-Black and half-Indian, with a Chinese accent, was probably shared by the majority of Americans. So, too, were his conceptions of the Afro-American. It may be therefore unjust to condemn Griffith for his screen renditions of social situations that reflected then current mores. Yet, when he did use the film for social protest, he did so with eloquence. The saving grace of *The Love Flower* was Griffith's visual impressions of moods, which were effective for the early 1920s. An example is a girl standing at the edge of the sea feeling the salt spray.

If while making these three potboilers Griffith was concurrently preparing and subsequently shooting *Way Down East,* then he can be excused for them. Shot on location in New England, *Way Down East* contains some of the most suspenseful sequences in motion picture history. The final ice-floe sequence is not artificial although spectacular, and it is exciting even today. The use of real ice, snow, and outdoor locations lends credibility to the melodramatic story. Pudovkin considered *Way Down East* a model of how background in a film can supplement and strengthen character and story.[18] For example, the climactic waterfall sequence is foreshadowed when the waterfall is seen earlier during a love scene.

From an antique stage melodrama for which screen rights cost $175,000, *Way Down East* is mid-Victorian in plot but enriched with

---

18. V. I. Pudovkin, *Film Technique*, translated by Ivor Montagu (London: George Newnes, Ltd., 1935), p. 129.

performance, atmosphere, and many filmic touches. In contrast to the three First National Films, *Way Down East* required much time to make. Griffith used multiple camera angles and placements, including a moving sled. Technique was not new, but the shots of the gossip hurrying to spread the news about virtuous but pregnant Lillian Gish are extremely effective and give a sense of emergency and impending doom. Griffith once again used exit and reentry into the frame. Absence of the previous stereotypes give *Way Down East* its authenticity. Stereotypes were not needed because the characterizations are in depth.

In *Way Down East* a typically innocent girl is seduced by a cad, this time after a mock wedding. She gives birth alone in a cold New England boarding-house. The child dies but is baptized by the mother in a moving scene. She falls in love with an upright farmer who rescues her from an ice-floe just before it crashes over the falls. The storm scene was photographed during an actual blizzard in Mamaroneck and certainly must have influenced Pudovkin for his ice-floe sequence in *Mother*. *Way Down East* was released September 3, 1920, and was second only to *The Birth of a Nation* in its commercial success.

It is almost impossible to believe that *Dream Street*, released by UA April 12, 1921, was made by the same man. Sets from *Broken Blossoms* appeared to have been utilized, but *Dream Street* is overlong and poor. In this Yellow Peril film, a Chinese gambling king covets a dancer who tells him—"After this, you let white girls alone." In addition to the "Chink," a "Negro" is seen, for comic relief. Griffith attempted to incorporate a symbolic struggle between Good and Evil into the plot. A Gypsy violinist as Satan and a Street Preacher doing the Lord's work portray the combatants. Many scenes depict the characters being swayed, literally, in either direction. There are few effects worthy of mention. A fade-out was used not only instead of a dissolve but also in the middle of a sequence, as in the middle of an embrace. The camera was defocused as a man died. Gauze was used over the lens to create fog. An exciting use of the close-up to depict panic in a theater was a hint that in a few years an Eisenstein could create the Odessa Steps montage. Griffith's cuts to hell and the Devil and then to Christ were repetitive of his early films.

Almost nine months later, the master returned with an old-fashioned, well-made spectacular (UA, December 28, 1921). *Orphans of the Storm* starred Lillian and Dorothy Gish as two orphans caught up in the French Revolution. The film contains two grandly suspenseful scenes: when Lillian Gish hears the singing of her blind kidnapped sister but cannot get to her, and the final big scene when Monte Blue as Danton saves her and her lover from the guillotine. Characters are two-dimensional, especially Robespierre as played by Sidney Herbert. Even Griffith made a brief appearance sipping champagne at a debauched soirée of aristocrats. The prologue of *Orphans of the Storm* compares the bloody events after the French Revolution to "present-day" Bolshevism. Titles refer to "Anarchy and Bolshevism of the Committee of Public Safety" and the "Revolutionary Government."

In *Orphans of the Storm* Griffith used a matched cut from a close-up of eyes to another close-up of eyes with the camera lens gauzed. For certain scenes, the camera was masked at top and bottom to give a wide-screen effect. At Versailles, the camera dollied back to give the feeling of spaciousness. When Louis XVI entered, Griffith panned the walls, reminding one of Resnais's *Last Year at Marienbad.*

One of the screen's early who-dunnits, *One Exciting Night* does not identify the murderer until its climax. Broadway actor Henry Hull portrayed the dashing young hero who wants to marry blackmailed Carol Dempster. Scotland Yard solves the case and the film ends on a bright note. A subplot featuring blackfaced Porter Strong as a comic Negro frightened by the mysterious events was not unusual for its day. Later, Negro actors were to replace white minstrel actors in such Hollywood mysteries of the thirties and forties as the Charlie Chan series, with its "funny" chauffeur, Mantan Moreland (who rolled his eyes "better" than Stepin Fetchit). Griffith's title during a tender scene: "Words cannot tell what he proposes in love"—is disappointing. A truly successful silent film made such descriptive titles unnecessary. *One Exciting Night,* released by UA October 2, 1922, lost money.

When Griffith left the studio and went out on location, he almost always produced a good film. *The White Rose,* which was opened in New York by UA May 21, 1923, was set in the bayous of Louisiana. A cynic might accuse Griffith of "arty" pictorialization, but the effect was that of a lovely postcard mailed from the Deep South. Mae Marsh stole the film as the girl seduced by a fallen minister. The scene with her using a discarded dog box for her baby is Griffith at his best. Later, Mae Marsh and her illegitimate child are harbored by friendly Negroes, servants of the minister's high-born fiancée. As Mae Marsh lies dying, the wealthy girl summons him. He discovers that this is the girl he had wronged, marries her, and he nurses mother and child like sick roses. A close-up of a rose closes the film.

Almost every schoolchild has seen footage from *America* (UA February 21, 1924). This spectacular was supposed to do for the War of Independence what *The Birth of a Nation* had done for the Civil War. It told the story of the American Revolution through two Colonial families, one Tory and one Rebel. Griffith exonerated the British for the war atrocities; instead the loyalists among the Americans are the culprits. In this story a Tory girl falls in love with a Rebel boy. She is rescued at the last minute from a British villain by a poor American farmer who had fought at Lexington and Concord. George Washington is portrayed as a Christ-like figure. He is shown in magnificent glory during Cornwallis's surrender. Washington is on a white horse, the camera faces the sun, which is blocked by the victorious General, giving him a terrific, shining glow.

*America* did not possess the believability of *The Birth of a Nation.* To Griffith's credit, he did not edit out the shot of Paul Revere's horse as it falls. This inclusion was the only believable part of the picture. No new techniques were used, although opening titles dissolve one to another.

Iris Barry has stated that Griffith's *Isn't Life Wonderful?* (December 24, 1924) "lacks the shock-value" of G. W. Pabst's *The Joyless Street.*[19] The former, shot on location in Germany in the summer of 1924, was made a year before its German counterpart. Yet it may have influenced Pabst[20] in his treatment of German post-World War I inflation. *Isn't Life Wonderful?* possesses a crisp semi-documentary style while the Pabst is a psychological interpretation. The latter may have more Freudian dynamite, but the Griffith contains the most subtle and remarkable images found in movies, according to James Agee.[21]

One of Griffith's finest chase scenes has the wounded war veteran and his fiancée running from thieves who finally steal their precious potatoes. Other outstanding sequences show people pushing on a meat-line as prices keep going up and the ripping of the Kaiser's picture by the Professor, who then kicks the pieces into a dust pan. A subjective shot of trees blowing in the wind, together with time-lapse photography of potatoes growing, mark the film as one of Griffith's most sophisticated ventures. Unfortunately, the irony of the title is missing from the story. Griffith's typical happy ending destroys the impact of the sullen existence of the characters. *Isn't Life Wonderful?* was Griffith's final silent film as an independent producer.

Griffith's first film for Paramount, which he joined as a staff director in 1925, was *Sally of the Sawdust.* It had no new or interesting film techniques. Comedy scenes were funny, due to the antics of W. C. Fields as a circus fakir who adopts an orphan. After many tribulations, some hilarious, the girl is united with wealthy relatives and Fields becomes a real estate agent. Griffith, in the closing title, compares this new occupation with the shell game and Fields' other circus gambling tricks.

*The Sorrows of Satan* came in 1926 for Paramount. Its street scenes and wedding shots are strictly Hollywood studio slickness, lacking any

19. Iris Barry, op. cit., p. 32.
20. Siegfried Kracauer, *From Caligari to Hitler* (New York: Noonday Press, 1960), pp. 169–70.
21. *Agee on Film,* edited by David Manning White (Boston: Beacon Press, 1964), p. 315.

realism. The love scenes are very bad—nothing is left to the imagination. They are a far cry from the old Griffith, when characters delicately stepped out of the frame for a kiss. The sole artistic touch is in the scene between Menjou as the Devil and Ricardo Cortez as the tempted one, when the pair walk in and out of pools of light. The Devil, of course, departs at the film's close because the hero repents. A final shot of Satan's "horrible" shadow vanishing is disappointing if one remembers Murnau's *Nosferatu* and its communication of terror four years earlier.

In 1927, Griffith signed with Joseph Schenck, the controlling force in UA, to work for Schenck's Art Cinema Corporation.[22] The master returned to Hollywood and made four films.

*Drums of Love* reunited Griffith with his old star from the Biograph days and *America,* Lionel Barrymore, who gave a brilliant performance as the hunchbacked Spanish nobleman whose handsome brother commits adultery with his young bride. The deformed giant kills his two beloveds at the close of the film. In an alternate ending the court jester kills Barrymore as the young lovers repent. Both finales are equally poor. The film contained several long moving camera shots, had some good action, and moved at a fairly rapid pace. Laboratory dissolves were used by Griffith for the first time. There is an effective subjective shot, from the brother's point of view, as he looks at the girl's body. The Art Cinema-UA release opened in New York January 24, 1928.

Griffith's first all-sound film (he had experimented with disc recordings previously) was *Abraham Lincoln,* starring Walter Huston, with a scenario by Stephen Vincent Benét. Typical of American history in the films of the 1920s, great Americans have no faults. It traces Lincoln from birth to assassination, emphasizing his well-known qualities. There is no dramatic continuity, plot, or sub-plot. Sound quality is poor and editing jumpy.

However, Griffith did use sound creatively. Off-camera sounds were utilized as well as sounds coming from the distance on long shots. The technique was similar to that of television drama in its early days. The camera dollied in on the person speaking, dollied out to a two-shot, widened for a group shot and came in on another person. Screen dialogue was not yet developed in 1930 when *Abraham Lincoln* was released by Art Cinema-UA, and there was a trace of stylized stage diction. Some scenes showed promise of a future film sound language, but Lincoln's monologues were mostly taken from his actual speeches and were wooden. Griffith was voted best director of 1930 for *Abraham Lincoln,* in spite of

22. Eileen Bowser, op. cit., pp. 78–80.

what Lewis Jacobs has called its "many moments of absurd sentimentality."[23]

*The Struggle* was Griffith's last film, made as an independent and released December 10, 1931, by UA. It was withdrawn after unfavorable criticism. The story is the old-timer about the family man who becomes a drunkard. Griffith opens with a montage of conversations concerning alcohol. Street and steel-mill scenes are well directed and photographed. Hal Skelly, as the father, does an admirable job, especially in delirium tremens. His wife's line—"Jimmie, your eyes are all shiny"—is typical of the script. *The Struggle's* good features are its realism and the quality of its sound track, the latter a tremendous improvement over *Abraham Lincoln.* Griffith reverted to stereotypes for humor in this quickly made film by inserting a Jewish bill collector into the story. If one were to criticize the happy ending, as the drunkard reforms and lives happily ever after, he should not forget the Academy Award-winning 1945 Billy Wilder film, *Lost Weekend.*

Sixteen years after *The Struggle,* Griffith died at the age of seventy-three. He had made 432 movies from 1908 to 1931, according to Agee, that had grossed $60 million.[24] Stern put the total number of films at a higher figure.

Aside from the huge gross of his life's output, Griffith's contributions to the art of the film are many. With Billy Bitzer, he enormously advanced the sophistication of the camera. He was a master editor. Screen acting in his hands moved ahead to far greater subtlety and expressiveness. Aside from many unforgettable individual characterizations, he provided spectacular scenes of great masses of people in action. He uplifted the taste of audiences and brought them from smelly, cheap nickelodeons to gilt palaces with huge screens and symphonic orchestras to provide accompaniment.

"A film," Griffith said, "is a cooperative effort between the director and the audience. A director shows a bit of human emotion; the audience fills in the rest. The better the film, the greater the cooperation between director and audience."[25]

Griffith at his peak let the content determine his film technique. His films integrated story, mood, title, and technique, blending schematically.[26] He may have carried Victorian morality long beyond its proper

23. Lewis Jacobs, *The Rise of the American Film* (New York: Harcourt, Brace and Company, 1939), p. 394.

24. *Agee on Film,* p. 398.

25. Homer Croy, op. cit., p. 75.

26. Paul Goodman, "Film Chronicle: Griffith and the Technical Innovations," *Partisan Review* (May–June 1941), pp. 237–40.

life-span,[27] but his themes of social consciousness are still valid. Although his recurring plots depicting the poor hero or orphan making good or the dire consequences of immorality or the evils of drink are unsophisticated by our contemporary existential non-standards, it cannot be overlooked that these concepts still rest in the subconsciousness of the American people. So, too, Griffith's Southern fundamentalist religious view that Christ in Heaven is pitted against the Devil in Hell is believed by millions of persons.

One must take issue with Lewis Jacobs who claimed that Griffith was interested only in money and prestige, that he did not keep up with the times, and that as soon as the great director did not move forward, he disintegrated as an artist.[28] Griffith crumbled as a craftsman only when he did not have sufficient time to produce his films and when he could not retain overall supervision of the work in progress. As a Hollywood studio staff director, Griffith was as out of place in the twenties as Ingmar Bergman would be in Hollywood today. Griffith was indeed aware of his artistic successes. He did not bumble through his films as many have suggested.

In an interview with Ezra Goodman shortly before his death, Griffith linked *Intolerance* to *Potemkin* and to *Triumph of the Will*.[29] Such an astute observation could have been made only by a person well aware of the vast potentiality of the cinema, its relationship to history, and its impact on audience attitudes in the twentieth century.

27. Herb Sterne, "Screen and Stage," *Script* (January 8, 1944), pp. 12–13.
28. Lewis Jacobs, op. cit., pp. 384–94.
29. Ezra Goodman, *The Fifty-Year Decline and Fall of Hollywood* (New York: Simon and Schuster, 1961), p. 8.

# Howard Hawks

HOWARD HAWKS *was born in Indiana in 1896 and died in Palm Springs, California, in 1977. During vacations from Cornell University he became a propman for Famous Players-Lasky in California. From the age of sixteen to twenty-one he had also been a barnstorming pilot and later served in World War I with the embryonic Army Air Corps. Returning to Hollywood after the war, he was hired as an editor, produced several films for director Allan Dwan among others, and worked in the story departments of Paramount and MGM. Taken on as a director by William Fox, he made his first feature,* The Road to Glory, *in 1926.*

*Hawks had also written the story for* The Road to Glory, *and, beginning with* Scarface *(1932), he worked on virtually every script for the films he directed (usually without screen credit) and produced most of the films as well. In all, Hawks made eight silent films, a few of which contain the seeds of his later career. But it was not until the coming of sound that Hawks's characteristic mixture of action and dialogue could be set free and refined.*

*In the early 1930s Hawks remarked that he and Josef von Sternberg were the only "real" directors in Hollywood. In great part the cleanness and directness of Hawks's visual world seems conceived as a counterstatement to Sternberg's more shadowy and textured nuances. In his films Hawks helped create an "American" style, indebted primarily neither to the nineteenth-century popular theater nor to expressionist drama, but drawing instead on the possibilitites for movement and characterization made available with sound film.*

*Hawks's main themes involve action, testing, courage, and professionalism, often within all-male groups like soldiers, fliers, cowboys, and gangsters, as in* The Dawn Patrol *(1930),* Only Angels Have Wings *(1939), and* Red River *(1948). When the challenges involve both men and women, the terms of the contest are more often verbal, with a definite physical undertone, as in* Bringing Up Baby *(1938),* His Girl Friday *(1940),* Ball of Fire *(1941), and* Man's Favorite Sport? *(1963).*

*Lured by his taste for both a strong story line and characters defined by action, Hawks has explored virtually every film genre. His own life as an airplane pilot and racing driver stands behind such films as* The Dawn Patrol, Only Angels Have Wings, Air Force *(1943),* The Crowd Roars *(1932), and* Red Line 7000 *(1965). He has made prison films (*The Criminal Code, *1931), detective films (*Trent's Last Case, *1929;* The Big Sleep, *1946), underworld films (*Scarface; Barbary Coast, *1935), "Grand-Hotel" films (*Twentieth Century, *1934), newspaper films (*His Girl Friday*), musicals (*Gentlemen Prefer Blondes, *1953), and Westerns (*Red River; Rio Bravo, *1959;* El Dorado, *1967;* Rio Lobo, *1970)—all directed with a concentration and sharpness that makes them exemplary in their genre. The* *framework of plot conventions allows Hawks to follow his own interests in action and dialogue without undercutting the story.*

*The one genre that might be called totally Hawks's own —"screwball" comedy—similarly uses the frame of conventional story as a precarious container for the energies of the sex war, in such films as* Bringing Up Baby, His Girl Friday, Ball of Fire, I Was a Male War Bride *(1949),* Monkey Business *(1952), and* Man's Favorite Sport? *The sex-war dynamics of the screwball comedies Hawks began to make in the late 1930s crossed with his male-oriented action films to produce such hybrids as* The Big Sleep *and* Rio Bravo, *in which the male ethic of pure action is complemented yet undermined by a female rhetoric of wit and sophisticated banter. Hawks's characters still exist on the surface of themselves, whether that surface is defined by body, words, or action. But the complex truth of that surface bears out the implication of Hawks's entire movie-making method: appearances are simple only for those who do not examine them very closely.*

*Although Hawks's films have received extensive critical attention in France, there are as yet only two books in English devoted solely to his career: Robin Wood's* Howard Hawks *(1968) and Peter Bogdanovich's monograph* The Cinema of Howard Hawks *(1962). Joseph McBride's anthology,* Focus on Howard Hawks *(1972), assembles many of the most important articles dealing with Hawks and contains an astute introduction, and Peter Wollen devotes an important part of his general discussion of the auteur theory to Hawks and John Ford in* Signs *and* Meaning in the Cinema *(1969).*

# Howard Hawks
# and the Action Film

## Manny Farber

The saddest thing in current films is watching the long-neglected action directors fade away as the less talented De Sicas and Zinnemanns continue to fascinate the critics. Because they played an anti-art role in Hollywood, the true masters of the male action film—such soldier-cowboy-gangster directors as Raoul Walsh, Howard Hawks, William Wellman, William Keighley, the early, pre-*Stagecoach* John Ford, Anthony Mann—have turned out a huge amount of unprized, second-gear celluloid. Their neglect becomes more painful to behold now that the action directors are in decline, many of them having abandoned the dry, economic, life-worn movie style that made their observations of the American he-man so rewarding. Americans seem to have a special aptitude for allowing History to bury the toughest, most authentic native talents. The same tide that has swept away Otis Ferguson, Walker Evans, Val Lewton, Clarence Williams, and J. R. Williams into near oblivion is now in the process of burying a group that kept an endless flow of interesting roughneck film passing through the theaters from the depression onward. The tragedy of these filmmakers lies in their having been consigned to a Sargasso Sea of unmentioned talent by film reviewers whose sole concern is not continuous flow of quality but the momentary novelties of the particular film they are reviewing.

Howard Hawks is the key figure in the male action film because he shows a maximum speed, inner life, and view, with the least amount of flat foot. His best films, which have the swallowed-up intricacy of a good soft-shoe dance, are *Scarface, Only Angels Have Wings, His Girl Friday,*

From *Negative Space* by Manny Farber (New York: Praeger, 1971). The first part of this essay appeared originally under the title "Underground Films" in *Commentary,* vol. 24, no. 5 (November 1957); copyright © 1957 by the American Jewish Committee; reprinted by permission of *Commentary* and the author. The second part appeared originally under the title "Howard Hawks" in *Artforum,* April 1969; copyright 1969 by California Artforum, Inc.; reprinted by permission of *Artforum* and the author.

and *The Big Sleep*. Raoul Walsh's films are melancholy masterpieces of flexibility and detailing inside a lower-middle-class locale. Walsh's victories, which make use of tense, broke-field journeys and nostalgic background detail, include *They Drive by Night, White Heat,* and *Roaring Twenties*. In any Bill Wellman operation, there are at least four directors—a sentimentalist, deep thinker, hooey vaudevillian, and an expedient short-cut artist whose special love is for mulish toughs expressing themselves in drop-kicking heads and somber standing around. Wellman is at best in stiff, vulgar, low-pulp material. In that setup, he has a low-budget ingenuity, which creates flashes of ferocious brassiness, an authentic practical-joke violence (as in the frenzied inadequacy of Ben Blue in *Roxie Hart*), and a brainless hell-raising. Anthony Mann's inhumanity to man, in which cold mortal intentness is the trademark effect, can be studied best in *The Tall Target, Winchester 73, Border Incident,* and *Railroaded*. The films of this tin-can de Sade have a Germanic rigor, caterpillar intimacy, and an original dictionary of ways in which to punish the human body. Mann has done interesting work with scissors, a cigarette lighter, and steam, but his most bizarre effect takes place in a taxidermist's shop. By intricate manipulation of athletes' bodies, Mann tries to ram the eyes of his combatants on the horns of a stuffed deer stuck on the wall.

The film directors mentioned above did their best work in the late 1940's, when it was possible to be a factory of unpretentious picture-making without frightening the front office. During the same period and later, less prolific directors also appear in the uncompromising action film. Of these, the most important is John Farrow, an urbane vaudevillean whose forte, in films like *The Big Clock* and *His Kind of Woman,* is putting a fine motoring system beneath the veering slapstick of his eccentric characterizations. Though he has tangled with such heavyweights as Book of the Month and Hemingway, Zoltan Korda is an authentic hard-grain cheapster telling his stories through unscrubbed action, masculine characterization, and violent explorations inside a fascinating locale. Korda's best films— *Sahara, Counterattack, Cry the Beloved Country*—are strangely active films in which terrain, jobs, and people get curiously interwoven in a ravening tactility. William Keighley, in *G-Men* and *Each Dawn I Die,* is the least sentimental director of gangster careers. After the bloated philosophical safe-crackers in Huston's *Asphalt Jungle,* the smallish cops and robbers in Keighley's work seem life-size. Keighley's handling is so right in emphasis, timing, and shrewdness that there is no feeling of the director breathing, gasping, snoring over the film.

The tight-lipped creators whose films are mentioned above comprise the most interesting group to appear in American culture since the various groupings that made the 1920s an explosive era in jazz, literature, silent films. Hawks and his group are perfect examples of the anonymous artist, who is seemingly afraid of the polishing, hypocrisy, bragging, fake educating that goes on in serious art. To go at his most expedient gait, the Hawks type must take a withdrawn, almost hidden stance in the industry. Thus, his films seem to come from the most neutral, humdrum, monotonous corner of the movie lot. The fascinating thing about these veiled operators is that they are able to spring the leanest, shrewdest, sprightliest notes from material that looks like junk, and from a creative position that, on the surface, seems totally uncommitted and disinterested. With striking photography, a good ear for natural dialogue, an eye for realistic detail, a skilled inside-action approach to composition, and the most politic hand in the movie field, the action directors have done a forbidding stenography on the hardboiled American handyman as he progresses through the years. . . .

Any day now, Americans may realize that scrambling after the obvious in art is a losing game. The sharpest work of the last thirty years is to be found by studying the most unlikely, self-destroying, uncompromising, roundabout artists. When the day comes for praising infamous men of art, some great talent will be shown in true light: people like Weldon Kees, the rangy Margie Israel, James Agee, Isaac Rosenfeld, Otis Ferguson, Val Lewton, a dozen comic-strip geniuses like the creator of ''Harold Teen'', and finally a half-dozen directors such as the master of the ambulance, speedboat, flying-saucer movie: Howard Hawks.

The films of the Hawks-Wellman group are *underground* for more reasons than the fact that the director hides out in subsurface reaches of his work. The hard-bitten action film finds its natural home in caves: the murky, congested theaters, looking like glorified tattoo parlors on the outside and located near bus terminals in big cities. These theaters roll action films in what, at first, seems like a nightmarish atmosphere of shabby transience, prints that seem overgrown with jungle moss, sound tracks infected with hiccups. The spectator watches two or three action films go by and leaves feeling as though he were a pirate discharged from a giant sponge. . . .

*Scarface* (1932) is a passionate, strong, archaic photographic miracle: the rise and fall of an ignorant, blustery, pathetically childish punk (Paul Muni) in an avalanche of rich, dark-dark images. The people, Italian gangsters and their tough, wisecracking girls, are quite beautiful, as varied and shapely as those who parade through Piero's religious paintings. Few movies are better at nailing down singularity in a body or face, the effect of a strong outline cutting out impossibly singular shapes. Boris Karloff: long stove-pipe legs, large-boned and gaunt, an obsessive, wild face; Ann Dvorak: striking out blindly with the thinnest, sharpest elbows, shoving aside anyone who tries to keep her from the sex and excitement of a dance hall. Besides the sulphurous, extreme lighting and so many feverish, doomed types, like Osgood Perkins as Johnny Lovo, top hood on the South Side until his greedier right-hand man Tony Camonte takes over, the image seems unique because of its moody energy: it is a movie of quick-moving actions, inner tension, and more angularity per inch of screen than any street film in history.

Crisp and starched where *Scarface* is dark and moody, *His Girl Friday* (1940) is one of the fastest of all movies, from line to line and gag to gag. Besides the dynamic, highly assertive pace, this *Front Page* remake with Rosalind Russell playing Pat O'Brien's role is a tour de force of choreographed action: bravado posturings with body, lucid Cubistic composing with natty lapels and hat brims, as well as a very stylized discourse of short replies based on the idea of topping, outmaneuvering the other person with wit, cynicism, and verbal bravado. A line is never allowed to reverberate but is quickly attached to another, funnier line in a very underrated comedy that champions the sardonic and quick-witted over the plodding, sober citizens.

The thing you remember most about Cary Grant's sexy, short-hop Lindbergh in *Only Angels Have Wings* (1939), a rather charming, maudlin Camp item, is his costume, which belongs in a Colombian Coffee TV commercial: razor-creased trousers that bulge out with as much yardage as a caliph's bloomers and are belted just slightly under his armpits. Except for a deadpan, movie-stealing performance by Richard Barthelmess, this movie about a Zeta Beta Tau fraternity of fliers in a South American jungle is a ridiculous film of improbability and coincidence, the major one being that Bat McPheerson, the blackest name in aviation, the man who betrayed Thomas Mitchell's kid brother and married Grant's old flame, should show up years later broke and in need of a job in Barranca, where buddies Grant and Mitchell are busting up planes on the strangest stalactite mountains.

*Red River* (1948), as a comment on frontier courage, loyalty, and leadership, is a romantic, simple-minded mush, but an ingeniously lyrical film nonetheless. The story of the first trip from Texas to the Abilene stockyards is a feat of pragmatic engineering, working with weather, space, and physiognomy. The theme is how much misery and brutality can issue from a stubbornly obsessed bully (John Wayne, who barks his way through the film instead of moving), while carving an empire in the wilderness. Of the one-trait characters, Wayne is a sluggish mass being insensitive and cruel-minded on the front of the screen; Joanne Dru is a chattering joke, even more static than Wayne; but there is a small army of actors (Clift, John Ireland) keyed in lyrically with trees, cows, and ground.

The very singular compact names that beat like a tom-tom through the above films are as eccentric and Hollywoodish as the character who makes them. They're summing up names, they tie a knot around the whole personality, and suggest the kind of bravura signature that underlines itself. Jeff Carter, Tess Millay, Mathew Garth, Guino Rinaldo, Buck Kennelley, Johnny Lovo, Molly Malloy, Cherry Valance are dillies of names that indicate a Breughel type who creates a little world of his own, outfitted in every inch with picturesque hats, insensitive swagger, and good-natured snobberies.

Howard Hawks is a bravado specialist who always makes pictures about a Group. Fast dialogue, quirky costumes, the way a telephone is answered, everything is held together by his weird Mother Hen instinct. The whole population in *Scarface,* cavemen in quilted smoking jackets, are like the first animals struggling out of the slime and murk toward fresh air. *Only Angels,* a White Cargo melodrama that is often intricately silly, has a family unit living at the Dutchman's, a combination bar, restaurant, rooming house, and airport run by a benevolent Santa Claus (some airline: the planes take off right next to the kitchen, and some kitchen: a plane crashes, the wreck is cleared and the pilot buried in the time it takes them to cook a steak; and the chief control is a crazy mascot who lives with a pet donkey and serves as a lookout atop a buzzard-and-blizzard-infested mountain as sharp as a shark's tooth). The wonderfully dour reporters in *His Girl Friday* and the mawkish cowboys in *Red River* are also strangely pinned in place by the idea of people being linked together in tight therapeutic groups, the creations of a man who is as divorced from modern *angst* as Fats Waller and whose whole moving-making system seems a secret preoccupation with linking, a connections business involving people, plots, and eight-inch hat brims.

The Mother Hubbard spirit gives the film a kind of romance that is somewhat WASP-ish with a Gatsby elegance and cool. Both the girls in *Scarface,* like Zelda Fitzgerald, would fling themselves away over a Russ Columbo recording of "Poor Butterfly." Ann Dvorak, dancing with a big, bland-faced clod who is bewildered by all her passion and herky-jerky cat's meow stuff, is so close to *Tender Is the Night* in her aura of silly recklessness. The sophomoric fliers of Barranca, like Fitzgerald's expatriates in Paris, are ravished with each other's *soignée:* Bonnie, playing real jazzy "Peanuts" with a whole saloon jammed around her piano cheering her on, is an embarrassing square version of supersquare Chico Marx. The feeling of snobbery in any Hawks work is overpowering, whether it is a Great White Father (Grant) patronizing a devitalized native with a gift watch or the female Jimmy Breslin (Rosalind Russell) breezily typing a socko story.

This romanticism, which wraps the fliers-reporters-cowhands in a patina of period mannerism and attitude, makes for a film that isn't dated so much as removed from reality, like the land of Tolkien's Hobbits.

It is interesting how many plots are interwoven into a scene. The whole last part of the *Front Page* remake is a fugue in fast humor, peculiar for the way each figure touches another in ricochets of wild absurdity. Molly Malloy, the killer's lady defender (''Ah come on fellahs, he didn't even touch me, I just gave him some tea, and he was shaking all over'') jumps out the window and is forgotten; her boyfriend, who has been entombed forlornly inside a rolltop desk, is dragged to his cell, presumably to be hung the next morning; Hildy Johnson finally gets maneuvered back to the *Morning Star* by her arch-heel editor; the mayor and the sheriff are politically destroyed for trying to bribe a fat Baby Huey, who turns up with a reprieve for the convicted killer. Then there's Louie, a terrific heist artist who steals a mother-in-law and gets mangled by a police car which was driving in the wrong lane. People who talk reams about great film comedy never mention this version of Hecht's play with its one twist, an elegantly played, pragmatic girl, sharp and immediately aware of everything in the ace reporter's role. It is a prime example of Hawks's uncelebrated female touch: the light flouncy foot, the antipomposity about newspaper problems, and the Mother Hen way of setting up family relationships. The ingenuity of its pragmatic engineering is that every gesture (she picks up the phone, it's funny) contributes to the plot, is laugh-provoking, and adds up to a supply of intricately locked humor so large that there's hadly time to relish any one gag.

The films have a musical comedy hokeyness joined to a freedom, a mellifluous motion, which is summed up in the line ''Wherever they roam, they'll be on my land,'' spoken as a couple of cows—the start of a mighty herd: the man's bull and the boy's cow—wander off into a nice, sparse landscape. But the deep quality in any Hawks film is the uncannily poetic way an action is unfolded. Sometimes this portrayal of motion is thrilling (the cattle going into Abilene), funny (Abner Biberman's harmless hood: ''Everybody knows Louie''). gracefully dour (Karloff's enigmatic cockiness in a bowling alley, like a Muybridge photograph), or freakishly mannered (Karen Morley sizing up Scarface's new pad: ''It's kinda gaudy, isn't it''), but it is always inventive, killingly expressive, and gets you in the gut. One blatantly colloquial effect is slammed against another. The last section of *Scarface* builds detail on detail into a forbidding whirlwind. As the incestuous duo shoots it out with the cops, slightly outnumbered eighty to one, the lighting is fabulous, Dvorak's clamoring reaches an unequaled frenzy (''I'm just like you, Tony, aren't I, I'm not afraid''), and there is an authentic sense of the primeval, life coming to smash the puny puffed-up egos.

Not many moviemakers have gone so deeply into personality-revealing motion, the geography of gesture, the building and milking of a signature trait for all its worth. Hawks's abandon with his pet area, human gesture, is usually staggering, for better or worse. Why should Cary Grant get away with so much Kabukilike exaggeration, popping his eyes, jutting out his elbows, roaring commands at breath-taking speed in a gymnasium of outrageous motion? Sometimes Hawks's human-interest detailing falls on its face: the beginning of a cattle drive with Wayne a tiny speck moving down a channel of earth, the Knute Rockne of Cattledom, and, then, those endless ghastly close-ups of every last cowboy, one after the other, giving his special version of a Yahoo.

*Scarface,* as vehement, vitriolic, and passionate a work as has been made about Prohibition, is a deadly grim gangster movie far better than *White Heat* or *Bonnie and Clyde,* a damp black neighbor to the black art in Walker Evans's subway shots or the Highway 90 photographic shot at dawn by Robert Frank. Nowhere near the tough-lipped mentality or hallucinatory energy of Hawks's only serious film, *His Girl Friday* is still better than a clever, arch, extremely funny newspaper film. It's hard hard to believe that anything in Chaplin or W. C. Fields has so many hard, workable gags, each one bumping the other in an endless interplay of high-spirited cynicism. But rating these close camaraderie films, teeming with picturesque fliers-punks-pundits and a boys' book noble humanism, in the Pantheon division of Art and giving them cosmic conceptions is to overweight them needlessly.

A director who's made at least twenty box-office gold mines since 1926 is going to repeat himself, but the fact is that Howard Hawks's films are as different as they're similar. In each action film, he's powerfully interested in the fraternal groups that he sets up, sticking to them with an undemonstrative camera that is always eye level and acute on intimate business, and using stories that have a straight-ahead motion and develop within a short time span. The point is that each picture has a widely different impact: from the sulphurous lighting and feverish style of *Scarface* to the ignorant blustering of John Wayne in a soft Western that doesn't have any pace at all. Within the devil-may-care silliness of his *Angels* picture, the difference in acting between Barthelmess (crafty and constipated), Thomas Mitchell (maudlin, weepy), and Jean Arthur (good grief!) is so violent as to suggest the handling of three directors.

Hawks, a born movie-manipulator who suggests a general moving little flag pins around on a battle map, is not very fussy about the pulp-story figures nor the fable-ized scenery into which he jams them. The opening shots of his Andes airline movie are supposed to "vividly create Barranca, the South American town" in and around which the "completely achieved masterpiece" is set. This operetta seaport, with boas of smoke hanging in swirly serpentines and pairs of extras crisscrossing through the fake mist, might be good for a Douglas, Arizona, high school production. In the next "vividly created" scene, Jean Arthur is being dim and blithe, snapping her fingers (the first of the block-headed swingers) in time with some fairly authentic calypso dancers who are being unbelievably passionate at ten in the morning. In such movies, where a broken-down Englishman or a drunken rubber planter is seated in the corner muttering "Only two more months and I get out of this godforsaken place," a Rhonda Fleming or Brian Keith (in something called *Jivaro*) is far classier than the dopy inner-tubes who so seriously act characters getting the mail through for seven straight days in Hawks's corny semicatastrophe.

Hawks gets exhilarating situations: the stampede in *Red River* is great, maybe because everyone shuts up during the panic. He can be very touching, as in Harry Carey Jr.'s death with four or five cowboys standing in straight-line silence in a strangely hollowed out terrain that suggests Gethsemane. Yet no artist is less suited to a discussion of profound themes than Hawks, whose attraction to strutting braggarts, boyishly cynical dialogue, and melodramatic fiction always rests on his poetic sense of action. It would be impossible to find anything profound in Rosalind Russell's Hildy, but there is a magic in the mobile unity of the woman: her very mannish pinstripe suits, the highly stylized way she plants a hand on her hip, and her projecting of the ultimate in sophisticated swagger, taking off her hat and coat and showing how a real reporter sets up shop. The genius of such action engineering is that Hawks is able to poeticize dialogue as well as faces and costumes, making a 100 per cent ordinary line—Hildy's parting shot to Earl Williams in his death cell: "Goodbye Earl and good luck"—seem to float in an air of poignant, voluptuous cynicism.

# The Genius of
# Howard Hawks

## Jacques Rivette

The evidence on the screen is the proof of Hawks's genius: you only have
to watch *Monkey Business* to know that it is a brilliant film. Some people
refuse to admit this, however; they refuse to be satisfied by proof. There
can't be any other reason why they don't recognize it.

Hawks's *oeuvre* is equally divided between comedies and dramas—a
remarkable ambivalence. More remarkable still is his frequent fusing of the
two elements so that each, rather than damaging the other, seems to underscore their reciprocal relation: the one sharpens the other. Comedy is never
long absent from his most dramatic plots, and far from compromising the
feeling of tragedy, it removes the comfort of fatalistic indulgence and
keeps the events in a perilous kind of equilibrium, a stimulating uncertainty
which only adds to the strength of the drama. Scarface's secretary speaks
comically garbled English, but that doesn't prevent his getting shot; our
laughter all the way through *The Big Sleep* is inextricable from our foreboding of danger; the climax of *Red River,* in which we are no longer sure of
our own feelings, wondering whose side to take and whether we should be
amused or afraid, sets our every nerve quivering with panic and gives us a
dizzy, giddy feeling like that of a tightrope walker whose foot falters
without quite slipping, a feeling as unbearable as the ending of a nightmare.

While it is the comedy which gives Hawks's tragedy its effectiveness,
the comedy cannot quite dispel (not the tragedy, let's not spoil our best
arguments by going too far) the harsh feeling of an existence in which no
action can undo itself from the web of responsibility. Could we be offered a
more bitter view of life than this? I have to confess that I am quite unable to

This material originally appeared as "Génie de Howard Hawks" by Jacques Rivette in
*Cahiers du Cinéma* (May 1953). Reprinted by permission of Grove Press, Inc. Translation by
Russell Campbell and Marvin Pister.

join in the laughter of a packed theater when I am riveted by the calculated twists of a fable (*Monkey Business*) which sets out—gaily, logically, and with an unholy abandon—to chronicle the fatal stages in the degradation of a superior mind.

It is no accident that similar groups of intellectuals turn up in both *Ball of Fire* and *The Thing*. But Hawks is not concerned so much with the subjection of the world to the jaded, glacial vision of the scientific mind as he is with retracing the comic misfortunes of the intelligence. Hawks is not concerned with satire or psychology; societies mean no more to him than sentiments do; unlike Capra or McCarey, he is solely preoccupied with the adventure of the intellect. Whether he opposes the old to the new; the sum of the world's knowledge of the past to one of the degraded forms of modern life (*Ball of Fire, A Song Is Born*); or man to beast (*Bringing Up Baby*), he sticks to the same story—the intrusion of the inhuman, or the crudest avatar of humanity, into a highly civilized society. In *The Thing,* the mask is finally off: in the confined space of the universe, some men of science are at grips with a creature worse than inhuman, a creature *from another world;* and their efforts are directed toward fitting it into the logical framework of human knowledge.

But in *Monkey Business* the enemy has crept into man himself: the subtle poison of the Fountain of Youth, the temptation of infantilism. This we have long known to be one of the less subtle wiles of the Evil One— now in the form of a hound, now in the form of a monkey—when he comes up against a man of rare intelligence. And it is the most unfortunate of illusions which Hawks rather cruelly attacks: the notion that adolescence and childhood are barbarous states from which we are rescued by education. The child is scarcely distinguishable from the savage he imitates in his games: and a most distinguished old man, after he has drunk the precious fluid, takes delight in imitating a chimp. One can find in this a classical conception of man, as a creature whose only path to greatness lies through experience and maturity; at the end of his journey, it is his old age which will be his judge.

Still worse than infantilism, degradation, or decadence, however, is the fascination these tendencies exert on the same mind which perceives them as evil; the film is not only a story about this fascination, it offers itself to the spectator as a demonstration of the power of the fascination. Likewise, anyone who criticizes this tendency must first submit himself to it. The monkeys, the Indians, the goldfish are no more than the guise worn by Hawks's obsession with primitivism, which also finds expression in the savage rhythms of the tom-tom music, the sweet stupidity of Marilyn Monroe (that monster of femininity whom the costume designer nearly deformed), or the aging bacchante Ginger Rogers becomes when she reverts to adolescence and her wrinkles seem to shrink away. The instinctive euphoria of the characters' actions gives a lyric quality to the ugliness and foulness, a denseness of expression which heightens everything into abstraction: the fascination of all this gives *beauty* to the metamorphoses in retrospect. One could apply the word "expressionistic" to the artfulness with which Cary Grant twists his gestures into symbols; watching the scene in which he makes himself up as an Indian, it is impossible not to be reminded of the famous shot in *The Blue Angel* in which Jannings stares at *his* distorted face. It is by no means facile to compare these two similar tales of ruin: we recall how the themes of damnation and malediction in the German cinema had imposed the same rigorous progression from the likable to the hideous.

From the close-up of the chimpanzee to the moment when the diaper slips off the baby Cary Grant, the viewer's head swims with the constant whirl of immodesty and impropriety; and what is this feeling if not a mixture of fear, censure—and fascination. The allure of the instinctual, the abandonment to primitive earthly forces, evil, ugliness, stupidity—all of the Devil's attributes are, in these comedies in which the soul itself is tempted to bestiality, deviously combined with logic *in extremis;* the sharpest point of the intelligence is turned back on itself. *I Was a Male War Bride* takes as its subject simply the impossibility of finding a place to sleep, and then prolongs it to the extremes of debasement and demoralization.

Hawks knows better than anyone else that art has to go to extremes, even the extremes of squalor, because that is the source of comedy. He is never afraid to use bizarre narrative twists, once he has established that they are possible. He doesn't try to confound the spectator's vulgar tendencies; he sates them by taking them a step further. This is also Molière's genius: his mad fits of logic are apt to make the laughter stick in your throat. It is also Murnau's genius—the famous scene with Dame Martha in his excellent *Tartuffe* and several sequences of *Der Letze Mann* are still models of Molièresque cinema.

Hawks is a director of intelligence and precision, but he is also a bundle of dark forces and strange fascinations; his is a Teutonic spirit, attracted by bouts of ordered madness which give birth to an infinite chain of consequences. The very fact of their continuity is a manifestation of Fate. His heroes demonstrate this not so much in their feelings as in their actions, which he observes meticulously and with passion. It is *actions* that he films, meditating on the power of appearance alone. We are not concerned with John Wayne's thoughts as he walks toward Montgomery Clift at the end of *Red River,* or of Bogart's thoughts as he beats somebody up: our attention is directed solely to the precision of each step—the exact rhythm of the walk—of each blow—and to the gradual collapse of the battered body.

But at the same time, Hawks epitomizes the highest qualities of the American cinema: he is the only American director who knows how to draw a *moral*. His marvelous blend of action and morality is probably the secret of his genius. It is not an idea that is fascinating in a Hawks film, but its effectiveness. A deed holds our attention not so much for its intrinsic beauty as for its effect on the inner works of his universe.

Such art demands a basic honesty, and Hawks's use of time and space bears witness to this—no flashback, no ellipsis; the rule is continuity. No character disappears without us following him, and nothing surprises the hero which doesn't surprise us at the same time. There seems to be a law behind Hawks's action and editing, but it is a *biological* law like that governing any living being: each shot has a functional beauty, like a neck or an ankle. The smooth, orderly succession of shots has a rhythm like the pulsing of blood, and the whole film is like a beautiful body, kept alive by deep, resilient breathing.

This obsession with continuity imposes a feeling of monotony on Hawks's films, the kind often associated with the idea of a journey to be made or a course to be run (*Air Force, Red River*), because everything is felt to be connected to everything else, time to space and space to time. So in films which are mostly comic (*To Have and Have Not, The Big Sleep*), the characters are confined to a few settings, and they move around rather helplessly in them. We begin to feel the gravity of each movement they make, and we are unable to escape from their presence. But Hawksian drama is always expressed in spatial terms, and variations in setting are parallel with temporal variations: whether it is the drama of Scarface, whose kingdom shrinks from the city he once ruled to the room in which he is finally trapped, or of the scientists who cannot dare leave their hut for fear of The Thing; of the fliers in *Only Angels Have Wings,* trapped in their station by the fog and managing to escape to the mountains from time to time, just as Bogart (in *To Have and Have Not*) escapes to the sea from the hotel which he prowls impotently, between the cellar and his room; and even when these themes are burlesqued in *Ball of Fire,* with the grammarian moving out of his hermetic library to face the perils of the city, or in *Monkey Business,* in which the characters' jaunts are an indication of their reversion to infancy (*I Was a Male War Bride* plays on the motif of the journey in another way). Always the heroes' movements are along the path of their destiny.

The monotony is only a facade. Beneath it, feelings are slowly ripening, developing step-by-step toward a violent climax. Hawks uses lassitude as a dramatic device—to convey the exasperation of men who have to restrain themselves for two hours, patiently containing their anger, hatred, or love before our eyes and then suddenly releasing it, like slowly saturated batteries which eventually give off a spark. Their anger is heightened by their habitual *sangfroid;* their calm façade is pregnant with emotion, with the secret trembling of their nerves and of their soul—until the cup over-flows. A Hawks film often has the same feeling as the agonizing wait for the fall of a drop of water.

The comedies show another side of this principle of monotony. For-ward action is replaced by repetition, like the rhetoric of Raymond Roussel replacing Péguy's; the same actions, endlessly recurring, which Hawks builds up with the persistence of a maniac and the patience of a man obsessed, suddenly whirl madly about, as if at the mercy of a capricious maëlstrom.

What other man of genius, even if he were more obsessed with con-tinuity, could be more passionately concerned with the consequences of men's actions, or with these actions' relationship to each other? The way they influence, repel, or attract one another makes up a unified and coher-ent world, a Newtonian universe whose ruling principles are the universal law of gravity and a deep conviction of the gravity of existence. Human actions are weighed and measured by a master director preoccupied with man's responsibilities.

The measure of Hawks's films is intelligence, but a *pragmatic* intelli-gence, applied directly to the physical world, an intelligence which takes its efficacity from the precise viewpoint of a profession or from some form of human activity at grips with the universe and anxious for conquest. Marlowe in *The Big Sleep* practices a profession just as a scientist or a flier does; and when Bogart hires out his boat in *To Have and Have Not,* he hardly looks at the sea: he is more interested in the beauty of his passengers than in the beauty of the waves. Every river is made to be crossed, every herd is made to be fattened and sold at the highest price. And women, however, seductive, however much the hero cares for them, must join them in the struggle.

It is impossible to adequately evoke *To Have and Have Not* without immediately recalling the struggle with the fish at the beginning of the film. The universe cannot be conquered without a fight, and fighting is natural to Hawks's heroes: hand-to-hand fighting. What closer grasp of another being could be hoped for than a vigorous struggle like this? So love exists even where there is perpetual opposition; it is a bitter duel whose constant dangers are ignored by men intoxicated with passion (*The Big Sleep, Red River*). Out of the contest comes esteem—that admirable word encompassing knowledge, appreciation, and sympathy: the opponent be-comes a partner. The hero feels a great sense of disgust if he has to face an enemy who refuses to fight; Marlowe, seized with a sudden bitterness, precipitates events in order to hasten the climax of his case.

Maturity is the hallmark of these reflective men, heroes of an adult, often exclusively masculine world, where tragedy is found in personal relationships; comedy comes from the intrusion and admixture of alien elements, or in mechanical objects which take away their free will—that freedom of decision by which a man can express himself and affirm his existence as a creator does in the act of creation.

I don't want to seem as if I'm praising Hawks for being "a genius estranged from his time," but it is the obviousness of his modernity which lets me avoid belaboring it. I'd prefer, instead, to point out how, even if he is occasionally drawn to the ridiculous or the absurd, Hawks first of all concentrates on the smell and feel of reality, giving reality an unusual and indeed long-hidden grandeur and nobility; how Hawks gives the modern sensibility a classical conscience. The father of *Red River* and *Only Angels Have Wings* is none other than Corneille; ambiguity and complexity are compatible only with the noblest feelings, which some still consider "dull," even though it is not these feeings which are soonest exhausted but rather the barbaric, mutable natures of crude souls—that is why modern novels are so boring.

Finally, how could I omit mentioning those wonderful Hawksian opening scenes in which the hero settles smoothly and solidly in for the duration? No preliminaries, no expository devices: a door opens, and there he is in the first shot. The conversation gets going and quietly familiarizes us with his personal rhythm; after bumping into him like this, we can no longer leave his side. We are his companions all through the journey as it unwinds surely and regularly as the film going through the projector. The hero moves with the litheness and constancy of a mountaineer who starts out with a steady gait and maintains it along the roughest trails, even to the end of the longest day's march.

From these first stirrings, we are not only sure that the heroes will never leave us, we also know that they will stick by their promises *to a fault,* and will never hesitate or quit: no one can put a stop to their marvelous stubbornness and tenacity. Once they have set out, they will go on to the end of their tether and carry the promises they have made to their logical conclusions, come what may. What is started must be finished. It doesn't matter that the heroes are often involved against their wills: by proving themselves, by achieving their ends, they win the right to be free and the honor of calling themselves men. To them, logic is not some cold intellectual activity, but proof that the body is a coherent whole, harmoniously following the consequences of an action out of loyalty to itself. The strength of the heroes' will power is an assurance of the unity of the man and the spirit, tied together on behalf of that which both justifies their existence and gives it the highest meaning.

If it is true that we are fascinated by extremes, by everything which is bold and excessive, and that we find grandeur in a lack of moderation—then it follows that we should be intrigued by the clash of extremes, because they bring together the intellectual precision of abstractions with the elemental magic of the great earthly impulses, linking thunderstorms with equations in an affirmation of life. The beauty of a Hawks film comes from this kind of affirmation, staunch and serene, remorseless and resilient. It is a beauty which demonstrates existence by breathing and movement by walking. That which is, is.

# The Lure of Irresponsibility: "Scarface" and "Bringing Up Baby"

## Robin Wood

### "Scarface"

It may seem perverse to approach the comedies via a gangster film of exceptional ferocity, almost the only Hawks film in which the protagonist dies. But *Scarface* belongs with the comedies.

There are interesting parallels between *Scarface* and Godard's *Les Carabiniers*. Though utterly different in style and method, both have leading characters who consistently perform monstrous violent actions which the films never condone, yet who retain the audience's sympathy to the end, and for similar reasons. Godard gives his Michelangelo the characteristics, not only of a primitive, but of a young child, an innocent immune from moral judgments because he has never developed moral awareness. Far from weakening the statement of horror and despair, this intensifies it.

Tony Camonte (Paul Muni), the "hero" of *Scarface*, is always touching and eventually pathetic, because he too is an innocent. Indeed, he captures and keeps more of the spectator's affection than Michelangelo; this is surprising, because Hawks allows us to see him killing sympathetic characters (Guino Rinaldo), where Godard keeps the slaughter in *Les Carabiniers* strictly impersonal; but Hawks's method, though consistently objective, allows us much closer to the characters than Godard's. There is one basic difference between the two films: *Scarface* remains firmly within the conventions of naturalism, whereas *Les Carabiniers* refuses all such limitations (thereby discovering limitations of its own). The difference is apparent in the "childlike" presentation of Tony and Michelangelo (and even in their names). Tony's primitivism is entirely credible naturalistically, where Michelangelo's infantilism is very stylized.

Tony is introduced as a squat shadow, evoking ape or Neanderthaler. His fascinated attraction to gaudy trappings (loud dressing gowns, ties, jewelry, etc.) recalls the savage's fondness for beads. His attempts at elegance—large acreage of handkerchief protruding from breast pocket, huge tie—are grotesque. With this goes his ignorance. When Poppy (Karen Morley) tells him that jewelry on men is "effeminate" he is boyishly delighted, automatically assuming a compliment. When she tells him his place is "kind of gaudy," his reply is "Isn't it though? Glad you like it." When he rises to power as Johnny Lovo's right-hand man, he wears a new shirt each day, sports an even fancier dressing gown than Lovo's, boasts to Poppy of having several more suits, "all different colors," jumps up and down on the bed showing it to her, saying, "It's got inside springs. Bought it at an auction." His attempts at seduction show a childlike *naïveté* which eventually, touching Poppy, becomes an important factor in her capitulation. His infantile confusion of values—woman and dressing gown placed on roughly the same level, half gaudy toys, half status symbols—anticipates interestingly Michelangelo's response to the *carabinier's* catalogue of the treasures of the world that he will bring back as loot.

This essential innocence is reflected in other characters. The fat Italian gangster Costillo, celebrating at a New Year's Eve party, paper-hatted amidst a debris of festoons among which is a discarded bra, boasts childishly of his prosperity (he is about to get shot), mentioning in the same breath the girl and the automobile that he can now afford. Guino Rinaldo (George Raft), when Cesca (Ann Dvorak) calls on him, is cutting out paper dolls; and it is he, the tough gangster, who is seduced by the sheltered Cesca. As Tony comes to kill Guino, Cesca is singing a comic song about a train driver, complete with "poop-poop" noises. Tony's illiterate secretary has continual difficulty with telephones: he is afraid of them, and at one point wants to shoot one. Both here and in *Les Carabiniers* we are made to feel the frightening discrepancy between the achievements of civilization and the actual level of culture attained by the individuals who are its by-products.

Characteristically—though, considering the ostensible subject of *Scarface,* remarkably—there is little sense of social context. Members of normal society appear only as the merest background figures (waiters in the machine-gunned restaurant, nurses held up in the hospital where Meehan is finished off). Considered too simply, *Scarface* appears a dangerously immoral film. It opens with an explicitly moralizing foreward about ". . . the intention of the producer . . . ," and halfway through there is an embarrassingly hammy scene (added by another director, apparently, as a safeguard against censorship) where a newspaper editor accused of sensationalism defends his position, arguing the need to expose outrages. But the film shows remarkably little society either to outrage or to defend. Hawks's "naturalism" is highly selective: he works by simply eliminating society. Hence in *Scarface* the ostensible subject—society threatened by gangsters—isn't really treated at all. We see almost nothing of the results of the outrages—bomb explosions, machine-gunning—in terms of human suffering. The police are uniformly unsympathetic. Hawks presents his gang wars as kids' games played with real bullets. A sardonic, macabre humor is seldom absent, and some of the outrages are treated as uninhibited farce: Gaffney's machine-gunning of the restaurant, with Tony's secretary struggling to cope with the telephone—an attempt continued, doggedly, throughout the attack, with boiling tea pouring out over his bottom through the bullet holes in an urn. The film communicates, strongly, a sense of exhilaration: Hawks actually encourages us to share the gangsters' enjoyment of violence. If Tony has the innocence of a child or a savage, he also has the energy and vitality that goes with it.

Yet no one with a sensibility more developed than Tony Camonte's could find *Scarface* ultimately immoral. The attitude to Tony is complex. If we regard him sympathetically, we never feel that he is being glorified. His pitiful end is implicit throughout. He is funny and touching because he is an overgrown child, emotionally arrested at an early stage, with no sympathetic awareness of others and no self-awareness. He dies when he loses his essential innocence—when, in a very shadowy, disturbing way, he begins to see himself, and his armor of boyish self-confidence, like his steel shutters ("I got nobody—I'm all alone—my steel shutters don't work"), is no longer any protection.

How, then, does Hawks "place" this monstrous innocence and its effects?—why, if the killings are often exhilarating and farcical, are they also so disturbing? Hawks faced a difficult problem: how to discover images or references which could be incorporated unostentatiously within the naturalistic conventions? Instead of inviting judgment on the gangsters for subverting the social order, Hawks disturbs our response to the film's humor with images and leitmotifs, very simple and traditional yet the more evocative because of it, with their accumulated associations. One thinks of the passage from Borges which Godard quotes at the start of *Les Carabiniers:* the writer returns increasingly to the "old metaphors" because they are enriched by past usage.

The image of the cross pervades the whole film. It is the first thing we see; every killing is accompanied (often unobtrusively) by a cross, sometimes formed by patterns of light or shadow; the scar on Tony's face is a cross. In the Scene of the St. Valentine's Day Massacre the camera moves down from seven crosses—the pattern in a wooden overhang—to show the seven victims. The majority of these are the multiplication-sign form of the cross—a straightforward sign for death, the crossing-out of a human being; but several take the traditional Christian shape. The pervasive image carries associative emotional overtones which contribute importantly to the effect of the killings. Individual instances carry their own overtones. Near the end of the film Tony, incestuously involved with Cesca without understanding the nature of his own feelings, kills Guino out of possessive jealousy; at the first meeting of Guino and Cesca, Guino is seen through a cross formed by the balcony edge and its support. The effect is very unobtrusive—Hawks never sacrifices the action of a scene to symbolism—but we are by that time sufficiently used to the association of the crosses with killings for it to carry an emotional charge. Lighting is of great importance in *Scarface:* in the scene where Gaffney (Boris Karloff) is shown the concrete results of the St. Valentine's Day Massacre, and he, among the most ruthless of the film's killers, is morally outraged, the accompanying cross is a radiant white. At another point the cross—Christian shape—is part of an undertaker's sign, shot from above so that it hangs over the body like a cross at a funeral. The associations give the killings a particular flavor of profanity.

For many of the killings in *Scarface* Hawks finds vivid epitomizing images. In the bowling alley Gaffney rolls a ball, the sound of gunfire tells us he has been killed, and then as the shot continues we watch the progress of the bowling ball until it knocks over all the ninepins. Gaffney will never know his throw was so successful. More than any face-contorting and stomach-clutching, the shot conveys the finality of death, in a manner no less moving for being detached and indirect. Later, when Tony shoots Guino for touching Cesca (they are in fact married), Guino dies while the coin he has flipped is still in the air: its falling to the ground, after all the previous occasions on which he has infallibly caught it, conveys the fact of his death with great intensity. The death of Tony's secretary makes similar use of habitual behavior: he dies, mortally wounded by bullets through the door he has just closed, struggling to cope with the telephone that has defeated him throughout the film. But all the comic quality has gone, removed with the ill-fitting hat he automatically takes off as he staggers back from the door: his illiteracy, his unquestioning devotion to Tony, his funny clothes, his total childlike inadequacy in coping with his environment, are no longer in the least funny, and we are left with a sense of terrible waste.

Other images and references in *Scarface* associate with the crosses. One in the historical data—the traditional associations of St. Valentine's Day giving the massacre an extra profanity—is neatly underlined by the killers' brutal talk about "bringing you a valentine." Earlier, Gaffney's attack on the restaurant was made under cover of a funeral procession, the machine gun hidden in the hearse. In two scenes flowers are used. Tony's men enter a hospital to finish off Meehan, survivor—though badly injured—of a previous attack. The intensity and terrible poetry of the scene are partly the product of its economy: no preliminaries, simply a brief sequence of shots of the gangsters, carrying bouquets, holding up terrified nurses in a corridor, opening a door beyond which is a heavily bandaged figure in a bed, with one leg strapped up, unable to move to cover, the leg support casting a cross-shaped shadow on the far wall. The figure is blasted with bullets, then a bouquet is flung in on the body as a parting cynicism. The scene (it is all over in a few seconds) epitomizes the disturbing power of the film. The tension and pace of direction and editing capture a sense of exhilaration, we respond to the uninhibited audacity of the gangsters, their freedom from all social and moral restraints, their ability to perform outrageous actions in the face of social institutions. At the same time the horror of the scene is overwhelming: only a Tony in the audience could find it *merely* exhilarating. As elsewhere in Hawks's work (*Monkey Business* offering the extremest instance), our yearnings for total irresponsibility are evoked to be chastised. Through the images of cross and flowers, the utter helplessness of the victim, the values appealed to are absolute rather than social; our horror derives from deeper sources than the violation of social stability.

The other scene centered on a flower is equally complex and disturbing. Guino Rinaldo brings Tony a rose as a token that he has killed a rival who ran a flower shop. Tony later in the scene gives it to Poppy, whom he is trying to seduce. The scene evokes the rose's traditional associations with love and beauty, tenderness and transience, and juxtaposes these with our knowledge of its actual *dramatic* significance.

Hawks, like Godard, uses the arts to suggest more developed values beyond the reach of the characters; though the examples in Hawks's film are again much simpler, and entirely integrated in the action. Tony's signature tune, whistled every time he kills (the sextet from Donizetti's *Lucia di Lammermoor*, "Chi me frena?" What restrains me?) gives his first appearance an almost surrealist quality: the squat ape-like shadow juxtaposed with the elegant phrases of Italian opera. His visit to the theater and his reactions to the play (*Rain*) anticipate *Les Carabiniers'* cinema scene. Tony does not, like Michelangelo, totally misunderstand the nature of the medium; but his attitude shows a similarly elementary contact. His dimly awakening sense of the existence of moral problems foreshadows his downfall: he is quite unable to grasp their nature, let alone cope with them. He tries to explain the play to his secretary, who prefers "shows with jokes." "This Sadie, she's a girl with a problem. . . . She's what you call disillusioned." He leaves the secretary to find out how the play ends while he goes to another killing that can't wait, and when he gets the garbled report, gives Sadie's solution (she "climbed back in the hay with the army") his delighted approval. His incomprehension of the issues (counterpointed with his further progress in bloodshed) beautifully defines the terrible innocence that permits him to kill and plunder, and which also allows him not to question his attachment to Cesca or his immediate ferocious jealousy of any man who comes near her.

In the scenes of Tony's muddled self-realization and subsequent death the film's moral force becomes finally evident. Far from being a "moral" ending hastily tacked on in an attempt to make an immoral film respectable, it is as inevitable as the ending of *A Bout de Souffle*. Tony is strong only while he remains unaware. The shooting of Guino and Cesca's ensuing outcry are crucial. Tony loses control over her because he is losing control over himself—we see from his facial expression, from his inability, now, to hold her, his dim, reluctant realization of what his real feelings for her are. When Tony's secretary dies struggling with the phone, it is Poppy on the other end. All Tony can find to say to her is a vague, confused, "I didn't know," which can refer simply to the dead secretary—Tony hadn't realized that he was hit—or to the realization of his own involvement with Cesca (which makes Poppy no longer of the slightest importance to him). The ambiguity prevents us from applying the words narrowly: they sum up Tony's whole appalling ignorance: after all the massacres, the audacities, the exhilaration, the success, they are all he can find to say for himself. After it, his reaction to Cesca's failure to kill him is "Why didn't you shoot?"—followed by a hysterical defiance of the encircling police which grotesquely parodies the exhilaration of the violence earlier in the film. His hysterical triumphant laughter coincides with Cesca's being struck by a bullet—which ricochets off the much-vaunted steel shutter, symbol to Tony of his invulnerability, which he is holding open at that moment. The cross that has accompanied all Tony's killings is appropriately, though ironically, there for the death of his sister; after which his disintegration into blind panic as the gas bombs explode around him—the rising and overpowering clouds of gas providing the perfect visual expression for his bewildered state of mind, the protective innocence punctured—stands as judgment on all his past.

The essential condemnation of Tony Camonte, like that of Michel Poiccard in *A Bout de Souffle*, whose anti-social behavior also conveys to the audience an irresistible exhilaration, is not imposed from any external moral standpoint (despite *Scarface's* foreword to the effect that "... Justice always catches up with the criminal who must answer for his sins"), but is arrived at empirically in terms of the character's own development. Tony and Michel condemn themselves, ultimately, because their behavior is self-destructive, not only in the simple, literal sense that it gets them killed, but because it denies them fulfilment of their basic needs. Both directors have the courage to treat their characters' rejection of responsibility and rush towards self-destruction inwardly, with the implicit admission that they are dealing with universal traits and urges. A dangerous method (both films have been accused of immorality); but valid morality must be based on honesty.

The comparison with Godard reveals Hawks's strength and limitations. At first sight *Scarface* seems richer than *Les Carabiniers*. It works brilliantly on a popular narrative level, a dimension that Godard's film doesn't pretend to. Beyond this is the essential stability of Hawks's character and the traditional nature of his art: his successful films are pervaded by a robustness derived from stable values—loyalty, courage, endurance, mastery of self and environment—whereas the emotion underlying and characterizing *Les Carabiniers* is a terrible despair, arising from Godard's exposure to the complexities and confusions, the disintegration of accepted values, inherent in contemporary society. *Les Carabiniers* is a statement about the modern world of a kind Hawks nowhere attempts. This defines him as an artist—it doesn't invalidate him. Hawks takes the state of civilization for granted in a way that has become increasingly difficult for the modern artist, and he has been helped in this by the availability to him of cinematic traditions which manifest themselves in the genres, but his inability to make statements about modern society limits his work, affecting particularly certain of the comedies.

It is with the comedies that *Scarface* unquestionably belongs. It has almost nothing in common with the adventure films (besides the enclosed group); it has almost everything in common with the comedies. The overlapping and combining of farce and horror points ahead to *His Girl Friday,* Tony's destructive innocence to that of Lorelei Lee; in *Monkey Business,* the juxtapositions of ape, savages, and children are clearly related to the presentation of the gangsters in *Scarface*. Above all, *Scarface* gives us the essential theme of Hawks's most characteristic comedies. If the adventure films place high value on the sense of responsibility, the comedies derive much of their tension and intensity from the fascination exerted by irresponsibility...

## *"Bringing Up Baby"*

*Bringing Up Baby* is perhaps the funniest of Hawks's comedies but not the best. Again and again, after no matter how many viewings, the spectator is delighted by small touches of comic business often beyond the critic's reach, since they defy verbal description: matters of gesture, expression, intonation. Consider the little scene where the delivery man brings Professor David Huxley (Cary Grant) the intercostal clavicle while David is speaking on the telephone to his fiancée: one or two laconic comments by the delivery man ("Don't let it throw you, buster") aside, the humor lies in the way the characters are standing, the way they look at each other, the way they speak. Or there is the moment when David, in an elaborately feminine negligée, opens the front door to Katherine Hepburn's aunt, a determined masculine-looking woman in manly tweeds, and, already driven to near-frenzy by the systematic humiliations to which he has been subjected, in answer to her question as to what he's doing dressed like *that,* gives a frenetic little leap in the air, waggles his arms, and shouts "I went gay suddenly." It is a moment that epitomizes many of the essentials of Hawksian comedy. There is the extremeness of it, in the context of the light comedy genre: we are almost in the world of the Marx Brothers. There is the sexual reversal, the humiliation of the male, his loss of mastery, which makes the comedies an inversion of the adventure films. Finally, there is the *resilience* of the male, his ability to live through extremes of humiliation retaining an innate dignity.

The inspiration isn't consistent. The tension throughout is in the Grant-Hepburn relationship; scenes involving minor characters are sometimes labored. Major Horace Applegate (Charles Ruggles), the effeminate and ineffectual big-game hunter, is interesting as a crazy-mirror reflection of the men of action, dominant and professional, who people the adventure films, but somewhat tedious in himself. Barry Fitzgerald's drunken Irish gardener seems predictable. Worse, the invention flags in the middle of the film, even in scenes involving the principals. During the first hour, with Hepburn ruining Grant's golf game with an important business connection, bringing every conceivable disaster upon him in a nightclub, then blackmailing him into helping her take Baby (her leopard) to Connecticut, the inspiration, both in script and direction, never lets up. But later, in the scenes where the two search for the missing leopard in the woods at night, conception and execution falter, the material is thin and directional inspiration more spasmodic. Incidents where characters fall down banks and get entangled in poison ivy are not very funny, nor do they add much in terms of thematic development. With the release of the dangerous circus leopard the film picks up again and the invention regains something of its previous density; but the sense of *élan,* once lost, is hard to recapture.

The real nature of the flaw in *Bringing Up Baby* lies deeper, and is far more revealing of Hawks's limitations and weaknesses. The structure is satisfyingly bold and symmetrical, with leanings towards allegory, built on oppositions. In the center is Professor Huxley, on the surface entirely dedicated to zoological research (the reconstruction of a dinosaur skeleton). On one side is his mousy, earnest, sexless secretary-fiancée, who refuses a honeymoon on the grounds that it would interfere with his work; on the other there is Susan (Hepburn). It is easy to see them as Duty (conceived as deadeningly dry and repressive) and Nature (conceived as amoral and entirely irresponsible); and tempting to simplify further (the film encourages it) and see them in Freudian terms as Superego and Id. David's dedication to his work *isn't* complete: in his extreme absent-mindedness, his inability to cope practically with situations, we feel inner forces working against it; and we note that *he* wants a honeymoon even if his bride-to-be doesn't. Hepburn erupts at moments when he is about to clinch a deal that will ensure his future; and each time she shatters to fragments the superficial order of his life. Once she has materialized, he is completely helpless against her. The entire characterization of Susan favors this interpretation. She is not so much *im*moral as *a*moral: she seems never to feel a twinge of guilt, never acknowledging responsibility for the comic disasters she precipitates. The opposition of the two women in the film's basic pattern is reinforced by the equally clear-cut opposition of animals, living and dead: the dinosaur skeleton (represented for us during most of the film by the intercostal clavicle) and the leopard, extensions, respectively, of David's way of life and Susan's. There is a fairly systematic progression in the film, from the world of the dominance of the Superego to that of the Id: starting amid the most civilized settings—museum, golf course, night club—the film moves to the country house of Susan's aunt, thence to the garden, thence to the woods; and there is a corresponding movement from light to darkness. We pass from the unnatural order of the museum to the natural disorder of the woods at night. One can see a parallel progression in the animals, dead dinosaur, pet terrier, tame leopard, wild leopard, though they are not introduced in quite that order (no one who sees the film will find it as crudely schematic as I have made it sound). The release of the semi-wild leopard, suggesting forces beyond anything Susan represents (even she is terrified of it, when she realizes it isn't Baby), clinches this sense of a descent into a dangerous, disordered world of nature.

The Grant and Hepburn characters exist on different levels of reality. The trouble is that they are also a man and a woman, and some of the slackening of tension in the scenes in the woods can be accounted for by the feeling that on this level Hawks simply didn't know what to do with them. This discrepancy between levels gives rise to doubts about the film's resolution, and the total outlook it expresses. With Hepburn as Id-figure the end works rather well. Grant, restored to order, is putting the finishing touches to his life-work, the dinosaur skeleton, at the top of a huge scaffolding. Hepburn reappears and climbs up to him; Grant admits that he has enjoyed their misadventures; and within minutes the entire skeletal structure has collapsed. The dry bones represent his lifework and are an image of his way of life, destroyed finally by the eruption of the Id. But it is impossible to see the film *only* like that: one is forced also to contemplate Hepburn as a suitable life-partner for him. One can only feel uneasy, and question whether the triumph of total irresponsibility the film appears to be offering as fitting resolution is in fact acceptable. There is no sense of a possible synthesis or even compromise; the only alternative to Susan is made so ridiculous as to be instantly discounted. Hasn't the temptation to irresponsibility, that gives *Scarface* and *Monkey Business* their tension and vividness, here got the better of Hawks's judgment?—as it is to do again, and more disturbingly, in *His Girl Friday*. And isn't the films facile ridicule of the stock figure of the Freudian psychiatrist rather revealing?

ALFRED HITCHCOCK *was born in England in 1897, the son of Catholic parents who educated him in Jesuit schools. He began his film work as a painter and letterer of intertitles for Famous Players-Lasky in London in 1920. He trained for a time (1922–1923) at the famous Ufa Studios in Berlin, where he came under the influence of German expressionism. He first worked as an assistant director and then made his mark as a director with a silent film,* The Lodger *(1926). Later he directed the first British sound film,* Blackmail *(1929).*

*Hitchcock achieved international recognition with a celebrated series of thrillers made in England between 1934 and 1938, including* The Man Who Knew Too Much *(1934),* The Thirty-Nine Steps *(1935),* The Secret Agent *(1936),* Sabotage *(1936),* Young and Innocent *(1937), and* The Lady Vanishes *(1938). He was brought to Hollywood by David O. Selznick in 1939. His first American film, still set in England with a British cast, was* Rebecca *(1940), a Gothic romance, but his love of public settings took on an American flavor with* Saboteur *(1942). From this point on he was very much an American director, who could elicit remarkable performances from Hollywood stars like Cary Grant, Ingrid Bergman, Joseph Cotten, Jimmy Stewart, and many others.*

*His thrillers of the mid-1930s, turned out on a relatively small budget, show a pronounced emphasis on visual detail, camera angle, and atmosphere that is a legacy of his silent films. His taste for macabre wit was also developed in this period, as well as an inclination for mixing murder with social comedy and an ability simultaneously to exploit a genre— usually the detective or spy story—as well as to parody it. While these films are well made and entertaining, Hitchcock's persistent thematic concerns emerge more clearly in the forties and fifties.*

*In the early 1940s his films take on a glossy, star-studded look, which disguises both his strict control over his actors and his careful manipulation of narrative rhythm. This he achieves by controlling audience awareness and by intricately tightening and relaxing tension. His taste for spectacular settings shows in the dénouement of* Saboteur *atop the Statue of Liberty, but it is already present in his use of the British Museum for the final chase scene in* Blackmail, *or of Albert Hall and a full symphony orchestra for the assassination scene in* The Man Who Knew Too Much. *His main interests shift, or perhaps intensify, with the technical experiments of* Lifeboat *(1944) and* Rope *(1948)—essentially one-set, single-take films—and the domestic and psychological explorations of* Suspicion *(1941),* Shadow of a Doubt *(1943),* Spellbound *(1945),* Notorious *(1946),* Rope, *and* Stage Fright *(1950). Gradually there emerges in these films an intense preoccupation with the nature of guilt, often the guilt of a seemingly innocent person, even a bystander—a theme summarized in the title of a later, "non-fiction" film,* The Wrong Man *(1956).*

*One of his brilliant plotting devices is the pairing or doubling of characters in films like* Shadow of a Doubt *and* Strangers on a Train *(1951), which enables him to develop the motifs of mistaken identity, "false" accusation, and the web of secret connection between the obviously guilty and the superficially innocent—the good citizen whose unconscious motives do not bear close examination. These two films, which are among his best, are noteworthy also for their villains, who are exceptionally insidious and charming, particularly as set off against a hero or heroine who is somewhat callow, two-dimensional and naïve. These linked characters represent the bland, civilized surface that conceals the violence within.*

*With use of color, Hitchcock projects such themes onto increasingly expensive and exotic settings—like the Riviera in* To Catch a Thief *(1955) and Mount Rushmore in* North by Northwest *(1959)—and often with a sure comic touch; indeed, a wry, macabre humor takes over completely* The Trouble with Harry *(1954) and* Family Plot *(1976). Yet for Hitchcock evil still appears in domestic and ordinary situations, whether the small town of* The Birds *(1963) or the isolated family motel, half Gothic and half banal, in* Psycho *(1960). The latter production is perhaps the masterpiece of this period and, along with* The Wrong Man, *is Hitchcock's only black-and-white film after* Dial M for Murder *(1954). Some later films, such as* Marnie *(1964),* Torn Curtain *(1966), and* Topaz *(1969), show a distinct falling off, but the archly perverse* Frenzy *(1972) was both a critical and a popular success.*

*Hitchcock has been appreciated by critics chiefly as a master of audience manipulation. The moral and technical roots of that manipulation were first analyzed closely by the French, especially Eric Rohmer and Claude Chabrol, and later François Truffaut, who explored the influence of Hitchcock's Catholic and family background on his themes of guilt and innocence. Many English and American critics with a strongly high-cultural bias and a distaste for the formulas of the genre film still find him merely a skillful technician and entertainer, limited by his commercial projects and incapable of portraying fully rounded human beings. Unlike the French and other pro-Hitchcock critics, they usually value his British films more highly, for their taste and their modest scale.*

*The French perspective on Hitchcock can be sampled in Eric Rohmer and Claude Chabrol,* Hitchcock *(1957), and François Truffaut's book-length interview,* Hitchcock *(1967), which touches all his films. Robin Wood's* Hitchcock's Films *(1969) concentrates entirely on the later work. A good sampling of criticism is Albert LaValley's* Focus on Hitchcock *(1972); see also James Naremore's* Filmguide to "Psycho" *(1973), Raymond Durgnat's* The Strange Case of Alfred Hitchcock *(1975), and Donald Spoto's* The Art of Alfred Hitchcock *(1977).*

# Alfred Hitchcock

## Lindsay Anderson

Prefatory Note
Some thirty years old, this piece has been well and truly overtaken by the fashionable "auteur" theorists, who have acclaimed Alfred Hitchcock as a philosophic master-artist, to rank with Goya and Dostoevsky. (The French are chiefly to blame for this inflation of the artist's pretensions. English-speaking intellectuals have always had an exaggerated respect for the French language.) There is certainly more to be said about Hitchcock than I found in 1949; but my youthful severity may still provide a useful corrective.

L.A.

As, geographically, Britain is poised between continents, not quite Europe, and very far from America, so from certain points of view the British cinema seems to hover between the opposite poles of France and Hollywood. Our directors and producers never—or rarely—have the courage to tackle, in an adult manner, the completely adult subject; yet they lack also the flair for popular showmanship that is characteristic of the American cinema. It is significant that the most widely celebrated of all British directors should be remarkable for just this quality. So much so indeed that, when his powers were at their prime, he emigrated to Hollywood; and today, when he returns to work again in a British studio, he carries with him the pervasive aura of Hollywood success, and stays at the Savoy Hotel.

Alfred Hitchcock's long career has been intimately bound up with the history of the cinema. He began in the early twenties, title writing, then joined Michael Balcon's first production company, first as assistant and art director, then directing on his own. Between 1925 and 1929 he made nine pictures, and established himself as the foremost British director of the day. His *Blackmail* was the first British sound film. During the thirties he went on to perfect his grasp of technique, win a Hollywood contract and the opportunity to exploit the finest technical resources in the world. Essentially he is a man of the cinema—one who has approached the film as an art through the film as an industry.

From *Sequence 9* (Autumn 1949). Reprinted by permission of the author.

His first two films are remarkable for their evidence of an immediate ease, an instinctive facility in the medium. *The Pleasure Garden* (1925) is a novelettish story—a good-hearted chorus girl befriends a vixenish young dancer, and ends up eight reels later menaced by her drunken husband, who believes himself incited to murder her by the ghost of his native mistress (whom he has drowned in the lagoon). The most enjoyable passages are at the start: the first shots of chorus girls hurrying down a circular iron stair, then out on to the stage, gyrating enthusiastically in the abandoned fashion of the period. *The Mountain Eagle,* another romantic melodrama, was set equally far from home, among the hillbillies of Kentucky; one is not surprised to find *The Bioscope* commenting that "in spite of skillful and at times brilliant direction, the story has an air of unreality."

Both these films were produced by Balcon in Munich; in 1926 Hitchcock returned to Islington to make his first picture in Britain, and the first opportunity to work on the sort of subject most congenial to him—the story of uncertainty, suspense, and horror amid humdrum surroundings. *The Lodger* was again a melodrama, but biased this time towards violence rather than romance. One winter evening, in a London terrorized by a homicidal maniac known as The Avenger, a handsome stranger arrives at a Bloomsbury lodging-house. He behaves strangely, creeping from the house at night, removing from his wall the portrait of a beautiful fair-haired girl (The Avenger attacks only blondes), and gradually the suspicion is built up that he is The Avenger himself. *The Lodger* is by no means a perfect thriller; it creates its suspense too often illegitimately: the innocent young man behaves like a stage villain, arriving out of the night heavily muffled and mysteriously silent. Playing chess before the fire with his landlady's attractive (blonde) daughter, he remarks with sinister emphasis, "Be careful, I'll get you yet," and picks up the poker—only to poke the fire vigorously on the entrance of a third person into the room.

This improbable development of the plot is partially disguised by the conscientious realism of its locales and characters: the authentic middle-class decors and homely atmosphere of the Buntings' house in Bloomsbury, the mannequins' dressing room at the couturier's where Daisy works, the flirtatious progress of Daisy's affair with Joe, the detective in charge of the case. Most remarkable, though, is the rapid, ingenious style of narration. From the opening—the close-up of a man's pale hand sliding down the bannister rail as he slips quietly out of a dark house—the camera seizes on the significant details which convey the narrative point of the scene. The result is a compression which gives the film continuous excitement.

For this compression, some credit is evidently due to Ivor Montagu, who was called in by the distributors when they found themselves dissatisfied with the first copy of the film. After specifying certain retakes, which Hitchcock shot, Montagu reedited the film and produced a version which the distributors accepted with delight. In view of later developments, however, there is no mistaking Hitchcock's primary responsibility for *The Lodger,* and for the ingenuity of its style in particular: A series of rapidly superimposed close-ups show alarm spreading as a new murder is reported; as the Buntings listen suspiciously to their lodger walking up and down in his room above them, we see a shot of the ceiling with his feet superimposed, walking to and fro, as though the floor were made of glass.

This inventiveness and visual dexterity was to form the basis of Hitchcock's style; they are the characteristics of a born storyteller, of one who delights to surprise and confound expectation, to build up suspense to a climax of violence and excitement. Strangely enough, though, the success of *The Lodger* did not lead Hitchcock to concentrate on this kind of film. He followed it with a return to romance, *Downhill,* which again starred Ivor Novello, as a noble boy who takes the blame for a chum's offense, is expelled from school ("Does this mean, sir, that I shall not be able to play for the Old Boys?"), and progresses downhill to the docks of Marseilles. There are interesting patches of technique: a delirium sequence as the hero is carried home on a cargo boat—scenes from his past superimposing and dissolving over shots of a gramophone playing in his cabin, the ship's engines turning over, the whole a powerful visual equivalent of discordant sound; and a daring subjective sequence as he lurches through the streets on his way home, the camera tracking and panning unsteadily to recreate his feverish impressions.

Three years, and six pictures, passed before, with *Blackmail* (1929), Hitchcock was able to find a story which suited as happily as *The Lodger;* in between there came a version of Noel Coward's *Easy Virtue* (which must have been almost as prodigious an achievement as Lubitsch's silent *Lady Windermere's Fan*), a boxing melodrama, a version of *The Farmer's Wife* and a couple of novelettes. Then at last Hitchcock hit on Charles Bennett's play, prepared a screenplay of it in collaboration with the author and Benn Levy, and shot it as a silent film. It was released, however, as Britain's first sound film, in part reshot and in part dubbed; it is thus of double interest—both for Hitchcock's uninhibited ingenuity in dealing with a new medium, and as a second example of his primary excellence in melodrama.

*Blackmail* is not as satisfactory as *The Lodger;* in construction it is less concise, less inevitable in progression. The connection of the first reel (the police at work) with the rest of the film is not well established; the scene in the artist's studio, in which Cyril Ritchard sings sub-Coward songs and attempts to seduce Anny Ondra is ludicrous in writing, setting, and handling; the famous chase, ending up with the blackmailer's fall through the dome of the British Museum, is too obviously tacked on to provide a spectacular climax. Also the film is weakened by the happy ending Hitchcock was forced (not for the last time) to substitute for the ironic fade-out he had planned.

Much of *Blackmail,* though, is excellent and survives in its own right. The everyday locales—a Corner-House restaurant, the police station, the little tobacconist's shop where the heroine lives with her parents, empty London streets at dawn—are authentic; the characters are believable; and at least one scene, between the blackmailer, the girl, and the detective, in which the detective does not know the guilt of the girl, the girl is too frightened to confess to it, and the blackmailer tries to play on the nerves of each, is worked up to a most successful tension. As in *The Lodger,* Hitchcock develops his story with a succession of felicitous, striking, or revealing touches, particularly remarkable in this instance for the ingenuity with which they exploit the new dimension of sound. The portrait in the artist's studio, for instance, of a malevolently smiling jester is used as a sort of dumb commentator on the story—the last shot shows the picture carried away down the passage of the police station while the walls re-echo to the sound of ironic laughter. Sound is used throughout with extraordinary freedom, for the period: to support continuity, as where the heroine, wandering in the streets after knifing her seducer, sees a man lying in a doorway, his hand dangling like the dead artist's; she opens her mouth to scream, and we cut to the scream of the landlady discovering the body of the murdered man. Two famous, and very effective, examples of the distortion of sound to convey a subjective impression of tension and near-hysteria occur as the girl sits miserably over breakfast the next morning. A garrulous neighbor is discussing the news: "I don't hold with knives. . . . No, knives isn't right . . . now, mind you, a knife's a difficult thing. . . ." Gradually all other words are mixed together in a monotonous blur, the word "knife" alone stabbing clearly out of the sound track over a close-up of the girl. "Cut us a bit of bread," says her father. The camera tilts down to a close-up of the knife; the girl's hand reaches out. Suddenly "KNIFE!" screams the voice, the hand jerks sharply up, and the breadknife flies into the corner of the room. A similar use of distortion and sudden crescendo conveys the girl's alarm at the sudden ringing of the shop bell: Instead of dying swiftly away, the sound of the bell is held for some four seconds, swelling up to a startling intensity.

Again like *The Lodger,* the films which followed *Blackmail* presented in the main a series of disappointments. *Juno and the Paycock* is straightforward filmed theater, well and respectfully handled; it is memorable however not so much for Hitchcock's contribution as for its perpetuation of some fine performances—in particular Sara Allgood's Juno, a figure that one sets beside Jane Darwell's Ma Joad for its grandeur and humanity. *Murder,* which followed it, is an odd mixture, with some effective sequences—a midnight murder in a sleepy village, an exciting climax in a circus tent, with the murderer (Esmé Percy as an epicene trapeze artist) hanging himself from the big top. Amongst the enterprising uses of sound are one of the first uses of an overlaid track representing the thoughts running through a character's head while he shaves, and a not altogether successful experiment in expressionism—an impatient jury chanting in chorus against its one dissenting member. Long stretches of the film, though, are theatrical in the extreme, clogged with dialogue and dominated by an excessively stagey performance by Herbert Marshall.

None of Hitchcock's remaining films for British International (the producers of *Blackmail*) achieved much success. In 1933 he left to direct an unhappy excursion into musical comedy, *Waltzes from Vienna.* His career seemed to have reached its nadir when, with his infinite capacity for surprise, he rejoined Balcon at Gaumont British, renewed his assocation with Ivor Montagu (associate producer) and Charles Bennett (scriptwriter), and directed in a row a series of films which were to mark his most memorable and enjoyable contribution to the cinema.

The team of Hitchcock, Bennett, and Montagu remained in collaboration for three years, during which, with Balcon as producer, it was responsible for *The Man Who Knew Too Much, The Thirty-Nine Steps, The Secret Agent,* and *Sabotage.* In 1937 Balcon and Montagu left Gaumont British, but Bennett remained to write *Young and Innocent:* In 1938 Hitchcock made his last good British film, *The Lady Vanishes,* from a script by Launder and Gilliat. All these films are melodramas—stories of violence and adventure in which the emphasis is on incident rather than on characters or ideas. Hitchcock had himself come to realize that this was the form ideally suited to his talent and his temperament. In his autobiography, Esmond Knight quotes an illuminating *cri de coeur* on the set of *Waltzes from Vienna:* "I hate this sort of stuff," groaned Hitchcock; "melodrama is the only thing I can do."

Melodrama does not, of course, preclude common sense; with the exception of *The Lady Vanishes,* with its Ruritanian locale and its deliberate light comedy accent, these films gain a particular excitement from their concern with ordinary people (or ordinary-looking people) who are plunged into extraordinary happenings in the most ordinary places. This gives them immense conviction, and enables Hitchcock to exploit to the utmost his flair for the dramatic value of contrast. Instead of dressing up the Temple of Sun Worshippers—which covers the headquarters of the gang in *The Man Who Knew Too Much*—he presents it as a drab little nonconformist chapel, bare and chilly, with a typically shabby congregation of elderly eccentrics. In *The Thirty-Nine Steps*, the head of the organization lives in a solidly respectable country house, and entertains the [gentry of the] County at cocktails after Sunday morning service. Verloc, the secret agent of *Sabotage,* runs an unpretentious suburban cinema. The pursuit in *Young and Innocent* winds up at a *thé dansant* at a seaside hotel. Similarly the people are conceived in common-sense, unglamorized terms; the leading players (one hardly thinks of them as stars) dress with credible lack of extravagance, get dirty, behave like average human beings— neither brilliant nor foolishly muddled. And supporting them are a multitude of equally authentic minor characters, maids, policemen, shopkeepers, and commercial travelers. This overall realism makes it all the more thrilling when the unexpected occurs—as it inevitably does: pretty maids lie to the police without blinking an eyelid, harmless old bird-fanciers are revealed as sabotage agents, old ladies who are playing the harmonium one minute are whipping little revolvers from their handbags the next.

The plots of these films are less important for themselves than for the way they are unfolded. They are all stories of violence and suspense, five exploiting in one way or another the excitements of espionage and political assassination (of these, *The Thirty-Nine Steps* and *The Man Who Knew Too Much* are perhaps the most completely successful and continuously exciting), the sixth (*Young and Innocent*) centering on the pursuit of a murderer by the young man accused of his crime. In most of them the tensions of mystery and intrigue erupt in a climax of public violence: The agents in *The Man Who Knew Too Much* are exterminated in a street battle which recalls the historic battle of Sidney Street; *The Thirty-Nine Steps* winds up with shooting during a Crazy Gang show at the Palladium; *The Secret Agent* has a train crash, *Sabotage* a timebomb exploding in a crowded bus, and *The Lady Vanishes* another gunfight, between the agents of a foreign power and a party of Britons stranded in a railway carriage in a central European forest.

These set pieces are not, however, isolated delights; the films are continuously enjoyable for the brilliance and consistency of their narration—a technique which shows the value of experience with the silent cinema and the necessity of unfolding a story in visual terms. Hitchcock has freely acknowledged his debt to Griffith; his own style, at its best, has always been firmly based on cutting. In a famous article on his methods of direction, published in *Footnotes to the Film,* he states his *credo* specifically: "What I like to do always is to photograph just the little bits of a scene that I really need for building up a visual sequence. I want to put my film together on the screen, not simply to photograph something that has been put together already in the form of a long piece of stage acting. . . ."

Besides being an admirable instrument for the building up of tension within the scene, Hitchcock's cutting contributes to the boldness and ingenuity with which his plots are developed, with continuous speed and surprise. (His scripts are preplanned, his films edited in the camera rather than the cutting room). We are precipitated at once into the middle of events— *Young and Innocent,* for instance, starts brilliantly, at the climax of a murderous quarrel. With a few happy strokes a locale is sketched in, an atmosphere established; the stories proceed with a succession of ingenious visual, or sound-and-visual, effects (the Hitchcock touch) as the celebrated continuity from *The Thirty-Nine Steps* [the chambermaid discovers the body and screams, but we hear the screech of a train emerging from a tunnel in the next shot]; or the ominously sustained organ note in *The Secret Agent* (a film packed with ingenious touches, and Hitchcock's favorite of the series), which announces the death of the Allied agent, strangled in the lonely little Swiss church.

Hitchcock's best films are in many ways very English, in their humor, lack of sentimentality, their avoidance of the grandiose and the elaborately fake. And these qualities were threatened when, in 1939, he succumbed to temptation and signed a contract to work in Hollywood for David Selznick. He was ambitious to make films for the vast international audience which only Hollywood could tap; also no doubt he was eager to work with the technical facilities which only Hollywood studios could provide. It was particularly unfortunate, however, that Hitchcock chose the producer he did; for Selznick is a producer who has always relied on pretentiousness, the huge gesture, the imposing façade, to win success (*Gone with the Wind, Since You Went Away, Duel in the Sun*). Almost in advance Hitchcock was committed to all that is worst in Hollywood—to size for its own sake (his first picture for Selznick was 2,000 feet longer than any he had directed previously), to the star system for its own sake, to glossy photography, high-toned settings, lushly hypnotic musical scores.

The negotiations with Selznick were carried on while Hitchcock was working on his last British film, *Jamaica Inn,* a dully boisterous smuggling adventure with Charles Laughton. It was curious and unhappily prophetic that his first film in Hollywood should also be an adaptation from a Daphne du Maurier bestseller, *Rebecca*—a less boring book, but equally Boots Library in its level of appeal. *Rebecca* is a very skillful and competently acted film: numerous imitations employing the same theatricalities of suspense—the great house dominated by a mysterious figure, the frightened girl, the sinister housekeeper—emphasize the smooth plausibility of Hitchcock's handling. But the film as a whole is not recognizable as the work of the Hitchcock of, say, *The Thirty-Nine Steps;* it is at once bigger and less considerable.

The films which followed it in the next four years are of uneven quality, and represent no progression, no real acclimatization. *Suspicion* (the next-but-two) was an attempt to reproduce the high-class tension of *Rebecca,* again with Joan Fontaine; it succeeds only in ruining a fine thriller by Francis Iles, the story of a sensitive, unattractive girl married and murdered for her money by a handsome wastrel. By dressing her hair with severity and intermittently fondling a pair of horn-rims and a book on child psychology, Miss Fontaine effected the conventional compromise between glamor and realism successfully enough to win an Academy Award; but the film lacks excitement or conviction. The English backgrounds (Hunting, Church) are pure Burbank; and the ludicrous happy ending—neither written by Iles nor desired by Hitchcock—sets the seal of failure on the film.

*Suspicion* was preceded by a comedy, *Mr. and Mrs. Smith* (of which one would welcome a revival), and a thriller, *Foreign Correspondent;* after it came another reminiscence of the Gaumont British period, *Saboteur.* The earlier of these, written by Charles Bennett in collaboration with Joan Harrison, has excellent sequences embedded in a diffuse and vexatious story. The assassination of an elderly statesman in Amsterdam is brilliantly staged: rain drizzling, the square thronged with umbrellas, the news camera which fires a bullet, the assassin's escape through the crowd of bobbing umbrellas. There is a pleasantly sordid scene many reels later in which the kidnapped diplomat is grilled in a Charlotte Street garret, while a terrified German girl (in thick-lensed spectacles) sobs in terror by the wall; and the climax is worth waiting for—a transatlantic airliner shelled and nose-diving into the sea (seen entirely from within the plane), water crashing through the pilot's window, passengers fighting hysterically,. and finally a handful of survivors clinging exhaustedly to a floating raft.

*Saboteur* is even more an affair of sequences, and is remarkable for its barefaced pilfering from almost every film Hitchcock had ever made. Its handcuffed hero and heroine (limp derivatives from *The Thirty-Nine Steps*) are pitched from one exotic location to another, individual episodes are directed with enjoyable virtuosity—the aircraft factory fire at the start, a gunfight in a cinema, the final megalomaniac climax on the Statue of Liberty—but the film as a whole has the overemphasis of parody.

It was not until 1943 that Hitchcock made a film which might be construed as an atttempt—his last—to justify himself as a serious director. Before writing the screenplay of *Shadow of a Doubt,* he and Thornton Wilder went to live for two months in the little Californian town of Santa Rosa, where their story was to take place. Most of the film was shot there. As a result it has an everyday realism that is reminiscent of earlier days; and in its opening stages, a subtlety of characterization distinctly superior to them. Its central character is Charlie Newton, handsome and debonair, who lives by marrying and killing rich widows. Hard-pressed by the police, he comes to Santa Rosa to stay with his sister (who idolizes him) and her family: her quiet, respectable husband, her beautiful adolescent daughter, who feels that there is some special, secret bond between her and her uncle, and two smaller children. The film is at its best in its first half, establishing the family and their town, the impact of Uncle Charlie's arrival on each of them; experimenting once again with sound, Hitchcock adopted for these scenes a technique similar to Orson Welles' in *The Magnificent Ambersons*, superimposing one conversation over another, dovetailing, naturalistically blurring and distorting. The strange bond which seems to unite Young Charlie (the niece) with her uncle is subtly conveyed; the acting is excellent: Joseph Cotten as Charlie, bitter, arrogant, his smooth charm concealing a spirit wounded and festering, the exquisite Patricia Collinge, his sensitive, overstrung sister, Teresa Wright as Young Charlie, youthful and mercurial, waiting for love. In its later reels the film falls away; there is not the progression and development necessary to a serious study, and as a simple thriller (which is all perhaps Hitchcock would claim for it) it fails to sustain excitement and surprise. It remains, all the same, his best American film.

After *Shadow of a Doubt* Hitchcock completed one more picture in Hollywood, then ventured across the Atlantic to make his contribution to the Allied war effort. This came in the form of two short French-speaking films for the British Ministry of Information, *Adventure Malagache* and *Bon Voyage*. Each tells its story—the former of resistance activity in Vichy-dominated Madagascar, the latter of underground work in France—economically (most scenes are played in a single set-up), tastefully, and not very excitingly. A project for Hitchcock to direct a film about German concentration camps, for which he viewed a large quantity of documentary material, eventually came to nothing. This visit to Britain inspired no renaissance of style, no return to reality.

Almost, in fact, it appears to have precipitated his flight from it. From 1945 onwards the quality one associates with Hitchcock films is neither their excitement, nor their power to entertain, but their technical virtuosity. The trend had indeed already started in 1943, when he followed up *Shadow of a Doubt* with *Lifeboat*. For an hour and a half the camera remains in a lifeboat carrying eight survivors from a sunken Allied ship and one German, who turns out to be the captain of the U-boat which attacked it. The virtuosity of the direction is undeniable, and in a theatrical way the film is effective; but the attempts to build the story into a propagandist allegory, stressing the feebleness of a democracy in comparison with a dictatorship, were as unconvincing as (at this stage of the war) they were unnecessary.

One remembers *Lifeboat* chiefly for its reintroduction of Tallulah Bankhead, and for some suspenseful episodes—a grim amputation carried out by the German with a clasp-knife, a realistically contrived storm.

*Spellbound,* with which Hitchcock returned to Selznick in 1945, also contains its entertaining passages of exhibitionism; its psychiatric background is futile and its Dali dream sequence merely pretentious, but one can enjoy the acid observation of the psychiatrists' common room, and some facile patches of melodrama revolving around razors, glasses of milk, and the like.

It is unfortunate that even these are marred by a tendency to overplay, to inflate, a tendency which in *Notorious* swelled to an obsession and produced a film which shares with its successors, *The Paradine Case* and *Rope,* the distinction of being the worst of his career. In these films technique—lighting, ability to maneuver the camera in hitherto unimaginable ways, angles—ceases to be a means and becomes an end in itself; *Notorious* is full of large and boring close-ups. For hundreds of feet Ingrid Bergman and Cary Grant nuzzle each other in medium close-up, a sequence of embarrassing (because so thoroughly fake) intimacy. *The Paradine Case,* maimed from the start by Selznick's creaking script and a heavy roster of stars, is lit with magnificent but inexpressive artifice, contains further nuzzling by Ann Todd and Gregory Peck, and moves at a pace slower even than that of *Notorious.* And with *Rope,* a debilitated version of Patrick Hamilton's play, which abandons all the resources of cutting and lighting on the pretext of an experiment in technique, we come pretty well to a full stop.

Different though the results are, the experiment of *Rope* resembles the stylistic elephantiasis of *Notorious* and *Spellbound* in its preoccupation with technique, to the detriment of the material. The films, as a result, are neither good nor entertaining. To such highbrow accusations Hitchcock has a ready answer. To quote from an acutely critical article by Lawrence Kane (*Theater Arts,* May 1949): "*Spellbound* cost $1,700,000 and grossed $8,000,000. *Notorious* cost $2,000,000 and had enough love in it to take in $9,000,000." "Beyond that," said Alfred Hitchcock in a 1946 interview, "there's the constant pressure. You know—people asking. 'Do you want to reach only the audiences at the Little Carnegie or to have your pictures play at the Music Hall?' So you compromise. You can't avoid it. You do the commercial thing, but you try to do it without lowering your standards. It isn't easy. Actually the commercial thing is much harder to do than the other. . . ."

Disregarding the latter irrelevant (and untrue) argument, the critic can only comment that Hitchcock's career in America has suffered from more than compromise with commercialism (a compromise to which he has been no more exposed than any other director of equivalent status). He is a director, in the first place, who depends considerably on his scripts; in the last ten years he has found no writer to give him what Bennett gave him at Gaumont British. It is not a coincidence that his collaboration with Thornton Wilder resulted in his best Hollywood film.

But *Shadow of a Doubt* hints at a more crippling limitation. When Hitchcock left Britain, it was, at least in part, because he felt that a chapter in his career was ended, and he was ripe for further development. And in certain directions, it is true, Hollywood has offered him vastly greater opportunities than Shepherd's Bush; there are sequences in *Foreign Correspondent* and *Saboteur, Shadow of a Doubt* and *Lifeboat* which outstrip anything in his earlier pictures for virtuosity and excitement. What these films lack is the wholeness of their predecessors. The Gaumont British melodramas succeed as works of art (however minor) because they attain a perfect, satisfying balance between content and style; the enlargement which Hitchcock's style has undergone in Hollywood has been accompanied by no equivalent intensifying or deepening of sensibility or subject matter.

Hitchcock has never been a "serious" director. His films are interesting neither for their ideas nor for their characters. None of the early melodramas can be said to carry any sort of a "message"; when one does appear, as in *Foreign Correspondent* and *Lifeboat,* it is banal in the extreme—"You'll never conquer them," Albert Basserman wheezes on his bed of torture, "the little people who feed the birds." In the same way, Hitchcock's characterization has never achieved—or aimed at—anything more than a surface verisimilitude; which, in a film where incident and narrative are what matters, is perfectly proper.

The method, though, appropriate to *The Thirty-Nine Steps* and *The Lady Vanishes,* is inappropriate to *Suspicion* and *Shadow of a Doubt.* In these the more deliberate pace, the constant emphasis on the players (dictated by the star system) directs our attention to the characters; their emptiness becomes apparent, and the dramas fall apart. *Suspicion* is not a failure simply because of its outrageous *volte face* at the end; the characters have never begun to live, so there is nothing really to destroy. In *Shadow of a Doubt* an atmosphere and a complex of relationships of some subtlety is established—only to dwindle conventionally instead of developing. *Notorious* presents an unpleasant but by no means uninteresting situation, which is thrown away largely because characterization is sacrificed to a succession of vulgar, superficial effects. In films like these, in *Rope* and *The Paradine Case,* even the old skin-deep truthfulness has been lost; Hitchcock's attitude towards his characters (as towards his audience) would seem to have hardened into one of settled contempt.

Hitchcock's progression from *The Pleasure Garden* to *Rope* is aesthetically pleasing; on the graph it would appear a well-proportioned parabola. But he does not oblige us by bringing his career to so satisfyingly geometric a close ("I am interested only in the future," he says). At the time of writing he has a period barnstormer, *Under Capricorn,* already completed, and a modern thriller, *Stage Fright,* almost finished. What is to be expected from these? Prophecy is always rash, but it is safe to assume that neither will present a dramatic reaction from the standards of showmanship which he has set himself in his "International" period; at their worst they will be heavy, tedious, glossed, at their best, ingenious, expert, synthetically entertaining. They will make a lot of money. Which, Hitchcock would reply, "is why they were made!" But at this point the wise critic resists the temptation to enter once again the vicious circle, and withdraws.

# Hitchcock

## Charles Thomas Samuels

Occasionally in all of his films and always in the best of them, Hitchcock is the master of evocation. Intellectual emptiness and spurious realism are preconditions for his effects. Since Hitchcock depicts a world in which anything can happen, and therefore everything is a threat, distinctions and priorities are forbidden.

Like Poe, the writer he most resembles, Hitchcock is obsessed by a small stock of situations which we can mistake for themes; but, as in Poe's case, these "themes" are only emotional stimuli born from the primitive stage of indiscriminate terror. Both men are sensationalists, but Hitchcock has the advantage of working in a medium that thrives on sensations which it can transmit with irresistible completeness. Sometimes Poe appears to be unveiling a metaphysical terror behind a physical threat, but since words can only point, and since Poe wielded one of the clumsiest pointers in English literature, he had to fall back on insinuation, validated by an aesthetic that argued for vagueness. Hitchcock's vocabulary is the very world from which he wants us to shrink, its items an inexhaustible stock of palpable terrors.

Yet Hitchcock never merely exhibits the sources of dread. As countless horror films and Hitchcock imitations prove, the naked ugliness is likely to excite only laughter. Not by accident do Hitchcock's excursions into direct brutality—*Psycho* and *The Birds*—contain his most elaborate contrivances, his most artful examples of aesthetic distance.

The secret of Hitchcock's terror lies not in the objects he employs but in the timing with which he presents them. He understands, as Poe understood, that emotion, which is imperious when it peaks, cannot be long sustained but may be extended through counterpoint. Like other romantics harassed by the essentially cognitive nature of language, Poe always yearned

Excerpted from "Sightings: Hitchcock" in *The American Scholar,* Spring 1970. Reprinted by permission of Lawrence Graver for the Estate of Charles Thomas Samuels. The full essay appears also in Samuels's *Mastering the Film* (University of Tennessee Press, 1977).

to transform himself into a musician—which, with a tin ear, he eventually became. For Hitchcock, no such transformation is required, since inherent resemblances between music and film have only to be exploited. Because a film is made from individual shots, the length of which is determined by editing, the filmmaker can control the speed of his revelation to a degree imperfectly approximated by the stage, with its cumbersome machinery, and unavailable to the writer (even the poet) who remains in thrall to the reader's attention span and rhythmic exactness. Therefore, by choosing precisely what we may see and hear at any given moment, by altering the amount of information and by varying the tempo at which it is conveyed, Hitchcock can play upon each spectator's emotions in much the same way that a piece of music plays upon his hands and feet.

Admiring interviewers seeking to pluck out the secret of Hitchcock's meaning forget that the secret is the absence of meaning, the absolute identification of meaning with effect. Thus Hitchcock asserted to Ian Cameron and V. F. Perkins (in *Movie,* January 1963), "I'm more interested in the technique of story telling by means of film rather than in what the film contains." And when his interlocutors touched upon a question that Hitchcock was normally happy to emphasize—box office receipts of, in this case, *Psycho*—the director pressed on with his shrewd self-analysis: "[The money] was a secondary consideration. *Psycho* is probably one of the most cinematic films I've made and there you get a clear example of the use of film to cause an audience to respond emotionally."

INTERVIEWERS: It was primarily an emotional response you were after from your audience?
HITCHCOCK: Entirely. That's the whole device. After all, the showing of a violent murder at the beginning was intended purely to instill into the minds of the audience a certain degree of fear of what is to come. Actually in the film, as it goes on, there's less and less violence because it had been transferred to the minds of the audience.

The key to *Psycho* is less Sigmund Freud than Richard Strauss. That is why most of Hitchcock's best films are devoid of meaning, peopled by mere containers of stress, and set against backgrounds chosen simply because their innocuousness counterpoints terror. Primitive in insight, Hitchcock is a sophisticated man revelling in pure form, whose films are ends in themselves and so can please both the plebes who want thrills and the cognoscenti thrilled by such an arrogant display of craftsmanship. That is why, like music, Hitchcock films are always most striking at the beginning and the end (introduction and coda), and why he sustains interest only when there are enough crescendos to provide rhythm, paralyzing reason and achieving kinesthesia.

*The Thirty-Nine Steps,* Hitchcock's first masterpiece (1935), exhibits his technique in its simplest form. Consider the first sequence showing Robert Donat entering a vaudeville pub where he enjoys the performance until it is interrupted by a shot. We divine no reason for Donat's presence and the pub itself seems utterly insignificant, yet Hitchcock's editing creates a rhythm of anticipation that makes the gunshot doubly effective. First he pans across the music hall sign as it is being illuminated (other directors simply start their films; Hitchcock emphatically begins them). Then, in a tilt shot that declares some approaching mishap, we see a man's back as he nears the box office. Increasing our curiosity, Hitchcock shoots his entrance at floor level, raising the camera only when Donat sits, but still not affording a frontal view. Immediately, the band strikes up, distracting our attention in a way that is obtrusive and therefore frustrating. He now cuts to a full view of the stage taken from the back of the theater, and from this to a close-up of the stage itself on which the mind reader is being introduced. Pans across the audience, in which Donat is casually revealed, and cuts between it and the stage, pile up new information and raise new questions (who is Donat? why is he here? what is his relationship to the mind reader? *et cetera*) with a speed that nearly defies formulation. The cutting and panning tempo now accelerates (that is, we get shorter and shorter bits of film alternately devoted to stage and audience), a movement augmented by the sudden exchange of questions and answers. Donat asks about the distance from Winnipeg to Montreal (whatever for? we wonder), someone challenges the mind reader's response, a fight breaks out in the hall, and Hitchcock further increases the editing speed. Suddenly we get a close-up of the gun; after a moment sufficient to inspire our surprise, it goes off. Then the frame fills with a mass of bodies seeking exit. Donat is pushed against a foreign woman; they talk, leave the hall, get a bus. Fade-out.

By showing the audience that the unexpected can occur, this scene builds up anticipation that will keep us tense even at moments that are relatively placid. This pattern of tension and relaxation, not the silly spy story, is what *The Thirty-Nine Steps* is "about." The film's next brilliant sequence moves from the primitive fear of the unexpected to the somewhat more sophisticated fear of false appearances. Having witnessed the death of his mysterious guest, after she had told him about the thirty-nine steps and the archdeceiver with the missing finger, Donat seeks refuge from the police, at a farmhouse near the residence of a man he believes will epitomize "the right side." At first, the farmer rejects Donat's plea for shelter, but he relents at the hero's offer to pay. When he thinks Donat has begun making love to his wife, however, he determines to take vengeance. This he does by informing the police of the fugitive's whereabouts, but not before the wife has informed Donat that a police van has arrived.

Beginning with a close-up of the wife's face after Donat flees, the sequence then dissolves into the sweating face of a policeman in the same position: protection is literally replaced by jeopardy. Immediately, Hitchcock cuts to long shots of the pursuit across the moor, intercut with close-ups of solitary policemen silhouetted against the sky—an alteration suggesting that Donat will come through. Still, the police outnumber him and he has no place to hide. Excited by pulsating music and Hitchcock's use of fast motion photography, we are desperate for Donat to gain admission when he finally arrives at the house of the "key man." Donat being let in by the maid is immediately replaced by the policemen being turned away by her saucy lies. Relieved at the ease of this getaway, we settle down as Donat enters a highly civilized drawing room, presided over by suave Godfrey Tearle. The houseguests turn out to include a sheriff, but this reminder of pursuit is cleverly evaded, as Tearle draws our hero to the window, through which we spy the police running in the opposite direction. The guests exit, Hitchcock moves in for a closer shot, and we are now back in a confined haven, very much like that of the farm. The relaxed Donat tells about his adventures, while the camera keeps Tearle in sharp focus and Donat in soft. At the end of his recital, Tearle holds up, for the camera's inspection, a hand missing one finger.

This *coup de théâtre* is effective because of Hitchcock's editing. The coincident use of close-ups and relatively slow pacing at the farmhouse and the mansion make them both valleys of rest below Donat's hill of effort. Moreover, Hitchcock controls the image size so as to emphasize the contrasting coziness of the farm and house scenes with the wide-open threat of the moor. For these reasons and others (like the splendid performances of Donat and Tearle, and of Wendy Hiller as the farmer's wife), the climax of the sequence is made tremendously powerful. Characteristically, the pace slackens immediately thereafter, as Tearle regretfully discusses his need to kill Donat, which creates an even greater shock when he does so. That is, he seems to have done so—until the next scene. The film's suspenseful rhythm is subsequently reinforced when Donat is joined in his ordeal by a woman, thus doubling the audience's apprehension, while also providing an opportunity for a different kind of suspense as the strangers are handcuffed to each other: will his bravery overcome her reluctance?

To this combination of exciting rhythm and speedy plotting, Hitchcock adds in his next major film a new kind of comedy rooted in national caricature, Hitchcock's only viable, because swift, means of creating people. Based on the famous story of a girl who can find no trace of her hotel companion on returning to their room, *The Lady Vanishes* (1938) features the shock of losing confidence in one's perception. Throughout the film, as Margaret Lockwood searches for Dame May Whitty (an incongruously mild-mannered spy of whose presence all signs have been erased), she encounters little help from her compatriots, who all have selfish reasons for denying that they saw the woman. Thus, for the British audience for which the film was made, national self-confidence is affronted in a way that parallels the affront to the heroine.

Pursued by the villains, Lockwood and Michael Redgrave turn to their British trainmates who, since it is teatime, must be massed in the dining car. This the villains have uncoupled and surrounded, but the occupants won't, at first, believe that they are in danger ("They won't do anything," one announces. "We're British subjects"); and when an emissary sent to entice them from the train reveals he went to Oxford, the poor dupes almost follow him. Only after a shot rings out do they acknowledge their error, rally round the protagonists, and simultaneously thrill the audience with affirmation of Miss Whitty's existence and of British grit.

Like *The Thirty-Nine Steps, The Lady Vanishes* offers a nonstop display of Hitchcock's speedy, evocative construction. But this film is even more brilliant in its reliance on visual details to create desired effects. Shortly after the first scene, for example, as they prepare to board the train, Margaret Lockwood is hit on the head by a falling window box intended for Dame May. Immediately, Hitchcock cuts to a subjective camera shot of blurred vision, further representing Lockwood's vertigo by superimposing a train wheel. The speedy progress of surrounding experience is then established by close-up shots of tracks as they merge and separate before the onrushing train. Then, from an objective shot of the compartment with Miss Lockwood waking up, Hitchcock again cuts to a subjective shot, as the heroine's "eyes" pick up Dame May, a smiling man, a veiled woman peering at her, and, at her side, a mother and daughter. A bit later she returns to the compartment and prepares for sleep. Quickly cutting to the famous shot of the train as it crosses a graceful but narrow and enormously high viaduct, Hitchcock visually implies the dangerous vulnerability of the heroine's position, which she does not yet understand. So Miss Lockwood closes her eyes once more, after panning across the compartment where the man is playing with the little girl, Dame May is humming, and all seems safe.

This shot fades, we again see the train laterally, and again move to tracks merging and separating in their measurement of time. Abruptly there is a frontal shot of the train as it effectively runs us over, a whistle shrilly blares, and Miss Lockwood wakes up, glancing about the compartment in a direction opposite to the one used before and coming to rest on an empty seat. This skillful use of visualized time and parallel subjective shots creates for the audience the heroine's terrifying sense of having lost her grip on reality and thus involves us emotionally despite the blatant preposterousness of the plot.

While sacrificing the tightness of these early films—each photographed in a studio—*North by Northwest* (1959) contains the boldest display of Hitchcock's mastery of emotional rhythm. Critics faulting this extravaganza as self-parody misjudge the seriousness of its models. *The Thirty-Nine Steps* and, more obviously, *The Lady Vanishes* are exercises in the terror of confinement; *North by Northwest* is Hitchcock's bravura answer to the question: how can you scare people in technicolor and a Vista-Vision screen? For this reason, the plot of the film is rooted in topography: the true star of *North by Northwest* is the United States map.

Therefore, Hitchcock's signatory appearance in this film is the most functional of his career. Materializing in the crowd of people as the credits are ending, Hitchcock reaches a bus that slams its door in his face just as we read "Directed by . . ." Like his creator, the hero of the film is a man with less than expected control over his environment.

At first, Cary Grant seems fully in charge, weaving through the crowd while dictating orders to his secretary that will simultaneously placate his girl friend and his mother, and climaxing his display of cool by commandeering a taxi—emblem of power throughout the New York scenes. Whizzing into the Plaza where he is greeted as a steady client, Grant seems on top of his world, which he is—until some thugs mistake him for someone else. From then on he becomes someone else—a man senselessly hounded through areas of differing dimensions.

*North by Northwest* is simultaneously humorous and frightening—not alternately one or the other like *The Lady Vanishes* and *The Thirty-Nine Steps*—because it lets the viewer in on the joke of its sheer contrivance. We get the bravura idea near the beginning of the film through a scene with Grant drunkenly careening down a narrow road in a car, since we all know that this is a standard movie conclusion. This scene is, moreover, a model of shifting tempi to enhance a mood and of the centrality of the landscape, for the horror of Grant's experience is equivalent to the narrowness of the road and the proximity of the sea at its side, a vision that comically sobers him enough to renew his self-control. Subsequently, he is trapped with his pursuers in an elevator from which he is literally saved by humor: the laughter his mother excites providing cover for his escape. Menace in tight quarters reaches its climax in the film when Grant visits the United Nations, citadel of civilized safety, only to see a man stabbed in the back.

Henceforth, menace moves outdoors (with the single exception of the auction room scene, borrowed from *The Thirty-Nine Steps,* needed to further the romance, borrowed from *Notorious*). Of the two set-pieces of outdoor menace, the crop-dusting sequence is the more adroit, making full use of the possibilities offered Hitchcock by his medium.

Sent to a rural bus stop, Grant finds himself on a wide open road, which Hitchcock emphasizes with aerial shots. Lack of music and the long-held emptiness of the setting also create a feeling that something tremendous is coming in a film so normally galvanic. Brilliantly, Hitch-cock builds suspense by exaggerating the eventlessness of the scene. For some time, Grant merely peers up and down the road; the rare car that crosses moves on without stopping. When a truck comes through, Grant is rewarded only by a mouthful of dust. Soon, however, another car appears from a side road, depositing a man. Now we get a long shot of two figures at opposite sides of an immense vista. Something must surely be up! After a moment of hesitation, Grant crosses the road, an action Hitchcock shoots subjectively, thus heightening our expectation, because subjective shots invariably provide dramatic emphasis. Then exquisitely laconic dialogue assures us that this man cannot be the threat we have feared. A bus now draws up and the man mounts its steps, but not before remarking, "Funny about that plane. Crop-dusting where there ain't no crops."

Having thrown us off so long and so completely, Hitchcock now explodes the violence, hurling Grant across the wide expanse, in which there is no cover, before the swooping, gunfiring plane. Suddenly, Grant notices a cornpatch and makes a run for it; the camera closes in on his triumphant face. But he (we) had forgotten: the plane is equipped with poison gas. How can Grant get away? Running into the road, he stops a truck, but almost at the cost of his life. The marauding airplane, however, can't brake as easily as the truck into which it crashes, as we crash into laughter at the delicious coincidence. Artistically, Hitchcock ends the se-quence with a wide-screen intersected by a forward motion of perpendicu-lars (people moving toward the debris) through which Grant moves back-wards in the opposite direction, But this too dissolves in laughter, when we dissolve into the hayseeds' truck, which Grant expropriated for his geta-way, parked on a posh Chicago street, to the obvious consternation of the traffic cops.

*North by Northwest* is a prime example of contentless virtuosity. It is also notable for showing, with peculiar clarity, the function of Hitchcock's cynicism. Matching his display that no object is innocent is his belief that no person is. The ubiquity of guilt and of corruption in Hitchcock's world, however, contrary to the view of solemn critics, are rarely moral observations but usually emotional cues. Since no one is very good in the typical Hitchcock movie, we needn't take sides and can root for naked skill. This, in turn, concentrates our feelings on action, which is what the director wants. "Audiences are strange," he has asserted. "I know their reactions so well I don't have to go to the theater anymore; the emotional anxieties are pretty well standard. And they do not necessarily relate to right and wrong." As evidence of this proposition, Hitchcock repeatedly cites the scene from *Psycho* where Tony Perkins is trying to submerge a car containing the woman he has just killed. Hitchcock maintains that spectators root for it to sink, and they do; because the victim has been revealed as a thief and fornicator and because the action is irresistible in its appeal (the car almost sinks, stops, causes Perkins a moment of panic, and then goes to the bottom, bringing him and us relief).

In *North by Northwest* the release of the spectator from moral considerations is patterned every bit as carefully as the release of Cary Grant from his sources of control. First, we have the flaming-haired bridge-playing mother whom her son can bribe. Then we have venality on the train: when Grant escapes by stealing a porter's clothes we applaud his cleverness, until the camera cuts to the "victim" in underwear counting his cash. Even later when anxiety seems the only desired response, Hitchcock provides a tiny moral shock: when Cary Grant escapes from a hospital room by invading that of another patient, she screams until putting on her glasses, at which point she begs him to remain.

Morality is more seriously neutralized in the film through Hitchcock's characterization of the ostensible "good guys," who not only risk Grant's life but do so with outrageous callousness. Upon being informed that Grant must play decoy in the fight against foreign agents, a nice-old-lady C.I.A. officer sighs, "Good-bye, Mr. [Grant], wherever you are," and Leo G. Carroll, our head man, hatches the plot while photographed against the Capitol. The crucial contribution made by such cynicism can be quickly perceived by comparing *North by Northwest* to *Foreign Correspondent,* a film nearly identical in plot that is washed out by patriotic sentimentality.

Hitchcock's cynicism makes an advantage of his moral indifference by freeing him and his audience to admire pure aggression, including the aggression of film form. But his fear that nothing is what it seems (of which the skepticism about moral distinctions is only one consequence) sometimes approaches the status of serious belief, and then we see, most dramatically, the special underpinnings of his work.

*Shadow of a Doubt* (1943), often described by Hitchcock as his favorite film, culminates notions that can be traced back to *The Lodger* (1926). That silent movie is one of Hitchcock's many teasing thrillers (like *Stage Fright* and *Vertigo*) in which the audience is crudely misled about a character's guilt, in this case a man who is suspected of being Jack the Ripper. Surrounding the silly puzzle are scenes of real interest that establish the moral inferiority to the presumed criminal of more respectable members of his society. The opening sequence, which is astonishingly fluent for the period, emphasizes the public's prurient interest in crime, and the closing sequence, although a bit florid, makes the public seem reprehensible in its vengefulness (a characteristic emphasized, here as elsewhere, by the scapegoat's innocence).

Unlike the hero of *The Lodger,* Uncle Charlie, in *Shadow of a Doubt,* is guilty of crimes attributed to him; but he is given idealistic, if cracked, motives in Hitchcock's evident desire to create an approximate—and highly ironic—moral parity between Uncle Charlie and the innocent niece who is his alter ego. Although she had longed for him to relieve the dullness of her middle-class life, she instantly determines to banish him after discovering his crime. This discomforts us not only because her professed love should at least make her consider protecting him, but because her motives for wishing him gone are hardly edifying: she fears that his presence will compromise her father's job at the bank and will disillusion her doting mother.

Throughout the film, Hitchcock pokes holes into the facade of respectability that he was initially careful to erect. When Uncle Charlie visits his brother-in-law at the bank, for example, and makes a joke about embezzlement, the brother-in-law cautions against such humor in such a place. Shortly after, when Charlie is introduced to a rich widow (his preferred class of victim), she reacts rather more libidinously than accords with her mourning. One of the family's best friends plots murders for his pastime, and the father enthusiastically joins in. Innocent small-town life involves a yearning for forbidden thrills, a point Charlie makes explicit in a cafe scene before the climax. When he is killed by his niece in self-defense, the thematic substructure of their relationship is perfectly externalized in action. In her attempt to preserve cherished insulation from a more mordant perspective on life, she turns lethal.

*Shadow of a Doubt* is erratically written (its collaborators running from Sally Benson to Thornton Wilder), but it almost succeeds in making a serious comment. Thus we get the first important example in Hitchcock of visual symbolism: in identical shots that introduce the protagonists in identical poses after setting has established the dramatic difference between their worlds. But Hitchcock ruins this subtle equation, not only through blatant details in the script (uncle and niece share first names and telepathic powers), but by his final submission to conventions of melodrama. Since these necessitate someone to root for, Hitchcock must ultimately dissolve the equation whose irony sustains the film. In totally amoral movies like *North by Northwest* rooting for the hero implies no disruptive judgment; in *Shadow of a Doubt* it is profoundly illogical.

Nevertheless, *Shadow of a Doubt* helps us measure the extent to which Hitchcock's art is based on his assumption that normality is merely a thin veneer covering a lust for thrills. Like the niece, we tolerate thrills just until they threaten permanently to taint our self-image, so Hitchcock obligingly neutralizes the threat with last-minute melodrama. But his concern for us is specious, only a reflection of his concern for the box office. ("I have too much conscience," he once said, "to make a film that would please only me and the critics.") Only our money commands his respect and nothing so validates his contempt for the rest of us as our willingness to pay for manipulation. Hitchcock's sensitivity to audience tolerance alone restrains his contempt; when that tolerance loosens, he makes *Psycho* and *The Birds*.

In the best of his films, however, contempt for respectable pretension is reflected, more fully than in *Shadow of a Doubt,* in the plot as well as in Hitchcock's formal aggression. Thus *Strangers on a Train* (1951) almost succeeds in joining Hitchcock's mastery of emotional rhythm to the other qualities that we associate with narrative art.

Made in 1951 after four straight flops, from a novel Hitchcock discovered for himself, *Strangers on a Train* is a happy instance of an impulse suddenly finding its proper form. Throughout his work, Hitchcock had used, strictly for emotive purposes, the device of one character's being accused of another's crime. Patricia Highsmith's novel, while itself a pretentious, even brazen affair, has the virtue of making this device accord perfectly with Hitchcock's most fundamental attitude: that everyone is latently a killer. In this film, the victim of false accusation is, in a sense, morally guilty. What is only hinted at in the niece of Uncle Charlie is explicitly and carefully developed in Guy Haines.

In the film, as in the novel, Haines is a rather unformed young man who learns of his homicidal impulses by meeting Bruno Anthony accidentally on a train. Bruno, who hates his father, offers to murder Guy's wife (a woman of little virtue) so that Guy can remarry, if Guy will react in kind. Normal restraints make Guy refuse Bruno's offer, but we see that it has definite appeal. Seeing this too, Bruno follows the wife to an amusement park and strangles her. Then, when Guy balks at fulfilling his part of the "bargain," Bruno strikes back.

Hitchcock's interest in this plot is suggested by the few changes he makes in its initial details. First, he turns Guy from an aspiring architect into a famous athlete and thus from a genuine talent blocked by an unsuitable spouse into a tennis bum coveting a patrician Senator's daughter (transformed from the novel's interior decorator to clarify the shadiness of Haines's motives). Then he shifts the setting to Washington, from which he draws ironic contrasts between civilization and the baser impulses, as in the wonderful shot of a dark-suited Bruno standing before an august white pillar of the Jefferson Memorial.

Further evidence of the story's appeal are the visual analogies to which it inspired Hitchcock. Appropriately, the film begins by equating its protagonists, since the first shots are of taxis drawing up to a railroad station and depositing two sets of feet that don't possess bodies until they bump against each other in the dining car. Then, throughout the reverse shots of Bruno and Guy in conversation. Bruno's face is barred with shadows cast by some venetian blinds while Guy's appears in white light. This contrast is exploited later in the film, after Bruno has murdered Guy's wife, when he is waiting across the street from his beneficiary's apartment. Bruno stands behind a metal gate, suggesting the expected consequence of crime, but he is composed and regularly photographed, whereas the agitated Guy soon appears in tilt. Heeding Bruno's call, Guy crosses, but, during the ensuing conversation about Bruno's father, Guy addresses him while standing clear of the gate. When some police unexpectedly arrive, Guy is forced to seek shelter, and we now see him at Bruno's side slashed by the same shadows as his alter ego.

Similarly, respectable society is tainted by prurience and hypocrisy, like the Senator's guests who are charmed by Bruno's discussion of murder but fearful of the scandal caused by his excessive zeal. In the final chase scene, when the police expropriate a cab, its old lady occupant is delight to be involved in a crime, and news of the murder has the effect of boosting the box office at the amusement park. On the other hand, Bruno, although a psychopathic murderer, is a figure of tremendous charm and even some semiserious moral ambiguity. Soon after entering the amusement park, he is accosted by a little boy who shoots a toy gun at him, to which he responds by bursting the child's balloon. But after the crime we see him guiding a blind man through traffic.

Before the end, however, Hitchcock has cut things down again to the dimensions of a thriller. In the novel, Guy actually kills Bruno's father, subsequently filling more than half the book with his anguish. In the film, Guy refuses to follow Bruno this far, preferring instead to incur the vengeful wrath that produces Hitchcock's most brilliant coda, in which Guy has to win a tennis match and reach the amusement park before Bruno has the chance to plant a clue that will convince the police of his guilt. No sequence in Hitchcock makes such brilliant use of the screen's fundamental method of producing suspense: parallel editing of simultaneous action. Moreover, the conclusion of the film, with Guy and Bruno struggling on a merry-go-round gone berserk, is both emotionally stunning and precisely suggestive of their entire relationship. For sheer invention, unfailing pertinence of every frame, and occasional suggestions of deeper purpose, *Strangers on a Train* is Hitchcock's masterpiece.

But, it will be said, the masterpiece of a low ambition. Such derogation is implied even in the applause of *Cahiers du Cinéma* critics and their numerous followers who have tried to elevate Hitchcock into the ranks of directors like Bergman, Antonioni, and Truffaut. Although recent film criticism is typified by mindless emphasis on visual effects (thus Nicholas Ray can be thought an important director and *Lola Montès* an important film), most critics are made nervous by effects without theme or psychological insight. As a result, visual signs are read as if they were literary symbols, and directors like Hitchcock, whose meanings are his effects, become no less elusive for cinephiles than for traditionalists.

Yet no other director is so badly represented by translation into the assertions and propositions that criticism, being a tendentious, pattern-making activity, can scarcely avoid. A Hitchcock film can only be appreciated while it is seen, and is therefore perfect for the so-called "new sensibility." A critic like Susan Sontag, however, wouldn't be caught dead discussing Hitchcock because he is so relentlessly lowbrow and frivolous about meaning, whereas the new sensibility is only frivolous about craft.

As a craftsman, Hitchcock ranks with the best. He has taught essential lessons to directors with greater aspirations because he has realized one of the potentials of film form. From the first, cinema theoreticians recognized the unparalleled power of film, its ability to make the audience both a crowd and a collection of separate individuals (riveted to the screen in darkness that conceals the depth of their enslavement). Propaganda, it was thought, must inevitably result, and no one would be completely impervious to the appeal of screened messages. The history of film, however, has shown the form equally resistant to ideas and ideology. For the essence of cinema is action, gesture, surface: natural inciters not of reflection but of perception and feeling. What Hitchcock has supremely understood is that the line between perception and feeling can be manipulated by the director, can be sustained or broken, quickened or retarded so that the spectator feels only what the filmmaker intends. Moreover, he has understood that no other medium can simulate action with most of life's reality but none of its limitations. As a result, Hitchcock has produced a new experience, a new kind of art. It is low but powerful; it does not exploit the full range of his medium, but it takes to the limit one of the things that film can do more fully than any other art. In Robert Warshow's phrase, film is the "immediate experience." No director knows that better than Hitchcock.

# Hitchcock and Moralist Narrative

## David Thomson

Hitchcock is a commercial genius: *Psycho* has one of the best profit/cost ratios in the history of the cinema. Very few directors can offer a body of work so imaginatively disturbing. In watching Hitchcock films one becomes conscious of issues of freedom, not only to the extent that the characters in the film enjoy it but in how far the spectator in the cinema is deprived of it.

Hitchcock is a contemporary of the commercial cinema. He was born in 1899, only a few years after Lumière's first show at the Regent Polytechnic; *The Great Train Robbery* or *Rescued by Rover* might have been the first film he saw. He began as a film publicist and turned to scriptwriting before aspiring to directing. In 1921 he completed *Always Tell Your Wife* at the Islington Studios after the director had fallen ill. He continued to work as assistant director and set designer at a time when film-making was largely unorganized by trade unions. Before sound broke into the middle of *Blackmail* he had directed ten silent movies, and did fourteen more sound pictures before going to America to make *Rebecca*. It is a life constantly involved with the cinema and it has produced an attitude perfectly in keeping with the ideals of the film industry. Talking about *Psycho* he invoked the standards of popular, unsophisticated entertainment: "To me it's a *fun* picture. The processes through which we take the audience, you see, it's rather like taking them through the haunted house at the fairground or the rollercoaster."[1] And in 1959, when asked "Quelle est alors la logique profonde de vos films?" he answered, "Faire souffrir le spectateur."[2]

Essential to every Hitchcock film is this awareness the director has of his spectator. It conceives of the spectator as an economic generalization

1. *Movie* 6, interview with Ian Cameron and V. F. Perkins.
2. *Cahiers du Cinéma*, no. 102, interview with Jean Domarchi and Jean Douchet. ["What then is the inner logic of your films?" "To make the viewer suffer."—EDS.]

and there is an element of sadism in the devices inflicted. In one way Hitchcock's films are un-cinematic: his images are most effective when most contrived. At the same time his work defines the nature of cinema more than any other director's. The chief contribution to this definition is the similarity of treatment he offers to his audience and to the characters in his films. And if Hitchcock evokes the voyeur in one it is, I think, because he regards his own characters in this way.

Speaking about his confessed inclination to torture his characters, Hitchcock said, "That scene in *Vertigo* where James Stewart forces Miss Kim Novak to alter her whole personality by altering her lipstick, hairstyle, even hair-tint—for me it has the compulsion of a striptease in reverse. The woman is made insecure by being forced to make up, not take-off."[3]

The setting of *Vertigo* is San Francisco and Hitchcock emphasizes the sheerness of that city. This is clearly relevant to vertigo—the complaint of the private detective played by James Stewart—but it is an image Hitchcock has already made us familiar with: the cliff-top and the staircase of Manderley in *Rebecca;* the steep streets of Quebec in *I Confess;* the staircase, guarded by a dog, that Farley Granger ascends in *Strangers on a Train.* More than specific instances of steepness there is Hitchcock's use of high-angle camerawork at moments of crisis and judgment. At the conclusion of the court proceedings in *The Paradine Case,* for example, the camera towers above Gregory Peck. Height is a metaphysical symbol for Hitchcock just as the fact that so many of his characters have "fallen" is a sign of their moral condition.

In *Vertigo* Stewart is hired by a friend, Tom Helmore, to keep a watch on his wife, Kim Novak. There is a long sequence in which he trails her through San Francisco and into the Californian countryside as she visits places associated with her Spanish grandmother. The grandmother committed suicide and Helmore has told Stewart that he fears his wife's own depression may be leading to this end. Ostensibly, the terms on which the film opens are those of a thriller, and the method of narration transmits these terms to the audience. But Hitchcock is not content that Stewart should be simply the ingenious and heroic detective of tradition or that we should be allowed to enjoy the thrills unaffected. Both Stewart and the spectator follow Novak in the same degree of ignorance, and when Stewart's interest grows into sympathy and love it is an expression of what many of the spectators may feel. Stewart rescues Novak from an attempt to drown herself and the pattern of pursuit changes to their traveling together. It is a love affair, but blighted by Novak's remoteness and the emphasis this gives to Stewart's original role as detective and watcher. When they

3. *Evening Standard,* March 24, 1965, interview with Alexander Walker.

visit the monastery where the grandmother died a distraught Novak runs away from Stewart up the bell tower. When he tries to follow vertigo disables him. He reaches the top only to see Novak's body in the courtyard below. Stewart is quietly condemned for negligence at the inquest and he has a breakdown.

Several months later, when his recovery seems good, he sees a girl in the street who resembles Kim Novak. At this point the difficulty of distinguishing the two Kim Novaks from the two characters she is playing is such that I must divulge the device behind the film. Hitchcock himself waits a little longer but still reveals it half an hour before the end of what started as a thriller, the twist of which one might have expected would be reserved for the last minute. The throwaway shows how little the "detective story" interests him compared with the moral psychology. The two Kim Novaks are, as our eyes tell us, one. More than that, Novak has not been Helmore's wife, but only a part of a conspiracy with him to accomplish the killing of his real wife. She had not been an unknowing object of pursuit but a decoy. Helmore had been waiting at the top of the tower with his unconscious wife whom he had thrown down; he had hidden with Novak and escaped when Stewart collapsed. To impersonate the wife Novak had been blonde, now she is brunette.

Just as Helmore has deceived Stewart, so Hitchcock has misled the spectator by ensuring that he gains information in exactly the same way as Stewart. Stewart's assignment to follow and the subsequent attraction he feels towards his object are the equivalents of the cinematic method. Because the central character is a detective and because the movie's main purpose seems to be the solution of a mystery, which on the available evidence presupposes a supernatural intervention in man's affairs, *Vertigo* progresses by what appears to be a factual gathering. The facts can be related to the ideal of pure cinema: what a person looks like, what she does, the manner of her gestures. It is in these terms that Stewart watches Novak and the entire visual material is directed to this information; cuts separate fact from fact rather than allowing them to elide with each other so that their certainty might be undermined by context. And, of course, Novak is behaving to the order of this method through her conspiracy with Helmore, which is the equivalent of her cooperation with her director.

The appearance of the second Novak is a crucial indication of *Vertigo*'s real nature, for Stewart's obsession with the Novak face and the associations of guilt he has with it override the detective in him. He attempts, as Hitchcock indicated in his interview, to recreate the appearance she had as Helmore's wife. When the transformation is complete and the second Novak stands in a sexually charged and quite non-naturalistic green light, the exact image of her earlier self, and the camera tracks a full circle of vortex round them while they kiss, we can see how deranged Stewart is. He notices only that his dream has been reincarnated and that it is possible for him now to exercise the desire he had felt earlier but which had been suppressed by the nature of his job. For Novak the position is ontologically precarious. She has herself fallen in love, but while in her first character the mechanism of deceit kept her from being frank, she now recognizes how far Stewart is obsessed. Finally she confesses to the trick. Furiously Stewart takes her back to the monastery and chases her to the top of the tower. Novak is startled at the top by the sudden appearance of a nun—black robes appearing from black shadow—and falls to her death. This death is accident, punishment and suicide of remorse and identification, so involved have the layers of duplicity become. For Stewart, left at the top of the tower, there is no prospect but madness. Hitchcock has even intimated that he expects Stewart might throw himself down. Vertigo has been made the symptom of delusion, indecision, guilt, sexual obsession and, finally, chaos.

I have found it more necessary to detail the sequence of events in *Vertigo* than in any other film.[4] As in *Psycho* the movement of plot hypnotizes; at the same time the overtly narrative aspect is a pretext for Hitchcock to uncover spiritual responses. The height of his plots is when the mystery is most inexplicable, so that the rational processes the characters have been following break into psychological fantasy. Cary Grant, stranded in a mid-West desert in *North by Northwest* is in such a position; the whole idea of *The Birds* is perhaps Hitchcock's boldest juxtaposition of the real and the abstract. It is this talent that enables him to appeal more than any other director to the most general and most exclusive of film audiences. The cynical use of *doubles ententes* is the director's own awareness of his width of appeal. When Anthony Perkins remarks to Janet Leigh in *Psycho* that taxidermy is his hobby, the horrible pun is a dare to the audience: how can such artifice coexist with a tension so compulsive? Why, in fact, do the most old-fashioned plots work in his hands?

Basically, the effectiveness lies in the paradox that Hitchcock's films purport to be a sequence of factual statements, but that these ''facts'' are subsequently revealed to be false. Because the method filters a continuum of experience into discrete items, the real source of disorientation is the insinuation of the film's form with the natural processes of watching a movie, particularly a movie from Hollywood in a circuit cinema. While Hitchcock seems the most penetrative talent the cinema has offered, his method is already stranded by events that have separated the film process

4. An excellent and more comprehensive analysis of *Vertigo* is to be found in *Hitchcock's Films* by Robin Wood (Zwemmer, 1965).

from the commercial structure that originally fostered it. In some ways Hitchcock, more than many of his contemporaries, adheres to an old-fashioned cinematic concept. His reliance on the conclusive "story" form is such that he has concentrated on making all its connections plausible, so that the story has become more and more isolated from a spectator's sense of external reality. The photographic images have consequently moved further towards the abstract and Hitchcock's most striking achievements have occurred when the counterpoint between reality and the abstract has been most disarming. Only a great talent could have done this and only a supreme showman could have continued doing it in Hollywood. As a result he has come to occupy the position of creative artist, and it is this that makes an anachronism. His films are concentrated on intention, and their elements have to be meaningful, whether the meaning is conveyed directly or by contradiction.

Hitchcock utilizes back-projection more successfully than most directors, and this is because the relationship between person and background in his films is conceptual rather than real. The isolated Cary Grant in the prairie in *North by Northwest* is as much a figure projected against a background as Stewart struggling to climb the vertiginous face of San Francisco or Anthony Perkins playing out his fantasies in the Gothic set of *Psycho*. All these situations are convergent on meaning and the result of calculation. Hitchcock has admitted just how important the process of planning and conception is: "Je ne regarde jamais dans le viseur. Je prends un crayon, et je dessine le plan suivant pour le chef-operateur lorsqu'il y a une difficulté. Mon film est terminé avant le tournage. C'est pourquoi j'ai mis un an à écrire *North by Northwest*. Si je vais aux rushes après, c'est pour voir si les cheveux et le visage d'Eva Marie Saint sont comme il faut. Je sais tout."[5]

The truly creative process then is one of solitary imagination and it is literary in the sense that much of it can be set down in a shooting script. It seems to me that Hitchcock conceives of his event and his way of presenting it simultaneously. That is the power of his best movies, but it is what today makes their meaningfulness increasingly claustrophobic. "Je sais tout" is an aspiration to sublimity that is sustained by enough of his movies even though it is a denial of the camera's potential.

5. *Cahiers du Cinéma*, no. 102. ["I never look through the view-finder. When there's a problem I take a pencil and sketch the next shot for the cameraman. My film is finished before it's shot. That's why I took a year to write *North by Northwest*. If I go to the rushes later, it's to see if Eva Marie Saint's hair and face look right. (Otherwise) I know everything."—Eds.]

# Inside Norman Bates

## Raymond Durgnat

The camera climbs towards a window like any other window. Documentary-style, a subtitle states time and date; but it really means: Here and Now, at this moment, without warning, imperceptibly, destiny entered these lives. On a hot day, during their lunch break, in an impersonal hotel bedroom, Marion Crane (Janet Leigh) and Sam Loomis (John Gavin) are half-naked and necking. The nightmare begins at noon. The heat, the bleached feel of the visuals, the half-nakedness, the time, evoke an atmosphere of unsatiated sensuality (indeed, the heavy petting of so many of Hitchcock's American films, from *Notorious* to *North by Northwest,* suggests a frustrating coldness, even, intercourse with neither orgasm nor emotional relief). In a very matter-of-fact way the lovers are discussing the man's divorce and the money they need if they are to marry. The general situation—half-stripping at lunchtime and then talking about cash—is vaguely offensive; yet they seem decent people, we accept and care about them. This ambiguity pervades their whole relationship. In some way Sam seems petulant, weak, unworthy; in others, Marion seems prim, tough, less concerned with unconditional love than with—respectability? Are they in love or only convinced they are? At any rate, we're not especially anxious for them to get married. In default of the money, she is tempted to break off the affair, and we are sufficiently disquietened to watch with something between curiosity and concern, rather with an eagerness for them to get married and live "happily ever after."

Marion returns to the sane, shallow, superficial people of the office where she works. It's not long before sex and cash are intertwined again. A fat client makes a rather coarse and vulgar attempt to flirt with her, brandishing a fat bankroll in her face. The other office girl, a plain and silly creature, is naïvely jealous of these gross attentions. "I expect he saw my wedding ring." Her self-consoling remark rubs salt in Marion's wound. We agree with her feeling that she is too pretty, efficient, sincere in love, to deserve to be worse off than this other girl. The fat customer brags that he wouldn't miss the money if it were stolen, and Marion's boss absolutely insists on entrusting it to her. Such smug, imperceptive responses all round reinforce our feeling that Marion has as much right to this excess money as its actual owner. These pinpricks accumulate into a kind of obsession and reinforce the confusion between her respectability (or pride) and her love (or sensuality). The money seems to offer a solution to all these "raw edges" of feeling. Her theft is (so to speak) an impulse born of converging obsessions, which suddenly click into place forming an irresistible urge. It is also a tribute to her daring, her strength of passion; there is an element of moral *hubris vis-à-vis*. There is also an element of *hubris vis-à-vis* her lover, as if in acting so boldly where he has been so weak she is taking over the initiative—and is not going to be thanked for her devotion. Soon she is driving hard away from the town, tormented not so much by conscience as by fear. We can't believe she'll get away with it, especially as criminals never do in American films. We hope she will, and there is still a get-out: The theft won't be noticed until Monday norning, she can always return the money. Will she go on to decide to return it, but lose it? Will someone else steal it from her? Will Sam betray her, by his weakness, somehow?

A big, brutal-looking motorbike cop with dark glasses trails her, suspiciously. His menacing figure recalls the lawbreakers of *The Wild One* and the motorcyclists of *Orphée* who ran men down in the name, not of justice, but of a law above the law, the brutal Will of destiny. He is "the law," but he has a special, *personal* brutality of his own. Is he really following her, or is she only imagining he is? The psychological pressures complicate and intensify. To shake him off, she exchanges her car at a garage run by a very obliging character, apparently the very antithesis of the cop. The cop is saying, "I remind you of punishment. Turn back!," the garagehand, "I make crime pleasant and easy, go on." She acquires a white car—the color of her underwear in the necking scene, the color of innocence and dissatisfied sensuality; but all her precautions are of no avail. The cop still tails her, a terrifying dark angel sent to give her a last chance. Or sent simply to torture her, to diminish her chances; for without him she has a weekend in which to repent. There is danger of, as it were, rape-by-justice. We sigh with relief when at last she shakes him off.

She is beyond the reach of the law—or fear—now. But—where is she? The rain pours down across the windscreen, blurring lights and creating a wavering landscape. She is what in *Orphée* is called *la Zone,* the no-man's-land between reality and the nightmare. The cop was both danger and safety. It is almost as if he were sent, after all, not to turn her back, but to make her drive on. The theological notion of double predestination provides a clue, "God sends sinners a chance to repent *in order that* by rejecting it, as he knows they will, they will damn themselves more thoroughly than ever." But as she reasons with herself, she is beginning to realize the futility of her theft—Sam is too sensible to accept the money. . . .

The rain forces her into a motel, managed by Norman Bates (Anthony Perkins). Norman is an engagingly naïve country youth, very honest, unconcerned with making money, almost a symbol of rustic virtue and country contentment. The whole film hinges on his sensitivity and charm—we tend to like him whatever his faults. His friendliness is all the more reassuring in contrast with the sinister atmosphere (the stuffed birds of prey, the Victorian house just behind the motel, where his petulant, tyrannical old mother lives). He seems tainted by the atmosphere, but the over-obvious horror clichés shift our suspicions from Norman to the atmosphere; they camouflage the inevitably stilted presentation of his relationships with Mrs. Bates; they contrast with the slick, modern, informal style of the film as a whole. Mrs. Bates comes from Norman's childhood and it's fitting that she should exist in an aesthetic idiom now considered childish—she would feel quite at home in James Whale's *The Old Dark House*.

Marion calls Norman's bird-stuffing a rather morbid hobby and says Norman resembles the dead birds of prey. Hitchcock plays fair with his audience, even while misleading us. True, he lets us believe in Mrs. Bates—but so do Marion and Norman. Maybe, as the psychiatrist says later, Norman was never entirely Norman, he faintly knew the truth about Mrs. Bates—but then again Mrs. Bates is very stilted, we only half-believe in her.

Norman cheerfully admits to his faults of character; he is a very reasonable, modest guy. Gradually Marion realizes that she is his superior, that, if unhappy, she is self-possessed, whereas his "contented" acquiescence in looking after his domineering mother has something weak and helpless. His wisdom about money and the example of his servitude help to free her from the power of her impulse. She realizes that what she stole was not love but only money, an attempt to avoid her problems. Norman is almost a sacrifical victim whose tragic example frees her.

But he is not a hopeless case. We feel that she owes it to him to return the favor. We want him to be freed from his horrible mother, for he is a decent fellow. There is something dissatisfying in Marion's decision simply to return, alone, to the everyday, with its little degradations, its mutually exclusive choices—while leaving Norman here, unhelped. A sort of bewilderment percolates through the audience at this weird, premature "happy ending." We are, so to speak, in another "zone."

The film elaborately establishes Marion's search for a hiding place for her cash. The search seems to turn her indifference to Norman into an entrenched cynicism, for he isn't the sort of lad to steal it. As she undresses, Norman watches through the peephole. We laugh very uneasily at his avid voyeurism, but it does not quite put him in our bad books, for he has been lonely and dominated by his puritanical mother and his spying on Marion represents a movement towards normality and freedom, which we want for his sake. This is almost a dissatisfying love scene (like necking for lunch). The erotic overtones are juicy, and please us. And we are pleased to feel the story moving again.

The "movement towards" Marion is intensified—with a vengeance—when Mrs. Bates with a knife upraised charges in and stabs her to death in the shower. The murder is too erotic not to enjoy, but too grisly to enjoy. Its ferocity and pornography are opposed, we are shocked into violent protest and horror, yet they force on the average spectator a rapid, hysteric, moral oscillation between protest and enjoyment. There is a Hays Code sort of moral in the air: "Look what thieving necking girls get," but her fate is also ironically unjust, for she had just resolved to return the money.

If the Peeping Tom episode is a "weak" yet eerie version of the hotel scene, the murder is a sarcastic exaggeration of it—her sensuality's satisfied now, all right. We feel guilty about enjoying this film, but we have to admit we're having our money's worth of fun and fear.

Mom would be a convenient scapegoat; but we are headed away from complacent hatred back into something subtler and far more uncomfortable by Norman's distress at her crime and his concern for her. In the next sequence, he begins mopping-up operations in the bathroom, the action of an exceptionally dutiful son. The presence of Marion's naked corpse is both erotic and extremely uncomfortable. The film offers us a "first-person" experience answering the question which so often occurs to crime fans, "Would I be able to get down to the practical details of clearing up the corpse and the blood"—a thought which appalls many people more than that of the actual killing. The answer the film gives is, "A sensitive and dutiful son like Norman can—therefore, so could you, if you really had to." We watch Norman doing it, and the feeling that we could too is gratifying to the worse side of our nature, but upsets the other.

Although there is a quietly disturbing contrast between Norman's usual sensibility and his matter-of-fact practicality on this particular chore, we feel that in his way he was on the edge of being "liberated" by his interest in Marion, that she slew Marion so as to keep him, and that in covering up for Mom, Norman is turning the other cheek, manifesting the equanimity and charity of a saint. The spectator's moral purity is being outflanked at both ends—by morbid, pornographic interest and by a sympathetic pity for charming Norman.

Not that indignation and disgust are lulled asleep. On the contrary. For example, there is a very precise mix between a close-up of the plughole down which our saintly voyeur is swabbing the blood and a close-up of Marion's open eye staring at us as if to say, "What about my feelings? Why don't you interview the dead?" She's peeping back at us from beyond the grave, from down the drain, with protest and indignation, eternal and colossal— or surprise and fear—or just nothing. This visual rhyme is not just a piece of sadistic wit, but a little essay in metaphor; it never does to interpret visual effects too definitely, but, e.g., the plughole is like an eye socket, the eye ("Window of the soul," as they say) is just a mushroom out of a black hole. There is a sense of total nothingness and if the "joke" provides a little hysteria which relieves the horror faintly, it insinuates a subtler unease: We must be mad to be laughing at a joke like this.

Norman chews candy as he watches the white car sink beneath the very black surface of the swamp behind the house. As the film uses psychoanalytical ideas, it's appropriate to use them on the film—the bathroom scene, very glossy and white, and devoted to the theme of cleanliness, is followed by a scene in which everything disappears into a black sticky cesspool. Norman has pulled the chain.

When the car sticks instead of sinking, we are alarmed, but when at last it disappears we heave a sigh of relief. Thank goodness! Norman is a good boy (despite the candy), it would be wrong to punish him, Marion's a corpse, it's no use crying over spilt blood, bury her quick, tidy up, get her out of the way! But when Norman tosses in the thick wad of cash, which he thinks is just an old newspaper, a cry of shock and regret is wrested from the audience. That valuable money, what a waste! Norman's saintly indifference to Mammon hurts us. We want to forget Marion probably because her murder shook us up so much. But the money had become "what she died for, what she hid," that is, virtually a substitute identity. Its derisive disappearance creates hysteria as again the narrative seems to "end."

Sam Loomis discusses Marion's disappearance with her sister Lila (Vera Miles). The visuals are grey and scruffy. The setting is Sam's wife's ironmongery store where callous chit-chat aobut insecticides is overheard and pitchfork prongs are visually prominent. The drab everyday is full of trivial or latent cruelty. The meeting of lover and sister is hostile, but their disputes are ironically complacent compared with the terrible truth. Lila seems more sensible, more adult than Marion, and perhaps more righteous—but also worried, subdued. A private detective, Arbogast (Martin Balsam) insists on introducing himself, and tells them that Marion has absconded with the money. They refuse to believe him. They detest his coarse, obnoxious approach—so do we, and, like Sam and Lila, feel he must be up to some dirty game. His cynicism doesn't fit Marion's case—although, in a sense, it is justified.

As he tracks Marion down to Norman's mansion we half want him to fail—for Norman's sake, and because he may be up to some cynical scheme of his own. . . . Just before he confronts Norman we realize that he is completely, admirably honest. In the battle of wits between Norman and Arbogast we sympathize with them both—Marion *must* be avenged, Arbogast is tough enough to uncover the truth; and yet Norman's motives are selfless, and perhaps Mrs. Bates will be more than even Arbogast bargains for. As he climbs the stairs towards the old lady's room, we realize clearly that his pushful cynicism, hitherto his strength, is now his weakness. He is formidable, and physically is probably Mom's match, but he is too naïve to be looking for whatever he'll find—and Mrs. Bates comes tearing out of her room with the superspeed of the superstrong insane and with repeated jabs of her knife sends him tumbling backwards down the stairs, dead, just like that. Is Mom invincible?

Another car sinks into the swamp, the narrative "ends" at another nihilistic moment.

The whole plot, which has twice ended so disastrously, starts again, as Sam and Lila come to investigate the disappearance of the investigator who came to investigate the disappearance of. . . . Probably by now most spectators have guessed that Mom=Norman. But we can't be sure, in such a film. The only thing we can be certain of is the imminence of violent death—again. What matters is not whether we know, but whether Sam and Lila find out—or get killed. They might. Heroes and heroines do, in this film. And if they do find out, what will happen to Norman—saintly accomplice of two—at least—crimes . . . ?

The determined, but prosaic and therefore perilously naive, couple call on the local sheriff (John McIntire) who explains that Norman is eccentric but harmless, that Mom has been dead and buried these ten years past, and so on. But we heard Norman persuade Mom to hide in the cellar and we saw Mom come tearing out of her room to kill Arbogast. The sheriff's clue is so wrapped up in complacency and ignorance that instead of clarifying our suspicions it confounds them further. The sheriff's suggestion opens up astounding new avenues of depravity: "If Norman's mother is still alive, then who's the woman buried up there in Green Lawns Cemetery?"[1] If they believe what the sheriff says, they will never go to the old house, and then how can Marion and Arbogast be avenged? But *if* they go there. . . .

1. Well might he ask.

Sam keeps Norman talking while Lila sneaks into the house to explore; clearly the most dangerous game to play, especially with a possible Mom waiting for her. As we can't make up our mind whether the danger is coming from in front of her (Mom) or from behind her (Norman), we're no longer thinking very coherently, and as we can't make up our mind what we want to happen to Norman, we yield to a helpless hysteria.

Norman grows more anxious and angry as Sam brutally presses him; he struggles to keep his temper, to quieten his tormentor's suspicions, while keeping Mom from breaking out in himself (if you know) or (if you don't) bravely protecting his Mom or (if you're not sure) both or neither or which? The scene almost shifts our sympathies round—such is Norman's sincerity—to: "brutal smug adulterer bullies sensitive kid into despair." After all, whether Norman is weak or maniac or both, he probably believes in Mom, he is only trying to obviate another climax, another killing, he is frantically on the side of peace.

Lila explores the house. Amidst the tension there is an unexpected intellectual interest, and pathos. Norman's rooms are a picture of his mind and everyday life. There is the record player with the classical L.P. (so out of place in this Gothicy house), there are the fluffy childhood toys which are presumably still played with. Norman is weaker-minded, more sensitive, than we thought, which makes him more pathetic (and more surprising—menacing?). Norman, mad with suspicion, rushes from the motel into the house as Lila takes refuge in the cellar—where, we know, Norman puts Mom in times of stress. And Mom does exist, there she is, horribly old, evil and withered, at a closer look she's dead and withered, but still grinning malevolently, she's a ghost, and when Lila turns, there's *another* Mom, grinning malevolently, very much alive, knife upraised. There aren't no Moms, there are two Moms, then the second disintegrates, the wig slides off, it's Norman. It's not simply the surprise that shocks; it's the intensity of terror and the obscenity of the disintegration. In rather the same way, when Mom came tearing out of her room at Arbogast, she had the notoriously terrible strength of the insane, and a visible virility quite obscene in an old lady; the explanation doesn't explain *that* away; it intensifies its impact because illusion and explanation coexist.

We are relieved to hear that everything is going to be comfortably explained for us by the police psychologist (Simon Oakland). As soon as we see him we begin to dislike his brash, callous, know-all manner; he puts our backs up as Arbogast did. We expect the clichés: poor mixed-up kid, it was all the fault of stern, possessive, puritanical Mom. But gradually we realize he's not saying this at all. It was Norman who was jealous, who imagined that his (for all we know) normal Mom was a promiscuous Mom and murdered and embalmed her and then imagined she was a jealous puritanical Mom and then lived out two false characters—nice normal Norman and nasty Mom. So much for rustic contentment. Norman was never, we gather, entirely Norman, i.e., even when he was being charming and we felt sorry for him, he knew deep down what he was doing. The psychologist's explanation takes away our explanation: What we thought was "deep," the "solution," is merely the topmost level of nastiness. He restores terror, guilt, injustice. Up till now Mom's gruesome appearance has been in accord with her character: "Well, if she's dead, she asked for it, look at how she messed up her tender and devoted son." Now all this is reversed, the coconut-faced corpse was once a sunny, apple-cheeked mother. The boy has literally turned her into his fantasy of her.

But if the psychologist, brutal and cynical, is the most intimate of private eyes, the joker is still to come. All we've had has been an intellectual, rational explanation. Now we see Norman sitting against a blank, white, hygienic wall. He is in full-face close-up, his madness is rammed into the cinema. Briefly our entire world is his face, the thoughts behind it, *his* world. We have little else with which to identify. An utter flatness, whiteness, simplicity, in short, eternity. He is cackling to himself, in Mummy's mummy's voice. She is jubilant because she is outwitting them all, pretending to be a sweet old lady who won't even hurt a fly. Mom has just killed Norman and disguised himself as him.

The Chinese sage wrote: "Now I do not know whether I was then a man dreaming I was a butterfly or whether I am now a butterfly dreaming I am a man." With Norman it's flies. His ricocheting self-punishment is so total that—well, we can hardly pity him, for there's no one left there to pity. And he or she or it seems to think it is escaping punishment, which is very immoral of him or her or it; but a nausea-*like* compassion makes itself felt. We are too thoroughly satisfied to hate.

The appearance of Mom's face under the madman's, and then of a skull under Mom's, has a climatic brutality, but also simplifies, liberates us from the baffling maze of malevolent Nothings which our sensitive boy has become. Needless to say, it is a simplification on the most nihilistic level: Are any of us realler than our skulls? There follows a shot of the police lifting Marion's car, wrapped in chains from the swamp. There is no "decent obscurity." And Nothing to the nth degree has killed real people whom we sympathized with. But we too hoped the car would sink (just as we hoped Marion would get away with the cash). We too have been accomplices after the acts—futile acts.

People leave the cinema, chuckling incredulously, groggy, exhilarated yet hysterical, half ready to believe that everybody in the world is as mad as Norman. A cathartic indulgence in pornographic murder is succeeded by an embarrassed humility, an unsentimental compassion towards insanity. The entire film is a prolonged practical joke in the worst of taste. If it weren't in bad taste, it would not be cathartic, embarrassing or compassionate.

It is not just a sick joke, it is also a very sad joke. Because it is outrageous, it exhilarates, but it is a very depressed film as well. The by-play with the money is strange and disturbing. It is produced as a weapon of seduction by a repulsive but normal male. Its victim resents the implied insult but yields to the money. The money, she felt, would enable her to find, all at once, respectability, sensuality, love. It becomes the last clue, a substitute identity, an antisoul. Marion who hoped to avoid choice, and sacrifice (the *hubris* of American optimism), is reduced to a nude body, a car, bankroll.

Everything piles up in the swamp—and is dredged up again. The film is not just a sick joke and a very sad joke, but a lavatory joke. It is a derisive misuse of the key images of "the American way of life": Momism (but it blames son), cash (and rural virtue), necking (and respectability), plumbing and smart cars. The reality to which Sam and Lila return is not a joyous one, but a drab shop of insecticides, pitchforks, and—in addition—a vision of horror. The plot inevitably arouses in the spectator a feeling that Lila and Sam could eventually, possibly, consolingly, fall in love. But there is no hint of it in the final image. Each is still alone. This is the sanity that balances the diabolical nothing which is the human soul. Marion, striving for everything, lost everything. Only Norman has defied society and superficiality and found "rest." Only Norman has found himself, and lost himself.

Like many films, *Psycho's* aesthetic method is not that of providing enlightening information about its characters; it provides just enough to confuse us; it works by luring the audience into becoming the characters, sharing and living out their experiences within them in carefully determined patterns. The characters tend to be alone on the screen. Even the conversations are filmed mainly in alternating close-ups. The close-up both enlarges (intensifies) and isolates (blots out the rest of the world). While each character is speaking the spectator sees, feels, becomes him and only him. The next shot wrenches him into becoming the *antagonistic* character. Our sympathies alternate rapidly—our feelings are poured into so many molds which are distended or smashed by contradictions, revelations, twists. Simple as the characters are, in principle, they are, because well acted, convincingly real. The atmosphere is hypnotic, the events so outrageous and managed with such brinkmanship of taste, the hints, allusions and subersive shifts of sympathy are managed with such sly tact, its constant emotional collisions are so quick, subtle and drastic, that the "sketchiness" of the characters no more invalidates them than it invalidates the plays of Racine.

In its powerful vagueness, it works on the spectator not unlike music. It is planned, felt out, in terms of varied motifs, of emotional chords and dissonances, of patterns. Hitchcock has a very refined sense of sly or brash emotional discords, of how to modulate and combine them. The coarse customer, the cop, Arbogast, and the psychologist are incarnations of the same force—unpleasant common sense. The trusting boss, the garageist, the local sheriff, Norman himself all agreeably further evil. The woman in the ironmonger's who is determined to kill insects painlessly is mirrored in Norman's final crone-voiced cackle that he won't even hurt a fly (Is absurd squeamishness the hypocritical form of homicidal mania?). Norman, in conversation, unwittingly frees Marion of the compulsive theft which Sam inspired in her. But Sam bullies Norman like the cop bullied Marion.

Lila is a more reasonable, but "joyless" double of Marion. Sam loses Marion to Norman but Norman is destroyed by Sam and Lila. Lila, in a sense, is Marion "come back"—a parallel to the "second Mom" in the basement. As Lila roams through Norman's rooms, she is almost the substitute mother, the young woman who is kind and normal and will therefore destroy him. Norman and Sam are both dark-haired, faintly resemble each other. Norman killed his mother because he thought she had a lover; and is destroyed by a young adulterer and his mistress's sister. The three penetrations to "the truth about Norman"—Marion's, Arbogast's, the young couple's—are like three movements in music—the first two themes are contrasted (a sensual theme involving a girl, an unromantic theme involving Arbogast, the third combining them—a young couple who aren't quite romantically connected).

All these patterns, like inversions of certain emotional chords, result from the film's simplicity of form, but they are like haunting harmonies placed on a simple, yet eerie melodic line. The cutting has a quick, ragged, Stravinskian rhythm.

The minor quirks and sins (adultery, a "thing" about insecticides) of the normal world are the tips of the horns of the real reality, concealed beyond, or below, the "zone." In *Psycho* nothing that isn't disturbing or tainted ever happens, and to enjoy it (as most people do) is to stand convicted, and consciously convicted, of a lurking nostalgia for evil (i.e., of thoroughly enjoying it in fantasy). Norman's big mistake is that he let his fantasies enjoy him. The film is a practical joke: It convicts all the spectators of Original Sin. One does not so much watch, as participate in, it, as one might in a religious ritual involving the confession and a—well, one cannot say that absolution is granted. On the contrary, we have to take what comfort, or discomfort, we can from the implied complicity.

Hitchcock may have had a Jesuit education, but surely *Psycho* isn't a Christian film; it has a Dionysiac force and ruthlessness; one might call it a Greek tragicomedy.

# Buster Keaton

BUSTER KEATON was born in the town of Piqua, Kansas, in 1895 and died in Hollywood in 1966. He came from a vaudeville background and joined the family act as a young child. By the age of three he was learning to do daring pratfalls without injuring himself, a skill that would enhance all his work in films. In 1917, when the family act broke up, he began a moviemaking stint with Fatty Arbuckle. He went on his own in 1920 and made a series of remarkable two-reelers; these were followed between 1923 and 1928 by ten uneven but brilliant feature films. He lost much of his creative freedom when he signed on with M-G-M in 1928, and his career declined irrevocably with the coming of sound. Only in the 1960s were his early films collected, released again, and rediscovered.

Because Keaton almost never smiled in films, he became more famous for his impassive face and flat straw hat than for the daring and coordinated movement of his whole body. It is by now commonplace to say that Keaton is athletic where Chaplin is balletic; yet this does scant justice to the extraordinary grace and ingenuity of Keaton's stunts, in which physical bravura is augmented by clever—hilariously too clever—mechanical contraptions. There's something typically American about Keaton's quixotic mastery over machines, his pragmatic ability to conjure them up or alter their nature on the spur of the moment. Keaton plays a character who is less a schlemiel (like Langdon) or an underdog (like Chaplin) than an ordinary American Joe, full of native pluck and resourcefulness. He can solve any problem, but often in a bizarre way that leads to further problems and even more elaborate solutions. His body is a perfectly honed instrument, which helps make his stunts look effortless and inevitable, despite the effort he puts into them.

The long dream sequence in Sherlock Junior (1924) particularly releases a surreal inventiveness that the more realistic films keep in check. Where Chaplin usually worked with obvious studio sets (in which he could exert full control), Keaton often filmed on location, and his work still has a fresh and natural outdoor look. In period films like Our Hospitality (1923) and The General (1926), he aimed at meticulous historical reconstruction, especially of the railroads. Like Chaplin he moved from the skits and routines of his two-reelers to more subtle drama and characterization in his feature films. Yet he often neglected the ongoing details of the story, and even had other directors handle them while he concentrated on the comic sequences, which became more complex without being any less funny.

The General, his most celebrated work, if somewhat different from the rest of the films, eschews the isolated comic highs of his funnier films but more than makes up for them in integrated drama, visual beauty, and warmth of historical coloring. Finally, unlike Chaplin's, Keaton's films steer clear of sentimentality and pathos. The films as a whole are less *emotional; getting the girl is much less important, since she is simply the necessary object of the quest, not the magical Grail that impassions and transfigures it. Extraordinary as he is, Keaton thus remains true to the ordinariness of his main character.*

*Gerald Mast's full study of Keaton can be found in* The Comic Mind *(1973), while James Agee's celebrated essay "Comedy's Greatest Era" (1949) was included in* Agee on Film. *Keaton told his own story in* My Wonderful World of Slapstick *(1967). Two useful critical studies, both titled* Buster Keaton, *are those by J. P. Lebel (1967) and David Robinson (1969). There is a biography by Rudi Blesh,* Keaton *(1966).*

# The Great Blank Page

## Penelope Houston

He had two spectacular advantages: his timeless American face, which means that in a costume picture (even in the absurd hearthrug and fur boots of *The Three Ages*) he never seems any more ridiculous than he intends to; and his chameleon classlessness. His indolent millionaires (in *Battling Butler* and *The Navigator*) or his pushing young men from Main Street (*Three Ages, Seven Chances*) never look as though they were making off in some richer boy's clothes. Chaplin's comic personality started from English class-consciousness; Keaton's was American and free. In disguise—at the beginning of *Steamboat Bill Jr.,* when he turns up in moustache and beret—he could look curiously seedy, like a weasel made up as a hairdresser's assistant. It is a great moment, made much of, when the moustache comes off and the Keaton face emerges: the great blank page, on which he could write every process of thought.

Imagine someone who has never seen a Keaton film, doesn't even know what he looks like. Would he leave *The Butcher Boy* (1917) curious about the identity of the pale young man who gets stuck in the molasses and later attacked by a ferocious schoolmistress brandishing a pistol? One suspects so, partly because Keaton's apprehensive good looks always make him stand out (comedy, on the whole, is not a profession of the handsome), and partly because even in his first screen appearance he draws attention to himself simply by not doing so. Everyone else is capering and jittering: Buster is just terribly puzzled that his hat should have become attached so irrevocably to his head.

The Arbuckle shorts blur into a confusion of glue, paint, whitewash, feathers, falling scenery, with Buster hovering like a small, anxious referee over Fatty's more obese and girlish cavortings. In a slightly repellent way, Arbuckle could be rather funny, tossing his curls as a terrifying St. Tri-

Excerpted from the article of the same title in *Sight and Sound,* vol. 37, no. 2 (Spring 1968). Reprinted by permission of *Sight and Sound* and the author.

nian's vision in *The Butcher Boy,* or twirling a tiny parasol—he seems to have found grotesque female disguise irresistible—in *Coney Island.* (This, incidentally, is the film in which Buster actually laughed: an error not to be repeated.) Buster appears as a dashing westerner, with six-gun and cigar, or a harassed surgeon, waving a chopper and heavily bloodstained. In *Backstage,* playing a bewigged Roman lady while Fatty lolls in a tiger skin, he suddenly looks unnervingly like Bette Davis. Elsewhere, he's to be seen making a wild and unmistakable Keaton entry on a bicycle, or abstractedly lubricating his horse's legs with an oilcan. There's one extraordinary moment: Arbuckle in *The Cook* (1918) doing the little dance with the rolls which Chaplin was to perfect seven years later in *The Gold Rush.*

Arbuckle was the right ally for Keaton (Buster himself always insisted on this) because his gags are planned as *film* jokes, and paradoxically because their styles were so different that the essentially solitary Keaton never risked becoming straight man to his stout partner. Watching these two-reelers, however, one realizes how hard they found it to keep them going, to think in terms of a single situation which could be spun out for twenty minutes. First reels tend to be better than second reels; invention runs out or (as in the case of *The Butcher Boy*) everything starts all over again.

Keaton *sans* Arbuckle was to perfect shorts which are intellectually satisfying as well as funny, because everything follows with blinding comic logic from one initial premise. This was still not the rule: the very curious *The Playhouse,* for instance, has two linked ideas, of an almost metaphysical oddity. In the first half, we're introduced to a whole theater peopled by Keatons—Buster playing all the parts, all the instruments in the orchestra pit, providing his own critical audience for himself. The point of the virtuoso joke depends on everyone's ability to recognize the second most recognizable comedian in the world. Then the film changes tack: the joke is Buster's inability, back in his natural character as stagehand, to recognize which of two identical twins is the one he loves, or even to acknowledge that there *could* be two girls looking alike. Crossly, he keeps finding he's caught up with the wrong girl. It isn't all that funny, but as a notion for a comedy it has all the abstract absurdity of Keaton at his most mathematical.

Over many of these 1921–22 shorts hangs a certain melancholy. They are ceaselessly funny, and so effortlessly inventive that Keaton throws away jokes anyone else would loiter over. One thinks of him casually striking a match on the cigar store Indian who promptly rounds on him with a tomahawk; or rolling himself up in a carpet and then rolling briskly downstairs in it; or as the blacksmith who feels that horses should be shod according to the procedures followed in shoe-shops. But the slapstick havoc is seldom entirely comic; and two great chase films, *The Goat* and *Cops,* both hinge on the feeling of fatalism with which Buster meets doom at every corner.

*The Goat* is the chase film which has everything. One feels that modern directors (Clive Donner, Blake Edwards, Dick Lester, etc.) who like to end comedies with chases ought to be made to watch it ten times through: not as a penance, however deserved, but as an object lesson in relevance and coherence and the importance of conveying, even in the silliest context, some sense of real danger. There is only one bad joke in the film: the uncharacteristic, because impossible, shot at the end when the lift goes rocketing through the roof. Good jokes include Buster queueing behind a couple of shop window dummies and restlessly surveying their immobility; Buster decorating the "Wanted Man" poster with a fur tippet, and then forgetting that he's trying to disguise his face and getting fascinated by the angles of the fur moustache; Buster unveiled as the lone rider on the model horse, whose plaster legs very slowly buckle under him; and the moment when he realises that he is sitting gaily down to dinner with the sheriff who has been hunting him, and escapes by hurtling off his chair, using some part of the sheriff as springboard, and diving straight through a fanlight.

Buster ends *The Goat* in triumph: the girl on his arm and the enemy routed. *Cops* is more extraordinary, because chance plays an even more malign role and the enemy is not a jovial village sheriff but an entire, impersonal city police force. Everyone always remembers the freezing instant when Buster appears all alone, a tiny figure at a distant crossroads, before the buffalo herd of policemen tear into the shot. But by this time Buster is inadvertently a thief (he thinks he has bought the load of furniture he is placidly trundling through the town) and inadvertently a bomb-thrower. The chase ends in triumph: all the cops in the police station, and the lone figure slipping out and locking the door behind him. Then along comes the girl, tosses her head, and Buster goes quietly back inside. To what doom is suggested by the last shot, of his tombstone.

Everything in *Cops* follows from Buster's righteous desire to please the girl and become a man of property. Having acquired the horse and cart, he at once converts it (as he does the balloon in *Balloonatics*) into a comfortable traveling home, littered with useful gadgets. He strikes up an endearing relationship with the barmy horse—the trusty, shambling grey, Onyx. In fact, he's an innocent householder, whose temporary home just happens to be wedged into the traffic jam of the police parade. The chase in *Cops* is not punctuated by the checks and whims of *The Goat:* this is Buster in full flight. And the coda—an exception to the rule that Keaton films have happy endings—is not merely wry and disenchanted. It is annihilating.

The chase films, once launched, pick up their own momentum: there is no chance of Buster turning round to explain to any pursuer that he is a much misunderstood man. My own favorite among the shorts, *The Boat*, starts from another premise: Buster brings fate thundering down on his head by sheer mulish devotion to an idea of himself as a boating man. This time he's married, with a practically-minded wife, and two small sons who wear the same flat hats and the same air of resignation to the unexpected. In the first scene, Keaton hitches the boat he has been building to his car, starts it up—and very slowly, like a card house, the family home crumbles as the boat is hauled out. This is not merely a comedian's destruction joke: as the whole front of the house comes adrift, the doll's-house furniture ranged around the surviving walls looks as forlorn as the wreck of a blitzed building.

There follows one of the most celebrated of all Keaton scenes: Buster standing proudly on deck, everyone helping in the launching, and the boat rolling slowly down . . . and down . . . and down, until only the flat hat bobs on the waves. But finally, irrevocably, the *Damfino* sets sail, a typical Keaton mobile home, with collapsible funnels and ropes to pull when passing under bridges. Mother cooks leather-hard pancakes; to spare her feelings the family, as one man, hide them under their hats. Then comes bedtime (the children wearing their hats with their nightshirts); and then the storm. Buster packs the others into a cupboard and settles down to fight it, upside down on his wildly tilting ship. And again it isn't exactly—or entirely—funny. There's the despairing, surrealist radio signal to the coastguard. "*Damfino,*" Keaton identifies himself. "Well if you don't, how can I?" is the only answer. And the characteristic moment when Keaton, bailing out with a teacup, suddenly reaches the point beyond sanity. Reason visibly snaps: the thing to do with a teacup is to drink out of it, not try to stem a flood, so he takes a gloomy swig.

Down goes the *Damfino;* her crew pile into a small bathtub, their last floating home. And then the younger boy, a true Keaton child if ever there was one, very gleefully pulls out the plug. Buster can do no more; but fate can, and the family walk from their foundering bathtub on to dry land. It is dark, lonely, a strange beach at night. They have lost the safety of home, and the dream of life at sea. Where are they going? *Damfino.*

*The Boat* has all the resilience, pig-headedness, and strangeness of the best Keaton films. It ends perfectly; but if it were to go on one has no doubt that this extraordinary family (wife and children behave like extensions of Keaton himself) would next be found setting up some ultra-ingenious desert island shack. The survival power of the Keaton character is never seriously in question. But the element of melancholy—Agee went so far as to call it melancholia—still bites. Keaton's humor is seldom destructive except at his own expense; and the collapse of the house at the beginning of *The Boat* seems to me one of the most strangely and sorrowfully and totally comic moments in cinema.

By now, the principles of Keaton films were set—of Keaton, that is, looked on as director rather than performer. There are obvious rules of construction, like the slow starts and all-out finishes. But I would suggest three basic elements of Keaton comedy, all in evidence in *The Boat*. First, there is the concern with plot, adventure, real hazards. I find the storm sequence reminiscent, of all unlikely things, of the hurricane in *Alone on the Pacific,* a comparison one could never begin to make if Buster were just a booby adrift in a studio mock-up boat. Second, there is the sense of place. In *The Boat* this is no more than the modest little harbor whose yachts and boathouses can be seen in the background of the launching sequence. But if this scene were staged in a studio tank, it could become just a pretty gag. Here it acquires the utter lunacy of some freakish happening in real life.

In other films, background takes on more value: the dusty, countrified streets of small towns, the Model Ts racing down country lanes, the railroad always somewhere near the center of town. (*Bonnie and Clyde* shots, one now finds oneself thinking, in an absurd time switch.) Even in the two-reelers, Keaton was clearly prepared to go to great trouble for the sake of a single shot: there's an extraordinary one, for instance, in *The Paleface,* which finds him on horseback in the middle of a great misty landscape of oil derricks, like something out of *The Red Desert*. But more significant than this is the sense of a world beyond the comedy: the river settlement of *Steamboat Bill,* the orchard alongside the millionaire's ornate encampment in *Battling Butler*. *Steamboat Bill* contains a shot which seems quintessential Keaton. He is standing in the foreground, gazing mournfully out at us; behind him, unobserved, the heroine has crept up and is dithering about whether to attract his attention. She is on the right of the frame; backward to the left stretches the riverside path, with people wandering about. The moment is caught and framed by the unconcerned presence of other people.

The third obvious Keaton principle is his fondness for keeping as much of the action as possible within a shot. It started, presumably, with a natural pride in letting the audience see that those leaps and falls and glissades of movement were all his own work. There could be no cutting, because to cut into the action would suggest a cheated effect. In *College,* when he's pretending to be no athlete, he runs towards the camera down a line of hurdles, knocking down every one; in *Steamboat Bill* he stands stock still while the falling house collapses around him; in *Seven Chances* he dances about the screen, slipping and dodging under a rain of falling boulders. He was prepared to risk his neck for an effect which might last twenty seconds on the screen. The camera had to get far enough back to take it all in, to exploit a connoisseur's satisfaction in the number of ways of staging a fall. And so he hit on the technique which happens to be most in line with modern, or at least 1960s, aesthetics. (It's interesting, though quite profitless and abstract, to speculate on whether this could have anything to do with the fact that at long last he seems to be *everyone's* favorite comedian.)

Though no one could call Keaton a theoretician of comedy, every published interview suggests that he had a total grasp of what he wanted to do, how an effect would come across, and what he expected from his co-directors. In his performances, he liked to build pyramids of action. He falls off a roof; gets caught up on a projecting pole; is catapulted off that into a room; slides along the floor; snatches at what turns out to be a fireman's pole; slithers down that to ground level and is at once off again. Here each cut flicks the action forward, so that the whole lunatic route from top to bottom of the building is as neat as an equation. But effects like this are perhaps less characteristic than the moments when the camera simply pauses, at a distance, waiting for Buster to emerge head first from a window or dash down a street.

What distinguishes his feature films qualitatively from each other is partly the sheer flow of comic invention (inexhaustible in *Seven Chances,* decidedly sparse in *Battling Butler*), and partly the extent to which he managed fully to realize a character. *The Three Ages,* for instance, is so limited by its parody form that it virtually breaks down into three interlocked two-reelers. Marvelous jokes—the first sight of Wallace Berry riding the mastodon, answered by Buster in his sea captain attitude on the back of a brontosaurus; the golf swing with the stone age club; his consternation when surrounded by those Thurberesque neanderthal women. But this is basic Buster; not much more.

So, though the college sweater and Harold Lloyd stance make a difference, is *College*—again tied to a rather rudimentary comic idea, about the bookish student, the least popular boy in the school, who wants to be an athlete. One sequence is as exhilaratingly daft as anything in Keaton: his hopeless imitation of the dashing sodajerk, which ends with the milkshake being slid nonchalantly along the counter—straight into the customer's lap. And the scene in which he practices javelin throwing (an immense wind-up, and the javelin thudding into the ground all of six inches in front of his feet) and pole-vaulting is a charming and very funny résumé of all college boy pictures. Again, the scene is made not just by the little ludicrously striving figure in the foreground, but by the feeling of space in the great empty stadium, with dusk coming on and the girl watching from the entrance.

# Buster Keaton's College

## Luis Buñuel

Here is Buster Keaton, with his latest and admirable film, *College*. Asepsia. Disinfection. Liberated from tradition, our outlook is rejuvenated in the youthful and temperate world of Buster, the great specialist against all sentimental infection. The film is beautiful as a bathroom, vital as a Hispano. Buster never tries to make us cry, because he knows that easy tears are valueless. Yet he is not a clown who makes us laugh belly laughs. We never for a moment stop smiling, not at him but from ourselves, the smile of health and olympian force.

In cinema we would always prefer the monochord expression of a Keaton to the variety of a Jannings. Filmmakers abuse this last, multiplying to the power $n$ the least contraction of his facial muscles. With Jannings sorrow is a hundred-faced prism. This is why he is capable of acting on a great fifty-meter close-up and if he's asked for "Still more!" he would show that with nothing but his face you could make a film called *Jannings' Expression, or the permutations of M wrinkles raised n to the power n*.

With Buster Keaton the expression is as modest as that of a bottle for example: although around the round, clear circuit of his pupils dances his aseptic soul. But the bottle and the face of Buster have their viewpoints in infinity.

There are rare souls who are able to accomplish their destiny in the rhythmic and architectonic gearing of the film. Montage—the golden key of the film—is what combines, comments and unifies all those elements. Can one aspire to greater cinematographic virtue? There are those who have sought to believe Buster the "anti-virtuoso," inferior to Chaplin, to reckon it some sort of a disadvantage, a kind of stigmata in him, what the rest of us reckon a virtue, that Keaton arrives at comedy through direct harmony with objects, situations and the other means of his work. Keaton is full of humanity: but of an actual and not a synthetic humanity . . .

From *Luis Buñuel: A Critical Biography* by Francisco Aranda, translated and edited by David Robinson. (New York: Da Capo Press, 1976). Reprinted by permission of the publisher.

Much is said about the technique of films like *Metropolis, Napoleon.* . . . No one ever talks about the technique of films like *College* and it is because it is so indissolubly mingled with the other elements that no one even notices, just as if you live in a house you do not take note of the calculated resistance of the materials which compose it. Superfilms serve to give lessons to technicians; those of Keaton to give lessons to reality itself, with or without the technique of reality.

School of Jannings: European school: sentimentalism, prejudices of art, literature, tradition etc. John Barrymore, Veidt, Mosjoukine, etc.

School of Buster Keaton: American school: vitality, photogeny, no culture and new tradition: Monte Blue, Laura la Plante, Bebe Daniels, Tom Moore, Menjou, Harry Langdon, etc.

# Keaton

## Gerald Mast

Like Chaplin, much of what Keaton became as an adult clown was shaped by childhood experiences. If Chaplin's childhood was a combination of homelessness, poverty, and hunger, Keaton's was quite the reverse. Although the Keaton family life was far from normal, the family did stay together—both on the stage and off. In the vaudeville act "The Three Keatons," Buster's father, Joe, held the boy's ankles and swept the stage with Buster's hair (Buster was billed as "The Human Mop"), after which he hurled his son across the stage, over the scenery, and into the flies (and, once, into the audience). Buster learned to suffer any kind of fall without injury. As an adult, Keaton injured himself seriously only once; he broke his leg when his foot got caught in one of the intricate, crazy machines that dominated his films (the moving staircase in *The Electric House*). Keaton's adult body was so resilient that he broke his neck during the filming of *Sherlock Jr.* without finding out about the injury until years afterward.

Keaton's delight in intricate machines also began in childhood. At their summer home in Muskegon, Michigan (the Chaplin family could not even afford a home, much less a summer one), Keaton and his pals rigged up various tricky devices. One of them was an outhouse whose boards collapsed at the tug of a string, exposing the busily seated occupant to the wind and world. Another was a tricky fishing line that fooled the victim by seeming to be attached to a huge fish; it was really hooked to a piling of the yacht club. (A modification of this fishing device appears in *The Frozen North*.) As a child, Keaton also discovered his love of sports—particularly baseball. As a star at M-G-M he organized a studio baseball team; and his love of baseball shows itself in two films (*College* and *The Cameraman*) in which the baseball sequences are among the funniest, most exciting moments.

Acrobatics, athletics, and machines—three essential ingredients of the great Keaton films. Buster received his nickname (he was christened

Joseph Francis Keaton) from his godfather, Harry Houdini, after the infant Buster tumbled down a flight of stairs without busting himself. On a single day of his one-year-old existence, Buster caught a brick on the head, got his finger caught in the wringer of a washing machine, and got caught up in a cyclone which swept him into the air and carried him hundreds of feet through the town. The cyclone practically leveled the Midwest town, but Buster survived all three catastrophes without serious injury. (He did, however, lose a joint of one finger.) The Keaton pattern had been established while he was still in swaddling clothes—impossible physical feats accomplished with miraculous success. In his films, Keaton never performed a physical stunt with the aid of any trick. Except for using a double once (to pole-vault into the girl's window in *College*), Keaton actually performed every stunt in every Keaton film. And he often doubled for stuntmen who were less proficient than he. Unlike Chaplin, he consistently caught the perfect performance of a gag in a single take. He would have to. Such stunts did not bear frequent repetition.

Whereas Chaplin's comic technique centered about his face, hands, and legs, each of which operated as separate entities, with individual limberness and subtlety, the Keaton comic technique centered about the body as a whole, a single physical object that could comport itself in space the way no physical object ought to have the right or power to do. When Keaton takes a fall, his body doesn't merely fall. It lifts itself several feet into the air and then hurls itself down onto the ground. When he does a flip, his body doesn't merely flip. It leaps into the air, tautens itself into planklike stiffness, then tucks in its knees and tumbles over itself in midair. The Keaton body is alternately, indeed simultaneously, both elastic and bone, the most malleable and the most tensile of physical substances. When The Three Keatons broke up in 1917, Buster could have gone on the stage by himself at $250 a week. Instead, he took a job in films at $40. His career in films paralleled Chaplin's. Keaton began his apprenticeship as a subordinate clown in pure knockabout farces. Whereas Chaplin began with Sennett, Keaton began with Arbuckle, a Sennett pupil, in highly Sennettesque romps. Keaton then, like Chaplin, went on to perfect his comic technique and cinematic ideas in two-reel films. Then, like Chaplin, Keaton reached his maturity in a series of features. Finally, like Chaplin, Keaton suffered disappointment, disgrace, and rejection by his public— although for reasons and under circumstances very different from Chaplin's.

## The Keaton Comic World

Keaton never took the world so seriously as Chaplin did. Whereas Chaplin's films, even his individual comic bits, are pointedly social, intellectual, concerned with hunger, humiliation, justice, and freedom, Keaton's films seem pointedly pointless. Keaton as an artist was never conscious of trying to say something; he merely tried to do something that he found funny.[1] In his autobiography Keaton belittles Chaplin's seriousness and intellectual pretensions. Keaton constantly tried to be a "good guy" with his "team"—gags on the set, drinks with the gang at the studio or at home, playing bridge, playing baseball—things that Chaplin did not do with his employees. Keaton's surface cheeriness shines through his autobiography in his refusal to say anything nasty even about those who ruined him. He went out of his way to be nice. And this niceness exists in his films—on the surface. They seem to be purely funny collections of gags and situations.

But beneath the surface there is more. The situations that Keaton found funny, the way he comported himself in relation to objects and the world, the stories he selected, and the way he solved his comic problems successfully in those stories—all these imply an attitude toward human experience, whether Keaton was conscious of it or not. The tension between surface and depths begins with the Keaton face—where discussions of Keaton always begin. The Keaton "Great Stone Face" has itself become a stony cliché. The fact that Keaton's face reflects no reaction to any event around him—no smile, no laugh, no tear, no puzzlement, no inquiry, no anticipation, nothing—lures some into assuming that Buster neither feels nor thinks. But the Keaton character is not unfeeling; and he is certainly not stupid. The Keaton character uses far more intellect, far more long-range strategy, than Charlie does. And that strategy is a product of thought.

In *The General* (1926), for example, two little town lads tag along behind Buster as he goes to visit Annabelle, his girl. They walk behind him into her parlor and sit down. Buster, without changing the look on his face, stands up, puts on his hat, and starts to walk toward the door. The two boys, of course, stand up to follow. Buster opens the door and the two boys walk out; Buster then closes the door behind them, takes off his hat, and goes back to sit beside Annabelle, again without changing the look on his face. The objective has been accomplished. Buster has performed a sensible action in a pragmatic way. And he has not tipped off a single maneuver; he plays his cards the way cards should be played. This initial bit of strategy in *The General* is merely the prologue to a whole film in which similar pragmatic strategies drive the plot.

Buster's unchanging expression is another strategy that helps him

---

1. J. P. Lebel makes the same point in his perceptive study *Buster Keaton* (London and New York, 1967).

survive. He does not kick, like Charlie; he feints. Behind the blank eyes and frozen mouth, the gears of Buster's brain are constantly clicking and turning. What it consistently comes up with is inevitably right in the circumstances. If the circumstances don't make any sense, well, that isn't Buster's fault. The face is a mask, a ruse, a cover for the ceaseless activity of the brain beneath.

The activity of the Keaton brain translates itself into action, not expression, as Chaplin's does. Whereas Lloyd's face shows all the mental activity that is taking place, and Langdon's face all the mental activity that isn't taking place, Keaton's body alone tells all. That body can either be in motion (kinetic) or at rest (latent).

At rest the Keaton body is a coiled spring; its perfect poise, its tense wariness, reveals its potential—even when covered with clothes. Keaton wears costumes beautifully. Many of his films effectively and purposefully use period costumes: the elegant gray cutaway and top hat in *Our Hospitality;* the formal top hat, white tie, and tails in *The Navigator, Battling Butler,* and *Spite Marriage;* the loose shirt, ascot tie, and flowing long hair of *The General. Battling Butler* is almost a male fashion show as Buster models a series of outfits for fishing, hunting, and camping.

The latent energy of the Keaton body that shines through his clothes becomes even more obvious when he is stripped to his shorts in *College* or *Battling Butler*. In those films, Keaton's body is so physically developed, so perfectly shaped and muscled, that he throws the whole premise of both plots (that Buster is physically weak and incompetent) under severe suspicion. Whereas Chaplin in shorts (*The Champion, City Lights*) still looks like a baggy-pants, puny weakling (the shorts are indeed baggy), Keaton in shorts is an uncaged and uncased jaguar.

The Keaton body in motion is equally elegant, poised, and commanding in its apparent ability to accomplish anything with the greatest ease and smoothness. Keaton performing a stunt was apparently no more taxed than Keaton at rest. Unlike Lloyd, whose technique makes every physical stunt look as difficult as possible, Keaton makes the most impossible physical stunts look like nonchalant, everyday activities: his smooth, effortless leaping from deck to deck in *The Navigator* and *Steamboat Bill Jr.,* from car to car in *The General;* the effortless swing over the falls that snares his lady love just as she plunges toward her death in *Our Hospitality*. Like his family's lifelong friend Harry Houdini, Buster Keaton makes the impossible seem easy. Unlike Houdini, Keaton shows us his body's magic while he performs the feat.

Keaton's real personality reveals itself not in facial expression but in posture and motion. Just as Chaplin thought words more limited, less communicative than mime and gesture, Keaton thought facial expression more limited than physical posture and motion. Keaton, unlike Chaplin, plays many different characters in his films, from different eras and different social classes: Rollo Treadway, Willie Canfield, Johnny Gray, Willie McKay, Jimmie Shannon, Alfred Butler. But beneath the different names and surroundings, all these Keaton figures reveal the same habits of mind—composed, careful, pragmatic, completely certain of the task to be accomplished, wildly imaginative in accomplishing it if that is the most sensible method, extremely flexible at responding to new obstacles, dogged about reaching the goal. All of these mental attitudes are clearly expressed by the Keaton body and without the Keaton face—or rather by the interplay of body and face, for the activity of the body plays in counterpoint to the inactivity of the face, leaving the spectator to infer what is going on behind that beautiful mask. The blank face is not a comic gimmick but a means of survival in a chaotic, dangerous world. It knows much more than it shows.

Psychological interaction and human motivation in the Keaton films are much more formulaic than in the Chaplin films. Motivation is far more literary; the plot demands a particular kind of action, and Buster's motivation is clearly to accomplish it. The desire to win the girl, to prove his mettle, and especially to stay alive are the three spurring drives. These formulas are further reasons that Keaton's films, unlike Chaplin's, did not require subtle and sensitive facial interactions. What the characters want and why are the basic stuff of the Chaplin films. What they want and why are obvious in the Keaton films; how they get what they want is the business at hand. For this premise, the body in motion is more useful than the expressive face. But unlike movement in the Sennett-style film, the Keaton body in motion is always directed in a specific manner toward a specific goal. It is not miscellaneous movement.

But blank-faced Keaton had other means to express himself than the body. Although that body is the center of the Keaton film world, many things revolve about that center. The Keaton body is a single object, indeed a small one, in space. The element surrounding Keaton is not society—a social role, definition, or assumption—as in Chaplin's films, but nature itself—trees, forests, oceans, the vast plains, cyclones, fire, rivers. Keaton is not a little guy set against malignant social forces, like Chaplin; he is a little guy set against elemental forces. And natural enemies, unlike Chaplin's opponents, are not necessarily malignant and oppressive. Nature is neuter. It is huge, violent, and overpowering. But it is also conquerable. Nature has no will. Only man has will. And Keaton films consistently reveal the triumph of human will and spirit over natural opponents. The Keaton comedies are more epic than Chaplin's because they show man in conflict with traditional epic forces rather than with individual men and social attitudes.

Keaton's camera reflects the change in emphasis. There is very little nature in Chaplin's films—even in *The Gold Rush* and *Sunnyside,* which use nature as a metaphor. Chaplin's camera works very close to the human players; human faces and bodies are Chaplin's photographic subjects. Keaton's camera works much farther away from the people; even Keaton himself is often only a distant figure in the frame, a human dot surveying the horizon with his hand on his brow. The Keaton film focuses on the interplay between man and nature. Every Keaton feature includes major sequences shot outdoors on location; most Chaplin films were shot on his studio lot. Keaton films were outdoor films; Chaplin films were not. (Even outdoor films such as *Sunnyside, The Pilgrim,* and *The Gold Rush* seem claustrophobic—intentionally.) The outdoors gave Keaton the space to move and the vast panoramas to contrast with his moving body, that small piece of elastic granite. Chaplin could generate a world of excitement from a single room (for example, *One A.M.*); Keaton films needed the world.

Little man juxtaposed with big universe—this was the Keaton theme, cinematic principle of composition, and basis of story construction. It also influenced the kinds of objects that Keaton chose to play against. Huge inanimate objects and living opponents were merely a manifestation of the hugeness of nature. Keaton played against a dinosaur, a waterfall, an ocean liner, a landslide, a herd of cattle, a locomotive, the entire Union and Confederate armies, a steamboat, a Tong war, a gang of bootleggers, a storm at sea, a tribe of Indians, and the entire New York police force. In most of the films, Keaton began playing against the enormous object and ended up playing with it. The object that dwarfed him at the film's beginning became an ally that he used to defeat others by the end.

Keaton conquered immense mechanical objects in addition to conquering immense natural forces; the two conquests were parallel and interrelated. Keaton's attitude toward machines is clearly two-edged—unlike Chaplin's monolithic contempt for escalators and assembly lines. Machines can pulverize little people; but people run machines, not the other way round. And people make machines, not the other way round. Once the principle of machines has been discovered, they can be tamed by men. Keaton sees both the brutality and the wonder of machines.

This attitude toward machines influenced his cinematic technique and makes the union between a mind like Keaton's and a mechanical medium like the movies particularly felicitous. Keaton favored the far shot, not only to juxtapose his individual body with the natural universe, but also to provide a distant view of how a particular mechanism works. The cinematic far shot provides the means to see both cause and effect, to see all the relevant elements, to illuminate the total process of a mechanism. And that is why Keaton's far shots are so memorable and so revealing—not just a little man on the vast plains of *Go West*, or a little man falling from a rope bridge in *The Paleface*, or a little man leaping from train car to train car in *The General*, but the principle of showing how a totality works.

In both *The Haunted House* (1921) and *The High Sign* (1920), a Keaton far shot reveals all four rooms of a house (one wall cut away) and exactly how the chase progresses from one to another. In *The Navigator* (1924), a far shot reveals both decks of an ocean liner and both aisles on each deck, so we can see exactly how a ship's hugeness can keep two lone passengers from finding each other. In *The General* (1926), another far shot reveals the Union train on a bridge between the Union and Confederate sides of a river. The bridge magnificently collapses and the train slides into the river, drowning the Union hopes.

Perhaps the most brilliant Keaton far shot to reveal a process (and what a process!) is in *Sherlock Jr.* (1924). A single far shot presents (1) a room where Buster is surrounded by thugs (Keaton has dissolved its fourth wall); (2) an open window with a paper hoop that Buster previously placed in it; and (3) the exterior of the house outside the window. In a single shot Buster dashes toward the window (1), leaps through it, through the hoop resting inside the window frame (2), somehow puts on a dress stuffed inside the hoop as he is tumbling through it in midair, rights himself on the ground outside the house (3), and begins to impersonate an old beggar woman, since he is now wearing a dress. Without the far shot, it would be impossible to believe that a human being could turn himself into a beggar woman while in midair tumbling through a hoop; it would also be impossible to believe that any comic acrobat could perform such a stunt. Apart from the mechanical performance of the stunt, there is the idea behind it. Who else would think of escaping his foes in such an incredible way and with such an incredible means to an incredible disguise? Keaton's far shot makes incredibility to the third power completely credible.

No director ever used the far shot with more strategic effectiveness (rather than just pictorial grandness) than Keaton. Keaton far shots turn human processes into mechanisms (Sherlock's leap through the hoop: pure Bergson) and reveal the human causes of mechanical effects (the chase in the *Navigator:* a mechanical game). For Keaton's physical comedy is essentially a synthesis of malleable human flesh and Bergsonian encrusted machine. While his human brain clicks away its strategies, his body becomes a perfectly designed machine for carrying them out. Where Sennett converts people into pure toys and Chaplin displays a limber flexibility that abhors the mechanical and inelastic, Keaton is both machine and man at once.

Keaton's interest in machines and mechanical processes also influences the way he handles the camera, that cinema machine. Keaton was far more interested than Chaplin in the camera apparatus, and he had more fun with it as mechanical toy. In *The Cameraman* (1928) Keaton demonstrates Buster's incompetence as a cinematographer by using double exposures and split frames to show a battleship gliding down Fifth Avenue. Buster's "newsreel" is an unintentional surrealistic joke. Perhaps Keaton's greatest use of the cinema as toy is in the short *The Playhouse* (1921), when Keaton plays every role on the vaudeville bill, as well as every member of the audience, with the aid of the masked lens and multiple exposure. Most delightful in mechanical terms are Keaton's impersonations of both members of a tap-dance duo; Keaton, as both hoofers, dances in perfect symmetry with what seems a mirror image of himself. And *The Playhouse's* pyrotechnics climax with Keaton's playing all nine (count 'em, nine) members of a minstrel act—from the interlocutor to Mr. Bones. He accomplished the dazzling technical trick by shooting the sequence nine times, with a perfect nine-piece mask over the lens (designed by Keaton's great mechanic-designer, Fred Gabourie), and with Buster occupying exactly the right spot in the frame each time.

Keaton's greatest cinema game, his clearest realization of the cinema's mechanical basis, is the famous montage sequence in *Sherlock Jr.* Buster plays a motion-picture projectionist. As he falls asleep in the projection booth, a transparent second self (double exposure) rises out of Buster's body and walks through the theater and up to the screen. After several failures, Buster's dream-ghost succeeds in entering the looking glass of a motion-picture screen. (Lewis Carroll is not so far away.) Once Buster gets inside the film screen, he finds he is at the mercy of film space and film time, not reality's space and time. As Buster stands in a single spot in the frame, the environment surrounding him undergoes the editing process. Buster remains fixed; he maintains his spatial continuity. But the universe does not as it instantaneously shifts from a desert, to an ocean, to a snowdrift, to a lair of lions. Buster knows who and what he is; he has complete control over himself and his actions. He merely is powerless to control the filmic montage that instantaneously changes his physical surroundings without allowing him to do anything about it.

This scene in *Sherlock Jr.* is very much at the heart of Keaton's style and imagination. The mechanical perfection of the stunt is extraordinary, but behind the mechanical ability to work the gag is the sheer marvel of even conceiving it. Such farfetched lunacy is not what Chaplin would do at all; it is too dependent on trick, too divorced from individual human feelings, too much a far-out stunt. But it is precisely the kind of imagination that Keaton reveals in film after film. However, the stunt would not have been suitable for any screen comic or character. Despite its apparent lack of humanness and personality it has a unique relation to the Keaton *persona*.

This relation is clear, at first, in the combination of sense and nonsense in the gag. The gag works not just because of the montage idea, but because a human being tries to make sense out of impossibly changing surroundings, the activities of the universe (in this sequence, a cinematic universe) make no sense, but Keaton goes about his business trying to make as much sense of it as he can, to deal with it in the most practical way he can devise. That conflict—between senseless surroundings and sensible Keaton—is what makes the montage sequence of *Sherlock Jr.* a uniquely Keaton gag.

Second, Keaton knows that he is toying with the differences between cinema and reality, with the different ways that cinema can scramble both time and space. For *Sherlock Jr.* is, above all, a movie about a movie—a film within a film within a film. This intention is especially obvious in the film's conclusion when Buster, returned to the reality of its projection booth from his glorious screen dream, must deal with his real girlfriend. To know how to conclude his story line with her, he must look at the motion-picture screen to see how it is done in the movie. And Keaton visually parallels the activities in the projection booth with those on the screen by shooting the scene through the window of the booth. Just as there is a frame around the movie screen, there is a frame around the scene in "reality." Keaton's imaginative brain has discovered both the ways that the cinematic universe defies nature and the way nature would try to copy cinema if it could. The film's story, gags, situations, and character all proceed from the same idea—the depiction of life-in-cinema and cinema-in-life.

As a further demonstration that Keaton's far-out stunts are highly personal and not just gimmicks, the opening sequence of the short *The Scarecrow* (1920) does very nicely. In this scene, Keaton and his roommate live in an efficiency cottage. Keaton literally makes that cottage as efficient as possible. Everything is on strings—matches, stove, dining table, salt and pepper shakers, napkins, milk, refrigerator. Everything is worked by pulling a string and setting the perfect machine in motion. At least two other films use the same mechanical gag: Snub Pollard's *It's a Gift* (1923) and Harry Langdon's *Three's a Crowd* (1927). In both of these later imitations of a Keaton machine, the comics and filmmakers work as hard as possible to show how funny, extraordinary, bizarre, and ingenious such mechanizations are. In Pollard's film, the machines define him as a silly, crazy inventor. Keaton's *Scarecrow* does exactly the opposite.

Keaton and his pal go about using the mechanical gadgetry as if it were as natural and ordinary as waking up in the morning, getting out of bed, and eating breakfast—which it is.[2] Keaton makes the unnatural perfection of his mechanical contrivances seem human and natural by showing the perfect coordination of Buster and pal in adapting to the needs and rhythms of the machine: handing each other the rolls, passing the salt and pepper, slinging the milk into the fridge. Keaton personalizes such a scene in his calm ability to assimilate the extraordinary and mechanical into the routine of normal life.

Almost all the great Keaton gags reveal this synthesis of impossible nonsense and pragmatic sense. In the short *Cops* (1922) Buster thrusts out his hand to signal for a left turn. A dog bites his wrist. Next time, Buster signals with a boxing glove hooked onto an expandable towel rack. Another very sensible machine. Unfortunately, the boxing glove smashes a traffic cop in the face. Later in the same film, Buster wants to light a cigarette. An anarchist tosses a bomb onto the seat of Buster's wagon. Buster calmly picks up the bomb, lights his cigarette with the burning fuse, and then tosses the "match" away. What else do you do with an unlighted cigarette and a handy bomb? Unfortunately, he tosses the "match" into the midst of a policeman's parade. Keaton, of course, has no control over the consequences of his sensible actions. A pragmatic maneuver can produce unforeseen and disastrous results. Conversely, a simple pragmatic maneuver can have monumentally effective results far beyond the intention of Keaton's strategy—as in *The General*. Such disproportion between act and result, intention and consequence is another blend of sense and nonsense. A man can control his actions, not their consequences.

There is similar sensible nonsense in the short *The Paleface* (1922), when Buster, tied to a wooden stake, is about to become fuel for the fire. Buster, however, succeeds in getting the stake out of the ground. Now he could run away—or attempt it. But how far could he get tied to a portable stake? So Buster sneaks up behind each Red Man gathering tinder and slyly conks him over the head with the stake. Much more sensible strategy.

The plots of Keaton's features usually juxtapose the sensible and the impossible. In *Our Hospitality*, Buster must go through a series of practical maneuvers to avoid being the next casualty in the Canfield-McKay feud. In *The General* he goes through a series of tiny practical maneuvers—chops

2. Keaton's first cinematic use of a domestic machine with strings was probably the 1919 Arbuckle film *The Garage*. This film contains so many Keaton elements—the machine, Buster's acrobatics, a human ladder that would recur in *Neighbors,* the Keaton pose with hand on brow surveying the horizon—that it reveals how far Keaton developed in his apprenticeship with Arbuckle.

wood, uses logs, boxes, rope, kerosene lantern, and the like—and in the process singlehandedly rescues his train and his girl from the Union Army and then wins a terrific victory for the South. In *The Navigator,* he goes through a series of practical maneuvers in the process of running an entire ocean liner by himself, repairing it when it gets damaged, and fighting off a whole tribe of jungle savages who attack it. Buster performs the ultimately impossible by merely performing the ordinary—step by step, bit by bit. Eventually a series of steps mounts to a heroic plateau; individual moments of sense add up to one impossible sum.

The first two reels of the Keaton features set up some character trait in Buster that makes it seem even more impossible for him to accomplish such feats: weakness (*Go West, The Three Ages, Our Hospitality, Battling Butler, College, Steamboat Bill Jr.*) and/or bungling incompetence (*Sherlock Jr., The Navigator, Seven Chances, The General, The Cameraman, Spite Marriage*). Buster, without erasing the general inadequacy established in the opening reels, shows how he can still perform impossibly heroic acts. Thus, the Keaton features begin slowly. Unlike the Chaplin films, which can start with a Charliesque bang of a gag, the early reels of the Keaton feature must establish the character Buster plays. Then the Buster character faces what might be called "the Keaton imperative." Buster *must* do something—something that the character he plays would never do, yet somehow must. The imperative can be thrust on him specifically: you must marry by 7:00 P.M. of your twenty-seventh birthday to receive $7,000,000 (*Seven Chances,* 1925); you must become an athlete before you can woo the pretty girl again (*College,* 1927); you must be a tough physical brute to wed the daughter (*Battling Butler,* 1926). Or the imperative can be simply a problem that Buster walks into and cannot possibly walk away from (and continue to exist): saving himself from murder and the girl from the falls (*Our Hospitality,* 1923); steering an ocean liner (*The Navigator*); taking a whole herd of cattle to market (*Go West,* 1925); saving his locomotive (*The General*); saving his father from a cyclone (*Steamboat Bill Jr.,* 1927); saving himself and his wife from gangsters (*Spite Marriage,* 1929).

Buster's successful accomplishment of the Keaton imperative reveals how close the Keaton comic world is to melodrama, and how influenced Keaton was by the master of melodrama, D. W. Griffith. Many of Keaton's films culminate in variations on Griffith's last-minute rescues (*Our Hospitality, Seven Chances, Sherlock Jr., College, Steamboat Bill Jr., Spite Marriage*). *The General* is a pure chase. Buster's last-minute rescue of Natalie Talmadge from the awesome waterfall of *Our Hospitality* seems a specific glance at Richard Barthelmess and Lillian Gish at the end of *Way Down East.* And if there is any doubt about Keaton's awareness of

Griffith, consider that in *Go West* Buster plays a character called "the Friendless One" and his lover's name—she merely happens to be a cow—is "Brown Eyes." Keaton loved parody, as so many of the two-reelers reveal: *The Frozen North* (parodies William S. Hart), *Convict 13* (parodies prison pictures), *The Playhouse* (parodies Thomas Ince's egotism).

Among Keaton's favorite targets for parody were cinematic plots, structures, and devices themselves. *The Three Ages* (1923) is a story of three identical love triangles in three historical periods, its structure an obvious parody of *Intolerance*. Keaton also makes the film overly symmetrical—for symmetry was another of Keaton's mechanical passions. In all three sequences (Stone Age, Roman, modern) the plots are identical (parents want girl to marry rich, strong suitor, not Buster) and the devices are identical—transportation (dinosaur, chariot, automobile); fortune-tellers; sporting contests (Stone Age golf, chariot race, football). Keaton also destroys seriousness with anachronism. When one of the dogs pulling Keaton's chariot in the big race poops out (it's snowing, so dogs are more practical than horses). Buster takes a "spare" dog out of the chariot's trunk; as the Roman fortune teller predicts Buster's future using two huge dice (marked with Roman numerals from I to VI), four Negro litter bearers drop their passenger and run over to shoot craps.[3]

*Our Hospitality* parodies "feud" melodramas. It even begins with an apparently serious melodramatic reel to set up the feuding milieu. Although some critics have thought this serious beginning an error, what better way to begin a parody of a melodrama than by setting up your target? *Sherlock Jr.* parodies the detective story and serious cinematic versions of that Conan Doyle hero's exploits—including the close-up of the elegantly gloved hand ringing the doorbell (see Stan Laurel's *The Sleuth,* 1922, for an identical shot) and the unbelievable death plots the crooks have hatched for poor Sherlock (dynamited pool ball, poisoned wine, and guillotine-like axe poised above a chair). *Seven Chances* parodies the domestic romantic comedy in which the young man is too shy to ask his girl to marry him. It culminates in an unbelievable chase as thousands of would-be brides and thousands of landsliding rocks chase Buster all over town, all the while pressing him toward that seven-o'clcock deadline. *Go West* parodies the cowboy film; *Battling Butler,* boxing heroism; *The General,* Civil War

3. Keaton's racial jokes, like Sennett's, are very impolite by today's standards. They are also very funny. Actually Keaton's "sick" jokes and racial jokes are neither sick nor bigoted. They do not stem from contempt or superiority but are simply comic magnifications of human observation. Race and physical deformity exist in the world. They are, therefore, perfectly suitable comic subjects.

romances; *College*, college pictures; *Steamboat Bill Jr.*, Mississippi river-boat romances.

Although the features are playful, they have an underlying moral edge. When Shakespeare parodied both classical heroism and medieval romance in *Troilus and Cressida*, he raised the serious and disturbing question of whether any virtuous human action is possible in a world where both love and honor are reduced to nonsense. Although Keaton consciously dealt in the completely comic, his films suggest serious human issues that cannot be laughed away. The artificiality of the code of honor in *Our Hospitality*, which demands on the one hand that the Canfields treat the guest in their home with courtesy and, on the other, that they murder him as soon as he steps out the door, is certainly the basis of many ingenious Keaton gags—coy and subtle attempts to stay inside the house, disguising himself in a dress to leave it. But that code of honor is vicious as well as comical. It is inhuman, respecting abstract forms rather than the human spirit. The word "honor" in the film is no more than a word, divorced from the realities that created both the word and the concept.

That a human being's worth is defined in so many of the films as physical prowess or material success is also central to Keaton's observation of the separation of form and essence. Like Chaplin, Keaton contrasted surfaces with more important realities. Where Chaplin's contrasts invariably center on social definitions of human respectability and success, Keaton's center on personal definitions of human integrity and accomplishment. In *The Three Ages*, the girl's parents in all three ages want a rich, powerful (both socially and physically) mate for their daughter. In *Sherlock Jr.*, the man who gives his sweetheart a $3 box of chocolates is superior to the man who spends only $1—even if the gentleman stole the $3. In *Battling Butler*, the girl's family values a man in boxing trunks and despises the same man in expensive suits.

The moral culmination of the Keaton cycle is *The General*, which contains all the typical values of the Keaton canon—and more. Once again Buster earns the contempt of his girl and her family. They assume that he is a coward and does not want to enlist in the Confederate Army. The fact is that he had tried to enlist but was rejected: the Army needs his pragmatic abilities as an engineer; he is worthless to them as a romantic warrior. The Lee family is blinder than the recruiting officer. They do not respect Buster as engineer, only as potential soldier. The rest of the film reveals that being an engineer is handier than being a soldier. Further, it casts doubt on all the clichés about war and romanticism, of which the American Civil War is perhaps the most splendid historical example. *The General* is anti-heroic, anti-romantic, anti-war, turning romantic illusions into comic bits.

The consistent Keaton motif is the ridiculing of all inhuman definitions of human worth. To define a man by his uniform, wallet, muscles, or family name is not to define him as a person. In his denigration of the value of clothes (despite his elegance in wearing them) and surface characteristics as a means of defining a man, Keaton is the opposite of Brecht (*A Man's a Man*) and therefore, of Chaplin (whose tramp's clothes *are* the tramp). What Buster accomplishes often has little to do with social and literary clichés about what certain *types* of men can accomplish. The Keaton character consistently shows how much a little, unheroic, unromantic man can do simply by going about his business in his own way, exercising his individual human abilities and will.

But beneath Buster's accomplishments there is not the same optimism, the same view of success as there is in Harold Lloyd or Douglas Fairbanks films. In several of the shorts, Buster fails to fulfill the Keaton imperative. In *Cops* (1922), his lady love demands that Buster make something of himself. What he makes is a public enemy, attracting the animosity of every policeman in New York City. After this dazzling performance in the negative, the girl rejects him for the final time. Buster walks back into the police station, choosing to suffer their physical punishment rather than the pain of his emotional loss. The film ends with a tombstone, Buster's porkpie hat hanging atop it. Similarly, in *Daydreams* (1922) Keaton's girl demands that Buster make himself a success. After his failure and her rejection, the film ends with yet another tombstone. *One Week* (1920) and *The Boat* (1921) end with disaster: the little house and ship that Buster spent so long putting together have been smashed or sunk.

Even the features exist in the shadow of disaster and the tombstone. In *College,* after Buster has successfully mastered athletics, his bullying rival, and his lady's affections, Keaton ends with a strange series of dissolves— Buster and wife with kids, the two as a pair of old folks, and then their tombstones in the cemetery. Though Keaton may have meant to imply their living "happily ever after," those two tombstones cast doubt on the whole value of the task he has mastered and the prize he has won.

Many of the Keaton features seem skeptical about that prize. In most, doubt arises primarily from the fact that the lady Buster wins isn't much worth winning. The Keaton women are literary personages; they have names such as Annabelle Lee, Mary Jones, Mary Haynes, and Betty King. They provide Buster with a literary motivation: the striving to win them. But they have little apparent value except that Buster wants them. Keaton takes no pains to give them any value, whereas Chaplin's women, metaphors in his symbolic system, do at least smile, reveal tenderness, sensitivity, and charm. In Keaton films, the only reason he seems to care about the lady is that the plot would have it so.

Keaton's denigration of his ladies was conscious: "There were usually but three principals—the villain, myself, and the girl, and she was never important. . . . The leading lady had to be fairly good-looking, and it helped some if she had a little acting ability. As far as I was concerned I didn't insist that she have a sense of humor. There was always the danger that such a girl would laugh at a gag in the middle of a scene, which meant ruining it and having to remake it." Although Lebel thinks that Keaton performs his heroic feats because he has been inspired by a lady, Keaton really accomplishes the heroic because he has to, "because it's there." Keaton's ultimate feeling for his leading ladies comes through in *Go West,* when he uses a cow as the ingenue. Are we to believe that a cow actually spurs Buster's heroic impulses? Not without also seeing Keaton's sense of parody. No wonder no Keaton ingenue made more than two features with him.

The two nastiest Keaton women are the ladies in *The General* (Marian Mack) and *Spite Marriage* (Dorothy Sebastian). In the earlier film, the lady rejects Buster, the man she supposedly loves, for his lack of courage. She, like everyone else in the film, is a victim of false romantic notions. When Buster discovers Annabelle Lee in the Union Army's headquarters, she immediately makes the romantic assumption: Buster has performed all his heroics for her. Ironically, he has only been chasing his train and happened to stumble on her as a surprise bonus.

This romantic bonus almost costs him his train and his life, for Annabelle is incompetent. She runs the train in reverse when it should go forward; she starts it up when it should remain still, and vice versa. She is even incompetent at throwing pieces of wood into the engine's furnace, rejecting a perfectly good one on the aesthetic grounds that it has a hole in it, and thereafter choosing the tiniest, most genteel wood chips she can find.

But she receives poetic justice for her incompetence. Buster dumps her in a burlap sack, hauls her about like a sack of oats or potatoes, and can only imagine her pain when a heavy wooden box gets piled on top of the sack. Although Keaton's strategy is designed to rescue her, it is also designed to be as painful and undignified for her as possible. When Annabelle throws the engine a tiny piece of wood, Buster mimics her. He finds an even tinier chip, daintily hands it to her, and calmly watches as she seriously throws it into the fire. He then drops the dainty pose, grabs her by the neck, and throttles her. But he stops himself—and instantly switches from strangulation to a kiss.

The lady in *Spite Marriage* is the bitchiest of all the Keaton women. She thinks Buster a foolish idiot, but she marries him to spite the man she really loves, who has rejected her. Buster also gives this lady a dose of poetic justice. The sweet thing gets drunk on their wedding night; Buster hauls her—again the woman becomes an inanimate object—out of the nightclub and into their bedroom. Then follows a hilarious ten-minute scene in which Buster tries to hoist her insensible body onto the bed. (For once, Keaton's ingenue is a brilliant physical comedienne.) And once again Buster reduces the lady love to a piece of wood or sack of potatoes. He bounces, belts, lifts, drops, pushes, twists, hurls, and prods this human bundle.[4]

If Buster's ultimate rewards are questionable, the feats that he performs similarly undermine the moral homilies, "The race goes to the swiftest," "If at first you don't succeed, try, try again," "Where there's a will there's a way," and all the other pap of American idealism. Buster employs extraordinary human strategy, performs extraordinary physical feats, and enjoys extraordinary amounts of luck. The effort itself, the accomplishment of miracles by a resilient man with a limber body and a limber brain, is far more important to Keaton than the winnings. Exertion, expenditure of energy, magnificent human effort are more valuable than their result. For what comes afterward is middle age, old age, and the graveyard. In philosophy as well as comic method Keaton emphasizes action, not its consequences.

The most "serious" element in the Keaton films is this assertion of human potential, which in turn implies the imaginative potential of the Keaton mind. As in the Chaplin films, the man who conceives the comic situations and gags is closely related to the man who performs them. The same qualities that produce a character who can outwit the Union Army, outslug a gang of mobsters, outsmart a tornado, or outrace an entire police force also produce the situations, the stories, the business, and the machines that the character plays in, with, and against. Keaton's creative ideas as a director, his inventive stunts, parallel his ideas as clown; although many comic films copied Keaton's gags, they were never so powerful or unique as Keaton's, simply because in conception as well as execution they lacked the Keaton mind, the unique Keaton view of the human mechanism—as mechanism.

The gags themselves are, of course, brilliant. In *Convict 13* (1920), Buster walks to the gallows; Keaton's close-up shows the three strands of string that will send the prisoner to his death when severed (another parody of *Intolerance*). Meanwhile Buster's fellow prisoners sit in a grandstand watching the execution; a vendor circulates among them selling peanuts. Who else but Keaton would have the audacity to turn death into a ball game? Who else could also make the idea funny? And Keaton does not let

---

4. That great sequence, from a rarely seen film, was so dear to Keaton's heart that he and his wife, Eleanor, performed it in Paris at the Medrano Circus in the mid-1950s.

the parallel simply hang there but tops it. As the razors slice the strings, the trapdoor opens beneath Keaton's feet, and he falls through with the drop that should break his neck. The gallows rope, however, is a rubber band, and Buster bobs up unharmed, like a jumping jack. The folks in the grandstand boo—as they would an umpire who has made a bad call or a shortstop who has made an error.

In *The Playhouse* (1921), two Civil War veterans go to see a show; one lacks a right arm, the other a left. In order to applaud an act, the two veterans must agree on who is worth a meeting of their remaining hands. Sometimes they agree; if not, one one-handed man sadistically keeps from his friend the means to applaud an act he liked. In that same film, Buster impersonates a vaudeville ape (perhaps modeled on "Peter the Great," a very intelligent ape that played on the bill with Keaton in London). Buster's imitation of a real ape is perfect—facial expressions, mannerisms, stance, posture, gestures, movements. Who else but Keaton could do it? Or would?

But great as the gags are, the best Keaton films do not rely on them alone. Although the short Keaton films are compounds of these individual, inventive gags, the Keaton features assimilate them into unified and coherent plots. Perhaps the late two-reeler *Cops* (1922) points the way most clearly toward the features. The film is tightly unified: one man gets into more and more trouble with more and more cops. The film's first shot foreshadows the action by making us think that Buster is behind bars; later a far shot reveals he is really talking to his girl from behind an impressive iron gate. Working with this suggestion, the film steadily puts Buster closer to actual prison bars. He mistakenly finds the wallet of a cop, who thinks Buster has stolen it. While trying to make an honest living as a furniture mover, he mistakenly loses a cop's furniture. He mistakenly punches a traffic cop in the face. And his biggest mistake is hurling an anarchist's bomb into the midst of a policeman's parade. Each of the mistakes is the result of circumstance; his intentions are always honest and sensible. These mistakes culminate in the precinct house. Although Buster successfully avoids the thousands of cops who have swarmed into that house after him, he walks back inside when his girl rejects him. Now Buster finally gets his bars and stripes for real.

To sustain a comedy longer than two reels, Keaton realized he needed to pay attention to plot; not a series of inventive gags, but Buster's exploits (of course loaded with gags) drive the longer works. Keaton films never used any other performer who was so interesting as Buster. (The two who came closest were "Big Joe" Roberts, in the shorts and early features, and little Snitz Edwards, in *Seven Chances, Battling Butler,* and *College.*) Buster and his individual deeds took on a new importance: "I realized that my feature comedies would succeed best when the audience took the plot seriously enough to root for me as I indomitably worked my way out of mounting perils.'' Keaton's most successful films are those with the strongest plots, with ''mounting'' rhythms, mounting troubles, and an irresistible, ''indomitable'' drive toward the climax. Unlike Chaplin's films, Keaton's rely on drive, suspense, story, increasing complexity, and tension.[5]

The weaker Keaton features have great moments but weak structures from a lack of rhythmic drive. *The Three Ages,* his first feature, is more like three two-reelers than a single film. Its anachronistic gags are delightful, but it substitutes a schematic symmetry for story. *College* also is too insistent on symmetry; there are obligatory (and rather predictable) attempts by Buster to run the dash, hurl the discus, broad-jump, pole-vault, and so on, just so he can perform all the same feats in the film's climax. *The Cameraman* also seems predictable and schematic, too pat in its difficulties and their solution. *The Navigator* seems perfect Keaton up to the repair sequence and the battle with the savages, which stretch the film for gags and a climax. *Go West* also wanders about the plains rather than driving in that straight Keaton line. Again, the film's parodic premise (what other cowboy fell in love with a cow?) often obstructs its narrative drive.

But *Our Hospitality* is a driving straight line (after the prologue establishing the melodramatic milieu), from the effete Buster on a wooden bicycle in the ''Big City'' (ironically a cow town at the time) to Buster avoiding death from the old feud, to Buster saving the feuder's daughter herself from death. *Sherlock Jr.* drives irresistibly from Buster's being falsely accused of theft, to his illusionary heroism as he imagines performing exploits on screen, to his discovery of the real thief, to his use of the movie screen to show him how to end his own movie now that his girl stands in his projection booth. If the real plot of *Sherlock Jr.* is sketchier and more predictable than it might be, its imaginary ''movie'' plot makes

5. The importance of excitement and suspense to the Keaton comedy might well seem to contradict one of the preliminary assertions that suspense and the comic climate are mutually exclusive. But as with Chaplin's uses of empathy and pathos, Keaton's use of suspense is subordinate to his overall comic aims—as well as a warning about overly rigid and inflexible definitions. Keaton's work is very close to melodrama—not only his parodies of melodrama such as *Our Hospitality,* but his use of the suspenseful rhythms of melodrama in films such as *The General* and *Spite Marriage.* But the primary difference from melodrama is indeed that Keaton uses its *rhythms* but not its probabilities—that is, he uses ludicrous characters, far-fetched gags, incredible events, situations, and twists. Mack Sennett demonstrated the closeness of the rhythms of the comic chase and the suspenseful ''race for life.'' It is that rhythm which drives the stronger Keaton films.

up in energy, breathlessness, and dazzling surprise for any thinness in the projectionist's story.

*The General* drives from Johnny's rejection for military service to his pragmatic chase after his locomotive; to his heroic return with his girl, his locomotive, and a warning to his comrades; to his induction as an officer in the Confederate Army for his bravery. Interestingly, *The General* is as symmetrical as *Three Ages* or *College*. The four parts of the film—refusal for induction in the Army, chasing the Northern train robbers, being chased by the Northern Army, induction into the Army—mirror each other. The difficulties Keaton encounters on his trip north—wooden obstacles on the tracks, a loose car as obstacle, diverting the train to a side track—are repeated identically in the return trip south. But the driving structure of *The General* assimilates symmetry as an aid to narrative unity, rather than emphasizing symmetry at unity's expense. Similarly, the symmetry of *Seven Chances*—all those sevens—is absorbed by the film's driving structure rather than slowing down that structure with obligatory patterning. *Steamboat Bill Jr.* and *Spite Marriage* (an overlooked and curiously neglected delight) also drive relentlessly from Buster's effete inadequacy to his climactic success.

A driving, "indomitable" narrative line; outrageously inventive physical gags that serve both the narrative and character; a tiny human figure with an amazingly agile, acrobatic body and a constantly alert, strategic brain; vast panoramas, clever parody, melodrama, romance, costumes, elegance, grace; camera tricks and visual surprises—these are the elements that fuse to form the Keaton comic world.

# Akira Kurosawa

AKIRA KUROSAWA was born in Tokyo in 1910, the son of a former soldier who had become a physical education teacher. After high school graduation he decided to become a painter, began to study Western painting, and later joined a Marxist discussion group in which he especially enjoyed the conversations about nineteenth-century Russian literature. In 1936, he answered an advertisement and got a job as an assistant director at Toho studios, where he worked with Kajiro Yamamoto, writing innumerable scripts and learning his trade.

Kurosawa's first film as a director, Sanshiro Sugata (1943), the story of a young man who becomes a judo expert, already embodies his characteristic mingling of the physical and spiritual in his themes and methods. Kurosawa's use of the wipe—almost a signature device—his interest in the patterns of nature, and his fascination with the moral conflicts of action, are also present from the first. In the next seven years Kurosawa made ten more films that established his reputation in Japan before Rashomon (1950) brought him to international attention. These films, like his later work, can be divided between epics of the past and almost neo-realist observations of contemporary Japanese life—on the one hand patterned and stylized explorations of the theatrical side of film and on the other more loosely told urban stories. Especially notable are They Who Step on the Tiger's Tail (1945), an adaptation of a Kabuki play; Drunken Angel (1948), his first film with Toshiro Mifune, the actor who was to become his habitual star; and Stray Dog (1949), a detective story in the manner of the French novelist, Georges Simenon, whom Kurosawa admires.

With Rashomon began the great period of Kurosawa's career. His films are equally powerful whether they are original scripts of adaptations, whether set in the mythic samurai past or in the gloomy present. In the civil servant of Ikiru (1952) as much as in the samurai of Seven Samurai (1954), Kurosawa explores the different ways individuals try to give value to their lives. Like many of the neo-realists, Kurosawa is fascinated by individuals who feel outside their society even as they attempt to preserve values that society has either lost or corrupted. Kurosawa pursues these themes in both "high and low" aesthetic forms. (High and Low is the title of a 1963 Kurosawa crime film starring Mifune.) His adaptations of works by such acknowledged great writers as Dostoevsky (The Idiot, 1951), Gorki (The Lower Depths, 1957), and Shakespeare (Throne of Blood, 1957, based on Macbeth) are no more serious or less personal than his samurai films, which are the Japanese equivalent of our American Westerns, from which they spring in part and which they help us to understand.

These varieties of form are not inconsistent for Kurosawa, since they deal equally with the isolated and the disenfranchised, whose sense of personal pride can be expressed only in passion and movement. His later

*films include two part-comic, part-serious send-ups of samurai stories,
Yojimbo (1961) and Sanjuro (1962), and two detective stories in modern
settings, The Bad Sleep Well (1960) and High and Low—all starring
Mifune.*

*Kurosawa often works with several cameras at once to capture an im-
mediacy of feeling and movement, even within plots or stories whose pattern is stylized. His feel for the uncertainties of nature complements his
understanding of the necessary artificiality of social form. With two recent
films, Red Beard (1965) and Dodeska-den (1970), he may be struggling
to find a new form. The contained power of his films in the 1950s and
early 1960s, the samurai moral bravado and the contemporary anguish,
seem to have collided irretrievably. Red Beard, the story of a young man
who becomes a doctor in nineteenth-century Japan, may preserve some
of the optimism of Kurosawa's other films about the process of education.
But Dodeska-den, a series of contemporary episodes set in a Tokyo shanty-
town, mixes realism and theater to imply that the only reality, embodied
in the character of the schizophrenic boy who believes he is a streetcar
conductor, is that created by the individual himself. This is a view of the
creative imagination strikingly opposed to that of Fellini: the insane and
the idiot set off against the con man and the clown.*

*In 1971 Kurosawa attempted suicide, was hospitalized, and recovered
to make a film with Soviet co-production titled Dersu Uzala (1975)—a
work remarkable for its stirring simplicity and visual beauty.*

*Presently available are film scripts for Rashomon (1969), Ikiru (1969), and Seven
Samurai (1970). The career has been treated in thorough and acute detail by
Donald Richie in The Films of Akira Kurosawa (1970); Richie and Joseph L.
Anderson place it in the context of the history of Japanese moviemaking in The
Japanese Film: Art and Industry (1959); likewise helpful are Joan Mellen's Voices
from the Japanese Cinema (1975), and The Waves at Genji's Door (1976).*

# Kurosawa's Camera and Style

## Donald Richie

### Camera

Kurosawa once said: "When I finally photograph something, it is merely to get something to edit," and among the elements of film-making it is the actual shooting which seems to command less interest, though not less labor nor less concern.

"Before I decide how to photograph something, I first of all think about how to improve whatever it is I'm photographing. When that is done, then I think how it can best be photographed, from what angle, etc. And each technique I use necessarily differs according to whatever it is I'm taking a picture of." In order to capture the desired image, "I explain what I want in detail, not only to the cameraman but also to all other members of the staff. We all work together to get what I want—but whether I get it or not, that is my own responsibility." Kurosawa has never used a production designer. "It is always I who frame the shot, who design the movement—though I usually also take the advice of anyone who happens to have a better idea than I do."

Kurosawa's first and most important criterion for photographing is the apparent actuality of whatever is going to be photographed. He has been known to halt production because his long distance lenses picked up nail heads in a period-film set construction. Once he tore down an entire open set because the roof did not look real enough. Whole weeks were spent in ageing the large *Red Beard* set, including the pouring of fifty years worth of tea into the cups to be used, thus properly staining them.

The search for apparent actuality goes to extremes. In *Yojimbo*, Mifune practices impaling flying leaves with his knife, and Kurosawa got someone skilled enough to do just that. In *The Hidden Fortress*, the escaping party are shot at by soldiers and dodge behind tree trunks just in time,

From *The Films of Akira Kurosawa* by Donald Richie. Published in 1965 by The Regents of the University of California. Reprinted by permission of the University of California Press. The title "Kurosawa's Camera and Style" has been provided by the Editors.

the bullets tearing at the bark. Kurosawa originally wanted the gunners to shoot at the actors—just missing them—but this proved too dangerous. He resorted to the method of (1) photographing the actors dodging behind the trunk, (2) allowing them to retire, but not moving camera position, (3) photographing the bullets raking the logs, (4) bringing back the actors, starting the camera, having them dash for the safety of the next log, etc.

At the spectacular conclusion of *The Throne of Blood,* however, such makeshift was not enough. He wanted arrows shot at Mifune. First he tried the two standard methods: (1) trick arrows planted in place spring up at the proper moment, (2) arrows already planted are pulled out with wire, the whole scene photographed backwards. This did not satisfy Kurosawa and so, after a conference with Mifune, he stationed real archers just out of camera range (about ten feet from the actor) and had them shoot real arrows, full force, point blank. The scene was carefully rehearsed with chalk marks on the floor for Mifune to follow and was then photographed. Some of the arrows were designed to miss the moving Mifune by an inch, and missed by just that much.

After the object to be photographed has thus been "improved" and made more real, Kurosawa is ready to decide how to photograph it. Though he accomplishes this in various ways, his considerations are usually: to do it in such a way that the meaning of the shot is enhanced, and/or in such a way that economy of action is created, and/or in such a way that the composition itself comments on the scene.

If the meaning of the shot is "flight" or "chase," Kurosawa usually uses a dolly, believing that a fast scene should be shot "fast" with lots of trucking shots cut together. On the other hand a "slow" scene (for example, Mifune's change-of-mind scene in *The Bad Sleep Well*) is often shot in one long take with no cuts at all.

If the scene is about "suspense," then Kurosawa will often use a pan (for example, the scene in *Stray Dog* where we think that Shimura's house is the home of a criminal, and then the camera pans to show us his happy family). If the scene is about "discovery," then he usually first shows the reaction (the faces of the cops in *High and Low*) and then cut or dolly or pan to the object (the dead bodies which they discover).

This is by no means invariable and, in any event, is part of the equipment of most directors. The incisive way in which these techniques are used is very Kurosawa-like, however, as are the additions. One such would be the very fast dollies of the forest scenes from *The Throne of Blood,* where the foreground is continually obscured by bushes, tree trunks, vines, etc., which alternately hide and expose the horsemen. The reason was that "I wanted to produce in the audience the same feeling that the characters have of being trapped." Very often, also, he will combine various techniques to create a new effect, and examples of this have been noticed in the discussions of *Drunken Angel, Ikiru, Seven Samurai,* and others.

Kurosawa is also interested in economy of action and sometimes will use a single prop of some kind to obtain it. This prop may be as large as the single room in *The Lower Depths,* a great cage in which the camera may roam, or it may be as small as the electric fan in certain scenes of *Record of a Living Being,* or the low table with the saké bottle in *Red Beard,* around which the camera set-ups are chosen.

There is a fine example of the use of a small prop in *One Wonderful Sunday.* The boy and girl eat their cookies in a vacant lot in which a very large section of concrete sewer pipe stands. They rest against it, they lean over it, she climbs into it—all in the most naturalistic way. At the same time the camera sees the pipe as a piece of sculpture. Details of it, different ways of seeing it, different set-ups emphasizing different parts of it—all hold the dialogue scenes together, create an economy of action. A more subtle example is the hay rack in *Sanjuro.* The scene is the barn with the two rescued ladies and the boy samurai. First the camera is beside it, then in back of it, then under it—each of the many cuts containing a different portion of the rack itself, this visible structure, visibly holding these scenes together.

Sometimes economy is achieved by having multiple actions occur within the frame of a single scene. In *Scandal,* for example, the upper half of the screen shows the unwitting couple in their hotel window; the lower half has the photographers taking the incriminating photo. In the courtyard scene in *Red Beard,* the talking children are in the upper left hand frame; the listening adults are in the lower right. Here, the composition of the scene comments directly upon the action by explicating it. Usually, Kurosawa's compositions are more subtle.

In both *Quiet Duel* and *The Bad Sleep Well* a wall is used in the center of frame—separating the lovers. In the second part of *Sugata* a standing pillar splits the screen with the priest (*satori* achieved) on one side, and Sugata (*satori* not yet achieved) on the other. In *Red Beard* a tree separates the girl who says she does not trust men from the young man who says he does not trust women.

A favorite Kurosawa composition has two or more people carrying on a conversation while facing different directions. *Yojimbo* is full of this; it is used to give the feeling of danger—both directions must be watched at once because the enemy is all around. Occasionally this composition is used (as it is in Antonioni's films) to indicate the difficulty of communication. In *The Quiet Duel,* when Mifune is trying to explain to Shimura, they face in opposite directions. Richer and more complicated are those compositions which insist not only upon the actors facing in different directions but also various diagonals; the most famous example is the outdoor scene in *The Lower Depths*.

Kurosawa also uses other attributes of the camera to make his point. He has used slow motion a number of times—two examples occur in *Seven Samurai*, the death of the madman at the beginning of the picture, and the death of the blustering samurai during the first fight with the swordsman. Again, slow motion is used for the advance of the forest in *The Throne of Blood*, and fast motion is used for Mifune's fall down the stairs at the end of that film.

The special attributes of long-distance lenses are also used: to pile up images of night-time Yokohama at the end of *High and Low;* to throw images at the audience, as in the horse fall in *Seven Samurai;* for humor, as when one of the bad men in *Yojimbo* carries Mifune in a tub and the lenses makes his fat legs fatter, and his breathless trot appears to get him nowhere at all.

Kurosawa will occasionally "stop the camera" by reprinting the same frame over and over again as in the montage sequence in *The Bad Sleep Well*. Or, he "stops" the actors and presents an actual but motionless scene (as in the end of the prize fight in the second part of *Sugata*). Or, he will use still photographs both as nostalgic evocation (*The Quiet Duel, Record of a Living Being, Ikiru*), and because (as in *The Bad Sleep Well* and *High and Low*) a presented photograph in a film looks "realer than real."

Kurosawa, oddly, has never availed himself of color (except for the short scene in *High and Low*), and his reason, as one might expect, is that it is not "real" enough. "Color film isn't good enough to take Japanese colors... at present the degree of color transparency is too high. Japan's colors are all dull colors, dense colors, and if I did a color film I would want to bring this out. The film that got the prize... *The Gate of Hell*—those colors were exotic, not Japanese."[1]

Kurosawa continually emphasizes texture, however, and this concern with texture is one of the things which gives the "Kurosawa look." To remember any of his films is, in part, to remember a texture: the sun-drenched whites and light grays of *Rashomon*, the coarse grain of *Record of a Living Being*, the blacks and dark grays of *Yojimbo*. In *The Bad Sleep Well*, one remembers the texture of brocade (the wife's kimono) against polished wood and, eventually, raw concrete; in *Throne of Blood*, pale white skin, dense white fog, the black texture of earth, the glint of black armor; in *Red Beard* it is the mellowed sheen of old wood, the sunlit textures of human skin.

1. Since this was written, Kurosawa has made two films in color, *Dodeska-den* (1970) and *Dersu Uzala* (1975).—EDS.

As we have seen in the discussion of *Rashomon,* Kurosawa's use of cinematic punctuation is entirely his own. He has found the wipe ideal for a change of scene that needs more than a cut; the fade is used only when a softening is desired; the dissolve usually means a great amount of time has past (except in the dissolves at the end of *Rashomon* and those in *They Who Step on the Tiger's Tail* where dissolves are used to show Benkei getting more and more drunk). The simple cut is most useful to him within the sequence itself. Punctuation is not a matter of deciding and letting the laboratory do the work. It is often in the script from the very first and is considered an integral part of the camera work of the picture.

Once all of the above has been more or less decided, Kurosawa is ready to shoot. He does so with at least three cameras shooting simultaneously, though this is by no means an invariable rule: many scenes in *Red Beard* used only one; the train sequence in *High and Low* used nine. The cameras themselves are kept as light as possible. "They have to be," Takao Saito, one of his cameramen, has said. "The ordinary director, if he doesn't like the scene, moves the actors around, but Kurosawa moves the cameras. Ordinarily, the director sits next to the camera, but Kurosawa is always moving in and out among his two or three. He must walk about four times as much as other directors."

Another cameraman, Fukuzo Koizumi, has said: "Nowadays, he more and more goes in for long shots, three or more minutes, and lets the actors play naturally, and out of this he selects the best shots. Often the cameras will have long focal-length lenses on them, one 350 mm. and the other 500 mm. [The standard is 50 to 75 mm.] What he really wants to get is the best possible shot." This search accounts, as we have seen in the discussion of *Record of a Living Being,* for the usual shooting ratio in the Kurosawa picture, which is 20 to 1 (i.e., one foot of film used for every twenty exposed)—a high ratio, about as high as Antonioni's, but by no means extravagant; certain TV films have been made at the ratio of 500 to 1.

Kurosawa's method of shooting causes lighting problems. Set and actors must be properly illuminated not for one camera viewpoint, but for three. In addition, telephoto lenses need more light than ordinary lenses. Ichiro Inohara, who usually lights the Kurosawa picture, has said: "We had to devise a special new tool—we call it the *yokan* reflector. Ordinarily, for outdoor daytime shooting we use silver paper-covered boards but this did not bounce light nearly far enough. Using long-distance lenses, we had to somehow light people three or four times further away than usual. Then we found that fine crinkled silver paper that *yokan* [Japanese bean-paste candy] comes in worked and so we use it.

"Kurosawa works on the principle that 'everything seen on the screen is of equal importance' and this means that the camera must be stopped way down. We have to shoot at, say, f. 22 on an ordinary f. 4.5 scene. This means that even our day scenes need more light than most director's night scenes.''

The director's feelings about "the best possible shot" extends even to the posters for his films, even to his stills. Masao Soeda, his still-man since *Drunken Angel,* has said: "The Kurosawa group never poses for stills. Instead, the still man, staying near the camera, carrying all kinds of cameras himself, must shoot the moving actors from the same angle that they will later be viewed on the screen. If you miss your chance just once, you rarely have the opportunity to take it over again. It is rather like being a newspaper cameraman. After everything is finished, Kurosawa looks through these hundreds of negatives and throws out all those he doesn't like.

"He doesn't know the meaning of the word 'compromise' and his search for the perfect extends all the way from the performances to my stills. This, of course, makes an endless succession of struggles and diffi-culties for his staff but, on the other hand, it opens up for all of us a whole world of creativity.

"He scolds, it is true, but we know he loves us. We really are his children in a way. There is a Japanese proverb: 'If you stand, you walk.' This is true. He makes us stand up to creativity, and he makes his own will ours. We walk. I don't want to give the idea that we idolize him, but, really, his strength is such that not one of us can but feel that terrifying charm which is truly his.''

### Style

A man's style is what that man himself is, and throughout this book we have seen what Kurosawa is through what he has done. One cannot become more intimate than that. Yet, there is always a difference between what a man does and what he looks like and acts like, and in Kurosawa this difference is so extreme that even now he remains a "mystery" to those who look for profiles, for personal "close-ups," for "the man" himself. I remember that *The New York Times Magazine* once commissioned me to do a profile on Kurosawa. I did not one but three, each one different though similar, and each one was rejected because my subject was "not in focus," because the "idea" of Kurosawa did not emerge clearly enough, because I could not capture his essence in ten pages. Most of this inability was due to my lack of skill, but some of it was because Kurosawa is an extraordinarily complicated person. Generalizations no more fit him than they do his films. The only way to understand Kurosawa is to understand his pictures.

He is not at all interested in anyone's understanding him as a person.

He has a happy home life with two charming children and a gracious wife; he has his friends and drinking companions; he has his relationships with the producers and the studio—this is quite enough personal understanding for him. Consequently he is not helpful in the slightest to anyone wanting to find out more about him than his films have already offered.

Personal observation does not add much. He is tall, very tall for a Japanese, and his face, like that of many sensitive men, centers around his nose. Flanked by large, generous ears, supported by a full, sensuous mouth, this nose—Kyoto-looking, traditionally aristocratic—indicates a sensitivity which is not suggested by the tall, lanky body, the big, capable, workmanlike hands.

Like many creators, he is not of a piece. He has a divided look: the face of a mystic, the body of a carpenter. Standing in the set, wearing the cap which is his single personal affectation, amid the ordinary furor and occasional chaos of movie-making, he is calm, patient, ruminative, sometimes softly smiling, or quietly indicating how it should be done—the personification of intellect.

One might ascribe this to Oriental impassivity, were there any such thing. Rather, it is the knowing tranquility of a man under control. He already knows what he is going to do, and he knows how to do it. At the same time, however, his hands are always busy.

He plays with his hands; rather, it is as though they play with each other, expressing themselves rather than him. While he watches, friendly and impassive, his fingers are always busy with something or other, searching out something manual, something to do. When he directs, his hands are continually moving; hands which look as though they should be kneading clay or planing a board, creating gestures which cannot help but be plastic. Kurosawa literally shapes his film from the empty air. And when a lighter refuses to light, or a ball-point pen to write, these hands with the patience of Red Beard himself will click the one and manipulate the other until it decides to.

Kurosawa's divided aspect is indicative of him as a person. He is a craftsman who works with ideas. One could carry the dichotomy further and introduce the heart-head schism. The former would then be concerned with "humanism" and Dostoevsky and would produce films such as *One Wonderful Sunday;* the latter would be all intellect and craft and create a film like *The Throne of Blood;* somehow the two would occasionally come together and the result would be *Ikiru.*

Such a simplification is not untrue but it leaves most of Kurosawa unaccounted for because, like most highly organized and complicated men, he is not accountable. Nor does he attempt to account for himself. "I am a director . . . that is all. I know myself well enough to know that if I ever lost my passion for films, then I myself would be lost. Film is what I am about.''

About how he became what he is, he says: "I don't know— influences, I guess. From the very beginning I respected John Ford. I have always paid close attention to his films and they've influenced me, I think. I finally got to meet him. It was in a London hotel and I was having a quiet glass of wine. He came over and said: 'Hey, Akira!'—bought a bottle of scotch and poured us out really stiff drinks. He'd remembered me from when he came here after the war with a group of Occupation people. In London he was very nice to me, sent me chrysanthemums [Japan's national flower] and treated me just like his own son. I like him—he is so mature, and besides that he looks just like one of the cavalry generals in his own pictures.

"Other influences . . . well, the first film that really impressed me was *La roue* of Gance, and the pictures of Howard Hawks and George Stevens which I saw when I was young. [Elsewhere he has also mentioned Frank Capra and William Wyler as "favorites."] And Antonioni. He's not influenced me but he is a very interesting director. . . . And, of course, Mizoguchi—of all Japanese directors I like him the best.''

He is not so approving of Japanese films in general. "My liking Mizoguchi, it might be nostalgia—after all I *am* Japanese . . . and he creates a world which is purely Japanese . . . and he really cares about people. So do I. That's the thing about most Japanese films, they don't care anything about people. Then they go and call it artless simplicity or something and terribly Japanese. Well, that certainly isn't my way. People abroad seem to like Japanese films right now, but I wouldn't count on it. Most Japanese pictures lack any real depth at all. Even programmers from abroad have depths which we don't approach. All Japanese culture has this thinness.

"I hear a lot about foreigners being able to understand my pictures so well, but I certainly never thought of them when I was making the films. Perhaps it is because I am making films for today's young Japanese that I should find a Western-looking format the most practical. In order for them to understand I have to translate, as it were. *Seven Samurai*, for example. Under Mifune's scenes I had Hayasaka put in a mambo. If purely Japanese music had been used I don't think the young people would have felt what the character was like, how much he resembled them. I really only make pictures for people in their twenties. They don't know anything about Japan or Japaneseness, not really. Oh, they will in time, but not now. Oh, I'm Japanese all right. I'm truly Japanese.''

He is right. And despite the fact that he has become a director of international status, that the Japanese critics are always calling him "Western''; despite the fact that we of the West see his films without once remembering that the people are something so strange as "Japanese," one of the ways to define Kurosawa's style would be to insist upon this Japaneseness.

Kurosawa comes from samurai stock, his father was one of the last of the old military educators. Whatever part heredity and environment may have played, Kurosawa himself embodies a number of these earlier qualities. In particular, in him is seen in a very pure form, that old-fashioned virtue of compassionate steadfastness, complete moral honesty, inability to compromise, and action through belief—all of which come under that single much maligned term: *bushido*.

Nowadays all one sees of it is in the *chambara* or the Kabuki, and in a very debased form indeed. It usually has to do with obligation, personal honor, self-sacrifice, and other uninteresting attributes. Originally, however, it was a code of ethics, based in part on zen teachings, which in its finest form became a philosophy, part of which might be paraphrased (from one of the original teachings) as "if your mind is clean, orderly; likewise will your environment be clean, orderly."

The follower of *bushido* could not blame environment for any lapse. He had to take full responsibility for wherever he was and for those with whom he was. Their state commented directly upon his own. He was the center of his universe and if it was less than habitable then this was his own doing. Consequently early *bushido* had much to do with spiritual enlightenment, with an acute sensitivity to things as they are, and was of an innate practicality.

Another maxim of the time was: "Face both man and nature and learn." Thus the man adhering to *bushido* was a continual student in the face of the world and his test lay never in what he planned or thought but in what he did. If the *chambara* now has a large stock of heroes, it is because most heroes believe that a man is solely and entirely what he does. Consequently, the samurai who understood *bushido* was no sword-slinger. Action is far too precious to waste. Further, any action which could not in some way be corrected (a way of fighting, a way of thinking) was valueless. The reason was not, as might be thought, that perfection ought to be attained; rather, it was that *bushido* as a philosophy insisted upon the fact that perfection was not only impossible, it was also a chimera and a dangerous one at that. *Bushido* leads nowhere, that is, it has no goal. It is just what the name implies, a way—a way of living, a process rather than a state. Anyone who thinks himself past correction is a fraud because it means he thinks of himself as an end result, an accomplished thing. This is impossible. *Bushido* did not lead to a perfected better life. It was, instead, a way of living. Further, it could therefore only be expressed through action, and the most profound of the samurai maxims was: "To know and to act are one and the same."

The application of *bushido* tenets to the films of Kurosawa is obvious. His heroes are always completely human in that they are corrigible. The Kurosawa fable shows that it is difficult indeed "to know"; but at the end of the picture the hero has come to learn that "to know and to act are one and the same." The Kurosawa villain is the man who thinks he knows, who thinks he is complete.

Since the similarities between Kurosawa's heroes and Kurosawa himself are many, one may observe the old-fashioned virtues of *bushido* in the director himself—which is just what we have done throughout this book. With his ascetic face, his swordsman's hands, Kurosawa might be thought of as the last of the samurai.

In contemporary Japan this quality is completely debased and a part of the fury of the critics, to whom (in Japan more than elsewhere) compromise is a way of life, might be caused by Kurosawa's commitment to these older virtues. At the same time, certainly, part of the success of *Seven Samurai, Yojimbo,* and *Sanjuro* with the Japanese audience is that they present this ethic at a time when it is almost forgotten, yet still retains its part—however small—in the national character. When Kurosawa says he makes his films for the young people, he also says that he is bringing back to them a spiritual heritage which was once theirs. Like all creators, Kurosawa is a moralist; like all stylists, he manages to hide the fact superlatively well.

Thus, though seeming to create infinite variety, there is, at the same time a unity, a completely responsible and ultimately serious attitude toward life which makes his films, despite their seeming differences, all of a piece. And this totality is the totality of the man.

The basis of the Kurosawa style, as we have seen again and again, . . . is a search for reality and an inability to tolerate illusion. The Kurosawa character, like that of its creator, is possessed by a need to know things as they are, to know life as it is—though both necessarily include suffering, since suffering is one of the ways through which one recognizes existence. Reality is, therefore, for Kurosawa, a very different thing from what usually passes for it.

"There are people," he has said, "who criticize my work . . . and say it is not realistic. But I feel that merely copying the outward appearance of the world would not result in anything real—that is only copying. I think that to find what is real one must look very closely at one's world, to search for those things which contribute to this reality which one feels under the surface. These are few and one uses them to create. These are the core around which the world moves, the axis on which it turns. The novels of

Dostoevsky, Tolstoy, and Turgenev show us what these things are. To be an artist means to search for, find, and look at these things; to be an artist means never to avert one's eyes.''

[In the films of Kurosawa one finds that these things include an awareness of oneself and an awareness of the world, and an awareness of the fact that the world and the self do not, cannot match. "I suppose all my films have a common theme. If I think about it though, the only theme I can think of is really a question: Why can't people be happier together?" To ask that question is to answer it—which is what Kurosawa has done in every one of his major films. They cannot be happy because they are people, *because* they are human.

[Kurosawa is a philosopher who works with film, and who affirms that in this weakness lies the essentially human quality. But, though weak, man can hope and through this he can prevail. Samurai and robbers may be revealed as one and the same but there are always the villagers who, after the great deeds are done, will plant the new rice with hope and confidence. Man must fight to retain hope in the midst of this hopeless world and in this fight all men are brothers.]

This is the central thesis of Kurosawa's films, most of which show the progress from despair to hope, and this is one of the reasons his films are so meaningful to the world. This thesis is also personal to the director, is an expression of himself as a man. "The director," he has said, "really always makes his film for himself . . . if he says he makes it for the public, he is really lying. If the film is liked by the public and seems made for them, this is because their ideas are the same as the director's and not the other way around. He cannot make a picture different from his own ideas, from his own emotions—that is, he cannot make it and be honest about it. It is impossible for him to make a film below his own level; impossible that he make a picture which caters to public taste. Whatever level a picture is made on, that is the director's own philosophic, intellectual, emotional, artistic level.''

# Kurosawa and His Work

## Akira Iwasaki

Akira Kurosawa has already been at work on his latest film, *Akahige (Redbeard),* for more than a year. Even allowing for a break occasioned by brief illness, this is unusually long for the making of a Japanese film, and the reason lies, above all, in the perfectionism which characterizes all Kurosawa's creative activity. For instance, on a site close to the Toho studios, he has had his architect build for him an exact replica of a charity hospital of the late Tokugawa Period, an old-style, one-storied building with a tiled roof. Not only is this structure faithful to the contemporary plans, but anybody willing to forego various modern comforts could actually live in it for months on end.

The film takes place in the period when Western medicine was first transplanted to Japan and began to take root. Those young medical students of the day who were dissatisfied with the traditional Oriental medicine imported from China many centuries previously would make their way to the port of Nagasaki, the only point of contact with Western culture in a Japan officially isolated from the rest of the world. There they would study for several years and, on their return to Edo, apply their knowledge of the most up-to-date medical treatment for the benefit of the common people. The hero of the film, the head of a charity hospital, known by the nickname of Redbeard, is such a man. He himself has been to study at Nagasaki in his youth, and it is at his hospital that the young Noboru, his at first rebellious but later faithful follower, unpacks his bags on his return from a similar mission. Undoubtedly, Kurosawa's interest was stirred by the prospect of portraying these two humanist scientists who stood at the dawn of Japan's modern age. Yet was there not, perhaps, another, more personal motive behind his choice of such a theme?

While it is Akira Kurosawa who today represents the Japanese art of the film in the eyes of the world, it does not follow that in Japan itself he is

From *Japan Quarterly,* vol. 12, no. 1 (January–March 1965). Translated by John Bester. Reprinted by permission of *Japan Quarterly* and the author.

considered a truly Japanese artist. Not a few Japanese, in fact, would ascribe his world fame precisely to his "non-Japanese" qualities.

In an exchange of letters between Kurosawa and myself, published by a Japanese magazine some time ago, Kurosawa declares:

"I am a man who enjoys Basho and Buson along with Dostoevski, who likes Sotatsu, Gyokudo, and Tessai in the same way as Van Gogh, Lautrec, and Rouault. . . . I collect old Japanese lacquerware as well as antique French and Dutch glassware. In short, the Western and the Japanese live side by side in my mind naturally, without the least sense of conflict."

To a certain extent, any average intellectual in Japan today could confess to being in the same position; the ordinary dilettante, indeed, can perfectly well combine Japan and the West without feeling bothered at all. However, for a creative artist of Kurosawa's caliber it is not such a simple matter. The two things, the Western and the Japanese, certainly do exist alongside in him, but their coexistence is marked by constant conflict and sparring and, when they do make contact and combine with each other, by showers of sparks and the generation of much heat and light. Compared with directors of an earlier generation such as the late Yasujiro Ozu and Mikio Naruse, who are reputed to be the most "Japanese" of all film-makers, and with whom Japan is part of the very fiber of their being, Kurosawa belongs to a more recent generation which must look to the West for help in defining Japan, which verifies and analyzes the one by constant reference to the other.

The very first scenario Kurosawa ever wrote (written while he was still an assistant director, it never reached the screen) was "The German of Dharma Temple," which portrayed the life in Japan of Bruno Taut, the celebrated German architect. The choice of subject bears witness to a constant preoccupation of Kurosawa's, from his youth right up to the present. It was Taut, one of the founders of the Bauhaus, who discovered the plain and simple beauty of the Japanese sense of form to which the Japanese themselves, over-familiar, had become apathetic, and brought it once more into the Japanese consciousness. The process constituted a second rediscovery of Japan by the Japanese; the first was the reawakening prompted by the American art critic Fenollosa at the end of the nineteenth century. Kurosawa, too, as a young art student was much occupied with the question of the precise meaning of "Japanese," and he felt an interest in Taut as pointing the way to an answer. He discovered in Taut an instructive counterpart.

It was via such devious routes as this that the modern Japanese who had experienced fascination and infatuation for Western civilization had to hunt after, or find his way back to, the truly "Japanese." In this sense,

"The German of Dharma Temple," though no more than a study, represents something essential in Kurosawa; it was an attempt by the youthful Kurosawa, using Taut as a medium, to come to terms with his own past. *Sanshiro Sugata* (1943)—his first film, which brought him his first success—tells how the hero, Sanshiro, is ordered by his teacher to spend a whole day and night up to his neck in a lotus pond, as a result of which he grasps the essential secret of judo. The film seeks to embody this surely Japanese idea of a truth to be attained through sudden enlightenment or through rigid self-discipline—an idea, incidentally, which is obviously related to the Zen concepts fashionable at the moment.

In *Red Beard*, Kurosawa's interest is directed toward the confrontation between Japan and the West in the feudal society of a century or so ago, and toward the ways in which the West prodded Japan into motion and Japan, on her side, gradually set about assimilating the West. The fact that the hero is known by the name Red Beard, which was applied to all Westerners at the time, is in itself symbolic. It is true that Red Beard is convinced of the superiority of Western medicine, and is forever studying so as not to be left behind by its constant advances, yet in other respects he is a Japanese through and through. This is demonstrated most clearly of all by the purely Japanese way in which he teaches Noboru, the pupil for whom he feels most affection and on whom he pins most hopes: he gives him not a single word of instruction or advice, but relies solely on silent practice and precept to convey his influence.

*Kumonosu-jo* (*The Throne of Blood,* 1957) is, of course, Kurosawa's version of *Macbeth*. In it, he consciously adopts stylistic elements from the *Noh,* yet this is no mere trick, no feeling of "Well, this is a Shakespeare classic, so let's have a bit of classic *Noh* style to match." Even if it was so at the beginning, in the course of long and careful rehearsals with all his actors—something no other director in Japan does—Kurosawa was led by his fastidious sense of style to the idea of giving the work unity as a Japanese film by the use of motifs from the *Noh.*

In making films, the Japanese are creating art in an imported medium with imported machinery and techniques. Where, then, do they come in as Japanese? Where is the evidence that they are Japanese? This is a question that constantly preoccupies Kurosawa. What makes it more difficult is the fact that the Japanese outlook he must express will not be genuine unless it loves not only Basho and Sotatsu but Van Gogh and Rouault as well. That theme, which first appears in "The German of Dharma Temple," persists through *The Throne of Blood* and right up to *Redbeard*.

It is not possible to discuss *Red Beard* stylistically, since nobody has seen it yet. *The Throne of Blood,* however, was an unprecedented work in that, although its subject matter was regrettably no more than a rehash of

*Macbeth,* stylistically it was an experiment with national and classical styles in the Japanese cinema.

The appeal of this style is that it views Japan through a kind of Western veil. It was for much the same reason that *Rashomon,* which first established Kurosawa as a director of international stature when it took the Grand Prix at the Venice Film Festival, won such praise among Western critics despite the fact that in Japan it was not considered such a great masterpiece—the Japanese critics voted it to fourth or fifth place among the films of that year.

The popular appeal of Kurosawa's films lies first and foremost in their ability to tell a good story. With only one or two exceptions, his films have all been commercial successes. Again in strong contrast with such ''Japanese'' artists as Ozu and Naruse, he is drawn toward everything that is unusual, nonroutine, or abnormal, and he relates these things via techniques that seek constantly to startle.

One day many years ago, a young clerk in a trading company, unknown both to him and the world at large, brought him a scenario to read. As he read, Kurosawa was fascinated by the way each scene presented a challenge to the audience and each sequence had its quota of surprise and suspense. Here, at last, was the ideal type of scenario for him. In this way, Shinobu Hashimoto became Kurosawa's most trusted staff writer, and the scenario in question appeared shortly as the film *Rashomon.*

Nevertheless, unlike a crafty veteran of commercial storytelling such as Alfred Hitchcock, Kurosawa does not attach the ultimate importance to storytelling and clever strokes in the unfolding of the tale. Rather he is concerned with the inner significance of the story.

*Rashomon* is too well known to need much discussion here. In it, Kurosawa sets forth four accounts of a murder which takes place in a bamboo grove, given respectively by a bandit, the samurai who is killed, the samurai's wife who is violated by the bandit, and a woodcutter who witnesses the incident. Through these differing accounts, he seeks to demonstrate the many-sided nature of truth and, at a deeper level, its essential relativity—the nonexistence anywhere of any absolute truth. It was the nihilism and mistrust of humanity apparent in the tale that were to drive the original author, Ryunosuke Akutagawa, to despair and suicide. Unfortunately, they are utterly at variance with the outlook of Kurosawa himself, who is a humanist at heart. So, in the final scene of the film, he cannot resist having second thoughts and making the woodcutter, prompted by the stirrings of conscience, take up an abandoned child with the intention of bringing it up. Thus he gives the final victory to good will and neighborly love, although this ending clearly does violence to the whole philosophy of the film.

The thing which distinguishes Akira Kurosawa from other Japanese directors—I would go so far as to call it his great achievement—is precisely that he is first and foremost a director of ideas. Kurosawa is fond of insisting that every artist has, ultimately, only one theme. In his own case, he says, it is the question of why men cannot live together more happily and with greater good will than they do. Of course, one should be wary of swallowing whole such self-revelations by artists, since the artist is prone to self-delusion and self-misinterpretation in peculiarly complex and involved forms. Nevertheless, Kurosawa's remark can be taken at its face value insofar as it suggests that all his works are born, originally, of an idea. Whereas Japanese film directors in the past have leaned heavily toward naturalism, basing their work on a narrow, personalized experience, Kurosawa's style is intellectual, and his emergence after the war marked the appearance of an utterly unfamiliar element in the Japanese film world.

The fact that his favorite author is Dostoevski is in itself enough to suggest his style. Most of his films have a theme expressible in one line, or even one word: good, evil, happiness, unhappiness, the beauty of love—problems that boil down in essence to the problems of the existence of man, its meaning and its forms. Some of his titles, such as *Ikiru* (*To Live,* 1952) and *Ikimono no Kiroku* (*Record of a Living Being,* 1955), frankly set forth this concern from the very start. In *Donzoko* (*The Lower Depths,* 1957) he sets out again to study the conditions for man's survival in, as it were, a sealed room, and it troubles him very little that his story leans heavily in its outlines on a work by a Western writer, Gorky.

Kurosawa is a research worker who places man in a test tube, provides certain conditions or applies certain stimuli, then waits to see his reaction. His films are the resulting case studies. For example, he unearths an honest workman who finds himself one Sunday morning with only 35 yen in his pocket, in a great city plagued with the inflation and black marketeering of the immediate postwar years. What joys and what sorrows will the day bring him and his sweetheart? This is the experiment that produced *Subarashiki Nichiyobi* (*One Wonderful Sunday,* 1947).

*To Live* is still more frankly a case history: What effect does the news that he has only six months to live have on a man? Will he give himself over in despair to debauchery and dissolute living, or will he try to pass his remaining days as gracefully and meaningfully as he can? Kanji Watanabe, a middle-aged government clerk, is singled out as the hero. Twenty-five years of his life he had spent sitting at a desk in a city hall, mechanically applying his seal to the documents placed before him: the classic type of the "hollow man" who cannot, not for one moment of that time, ever be said to have "lived." One day at the hospital, he is told that he has stomach cancer and is given only three or four months to live. For the first time he becomes conscious of life, and begins to dwell on its significance. In the face of death, the man who for decades has not lived begins to live for the first time. He stops applying his seal mechanically to his official documents, conceives an affection for a girl young enough to be his granddaughter, and devotes every hour of his short remaining life to constructing for her a park no larger than a pocket handkerchief in a corner of the city. The evening of the day on which the park is completed finds him seated on a swing flecked with snow, ready now to meet his end with tranquility. The small flame that has flared momentarily at the end of a small man's life is yet, for all its smallness, a sign that Kanji Watanabe has lived.

If *To Live* is Kurosawa's finest work, *Tengoku to Jigoku* (*High and Low,* 1963) is comparatively confused. He uses the second-rate American mystery on which it is based merely as a springboard for his ideas on and criticisms of the modern age. In form a crime film, it is in that sense a struggle of wits and of wills between detective and criminal, a guessing game played between director and audience. In fact, however, Kurosawa uses this interest as a way of presenting his objections to and mistrust of the contemporary social structure. Here are the pitiless rules of modern capitalism. Here are the extreme material abundance and the absolute poverty that is its reverse face—though Kurosawa, carefully avoiding class references, refers to the contrasting sides of life simply as "heaven" and "hell." Here, too, is a modern Raskolnikov, who, living in the midst of it all yet priding himself on his superhuman wisdom and morality, takes his revenge on the social structure, and, in order to demonstrate the absolute infallibility of his own brain, resorts to murder and extortion. Set against this figure of evil is an honest manufacturer who is forced to give up all his property for the sake of his chauffeur's son, kidnaped by mistake for his own. The question that Kurosawa poses here is how far man is responsible for his neighbor and for the life and safety of others who are human like himself. He goes further and raises the question, Is not a man who is rich *ipso facto* guilty of a kind of original sin?

In *High and Low,* unfortunately, the question does not get across very strongly. Some, possibly correctly, have seen in the film a compromise with commercialism. In the earlier *Warui Yatsu Hodo Yoku Nemuru* (*The Bad Sleep Well,* 1960), however, Kurosawa had dug boldly to the roots of the major evils afflicting modern Japan—graft, bureaucratism, corruption within the political parties, and big-time Capital pulling the strings of government. In *Red Beard,* Kurosawa makes it clear that the enemy confronting both Red Beard himself and Noboru is not simply disease but a political setup which creates poverty and ignorance without the means to remedy them.

Even the characters who appear in Kurosawa's films seem to be internalized, to have passed through the filter of his intellect, and in the actors Toshiro Mifune and Takashi Shimura he has found the ideal vehicles for his ideas. Again and again they appear: the consumptive gangster Matsunaga with an inner loneliness belying outward swagger, and the boozy doctor Sanada who tends him so carefully, cursing him vilely all the while (*Drunken Angel,* 1948); the corrupt lawyer Hiruta who will stoop to any infamy in order to get money for the treatment of the consumptive daughter whom he worships (*Scandal,* 1950); Nakajima, the old man who in his opposition to nuclear tests—"Dying is one thing, but I'm damned if I'll be killed"—proposes to abandon family and wealth and go to live on the other side of the globe, and who ends up in a room in a lunatic asylum, pointing to the sunset and crying, "The world is on fire!" (*Record of a Living Being*); or Sanjuro, who turns up out of nowhere, weeds out the petty gangsters who lord it over the local community, then drifts off to the next small town in the same way he came (*Yojimbo,* 1961; *Tsubaki Sanjuro,* 1962).

Kurosawa always speaks of *Hakuchi* (*The Idiot,* 1951) with the greatest affection, though it is generally accounted one of his failures. Here, as in his version of *Macbeth,* it was an intellectual outlook on mankind already laid down in the original work that attracted his interest and stimulated his creativity. With *The Lower Depths* (1957), the thing that inspired him was the way Gorky takes the ordinary Russian people toward the end of the Czarist era and, placing them in an isolated setting, uses them as a kind of pure culture for his experiment. During a conversation I had with him in Warsaw last year, Andrzej Wajda, the great Polish director, who had high praise for Kurosawa, remarked that Nishi, the hero of Kurosawa's *The Bad Sleep Well* (1960) was a reincarnation in modern Japan of Hamlet. It had never occurred to me personally, but the remark undoubtedly revealed a grasp of the spring of Kurosawa's creativity.

Nor is it only Kurosawa's characters that are intellectually conceived. The settings in themselves seem somehow removed from the ordinary, everyday dimension. The very air is denser, the air pressure greater than in the atmosphere we normally breathe, sounds fall on the ear an octave higher than their usual pitch, and physical movements are speeded up or slowed down abnormally. Without such an atmosphere and such a setting, in fact, his characters would be incapable of acting freely or naturally. His films, simply described, are dramas of violent emotions, their traumatic effect heightened still further by exaggeration, emphasis, and extremes. Kurosawa himself admits to a preference for the harsher aspects of nature—for the glitter of high summer and the asperity of mid-winter, for torrential rains and blizzards. They provide his films with their natural backdrop and, of course, with their psychological background as well. They are the reverse of the conventionally "Japanese"—of the equivocal, the understated and the unadorned. He rejects the traditional "boiled-rice-and-green-tea" austerity so beloved of Ozu and Naruse: "I want my films to be like a steak spread with butter and topped with good, rich, broiled eels."

I have described his style as intellectual, a label which he gives to his work himself. Yet, in another aspect, the excellence of his work derives from the acuteness with which he constantly observes, remembers, and records the external world. He keeps an avid eye on the society and men about him, ever ready to summon actuality to amend his ideas for him.

During the filming of *Rashomon,* while Kurosawa's staff was at a loose end in its Kyoto hotel waiting for the completion of an open-air set, the half-ruined gateway that was to become famous all over the world, they saw a 16-mm. film of an expedition to Africa. One shot showed a lion staring at the cameraman from the edge of the jungle. "Look, Mifune!" cried Kurosawa. "That's how Tajomaru should be!" In that instant, he had seen the bandit Tajomaru as he was to appear in the film, peering out at the woman with piercing eyes from the bamboo grove. Around the same time, Masayuki Mori, who played the part of the murdered samurai Kanazawa no Takehiro, saw a film featuring a black panther at one of the local cinemas, and at his recommendation they all went to see it. When the panther at last appeared, Machiko Kyo, the actress who played the part of the young wife Masago, covered her face with her hands in alarm. It was this gesture that crystallized in Kurosawa's mind the image of Masago, confronted by the two men fighting over her like wild beasts in a thicket.

Kurosawa always insists that no amount of intellectualization can substitute for the living human being. When he succeeds, it is because the careful eye he keeps trained on reality is preventing ideas from running away with him.

When Kurosawa begins writing a scenario, he has no idea of what the final scene will be; intellectual though his first inspiration may be, he abhors intellectual conclusions. He creates the setting and gives his characters their personalities, but from then on it is the characters themselves who, with unpredictable results, take over the action. A single passing remark is enough to set his heroes and heroines on a completely different

course, and he is obliged to follow them wherever they lead. It is this kind
of realism in the course of creation that gives a sense of actuality to the
nonrealistic worlds he creates.

Unfortunately, a work produced in this fashion sometimes ends up at a
point that conflicts with the film's original intellectual point of departure.
At such times, the original idea is left stranded and without support. At the
end of *Rashomon,* the itinerant priest who has listened to the whole story
states that, thanks to the woodcutter, he has regained his temporarily
shaken faith in humanity—a conclusion utterly out of keeping with the
main theme the film has gone to such trouble to expound, the relativity of
truth and the perfidy of man. At the end of *Seven Samurai* (1954), Kambei,
the most clever strategist of the band, who has rid the farming village of the
wandering samurai who have been preying on it, muses to himself as he
rides away: The samurai have passed away like the wind, while the peasants, like the earth itself, go on forever—a patently forced moral that
blends ill with what has gone so far. It is, as it were, a vestigial reminder of
the original idea that moved Kurosawa to make the film.

# "The Seven Samurai"

## Tony Richardson

Akira Kurosawa's brilliant new film is a long, episodic reconstruction of an incident in sixteenth-century Japan. A peasant village is harried by brigands; in despair the villagers decide to hire professional soldiers to defend them; after recruiting difficulties, seven are collected; they organize the village's defense and succeed in wiping out the bandits completely. This basically simple plot Kurosawa elaborates in two ways. He introduces a profusion of incidents and subplots—the youngest samurai falling in love with a village girl disguised by her mistrustful father as a boy, the attempts of a wandering, humorous braggart to be accepted by the others as a samurai; and he gives to each of the many characters an intensely differentiated individual personality—the mature, kindly, self-less leader, the unassuming but obsessive professional swordsman, the traditional braggadochio.

In *The Seven Samurai* (Films de France), and in the light it throws back on *Rashomon,* Kurosawa's method and personality emerge clearly. He is, above everything else, an exact psychological observer, a keen analyst of behavior—in a fundamentally detached way. His handling of the young lovers is typical of this. He notes and traces with precision and truth their first, half-terrified awareness of each other sexually, the growth of mutual attraction, the boy's *gauche* admiration, the girl's aching and almost frantic abandonment; what he fails to do is to convey any feeling for, or identification with, the individuals themselves. He strives for this, he uses other images to heighten their scenes—the flower-covered hillside, the sun filtering through the tops of trees (an echo of its more successful use as an orgasm metaphor in *Rashomon*), the dappled light swarming like insects over them as they lie together in a bamboo hut—but somehow these remain perfunctory, a little cold, lacking in real poetry.

In this it is not unrewarding to compare Kurosawa with Ford—by whom, report has it, he claims to have been influenced. There are many

From *Sight and Sound,* vol. 24, no. 4 (Spring 1955). Reprinted by permission of the author.

superficial resemblances—the reliance on traditional values, the use of folk ceremonies and rituals, the comic horseplay—to Ford in particular and to the Western in general. The fast, vivid handling of the action sequences, the staccato cutting, the variety of angles, the shooting up through horses rearing in the mud, are all reminiscent of recent films in this genre. But the difference is more revealing. The funeral of the first samurai, killed in a preliminary skirmish, is exactly the sort of scene to which Ford responds, with all his reverence and honor for times past and the community of beliefs and feelings which they embodied. Kurosawa uses the scene in two ways, first as a further observation of the character of the "crazy samurai"—who, in a defiant attempt to satisfy his own feelings of frustration and impotence, raises the flag the dead man had sewn—and secondly, as an effective incident for heightening the narrative tension: the bandits launch their first onslaught during the funeral. One of the love scenes is used in a similar way, and in both cases one feels an ultimate shying-away from any direct, committed emotion—except anger.

Of course, to say Kurosawa is not Ford is critically meaningless; the comparison has value only insofar as it is a way of gauging the film's intentions, and its realization of them. What made *Rashomon* so unique and impressive was that everything, the subject, the formal structure, the playing, even perhaps the period, allowed for this exterior approach to behavior. In *The Seven Samurai* Kurosawa is striving for something different, a re-creation, a bringing to life of the past and the people whose story he is telling. Here, for all the surface conviction of period, the perceptive observation, the raging vitality and the magnificent visual style, the film doesn't quite succeed. All the elements are there except the depth and the generosity of life. One feels that each incident is too carefully worked into the texture as a whole. The Donskoi of the *Gorki* trilogy is a much simpler and, in many ways, more ordinary personality; but he achieved, almost without realizing it, what Kurosawa labors for. Life itself seems to have taken over from Donskoi, carrying him along on its great stream, but Kurosawa has engineered a stunning aqueduct along which it must flow. Only in his handling of the "crazy samurai" does it occasionally overflow. Toshiro Mifune, gibing at the samurai, waving, in mocking triumph, a fish caught in a stream, and—another Falstaff—bullying his hopeless recruits, brings to his portrayal a reckless and at moments out-of-hand gusto. It is a splendid performance, losing no opportunity, and it only fails to integrate a gratuitously introduced class motivation—he is really a peasant wanting to be a samurai. (The fault here lies with the script rather than the performer.) This is perhaps a momentary and rather glib contemporary analogy out of keeping with the rest.

These ultimate reservations should not, however, prevent us from recognizing the film's astonishing qualities. Incident after incident is created with biting precision for the whole 2½-hour length (the exported version, incidentally, is an hour shorter than the original)—the villagers shunning the samurai on their arrival only to tumble toward them in panic as the alarm is sounded, the capture of a thief and, brilliantly suspended in slow motion, his death, a brief and wonderful sketch of a farmer's wife abducted by the brigands stirring, guilty but sated, in her sleep. On a different level, Kurosawa is a virtuoso exponent of every technique of suspense, surprise, excitement, and in this he gives nothing to his Western masters. Only in his handling of the series of battles is there a hint of monotony. He knows exactly when to hold a silence; how to punch home an extraordinary fact with maximum effect; and his use of the camera is devastating—dazzling close-ups as the village deputation, overawed and desperate in their quest for samurai, scan the crowded street, or wild tracking shots as the drunken Mifune stumbles after his assailant. Visually the film makes a tremendous impression. Kurosawa can combine formal grace with dramatic accuracy, and many scenes create a startling pictorial impact. The raid on the bandits' hideout, when their slaughtered bodies are hurled, naked and haphazard, into the muddied pools outside their burning hut, is not unworthy of the Goya of *Los desastres*. The final effect, indeed, of *The Seven Samurai* is not unlike that of [Flaubert's] *"Salammbô,"* a triumph of rage and artifice; and one's final acknowledgment is not of the intrinsic fascination of the material but the wrested skill of the artificer.

# "The Seven Samurai"

## Donald Richie

Kurosawa had long wanted to make a real *jidai-geki,* a real period film. Though, at this time, fully half of all Japanese films made were *jidai-geki,* the "real" ones were very rare. Most of them were (then as now) *chambara,* simple sword-fight films. Japanese critics are fond of comparing the *chambara* with the American Western (the *seibu-geki*) and the comparison is appropriate. But, just as there are meaningful Westerns (*The Covered Wagon, Cimarron,* and *Stagecoach*), so there are meaningful *jidai-geki.* One can, in fact, trace the development of the "real" Japanese period films from the early pictures of Daisuke Ito and Mansaku Itami, through Sadao Yamanaka and Kenji Mizoguchi, to Masaki Kobayashi, and Kurosawa himself. These latter are "real" because they do not stop at simple historical reconstruction, inhabited by stock figures (which is true of costume pictures all over the world), but insist upon the validity of the past, and the continuing meaning of the historical. That the rule should be otherwise in Japan (so famous for its being a museum in which nothing is thrown away, almost notorious for its regard for the past, practically infamous for its historical sense) is surprising, but otherwise it is. The ordinary *jidai-geki* has no more vital connection to the past than does any Steve Reeves epic.

Kurosawa, then, wanted to present the past as meaningful, but do it within the framework of the *jidai-geki* (something he was to do again in *The Hidden Fortress,* in *Yojimbo,* and particularly in *Sanjuro*); at the same time, he says, he wanted to make a picture that was also completely entertaining. (He did not consider *Rashomon* either a *jidai-geki* or entertaining.) This is what he meant when he said: "Japanese films all tend to be *assari shite iru* [light, plain, simple but wholesome], just like *ochazuke* [green tea over a rice, a dish the *assari* connotations of which are so celebrated that Ozu—"the most Japanese of all Japanese directors"—used

From *The Films of Akira Kurosawa* by Donald Richie. Published in 1965 by The Regents of the University of California. Reprinted by permission of the University of California Press.

it as a film title once] but I think we ought to have both richer foods and richer films. And so I thought I would make a film which was entertaining enough to eat, as it were."

Entertaining it certainly is: convincing, thrilling, meaningful, compelling. It remains (along with *Ikiru*) the director's own favorite. At the same time it is completely serious. Most filmmakers believe that to be entertaining you also have to be amusing, just as most musicians believe that to play fast you must also play loud. Kurosawa knows otherwise. He also knows that nothing compels (particularly in a film) more than immaculate realism, and that this is even more true in a historical film where the reality has long vanished, and we are used to seeing only the slipshod reconstructions and interpretations of others—something the director particularly holds against the ordinary period film. In this regard Kurosawa's remarks on Mizoguchi are interesting.

"His greatness was that he never gave up trying to heighten the reality of each scene. He never made compromises. He never said that something or other 'would do.' Instead, he pulled—or pushed—everyone along with him until they had created the feeling which matched that of his own inner image. An ordinary director is quite incapable of this. And in this lay his true spirit as a director—for he had the temperament of a true creator. He pushed and bullied and he was often criticized for this but he held out, and he created masterpieces. This attitude toward creation is not at all easy, but a director like him is especially necessary in Japan where this kind of pushing is so resisted. . . . Of all Japanese directors I have the greatest admiration for him but, at the same time, I can't say that everything he did was equally good. If he portrays an old merchant you get marvelously successful scenes, like those in *A Tale from Chikamatsu,* but he was no good at samurai. In *Ugetsu,* when you get to the war scenes it just isn't war. A long time ago he did *Chushingura* and he left out the last scene [the great vendetta with much fighting and swordplay] which isn't surprising at all. Our historical worlds are actually different. His central figures are women and the world he describes is largely either that of women or of merchants. That is not my world. I think I am best at delineating *bushi* [warriors, samurai]. . . . But, in the death of Mizoguchi, Japanese film lost its truest creator."

Certainly the realism of the Mizoguchi historical film (a realism shared with Yamanaka and Itami) is enormously compelling but of equal importance is Mizoguchi's almost continual insistence that history be regarded as contemporary in that its problems were no less unique, no less personal, than are ours, and further—given the perspective of history—we are more likely to appreciate something of ourselves when it is given us out of our own historical context. . . .

Those who want to see *The Seven Samurai* as a social epic in the Soviet manner (the "Soviet manner" of the 1930s) have excellent reason for doing so. The picture *is* about groups of people and their social actions. But to see it only as a Russian-style social epic is both to ignore the ending (something no Russian in the 1930s would have filmed) and to neglect the fact that the film is not only about people—it is also, and mainly, about persons.

It is about the seven samurai as individuals (though Kurosawa does not so individualize the bandits, and there are only a few of the farmers who are given personal profiles) and, as an adventure story, is entirely about *their* exploits and how *each* reacts to this great adventure. For these are no ordinary samurai, and no ordinary men.

We first see Takashi Shimura having his head shaved. This usually means either punishment (for a samurai to lose his topknot means that he is déclassé and no longer a samurai) or that he is going to leave the world (to become a priest). As the watching Mifune discovers, however, it is neither. In what seems to be return for two balls of rice, he will save the child of a farmer, kidnapped and held prisoner by a madman. Shimura is given a priest's robe and the rice balls. He approaches the house where the madman is holding the child, impersonates a priest, catches the kidnapper off guard, kills him and saves the child. The parents are happy, the local farmers are full of congratulations. Then they all go away, back to their work.

The farmers searching for samurai to help them, decide that this is one they want. But he is also being followed by young Kimura, who begs to become his disciple, and by Mifune who can make nothing whatever of such apparently unmotivated goodness. Finally one of the farmers kneels in front of him and pleads. Shimura sees that one or two samurai would be useless—seven would be needed, and besides:

> It isn't easy to find that many reliable samurai . . . particularly when the only reward would be three meals a day and the fun of it. Besides I'm tired of fighting. Maybe I'm getting old.

The farmers are so disappointed that they begin to cry. A laborer makes fun of them, saying:

> I'm certainly glad I wasn't born a farmer—rather be born a dog than a farmer. Take it from me, a dog has a better life. Look, why don't you just go hang yourselves—all of you farmers. You'll be much better off. . . . And you, samurai. You know what these wretches eat? Millet! Because they'll be saving all

their precious rice for you. They'll be giving you all they have—
their very best.

This decides Shimura because he is the kind of man who makes decisions
in this way. In the same way he allowed himself to be shaved and to save
the child, for no reward at all. It is as though by personal example he will
set the world right, and this is what so captivates Kimura and intrigues
Mifune. . . .

 Few things surprise Shimura. He is like the pilgrim-priest in *The
Lower Depths* because he knows better than to hope. All a man can do, he
seems to say, is to do his best. If he does his best for himself that is one
thing; but it is better to do your best for others: even if the task is dangerous
and without reward; even if (as here) it is absurd. Still, it is better to have
done it. The farmers are saved (whatever that means); the village still
stands (whatever that means); and these three are alive (whatever that
means). Something has been accomplished, and if it is meaningless then
that is small concern of ours.
 This is heroism, and of a kind that particularly appeals to Kurosawa. It
is stoic, hopeless in the strongest possible sense, and generous. It is for this
reason that Shimura has become a leader, and it is why his character so
interests his men that they are willing to die for him. He knows that men
are individuals; he knows that all social actions are collective; he recognizes the gulf that exists between these two—and he still chooses to act.
 The other samurai share something of this. Obviously, or they would
not have been attracted to the pointless adventure. Inaba most closely
resembles Shimura and it is he who becomes second-in-command; and it is
he who finds Chiaki. Finds him chopping wood, an occupation unheard of
for a samurai.

CHIAKI: Yah! [Giving the samurai cry as he brings down the ax as though it
were a sword, neatly chopping the log in half. After a bit he becomes
irritated that Inaba is watching.] Haven't you even seen anyone cut
firewood before?
INABA: Yes, but you seem to enjoy it.
CHIAKI: I guess I'm just made that way. Yah! [Slices firewood.]
INABA: You're very good.
CHIAKI: Not really. It is a lot harder than killing enemies. Yah!
INABA: Killed many?
CHIAKI: Well, you see. Since it is impossible to kill them all—yah!—I
usually run away.
INABA: A splendid principle.
CHIAKI: Thank you very much. Yah!

INABA: By the way, you wouldn't perhaps be interested in killing twenty or thirty bandits?
CHIAKI: Yah! [But he is so surprised that he completely misses the log.]

Minoru's ideas on war are very close to those of Kato who at one point tells what he thinks:

> All right, now remember. [To the farmers.] War is mostly run.
> We are going to run, both in offensive and defensive. When you
> can't run in a war—that is when you get killed.

At an extreme from such practicality is the swordsman, Miyaguchi. He is a complete professional; we know this because we have seen him fight. He says very little, is closed, and—like his sword itself—only uses himself when he needs to. We know that he is lethal, though peaceful, and there is one beautiful scene of him alone in the forest where he carefully picks a single flower and looks at it. He incorporates the true spirit of *bushi*—something which none of the others do. He is killed, ironically, by a bullet.

The youngest samurai, Kimura, has an enormous veneration for the swordsman, even more than for Shimura. When the latter comes back with the gun, strolls into camp, and prepares for sleep, Kimura approaches him, eyes shining, and says: "You are a wonderful person,"—at which, for the only time in the picture, the swordsman smiles.

He, too, is attracted by the boy and the only time he displays any curiosity is when the boy meets and gives his rice to a girl. Kimura had originally met her in the forest while he lagged behind picking flowers. Since she has had her long hair cut short by her father, he takes her for a boy—which was the father's intention, since he mistrusted the samurai. She is also picking flowers and they accidentally meet:

KIMURA: If you're a boy, why aren't you out drilling with the rest? Picking flowers at a time like this! [He suddenly remembers that he too has flowers in his hand.]

The others treat Kimura as the child they think he is, though there are some indications that he is growing up. Shimura and Inaba are going out for night partol. Kimura is sleeping beside them.

SHIMURA: Well, shall we go?
INABA: Shall we wake him?
SHIMURA: No. Let the child sleep.
KIMURA: [In his sleep.] Shino!

SHIMURA: What's that? Shino is a girl's name, isn't it?
INABA: Yes, indeed. Not a very childish remark for a sleeping child to make, is it?

Later, he makes love for the first time, and the very next day, kills his first man. He himself has become a man. Yet, when the swordsman is suddenly killed by a stray shot, he kneels into the mud and weeps as though his heart is breaking. Shimura looks at him. The boy remembers to ask if there are any more bandits. No, there are no more. Then he flings himself to the ground, sobbing, while Shimura looks. The child is not quite yet a man.

It is, indirectly, through the swordsman and the boy that Mifune dies. Like all the rest of the samurai he wants the regard of Shimura, and he also (like the swordsman) enjoys the adulation of the youth. When the latter begins telling him how wonderful the swordsman is, Mifune is sarcastic, but it is just after that that he goes out and gets the gun. And when he sees the boy weeping, it is he who goes after the bandit chief, and kills him—though he himself is killed in the attempt.

And bravery is not at all natural to him. To be sure, it is to no one, it must be acquired, but Mifune has acquired little enough of it. A buffoon, a standard joke to the rest, it is nonetheless he who kills the final and most important bandit—as though, by this action, he will vindicate himself in the eyes of both the leader and the boy.

Unlike the others, he is no warrior. Indeed, if things had happened differently he might just as well have been one of the bandits. But his parents were killed by bandits, and he was orphaned. This is shown in a single scene where, during the burning of the mill, the dying mother gives her living child to him. He holds it in his arms, astonished, up to his thighs in the stream, the burning mill behind him, then suddenly sits down in the water and bursts into tears:

SHIMURA: She was speared. What enormous will she had to come this far afterwards. Well, bring the child, let's go back. What is the matter with you?
MIFUNE: [Looking at the baby in his arms, crying.] This . . . baby. It's me. The same thing happened to me. The very same thing! [Sobs, holding the baby.]

Mifune is also a farmer's son, and though he has come a long way from the soil he has never forgotten the enmity traditional not only between farmer and bandit, but also farmer and samurai. At one point he hopes to please his comrades by bringing them armor which he has found hidden away in the village. The others are solemn because they know that the armor was stolen from samurai whom, perhaps, the villagers themselves murdered.

MIYAGUCHI: I'm beginning to want to kill every farmer in this village.
MIFUNE: What do you think farmers are? Saints? They are the most cunning and untrustworthy animals on earth. If you ask them for rice, they'll say they have none. But they have. They have everything. Look in their rafters, dig in the ground, you'll find it. Rice in jars. Salt. Beans. Saké. Look in the mountains, hidden farms everywhere. And yet they pretend to be oppressed. They are full of lies. When they smell a battle they make themselves bamboo spears. And then they hunt. But they hunt the wounded and the defeated. Farmers are miserly, craven, mean, stupid, murderous beasts. [Tears in his eyes.] You make me laugh so hard I'm crying.
But then, who made animals out of them? You. You did—you samurai. All of you damned samurai. [He picks up a handful of arrows and throws them at the wall.] Each time you fight you burn villages, you destroy the fields, you take away the food, you seduce the women and enslave the men. And kill them if they resist. You hear me—you damned samurai? [He begins to cry.]
SHIMURA: [Quietly, with great sincerity.] You're a farmer's son, aren't you?

He is a farmer's son but he dies as a samurai. And it is perhaps he whom the others will miss the most, precisely because he was so weak, so very human. Shimura appears almost superhuman, but Mifune is completely human. And it is he who therefore sees the dilemma that even Shimura has missed. Aren't, then, samurai and bandits to be equated?—aren't the actions of each equally absurd?—and don't they really do much the same things?

It is a startling question. One which Kurosawa has asked in *Stray Dog* and will ask again in *High and Low*. Good and bad might be identical. The farmers would find it so. They are almost as distrustful of the samurai as they are of the bandits. For them it is plainly a choice between evils. We are thus prepared for the final scene.

The opening sequence with Shimura has shown a gratuitous action, one for which he expects neither reward nor acclaim. The laborer, and now Mifune, have indicated that one need not expect to find generosity, gratitude, or other such civilized luxuries among the peasants. And at the end, therefore, when the three remaining samurai are ignored by the farmers who are, obviously, only waiting for them to leave (and in a scene carefully prepared since it was just these three—Shimura, Kato and Kimura—who were present when the leader asks Kato: "Tired of fighting?"), Shimura may say.

SHIMURA: And again we lose.
KATO: . . . ?
SHIMURA: We lose. Those farmers . . . they're the winners.

What did Shimura hope to win? He knew the entire venture was quixotic, he knew it would be without reward, he knew that its only profit was in the "fun of it." To be disappointed in the farmers was to have hoped, and this is something which, until now, he has not allowed himself. Yet he had hoped to win, and further had hoped that this winning would somehow change something. He has become human enough to confuse ends and means and forget that everything is means and that there is no end. The true wisdom (cold, comfortless) would have been to enjoy the "fun" while he had it, to (put in a way which Kurosawa would never be guilty of saying) realize that *being* is the sole end, and that *becoming* turns into snare and delusion if looked for, hoped for.

This does not mean, of course, that *becoming* is impossible. Indeed, it is impossible *not* to *become*. Nor does this mean that wishes and will have no power—indeed, they have considerable power, as *Ikiru* has indicated. But what disappoints is when one allows the illusion (the unfulfilled wish) to supersede reality (ungrateful peasants, dead comrades). . . .

Like the Russians (Eisenstein, Dovzhenko) to whose epics *The Seven Samurai* has often been compared, Kurosawa—here perhaps more than in any other single film—insisted that the motion picture be composed entirely of *motion*. The film opens with fast pans of the bandits riding over hills, and ends with the chaos of the battle itself, motion so swift we can almost not see it at all. There is no shot that does not have motion, either in the object photographed, or in the movement of the camera itself. The motion may be small (the quivering nostrils in the long-held image of the village elder) or it may be great (the huge, sweeping frescoes of the charges) but it is always there.

At the same time, another kind of motion is present. Kurosawa, always an economical filmmaker, uses a number of shortcuts which hasten the pace of the story itself. When the farmer first approaches Shimura the continuity is:

> Farmer, face down in the dirt, Shimura looking / cut / new location, an inn, and Shimura is saying to the farmer: "It's impossible."

All obvious retelling is left out, all obvious continuity linkage (the two of them walking to the inn, for example) is rigorously excluded. Again, Inaba (sensing that Kimura is waiting with the stick just inside the door) stops outside.

He says: "Oh, come now. No jokes," / cut / inside the inn, he and Shimizu are sitting down and he is saying: "Well, it sounds interesting."

Sometimes scenes are telescoped and put into one. There is a beautiful example of this during the funeral of Chiaki. All are gathered around the mound and Mifune dashes back to get their banner (which Chiaki had made) and climbs a roof to put it on the ridge-pole—a gesture of defiance. He suddenly looks at the hills and there, as though in answer (a marvelous image), come wave after wave of bandits, riding down on the village, heralding the first of the major battles. As Mifune looks, there is a wide pan which moves from village to hills. At the same time the sounds of weeping turn to cries of alarm from the villagers, to cries of exultation from the samurai—who now want to fight. Within this single scene not only has action been carried forward but—as though the pan had caused it which, in a way it did—the entire mood has been changed, in just two seconds, from abject sorrow to the most fierce joy.

Another means of telescoping is through the interlinking of very short (usually funny) scenes, connected with wipes, that Kurosawa has used from *They Who Step on the Tiger's Tail* onward. It is seen at its funniest both here and in *Sanjuro*. The samurai are being taken to the village, and their journey is seen in a mosaic of tiny scenes the point of which is that they are being followed by Mifune who, taciturn, apparently stupid, wants to join them, and at the same time cannot bring himself to. The entire sequence (covering a seemingly enormous journey) takes just three minutes and at the end Mifune, looking down at the village, utters his ironic and prophetic remark which (in retrospect at any rate) makes him appear much more human, much less of the clown: "Whew—what a dung pile. I'd certainly hate to die in a place like that."

All of these shortcuts and telescopings, all of this motion on the screen, means that the picture moves very fast indeed. It is so swift that Kurosawa has availed himself of at least several devices to insure that he does not lose his audience. The first of these is the banner and, at the same time, a list which Shimura draws up in which the number of circles indicates the number of bandits. Like the bullets in *Stray Dog*, like the money in *One Wonderful Sunday*, the viewer keeps score, as it were, by seeing how many down, how many to go. Each scratched circle means one less bandit.

Another way in which Kurosawa keeps his audience up to the pace he has set is by a full explication of the visual surroundings. In the original version of the picture, this is even stronger, but even in the cut version (which is all that other countries ever see of this picture) this explication is very strong. He begins with a map (as he does in *Stray Dog,* in *The Hidden Fortress,* and in *High and Low*)—a map which Shimura has drawn and which is a bird's-eye view of the village. Kurosawa loves bird's-eye views, and he is particularly fond of anything which will show all the ingredients of a certain situation, which will allow you to spread them all out before you and try to put them together. It is like the watchmaker's interest, the cook's interest—the finished thing is all very well but how it got finished is the most interesting thing. Consequently we learn all about the various sections of the village and (as with the room in *The Lower Depths*) we get to know it extremely well, better perhaps than most places we actually visit. In the same way we watch the samurai, first hear of their plans, and then see them in action (much as we, fascinated, watch the police force in *High and Low*) and then judge the results. As always, Kurosawa is particularly careful to show us *how* a thing happens.

Finally, in the last reel, we are shown *how* a battle occurs. It resembles what we have been prepared for, but at the same time it is entirely different. Shimura speaking in measured tones and pointing to his map is one thing; this inferno of men and horses, rain and mud, is quite another thing. Reality is very different from illusion.

Even on a technical level, quite removed from the context which gives it its final meaning, this last reel is one of the greatest of cinematic accomplishments. It is chaotic but never chaos; disordered but orderly in its disorder. The rain pours down; bandits dash in; horses neigh and rear; Shimura poses, bow ready; Mifune slashes; an arrow thuds home and we glimpse it only for the fraction of a second necessary; riderless horses rear in terror; a samurai slips; Mifune grabs another sword. All of these images and literally hundreds more are crowded into a final reel which galvanizes the screen. (Having already given us plenty of excitement in the earlier battles, here Kurosawa does himself one better and uses telephoto lenses—a rarity in 1954—to bring the action directly into the laps of the audience. The first of these telescopic shots is a horse fall which seems to occur directly where the camera is and rarely fails to evoke a gasp from the audience.)

At the same time, in the final reel, we again see that what keeps this film (and all of Kurosawa's films) so completely vital is, after all, the cutting, and consequently the tempo. We have had indication of this before in the film. In the hunting-for-the-samurai section, a set piece like the journey-to-the-village which follows, Kurosawa shows us the four farmers in two pairs, each searching through the same town. In between each image of a pair of farmers looking from right to left, or left to right, their eyes following the samurai, sweeping pans of the samurai themselves are intercut. Thus the sweeping pans are answered by sweeping movements of the eyes of the peasants. The delight of this sequence (the delight of the hunt, of the unknown, accompanied on the sound track by music unmistakably of that intent), lies in the very brevity of each shot. Each is no longer than two seconds. Thus, even in a simple sequence such as this, expectation and excitement are generated through the cutting.

Mifune's fine scene with the armor is another example of Kurosawa's editing. It plays so very well and is so powerful that it is only on re-seeing that one notices, first, that Mifune acts directly into the camera (which is one of the reasons for the power—as in the final close-up in *The Lower Depths*) and second, that each shot of Mifune is a bit shorter than the one which went before. The tempo is accelerated by the cutting, and these long scenes become shorter. The next to last (Shimura) and last (Mifune) are the conventional one-two shots, each lasting for a conventional amount of time.

Another example of creative cutting is the raid on the bandits' fort. There is a broad downward pan. First we see mountains, then below it the road along which the three horsemen are galloping. The pan does not turn sidewise with the horsemen, however, nor does it stop (as one might expect)—rather, it continues on down, leaving the road (and the action) behind. At the same time, as the road disappears at the top of the frame, a slow lateral wipe (left to right) begins. This is the waterfall scene, and the samurai are already at their destination. The effect on the screen is, oddly, diagonal. Two essentially unrelated scenes have been perfectly connected, and we accept cause and effect though there is actually a great and purposeful lapse in the continuity. This fine effect of continuous movement is achieved entirely in the editing, since it would be impossible to obtain it photographically.

Sometimes sound enforces the cut. On the first day of the battle, there is a good example:

> The samurai, all asleep / cut / enormous close-ups of horses running, the bandits approaching, hoofs thundering on the sound track / cut / all asleep, but the swordsmen has heard (though we hear nothing) and stands up / cut / racing horses and hoofbeats / cut / all the samurai are standing and waiting; we hear hoofs very faintly and then, in the far distance see the dust raised by the horses.

These are only four shots and each is slightly shorter than the other. By the time the battle begins, we are quite prepared for it, and the editing has done it. . . .

What one remembers best from this superbly economical film then are those scenes which seem most uneconomical—that is, those which apparently add nothing to it. There is a short cut during the burning of the bandit's fort where we watch a woman awaken, see the fire, and yet refuse to warn the others. (She is the wife of one of the farmers, raped and carried away by the bandits.) The scene is beautiful enough, this hopeless farm woman, clothed in stolen silk, half obscured by the wisps of smoke—but Kurosawa renders it utterly mysterious (and completely right) by inserting beneath it the sound of the Noh flute with unearthly effect—a trick he later repeated, less gratuitously, in *The Throne of Blood* and *The Hidden Fortress*.

Again, there is the short scene where a prisoner has been caught, and the oldest woman in the village—she who has lost all of her sons—is called to come and murder him. She marches slowly forward, a hoe in her hand, terribly old, terribly bent, a crone. And though we sympathize, the image is one of horror—it is death itself because we have seen, and will see, men killed and think little of it, but here is death itself with a hoe, mysterious, unwilled. Or, those several shots of the avenue of cryptomerias, and two bonfires, one far and one near. This is where the bandits will come but we do not yet know this. Instead, the trees, the fires, the night—all are mysterious, memorable. Or, that magnificent image which we see after Mifune has rescued the baby and burst into tears. The mill is burning and Mifune is sitting in the stream, looking at the child and crying. The next scene is a simple shot of the waterwheel turning, as it always has. But the wheel is on fire. Or, that curiously long close-up of the dead Mifune. He has stolen some armor but his bottom is unprotected. Now he lies on a narrow bridge, on his face, and the rain is washing away the dirt from his buttocks. He lies there like a child—all men with bare bottoms look like children—yet he is dead, and faintly ridiculous in death, and yet he was our friend for we have come to love him. All of this we must think as we sit through the seconds of this simple, unnecessary, and unforgettable scene.

Or, my favorite among all of these magical images, that following Shimura's saying that the bandits are all dead, and Kimura's sinking, weeping, into the mud. The screen slowly darkens. It is as though the end has come, and one hopes it has not, because this, somehow, is not enough and because, even more strongly, we do not want to leave these men yet. The screen gets darker and darker. They are lost in the gloom. We sit in the darkness and then we hear music. It is the music of the farmers, and the screen lightens to reveal one of the most delightful and heartbreaking of sequences: the rice planting.

It is seen as dance, which indeed rice planting is in Japan. A small orchestra (flute, drums, bells, singer) accompanies the girls as they plunge the new shoots into the wet earth, all in unison. Since this is the way rice is actually planted, we accept it as real. At the same time, after the uproar, pain, horror, grief of the final battle, we had not expected a divertissement. Strictly speaking, the entire rice-planting sequence is unnecessary to the film; not speaking strictly at all, it is vital—perhaps because it relaxes, with its very beauty and its anticlimax. Nerves have been played upon and wrought up to an extent completely unusual in an action picture, and suddenly—childlike beauty. When tears flow in *Seven Samurai,* they flow here.

Then comes the great final scene with its reminiscence of the opening scene, followed by Shimura's profoundly ironic remark, and the picture ends on the splendid image of the high grave-hill with four naked swords stuck into the top, and three mere men standing below. And, under this, the child-like music of the peasants fades and is replaced by the music associated with the samurai.

Kurosawa has given us beauty in the midst of knowledge, a kind of reassurance while questioning all reassurances. At the same time that he questions deeds, hopes, thoughts, he has purposely played upon our emotions and we, too, have become open and child-like. More, in this profoundly subtle and mysterious final sequence (samurai and peasants; fighting and rice planting; silence and music; darkness and light), he has indicated hope. We are all, after all, human; we all feel the same—we are all peasants at heart.

# Fritz Lang

FRITZ LANG was born in Vienna in 1890. The son of a noted architect, he trained in architecture, then studied painting, and in his early twenties traveled extensively in Europe, Africa, and Asia. Wounded in World War I, he began to write scripts in Vienna for producer-director Joe May, acting in a few films as well. Although he had already become well known in Germany, his first international success was Destiny (Der müde Tod, 1921). Lang's silent period is marked by his interest in fantasies of the past, present, and future: the German legends of Die Nibelungen (1924), the metaphysical gangsters of Dr. Mabuse (1922) and Spione (1928), and the elaborate technologies of Metropolis (1927) and The Woman in the Moon (1929). On many of these projects Lang collaborated with his wife, Thea von Harbou, a novelist and scriptwriter.

M (1931, starring Peter Lorre), Lang's first sound film, was an elaborate venture into creating a world of significant sound as enclosed and paranoid as the symmetrical and patterned visual structures of his silent films. The Testament of Dr. Mabuse (1933), in which Lang drew upon the characters of his earlier films to identify the gangster-psychiatrist Mabuse with the Nazis, unexpectedly delighted Hitler's propaganda chief, Josef Goebbels, who nonetheless had the film banned. When Goebbels told Lang of Hitler's admiration for Metropolis and offered him the job of head of the German film industry, Lang agreed and instantly fled Germany, leaving behind his wife, who had already become a Nazi Party member.

With one film made in France (Liliom, 1934) behind him, Lang was hired by David O. Selznick for M-G-M. His American films, which began with Fury (1936), a commercially and artistically successful story of mob violence, are characterized by an adaptation of expressionist visual methods to more realistic situations, often involving a theme of personal betrayal, obsession, or vengeance—a pattern first explored in M. The fantastical spies and criminals become in the American films the corrupt government, the indifferent society, the Mafia-like gang, or—in World War II films like Man Hunt (1941) and The Ministry of Fear (1944)—the Nazis themselves. Like Hitchcock, Lang is interested especially in the individual who is caught in a web of overwhelming forces and can achieve some sort of control only by drawing on an antisocial, even pathological, strain in his own nature.

Lang's fascination with formal visual pattern, which went back to his early days in the Ufa studios in Germany (whose productions were famous for intricate sets and décor), often appears in his American films as an exploration of genre patterns. He made three somewhat eccentric but stylish Westerns—The Return of Frank James (1940), Western Union (1941), and Rancho Notorious (1951)—all notable for their use of color and natural spectacle. But Lang's concentrated visual power appears best in his city films, with their almost overpowering images of entrapment amid sky-

*obliterating buildings and labyrinthine streets. Perhaps the best example of Lang's American style is* The Big Heat *(1953). Here, as in* While The City Sleeps *and* Beyond a Reasonable Doubt *(both 1956), Lang's penchant for apocalyptic social criticism verges on attacking the idea of society itself, as he simultaneously expresses a fear of the anarchy of individual nature and an anger at the oppressiveness of social order.*

*The relative commercial failure of the two 1956 films caused Lang to leave American studio filmmaking, disgruntled especially with his lack of control over his projects. Returning to earlier themes, he remade two scripts from the 1920s—The* Tiger of Eschnapur *and* The Indian Tomb—*and ended his film career with yet another Mabuse film—*The Thousand Eyes of Dr. Mabuse *(1960), all French-German-Italian co-productions. Lang appears as the archetypal great director contending with commercial pressures in Godard's* Contempt *(1963). He died in 1976.*

*Scripts have been published of both* M *(1968) and* Metropolis *(1973). For* Metropolis *Thea von Harbou's original novel (1927) is also available. Critical works about Lang include those by Peter Bogdanovich (1967), Paul M. Jensen (1969), and Lotte Eisner (1976). Frequent comments about Lang and his films are contained also in Eisner's* The Haunted Screen *(1969) and Siegfried Kracauer's* From Caligari to Hitler *(1947).*

# The Style of
# Fritz Lang

## Georges Franju

Lang, whether or not he is shooting from a script by Thea von Harbou, seems haunted by an ideal of justice and a balance that transcends human affairs.

When he first began making films, Lang chose the mythological, archetypal subjects typical of the German school in that era, and he handled them in an equally typical epic fashion. Even then, however, his sociological bent was visible; but he was unable to isolate humanity—or rather, to consider humanity its own means and end. He quite naturally could not apply his ideas of equality and reform—both functions of the realism which is a marked characteristic of his later work—to material that was basically romantic in nature.

The concept of balance occurred for the first time in *Destiny,* a highly symbolic and extraterrestrial work. The film tells the story of a young woman (played by Lil Dagover) whose tremendous spirit lifts her above almost overwhelming contrary forces, and at the end of a series of terrible trials she moves the celestial authority to pity.

This celestial judgment in *Destiny* became the prototype and example. In his second film, *Mabuse the Gambler,* Lang passed on to a study of aggression in the form of scientific nihilism. Then *Metropolis* gave him the opportunity to focus upon an organized, conceptualized world the dichotomy implied in the other films, bringing man face to face at last with his own nature. This is the first stage in the sociological evolution of the theme.

Five years later, Lang's obsession with the tribunal made its appearance, and he was able to launch a frontal assault upon the real world, by

From *Cahiers du Cinéma,* no. 100 (November 1959). Revised by the author from an article that first appeared in CINEMAtographe (March 1937). Translated especially for this volume by Sallie Iannotti.

opposing to the idea of transcendent justice the actuality of the man-made laws determining our daily lives.

For the first time Lang openly attacked the official representation of authority, and in particular, those officials who dispense justice—a justice, moreover, regimented by laws—and the laws themselves resting upon privilege, mindless tradition, and stupidity. For the courts, in Lang's vision, are intrinsically human, and the right to judge others is shot through with private interests. Decrees, codes, and rules are revised to suit the moment and the result is often chaos, contention, and error. When this happens, those forces existing upon the margins of society—the pariahs, the cripples, the thieves—inherit the problem of constructing a new justice.

Lang's sympathies always lie with the little man, the man of low condition, who, by whatever means at his disposal, is willing to combat the dogmas of a stultified society.

I am speaking, of course, of *M,* Lang's first sound film (deliberately passing over the minor films that followed *Metropolis*). It is significant, particularly in view of Lang's interests and the fact that sex murder generally carried the death penalty, that Peter Lorre, through his defense counsel, pleads his cause in terms which cannot fail to place responsibility squarely upon an indifferent and narrow-minded society. More interested in revealing himself than in evoking the excuse of his insanity, which in intellectual circles would constitute an extenuating circumstance, Lorre bares his wounds to a horrified bureaucratic, bourgeois world which looks upon him as an aberration, a little dreg in the cup of creation. At the end of the film the "vampire" is snatched from the jaws of his mock judges and brought to a conventional court. But these magistrates in Lang's view are no more qualified to pass judgment than the underworld, and their verdict is never revealed.

In his next picture, Lang, still pursuing his constructive-destructive thesis, still aggressive and critical, turned once more to that awesome old tyrant Mabuse, and created an almost evangelical testament against the prejudices, incrustation, and basic injustices of the Nazis (*The Testament of Dr. Mabuse*). Once again, however, the guilty protagonist, because of his madness, escapes punishment. Mabuse (played by Klein-Rogge) trades the guillotine for the padded cell, and in fact actually reaps a sort of revolutionary esteem.

With *Liliom* (adapted from a play by Molnar) Lang returned to the heroic era of celestial justice. This time preferring suicide to imprisonment, the hero, Liliom Zadewski, escapes the intervention of the courts and is sent instead to Heaven, where an angelic and competent commissioner sets about his social and moral rehabilitation.

It is too soon, I think, to remark upon the judicial preoccupations of

*Fury,* Lang's newest production (and among his worst, in my opinion). Certain critics seem to have found in it a protest against lynching, but I tend to see here, once again, an indictment against arbitrary arrest. This, it seems to me, is the idea behind the events in the film. In any case, when Spencer Tracy accuses the court of destroying his faith in justice, he summarizes one of the preoccupations that make up the force and original-ity in Lang's work.

## Principles of Editing

The basis of a well-constructed, well-edited screenplay is, of course, a disciplined relationship among the images, the succession of shots, and the rhythms established from unit to unit. Lang, however, uses a system which I call intuitive editing, a stylistic device he first employed, I believe, as early as 1921—in an era, moreover, when even the best directors limited themselves to an orderly development in the narrative, or sought artistic enlargement in the expressionism of the performances and the impres-sionism of the camera.

The simplest example of this intuitive technique is found in the open-ing sequence of *Destiny:*

Opening shot: Iris diaphragm. A man Standing by a country crossroads.
Fade out . . . Fade in: A thicket. A coach drives by.
Subtitle: Anywhere, at any time. Two lovers on their wedding trip.

And that's all. But it is enough, and we understand that, juxtaposed in this fashion, the coach will encounter the man at the crossing.

Lang uses this technique—the conditional arrangement of shots, creat-ing place and time solely through editing—in many of his films. Near the beginning of *M,* for example, there is a scene which creates such a sense of contribution in the viewer, such a feeling of intuitive perception (yet or-dered and derived) that he cannot help but feel here, indeed, he has touched the wellspring of dramatic emotion. We are shown, by a shot to the clock, that an hour has gone by. There is a recurring image of an empty place at the table and an empty chair. We begin to lose hope that Elsie will return to her mother. Then the camera plunges into the stairwell, and we know we cannot hope any longer. The sight of this simple stairway—steep, narrow, bleak—is decisive. We, the audience, are caught up by a sense of doom. Little Elsie will never climb these stairs again. And the following se-quences confirm our presentiment.

In other films Lang uses a similar mechanism, one that acts upon us not through the narrative, in reflection and reason, as in the scenes above, but through a rupture in the narrative that produces a reflex response. Early in *Liliom* a quarrel breaks out between Boyer and Rignault. After we see them fighting, a pan shot focuses upon a crowd of bystanders who are laughing uproariously. Then, abruptly, all heads turn in unison, and the emotional atmosphere of the scene changes completely as their expressions alter. We know that something dreadful has taken place over there, but what? A reverse pan shot to one of the friends, knife in hand, on the point of stabbing the other.

In this way, using intelligent and dramatic cutting to reveal the image of the emotion before showing the action that stirred that emotion, the director makes his point far more forcefully than if he had merely followed a strict narrative line. Our very ignorance of the cause provokes a strong reflex of feeling.

Lang probably introduced this technique in *Destiny,* in the scene at the inn. In any case, it appears, in addition to the scenes I have mentioned, in *The Testament of Dr. Mabuse* (the scene in the amphitheater) and once more in *M* (the arrival of the police to the basement room).

## The Mise-en-Scène

At first glance, *The Saga of the Nibelungs* seems singularly theatrical in concept, and even in its effects, which are closely tied to the sets and background in a manner associated with the stage. Yet actually this transposed legend is constructed entirely by the one element most essential to the cinema: the action of the camera. The subtlety of this instrument and the sobriety that marks Lang's use of it do not diminish the effective action in the slightest. No matter how well-equipped a theater might be, it could not possibly give a comparable treatment to this story. Nothing on the stage could equal, for example, the evocative power of the filmed image of the treasure entering the courtyard at Worms: this power is solely the function of camera action—a tracking shot that zooms down into the view. Again, the sequence of the chase in the forest depends upon a long shot. And in another—the unforgettable close-up in the forge—a feather drifts down in slow motion and is split upon Siegfried's sword. All pure cinema, pure products of the photographic lens, unattainable except through the artificial eye of the camera.

The very atmosphere of the film depends upon a physical system impossible on the stage: dwarfs turn to stone, mists swirl in the forest, a plain stretches out across the screen, in flames.

When *M* appeared, critics were quick to find fault with the courtroom scene. Even as they acknowledged its undeniable drama, they found it lacking in cinematographic qualities. It existed, they claimed, purely as a gratuitous effect. Yet this scene, which intercuts statistical and decorative elements very intelligently, could not have stirred audiences to a fever—as it did—if its message had not been, in the end, both final and inevitable. Those animate and inanimate forces came to a head in a manner that was *filmic*—far more filmic than theatrical.

There are, unquestionably, many reminiscences of the theater in Lang's pictures. "I see three bicycle riders," in *Liliom;* in *M,* the young beggar on Lorre's trail says to the blind man: "I see him. He's stopping . . . now he's going on again." These are rather clear examples and in the best stage tradition. Yet, why shouldn't the cinema incorporate elements of the stage?

In this article I have limited myself to an examination of a style and the elements which compose it. These elements are readily accessible to analysis, of course. But the ideas behind them, though they make themselves felt, are far harder to define. Perhaps the moving spiritual force behind Lang's films is best described as the search for energy, for the living force. It is a universal, even cosmic, concern, one of the great imponderables. No doubt this search is at the bottom of Lang's fascination with spectaculars. Great epic spectacles like *Metropolis* and *Woman on the Moon,* to name only two, allow a certain free play to the imagination. There are sequences in these films that are charged with tremendous power—the flood in *Metropolis,* or the rocket blasting off in *Woman on the Moon.* Though they are surely among the most beautiful moments in cinema, they are really not worth examining in detail. It is important, however, to remember that every type of spectacular events and disasters one can imagine have been used at one time or another by Lang, among them flood in *Metropolis* and *Mabuse,* explosion in *Spies* and *Mabuse,* and conflagration in *Destiny* and *Fury.*

The setting and décor are of primary importance in all these works. Elements of the background in many of these films take on the force of characters in themselves. The first one that comes to mind is the glass cabinet in the orthopedist's office which appears in the middle of *M,* as Lorre stops there to wait for a little girl. This glass cabinet is a decorative detail very typical of Lang's style—an ordinary object, remarkable only for a little black and white revolving spire, whose motion is seemingly infinite. And beside it, in contrast, a balance pointer which moves from side to side at a slow regular pace. In the same manner the nude mannequin in the shop window in *The Threepenny Opera* is typical of Pabst, and the haberdasher's display case is representative of René Clair in *The Italian Straw Hat.*

## Acting

In all these films, performances are characterized by extreme attitudes, energetic expressions, and nervousness of gesture. It is difficult to determine whether Lang discovers personalities, or exploits them. Whichever the case, the chilling magnetic charm of Brigit Helm, the mesmerizing presence of Bernard Goetzke, the physical power of Klein-Rogge, the intensity of Peter Lorre—these suggest a determination to impose a sense of force, not so much through the varied talents of the actors as through the evocation of archetypes, chosen for their dimensions. This, of course, calls for certain physical characteristics, a radiant active power, for example, as seen in Klein-Rogge as Mabuse, or a passive power (Sylvia Sydney in *Fury*). It is a problem, no doubt, to find actors whose physical attributes tally exactly with the role, but it also means that the director must spurn the rules of the drama school, and its methods, which stress finely shaded psychological interpretations.

For Lang, in effect, the role is not carried within the character, but upon it. His cinema is less an art of externalizing interior qualities than one of creating the appearance of a certain exterior in itself. It really does not matter to us if an actor is sincere provided his portrayal is true. It has to be, however, absolutely true. Anyone who confuses ''apparent truth'' with the ''appearance of truth,'' that is, the embodiment of a quality as opposed to the representation of it, should make a point of seeing Bernard Goetzke's magnificent creation of Death in *Destiny*.

A safecracker, let us say, is not on the whole readily distinguishable from an academician. Only his hands are peculiar to his art. Therefore to them and to them alone Lang gives the task of characterization.

Certainly a concern with truth is unmistakable in these details of personal significance. It has become, indeed, a sort of personal signature for Lang. We have already observed his affinity for the riffraff, if there is such a thing, when respectability is in such bad odor. But it's not really a matter of simple affinity, which is hardly forceful enough to justify his glorification of alienation and crime. Lang sanctifies, so to speak, the underworld of crime. But to give him his due, his chosen spokesmen from this world are never weak or lacking in courage. Instead, these individuals often assume a very high-class polish. Lang seems to delight in this; and so, some gangland boss, as in *M,* might wear sleek black gloves or a young thug might appear to be the boy next door with a dash of distinguished debauchery. All in all, this super-criminal world emerges as so intelligent, and so very admirably organized, capable of giving such an impression of strength, culture, and breeding, that its omnipotence cannot be questioned.

In short, a world of self-willed individuals, projecting, as a group, a powerful magnetism which leads us back to the idea of energy, life force:

spiritual and physical energy which touches our hearts from time to time—and our nerves always.

This study, perhaps, should have been entitled "Nerves at the Edge." It calls to mind a simple interpretive action; a signal, a gesture: Sylvia Sydney, in anguish, strikes her temples with her fists (*Fury*). This gesture is found, executed in exactly the same manner, the same rhythmic little blows, same clenched fists, in *Destiny*. It passes through *The Spies* (the scene in the taxi), *Woman on the Moon* (the scene in the space ship), *The Testament of Dr. Mabuse* (in the printing house). This little gesture is evidence of the spirit of precision in the director, a characteristic of an almost obsessional purpose. The affirmation of a very personal conception, manifested cinematically by style.

# "Metropolis"

## Luis Buñuel

*Metropolis* is not one film, *Metropolis* is two films joined by the belly, but with divergent, indeed extremely antagonistic, spiritual needs. Those who consider the cinema as a discreet teller of tales, will suffer a profound disillusion with *Metropolis*. What it tells us is trivial, pretentious, pedantic, hackneyed romanticism. But if we put before the story the plastic-photo-genic basis of the film, then *Metropolis* will come up to any standards, will overwhelm us as the most marvelous picture book imaginable. Imagine, then, two antipodean elements held under the same sign, in the zones of our sensibility. The first of them, which we might call pure-lyrical, is excellent; the other, the anecdotal or human, is ultimately irritating. Both, simultaneously, successively, compose the latest creation of Fritz Lang. It is not the first time that we have noted such a disconcerting dualism in the works of Lang. For example: in the ineffable poem *Destiny* are interpolated disastrous scenes of a refined bad taste. Even though we must admit that Fritz Lang is an accomplice, we hereby denounce as the presumed author of these eclectic essays and of this hazardous syncretism his wife, the scenarist Thea von Harbou.

A film, like a cathedral, should be anonymous. People of all classes, artists of all kinds have contributed to raising this monstrous cathedral of the modern cinema. All trades, all the engineers, crowds, actors, writers; Karl Freund, the ace of German cameramen with a pleiade of col-laborators, Ruttmann, creator of the "absolute" film. At the head of the architects is the name of Otto Hunte: it is to him and to Ruttmann in fact that we owe the most striking visualizations in *Metropolis*. The scenic artist, last of the theater's legacies to the cinema, scarcely plays a part here. We sense his hand only in the worst of *Metropolis*, in the emphatically named "Eternal gardens" with their lunatic baroque and striking bad taste. The architect will henceforth forever replace the designer. The cinema will be the faithful interpreter of the boldest dreams of architecture.

From *Luis Buñuel: A Critical Biography* by Francisco Aranda, translated and edited by David Robinson (New York: Da Capo Press, 1976). Reprinted by permission of the publisher.

In *Metropolis* the clock has only ten hours, which are those of work, and the life of the whole inner city moves to this compass of two times. The free men of *Metropolis* tyrannize the workers, nibelungs of the city, who work in an endless electric day in the depths of the earth. All that is lacking is the simple gearing of the Republic, the heart, the sentiment that is able to unite such extreme enemies. And in the dénouement we see the son of the director of *Metropolis* (Heart) unite in an eternal embrace his father (Head) and the general overseer (The Arm). Mix these symbolic ingredients with a good dose of bloodcurdling scenes, with stylized theatrical playing. Shake the mixture well and we have arrived at the content of *Metropolis*.

Yet on the other hand . . . What a captivating symphony of movement! How the engines sing amidst wonderful transparent triumphal arches formed by electric charges! All the glass shops in the world romantically melted into reflected light could nestle over the modern canon of the cinema. Every most furious glint of swords, the rhythmic succession of wheels, pistons, of uncreated mechanical forms is an admirable ode, a new poetry to our eyes. Physics and chemistry are miraculously transformed into rhythm. Not a moment of retardation. Even the titles, already rising and falling, revolving, hazy, melting by and by in light or disintegrating into shadows, unite in the general movement and themselves become images. In our judgment the capital defect of the film rests in the author's failure to follow the line shaped by Eisenstein in his *Potemkin,* which presented us with one actor alone, but full of novelty and possibilities: the mass. The matter of *Metropolis* calls for it. But instead we suffer a series of characters, full of arbitrary and vulgar passions, charged with a symbolism to which they in no way respond. This is not to say that there are no crowds in *Metropolis;* but they seem to respond more to a decorative need, to a gigantic ballet; they aim to delight us with their admirable and admired movement rather than to show us their soul, their exact obedience to more human, more objective motives. Even so there are moments—Babel, the workers' revolution, the final persecution of the automaton—in which both extremes are admirably accomplished.

Otto Hunte astounds us with his vision of the city of the year 2000. It might be mistaken, even antiquated in relation to the latest theories about the city of the future, but, from the photogenic point of view, its emotive force, its remarkable and surprising beauty are unparalleled; of such technical perfection that it can be studied minutely without the possibility of recognizing the *maquette*.

*Metropolis* cost ten million gold marks to make; with actors and extras, some 40,000 people took part in the production. The actual length of the film is 5,000 meters, but some two million meters were shot. The day of its premiere in Berlin stalls cost eighty gold marks each. Is it not demoralizing, taking into account such extraordinary resources, that the film did not turn out a model of perfection? From the comparison of *Metropolis* and *Napoleon*, the two biggest films which the modern cinema has produced, with other much humbler but also more perfect and purer works, comes the useful lesson that money is not the essential of modern cinema production. Compare *Rien que les heures,* which cost a mere 35,000 francs, and *Metropolis.* Sensitivity, paramount; intelligence, paramount, and everything else, including money, comes after.

# "Metropolis" and "M"

## Siegfried Kracauer

### "Metropolis"

Outstanding instances of grand-style manner were the three films Fritz Lang produced during the stabilized period. They dealt with thrilling adventures and technical fantasies symptomatic of the then current machine cult. The first of them was *Metropolis,* an Ufa production released at the beginning of 1927. Lang relates that he conceived the idea of this internationally known film when from shipboard he saw New York for the first time—a nocturnal New York glittering with myriad lights.[1] The city built in his film is a sort of super New York, realized on the screen with the aid of the so-called Shuftan process, an ingenious mirror device permitting the substitution of little models for giant structures.[2] This screen metropolis of the future consists of a lower and an upper city. The latter—a grandiose street of skyscrapers alive with an incessant stream of air taxis and cars—is the abode of big-business owners, high-ranking employees and pleasure-hunting gilded youth. In the lower city, shut off from daylight, the workers tend monstrous machines. They are slaves rather than workers. The film elaborates upon their rebellion against the master class in the upper world, and ends with the reconciliation of the two classes.

However, what is important here is not so much the plot as the preponderance of surface features in its development. In the brilliant laboratory episode, the creation of a robot is detailed with a technical exactitude that is not at all required to further the action. The office of the big boss, the vision of the Tower of Babel, the machinery and the arrangement of the

1. Information offered by Mr. Lang.
2. Information offered by Mr. Shuftan.

From *From Caligari to Hitler: A Psychological History of the German Film* by Siegfried Kracauer. Copyright 1947, © 1957 by Princeton University Press; Princeton Paperback, 1966. Reprinted by permission of Princeton University Press. Title supplied by the Editors.

masses: all illustrate Lang's penchant for pompous ornamentation.[3] In *Nibelungen,* his decorative style was rich in meaning; in *Metropolis,* the decorative not only appears as an end in itself, but even belies certain points made through the plot. It makes sense that, on their way to and from the machines, the workers form ornamental groups; but it is nonsensical to force them into such groups while they are listening to a comforting speech from the girl Maria during their leisure time. In his exclusive concern with ornamentation, Lang goes so far as to compose decorative patterns from the masses who are desperately trying to escape the inundation of the lower city. Cinematically as incomparable achievement, this inundation sequence is humanly a shocking failure. *Metropolis* impressed the German public. The Americans relished its technical excellence; the English remained aloof; the French were stirred by a film which seemed to them a blend of Wagner and Krupp, and on the whole an alarming sign of Germany's vitality.[4]

Lang's subsequent film, the mystery thriller *Spione* (*The Spy,* 1928), shared two traits with his *Dr. Mabuse.* It featured a master spy who, like Mabuse, led several different lives: besides the spy, he was also the president of a bank and a music-hall clown. And exactly like *Dr. Mabuse,* this new film refrained from conferring moral superiority upon the representatives of the law. Espionage and counterespionage were on the same level—two gangs fighting each other in a chaotic world. Yet there was one important difference: while Dr. Mabuse had incarnated the tyrant who takes advantage of the chaos around him, the master spy indulged in the spy business for the sole purpose, it seemed, of spying. He was a formalized Mabuse devoted to meaningless activities. By emphasizing this figure, the film reflected the neutrality prevalent during that period—a neutrality which also manifested itself in the absence of any distinction between legal and illegal pursuits and in a prodigal abundance of disguises. No character was what he appeared to be. This constant change of identities was appropriate to denote a state of mind in which the paralysis of the self interfered with any attempt at self-identification. As if to fill the void, Lang piled up sensations which conveyed no meaning. His imaginative virtuosity in shaping them reached its climax with a train wreck in a tunnel. Since it proved impossible to stage the catastrophe in life-size proportions, he gave the impression of it through confused mental images of the persons involved in this shock situation.

*The Spy* would have been a true forerunner of the Hitchcock thrillers if

3. Cf. Rotha, *Celluloid,* pp. 230–32; "Die entfesselte Kamera," *Ufa-Magazin,* March 25–31, 1927; Jahier, "42 Ans de Cinéma," *Le Rôle intellectuel du cinéma, p. 62.*

4. While H. G. Wells damned *Metropolis* as "quite the silliest film" (Rotha, *Film Till Now,* p. 194), Conan Doyle was enthusiastic about it (cf. "Was is los?") *Ufa Magazin,* April 15, 1927).

Lang had not fashioned it after the pompous manner of *Metropolis,* so that empty sensations took on the air of substantial revelations. Virtuosity alienated from content posed as art. In accordance with this pretense, Ufa issued a volume that was a triumph of bookbinding though it contained nothing but the Thea von Harbou novel from which *The Spy* had been made.[5]

In his third film, *Die Frau im Mond (The Girl in the Moon,* 1929), Lang imagined a rocket projectile carrying passengers to the moon. The cosmic enterprise was staged with a surprising veracity of vision; the plot was pitiable for its emotional shortcomings. These were so obvious that they discredited many an illusion Lang tried to create by showy virtuosity. The lunar landscape smelled distinctly of Ufa's Neubabelsberg studios . . . .[6]

[In *Metropolis,* however,] the paralyzed collective mind seemed to be talking with unusual clarity in its sleep. This is more than a metaphor: owing to a fortunate combination of receptivity and confusion, Lang's scriptwriter, Thea von Harbou, was not only sensitive to all undercurrents of the time, but indiscriminately passed on whatever happened to haunt her imagination.[7] *Metropolis* was rich in subterranean content that, like contraband, had crossed the borders of consciousness without being questioned.

Freder, son of the mammoth industrialist who controls the whole of Metropolis, is true to type: he rebels against his father and joins the workers in the lower city. There he immediately becomes a devotee of Maria, the great comforter of the oppressed. A saint rather than a socialist agitator, this young girl delivers a speech to the workers in which she declares that they can be redeemed only if the heart mediates between hand and brain. And she exhorts her listeners to be patient: soon the mediator will come. The industrialist, having secretly attended this meeting, deems the interference of the heart so dangerous that he entrusts an inventor with the creation of a robot looking exactly like Maria. This robot-Maria is to incite riots and furnish the industrialist with a pretext to crush the workers' rebellious spirit. He is not the first German screen tyrant to use such methods; Homunculus had introduced them much earlier. Stirred by the robot, the workers destroy their torturers, the machines, and release flood waters which then threaten to drown their own children. If it were not for Freder and the genuine Maria, who intervene at the last moment, all would be doomed. Of course, this elemental outburst has by far surpassed the

5. Program brochure to the film; Rotha, *Film Till Now,* p. 193, and *Celluloid,* p. 223; Herring, "Reasons for Rhyme," *Close Up,* Oct. 1929, pp. 280–81.
6. Rotha, *Celluloid,* pp. 232–37; Dreyfus, "La Femme sur la Lune," *La Revue du Cinéma,* May 1930, pp. 62–63; "Frau im Mond," *Close Up,* Nov. 1929, pp. 443–44; Jahier, "42 Ans de Cinéma," *Le Rôle intellectuel du cinéma,* p. 62; Arnheim, *Film als Kunst,* p. 180.
7. For the mixture of story ingredients in *Metropolis,* see article by Willy Haas on this film (*Kinematograph,* Jan. 11, 1927), quoted by Zaddach, *Der literarische Film,* p. 62.

petty little uprising for which the industrialist arranged. In the final scene, he is shown standing between Freder and Maria, and the workers approach, led by their foreman. Upon Freder's suggestion, his father shakes hands with the foreman, and Maria happily consecrates this symbolic alliance between labor and capital.

On the surface, it seems that Freder has converted his father; in reality, the industrialist has outwitted his son. The concession he makes amounts to a policy of appeasement that not only prevents the workers from winning their cause, but enables him to tighten his grip on them. His robot stratagem was a blunder inasmuch as it rested upon insufficient knowledge of the mentality of the masses. By yielding to Freder, the industrialist achieves intimate contact with the workers, and thus is in a position to influence their mentality. He allows the heart to speak—a heart accessible to his insinuations.

In fact, Maria's demand that the heart mediate between hand and brain could well have been formulated by Goebbels. He, too, appealed to the heart—in the interest of totalitarian propaganda. At the Nuremberg Party Convention of 1934, he praised the "art" of propaganda as follows: "May the shining flame of our enthusiasm never be extinguished. This flame alone gives light and warmth to the creative art of modern political propaganda. Rising from the depths of the people, this art must always descend back to it and find its power there. Power based on guns may be a good thing; it is, however, better and more gratifying to win the heart of a people and to keep it." The pictorial structure of the final scene confirms the analogy between the industrialist and Goebbels. If in this scene the heart really triumphed over tyrannical power, its triumph would dispose of the all-devouring decorative scheme that in the rest of *Metropolis* marks the industrialist's claim to omnipotence. Artist that he was, Lang could not possibly overlook the antagonism between the breakthrough of intrinsic human emotions and his ornamental patterns. Nevertheless, he maintains these patterns up to the very end: the workers advance in the form of a wedge-shaped, strictly symmetrical procession which points towards the industrialist standing on the portal steps of the cathedral. The whole composition denotes that the industrialist acknowledges the heart for the purpose of manipulating it; that he does not give up his power, but will expand it over a realm not yet annexed—the realm of the collective soul. Freder's rebellion results in the establishment of totalitarian authority, and he considers this result a victory.

Freder's pertinent reaction corroborates what has been said about the way in which the street films as well as the youth films anticipate the change of the "system." Now it can no longer be doubted that the "new order" both series foreshadow is expected to feed upon that love with which Asta Nielsen's prostitute overflows, and to substitute totalitarian discipline for the obsolete mechanical one. In the case of *Metropolis,* Goebbels' own words bear out the conclusions drawn from this film. Lang relates that immediately after Hitler's rise to power Goebbels sent for him: "... he told me that, many years before, he and the Führer had seen my picture *Metropolis* in a small town, and Hitler had said at that time that he wanted me to make the Nazi pictures."[8] ...

### *"M"*

Fritz Lang told me that in 1930, before *M* went into production, a short notice appeared in the press, announcing the tentative title of his new film, *Mörder unter uns (Murderer Among Us).* Soon he received numerous threatening letters and, still worse, was bluntly refused permission to use the Staaken studio for his film. "But why this incomprehensible conspiracy against a film about the Düsseldorf child-murderer Kürten?" he asked the studio manager in despair. "*Ach,* I see," the manager said. He beamed with relief and immediately surrendered the keys of Staaken. Lang, too, understood; while arguing with the man, he had seized his lapel and caught a glimpse of the Nazi insignia on its reverse. "Murderer among us": the Party feared to be compromised. On that day, Lang added, he came of age politically.

*M* opens with the case of Elsie, a schoolgirl who disappears and after a while is found slain in the woods. Since her murder is preceded and followed by similar crimes, the city lives through a veritable nightmare. The police work feverishly to track down the child-murderer, but succeed only in disturbing the underworld. The city's leading criminals therefore decide to ferret out the monster themselves. For once, their interests coincide with those of the law. Here Thea von Harbou borrows a motif from Brecht's *Dreigroschenoper:* the gang of criminals enlists the help of a beggars' union, converting its membership into a network of unobtrusive scouts. Even though the police meanwhile identify the murderer as a former inmate of a lunatic asylum, the criminals with the aid of a blind beggar steal a march on the detectives. At night, they break into the office building in which the fugitive has taken refuge, pull him out of a lumber room beneath the roof, and then drag him to a deserted factory, where they improvise a "kangaroo court," which eventually pronounces his death sentence. The police appear in time to hand him over to the authorities.

Released in 1931, this Nero production found enthusiastic response everywhere. It was not only Lang's first talkie, but his first important film after the pretentious duds he had made during the stabilized period. *M*

8. "Fritz Lang," *New York World Telegram,* June 11, 1941.

again reaches the level of his earlier films, *Destiny* and *Nibelungen,* and moreover surpasses them in virtuosity. To increase the film's documentary value, pictorial reports on current police procedures are inserted in such a skillful way that they appear to be part of the action. Ingenious cutting interweaves the milieus of the police and the underworld; while the gang leaders discuss their plans, police experts, too, sit in conference, and these two meetings are paralleled by constant shifts of scene which hinge on subtle association. The comic touch inherent in the cooperation between the lawless and the law materializes on various occasions. Witnesses refuse to agree upon the simplest facts; innocent citizens indict each other fiercely. Set against these gay interludes, the episodes concentrating upon the murders seem even more horrifying.

Lang's imaginative use of sound to intensify dread and terror is unparalleled in the history of the talkies. Elsie's mother, after having waited for hours, steps out of her flat and desperately shouts the child's name. While her "Elsie!" sounds, the following pictures pass across the screen: the empty stairwell; the empty attic; Elsie's unused plate on the kitchen table; a remote patch of grass with her ball lying on it; a balloon catching in telegraph wires—the very balloon which the murderer had bought from the blind beggar to win her confidence. Like a pedal point, the cry "Elsie!" underlies these otherwise unconnected shots, fusing them into a sinister narrative. Whenever the murderer is possessed by the lust for killing, he whistles a few bars of a melody by Grieg. His whistling threads the film, an ominous foreboding of his appearance. A little girl is seen walking along: as she stops in front of a shop window, the weird Grieg melody approaches her, and suddenly the bright afternoon street seems clouded by threatening shadows. Later on, the whistling reaches the ears of the blind beggar for a second time and thus brings about the murderer's own doom. Another fatal sound is produced by his vain effort to remove, with his jackknife, the lock of the door which has slammed behind him after his flight into the lumber room. When the criminals pass along the top floor of the office building, this jarring noise reminiscent of the prolonged gnawing of a rat, betrays his presence.[9]

The film's true center is the murderer himself. Peter Lorre portrays him incomparably as a somewhat infantile petty bourgeois who eats apples on the street and could not possibly be suspected of killing a fly. His landlady, when questioned by the police, describes this tenant of hers as a quiet and proper person. He is fat and looks effeminate rather than resolute. A brilliant pictorial device serves to characterize his morbid propensities.

9. Arnheim, *Film als Kunst,* pp. 230, 252, 300, comments on several devices in *M.* Cf. Hamilton, "M," *National Board of Review Magazine,* March 1933, pp. 8–11.

On three different occasions, scores of inanimate objects, much more obtrusive than in *The Blue Angel,* surround the murderer; they seem on the point of engulfing him. Standing before a cutlery shop, he is photographed in such a way that his face appears within a rhomboid reflection of sparkling knives. Sitting on a café terrace behind an ivy-covered trellis, with only his cheeks gleaming through the foliage, he suggests a beast of prey lurking in the jungle. Finally, trapped in the lumber room, he is hardly distinguishable from the tangled debris in which he tries to evade his captors. Since in many German films the predominance of mute objects symbolizes the ascendancy of irrational powers, these three shots can be assumed to define the murderer as a prisoner of uncontrollable instincts. Evil urges overwhelm him in exactly the same manner in which multiple objects close in on his screen image.

This is corroborated by his own testimony before the "kangaroo court," an episode opening with a couple of shots which render perfectly the shock he experiences at that moment. Three criminals, insensitive to the murderer's frantic protests, push, drag and kick him forward. He lands on the floor. As he begins to look about, the close-up of his face—a face distorted with rage and fear—abruptly gives way to a long shot surveying the group of criminals, beggars and street women in front of him. The impression of shock results from the terrifying contrast between the wretched creature on the floor and this immovable group which, arranged in Lang's best monumental style, watches him in stony silence. It is as if the murderer has unexpectedly collided with a human wall. Then, in an attempt to justify himself, he accounts for his crimes in this way: I am always forced to move along the streets, and always someone is behind me. It is I. I sometimes feel I am myself behind me, and yet I cannot escape. . . . I want to run away—I must run away. The specters are always pursuing me—unless I do it. And afterwards, standing before a poster, I read what I have done. Have I done this? But I don't know anything about it. I loathe it—I must—loathe it—must—I can no longer. . . .

# "Fury"

## Graham Greene

*Fury* is Herr Fritz Lang's first American picture. The importation of continental directors is always a nervous business. Hollywood offers so much in
the way of technical resources (so that a witty playboy like Lubitsch gains
by the translation), so little help, among the yes-men and the entertainment
racketeers, to the imagination. *M,* until *Fury* Herr Lang's best film, the
study of a child-murderer, could hardly have passed the Hollywood execu-
tives; *Metropolis, The Spy, Dr. Mabuse,* these melodramatic pictures of
Herr Lang's apprenticeship, on the other hand, might possibly have been
made with even more chromiumed efficiency in America; and I visited
*Fury* in some trepidation lest Herr Lang had been driven back to melodrama (melodrama, of course, infinitely more expert than, say, Mr. Hitchcock's). But *Fury,* the story of how a mob in a small Southern town lynches
an innocent man who has been arrested under suspicion of kidnapping, is
astonishing, the only film I know to which I have wanted to attach the
epithet of ''great.'' There have been other films—*Kameradschaft* comes
first to mind—where a generous theme, a sense of spiritual integrity, has
somehow got conveyed *in spite of* the limitations of the screen, but no other
picture which has allowed no value to slip, which has conveyed completely
by sound and image better than by any other medium the pity and terror of
the story. (The last third of the picture leading up to a neatly contrived
happy ending is not on the same level, though the picture never falls below
finely directed melodrama.)

Mr. Spencer Tracy as the victim, a garage-keeper, a simple honest
kindly creature saving up to be married; Miss Sylvia Sidney as his girl, a
teacher in the Southern town; Mr. Edward Ellis as the Sheriff, harsh,
upright, ready to defend his prisoner to the last tear-gas bomb, with his
own life if necessary, but belonging nevertheless to the same township as

the mob, knowing it as individuals, each in his home, his office, his barber's chair, refusing at the trial which follows the lynching to identify a single culprit: all these give their finest performances. Miss Sidney in particular. She has never more deeply conveyed the pain and inarticulacy of tenderness. No film passion here, no exaggeration of the ordinary human feeling, as the two lovers shelter under the elevated from the drenching rain, say good-bye at the railway station with faces and hands pressed to wet fogging windows: it is the ordinary recognizable agony, life as one knows it is lived. And the same power to catch vividly the truthful detail makes the lynching of almost unbearable horror. I am trying not to exaggerate, but the brain does flinch at each recurring flick of truth in much the same way as at the grind-grind of an electric road-drill: the horrible laughter and inflated nobility of the good citizens, the youth leaping on a bar and shouting "Let's have some fun," the regiment of men and women marching down the road into the face of the camera, arm in arm, laughing and excited like recruits on the first day of a war, the boy singing out at the Sheriff, "I'm Popeye the Sailorman," at last the first stone, until the building is ablaze, the innocent man is suffocating behind the bars, and a woman holds her baby up to see the fire.

Any other film this year is likely to be dwarfed by Herr Lang's extraordinary achievement: no other director has got so completely the measure of his medium, is so consistently awake to the counterpoint of sound and image. . . .

# Fate, Murder, and Revenge

## Peter Bogdanovich

*... Listen to the legend of Chuck-A-Luck, Chuck-A-Luck—*
*Listen to the wheel of Fate;*
*As round and round with a whisperin' sound it spins,*
*It spins the old, old story of HATE,*
*MURDER*
*AND REVENGE ...*

*"The Legend of Chuck-A-Luck"*
(*from* Rancho Notorious)

Except in France, very little of value has been written about Fritz Lang's American films, though they make up over half of his work. The conventional opinion (as voiced by Gavin Lambert's 1955 *Sight & Sound* articles) is that after his first two pictures in Hollywood (*Fury, You Only Live Once*), Lang went into decline, with only occasional flashes of his former talent and personality. This is as tedious and inaccurate a cliché as the theory that Hitchcock's British films are better than his American ones, that John Ford never made another movie quite as good as *The Informer,* or that Orson Welles hasn't done anything worth discussing since *Citizen Kane.*

Whereas Lang's American work is generally accessible, his German films are extremely difficult to get to see and most criticism is based on opinions formed years ago; the German films therefore are enriched by the tricks of memory, and the more "common" American ones simply don't stand a chance. That something made *now* could possibly be better than something made *then* also seems inconceivable to most "liberal" critics. (Lang's own preferences are strongly influenced—as he admits—by the circumstances surrounding the making of the films, and on their success or lack of it.) There is oneupmanship operating here too: if a reader is told that *Spione* (1928) is much better than *The Big Heat* (1953), the critic isn't likely to be challenged, because the reader's chances of seeing *Spione* are poor. But that's how values in film history are set. One wonders how long it has been since the *critic* saw *Spione*.

More informative and to the point is Andrew Sarris' observation that "both *Metropolis* [1927] and *Moonfleet* [1955] . . . share the same bleak view of the universe where man grapples with his personal destiny, and inevitably loses" (*Film Culture,* no. 28, Spring 1963). Lang's work has been remarkably consistent over the years, both in theme and outlook: the fight against fate continues from *Der Müde Tod* (his first success in Germany) to *Beyond a Reasonable Doubt* (his last American picture). And the "Chuck-A-Luck" song that expresses the moral of *Rancho Notorious* (1952) could as easily be applied to *Die Nibelungen* (1924):

> . . . Revenge is a bitter and evil fruit
> And Death hangs beside it on the bough.
> These men who lived by the code of hate
> Have nothing to live for now . . .

It could be argued that Lang's American films are better than his German ones; certainly they are meaningful to a larger audience. As Hitchcock has said, "When we make films for the United States, we are automatically making them for all the world—because America is full of foreigners." (*The Cinema of Alfred Hitchcock,* 1963). More succinctly, he advised Truffaut when making films always to "remember *Japon* . . ." In his own way, Lang quite consciously did the same. By changing the German super-hero into the American common man, he gave his work not only a wider appeal but more emotional impact: a far bigger audience can identify with the protagonists of *Fury* (1936) or *The Big Heat* than with the people of *Die Nibelungen*.

The shift from silence to sound was also a turning point for Lang. In its documentary nature, his first talkie, *M* (1931), is as different from his preceding German work as are his subsequent films in America. One feels, in fact, that given equal freedom and the differences in milieu, Lang might well have made *M* the same way in Hollywood as he had in Berlin. Not only is *M* still his most famous film (and personal favorite), but, significantly, it is the only one that *could* be remade in an American locale— which Joseph Losey *did* in 1951 (for certain sequences, shot by shot).

In the first two American films, Lang clearly phrased his main themes, on which he was to play variations through most of the twenty other pictures he made here. *Fury* deals as much with the sickness of revenge, of hate, as it does with the iniquities of destiny—the merciless-ness of which gives *You Only Live Once* (1937) its near-classical dimen-sion: Eddie (Henry Fonda), the three-time loser, is as doomed from the start as Oedipus; but for Lang, it is not the outcome that matters in a struggle against fate, it is the fight itself. Long after the social aspects of these films—dangers of lynch mob mentality, society's injustice to ex-convicts—are forgotten, the more universal qualities will continue to have strength and poignancy.

Their social commitment, however, is exactly what makes these two films so popular with Lambert and other Grierson-minded critics who will dismiss Sternberg as a "photographer," and discuss art in terms of "im-portance" and morality; the visual aspects tend to be ignored if there is—for them—no greater meaning attached. A film is not examined for how much of the artist is exposed, but for how much of society. Therefore—because it is a personal tragedy that does not in any way indict the world at large—*Scarlet Street* (1945), according to Lambert, is "only an exercise in low-life. Its texture is brilliant but no more than decorative in its significance; and for this reason its essential thinness becomes increas-ingly apparent," whereas *The Big Heat*—because it could be interpreted as a study of city corruption—"is a minor but frequently brilliant film that stands comparison with his best work." However, it could equally be argued that *Scarlet Street* is nearly flawless, whereas *The Big Heat* is marred by several "average family" scenes (Glenn Ford, his wife and child) that ring false because Lang has little interest in anything approach-ing normality—in fact, he denies its existence. On the other hand, all the characters in *Scarlet Street* are believable because each in his own way is warped by life, and the crippled—physically, emotionally—are Lang's true métier. The finest scenes in *The Big Heat*—in all his pictures—are the ones that deal with the insulted and injured.

Lang remarked once in conversation that he considers *You and Me* (1938) his worst film. Certainly it is the least successful considering its ambitions; on the other hand, it is much more personal and interesting in its failings than *The Return of Frank James* (1940) or *American Guerrilla in the Philippines* (1950) are in their reasonable effectiveness as genre pic-tures. The Brechtian flavor he was trying to capture eludes him—except in the excellent opening montage about pickpocketing, and in a sardonic, memorable sequence in which a group of ex-convicts reminisce with nostalgia about their days in prison. Otherwise, the attempts at lightness and dialect humor are labored and unappealing, and the visual wit that distinguished his French adaptation of *Liliom* (1934) is missing.

Brecht's influence is naturally apparent in *Hangmen Also Die!* (1943), since the playwright collaborated on the screenplay with Lang, but it also appears, not so predictably, in *Rancho Notorious*, a fascinating Western in which the story is told through—and takes the subtle form of—a ballad. There is, too, an individuality here, a driving forward motion, that is missing from his other Westerns, *The Return of Frank James* and *Western Union* (1941)—both assignments, mainly interesting today for their use of color (first times for Lang) as well as an authenticity of detail and atmosphere. Though entertaining (especially the second), one could imagine Henry King (who made the original *Jesse James*, to which Lang's film was a sequel), or DeMille (whose successful 1939 *Union Pacific* no doubt led Fox to produce *Western Union*) making the same projects. *Rancho Notorious*, however, is uniquely Langian—visually, temperamentally, thematically; a man whose sweetheart has been raped and murdered *lives* for his revenge; once it has been achieved, life becomes meaningless: hate, which drove him "like a whip," has burned out his soul. Despite budgetary limitations (resulting in some unfortunate backdrops), it is among Lang's finest pictures.

With *Man Hunt* (1941), Lang began a series of four anti-Nazi films (*Hangmen Also Die!*, *The Ministry of Fear*, 1944, *Cloak and Dagger*, 1945), each characterized by an intense personal involvement, a vivid awareness of the fascist mind, missing from other similar movies of the period. Not only had Lang known these types in Germany, but several of his early films, (*Dr. Mabuse der Spieler*, 1922, *Spione*, even *Die Spinnen*, 1919–20), had forecast the Hitler calamity in their portraits of diabolical super-criminals planning world domination. Lang's last film in pre-war Germany, *Das Testament des Dr. Mabuse* (1932), was actually a thinly veiled anti-Nazi picture (the world's first), which as a result was banned by Goebbels and never received much exposure anywhere. With Hitler's plots a reality, Lang brought a venom and savagery to these American pictures as well as a kind of universality that transcends the propaganda of the day: *Man Hunt* today retains its pathos just as *Hangmen Also Die!*—the most personal of the quartet—has an anger unaffected by time.

Alternating with these pictures of Nazi terror, Lang created three other equally chilling nightmare worlds: *The Woman in the Window* (1944), *Scarlet Street* and *Secret Beyond the Door* (1948) are remarkable studies in the inexorableness of fate. The first (though Lang defends it) and last are marred by unsatisfactory endings that tend to dissipate the mesmerizing force of everything that has preceded the "awakening." *Scarlet Street*, however, is one of his best films—a devastating portrait of a good and talented man hopelessly—fatefully—bewitched by a frivolous woman and her lover (the *femme fatale* had been the subject of several of Lang's earliest pictures). With a pervasive sense of doom, great visual density and narrative power, it shares with *You Only Live Once* its formal perfection as well as its painful sadness.

Lang began his last decade as a Hollywood director with *American Guerrilla in the Philippines*—the only one of his movies that could properly be called "routine"—and with *House by the River* (1950), perhaps his least known work; filled with striking imagery, and consistent thematically (a man accidentally murders a girl, then tries to escape the trap fate has set for him), it deserves resurrection. The same is true of *Clash by Night* (1952), an explosive picture (the result of Clifford Odets' dialogue combined with Lang's camerawork) which begins with a fishing-to-canneries sequence that would put most documentary filmmakers to shame.

Lang cannot approach a project casually; he enjoys making films too much. Even such a relatively minor work as *The Blue Gardenia* (1953) contains as corrosive a view of society as any he has shot—all the more insidious because the surface is so normal, the people so plain. In *While the City Sleeps* (1956), this seemingly civilized exterior reveals a cancerous center: unlike Haghi (of *Spione*), the monsters are not disfigured super-criminals plotting from subterranean cellars, but well-dressed citizens in the mainstream of life. These people who vie so ruthlessly for the editorship of a large city newspaper are much more brutalized and corrupt than the psychopathic murderer they are hunting. (Just as in *Beyond a Reasonable Doubt* [1956], the puritanical woman who betrays her lover at the end commits an act more cold and reprehensible than his passion-murder of a stripper.) The sick boy (in *City*) who pleads, "Please catch me before I kill more!" has a self-awareness, a humanity even, that does not exist in his pursuers; but the psychic destruction they cause goes unpunished, the real sickness of society is not cured.

As a creator of nightmares, Lang has few peers; his world—whether it's the eighteenth-century England of *Moonfleet* or the middle-class railroad community of *Human Desire* (1954)—is one of shadows and night—ominous, haunted—filled with foreboding and violence, anxiety and death. The tears he elicits for the damned figures who inhabit it—the couple in *You Only Live Once,* the whore in *Man Hunt,* the artist in *Scarlet Street,* the moll in *The Big Heat*—are born from the depth of his personality; in his words, they have "all my heart."

# Loving Fritz Lang

## François Truffaut

> *The Big Heat.* American film directed by Fritz Lang. Screenplay
> by Sydney Boehme. Photography by Charles Lang. With Glenn
> Ford, Gloria Grahame, and Jocelyn Brando. Columbia Pictures,
> 1953.

Whenever the film critic sits down to analyze in depth the work of a
particular director, he has to accept a stiff handicap at the very outset. For,
while the literary critic may hie himself to the nearest library to consult the
complete works of his subject at will, it is rare to find all the films of any
director on view at one time. Yet at this moment, December 1953, a
marvelous fate has seen fit to bestow upon us a veritable cornucopia of
Lang. His newest film, *The Big Heat,* has just appeared; *Rancho Notorious*
and *Cloak and Dagger* are showing in various quarters of the city; *Scarlet
Street* is playing at the Parnasse, and the Cinémathèque is presenting on
alternate evenings Lang's last German film, *The Testament of Dr. Mabuse,*
and his first American picture, *Fury.*

    Throughout all these films runs a thread of solitude, a favorite theme:
Man fighting alone in a half-hostile, half-indifferent universe. Even the
titles of Lang's pictures—*M, Fury, Man Hunt, You Only Live Once*—
proclaim the director's fidelity to a single vision. A man becomes entangled in a conflict. Almost, at first, by accident, or, if he is a cop, a soldier,
or a philosopher, by simply going about his normal business. Before long
he becomes sick and tired of the battle; it seems to him almost pointless to
carry on, and he is on the verge of abandoning his efforts. This is the crux,
the turning point. And at this moment, inevitably, an event occurs to force
the protagonist back into the action; only now he is in it to the hilt. The
pivotal event is nearly always a death. Someone outside the original conflict is killed, usually a woman, often a woman the hero loves (Joan

From *Cahiers du Cinéma,* vol. 6, no. 31 (Jaunary 1954). Translated especially for this volume
by Sallie Iannotti.

Bennett in *Man Hunt,* Kennedy's fiancée in *Rancho Notorious,* Jocelyn Brando in *The Big Heat*). From this point the conflict is strictly personal; what began accidentally or as a duty to a political or social cause becomes an obsession with revenge. Walter Pidgeon at the beginning of *Man Hunt* almost makes sport of Nazi barbarism. But then Joan Bennett dies and the game becomes a deadly reality. Hitler has killed her; therefore Hitler must die. Similarly, Glenn Ford in *The Big Heat* must leave the Police Department in order to avenge himself more directly.

Lang's universe has the high morality, the rules and ethics, of a cosmic game. Certainly conventional morality cannot be found here, and the forces of our social conventions—police, army, even the Resistance—are portrayed as contemptible, weak, and dispirited. In fact, society and honest folk in general take quite a beating in Lang's films. His protagonists, in one sense, represent the interests of society—which is why espionage plays such a marvelous part in his pictures—though it is hardly an obvious connection or the stuff of melodrama, since the hero is seeking restitution solely for himself. He is not the defender of the weak nor the champion of the oppressed; he makes no great claims, but, in fact, avenges a single victim in each film. Lang is interested primarily in the uncommon figure, the exception to the masses, found in the unassuming guise of a trainer, a cop, a spy, or an unsophisticated cowboy.

A highly moral universe, I suggested earlier. A conventional universe, some critics will reply, and not entirely without justification. Lang uses his plots to make a game of conventions, and then plays by the rules. His characters, thrown into the action, are teased by a reality which hovers continually on the edge of irrationality and defiance. They are swept along in their private darknesses to the very limits of their being, to the very limits, indeed, of humanity, where the bad becomes truly evil, and the good achieves the sublime.

What Lang is striving for, of course, is the complicity of the audience—both in and out of the action. Indeed, the spectator would have to be tragically impassive not to feel once in a while the omnipotence of the creator in himself, a creator who raises up and cuts down at will. So if, in the last analysis, Fritz Lang plays a kind of god in his films, we cannot really reproach him too much. He is too fine an artist not to know exactly when to submit to the natural course of the narrative and when to control it. He dominates and is dominated in perfect sequence.

There is a movement afoot in cinema these days that seems to take pleasure in obfuscation and the promotion of "cool." To this aloof detachment I offer the antidote of Lang's work. For Lang is a moral preacher, in his own peculiar way, a filmmaker with a dash of Balzac. He is not afraid to make decisions; he takes a stand, he draws conclusions. In his films each frame answers the questions: How? Why? His men and women frankly love one another; his earth is round, it turns upon its axis; two and two invariably add up to four.

*The Big Heat* is a fine film—physically and emotionally very satisfying. In many ways it is a precise re-enactment of *Rancho Notorious* in thriller form. Lang works admirably with actors, and perhaps even better with actresses. In this picture he gives Gloria Grahame a chance to perform at her best. She is able to endow even the simplest actions with a poignant significance; she walks, she dances, she talks on the telephone, with flair. And then, in a series of events that is almost unbelievably painful, she is mutilated, masked, and dies. A certain high-strung tension always exists in her performances, and in this film it is absolutely perfect.

The narrative itself is beautifully simple, and as always with Lang, of the utmost violence.

"*The Big Heat,*" Louis Chauvet writes. "Not bad. Not terribly good. The old Fritz Lang is gone. We've all known it for several years. The man who brought us *Metropolis* hasn't a trace of that grand symbolism left; and only a drop of the old expressionism." What sophistry! But this is the attitude the pedants are taking, and the time has come to dispose of it once and for all. Looking at Lang's entire work, it seems impossible not to notice how much of Hollywood appears in his German films. *Spies,* for example, or *Metropolis,* or *The Testament of Dr. Mabuse*—all those spectaculars. Conversely, Lang strives to keep a great many of his germanic effects in his American pictures—certain sets, certain lighting effects, the tasty vistas, lively camera angles, Gloria Grahame's mask-like bandage, and so on.

Of course it is hard not to be irritated when many of our fine European directors defect to Hollywood; and it is tempting to read into this exodus a symbol of failing genius on the part of the exiles. But this theory becomes fatuous when the same critics (who seem to labor under a special grace for the blind) accept the contrary prejudice and declare that the best of Hollywood is inspired by European talent—Hitchcock, Lang, Preminger, Renoir.

Another legend has it that the American director is a sharp operator, an astute jack-of-all-trades who does the best he can with material forced on him by that all powerful ogre, the producer. Yet if this is the case, it seems strange indeed that Lang's American pictures, written by a dozen different script writers, tell essentially one great story.

This would suggest, I think, that Fritz Lang is truly the *auteur* of his films, and if his themes and borrowed stories take on an ordinary guise, the banal illusion of a thriller, a war flick, a Western, this in itself might be considered the sign of a certain integrity—a cinema which denies that greatness must adorn itself in a certain enticing package.

At any rate it can certainly be said with assurance that in order to create cinema, it is necessary to create illusion. Or, from a slightly different angle: if you want to talk turkey with the producer, you'd better go in disguise. Now, the film in simple and insignificant guise bears close scrutiny, for disguise often masks a quality that is its opposite in nature. Indeed, I personally prefer the director who uses a surface that is normal, and people so plain . . .

Ah yes, we should love Fritz Lang. Toast the premiere of each new film, rush to see it, return again and again, and wait impatiently for the next (which will be, I believe, *The Blue Gardenia*).

**Note.**   The novel by William P. McGivern, from which *The Big Heat* was adapted, appeared in France under the title *Coups de torchons*. It is a trashy bit of hackwork, infinitely inferior to the film despite the film's fidelity to the original story. In brief, the picture is believable, and the book is not. This is true also with such films as *Big Sleep* and *Dark Passage*. We owe to American censorship the fact that Marlowe is not a pederast and that the characters are all predominantly either good or bad. A moralistic censorship requires the proposal of an obvious moral. Yet if this film had been attempted in France, with Lang's script indicting the French police and judiciary system, even if it had kept the final scene, when Glenn Ford rejoins the police force, it would not have gotten past the pre-censors. So, as Rossellini said: Where is liberty?

# Jean Renoir

JEAN RENOIR was born in Paris in 1894, the second son of Auguste Renoir, the Impressionist painter, and, as a child and teen-ager, the frequent subject of his father's paintings. During World War I he served in the French Cavalry and as a reconnaisance pilot in the Air Force. After marriage in 1920 to Catherine Hessling (one of his father's models), Renoir was a ceramicist for almost four years, until he became convinced by Stroheim's Foolish Wives and Volkov's Le Brasier ardent that a French national cinema, taking its subjects from French life, was possible. Filled with enthusiasm, he wrote a script for a film to star Hessling. But he became dissatisfied with Albert Dieudonné's direction of the film and began his own directing career with La Fille de l'eau (1924), financed by the sale of several of his father's paintings. He made six other substantial silent films, including most notably Nana (1926), based on Zola's novel, a film of the theater with lavish interiors that complement the natural settings of La Fille de l'eau.

By the end of the silent period, Renoir had earned a reputation for extravagance reminiscent of his idol, Stroheim. But he quickly made a short sound film, On purge bébé, that convinced producers that he could deal with the new medium cheaply and efficiently. Thus began the period of his greatest creativity—fourteen films from 1931 to 1939, two years before he would leave France in the wake of the Nazi occupation. The stylistic variety of Renoir's films of the 1930s is often astonishing; the dark shadows and grim social melodrama of La Chienne (1931), the misty crossroads of the detective story La Nuit du carrefour (1932), the sunny energy of the satiric Boudu Saved from Drowning (1932), the fatalistic pessimism of Toni (1935). In all these films no mood is unrelieved by contrast, no character single-minded enough to avoid conveying a personality larger than the plot requires.

During this time Renoir often worked with the same équipe or group of technicians and performers, and one film, The Crime of M. Lange (1936), celebrates the possibility of a self-sustained artistic community (writing, illustrating, and publishing a magazine devoted to stories of the American West). Also during this period Renoir adapted films from plays (Boudu; Chotard and Company, 1934; The Lower Depths, 1936) and from novels (Madame Bovary, 1934; La Bête humaine, 1938). His two masterpieces are La Grande Illusion (1937, in which Stroheim plays a major role) and La Règle du jeu (1939). The two titles—the great illusion and the rules of the game—suggest the interplay between nature and artifice that is the hallmark of Renoir's style and themes throughout his career.

After leaving France for the United States, Renoir made five films, generally much darker in tone and treatment than his earlier films, although obviously descended from the pessimism of La Règle du jeu about *the place of passion in a social world.* The River *(1950), filmed in India, was Renoir's first film in color and a triumphant return to themes of exuberance in natural processes. Three films of the 1950s*—The Golden Coach *(1953),* French Cancan *(1955), and* Elena et les hommes *(1956)— bring this new energy and optimism into the world of theater and artifice, now less a retreat from the world than a new source of value.*

*Renoir's interest in new visual techniques, especially marked in his silent period by* The Little Match Girl *(1928), was rekindled again in 1959 when he made two films for television*—The Testament of Dr. Cordelier *(in black and white), and* Picnic on the Grass *(in color).* The Elusive Corporal *(1962), a dark sequel to* La Grande Illusion, *dealing with prison-camp escapes in World War II, and* The Little Theater of Jean Renoir *(1969), a four-section film made for television that displays Renoir's work in a variety of moods and methods, were his final films.*

*In addition to their visual qualities, their themes, and their experiments with a looser narrative construction, Renoir's films are remarkable also for the way in which many of them are shaped around the qualities of a particular actor or actress—a method first developed most concertedly in* Boudu *with Michel Simon, and followed with Jean Gabin, Anna Magnani, Ingrid Bergman, and others.*

*The scripts of* La Grande Illusion *and* La Règle du jeu *have both been published in English (1968, 1970). Renoir has also written a novel,* The Notebooks of Captain Georges *(1966), plays, a biography of his father, and a recent autobiographical work,* My Life and My Films *(1974). Works on Renoir available in English include those of Pierre Leprohon (1971), Leo Braudy (1972), André Bazin (1973), Raymond Durgnat (1974), and Penelope Gilliatt (1975).*

# The French Renoir

## André Bazin

The most immediately noticeable paradox in Renoir's style, and the one which almost always trips up the public, is his apparent casualness toward the very elements of the cinema which the public takes most seriously: the scenario and the action. Slip-ups in detail and even casting "errors" abound in the films of the renowned "realist."

It will be argued that, on the contrary, Sylvia Bataille and Jeanne Marken in *A Day in the Country,* Pierre Fresnay and Erich von Stroheim in *Grand Illusion,* and Jean Gabin and Simone Simon in *The Human Beast* are perfect examples of actors made for their roles. This is true enough. It is certainly not the case, however, for Jacques Brunius and Renoir himself in *A Day in the Country.* None of the major actors in *The Rules of the Game* is in his element (with the exception of Gaston Modot and Paulette Dubost). And who would claim that the cast of *The Lower Depths* stepped from the Gorki play? Gabin as a hero in a Russian novel is a long shot at best; and it would be difficult to conceive of a more spectacular bit of miscasting than Valentine Tessier in *Madame Bovary.* She is appropriate as the Emma at the end of the film, but her obvious maturity makes it difficult to believe in her virginity earlier and certainly impossible to accept her as the extremely young Emma at the beginning of the story. In the film she is not made to age physically in the slightest.

One could go on forever citing similar examples, for Renoir seems to take pleasure in making unlikely choices in about three-quarters of his casting. Rather than give up an actor who appeals to him in spite of what the script calls for, Renoir seems to be able to modify the scenario in order to justify his choice.

Even more than the casting "errors," Renoir's direction of his actors gives the impression of an almost annoying nonchalance. The casting is

From *Jean Renoir* by André Bazin. © 1971 by Janine Bazin and Editions Champ Libre. Translation by W. W. Halsey and W. H. Simon © 1973 by Simon & Schuster, Inc. Reprinted by permission of Simon & Schuster, Inc., and Harold Matson Co., Inc.

tangential to the roles, but more than that, the style of acting seems to be irrelevant to the dialogue and the dramatic situation. Given a certain scene to film, Renoir frequently seems to treat it as nothing more than a pretext for a completely new and original creation. The party in *The Rules of the Game* is a perfect example. In *Tire au flanc* (a very revealing little sketch), Renoir's indifference toward the scenario is apparent throughout. Each scene uses the Mouézy-Eon story merely as a take-off point, rapidly developing into a sort of *commedia dell' arte*, a phenomenon reminiscent of the way Chaplin passes imperceptibly from the simple repetition of a gesture to its pure choreography.

Renoir showed a similar disregard for the script in shooting Boudu's first suicide attempt from the Pont des Arts. Rather than hire extras he simply filmed the group of curious observers attracted by the moviemakers. To understand why this approach is so appropriate for the scene, one must realize that the overriding purpose of the scene is to make fun of the world. With that aim in mind, there would be no other way to film it. As a final example of Renoir's cavalier approach to filming, remember that *The Lower Depths* was shot along the banks of the Marne, with the false beards and wigs of the Parisian muzhiks not even properly attached, at least figuratively speaking.

In short, Renoir directs his actors as if he liked them more than the scenes they are acting and preferred the scenes which they interpret to the scenario from which they come. This approach accounts for the disparity between his dramatic goals and the style of acting, which tends to turn our attention from these aims. This style is added to the script like rich paint liberally applied to a line drawing: often the colors obscure and spill over the lines. This approach also explains the effort required to truly enjoy half the scenes Renoir directs. Whereas most directors try to convince the viewer immediately of the objective and psychological reality of the action and subordinate both acting and directing to this end, Renoir seems to lose sight of the audience from time to time. His players do not face the camera but each other, as if acting for their personal pleasure. One senses that they become their own private audience, enjoying little inside jokes among themselves. This impression is strong in *A Day in the Country* (Brunius's dance) as well as in *The Rules of the Game,* and in *The Crime of M. Lange,* where Marcel Duhamel and Paul Grimault act like a couple of conniving friends slipped into the real cast.

A glance at the credits of Renoir's films is sufficient to indicate how little regard he had for union codes or specialized labor. Pierre Lestringuez, a scenarist for *Nana* and *Marquitta,* is an actor in two other films. André Cerf was both assistant and actor in *Le Petit Chaperon rouge,* along with

Pierre Prévert. And Renoir himself was not hesitant about appearing in his own films.

The party at the château in *The Rules of the Game,* an elaborate game organized for the pleasure of the people making the film, is symbolic of all of Renoir's French work. What is more, this aspect of Renoir's films is almost certainly one of the major reasons for their commercial failure. To appreciate a Renoir film, one has to be "in," one has to catch the winks exchanged between actors and the knowing glances tossed over the camera. And the spectator who does not pick up the invitation to play the game necessarily feels a bit left out. It is not surprising to note that Renoir's most commercially successful films are the ones where this sort of internal play is the least marked, the films which direct themselves most openly to the public: *The Human Beast* and *Grand Illusion.* The presence of major stars in these films was a further guarantee against incongruities in the casting, ruling out any possibility of the kind of inside jokes so dear to the less-known actors. At the other end of the scale lies the classic example of a film which demands considerable participation from its viewers: *The Rules of the Game.* The title itself is indicative of the nature of the film.

These remarks could be taken as reservations in my assessment of Renoir. Movies, after all, are not made for the people who produce them. But we should not push this line of reasoning too far, for it might lead us to consider Renoir's work as nothing more than a sort of modern-day *théâtre de salon,* a minor form dedicated to a limited audience. And to accept this judgment is to deny both Renoir's "realism" and the most striking elements in his work: the power, the fullness, the variety, and the creativity, to say nothing of the international influence of his long career. These are qualities hard to reconcile with a desire simply to entertain one's friends.

My point is that Renoir's tendency to hesitate between the scene in the script and the one he ends up making is only a dialectical moment of his realism. The party at the château is a game, but it is nevertheless a game whose absurd rule is to die of love. Roland Toutain, struck full force by a shotgun blast, rolls to the ground much like the rabbit we have just seen writhing in agony in front of the society folk, who like to kill in comfort from their hunting blinds. If Renoir is enjoying himself, if he entertains us by pushing his actors to the limits of parody, if he seems to linger over apparently incidental attractions, it is only the better to impress us with a sudden revelation of truth when we are no longer expecting it.

One of the most beautiful sequences in all of cinema is the moment in *A Day in the Country* when Sylvia Bataille is about to accept the advances of Georges Darnoux. The scene opens in a light, comic vein which one would logically expect to turn bawdy. We are ready to laugh, when suddenly the laugh catches in our throat. With Sylvia Bataille's incredible glance, the world begins to spin and love bursts forth like a long-stifled cry. No sooner is the smile wiped from our faces than tears appear in our eyes. I can think of no other director, except perhaps Chaplin, who is capable of evoking such a wrenching bit of truth from a face, from an expression. Think of the look on Nadia Sibirskaïa's face when René Lefèvre makes awkward advances to her on the bench in *The Crime of M. Lange* or the ridiculous grin that spreads across Dalio's face when he shows off his calliope to the guests in *The Rules of the Game*.

Renoir's sense and taste for comedy is deeply rooted in his awareness of human tragedy. The temptation to parody, the tendency to enter into a sort of game with his actors, is only a preliminary modesty or hesitation necessary to the dialectic of game and rules, of pleasure and love, and love and death. I mentioned earlier that the acting in Renoir's films is frequently inappropriate for a certain scene, much like a color not quite right for a given drawing. But this apparent incongruity only serves to set off the dazzling moment which will reveal how right Renoir has been all along. We say to ourselves that the actor is definitely not the character up until the instant when all falls into place and he becomes the perfect incarnation of that character. In this way Renoir moves from an original discordance to an incomparable human harmony. The need which brings the actor and the character together lies deeper than superficial appearances. The truth which illuminates the faces of Renoir's actors, is testament to a veritable revelation.

The cinema as a whole still suffers from the mentality of the kind of people who like slick color prints. It confuses the beauty of the model with that of the painting, whereas the painter's aim is not to depict a particular woman but to reveal a universal beauty. Renoir does not choose his actors, as in the theater, because they fit into a predetermined role, but like the painter, because of what he can force us to see in them. That is why the most spectacular bits of acting in his films are almost indecently beautiful. They leave us with only the memory of their brilliance, of a flash of revelation so dazzling that it almost forces us to turn our eyes away. At moments like these the actor is pushed beyond himself, caught totally open and naked in a situation which no longer has anything to do with dramatic expression, in that most revealing light which the cinema can cast on the human figure more brilliantly than any other art except painting.

Parenthetically, one can see by what I have just said how much Renoir owes to the crucial influence of von Stroheim. But if Stroheim came eventually to a sort of obscenity in acting, it was by a different route. While Renoir pretends to play with his actors so as to catch them unawares, Stroheim proceeds with an unrelenting insistence and obsessive patience which pushes acting to its limits.[1] Stroheim's influence is nonetheless curiously apparent in Renoir's last silent films and as late as *La Chienne* (1931). It is perhaps most striking, because unexpected, in *Tire au flanc* (1929), which includes a fabulous bit of pure Stroheim: the scene of the lieutenant picking a rose for the prisoner's wife, while the prisoner tries to observe the painful scene through his small barred window.

It is of course only a critical ploy which allows us to distinguish the direction of the actor from the interpretation of the scenario. The elements of *commedia dell'arte* which creep into the acting or the discrepancy between a given role and the way it is acted are examples of the liberties Renoir takes with a story. They are probably also reasons for the misunderstanding between Renoir and his public. The spectator wants to believe in the story that the actor brings to life. Psychological or physical verisimilitude is less important for him than respect for a certain dramatic logic, for a formal verisimilitude based on the conventions of storytelling. But it is precisely this sort of formal logic of which Renoir is incapable. What counts for him is not verisimilitude but accuracy of detail, and to achieve this he frequently takes dramatic shortcuts. Thus at the beginning of *The Human Beast* the pretext of the fat industrialist's little dog is rather unbelievable, all the more so since it is presented in a comic interlude. What Renoir needed was a justification for Ledoux's approach to his wife's godfather, and he seized upon the first excuse that came along. Even at that he could have made an effort to make us believe in the incident, but the little track-side episode amused him and he did not care that it revealed in his hero a courage and sympathy that would be belied by the following sequence.

Furthermore, we know how Renoir works, how important improvisation is to his technique. We know how he rewrites and polishes scenarios in advance only to modify them a final time on the set. These are hardly methods conducive to the development of dramatic logic and verisimilitude. But they are fertile indeed in the hands of a Renoir, who can infuse them with pure cinematic inspiration.

Renoir brings to the screen not a story but themes, for which the scenario is ultimately nothing more than a physical support, like props for a

---

1. Bazin wrote elsewhere that "It is certainly von Stroheim who is the most firmly opposed to both pictorial expressionism and the artifices of montage. In his work reality yields its meaning like a suspect under the relentless grilling of a police inspector. The principle of his *mise en scène* is simple: Look at the world close enough and insistently enough until it eventually reveals its cruelty and ugliness. Theoretically one could imagine a von Stroheim film composed of a single shot as long and as close as you like." André Bazin, *Qu'est-ce que le cinéma?*, vol. 1, p. 135.—Trans.

set. His themes are visual and plastic: the theme of water, for example, which we find throughout his work, from *La Fille de l'eau* to *The River*, the Marne of *Boudu* and *A Day in the Country*, the swamp of Sologne in *The Rules of the Game*, the Louisiana bayous of *Swamp Water*, the flood in *The Southerner*. Or they are dramatic and moral themes, such as the theme of the hunt in *The Rules of the Game*, or the metaphor of man and machine, which is the organizing principle in *The Human Beast*. This latter is by no means an abstract metaphor. It is earthy and physical, as in the scene where Jean Gabin, attentive and friendly but sensual as well, caresses his locomotive, *La Lison*. If we interpret the film as nothing more than a love story played against the realistic backdrop of the railroad, and poorly played and put together at that, we have not understood it at all.

By the same token, to grasp the subtle organization of *The Rules of the Game* we have to go from the general to the specific, from the action to the plot and from the plot to the scene. To grasp the scheme of the film, we must see the music boxes, the bearskin which gives Octave so much trouble, the agony of the little rabbit, and the game of hide-and-seek in the corridors of the château as the essential realities of the film from which unroll the dramatic spirals of each particular scene. This accounts for the integrity and independence of each scene relative to the scenario as a whole. But it also explains the unique quality and orientation of these scenes, which develop cinematically in concentric layers, much like the grain of sand within an oyster gradually growing into a pearl.

It is precisely this treatment that makes *The Rules of the Game* Renoir's masterpiece, for in it he has succeeded in dispensing entirely with dramatic structures. The film is nothing more than a tangle of reminders, allusions, and correspondences, a carrousel of themes where reality and the moral plane reflect one another without disrupting the movie's meaning and rhythm, its tonality and melody. At the same time, it is a brilliantly constructed film in which no scene is unnecessary, no shot out of place. *The Rules of the Game* is a work which should be seen again and again. As it is necessary to hear a symphony more than once to understand it or to meditate before a great painting in order to appreciate its inner harmonies, so it is with Renoir's great film.

The fact that *The Rules of the Game* was so long misunderstood is not simply the result of its originality and the public's psychological inertia, but also because it is a work that reveals itself only gradually to the spectator, even if he is attentive. *Citizen Kane* is a similar film in this regard. In retrospect it is surprising how obscure the Orson Welles film seemed when it first appeared, and hard to believe that nine out of ten critics found it impossible to recount the plot correctly. If there is any film which seems to us today to be simple (though ambiguous, it is certainly not obscure) and perfectly constructed, it is *Citizen Kane*.

From a dramatic point of view, the death of Toutain, running toward the greenhouse in *The Rules of the Game,* is a coincidence difficult to accept. The mistaken identity is too easy. If we accept this kind of turn of events anything could happen to anyone. But Renoir makes the whole sequence indispensable to his movie, and marvelously apt, through the metaphor of the hunt, which implicitly alludes to the case of mistaken identity in *The Marriage of Figaro* and reminds one of the tragic ending of Alfred de Musset's *Les Caprices de Marianne*. It is the glimpse of a rabbit rolling over dead and the memory of Beaumarchais and de Musset which elevate the hero's death and make an apparent coincidence into an aesthetic necessity.

In other words, Renoir does not construct his films around situations and dramatic developments, but around beings, things, and fact. This assertion, which explains his method of handling actors and adapting the scenario, also gives us the key to understanding his method of filming. Just as the actor does not "play" a scene which itself will be just another episode in the scenario as a whole, so the camera does not simply record the dramatic relationships and underline the main lines of the plot; on the contrary, it focuses on whatever is original and irreplaceable in the scene.

In this way Renoir reminds us that he is his father's son. It would be a mistake to look for the heritage of Auguste Renoir in the formal, plastic elements of his son's movies. For it is precisely here that painting had its worst influence on the cinematic image. And the stunning pictorial quality of Jean Renoir's work is by no means the result of his photographic composition, but of the originality of his vision and the ideas behind his images. What is more, if *A Day in the Country* plays at evoking the subject matter and the lighting of the Impressionists, it is out of an exceptional coquetry which only proves the rule. Renoir is playing at being his father, just as he plays at being Beaumarchais and de Musset in *The Rules of the Game*. It is a discreet and playful homage, which is significant not simply as a conscious imitation but as witness to the sensitivity and love which the films of Jean and the paintings of Auguste have in common. Jean made the ideal movies which Auguste himself would have made if he had abandoned his brushes for the camera.

Jean Renoir's pictorial sense is expressed above all in the attention he pays to the importance of individual things in relation to one another. He does not sacrifice the tree to the forest. Herein lies his true cinematic realism, rather than in his penchant for naturalistic subjects.

To define a film style, it is always necessary to come back to the dialectic between reality and abstraction, between the concrete and the ideal. In the final analysis, the principle of a director's style lies in his way of giving reality meaning. It should be kept in mind that the art of the film, so often considered the most concrete of all, is also the most easily abstracted. Look carefully at bad films and you will see that they are composed of nothing but symbolism and signs, of conventions, of dramatic, moral, and emotional hieroglyphs. It is this fact which lends a certain validity to the common sense critical standard which considers "realism" as a criterion of quality. The word "realism" as it is commonly used does not have an absolute and clear meaning, so much as it indicates a certain tendency toward the faithful rendering of reality on film. Given the fact that this movement toward the real can take a thousand different routes, the apologia for "realism" *per se,* strictly speaking, means nothing at all. The movement is valuable only insofar as it brings increased meaning (itself an abstraction) to what is created. Good cinema is necessarily, in one way or another, more realistic than bad cinema. But simply being realistic is not enough to make a film good. There is no point in rendering something realistically unless it is to make it more meaningful in an abstract sense. In this paradox lies the progress of the movies. In this paradox too lies the genius of Renoir, without doubt the greatest of all French directors.

Renoir the moralist is also the most "realistic" of film makers, sacrificing reality as little as possible to the thrust of his message. The last scenes from *Boudu* could serve as the epigraph to all of Renoir's French work. Boudu, newly wed, throws himself into the water. Dramatic or psychological logic would demand that such an act have a precise meaning. Is it despair, suicide? Probably not, but it is at least an attempt at escape. Boudu is fleeing the chains of a bourgeois marriage. This interpretation, although more ambiguous, would still lend a certain meaning to the shot. Boudu's fall would remain an *act.* But Renoir, like his character, quickly forgets the *act* in favor of the *fact,* and the true object of the scene ceases gradually to be Boudu's intentions and becomes rather the spectacle of his pleasure and, by extension, the enjoyment that Renoir derives from the antics of his hero. The water is no longer "water" but more specifically the water of the Marne in August, yellow and glaucous. Michel Simon floats on it, turns over, sprays like a seal; and as he plays we begin to perceive the depth, the quality, even the tepid warmth of that water. When he comes up on the bank, an extraordinary slow 360-degree pan shows us the countryside he sees before him. But this effect, by nature banally descriptive, which could indicate space and liberty regained, is of unequaled poetry precisely because what moves us is *not* the fact that this countryside is once again Boudu's domain, but that the banks of the Marne, in all the richness of their detail, are intrinsically beautiful. At the end of the pan, the camera picks up a bit of grass where, in close-up, one can see distinctly the white dust that the heat and the wind have lifted from the path. One can almost feel it between one's fingers. Boudu is going to stir it up with his foot. If I were deprived of the pleasure of seeing *Boudu* again for the rest of my days, I would never forget that grass, that dust, and their relationship to the liberty of a tramp.

This has been a rather long and lyrical treatment of a scene in which nothing happens. I could choose many others, each of which would bring out Renoir's feeling for the appearances of things, or at least the important role that these appearances play in his art.

A particular predilection for water is easily discernible in his work. I have just cited one example. Water evokes a theme of *mise en scène* which has become a screen classic: the boat scene which poses all sorts of complicated technical problems, such as the changing of camera angle, the dolly out and the other movements of the camera, and the sound recording. Often directors content themselves with a series of general exterior shots intercut with close-ups shot in the studio against backgrounds simulated by the transparencies. This technique would be unthinkable for Renoir, for it necessarily dissociates the actors from their surroundings and implies that their acting and their dialogue are more important than the reflection of the water on their faces, the wind in their hair, or the movement of a distant branch. All of Renoir's boating scenes are shot entirely on location, even if he has to sacrifice the shooting script to do so, and their quality is a direct result of this technique. A thousand examples could illustrate this marvelous sensitivity to the physical, tactile reality of an object and its milieu; Renoir's films are made from the surfaces of the objects photographed, and his direction is frequently but a caress, a loving glance at these surfaces. His editing does not proceed from the usual dissection of the space and duration of the scene according to a pre-established dramatic formula. Rather, it follows the dictates of his roving eye, discerning, even if occasionally distracted or willfully lazy.

Throughout the entire last part of *The Rules of the Game* the camera acts like an invisible guest wandering about the salon and the corridors with a certain curiosity, but without any more advantage than its invisibility. The camera is not noticeably any more mobile than a man would be (if one grants that people run about quite a bit in this château). And the camera even gets trapped in a corner, where it is forced to watch the action from a fixed position, unable to move without revealing its presence and inhibiting the protagonists. This sort of personification of the camera accounts for the extraordinary quality of this long sequence. It is not striking because of the script or the acting, but as a result of Renoir's half amused, half anxious way of observing the action.

No one has grasped the true nature of the screen better than Renoir; no one has more successfully rid it of the equivocal analogies with painting and the theater. Plastically the screen is most often made to conform to the limits of a canvas, and dramatically it is modeled after the stage. With these two traditional references in mind, directors tend to conceive their images as boxed within a rectangle as do the painter and the stage director. Renoir, on the other hand, understands that the screen is not a simple rectangle but rather the homothetic surface of the viewfinder of his camera. It is the very opposite of a frame. The screen is a mask whose function is no less to hide reality than it is to reveal it. The significance of what the camera discloses is relative to what it leaves hidden. But this invisible witness is inevitably made to wear blinders; its ideal ubiquity is restrained by framing, just as tyranny is often restrained by assassination.

Another scene which I would like to use as an epigraph is the shot from *The Rules of the Game* after the chase by the pond, where Nora Grégor, fooling about with a little spyglass, happens to spot her husband kissing his mistress. Just as it was chance that brought the husband into her field of vision, so it is chance that determines to a certain degree what part of a scene the lens will uncover. And, paradoxically, it is this chance which makes the perspicacity and the vigilance of the eye so important. The point of view of the camera is not that of the novelist's omniscient third-person narrator; nor is it a stupid, unthinking subjectivity. Rather it is a way of seeing which, while free of all contingency, is at the same time limited by the concrete qualities of vision: its continuity in time and its vanishing point in space. It is like the eye of God, in the proper sense of the word, if God could be satisfied with a single eye. Thus when M. Lange decides to kill, the camera stays in the courtyard with Jules Berry, watching through the windows of the stairway as René Lefèvre descends from one floor to the next, faster and faster, as if pulled along by his resolution. He emerges suddenly onto the stoop. At this point the camera is between the two protagonists, with its back to Berry. Instead of panning to the right to follow Lange, it swings deliberately 180 degrees to the left, sweeping the empty set to center once again on Berry, placing us at the side of the victim just as Lefèvre comes back into our field of vision from the left.[2] The

2. A look at what would have been the traditional handling of this scene will make clear exactly what I mean. Two approaches seem likely: (1) A continuous shot, a pan or dolly shot following René Lefèvre across the courtyard to the right, from the stoop to the fountain where Berry is standing. (2) Better, a discontinuous, edited sequence. René Lefèvre emerges from

intelligence of this bit of camera work is all the more admirable for the fact that it is doubly audacious, doubly effective. On the one hand, the whole scene rests on a continuity of point of view expressed by a camera precisely located in the center of the action. On the other hand, the personified camera takes it upon itself to turn its back on the action in order to take a little shortcut. Only in the work of F. W. Murnau can one find similar examples of a camera movement so liberated from the characters and from traditional dramatic geometry.

Technically this conception of the screen assumes what I shall call lateral depth of field and the almost total disappearance of montage. Since what we are shown is only significant in terms of what is hidden from us and since therefore the value of what we see is continually threatened, the *mise en scène* cannot limit itself to what is presented on the screen. The rest of the scene, while effectively hidden, should not cease to exist. The action is not bounded by the screen, but merely passes through it. And a person who enters the camera's field of vision is coming from other areas of the action, and not from some limbo, some imaginary "backstage." Likewise, the camera should be able to spin suddenly without picking up any holes or dead spots in the action.

What all of this means is that the scene should be played independent of the camera in all its real dramatic expanse and that it is up to the cameraman to let his viewfinder play over the action. Reframing, then, is substituted as much as possible for a switching of points of view, which not only introduces spatial discontinuity, a phenomenon foreign to the nature of the human eye, but also sanctions the concept of the reality of a shot on a single plane, the idea of each shot as nothing more than a unit of place and action, an atom which joins with other atoms to make the scene and then the sequence. When a film is made in this way, with each shot lit and played separately, the screen hides nothing, because there is nothing to hide outside the action being filmed. And as cleverly as these separate bits are stitched together, they cannot fool the attentive spectator. The little moment of hesitation at the beginning of a first line, the little something in the fixed nature of the camera and above all in the framing, where nothing is left to chance—everything betrays the existence of a preconceived "shot."

Never do we have this feeling in *The Rules of the Game*, where the action plays hide-and-seek with the camera and the set, passing from the

---

the stairway and heads toward the camera. Cut to Jules Berry behind the camera. Lefèvre re-enters the camera's field of vision.

In both cases the approach would be purely descriptive, directly determined by the action and the position of the actors.

pantry to the second floor, from the great salon to the smoking room, from the pantry to the corridors. In all this ceaseless action the slightest detail in this great complex of reality never ceases to be a living part of the rhythm, whether it is before our eyes or far away.

I should mention here how and why this deliberate use of realism which goes beyond the image itself to include the very structures of the *mise-en-scène* brought Renoir to the use of depth of field ten years before Orson Welles. Renoir himself explained it in the famous *Le Point* article:

> The farther I advance in my profession, the more I am inclined to shoot in deep focus. The more I work, the more I abandon confrontations between two actors neatly set up before the camera, as in a photographer's studio. I prefer to place my characters more freely, at different distances from the camera, and to make them move. For that I need great depth of field . . .

This modestly technical explanation is obviously only the immediate and practical consequence of the search for style which we have struggled to define. Simple depth of field is only the other dimension of the "lateral" liberty which Renoir requires. It is just that our commentary proceeds from the screen, whereas Renoir's explanation starts at the other end of his creation, with the actors.

But the function of depth of field is not only to allow more liberty to the director and the actors. It confirms the unity of actor and decor, the total interdependence of everything real, from the human to the mineral. In the representation of space, it is a necessary modality of this realism which postulates a constant sensitivity to the world but which opens to a universe of analogies, of metaphors, or, to use Baudelaire's word in another, no less poetic sense, of correspondences.

The most visual and most sensual of film makers is also the one who introduces us to the most intimate of his characters because he is faithfully enamored of their appearance, and through their appearance, of their soul. In Renoir's films acquaintances are made through love, and love passes through the epidermis of the world. The suppleness, the mobility, the vital richness of form in his direction, result from the care and the joy he takes in draping his films in the simple cloak of reality.

# Renoir's Anecdotal Narrative

## David Thomson

In Jean Renoir's biography of his father there is a glowing sense of family. In both Auguste's paintings and Jean's films this ambience is broadened to embrace servants, friends, acquaintances and passers-by. The society achieved is felt to be counterbalancing and thus there is a great generosity toward individual action. It is not a censorious society and we have seen how the equivalent of Auguste's busy crowd scenes is the depth of Jean's focus and the movement of his camera so as to connect people and associate their motives. A conclusive narrative is alien to such feelings, but the passing anecdote is perfectly suited to it. For in a circle of friends stories and jokes will be told about chance events without any extrusion of possible implications or verdicts. The fact of society will always outweigh incidents that seem to betray its unity.

The consciousness of the narrator must be found within this society and the only detachment from events that it exhibits is one of tolerance. As in Guy de Maupassant's work the storyteller is often a participant, for even though Renoir's movies are never first-person the camera is so closely identified with the characters that it conveys the same enjoyment in the fortuitousness or irony of events as Maupassant's stories. In both there is more sense of the inevitable human conclusions to human affairs than the assertion of destiny or government. The society is free but equal; its members can enjoy the same things and make the same mistakes.

In his concentration on brief interludes in human life that carry no more meaning than their own action and in his tendency to the precise description of a visual experience of an event, Maupassant is a writer whose work preludes the invention of cinema. The conclusion of *Cemetery Walkers,* for instance, in which the storyteller, while strolling in a cemetery, sees a repetition of the seduction once practiced on him is very like the plasticity and spatial relationship of a scene from a Renoir movie. Every visual event has charm, beauty or distinctiveness that generates response before an intellectual judgment can be worked out. Thus the first intrusion of Boudu into the bourgeois household of the bookseller Lestingois is a panning shot with him as seen through a telescope from the house. At first Lestingois is moving the telescope idly to look at girls' legs but it takes on intention and excitement to cover Boudu's progress. Lestingois's opinion "He is magnificent" is at one level an emotionally paternal gesture from the bourgeois but it is also an immediate reaction to a visual event that persuades him to go to Boudu's aid when he sees him jumping into the Seine.

Part of the irony of *Boudu* comes from the prompt humanity of this action. Boudu is taken in to the household, dressed in Lestingois's clothes and fed at his table. He brings chaos. His table manners are appalling: told to sprinkle salt on spilled wine, he pours wine on spilled salt. He overthrows the social system of the household by interrupting Lestingois's access to the maid's room and seducing his wife. One quiet afternoon Lestingois's wife wants Boudu to renew his attentions and in his embarrassed struggle they fall through a doorway to discover Lestingois and the maid enjoying each others' attentions. The odd conclusion to this is that Boudu shall marry the maid, a palatable fate for her because she likes him and because he has won first prize in the lottery on a ticket Lestingois gave him. The wedding party is rowed down the Seine. Boudu sees a flower and reaches for it. The boat overturns and he is away.

There is no suggestion that this is a deliberate action on Boudu's part. Just as he was content to live where he woke up to find himself, he swims ashore and resumes the tramp's life, not returning to his wife and his money because of the complication and because he goes where events take him, which is the sole discipline, of course, of Renoir's camera. There is no meaning to Boudu, he is an animal of the human species. The camera observes his behavior. Thus that original panning shot, his habit of sitting jammed between doorposts, his behavior at table and his unconnected strolls through the odd spatial arrangement of the Lestingois household. This is why earlier I described the final pan as a movement of Boudu's soul, for the whole identity of the narrative is closer to Boudu than to any other character. Even so, the others are seen in the round. Lestingois is generous, his wife, though neurotic, is passionate, and the maid is good-humored.

Boudu's intrusion has disrupted their system but has not brought them under the eye of eternity. The humor of the blundering of one adulterous couple on another is sustained by this equal treatment of people and by the photographic acceptance of human behavior. Its effect makes a striking contrast with that moment in *La Notte* when the two couples come face to face, and an interesting foresight of the conclusion of *La Règle du jeu* when suspicions of adultery held by the house party guests and the servants mingle and a tragedy occurs out of proportion to the circumstances but still credible and, in part, funny.

Repeated viewings of *La Règle* confirm the impression of integrity in the film and its perfect embodiment, Renoir's own presence. Detailed significance—audio-visual events that in a narrative sequence become evidence of meaning—continues to accumulate without ever disturbing the film's unique sense of disorganization. The apparent source of stability, Octave, is himself finally entangled by events, even playing a main but unwitting part in the tragedy; and this is a metaphor of Renoir's admission that the director, supposedly the authoritative and manipulating figure, is as much victim as originator of circumstances.

Sequences are joined not by an exclusive narrative bond, as limiting as a spotlight, but by means that accommodate an expanding social and physical contingency. The voice of the commentator at the airport is cut to the same voice on the radio in Nora Grégor's bedroom. We later discover Dalio listening to the radio and at the house party several guests refer to Jurieu's outburst. The story does not advance with the addition of characters; instead, possible relationships are uncovered. The chaos of the confused chase at the end of the film is thus a parody of physical action that represents an impossibly huge totality of relationships that occur and subside with great rapidity under the increasing pressure.

The Feydeau-like sexual pursuit emerges from the masquerade, an attempt by the characters to put an elegant gloss on their lives. That the butler is called Corneille and that he nimbly arranges the disposal of fainting bodies maintains the theatrical self-consciousness during the collison of coincidences. And yet finally the butler's finger snap that commands a minion is replaced by the nervous run of a middle-aged man as he goes to bring in Jurieu's corpse. The instant of physical shock seems to answer the previous balletic flow of chase. The comparison of people with Dalio's mechanical toys has been made consciously by Renoir, but not to the extent that every instance is planned.

That there is a small stage within the house, the rehearsed sketches of which are overrun by the spontaneous and dangerous farce, is a deliberate image of the confusion between conceptions of life and the intractable reality. There is detail to support the enactment of this idea: the toy birds on the floor that recall the game birds shot down; Octave walking across the terrace to find Jurieu's body being photographed in exactly the same way as when he impersonated the performance of Nora Grégor's father. As in *Boudu* the doorway is made a means of discovery and yet, though in *Portrait of a Lady* Isabel's view through a doorway is carefully selected for us by James, in *La Règle* there are so many doorways revealing so many things that one is not conscious of arrangement. It even seems possible that the characters have been let loose. The illusion of reality is complete enough to carry over to our attitudes towards the character, as well as the presence, of people, and to convince us of the illusoriness of universal meaning. Renoir has reproduced our experience of life by making his subject the individual means of understanding within a massive, disordered society. The images in *La Règle* are of an infinity within which "tout le monde a ses raisons" and the preference is "pour que chacun les expose librement."

Renoir takes a major step of withdrawal in allowing the spectator to come to terms with the material in the way that he has done himself. But this permissiveness is still part of an invocation to enjoyment and fulfilment that is a complete philosophy for all: that we be tolerant. For Renoir the camera remains a tool to be used in the description of life, whereas for Godard it is an expansion of communication and life itself. Renoir is a classical example of the humanistic, social culture, like Mozart or Bonnard. Distinctive of this classicism is the sense we have of the unity of man and subject so that neither choice nor calculation seems to have taken place. The events themselves are so entire as to be inscrutable: as Pascal said, "where one expected to discover a style, one finds a man." The supreme stylistic quality is a natural ease so commanding that it can accomplish the credible enactment of considerable stylization. Thus Mozart makes opera a realistic form, Bonnard adopts a harmony of color unknown in nature and Renoir conspires towards the beguiling balance of spontaneity and theatre. In all these cases the work is non-reasoning, content to continue the manifestation of integration, accepting it as calmly as seasonal renewal and the movement of the stars. Art is not a proper description: such work is reality itself.

The movement from *Boudu* to *La Règle du jeu* is one of evolution for Renoir. For in *La Règle* the theatrical level of spontaneous events is much more conscious and his own presence indicates the dawning of the idea that a social circle has directors, just like films. Since the war the theatrical reflection in his films has increased—as in *Le Carrosse d'or* and *French Cancan*—as has the emphasis on a producer who simultaneously organizes and becomes involved in events. Like Lang's this is a reduction of the actual that carries the cinema from a concern with verisimilitude to an awareness of epistemology.

Renoir's American films, influenced no doubt by the more schematic scenarios and the more precise camera work in Hollywood, have a far less involved style than that of *La Règle* and a much more direct statement of philosophical issues. The didactic ambiguity of *The Woman on the Beach* and the abstract sparseness of characterization are such as even recall Lang. With Renoir's return to Europe the philosophical consciousness is retained but the unpredictability is regained to achieve the exquisite late masterpieces: *The River, Le Carrosse d'or, French Cancan* and *Elena et les hommes.*

*Carrosse d'or* and *Cancan* are primarily concerned with performance and the metaphor it makes of a human relationship. The opening shot of *Carrosse d'or* is a track forward across the proscenium arch of a theater, at which moment the set magically becomes reality. Metamorphosis proliferates: every character is observed as a performer and it is the accredited actress, Anna Magnani, who is most able to live without affectation; the children and clowns of the *commedia dell'arte* troupe make the most mundane actions balletic, ushering on the other players like Corneille in *La Règle;* the action of the film is a succession of masquerades and dissimulations which thrust dramatic roles on the characters. Even the seemingly ordinary events are shaped to conform to a pattern of theater: thus the clothes of aristocrat, soldier and bullfighter are as much costume as any on the stage and bystanders make compositions from Goya, Velazquez, and Picasso, spontaneously and yet as formally as the troupe.

At the center is Anna Magnani, the only one of the players who moves from theatre to life, as shown by the way she changes her costume for normal clothes. Like a character in the play she is loved by three men and, although successful as an actress—which in her terms means winning the audience, and thus the three men—she only manages to embarrass their affairs, as if the magical qualities of an actress could not settle to ordinariness. At the end of the film she is alone on the stage and speaks to the lovers she has lost, admitting that she cries a little. This moment is the complement of that in *French Cancan* when Jean Gabin rebukes the women he has loved and produced by saying that the theater is his love and that he will continue to look at people for their aptitude in it. This is not a hardened show business attitude but an allegory of life sustained by the interchangeability of *Carrosse d'or.* The acceptance of performance and the enthusiasm for it, and the realization that style is character just as appearance is nature is, in Renoir's eyes, a fitness for the illusoriness of life. It involves an acceptance of human weakness and delusion that is asked of his audience by Renoir in the quotation from Beaumarchais in the prologue to *La Règle:* "Si l'amour porte des ailes, N'est-ce pas pour voltiger?"[1]

1. *The Marriage of Figaro,* Act IV, Scene x. ["If love has wings, is it not to fly?" —Eds.]

# Renoir and Realism: The Thirties

## Raymond Durgnat

Renoir's work exerted a powerful influence toward realism, as it was again to do for a subsequent generation, that of the *nouvelle vague*. But there are degrees of realism. His drive for literal realism—the direct recording of sound, the use of locations, the choice of nonprofessional actors—reached its apogee between *La Chienne* and *Toni;* he fed many of the lessons learned back into his more conventionally set-up productions; he came nearer still to Zavattini's definition of neo-realist subject matter with *La Vie est à nous* and with *La Marseillaise,* which certainly possess an alfresco air, but were scarcely known outside France and weren't the films which exerted the influence, re-emerging only in the wake of Renoir's celebrity in the '60s. Even Renoir's most realistic films represent, as we have seen, a middle way (rather than a compromise) between the "Epsteinesque" documentary and the studio fiction film. It is no doubt for this reason that they proved more influential.

Contemporary critics, wishing to distinguish between their notions of documentary realism, described the French compromise of the late '30s as "poetic realism." Exactly what "poetic" means is far from clear— perhaps it means "lyrical," an effect, which is, after all, quite possible within the means of prose. At any rate, Renoir seemed then one among a group of directors who were represented, pleasantly and uncontroversially, as typifying the humanity and artistry of the French spirit, compared to the brashness and glamour of Hollywood. Nor was Renoir accorded a unique place, or recognized for his individual characteristics, among Carné and Clair (who were both reckoned to be more perfect), Duvivier, Vigo, and Pagnol. When, in 1949, Gavin Lambert singled him out, following the long-delayed English release of *La Règle du jeu,* it was to speak of "the most distinguished unsuccessful career in cinema. Curiosity, tolerance, understanding have sustained Renoir, lack of concentration seems too often to have dominated him. One can only remember two unflawed successes, *Partie de campagne* and *La Règle du jeu."* The choice of examples, while distinctly ironical, is probably inspired by the fact that it's just these two films which, of the Renoir films known in England, least resemble the pessimistic poetic realism or populism of his contemporaries.

The difficulty which Renoir posed for critics was the way in which his interest was constantly flickering from the narrative point to the *temps-mort,* from the obvious climax to some adjacent distraction or unemphatic theme. In consequence his most conspicuous purpose was accomplished always a little roughly, or flatly, or tentatively, or unconvincingly. "Lack of concentration" there is indeed (although hindsight reveals the Carné-Prévert symbiosis as a balance of cross-purposes, and not at all the harmony it was then supposed to be). But why did Renoir's camera linger on figures peripheral to the main action? Why did his photographic palette lack the perfect monotonality of Carné's? Was Renoir a wayward child, or only erratically gifted and always a little clumsy?

Apart from the pressure of Renoir's view of reality, his interest in realism never excluded his awareness of spectacle. Its most conspicuous reassertion is the screen-within-a-screen of *Les Bas-fonds.* Even within the conventions of '30s realism, the effect is acceptable, since it merely exaggerates the silent screen's iris effect, or the later convention of a track-back to long-shot. Yet unless one apprehended some other significance one would have to wonder if Renoir hadn't proved childishly unable to resist a striking gimmick. For the effect is a bold defiance of a basic convention of illusionism, that the film must be as self-effacing as possible, must not acknowledge itself to be a film. The convention was accepted by film-makers, public and critics alike; filmgoers of the '40s can remember the impatience to be done with those seemingly endless credits and plunged into the dream, while even the dawning of flashbacks, beloved by producers for the sake of neat construction, would provoke audible resentment, as one dream-narrative was disrupted by another.

Yet these conventions, acceptable insofar as convention implies a tacit agreement to certain procedures, were never absolute. Comedies and musicals always enjoyed a degree of exemption; the star was not considered as an intrusion into the illusion; and the public never shared that grand delusion, which has stumbled from the primitive dogmas of the document-artists to its fascinatingly sophisticated development in Siegfried Kracauer's theories, whereby fantasy and photography are somehow incompatible. Renoir always distinguished interior and exterior realism, with the latter merely a means to the former. As we have seen, *Charleston* allows the consciousness of spectacle to predominate over the illusion of realism, in the Méliès tradition. In *Les Bas-fonds* the film comes to frame the vanishing reality. The reality disappears into and also with the film, as if to say, "Life is, after all, only a dream. A dream one must live seriously—yet, as it ends, it flies, as dreams must, into the night... " Later, of course, Renoir will allow a similar message to permeate by orthodox, "realistic" means, his Technicolor films of the '50s.

With "Socialist realism" his interests keep interweaving rather than coinciding. His sense of class groupings can bring him very near to it, and some such label is highly relevant in the case of *Lange* (if one allows it a comic spirit), in the case of *La Vie est à nous* (if one includes within it the more sensitive examples of propaganda) and *La Marseillaise* and *La Grande Illusion* (if one allows it a didactic optimism). Yet none of these films would qualify if one insisted, against the weight of Socialist critical opinion, that Socialist realism, should have led the artist to prophesy, correctly, the inefficacy of both Communist Party and Popular Front policies (in the context of which the individual might allow himself to take evasive action, to abandon an idealistic and not altogether natural identification with long-range historical inevitability, to adapt himself to short-range historical inevitability, leave political defeat to look after itself, and *cultiver son jardin*). From this viewpoint the evasive sense of Renoir's adaptation of Gorky's play is the most realistic. One is reminded how widely Renoir's realism is permeated by a desire not to propagandize, in the accepted sense, but to intervene; and that his films, far from being purely realistic, often contain a powerful didactic strain. All but the Gorky of his Popular Front films conclude by showing the French doing what they should have done, and didn't.

In practice Socialist realism can appeal to the precedent of Jack London's *The Iron Heel,* and accommodate, as *sufficiently* realistic, the didactic prophecy which turns out to be wrong—the self-negating prophecy. But it then becomes difficult to exclude Renoir for retaining many of the options of the best in liberal bourgeois individualism (*Chotard et cie*) or anarchism (if this is the sense of *Les Bas-fonds*).

Its arguable that Renoir comes nearest to Socialist realism in the fullest and most conscious sense in *Partie de campagne*—despite its petit bourgeois setting and its lyricism which make it seem a "holiday" film after *La Vie est à nous*. It is also the clearest example of what Alexandre Arnoux describes as Renoir's "double allegiance," on the one hand to the tradition of Zola in literature, and on the other to a thoroughly cinematic transposition of impressionistic subject matter, which so often celebrated the freest aspect of bourgeois society as it was, and so could seem to celebrate it even as it made the most of a discreet escape from it. In fact, the two traditions are not so completely distinct. Maupassant often brings a critical asperity to the holiday mood of impressionism (vide Ophuls's *Le Plaisir*), while Courbet, Degas, and Toulouse-Lautrec often venture, like Renoir, into intermediate territory. François Poulle interestingly argues that Renoir's entire career evinces a failure to reproduce and develop the accusatory realism of Zola.

At any rate, the bitterness of *Partie de campagne* is exceeded only by that of *La Bête humaine,* which, whatever its relationship to "old Zola," terminates an era of Popular Front optimism, and leads to the exclusion of the "solid working class" from *La Règle du jeu.* Which film restores us to the social pattern of *La Fille de l'eau,* with the well-off bourgeois, the poacher with a sense of hierarchy, and the respectable "villager" who lets the worst violence loose. But no one can save *Le Fils de l'air.*

We have commented on the shift from Michel Simon as star-emblem in Renoir's "bourgeois" period, to Jean Gabin as his proletarian hero, with his forceful and embittered masculinity. Something of Legrand's shyness remains in Toni, in Lange, in Bonnier, in Louis XVI, in Roubaud. The dreamlike air of *La Nuit du carrefour* recurs in *Les Bas-fonds,* and the reality of nightmare in *La Petite Marchande d'allumettes.* In all three films, a hideous social structure intersects with an internal incoherence. Insofar as Legrand expresses a loss of confidence in bourgeois solutions, Lantier expresses a loss of confidence in proletarian alternatives. In that film, Lantier is matched by Cabuche, the innocent bewildered. And in *La Règle du jeu* Octave represents precisely the mid-point of Maigret and of Boudu. The role, first meant for Pierre Renoir (Maigret), almost assigned to Michel Simon (Boudu), is played by Jean Renoir. It is as if the two alternative identities of an earlier period had coincided, and compromised.[1] Maigret is no longer a detective, but drawn into a giddy involvement; Louis XVI has been freed from his formality; conversely, Boudu has acquired a great many social graces. The coalescence is reflected in the film's classicism, implying a close, fine interaction of impulses. The clarity with which it emerges, and a possible development, through *La Tosca,* to the baroque, are obscured by Renoir's departure for Hollywood.

It is, after all, through peasant and artisan roots, and a social experience stretching from a household-full of domestic servants to the *haute bourgeoisie,* that Renoir derives his liberalism. It becomes easier to see how long and devious a journey his was, not to the Popular Front, which was his only natural allegiance, but to exclusively proletarian themes. Few

1. There are lean Boudus, as well as plump ones—Pomiès, Brunius—while the most miserable of the constrained characters is the lean and bony son-in-law-to-be of *Partie de campagne.*

of his films assert the virtues and values of the family. It is the interactions between individuals of different social classes that remain his theme. An understanding of this aspect of Renoir has been complicated by the prevalent confusion of *proletarian* themes with *Populist* themes (using Populism in the film, not the political, sense).

Normally, I take it, "Populism" emphasizes a wide range of "little people," including, on the one hand, small peasants, small shopkeepers, white collar workers, "decayed gentlewomen" living on small investments in shabby gentility; and a *lumpenproletariat* of criminals, vagabonds, poachers and so on. The intermixing of all these classes, in the street, in fairgrounds, in cross-section sets enabling the camera to peep in through the windows at separate little worlds hilariously unaware of or exasperated by their neighbors, is, of course, one of the delights of the Populist film. A proletarian film would have a narrower class as center of focus, although it's reasonable to describe some Populist films as proletarian by implication. A notable example is *Les Bas-fonds* which hasn't a single representative of the "solid working class" in it, but a variety of fringe personages—a burglar, a prostitute, a disgraced baron, a landlord and his family, and unemployed characters whose artistic, or philosophical traits loom large—almost, indeed, a "decayed bourgeoisie." Nonetheless the film has enough feeling of a middle/lower class helplessness to align this Populist joblot of bums with a proletariat; and spiritual self-respect is defined in terms of a proletarian, not a bourgeois, status. Much the same argument applies to *La Marseillaise;* and one might almost make out a case that *Chotard et cie* is a Populist film, because, although old Chotard is on the fringes of the civic establishment, he maintains so many characteristics of the peasant-turned-petty bourgeois—which provides many of the quieter jokes. It is possible that the proletarian elements in Renoir's films derive from their director's responsiveness toward such collaborators as Prévert, Gabin, and Carette, and less from Renoir's intimate observation than the Populist fringe (Legrand, Boudu, Cabuche), a little sentimental, often consciously so, but nonetheless honestly man-to-man and not patronizing.

In *La Grande Illusion* the mechanic turns officer turns peasant. Renoir is always interested in those interstices in which a man can come to own his "two acres and a cow," to possess a modest independence, within which to be a Boudu with roots. Not surprisingly, throughout his long career he has consistently turned his back on safe success (Lestingoisism) and struck out for independence, for an *artisan* independence, in which there is no clear line between the working owner, the foreman, and the trusted workman who, far from being exploited, was expected to marry into the family. That image is insistent, for it paraphrases the psychological and social freedom of Renoir's childhood home. Indeed, it is just that idyllic image which Renoir, in *Partie de campagne,* attacks, as if to remind us, and perhaps himself, of the prevalence of its abuse. In a sense, this is a tardy addition to his reflections on the bourgeois ethos. Throughout his Popular Front period, the emphasis is on intermingling, egalitarianism and a kind of collective anarchism which is not at all exclusive. Far from any dictatorship of the proletariat, there is a pointed admission of the poor priest, the rich Jew, the doomed aristocrat, the white-collar worker.

While Renoir has several working-class heroines, his proletarian heroes tend to be less typical. Lange is a clerk, Maréchal is an officer, who turns peasant and is thus doubly déclassé. Lantier is hardly typical, although common-sense, and the presence of Carette (as Pecqueux) beside him, effectively dampens any anti-proletarian overtones. Generally, his heroes are "compendium" figures, who suggest the urban proletariat along with other lower-income groups. Valentine in *Lange* is a petit bourgeois capitalist, but what matters is the class from which she has arisen, and her "proletarian hips." Much the same is true of Bonnier in *La Marseillaise;* what matters is not the apparent status of his house, but his debts, and the overall air of "self-consciously respectable lower-class." This end of the lower-class range fits the Popular Front program extremely well, and seems to give Renoir a more direct expression of his own experience and temperament. If a certain emptiness seems to make itself felt in certain images of *La Vie est à nous,* as of *La Marseillaise,* it is because of Renoir's temperamental aversion to the kind of hardened, cramping bitterness before which his camera hesitates in *La Nuit du carrefour* and which Gabin's mouth and glance bring with them. But Renoir's is a genuine duality, not an equivocation. He finds similarly dual heroes in America, where they prove far more controversial, by their contrast with the lavish helpings of the optimism, opulence, heroism, or myths of tough and innocent frugality with which Hollywood, by 1945, almost universally edulcorated its Populist themes.

# Renoir in Calcutta

## Satyajit Ray

"Mr. and Mrs. Renoir are occupying the Royal Suite on the second floor," informed the receptionist of the Great Eastern Hotel.

My decision to see Renoir at his hotel was a more or less desperate one. Although his arrival in Calcutta had been marked by a conspicuous lack of publicity, the stir it had created among local students of the cinema was considerable. For this was no chance visit, no casual passing through en route to important missions elsewhere. Renoir's mission was here, in Calcutta. He had come with the professed intention of making a film of Rumer Godden's novel *The River* against authentic backgrounds in Bengal. In all likelihood, therefore, his stay would be an extended one.

But fame invests a man with an aura of unapproachability, and I had all but despaired of a chance of meeting the great director when I stumbled upon Clyde DeVinna. A wizened, wisecracking American, DeVinna had acquired some reputation and a great deal of experience in the early nineteen-thirties by photographing *Trader Horn*. He was now considered something of an expert in outdoor photography, and had been engaged to supervise the preliminary shooting on *The River* (in monopack Technicolor). DeVinna had allayed my misgivings by cheerfully asserting that "John is a great guy, a great individualist, and *very* approachable. You can see him any day at his hotel in the evening."

As it turned out, Renoir was not only approachable, but so embarrassingly polite and modest that I felt if I wasn't too careful I would probably find myself discoursing upon the "Future of the Cinema" for his benefit. There were so many things I wanted to ask him. Why did he want to make *The River?* Did he enjoy making films in Hollywood? Was he thinking of going back to France? But when it came to asking them, I found that I was hopelessly mixed up, and came out with something inane like—How did he like India?

From *Portrait of a Director: Satyajit Ray* by Marie Seton. © 1971 by Marie Seton. Reprinted by permission of Indiana University Press and Hope Leresche & Sayle. First published in *Sequence*, no. 10 (January 1950).

Renoir replied with great seriousness: "That I will tell you when I have known it better. At present I am only beginning to understand the city of Calcutta, which I find very interesting."

I didn't have to ask many more questions that evening, for Renoir had a great deal to say about the two or three trips he had already made around the city and on the Ganges. The river, with its old-fashioned boats, had charmed him, and he was fascinated by all the colorful things he had seen. "You know," he said, "India seems to have retained some of the charm and simplicity of primitive life. The way the boatmen pull the oars, and the farmers plough the fields, and the women draw water from the wells, they remind you of old Egyptian murals and bas-reliefs."

Renoir had met a family of refugees who had come all the way from Pakistan by boat. "And they had all sorts of fantastic adventures on the way," he said, "I'm sure their story would make a very good film." I said India was full of such stories which simply cried out for filming. "And no doubt they are going to be made," said Renoir with naive conviction. I said No, because the Indian director seems to find more inspiration in the slick artificiality of a Hollywood film than in the reality around him. "Ah, the American film..." Renoir shook his head sadly, "I know it's a bad influence."

Soon after this, attending a reception given in his honor by the Calcutta Film Society, Renoir submitted himself to a barrage of questions ranging from the most absurd to the most abstruse, all of which he answered with great ease and candor in his charming broken English. Asked about *The River*, Renoir said that he had chanced upon a review of the novel in *New Yorker*. The outline of the story, as *New Yorker* gave it, had seemed to him to contain the elements of an interesting film. A reading of the novel had confirmed the impression, and Renoir had set about preparing a treatment, shelving for the time being a project on a life of Goya which he had previously thought of making in Italy.

I had not read the novel, and had no idea what the story was about, except that it had something to do with a river in Bengal (presumably the Ganges). But after all the nightmarish versions and perversions of India perpetuated by Hollywood, I was looking forward with real eagerness to the prospect of a great director tackling the Indian scene. It was therefore an acute disappointment to hear Renoir declare that *The River* was being made expressly for an American audience, that it contained only one Indian character—a servant in a European household, and that we were not to expect much in the way of authentic India in it. Of course the background would be authentic, since all the shooting was to be done on location in

Calcutta. I couldn't help feeling that it was overdoing it a bit, coming all the way from California merely to get the topography right . . .

"What goes wrong with the great continental directors when they go to Hollywood?" This was a question many of us had in mind but few had the temerity to ask. But when it did come Renoir's eagerness to answer it surprised and relieved us. "I'll tell you," he said, "I'll tell you what happens to them. It is the American mania for *organization* which frustrates them. You have heard of this mania of course, but you know nothing unless you have seen it in action. Suppose you are in the United States, and you want to go somewhere. So you go to a station to catch a train. And what do you find? You find the train arrives on time. *Exactly* on time. Now this is very strange. In France the trains don't run on time. You are not used to this punctuality, and it makes you feel uneasy. Then you go to work in a studio. You are on the floor, ready to begin work. And what do you find? You find you have to go by the schedules, and so many of them. Which means you are supposed to run on time too. And then they begin to check. They check the sound and double-check it, so that you get perfect sound, which is good. Then they check and double-check the lighting, so you get perfect lighting, which is also good. But then they check and double-check the director's inspiration—which is not so good!"

Renoir feels that the best intentions are apt to be thwarted in Hollywood owing to certain immutable factors. He mentioned the star system, the endless codes of censorship, and the general tendency to regard films as a mass-produced commodity, as being the three most obvious. Once in a rare while a director was lucky enough to find the right story, the right sort of players (not stars) to act in it, and the right sort of artistic freedom to make it, and the result was a worthwhile film. Only once, when he made *The Southerner,* was Renoir able to work in such ideal conditions in Hollywood.

Renoir also believes that the best films of a country are produced in times of stress; that an atmosphere of smug self-complacence is bad for the cinema. "Look what the war has done to Italian films," he said. "Look at *Brief Encounter.* I don't think a great film like that would have been possible without all those air raids London had to suffer. I think what Hollywood really needs is a good bombing . . ."

"Look at those flowers," said Renoir, pointing at a *palas* tree in full bloom. It was the first of several occasions on which I was fortunate enough to accompany him on his trips in search of locations. "Those flowers," said Renoir, "are very beautiful. But you get flowers in America too. Poinsettias, for instance. They grow wild in California. But look at the clump of banana trees, and that green pond at its foot. You don't get that in California. *That* is Bengal."

One could see that while searching for locations, Renoir was also searching for *la couleur locale,* for these quintessential elements in the landscape which would be pictorially effective as well as being truly evocative of the atmosphere of the country. As he put it: "You don't have to show many things in a film, but you have to be very careful to show only the right things."

For a man of his age and dimensions, Renoir's enthusiasm and energy are phenomenal. He would trudge across miles of impossible territory to find the right viewpoint for the right locale. At times the absorption in his work was so complete that his wife would have to administer some gentle admonishment like "You shouldn't be out in the sun so long, Jean", or "Jean, you haven't forgotten that appointment at six o'clock have you?"

During these trips Renoir spoke a great deal about himself. Of his youth; of his father, and the other great figures of the impressionist movement; of ceramics—his other great passion besides the cinema; and of the cinema itself. It was during the first world war, while convalescing in a hospital from a leg wound, that Renoir had first toyed with the idea of a possible career in the films, although the actual apprenticeship was to come later, after he had gone through a spate of journalism. While he spoke in glowing terms of the *avant-garde* movement, Renoir characterized the entire silent period of the French commercial cinema as being largely stagnant and ineffectual. With the coming of sound, however, there was a sudden and magical transformation. As Renoir put it: "It was as if someone had opened a secret door of communication between the filmmaker and his audience. It was a great feeling. Everything we did the audience understood. The French cinema could not have made those enormous strides towards maturity without this wonderfully perceptive audience. They helped us all along the way, and I for one feel grateful to them."

The rich period lasted till the occupation, after which—although there was no loss in technical quality since the Germans were anxious to prove their munificence in regard to cultural activities—there was an inevitable falling off in content.

Of his early films, Renoir spoke of *La Chienne* as being one of his favorites. "It is a pity they had to remake it in Hollywood, and so badly," he said. (This second version, directed by Fritz Lang, was called *Scarlet Street.*) Among the great masterpieces of the late 'thirties, Renoir had a special affection for *La Règle du jeu* because it was entirely his own creation. He even acted a role in it. The case of *Partie de campagne* was peculiar. It appears that Renoir had wanted to experiment with the short story film. For ease of commercial exploitation, two such short films would have to be made, and Renoir had started on the Maupassant story, hoping to follow it up with a second one. But, unfortunately, the film had to be abandoned before it was quite finished. All through the occupation the negatives lay hidden away by a friend to prevent destruction at the hands of the Nazis. It was only after the liberation that prints were made and the film released with explanatory titles filling the gaps in the narrative.

Renoir himself had yet to see *Partie de campagne*. For on the very day the Germans had marched into Paris, Renoir had marched out, taking with him his wife, and just such of his worldly belonging as could be got into one small suitcase.

From Paris to Hollywood. The inevitable trammels of adjustment apart, Renoir had found life in California pleasant enough. The climate was good, and there were good friends. Chaplin—*le maître*—the mere mention of whose name would make him beam, was one of the best. Renoir was sorry for him. "He is a sad man now," he said. "Nobody understands him in America." I asked him if he was aware of his (Chaplin's) future plans. Renoir said: "Well, the last time I met him he was thinking of a musical burlesque in which the characters would represent contemporary political figures. But I don't think he'll make it, because he also seemed very anxious to displease nobody, and you can't make a film like that and displease nobody."

Of the five films he had made in Hollywood, Renoir never mentioned *The Diary of a Chambermaid* or *Swamp Water*. He had made *This Land Is Mine* as a rejoinder to the notion then prevailing in America that the resistance movement in Europe was a myth, and that every person in an occupied country was a collaborationist. *The Southerner* he had enjoyed making mainly because it was a bit of authentic America, and the people in it were real. He considered it his best American film.

*The Woman on the Beach* was something of a misadventure. Originally what interested Renoir in the story was the character of the woman who "lived only for love." But after he had begun to make the film, he had discovered to his chagrin that the Codes prevented him from developing the character in the way it needed to be developed. As a result, in situations which called for a forthright emotional treatment, he had to fall back on subterfuge and extraneous technical claptrap (hence the near-surrealism of the setting and the distracting dissonances of Hanns Eisler's score).

To Renoir, there is nothing more important to a film than the emotional integrity of the human relationships it depicts. Technique is useful and necessary in so far as it contributes towards this integrity. Beyond that it is generally intrusive and exhibitionist. "In America," said Renoir, "they worry too much about technique, and neglect the human aspect."

I asked Renoir what he thought about the recent American trend towards documentary realism. "That is nothing new," he said. "I shot most of *La Bête humaine* on location in Le Havre. I built very few sets for *The Southerner*. But I am not dogmatic about it. I think a set is a useful and necessary thing at times. And in any case, if the people don't behave in a realistic manner there is no point in having them perform against real backgrounds. I have also heard theories about using non-professional actors. This I don't understand at all. Can you think of a non-actor replacing Raimu or Gabin? I can't. Personally, I have a great respect for the acting profession." For all his vast experience, Renoir is surprisingly free from aesthetic dogmas. I think he summed up his attitude beautifully when he said: "Each time I make a new film, I want to feel like a child who is learning about the cinema for the first time."

The day before he left for Europe, I saw Renoir again at his hotel. He was taking with him a trunkful of mementoes, some of which had been given him by his admirers, and some he had picked up himself at bazaars and curio shops. In the four weeks of his stay in Calcutta he had travelled, and observed, and reflected. Bengal had grown on him. The enchantment and novelty of the landscape on the one hand, and the picture of filth and misery and poverty on the other. I had watched him go into ecstasies over a simple hut, and pass into gloomy despondency at the sight of a beggar. The visit to a coalmine had stirred him so deeply that he had talked of it for days on end. And he had said: "If you could only shake Hollywood out of your system and evolve your own style, you would be making great films here."

He was to return to Calcutta with his unit in November, which is the best time for shooting outdoors in India. Of course the script had to be rewritten. "This time, when I'm in London, I must sit down with Rumer Godden and discuss the story. I may want to make some changes in it; add some new characters, maybe. Maybe an Indian family to show the contrast between their way of life and the Indians." It would be a good idea . . .

As I came away from the hotel that evening, I felt convinced that there was any amount of creative vigor still left in Renoir. Perhaps *The River* would mark the beginning of a fresh and vital period after all the disappointments of Hollywood. As he had now become an American citizen, the chances of returning to Paris were somewhat remote. The important thing, however, was to get away from the synthetic environment of Hollywood, and India was as good a refuge as any. There is no doubt that here Renoir would get his freedom. There would be no schedules to distract him, and no checking and double-checking of inspiration. And of course, out here, the trains never will run on time.

# Renoir's Theater Films of the 1950s

## Leo Braudy

With *Le Carrosse d'or* (1953), *French Cancan* (1955), and *Elena et les hommes* (1956), Renoir returns to a conception of the theatrical image more vital than either the darkly enclosed social world or the exuberant nature of the American films would have allowed. In these films the theater becomes an image of renewal rather than refuge and separation, perhaps as a result of the distancing devices first formulated in *Diary of a Chambermaid* and *The Southerner* and more subtly developed in *The River*. Like some of the films of the 1920s, these theater films of the 1950s distinguish between those characters who imprison themselves unconsciously and those who find a greater freedom in conscious enclosure and stylization. A character like Camilla in *Le Carrosse d'or* is a more direct descendant of the lighthearted characters played by Georges Pomiès in *Tire-au-flanc* and *Chotard* than of the melancholically theatrical Madame Bovary. Instead of pessimistically accepting the limits of theater like Boeldieu and La Chesnaye, she is an actress who delights in her profession. Unlike the theatrical characters of earlier films, who tended to be victims, the three theater films of the 1950s present theatrical characters whose control is based on their understanding of the frame in which they are caught. If there is an edge of sadness, these films are dark comedies rather than tragedies mingled with farce.

Although Renoir's American films are usually considered to be the work of a period of isolation away from his "roots" in France, they in fact directly presage his concerns in the first films made after his return to Europe in the early 1950s. The key to the change is the way in which the

Reprinted from *Jean Renoir: The World of His Films* by Leo Braudy. Copyright © 1971, 1972 by Leo Braudy. Reprinted by permission of Doubleday & Company, Inc. and Robson Books Limited. The title "Renoir's Theater Films of the 1950s" has been supplied by the Editors.

fatal implications of the theatrical frame that had been enforced in the 1930s, even when the frame itself was viewed positively, has been transformed into an image of freedom *through* theater. The change occurs because the emphasis falls on the aesthetic freedom within the frame rather than the human constriction, which, as films like *Toni* and *La Bête humaine* imply, can occur just as easily in nature as in theater. Although both nature and theater can be tyrannical, nature offers no order and theater no inner energy. The way to the theater films of the 1950s is paved by *The Southerner* and *The River,* in which Renoir comes to terms with and deals with the energies of nature. In the former, in the spirit of the title of the book from which the film is adapted—*Hold Autumn in Your Hand*—nature is controlled through understanding; in *The River,* through art.

Both methods are used in the theater films of the 1950s. All three of the films are free reconstructions of the past; no fatality of time or nature inhibits their vision. And all three deal in some way with artistry. *Le Carrosse d'or* involves a *commedia dell'arte* troupe in eighteenth-century Peru, while *French Cancan* deals with the efforts of the entrepreneur Danglard to found the Moulin Rouge and revive the cancan. *Elena et les hommes* absorbs this positive view of artistic order and intermingles love and politics amid the intrigues of the early years of the Third Republic.

Pauline Kael has called *Le Carrosse d'or* "a comedy of love and appearances," and the framing of its action within the curtains and proscenium of a stage emphasizes the primacy of the theatrical view of reality that dominates the film. Unlike the puppet-show frame of *La Chienne,* which served to emphasize detachment and contrast between the security of art and the chaos of life, the frame in *Le Carrosse d'or* defines a perspective that dominates the film, with its sets within sets, and their elaborate and obvious ceilings. The given of the film is enclosure; when the troupe moves into the courtyard of the inn, they immediately begin varying its inner space with curtains and hangings. When they play, the footlights appear at the bottom of the screen. All characters fall into postures naturally, framing themselves in windows or stopping in mid-gesture. The camera sits back from them in their settings and again shows their feet, in the process miniaturizing them and for a moment making their world a precious and intricate bauble, like Pope's "moving toy-shop of the heart."

The romances of Camilla (Anna Magnani) with her three lovers form a delicate counterpoint to the main theme of the ownership of the coach, this awesomely grotesque and gilded monster, which, like La Chesnaye's mechanical birds in *La Règle du jeu,* is an image of the art of film itself. Each of the lovers represents an aspect of the world that Camilla must include. Ramon the bullfighter participates in a kind of theater that is directly competitive with her own. When he comes into the audience of the troupe's show, he must divert all the attention away from the actors to himself. Don Antonio, the Viceroy, comes to the performance disguised, and his daily life of elaborate wigs and conferences is the public world's equivalent of the formalities of theater. Only Felipe, Camilla's lover within the troupe, asserts the values of what he calls reality. But these values are in this context attenuated and unbelievable. It may be idle to speculate on Renoir's casting, but in fact Paul Campbell, who plays Felipe, is the most wooden actor in the entire film, most so when he tells Camilla he loves her for herself and not for the characters she plays. In *Le Carrosse d'or* the would-be actor must fail. Don Antonio loves Camilla for the relief from the orders of his public life she can give, while Ramon sees in her a worthy companion in the public eye. No one, indeed, loves Camilla for what she thinks is most authentic in her nature, her theatrical self.

Like the coach, Camilla is the object of every one's demands and possessive assertions. She must elude the forms of the various worlds that try to entrap her to assert her own form and her own world. In a more seriously weighted film the implied questions could be harsh: does the coach belong to the state or to the actress? where, in short, can art survive? But this is a comedy. "The coach doesn't belong to any of us. It's a symbol," says one of the characters. The world is a stage, the state is staffed with comic fools, and the theatrical can absorb the rest of the world into itself. The separate demands of politics and art are easily reconciled by the archbishop, that master of baroque ritual. *Le Carrosse d'or* rides through a world of ormolu fantasy, happily protected from the rhythms of a world outside art. One exception may occur when Ramon the matador tells Camilla about his adventures among a tribe of Indians, a simple, natural people who live by a river. For a moment Camilla's face looks lined and older. But she quickly reassumes the style and glitter of art. Art is a balm for the pains of life. At the end of the film, when the proscenium frame has reasserted itself, Camilla stands alone at stage center, without her three lovers. Does she miss them, she is asked. "A little," she answers. Art may be self-sufficient, but it is also lonely and self-absorbed.

In *French Cancan* and *Elena et les hommes* the separation between theater and history is more acute because history has become a more oppressive force than it was in the purer theatrical world of *Le Carrosse d'or*. In these two films the aristocratic detachment from history that furnished the pathos in the court scenes of *La Marseillaise* has become a way of understanding history from the outside. In *French Cancan* there are wry analogies between the founding of the Moulin Rouge and the founding of the Third Republic; in *Elena,* also set in these early years of the Third Republic, the shift of value from history to theater seems to have become complete. The outside world of politics impinges comically and cryptically on *French Cancan,* more oppressively on *Elena.* The central focus has shifted from Camilla, the actress and role player, to Danglard, the producer and impresario. Instead of merely being within the theater, the main character now constructs and invents the entire theater, presenting *l'illusion de grande vie* for the public, like the illusions manufactured by the ministers who arrive for the dedication of the Moulin Rouge. But Danglard's role is not defined in the social terms of politics and governments. Like Camilla, he is alone at the end of the film. As he tells his jealous mistress, Nini, he exists not for her but for the audience. Backstage he sits in a large prop chair and swings his foot to the music, while on the other side of the curtain the crowds cheer and the camera sits firmly before the dancers, enjoying their performance as a good spectator should. With the film's end we are outside the new glittering Moulin Rouge and the camera pulls back until it has a long shot like those we have seen in the course of the cabaret's construction. A momentary stasis, and then a drunk reels by, dances a bit, and takes a bow.

Toward the beginning of *Elena et les hommes* Elena (Ingrid Bergman) and her fiancé, Martin-Michaud the shoe manufacturer, take a coach to the Bastille Day celebrations. The first view of the crowd we get is from the inside of the coach, a totally black background with one window cut in it, through which we see the surging crowd while someone tells them through the window that they can't proceed any further. The door opens. Elena gets out, and is immediately swallowed up by the surging, exuberant crowd. She seems to have moved from the interior of her apartment in the first scene, through the enclosed coach, to be finally pulled outside into the crowd. But in fact the crowd is only a larger version of the theater of her own life. In the first scene she remarks that she dismissed her last lover because she had succeeded in inspiring his opera *Héloise and Abelard* and need not do any more. In the rest of the film she similarly inspires the political world, as she is enlisted to use her wiles to convince General Rollan (Jean Marais), a Boulanger-like figure, to take over the government of France. Like Lisbonne, the journalist "who gave Sarah Bernhardt her start," now a publicist in Rollan's shadow cabinet, Elena moves easily from art to politics.

But the point of the film is that her values are actually reversed. It is politics that are reducible to mere theater, while love and art are the real world. And the world of *Elena* is filled with theatrical allusions and situations that emphasize its own commitment to the reconstruction and replacement of politics by theater and what it has come to represent for Renoir. A street singer comes in to sing choruses of the song "Méfiez à Paris" and hands out broadsheets of the song announcing that it was written by Jean Renoir and Joseph Kosma. Two women appear as a kind of chorus commenting on events and talking up the good old days, not in terms of politics, but in terms of the attitude toward women. Like the man and woman chorus in *French Cancan,* who sit in a sidewalk café and watch the construction of the Moulin Rouge, these women whimsically allude to the past when things were better. Yet these comments are part of a film that asserts its own vision of a real past, transmuted by art.

Elena herself is diverted from these values because she believes it is her "duty" to France to take part in the Rollan intrigue. She rejects Henri (Mel Ferrer) and goes off to Martin-Michaud's country home, where the complaisant shoe manufacturer, who is basically worried only about tariff control, allows her time and space for her mission. The house is a maze of rooms strung together by farce, with people running in and out, reminiscent physically of the movement through rooms in *La Règle du jeu,* but without the sinister overtones of disruption and chaos. In Martin-Michaud's house, theater makes social and political uneasiness comfortable. The battle-front of the Franco-Prussian War is actually only a few miles and at one point Elena and Henri are arrested as German spies. But within the house itself farce reigns, and the camera, instead of looking through the rooms at eye level, as it tended to in *La Règle du jeu,* takes the position of cinematic theater, about eight or ten feet above the floor, so that it can see into more than one room at once, emphasize the background, and in one shot include the various artificialities of form that surround Elena's attempt to bring Rollan to politics through love.

André Bazin has said that "all the work of Jean Renoir is a quest for the realism of the end of the nineteenth-century." But in the light of *French Cancan* and *Elena* this realism cannot be said to have any direct relation to the actual public world of that time. Theater triumphs in both films because it offers an alternate and better world to the world of politics and patriotism. It is a deeper "patriotism," like the international order of art that is asserted amid the warring languages of *La Grande Illusion.* When the observation balloon breaks loose in *Elena* and lands in Germany, we are shown the French and German newspapers, which each react in their own chauvinist way; there is no difference between them. And perhaps we are meant to remember that Gambetta escaped from the siege of Paris by balloon.

Renoir's world of art, expressed in these films as theater, has taken over history for its own, and made it into something quite different. As Henri says to Elena toward the end of the film, the greatest gift of French civilization to the world is love, not politics or anything else. Elena still thinks of theater only in terms of play-acting. They must stand before a window and pretend to the crowd below that it is Elena and Rollan rather than Elena and Henri, so that Rollan can make his escape. Elena is upset at having to perform this charade with Henri and she uses the theatrical metaphors of Marie Antoinette in *La Marseillaise:* "Je propose un entr'acte." But through this particular bit of theater she discovers that she has been submerging her real love for Henri. Through pretending they have come to reality. And the agents of their reconciliation have been the gypsies, who appear abruptly in the world of *Elena et les hommes,* like fugitive prophets from beyond the world of political maneuver. The head of the gypsy troupe calls himself its artistic director; and while Henri talks to them, tumbling and juggling go on in the background. Like the *commedia dell'arte* troupe of *Le Carrosse d'or,* the gypsies have magically appeared to redress the balance of politics and art. They turn bad theater into good theater. "La comédie est terminée," says Miarka (Juliette Greco), the gypsy girl who has wandered through the scenes, mainly unnoticed by the self-absorbed principles. She sits on the windowsill, watching Elena and Henri leave together, and she sings them away from this world. They have gone, and the crowd in the street has gone. Like Camilla at the end of *Le Carrosse d'or,* Danglard backstage in *French Cancan,* Miarka, the singer and reconciler, is finally left alone. But she is not the last image in the film. Instead we see a newspaper account of the marriage of Henri and Elena, in which a parenthesis identifies Elena as Ingrid Bergman. Theater has done its work, even to the extent of restoring "reality."

Most critics have considered these three films of the 1950s to be Renoir's recommitment to a sense of spectacle in cinema after the social consciousness of the 1930s. But what is striking about his own remarks about them is the frequency with which minimizing words appear, words like *croquis, pochade, esquisse,* and *divertissement.* In fact Renoir seems to believe that the time of spectacle has come to an end, that the world is suited only for briefer epics that contain rather than expand. The image that he constantly invokes for such limitation is the image of theater, for theater is conscious limitation that enriches what lies within its boundaries. In this way, the constantly escaping prisoners of *Le Caporal épinglé* (1962), a film with little theatrical allusion beyond some framing shots, reflect the theme of theater. The prisoners escape, but they are never quite sure what they are escaping from: some find a brief solace in imprisonment; others constantly escape and find no solace at all. In *Le Testament du Docteur Cordelier* (1959), where the visual allusions to theater are also very sparse, the same mood of pessimism is present. Theater in *Le Déjeuner sur l'herbe* (1959), in the person of Gaspard, the panic flutist, can bring together the worlds of science and nature under the shadow of the proscenium arch of the Temple of Diana; and it is part of Renoir's whimsy to have traveled from Corneille, the major-domo in *La Règle du jeu,* to Rousseau, the major-domo in *Le Déjeuner sur l'herbe.* But in *Cordelier* and *Le Caporal épinglé,* the mood is not so exuberant or conciliatory. Their themes are those of limitation that the theatrical allusion has helped Renoir to nurture, but the mood is more reminiscent of the gloom of the *genre noir* films of the 1930s.

*Le Carrosse d'or, French Cancan,* and *Elena et les hommes* in no way settle the issue of the uses of theater. They form instead an artistic counterpoint to the social and psychological issues of limit and confinement Renoir explores in *Cordelier* and *Le Caporal épinglé*. It is worth remarking that Renoir's use of theater departs totally from the use of theater in two other notable theater films, Marcel Carné's *Les Enfants du paradis* (1944–45) and Max Ophuls' *Lola Montès* (1955). Both combine a plot that occurs in a theatrical context with some reconstruction of a historical period. But in neither is the theatrical more than an extra mask. In *Les Enfants du paradis,* the relation between the characters and the theater is the usual "vesti la giubba" laughing on the inside/crying on the outside melodrama. Any "metaphysic of theater," defining what theater means in relation to the world of film, seems lacking.

*Les Enfants du paradis,* even though a theater film, is very crowded. But the crowds have little meaning. The crowd at the end of that film, for example, into which Baptiste loses Garance, could just as well be the crowd at the end of *The Bicycle Thief,* which anonymously swallows up the characters. Renoir's sense of crowds and the violation of theatrical space they imply, for example in the Bastille Day scene of *Elena,* is totally lacking from Carné's film. Theater is mere varying artifice or exotic milieu to Carné; he sees neither its limitations nor its potentials. Perhaps under the influence of Renoir's theater films, Ophuls uses the theatrical as a metaphor of Lola's life in society, through a series of circus tableaux, complete with artificial scenery and cardboard balustrades. But his treatment displays primarily the charming "world is a movie set" sentimentality of his earlier films, like *La Ronde*. Ophuls does exploit a relation between social and theatrical artifice, but the last shot in *Lola,* that long track backward (with which Andrew Sarris was perhaps so rightly entranced) fuzzes over with glib irony the actual need of an artist to be paid for his work. Renoir's own attitude toward theater and the place of the artist, actress or entrepreneur, within it, is at once more magical and more hard-edged. His understanding of the vitality of artifice perhaps owes something to the lessons of American musical comedy, and works like Vincente Minnelli's *The Pirate* (1947). Instead of either the disdain for theater of the "cinematically" oriented directors, or the crippling respect for theater of the wordy scriptwriters and posturing actors, Renoir preeminently knows how to use theater. In its many mutations of theme and method, from the start of his career, it has furnished an ever-replenishing refuge of order amid the freedoms of nature.

# Roberto Rossellini

ROBERTO ROSSELLINI was born in Rome in 1906, the son of an architect and builder, and died there in 1977. In his youth he was fascinated by mechanical devices, a passion that in later years emerged through the invention of several special pieces of filmmaking equipment. As a young man he attended the movies often—especially in two theaters built by his father—and was struck most memorably by two King Vidor films—The Crowd (1928) and Hallelujah! (1929). Working out of a small studio he had set up in a family villa, Rossellini made several shorts, often involving some sort of natural observation.

Attracted by the theories of documentary filmmaking being put forward by Alessandro Blasetti and by Francesco de Robertis, director of the government-sponsored Centro Cinematografico del Marine, Rossellini joined the Centro and made three features for the official film industry, experimenting with nonprofessional actors and a fictionalized documentary technique. Open City (1945) was his first independent film. Produced while the Nazis still occupied Italy and made often with hidden cameras and stolen film, Open City brought Rossellini to international attention. Applauded for the intensity of its realism, the low cost of its production ($19,000), and the performances of its new stars, Anna Magnani and Aldo Fabrizi, Open City also helped re-establish the moral stature of Italian culture after the long twilight of the Mussolini period. In Paisan (1946) Rossellini experimented still further with conventional film form by telling the story of the American liberation of Italy through a series of vignettes, each dealing with an effort at communication and the breaking of barriers. The third film in this postwar trilogy—Germany, Year Zero (1947)—has only rarely been seen in the United States.

Rossellini's career went into an eclipse with the 1950s, due principally to a boycott of his work encouraged by the American Catholic Church. This had been touched off by the supposed "blasphemy" of the short film The Miracle (1948) starring Anna Magnani and was fueled by reports of his celebrated liaison with (and later marriage to) Ingrid Bergman, which began with the filming of Stromboli (1949) and continued through several cinematic and theatrical collaborations into the late 1950s. The Miracle, Stromboli, and The Little Flowers of St. Francis (1950) all deal with the way spiritual values irradiate everyday life. But Rossellini's anti-institutional definition of religion created more enemies than an anti-religious position might have. In general his works of the 1950s ignore political and public themes to concentrate on individual spiritual and emotional situations. Voyage in Italy (1953) and Fear (1954) (both starring Bergman) are striking explorations of anguished middle-class marriages of convenience. These films, much admired by Godard and other French critics, were

653

*important forerunners of the work of Antonioni and Rohmer. They had a major influence on the young filmmakers of the New Wave.*

General della Rovere *(1959, starring Vittorio De Sica) marked a triumphant return for Rossellini to the critical and popular acclaim received by his earlier works, perhaps because he was once again telling a story of World War II. But the realism of the setting of* Della Rovere *stands in such sharp contrast to the con-man fantasies of its central character that he finally must become what he has been pretending to be. Rosselini's interest in the intersection of the individual and the historical moment appears in many other films he made in the 1960s, few of which have been seen here.* Della Rovere *brought Rossellini back to a world of society and politics, now complicated and enriched by the individualist documentary of the self he had explored with Bergman in the 1950s.*

*A new factor was Rossellini's increasing interest in the methods of television, which he had explored most extensively in a series of programs about India (1958). From the middle 1960s onward he has pursued his "love of what happens next" in a series of long documentaries about processes and people. The first of these was* The Iron Age *(1964) and the most successful* The Rise of Louis XIV *(1966), both historically organized statements of Rossellini's belief that the documentary facts of science and history must take on a human shape before they can be considered "real." Subsequently Rossellini also made long television films about the Apostles (1968), Socrates (1970), St. Augustine (1972), Pascal (1972), and the Medici family (1973).*

*A useful account of Rossellini's career film by film has been written by José Luis Guarner (1970), and the screenplays of* Open City, Paisan, *and* Germany, Year Zero *have been published under the title* Rossellini: The War Trilogy *(1973). See also André Bazin's essay "An Aesthetic of Reality" in* What is Cinema? *vol. 2, translated by Hugh Gray (1971).*

# Rossellini: From "Open City" to "General della Rovere"

## Leo Braudy

Roberto Rossellini was the first representative of Italian neo-realism to make an impact on an international public. Of all those directors, he was the most interested in exploring the film theoretically, and he has also been the most prolific, making more than twenty-five features, many shorts, and, in recent years, part-directing and part-producing several films for television on the order of *Man's Struggle for Survival* (*La Lotta dell'Uomo per la sua sopravvivenza,* 1967), a history of man from the caves to space travel, in twelve one-hour episodes. But, unlike Fellini, Antonioni, Visconti, and De Sica, Rossellini has never re-achieved the heights of renown he had with *Open City* (1946) and *Paisan* (1947). *General della Rovere* (1959) and *The Rise of Louis XIV* (1966) were widely acclaimed; yet Rossellini remains aesthetically the most elusive of the neo-realists, still basically an art house director in the United States, despite the European success of his television films.

Although Rossellini has been one of the few filmmakers who has not been hesitant to offer general formulations of his aims, the very openness of those formulations, their quality of improvisation, the willingness they express to respond, adapt, and change, indicates some of the difficulty in tracing the continuities of his career. When *General della Rovere* appeared in 1959, it was greeted with relief as a triumphant and welcome return to the neo-realist observation of milieu that had made Rossellini famous; *Variety* called it "his first saleable film in years." In the 1950s the more personal and subjective content of his films had combined with the censoriousness of American gossip columnists over his affair and later marriage to Ingrid Bergman as well as the opposition of the (Catholic) Legion of Decency to *The Miracle* (1948) to keep most of his work out of the

This material is here published for the first time, by arrangement with the author.

American market and make it seem opaque or outré to the Europeans.[1] But the public, whether popular critical or popular, often finds it easier to like what it can label, and the surface similarities between *Della Rovere* and Rossellini's early films implied a return to familiar truths.

In fact, Rossellini's career furnishes one of the most profound and complex continuing meditations we have on the meaning of realism in film style and content. The boundaries between phases in Rossellini's career may be more a matter of convenience than critical theory, but the evolution is continual. The proper image might be derived from some of Rossellini's own—a street that passes through very different parts of town, sometimes widening to a highway, sometimes contracting to a cowpath, sometimes underground, sometimes elevated, without any easily recognizable goal or basic nature except the enjoyment of the passage itself. *General della Rovere* is less a return to earlier themes and preoccupations than a new section of this continuing road.

Rossellini's first three postwar films—*Open City (Roma, città aperta,* 1945), *Paisan (Paisà,* 1946), and *Germany, Year Zero (Germania, Anno Zero,* 1947)—all explore documentary methods in stories that deal with the problems of collective action. But *Germany, Year Zero,* with its story of a young German boy trying to make sense of the rubble of his world, already announces the themes of Rossellini's second, more individualistic period when, often working with Ingrid Bergman, he develops a kind of documentary of the self, moved by what in one interview he calls "*l'amour du prochain,*" the love of what happens next. *General della Rovere* both expands these themes and points toward the films of the 1960s, when Rossellini once again explores the relations between an individual and his society and history, not this time in the context of war and disruption but as part of an overwhelming desire to bring man and society, art and science, together in a new understanding created and mediated by film.

Much of Rossellini's training and experience had been in varieties of documentary film. Several of his early amateur shorts (made between 1936 and 1941) dealt with nature, and his first two features *The White Ship (La nave bianca,* 1941) and *A Pilot Returns (Un pilota ritorna,* 1942) are story-documentaries, arraying factual material on a fictional framework. These early works show Rossellini's basic impulse to go beyond a merely ritual invocation of documentary "reality" to experiment with more vol-

1. A rich account of Rossellini's problems with *The Miracle* is contained in a long essay by Richard Corliss on Catholic film censorship in the United States, "The Legion of Decency," *Film Comment, 4* (Summer 1968), pp. 24–61. In the moralistic atmosphere of the American 1950s, the scandal even reached the Senate floor, where Senator Jackson called Bergman "a powerful force for evil." On April 19, 1972, Senator Percy entered an apology for these remarks into the *Congressional Record.*

atile mixtures of fact and fiction. Many young documentarians of the 1960s, who may have thought they were applying the lessons of neorealism, were shocked when Rossellini specifically rejected the "*cinéma vérité*" methods of Jean Rouch, Ricky Leacock, and the Maysles brothers because of what he called their "worship" of the camera: "This mythmaking is infantile. . . . To find the truth, you have to have also a moral position. You have to have a critical judgment."[2]

Rossellini attacked what he believed was a cynical decision to separate the director's point of view from the film and ignore its presence, and he indicted the pretense, whether sincere or disingenuous, that the director merely recorded the meaning already present in what his camera focused on. Although he had not worked in a studio for ten years (1945–1955) and considered them "the great enemy of the cinema . . . monsters of perfection and comfort," he did not believe that the highest goal of film was to be as much a window as possible. Rossellini accepts the need for stylistic self-denial to achieve what he calls an "impassiveness" that allows his material to flow into its most typical shapes. Self-conscious style draws too much attention away from what is being filmed: "Beautiful shots! They make me sick! A film has to be well constructed. That's the least you could expect of a man who makes movies. But a shot alone doesn't have to be beautiful."[3] Rossellini would probably agree with Truffaut's remark about *The 400 Blows:* "I had so many scruples that I filmed humbly, as if it were a documentary."[4] Rossellini's involvement as a director combines a humbleness of situation and an assertiveness of perspective. Before one looks at reality, he implies, one must have a moral vision; otherwise the facts remain inert.

Such a directorial style—with its emphasis on directness, sincerity, and lack of artifice—seemed especially suited to the historical and political moment of the liberation of Italy from the German occupation forces. In *Open City* and more concertedly in *Paisan,* Rossellini draws upon the methods of documentary to evolve new ways of telling a story through unconditioned images. His method is a kind of collage—the presentation of settings and characters so juxtaposed as to give the spectator a sense of the wholeness of the world he is watching at the same time that he is keenly aware of its variety and disjunctures. The spectator knows that liberation will come, and so there are strong images of potential liberation in both *Open City* and *Paisan.* But there is an equally strong sense of despair and incompleteness as well.

2. Interview conducted by Fereydoun Hoveyda and Eric Rohmer, *Cahiers du Cinéma*, no. 145 (July 1963), pp. 6–7. Unless otherwise noted, all translations are my own.
3. "Dix ans de cinema," *Cahiers du Cinéma*, no. 8 (August–September 1955), p. 8.
4. Interview with Dan A. Cukier and Jo Gryn, *Script*, no. 5 (April 1962), p. 9.

*Open City* presents a world defined by dislocation and disparity. The war has made gaps in the lives of Rossellini's characters. Social gaps appear in the juxtaposition of life in a large working-class apartment block, where Pina (Anna Magnani) lives, with life in the luxury apartment shared by Marina (Maria Michi) and Lauretta (Carla Rovere), Pina's sister. Personal gaps appear as well, to underline the abrupt dislocations of the social and visual worlds. Marina, an unemployed actress and drug addict, is the former mistress of Manfredi (Marcello Pagliero), an engineer who has become a Communist and member of the Resistance. Manfredi's friends continue to call him by the honorific "Engineer"; but his only work is now in the Resistance. Defining oneself through work must give way to the demands of acting in history. Don Pietro, the priest, first seen playing soccer with the children of his parish, must also become a Resistance fighter, ally himself with the Communist Manfredi, and finally be executed for his activities. Children must grow up before their time. In one scene Rossellini shows a group of boys returning home only to be cuffed by their unknowing fathers for staying out too late at night; in fact, they have been performing acts of sabotage against the Germans.

The normal events of life—birth, death, marriage, schooling, shopping—are all transfused and distorted by the context of war. Rossellini carries this sense of disruption even into the tone of the film, especially in a brilliant sequence in which German troops come to search the apartment block for men to impress into the army or the work camp. Pina and Francesco (Francesco Grandjacquet) had meant to marry, but the war intervened: "We thought it would end soon and we'd see it only in the newsreels." The plans for the marriage have all at last been made, but when the Germans come, Francesco is rounded up. Meanwhile, Don Pietro and Marcello, Pina's son, force their way into the building, ostensibly to minister the last rites to Pina's bedridden father, but actually to stop Romoletto, the crippled leader of the children's gang, from attacking the Germans with a bomb and a machine gun. They race to the roof, persuade Romoletto to give up his weapons, and then race down the stairs to the grandfather's room, just ahead of the ascending Germans. The grandfather wakes up, sees the priest, and begins loudly insisting that he's not dying.

In the next shot, the Germans have entered the room, and the old man is beatifically lying there with his eyes closed. Only after the Germans leave are we visually let in on the fact that Don Pietro has hit the old man over the head with a frying pan, and hidden the bomb and machine gun under his bedclothes. But downstairs a wailing begins. The Germans have found Francesco and are taking him away with many others. In a shot whose beauty is inseparable from the intensity of Anna Magnani's performance, Pina runs after the truck and is shot. After the impact of her death is felt by Don Pietro and the crying, kicking Marcello, Rossellini cuts to the trucks that had just left. They are attacked by the Resistance and the prisoners escape. Pina need not have died at all.

Because the movement of these scenes is so rapid, the mixture of comic and tragic elements seems very natural, and even that particular tone that might be called sentimental is qualified by the sense of detached, almost cold, observation that the camera conveys by its framing and its movement. Once again, the defining term is disparity, disparity between the life of the family and the war outside, between the normal jobs and roles of society and those the war forces on one, between the genial and comic parts of life and the grim and despairing. One part of *Open City* that has been often criticized is the placing of the Gestapo chief's office right next door to both a torture chamber and a sybaritic sitting room. But Rossellini's Rome is as much a psychic landscape as it is a real city, and in this interior, where the evil forces attempt to manipulate reality by drugs and torture as well as ideology, the unnaturalness of the relation of the rooms bespeaks the ultimate unnaturalness of the Nazi-created society.

In the outer world, Rossellini allows objects to reveal their meaning with less restriction. The execution of Don Pietro takes place out in a kind of fenced field. While the detail of shooting him in the back seems forced, the rest of the scene attempts a more successful casualness. The young boys of Romoletto and Marcello's gang have come to watch the execution. After it is over, they walk off in pairs, some arm in arm, back toward Rome, with the dome of St. Peter's rising above the distant city in the background. Despite the gloom of Don Pietro's execution, *Open City* does end with some hope, the image of potential embodied in a world where children can behave as children and not be forced to grow up too soon.[5]

*Paisan,* Rossellini's next film, draws much more on traditional documentary and newsreel method than does *Open City* and yet at the same time shows the kind of formal artistry typical of Rossellini's later films, the ability to build narrative as much through omissions as through linear, causal, plot. The film is organized in six sections, each dealing with part of the Allied invasion and liberation of Italy. The first occurs in Sicily during the early American landings; the second in Naples, after the American occupation of the city; the third in Rome, six months after the American entry into the city, but with a flashback to the liberation; the fourth in Florence, while the city is still divided between the Germans and the

5. The image of the child in neo-realist films, with its ambiguous implications for a future world beyond the scope of a particular film, appears often in the films of Rossellini, De Sica, and Fellini. Two of Rossellini's films—*Germany, Year Zero* and *Europa '51*—contain child-suicides.

Allies-supported partisans; the fifth in a monastery in the Apennine Mountains in Romagna, after the Germans have left the area; and the sixth in the Po Valley, while the Germans still control much of the area. These six episodes are held in place by a familiar documentary framework, including a strong voice-over narration and animated maps that chart the Allied advance. Where *Open City* included footage that appeared to be documentary, but was often either staged or shot clandestinely, *Paisan* uses documentary footage in the basic meaning of the term—that is, film made as a document of an actual and significant historical event, like the invasion of Sicily or the liberation of Rome. The film in fact begins with a precise date: July 10, 1943.

Let me briefly sketch the plots of the different episodes. In the first, a Sicilian girl and an American soldier try to make some contact without understanding each other's language very well. He is killed when the Germans see him light a cigarette. She hides and later takes a gun and shoots a German. The Americans return to find their friend dead and believe the Sicilian girl has betrayed him. But in the last shot we see her lying dead at the bottom of a cliff where the Germans have thrown her in retribution. In the second episode a young Neapolitan boy "buys" a drunk black American soldier, begins to grow fond of his purchase, but finally steals his shoes after warning him not to go to sleep. Somewhat later, the soldier, now sober and revealed to be an M.P., accidentally meets the kid again, stealing supplies from a truck. He takes the boy home to get his shoes back, discovers the caves outside Naples where the boy lives with thousands of other homeless Italians, and leaves without retrieving his shoes.

In the Rome of the third episode the American soldiers enter the city to music, goodwill, and applause. Six months later, Maria, a prostitute, picks up a soldier after a raid on a bar she has been in. Through his drunken reminiscences, she realizes that he is the same soldier that she gave a drink of water to and shared a few words in rudimentary Italian and English in the first happy days of the Liberation. She tries to tell him this, but he is too drunk to understand. She slips her address into his pocket with a meeting time on it, and appears there the next day, dressed in clothes more innocent that those she wore the night before. But he has forgotten and thrown the paper away as only a whore's address.[6]

In the Florence of the fourth episode, an American nurse helping to care for injured partisans asks after an artist friend of hers and discovers that he is Lupo, the Florentine Resistance leader. With another friend, who

6. This episode is parodied in the Rome section of *Catch-22*.

is trying to get back to his family, she enters divided Florence by way of the deserted Uffizi galleries. After labyrinthine wanderings in the city, she comforts a dying Resistance fighter who tells of the despair in Resistance ranks since Lupo died that day.

The fifth episode takes place in a Romagna monastery, where the monks are put into an uproar when they discover that of the three American Army chaplains they have given their hospitality to, one is Protestant and another is Jewish. In the final episode, which takes place in the Po Valley, American advisors to the partisans have been ordered to keep fighting, even though the Germans have them isolated. A group of local people who have given shelter to the partisans and the Americans are killed, and the Germans capture the rest. When on the next day the Germans begin to execute the partisans, an American protests and is shot. The last image of the film is the tightly-bound partisans being pushed, one by one, into the Po River to drown. The voice-over promise of an Allied victory in the spring seems little consolation.

The bare sketches I have given here convey something of the similarities and interrelations of the episodes, but little of the richness of Rossellini's detail: the snobbishness of the town Fascist in the Sicilian episode, who refuses to believe the parents of the Italian-American soldier come from the area; the scene in the Naples episode when the black soldier drunkenly disrupts a puppet show about the victory of the white Crusaders over the black Saracens by leaping onto the tiny stage to slug it out with the head Crusader; the hallucinatory feeling of deserted Florence and the detached comments on its art and architecture made by two observing British officers; the details of monastery life in Romagna; the energetically cooked meal of eels in the Po episode. All this rich texture plays against the limiting simplicities of the documentary maps and the explanatory narration, while each episode somehow reflects and comments on every other one. In essence they are all about encounter, the encounter of strangers, strangers to culture, to feeling, and to language—all in search of some attempted relation, the linking with some "paisan." Many of these attempts fail, and the episodic structure of *Paisan,* so appropriate for a documentary about widely scattered parts of a large human movement, at once reflects on the immediate failures and the dreams of possible success. Thematically, this episodic film is fascinated by the failures of relations between people, their separations and their misunderstandings. Visually, *Paisan* is conceived as a counterpoint between enclosures, their collapse, and their reassertion.

André Bazin, who was a great admirer of *Paisan,* believed that the key to the film was the way it showed a succession in events without striving to relate them. In one essay he called this method Rossellini's ability to convey the "lacuna in reality," the ellipsis in natural events.[7] According to Bazin, the three basic elements of neo-realism were the use of nonprofessional actors, natural setting, and just this kind of narrative structure, which respects "the actual structure" of events. In another essay he found a common element in the work of Rossellini, De Sica, and Fellini to be "the pride of place they all give to the representation of reality at the expense of dramatic structure."[8] All of Rossellini's films, says Bazin, teach us something new about the basic nature of reality, showing it as if for the first time.

But in such a formulation Bazin generally ignores the ambivalence essential to any film or any work of art that attempts to convey the impression of naturalness through the techniques of realism. That ambivalence derives directly from what Rossellini calls the "morality" with which one must seek out facts, in short, point of view, whatever results when the director's eye and mind look upon the world. Without considering the nature of this "morality," it is difficult to answer questions about the later, more surrealist and illusionistic, direction of the work of the neo-realist directors: De Sica's interest in folktales, Fellini's in theatricality and spectacle, and Rossellini's in the role of illusion in the creation either of a viable society or of a world.

The episodes in *Paisan* are more than vignettes snapped through the camera's window; each contributes to the "artifice" of the entire film, in which the three worlds of the Italians, the Americans, and the Germans individually and collectively impinge on one another. Because the main interest has shifted from the confrontation of Italian and German in *Open City* to the interplay of Italian and American in *Paisan,* none of these worlds is monolithic. Within his general terms, Rossellini varies the individual expressions, even experimenting with varieties of tone as well: the bittersweet sentiment of the Neapolitan story with its encounter of black soldier and street urchin; the irony of the Rome encounter of soldier and prostitute; the humor of the Romagna episode, with its confrontation of Catholic monks and "heathen" chaplains; as well as the more pessimistic tones of the Sicily, Florence, and Po episodes.

*Paisan* basically concentrates on the working out of such human relations amid the timelessness of the Italian landscape. And the setting of Italian geography and cities is important not because it is natural or "documentary" but because it is a setting, a mute and passive context that yet by its presence transmits a value and a nuance to the human activity

---

7. "De Sica: Metteur en Scène," *What Is Cinema?* vol. 2, p. 66.
8. "*Cabiria:* The Voyage to the End of Neorealism," *What Is Cinema?* vol. 2, p. 87.

taking place within it. The wrecked Sicilian castle, the slums of Naples, the prostitute's apartment in Rome, the deserted and rubble-strewn streets of Florence, the Romagna monastery, and the marshes of the Po—all are potential human spaces that have been disrupted or destroyed by the war. Throughout *Paisan* the sense of space created by Rossellini in the various episodes is the most palpable element in the film, a kinetic and psychological equivalent to the film's more obvious theme of the response of the various sections of Italy to the liberation brought by the Allied armies.

Liberation, Rossellini implies, involves disruption as well as freedom. The film begins with the disruption of space, the invasion of Sicily and the entry by night of a group of American soldiers into a Sicilian church where the town has gathered. If the sense of space in *Paisan* is considered, it is fitting that only the Romagna monastery episode ends with any unequivocal optimism. The American Catholic chaplain calls it a moment of serenity in the turmoil of the war. Amid the general disruption its walls constitute a real human refuge and setting, created and maintained with dignity by the sometimes comic and foolish men who live there.

But such comic benevolence is only an idyll in *Paisan,* for Rossellini is much more fascinated by disorientation. We enter *Paisan* in the darkness of the Sicilian attack, and Rossellini never gives us a clear sense of the spatial relations of the area. The castle is first held by the Americans, then by the Germans, and then again by the Americans, although neither group is quite sure of the existence of the other. The spectator of the film does not first grasp the general scene and then its components, but must work instead from the components into a general but always provisional understanding of what in fact is going on. Rossellini described the method in an article reviewing his work in the ten years since *Open City:*

> Usually, in traditional cinema, you cut a scene in this fashion: first, an establishing shot, define the ambiance, discover an individual, get closer to him, medium shot, head-to-hips shot, close-up, and you begin to tell his story. I work in exactly the opposite way: a man is displaced, and, thanks to his displacement, you discover the milieu he finds himself in. I always begin with a close-up; then the camera movement that accompanies the actor discovers the ambiance. ("Dix ans de cinéma," p. 9)

*Paisan* may be one of the few successful collective films—that is, a film in which there is no central hero or heroine but in which the film itself and the world the film comprehends is the center of interest. Rossellini accomplishes this with the calm and unobtrusiveness that is the hallmark of his style, that lack of directorial assertiveness Truffaut calls humble.

Through the episodic and open construction of *Paisan* at all levels, Rossellini forces the spectator to make connections that are there to be made.
*Paisan* presents a picture of what the liberation of Italy meant on many
different levels of society, and all the details of its creation—its episodes,
its editing, its individual shots—first clearly mirror and then elaborately
comment upon Rossellini's basic themes. An extraordinary film in itself,
*Paisan,* with its unique mixture of truth and story, moves far away from
the style of documentary established in England and America in the 1930s
to become the not-so-distant ancestor of a triumph of documentary form
like Marcel Ophuls' *The Sorrow and the Pity* (1969).

In *Open City* and *Paisan* Rossellini is fascinated by the aesthetic and
political implications of collective action. But however heroic the collective
actions may be, and whatever ultimate victory they look toward, the outlook
for individuals is a gloomy one. In *Open City* Manfredi dies by torture and
Don Pietro is executed. In *Paisan*'s last episode, both American guerrillas
and Italian partisans are killed by the Germans, even after the successes
shown in the other episodes and at almost the same moment that we hear
narration that foretells the end of the war. The pragmatic value in collective
heroism is the alliance of otherwise ill-assorted people in common cause
against their enemy; the ideal value involves the continuation of the alliance
after the enemy has been defeated. In this sense the moral status of Manfredi and Don Pietro does not differ very much from that of the crew of
the battleship in *La nave bianca;* they are less individuals than priest and
engineer, Catholic and Communist, leagued together against the Nazis.
Their personal deaths are less important than the examples they furnish to
others, like the children who imitate their Resistance activities and watch
Don Pietro's execution at the end of the film. Robert Warshow has remarked
that in *Open City* "heroism is presented not as the capacity to act but as
the capacity to suffer; the priest and the Communist are one, and the activity
of the underground leads not to victory but to sainthood."[9]
But Rossellini does not leave this heroic martyrdom unqualified. The
overall feeling of *Paisan* already involves the actual incompleteness of
Liberation, the gaps between people, the missed connections, both political
and personal, and the difficulty of creating a society in which all have
individual place and value. The vignettes of *Paisan* contain some admirable
characters; yet the episodic nature of the film increases the feeling that the
world is fragmented and there is no one, no person, no example, who
can establish coherent values in the old way. Past actions change things

9. *The Immediate Experience* (New York: Doubleday, 1962), p. 191. The quotation comes
from an essay on *Paisan* published originally in *Partisan Review,* July 1948.

irrevocably, and the dream of the past nurtured by the prostitute who wants to return to her innocence is only a more bitter version of the dream of Catholicism nurtured by the monks who want to save the Protestant and Jewish chaplains by conversion. What actions, feelings, or perceptions still carry the sanction of traditional value? In almost all the episodes of *Paisan* there is a dream of union that is thwarted; the monastery can remain serene only because it is separated from the world, and even there comic disruptions occur. History in *Paisan* seems too large for anyone, especially the film-maker, to hold more than a piece of—a definite withdrawal from the implication in *Open City* that an unambiguous morality can guide political and personal decisions.

A clue to Rossellini's attitude might be found in an odd little film he made in the same period called *La macchina ammazzacattivi (The Machine That Kills the Wicked,* 1948), which tells the story of a small-town Italian photographer who is given, supposedly by a saint, a camera that has the power to kill. He immediately begins exterminating everyone in town he considers evil. Here in essence is the supposed moral mission of neo-realism: the world purified through the camera. But Rossellini's actual point—which the hero of the film gradually realizes—is the difficulty of telling who should be disposed of by the avenging camera, and who in fact is the authority that put the magic camera into his hands. (The "saint" turns out to be a minor demon trying to curry favor with the Devil.) Could this fable have been a kind of apologia for Rossellini's career up to that point? In terms of his later films, it certainly points the way toward a closer focus on individuals, a less grandiose statement about moral issues, and a delicate regard for the camera as the instrument of his vision. *La macchina ammazzacattivi* and *Paisan* complement each other as aesthetic and political expressions of the realization that a morally irreproachable point of view does not insure a clear understanding of the world. The real difference between Rossellini and the documentarians whom he later attacks is defined by the implicit denial of *La macchina ammazzacattivi* that the camera eye is morally neutral.

During the 1950s, Rossellini was to tread a solitary path, both aesthetically and personally. The elements of historical documentary in both *Open City* and *Paisan* give way to a documentary of the self that focuses on isolated and often embattled individuals (*St. Francis* is a partial exception that I'll discuss later) who to an extent parallel Rossellini's own position as a filmmaker. Without the pressure of the historical reality of the war, Rossellini asks, how are the shapes of individual lives created? Many of Rossellini's most striking films of the 1950s deal with women alone, either by themselves or in marriages, struggling to assert some individual integrity and self-definition. Both *The Miracle* and *Stromboli* concentrate on a woman in an extreme situation. In *The Miracle* Anna Magnani plays Nanni, a simple-minded goatherd, who lives with other beggars on the steps of the cathedral of a small Italian hilltown. She has intercourse with a traveler whom she believes to be St. Joseph (played by Fellini). When she discovers that she is pregnant and announces the "holy" birth to the townspeople, they mockingly parade and then throw garbage at her. In *Stromboli* Karin (Ingrid Bergman) marries Antonio (Mario Vitale), a fisherman from the rocky island of Stromboli, in order to get out of an internment camp, after she has been refused a visa to Argentina. But she hates the life of the island village and her foreign ways arouse the hostility of the townspeople and her husband as well.

Characters like Nanni and Karin are battlegrounds between the demands of the self from within and the demands of a society from without, demands for conformity, for rationality, for all varieties of individual submission. Nanni is crazed and poor, the butt of jeering crowds. But she has some vision that carries her along, something inwardly authentic, no matter how outwardly ridiculous it may seem. Says Rossellini, "She is a crazy woman, but, in the middle of her mental confusion, she has a faith, deluded if you like, but a faith."[10]

Nanni has a faith; Karin finds a faith. And it is somewhat artificial to call them by the name of the characters, since Rossellini's camera insists on the interaction between the actresses, Magnani and Bergman, and the parts they play. In both *The Miracle* and *Stromboli* the camera is attracted to the central character as a dilemma to be understood, but never totally fathomed. Rossellini delves into the potential emotional energy that both Magnani and Bergman project, even when they seem most calm and happy. The camera circles around Magnani in *The Miracle* or it seeks out Bergman amid the rocky cliffs of Stromboli in an effort to respond to some subterranean mingling of actress and character, the mysterious knot of artifice and nature.[11]

The essence of faith for both characters involves a relation between themselves and nature as much as between themselves and God. In her delusion Magnani understands this natural world, while Bergman in her rationality must come to terms with it. In one scene in *The Miracle*, Magnani wakes from the sleep induced by "St. Joseph," picks up a load of firewood she has been collecting, and moves off, hidden by the wood, with its still leafy branches. She is like a moving tree, more part of

10. "Dix ans de cinéma," p. 8.
11. *The Miracle* was originally half of a two-part film called *L'Amore*. In the other part Magnani played the single role in Cocteau's *La Voix humaine*. *The Miracle* first appeared in the United States as part of a three-part film called *Ways of Love* that also included Jean Renoir's *Partie de campagne* and Marcel Pagnol's *Jofroi*.

the nature that surrounds her than she is a part of the town world to which she descends, with its narrow streets and hostile people. Bergman is just as isolated as Magnani. But she has none of the consolation of either nature or inner faith. She marries the fisherman to get out of the internment camp, but finds herself in what she considers to be a natural prison, when she had looked for a refuge. Whereas Magnani's confinement in the town is in opposition to nature, Bergman believes that the natural life of Stromboli has been created to confine her. She continually wears shoes, while her husband invariably goes barefoot. In the tuna-fishing sequence, the fish leap about in the nets, to be gaffed by the fishermen. Bergman is horrified, seemingly at the violence, but underneath because she sees their entrapment as an image of her own. When her husband nails their house shut to keep her from running away to the other village and escaping, he has fulfilled all her fears.

Both *The Miracle* and *Stromboli* end with a long climb: Magnani climbs endlessly up the stairs cut into the mountain to the monastery where she wants to bear her child; Bergman climbs up the volcano of Stromboli to get to the other island village, where she can find a boat to the mainland. Are these climbs "symbolic"? Is the fact that Bergman wears shoes while her husband goes barefoot "symbolic"? Perhaps they are, but not in the way symbols exist in literature, or the way objects gain significance in expressionist films.[12]

In realistic films such as Rossellini's, "symbols" tell us more about character than they do about some hidden substratum of the film the characters are unaware of. André Bazin has written that Rossellini's world is anti-psychological. But I think we can certainly call psychological the way that Rossellini externalizes the inner natures of his characters through symbolic or significant action, instead of allowing such meaning to come from the impositions of the director. Bergman *chooses* to wear her shoes; the meaning of that act is part of the fabric of the film. In the same way she chooses to interpret the tuna fishing as an image of imprisonment and death, and she chooses to climb the volcano, even after a recent eruption, through some combined psychic and literal necessity. Too many appreciators of Rossellini and neo-realism would agree with José Luis Guarner's remark that the tuna fishing in *Stromboli* is "merely a question of providing realism and giving a feeling of actuality to what might merely have been reconstruction."[13] It is true that *Stromboli* also employs a documentary-like voice-over narration. But the tension in the film is be-

12. Compare, say, Rossellini's use of stairs with the use of stairs in a German film of the 1920s, such as Fritz Lang's *Destiny* or *Metropolis*.
13. *Roberto Rossellini* (New York: Praeger, 1970), p. 108.

tween the detached documentary view of this quaint little island and Bergman's struggle for a life that she believes is personally authentic.

If there is a false note in the film, it occurs at the end, when the fumes from the eruption have caused Bergman to fail in her flight, and she cries out for help from God. The narration tells us with what I feel is a sonorous insincerity that putting her faith in God has reconciled her to life in the village and she returns down the mountain the way she came. To entrust the resolution of the film to a narrative voice that identifies faith with the acceptance of a hostile society seems to be a misguided artistic choice, with little feeling for the integrity of the outcast that Rossellini shows in *The Miracle* or little appreciation as yet for the way later films such as *Voyage in Italy* and *Fear* explore the evasions and self-falsifications of bad marriages. Bergman's submission in *Stromboli* denies everything that until that point had been attractive about her character. It is to Rossellini's credit that he never shows her returning home.

*Voyage in Italy* (1953) and *Fear* (1954) continue and elaborate the effort made in *Stromboli* to anatomize the relationship between husband and wife from the woman's point of view. Both are stark, bare films, with little of the visual beauty of Rossellini's earlier films, perhaps because here he is more directly concerned with the inner life of his characters. Ingrid Bergman plays the wife in both films. In *Voyage in Italy* she and her husband (George Sanders) come to Naples to sell some property and see Italy. Under the pressure of being together with nothing particular to do, the seams in their marriage begin to open. In *Fear* Bergman has taken over the control of her husband's factory while he was in a concentration camp (the film is set in Germany). When he returns, she retains control, while he works in his laboratory. As the film begins, she is engaged in an affair. A young girl who claims to be the girlfriend of her lover starts to blackmail her; but the young girl turns out to be an agent coached by Bergman's husband.

*Voyage in Italy* ends in a reconciliation at the San Gennaro festival in Naples; *Fear* ends in a reconciliation in the factory laboratories as Bergman is about to commit suicide. But both films are about the lack of connection between these husbands and wives. *Voyage in Italy* contains some of the most abrasive scenes between a man and a woman that have ever been filmed. But it is an abrasion without obvious conflicts, an abrasion of boredoms, spawned by the inconsequential, space-filling dialogue that will be echoed in Antonioni's *L'Avventura*. The final reconciliation of the couples in *Voyage in Italy* and *Fear* is just as unconvincing as the reconciliation at the end of *Stromboli,* but because it is truer to the bleak spirit of the films, its inadequacy remains authentic.

In both these films Rossellini exploits that character that Ingrid

Bergman often projects: the potentially insane erratic person, held in check only by her self-conscious will and by her reason. Both films take place in a modern world, where nature no longer has any power. In *Voyage in Italy* Bergman tours Naples and Pompeii and tries to take a picture of the ionization process that occurs in small pockets of the quiescent Vesuvius (part of the same volcanic chain as Stromboli). The Bergman of *Fear* is even more in apparent control, even more interested in the rational and scientific ordering of things, no matter how she fails at relationships. No longer can there be the walking, climbing struggles of *The Miracle* and *Stromboli*. Movement in *Voyage in Italy* and *Fear* takes place in cars. In the first scene of *Voyage* Bergman and Sanders reveal the nature of their relationship while she drives their car down toward Naples. In *Fear* she also drives quite a bit, especially through the gate of her factory, duly saluted by the guard, or out to the country to see her children.

In *The Flowers of St. Francis* St. Francis tells Brother Ginepro (Junípero) not to talk but to act. In *Voyage in Italy* and *Fear* there is little action and only empty talk. Man has been displaced from nature by the modern age, and there seems to be no way back. The lovers Bergman in *Voyage* sees on the streets of Naples are as far from her as the intertwined bodies she watches being excavated from the soil of Pompeii. The reconciliations at the ends of the two films ring hollow because they do not represent any new energy in the relationships, only a desire to try again. The San Gennaro crowd that brings Bergman and Sanders together at the end of *Voyage in Italy* works just as hard and just as unconsciously to separate them.

*The Flowers of Saint Francis* (1950) was made after *Stromboli* and before *Voyage in Italy*.[14] I take it out of chronological context primarily because I don't want to suggest by my own discussion that Rossellini works linearly, each film following a uniform development of method and meaning. But it is also suitable to take *St. Francis* out of chronological order because it represents an effort by Rossellini to get away from the contemporary world embodied in most of his films of this period and to present an idealized but not idyllic past. *St. Francis* begins with a montage of the painting of the period, while a voice-over commentary—once again a pseudo-documentary induction—tells us how this art actually describes a world of social turmoil. Then the story of the Franciscans opens with a long scene of St. Francis and his brethren walking down a road in the rain, returning to their church of Saint Mary of the Angels. It is difficult to recount the casual delicacy with which Rossellini displays these images of

14. Its literal title is *Francis, the Jester of God;* the literal title of *Stromboli* is *Stromboli, the Land of God*.

the rain-soaked monks, in the muddy road or crossing a stream, talking about God.

One could cast the film into three parts, according to the kind of space it defines. In the first the monks look for shelter from the rain. Then they return to their own church, continue its construction, and live together. Finally Brother Ginepro goes out to encounter Nicolaio, a ferocious warlord who is laying siege to nearby Viterbo. Partially prepared by this entrance into a world and a history that lies outside their timeless spirituality, St. Francis finally sends each of the monks out to a different part of Italy to carry his message.

The images of *St. Francis* almost effortlessly express the spiritual dimension of Rossellini's exploration of the limits of refuge (so much a theme of *Paisan, The Miracle,* and *Stromboli*) and the need to open that interior space into the world. The part-mindful, part-unmindful relation of the monks and the rain underlines their relation to nature much better than the invocations of "Brother Bird" and "Brother Fire," at the same time that it gives those words a visual substance and justification. The action of the film, the movement of the characters, gives the film its spiritual justification and validity. The monks have a place in the world because they embody what is for Rossellini the redemptive behavior of children, innocent and exuberant, without the modern melancholy that plagues the young boy of *Germany, Year Zero*.

When Ginepro goes into Nicolaio's camp, he is incredibly manhandled in some striking scenes that, without real violence, give a sense of the flexibility and physicality of Ginepro's nature at the same time that his smiling endurance shows his spirituality much more vividly than would a clichéd endurance of torture. Ginepro's openness is contrasted visually with Nicolaio's enclosure. For most of the time that we see the ferocious leader, he is strung up while he has his armor fitted, a metal shell with an empty, roaring interior. Ginepro succeeds in influencing Nicolaio to lift the siege when he shows that he is unfazed by Nicolaio's theatrical villainy.

The entrance into history Ginepro makes at Nicolaio's camp is therefore an entrance into a world of noises, crowds, and appearances. But it is an entrance that must be made. The values of childhood—innocence, clarity, spirituality, closeness to nature—cannot remain cloistered and fabulous. The action of *St. Francis,* with its final commitment to the world, seems therefore to be a refutation of the otherwise fabulous and idealized quality of the film in the context of Rossellini's other work. But the paradox works perfectly. *St. Francis* may be more successful and have more definition as a complete work than Rossellini's more problematic and less certain modern films. Yet it is not a myth of refuge, like the monastery in *Paisan,* but a myth of initiation into a more problematic world, a myth in which the potentially cleansing and renewing part of human nature is brought into history.

The energies and interests of *General della Rovere* (1959) have more to do with the commitment of *St. Francis* to a real world of society and history than they have with the failures of communication and community portrayed in the Bergman films. The central character of *General della Rovere* is a compulsive gambler and con man named Bardone (*alias* Grimaldi), who is forced by the Germans to assume the name and role of General della Rovere, a high Resistance officer, to escape being put into jail himself. Like St. Francis, Bardone/della Rovere participates in a myth of entrance into history. But it is a myth he ultimately creates and authenticates himself. For perhaps the first time in his films, Rossellini in *della Rovere* both explores the value of appearances (rather than their inferiority to nature) and examines the possibility that men may live more by the creation of such myths than by the facts of everyday reality.

In one interview, Rossellini tells the story of a Neapolitan family that made a great deal of money on the black market. But instead of using the money to raise their general standard of living, they bought for themselves elaborate coffins, decorated with gold, in order, says Rossellini, to present themselves before God with dignity. Rossellini is attracted to this story, it seems, because it embodies the theatrical impulse of all realistic artists. First comes the choice of subject, the concentration on its details, but then too comes the need to transcend, to find the transcendent or the uncommon within the everyday. Even Norman Rockwell, for example, rarely paints a scene from daily life so often as he paints a special event, when his subjects move outside their normal selves, to go to church, to play music after business hours, to take off their everyday clothes and personalities and be for a moment released and somehow transcendent. Bardone as con man and later as licensed della Rovere embodies precisely this relation between the commonplace and the heightened. Played by Vittorio De Sica, he is the image of the suave matinee idol who lives in a world that is unresponsive to his sense of himself, and so must play the fraud and the hypocrite.

The physical world of *General della Rovere* is reminiscent of *Fear,* with its stark night scenes, its narrow hallways and overcrowded rooms. A large part of Rossellini's visual achievement in the film consists in these interiors, constructed and photographed with so much feeling and intensity that every space seems a potential image of the inside of a character's brain, in much the same way that the more open, natural settings of *The Miracle, Stromboli,* and *St. Francis* had a metaphysical relation to the minds of the characters that walked within them. These rooms are the compartments of Bardone's life. We first see him on the street, where he unctuously gives directions to the German Colonel Müller (Hannes Messemer). Bardone is a man in perpetual transit, moving from place to place, sometimes a guest, usually an intruder. Even though we later see him in his own home, he doesn't seem to belong there either. First he argues with his mistress Valeria (Sandra Milo, already the overblown fantasy woman Fellini will cast her as in $8\frac{1}{2}$ and *Juliet of the Spirits*). Then he stands cramped in the narrow hall, making telephone calls, setting up deals between Italian families and the Germans who in some way threaten their sons—always the intermediary, bilking both sides. He has no ideals beyond an ideal of self-presentation, and when he is found out and arrested for his illegal activities, he seems destroyed.

But Colonel Müller, who has ultimate authority over his case, sympathizes with Bardone and offers him the alternative of impersonation, a deal suited to his talents. The real General della Rovere has been mistakenly shot, despite a plan to trail him and learn the secrets of the Resistance. Bardone must leave the sidelines and participate in history, but under an assumed name. At first Bardone enjoys the role, for it is perfectly suited to his consciously showy personality. Even though he is put into prison so that he can find out the names of the Resistance members, he spends most of his time luxuriating in the applause of the other prisoners for "his" exploits. Inspired by the presence of Bardone/della Rovere, one prisoner commits suicide rather than be executed. Gradually Bardone realizes that the role of della Rovere only shows more acutely the emptiness of his real nature, the disparity between his distinguished good looks and what he actually is. Spatially and visually, the realization is imaged in the distinction between the unacknowledged prison of his conman's life in hallways, bureaucratic offices, and small cafés, and the actual prison where he is now confined and where he begins to achieve some ideal of self-definition.

The end of the process occurs when the actor has become the role and Bardone leaves his real identity behind to take on the ideal identity of della Rovere; he has become the person the other prisoners have the faith to believe he already is. In revenge for the assassination of the Fascist leader of Turin, Müller is forced to choose ten men to be executed. He includes Bardone so that Bardone can finger Fabrizio, a high member of the Resistance, whose identity has been narrowed down to the other nine men. During the night before the executions, Fabrizio makes himself known to Bardone. But the next morning Bardone refuses to tell Müller who Fabrizio is and virtually runs out to be executed, but not before he gives the startled Müller a note for his (that is, della Rovere's) wife that reads "I love you. Viva Italy."

The theatricality and flamboyance of this action is an integral part of its meaning. *Open City* defined the years of Resistance to the Germans as a time when ordinary men could transcend their everyday lives and become heroes by associating themselves with an ideal of politics, morality, and community. By *General della Rovere* Rossellini seems less interested in collective heroism than he is in individual identity, and the standard of nature is less important than the possibility that self-conscious artifice may be a way out of the prison. One odd detail completes the picture. On the wall behind the ten men tied to posts to be executed is a painted version of the nearby skyline of Turin. The real city has vanished for Bardone/della Rovere. The stylization remains to mark the value of theatricality and gesture as a means of heightening the reality and truth of ordinary lives.

After the domestic and personal worlds of most of Rossellini's films of the 1950s, with their intimate settings and problems apart from history, *General della Rovere* represents a renewed attempt to integrate individual action with a historical moment. The theme, and the method, had been present in films like *Open City* and *Paisan*. But the importance and novelty of *della Rovere* for Rossellini's career derives directly from its acceptance of artifice—role playing, the assumption of disguise—as a way toward moral truth. In his earlier films, he did not seem especially interested in bringing together his fascination with his characters and his fascination with the performers (usually actresses) who play them. The character lay on the surface, but underneath was always the virtuosity of the actress, and potentially both her desire and her ability to play roles. An essential part of the character of Nani in *The Miracle* is that the other half of *L'Amore* shows Magnani in the role of a sophisticated urban woman in *La Voix humaine*. (At the end of the credits is a statement that "This film is an homage to the art of Anna Magnani.") Similarly, in almost all the Bergman/Rossellini films, the character played by Bergman is also trying to play an uncongenial personal or social role. In *Stromboli* she descends in class and changes in culture to marry the island fisherman; in *Voyage in Italy* she tries to play the tourist and guest, even while the problems of her marriage keep breaking into that leisure-time, special occasion, world; in *Fear* she has taken over her husband's role in running the factory and is also conducting an affair in which she generally plays the masculine role.

Rossellini's point of view in such films seems to stress the need to accept natural roles and reject unnatural ones, especially those that are the product of contemporary society, and sources of only external satisfaction. St. Francis and his monks can enter the world because they do it in purity and innocence. *General della Rovere* introduces the idea that role playing and disguise can lead to a liberation and realization of the self. By stressing De Sica playing Bardone playing Grimaldi playing della Rovere, it brings together for the first time in Rossellini's films his double interest in the naturalness of his characters and the artifice of his actors and actresses, and looks forward to the elaborate exploration of role playing and artifice that Rossellini will conduct in *The Rise of Louis XIV*.

# Rossellini's Materialist Mise-en-Scène of "La Prise de pouvoir par Louis XIV"

## James Roy MacBean

Rossellini's *La Prise de pouvoir par Louis XIV* is not a film *about* Louis XIV. Rather, as the title (in the original French) clearly indicates, it is a film which examines the *taking of power* by Louis XIV. The film's principal focus, then, is not Louis himself, but the mechanism of power as understood and manipulated by Louis XIV.

The distinction is crucial, I think, for depending on the focus of investigation, one raises very different types of questions. Rossellini himself has revealed that each of his films is an attempt to answer a specific question: and he acknowledges that the question at the base of *La Prise de pouvoir par Louis XIV* was not "What was Louis like as a person?" but rather "Why did people at the court of Louis XIV dress the way they did?" An interesting question—and one which the film answers very clearly. But perhaps intelligence consists not so much in coming up with the right answers as in asking the right questions, that is questions which open up some fruitful lines of investigation by raising further questions. In the case of *La Prise de pouvoir par Louis XIV,* for example, Rossellini's question about fashion styles may have served him as a point of departure; but the film as a whole is by no means limited to a dramatization of the answer that "fashion styles were deliberately set and cultivated by Louis XIV as part of an overall political strategy." On the contrary, perhaps the greatest of this film's many merits is that Rossellini places the answer to his original question within the larger context of a clear materialist examination of the basic socioeconomic situation of seventeenth-century France, and implicitly places the whole epoch within the ultimate context of the *process* of history itself.

To accomplish this, Rossellini resolutely avoids the crudely psychologizing interpretations and melodramatic structures of Hollywood's historical epics; and he rejects as well the lyrical excesses of Eisenstein's emotionalized reconstructions of historical events. Utilizing simple camera setups with very little movement of the camera, long takes, and a discreet but very effective use of the zoom lens, Rossellini maintains a cautious, alert distance from his historical material—thereby enabling us to experience, for once, the *strangeness* of a historical period that is not our own. This strangeness, however, is not to be confused with exoticism—especially the Cecil B. DeMille brand of exoticism where postcard images of "local color" (often Hollywood plastic) are shamelessly exploited, and every historical utterance is delivered with heavy-handed flailing by ham actors who dream of an Oscar.

Wisely, Rossellini relies primarily on nonactors in this film (Jean-Marie Patte, who plays Louis XIV, is a French post office functionary); and, preferring understatements to histrionics, Rossellini eschews the big scenes of emotional intensity that are the stock in trade of most historical films and lets us experience instead the subtle tensions of the daily, mundane deeds of history. And even when dramatizing the high points of Louis's *prise de pouvoir*—like the arrest of Fouquet—Rossellini evokes from Jean-Marie Patte a curious and penetrating sense of the dogged determination and single-minded effort involved in being (or playing) Louis XIV. Moreover, in close collaboration with historian Philippe Erlanger (who is credited with the script of this film), Rossellini brilliantly develops what I would call a *materialist mise-en-scène* in which *things*—the material objects of seventeenth-century France—are not mere props and backdrops for the drama, but share equal billing, as it were, with the human figures.

Rarely, if ever, has a work of art been so solidly rooted in *things;* and rarely, if ever, has an artist explored so vividly and yet so profoundly the role of *things* in the making of history. Significantly, the closest artistic antecedent I can think of for this film is Bertolt Brecht's *Galileo,* a play in which the dynamics of history are also explored from a resolutely materialist point of view.

Rossellini's eye for detail in this film is masterful. But the details are not mere flourishes added on to the major dynamics of the film; on the contrary, it is largely through the details—the cardinal's bedpan, the bloodletting, the king's morning toilet, the pastimes of the court, the preparing and serving of the king's dinner, and, of course, the all-important articles of clothing—that we begin to understand the way in which man's social existence is intimately tied to and strongly determined by his relationship to things.

But Rossellini examines as well the way in which man, starting with a concern for things, takes a detour—in his dealings with other men—into the world of *appearances*. "One rules more by appearances," declares Louis XIV, "than by the way things really are" (*la nature profonde des choses*). True enough, in one sense—and certainly the film documents the masterful manipulation of appearances that characterizes Louis XIV's reign. Nonetheless, that sophisticated web of appearances which Louis weaves around himself is by no means unrelated to "the way things really are." Quite the contrary, it is part of an overall strategy to *change* "the way things really are" while diverting people's attentions from this material reality. . . .

Throughout the film each successive sequence has a twofold function in which information is presented to advance the chronological story-line and, at the same time, to analyze different aspects of the historical period. That the former is often less important than the latter is illustrated best, I think, by the doctors' examination of the ailing Mazarin. In terms of story-line, this sequence is disproportionately long: all we really need to know is who Mazarin is (and the film doesn't really supply this information until the following sequences) and not *how* he died but simply *that* he died. But Rossellini is interested in aspects of history other than merely "who did what."

So the doctors' examination of Mazarin becomes Rossellini's examination of the state of man's scientific knowledge in seventeenth-century France. And what more telling index could there be of man's knowledge than his knowledge of his own *materiality?* The doctors take the patient's pulse . . . or roughly ten seconds worth. (In 1661—the year of Mazarin's death—the fact that blood circulates through our bodies was still a very recent discovery, the ramifications of which were only beginning to be understood.) They run their hands along the patient's nightshirt and bedding, then sniff their fingertips—presumably to evaluate the odor of the patient's sweat. Then they examine the . . . . The word is not spoken, out of *délicatesse;* but the request is immediately understood, and the cardinal's bedpan is quickly fetched from beneath the bed and handed to the chief consultant, who holds it up to his nose, shaking it gently to stir up the contents, sniffing it in short, businesslike inhalations.

After several moments, he passes the bedpan to a colleague, accompanying this move with a telling arching of the eyebrows; and, turning to the cardinal's resident physician, he concludes: "He must be bled." The other consultants quickly voice their agreement. Informed that the patient has already been bled several times that day and may be too weak to be bled again, they reply that "the human body contains 24 liters of blood and can lose 21 liters and still live." And to reassure the resident physician, they support their argument with analogies in the form of aphorisms: "The deeper you have to go to get water from a well, the better the water" and "The more milk a mother gives, the more milk she has to give."

The cardinal is lifted from bed, placed in a chair, and bled from the ankle. As he faints, the blood is collected in a small pot. Repeating the same procedure as with the cardinal's urine, the chief consultant grimaces resignedly: "Unless there's a miracle . . . ."

Finally, the renowned physicians withdraw. Outside the cardinal's chamber they discuss several treatments that might be tried in desperation. "Perhaps His Eminence needs to be purged of his 'bad humours,'" suggests one doctor. "But I already gave him rhubarb," counters the resident physician. "Precious stones," suggests one; "A mother's milk," suggests another. But they admit they have never tried these measures and don't really have any faith in them. The scene ends.

Quite tangential to the film's story-line, this sequence is absolutely central to the film's basic preoccupations. The dialectic between objective and subjective factors, between things and man's perception of their appearances, is *mise en scène* in the cardinal's death chamber. The doctors recognize the importance of the material things of this life—like our bodies. But at this stage of history they can only examine what is externalized—like urine, sweat, blood, and the general outward appearance of the patient—and their basic tools are their senses of sight, smell, and touch. Their information is limited to sense data. They can smell the urine, but they cannot yet perform a chemical analysis of the urine. Sense data is a prerequisite and an important part of analysis, but alone it often does not accomplish very much. And while we concentrate on the outward appearances of things, things go their own way—they degenerate, decompose, and are transformed into something else. And when *we* are the things that degenerate, decompose, and are transformed into something else, all the other *things* that we accumulated in our lifetime are then passed on to someone else. We make out a will to determine who gets what.

Enter the Church. Mazarin—himself a cardinal—is dying. He must be confessed and prepare himself for death. In the eyes of the Church this means settling his accounts in the material world in order to enter the realm of the spirit. "Settling accounts" is a business term. Entering the realm of the spirit is a business deal. There is an entrance fee. The Church sends a business representative to hammer out the terms of the bargain. . . .

But the twenty-two-year-old Louis XIV has no intention of remaining *only* a symbolic figure. In a conversation with the queen mother, Louis pours out his frustrations and very petulantly asserts his determination to change things. Power, he tells his mother, is shared by too many hands. The Parliament is getting too strong; it might get the idea of turning against its master. Louis fears the recurrence of the infamous *Fronde*—a rebellious coalition of bourgeois parliamentarians and dissident nobles who challenged the monarchy and ravaged French politics from 1648 to 1653, even forcing the royal family to flee Paris on several occasions.

The problem, Louis insists, is that the nobles of the court, living far from their lands, are in need of money and therefore turn to the bourgeoisie—putting themselves in debt at the hands of bourgeois creditors. "It's reached the point," he declares with disgust, "where *honneur* is for sale just like sugar or tobacco." "Power, today, equals *money*." Insisting that the selling of titles must cease, Louis sums up his aspirations: "What I want is that everyone should keep in his place!"

And the king's place, it is clear, is at the helm of his country, actively steering the ship of state. Everyone else—even his own mother—may be convinced that Louis is a self-indulgent, spoiled fop who will quickly tire of the responsibilities of government; but Louis XIV intends to fool them all and govern in his own right. . . .

Louis's goals have an anachronistic, backward-looking quality about them. In desiring that "each person must derive all from the king," Louis seeks nothing other than a return to the central institution of the early feudal age, where the basic social contract was the sacred pact of personal indebtedness and devotion that bound each subject to the king. And just as the planets revolve around the sun in fixed orbits, Louis would have his subjects revolve around him in a clearly defined hierarchy where "everyone would keep his place." In short, Louis's ideals are the ideals of a feudal age long past. Even his attempt to restore the monarchy to active rule is an attempt to stem the tide of history—as his mother has earlier in the film pointed out to him.

How strange it is, then, that the resolutely forward-looking proposals of Colbert should seem to fit in so well with the anachronistic ideals of Louis XIV. As the saying goes, politics makes strange bedfellows. But then so does history—and it is often only through the light of history that we can see how strange certain political alliances really were.

The brilliance of Rossellini's artistry, however, is that he knows how to visualize not just historical events themselves, but also the *internal contradictions* of a given historical situation. And here, in the meeting of the minds between Louis XIV and Colbert, one of the primary internal contradictions of class struggle in seventeenth-century France is subtly brought to the fore. The bourgeois, practical-minded outlook (here personified by Colbert) is concerned with *things;* while the aristocratic spirit (here personified by Louis XIV) is excessively preoccupied with *appearances.* And although, as the session with the tailor indicates, Louis XIV is a masterful manipulator of appearances for political effect, nonetheless he seems very limited in his ability to comprehend the economic (and ultimately political) consequences of the scheme he elaborates.

As Louis carefully specifies the number and placement of ruffles and feathers on the outlandish costume he intends to impose on the court, he explains to Colbert that these extravagant costumes will cost the nobles roughly one year's income apiece—thus bringing in a substantial income for the state treasury at the same time that the financial power of the potentially dissident nobles will be drained. Then, to placate the nobility and to keep them out of the hands of ambitious bourgeois creditors, Louis reveals that he will personally undertake—with funds from the state treasury—the housing and feeding of the court at the newly planned palace of Versailles.

Throughout this session with the tailor, Colbert keeps silent and lets Louis do all the talking. Louis's plan is so bold and Machiavellian in design that even its excesses are fascinating. But the look on Colbert's face, so evidently cautious and skeptical, tends to highlight, by contrast, the inconsistencies and excesses of a scheme which financially entails giving back with one hand more money than the other hand just took in, and which requires that enormous sums of money be pumped continuously into an almost totally nonproductive sector of the economy. Through the stolid presence of Colbert we begin to sense that while in the short run Louis's concern with appearances may seem to complement and reinforce Colbert's concern with things, in the long run the forces of history have them headed in two very different and conflicting directions.

And, in fact, it is perfectly clear from the perspective of history that Colbert's practical development of French industry and commerce served to accelerate the very patterns of social change—particularly the rise of the bourgeoisie—that Louis deplored and sought to reverse. Moreover, Louis's own policy of hosting the nobility at Versailles while ruining them financially eventually ruined the state's finances as well; and life at Louis's extravagant court, with its single-minded concern with appearances, so distracted the nobility from the material world of things (except as luxury items for conspicuous consumption) that by the end of Louis's reign this once mighty economic class no longer played a vital role in the system of production and was, as Marx put it, reduced to a mere "parasite" in the new industrial and commercial economy dominated by the bourgeoisie.

All of this is simply implicit, however, as far as the film is concerned, for Rossellini traces only the ascendancy of Louis XIV from 1661 to the mid-1680s. Nevertheless, the film as a whole, and particularly the later sequences dealing with Versailles, suggests quite clearly that despite the flamboyance of Louis's court, his reign is by no means a healthy, fruitful flowering of the French monarchy. Rather, it is simply the last flowering—dazzling in its sickly hues—of a dying plant artificially kept alive in a hothouse. . . .

Louis imposes his will unabashedly, gradually transforming the ceremonial functions of the court into a quasi-religious cult over which he presides as the living incarnation of the divine. Louis XIV becomes the "Sun-King"; all eyes are focused on him, and every glance or word which he deigns to address to one or another of his subjects is a life-giving ray of sunlight.

Absolutely faithful in each detail, Rossellini depicts the daily ritual of the king's *grand couvert*—the evening meal at which Louis, seated alone at a raised daïs, eats a dinner consisting of several dozen courses prepared and served by a legion of domestic servants, while the entire court stands respectfully and engages in courtly gossip. And when Louis XIV majestically demands some musical accompaniment, Rossellini's camera obediently follows a court functionary as he makes his way amid the gathered nobles to communicate the king's orders to the musicians, who are seated in a tiny balcony at the rear of the long, narrow hall. At the appointed signal, the musicians pop up like so many choirboys; and the camera's perspective from behind the king clearly emphasizes the churchlike atmosphere—with Louis seated at the raised altar, the focus of everyone's devotion.

Then, in a brief concluding sequence, Louis XIV is seen taking a short stroll, followed by his sycophantic retinue, in the ordered gardens of Versailles. Entering the palace, Louis momentarily withdraws to a private salon. In a scene that somewhat paradoxically recalls Brecht's famous dressing of the pope in *Galileo,* Louis XIV removes, one by one, the numerous articles of clothing that are the outward symbols of his power. But as the gloves, sword, wig, medallion, vest, and various collars and sleevelets are removed, it is questionable whether Louis—although perhaps a tiny bit more "human"—is any the less majestic. So painstakingly has he woven the web of appearances around his person that he has now almost completely identified himself with the fabulous demigod of his public image.

The private, intimate Louis XIV—we suddenly realize—has never existed! Eating, sleeping, participating in the hunt, presiding at court, even lovemaking, have all been political functions: for the sake of his public image, every act of Louis's daily life—no matter how trivial—has been carefully executed with a calculated aura of serene omnipotence. Only now—when we see him *alone for the first time in the film*—can Louis allow himself a brief moment of privacy: and even here, the private Louis and the public Louis XIV are barely distinguishable.

Almost totally absorbed now in the artificial rituals of the court at Versailles, Louis XIV is also almost totally isolated from his fellow men and the real world of things. In his lofty solitude, he can take comfort only in the spiritual ruminations of La Rochefoucauld, whose book of maxims Rossellini depicts Louis as meditating over endlessly—presumably finding in their Delphic ambiguity an inspirational pastime for his godlike aloofness.

# Josef von Sternberg

JOSEF VON STERNBERG, born Jonas Sternberg in Vienna in 1894, left with his mother at the age of seven to join his father, who had previously emigrated to the United States. Sternberg was to return to Vienna a few years later; then, some years after that, he settled permanently in the United States, although with several subsequent periods of work in Europe. Sternberg first came to film through his interest in graphic art, sketching, and painting. During World War I he worked on training films for the Army Signal Corps and after the war became the assistant to Emile Chautard, a French actor turned American director, working as writer and assistant director on several films.

After a brief period in London, Sternberg returned again to the United States, this time to Hollywood, and there independently made The Salvation Hunters (1925), which he also wrote and produced, for a cost of less than $5,000. After the film was seen by Charles Chaplin, Mary Pickford, and Douglas Fairbanks, Sternberg's reputation was made. Chaplin even hired Sternberg to direct The Sea Gull (not a version of the Chekhov play), but was disappointed with the results, and the film was never released.

After a few more abortive projects, Sternberg made Underworld (1927), with its American version of the fascination with crime and criminals that was already so marked in German and English films. Underworld owes its strength more to Sternberg's sense of streets and settings than to the actual history of Prohibition, and it launched him in a successful association with Paramount that was to last through eight films until 1935. The Blue Angel (1930) was not his first sound film, but it became his most familiar and most successful one, through the concentrated efforts of Paramount and Ufa, the German film trust that co-produced it. Made simultaneously in German and English versions, The Blue Angel also began the collaboration between Sternberg and Marlene Dietrich that was roughly to parallel his period at Paramount.

As with Erich von Stroheim before him and Orson Welles later, an essential ingredient of Sternberg's artistic make-up was the atmospheric publicity of the ''great director,'' exotic in appearance and personal style, filled with high-flown projects, prodigious and profligate with his talents and other people's (usually producers') money. The almost mystical relation Sternberg had with his star Dietrich enhanced the ambience of expressionist perversity and sexuality that already enveloped him—all delicately screened through the texture of his décors.

In fact, the director-actress relationship seems to have furnished an armature for Sternberg's virtuosity with the camera and sets that was hard to recover after the two parted. The only director to be admitted into the American Society of Cinematographers, Sternberg defined his directorial strength through the self-sufficient, almost sealed-off, quality of his film *worlds and the visual intricacy of their structure. The mystery of Dietrich's personality served to keep such elaborations from becoming mere decoration. Sternberg's sense of the existence of character beyond costume was therefore enhanced by the well of uncertainty and enigma he discovered in the screen image of his star.*

*The creation of the mythic actress before the camera perhaps necessarily superseded the creation of the mythic director behind the camera; and the strange clash between the moody settings and the wooden acting in* An American Tragedy *(1931) argued Sternberg's need for the inspiration of a performer.* An American Tragedy *was the only film he made without Dietrich in this period until* Crime and Punishment *(1935), another literary adaptation.*

*Feeling that he and Dietrich had done all they could together, Sternberg left Paramount in 1935 and began an almost twenty-year postscript to a career that had lasted only ten years at a high level of achievement. His ill-fated effort to film Robert Graves's* I, Claudius *(1937) was typical of many projects Sternberg began and for various reasons was forced to give up; it was, as Andrew Sarris has said, "his last, lost chance to recoup all his former reputation." (The story has recently been told in a BBC documentary film.) More reminiscent of Sternberg's earlier style was* The Shanghai Gesture *(1941), but it was less an elaboration than a self-parody.*

*Sternberg made no films between* The Shanghai Gesture *and* Jet Pilot *(1951, not released until 1957) except a government-sponsored documentary* The Town *(1943).* Macao *(1952) and* Anatahan *(1953) returned Sternberg to the exotic, dream-like East that had inspired so many of his earlier films.* Anatahan *in particular, with its enclosed world and narration spoken by Sternberg, is a fitting final film for a director whose best work had always maintained a firm balance between public statement and private obsession. Sternberg died in 1969.*

*Sternberg's autobiography,* Fun in a Chinese Laundry, *was published in 1965.* The Blue Angel, Morocco, *and* Shanghai Express *have appeared in script form. Critical works on Sternberg include those by Andrew Sarris (1966), Herman G. Weinberg (1967), and John Baxter (1973). See also the section dealing with* The Blue Angel *in Kracauer's* From Caligari to Hitler *(1947).*

# The Sternberg Style

## John Baxter

In his last years, a group of us asked Josef von Sternberg whether, among his many activities, he had found time for a hobby. "I have a hobby," he replied. "Chinese philately." Why that? "I wanted," he said in a tone that suggested we should have known, "a subject I could not exhaust."

There is much of Sternberg in this story; his love of the epigram, the suggestion of obscure personal disciplines far beyond normal men, that affinity for the exotic that dominated his artistic life. Yet the most revealing thing is that it is an anecdote, one of hundreds that surround Sternberg and his career, obscuring our view, diverting our attention and turning critical study aside. His public mask was the finest work of Sternberg's career and he died with it unpenetrated.

Who was he, this small—five feet five inches—stooped Viennese Jew with the disconcerting pale eyes and quiet, metallic voice? A poet, "a hard-boiled egg," a pornographer, charlatan, martinet, genius, fraud; he was called all these, and by people normally given neither to rhapsodies nor outbursts of rage. To every adjective Sternberg remained imperturbably aloof behind a barrier of evasion, enigmatic half-statement and a few boldly reiterated generalizations that frustrated even the most persuasive biographer. By refusing to be recorded, discouraging researchers, and demanding large sums even for simple radio or TV interviews, he ensured a body of critical evidence unrivaled in vagueness and contradiction, to which his autobiography *Fun in a Chinese Laundry* was an unhelpful addition.

But before his death in 1969 Sternberg saw his policy's final vindication. If he had not outlived all his enemies he had at least worn them down, and today few critics, even those most hostile to him while he lived, would deny him his place as one of the supreme artists of the cinema. Unfortunately this delayed recognition of his work has led to a sometimes unfortu-

Reprinted from *The Cinema of Joseph von Sternberg* (1973) by John Baxter, by permission of A. S. Barnes & Company, Inc.

nate canonization, writers accepting uncritically the numerous doubtful statements by and about the director and his career, a process that ill-serves Sternberg's films and reputation.

It often seems a fragile body of work and an insecure reputation. Of the twenty-seven features on which he actually began shooting, seven were taken over by other directors and partly or wholly reshot, another was suppressed entirely by its producer, a further production never completed. Of some films that did reach the public Sternberg complained that a failure to give him control over script or casting had frustrated his creative efforts, though we shall see that his curt "There is nothing of me in it" was more often an expression of pique than a genuine repudiation. No evasion, untruth, or misdirection can invalidate his remarkable work. Rich and evocative, it mocks our pettiness and his.

The key to Sternberg's genius, as well as to his bizarre personality, lies in his early life, and in the pressures of an aimlessly expanding America in the 1910s that turned a wandering alien into an artist of international repute—and notoriety. Privation in childhood and adolescence deeply marked the young Sternberg, causing him to hide his lack of education with pedantry and an arrogant display of erudition, disguise his sensitivity under an armor of feigned indifference, direct his energetic and passionate temperament entirely into art. He seldom, even in old age, relaxed the guard that had protected him for seventy years from the world.

Born Jonas Sternberg in Vienna on May 29, 1894, he had a disordered childhood. As part of a poor Orthodox Jewish family he was subject to the emotional and intellectual pressures of a rigorous faith. Forced by his overbearing father Moses to study Hebrew in addition to his normal schoolwork, he was denied all books in an attempt to concentrate his mind on a language for which he had little facility. When Jonas was three, his father left for the United States, sending for the rest of the family four years later. By the time he was ten they were back in Vienna. His mother never left Europe again, but when he was fourteen Jonas returned to America, this time for good. Later in life, he confided to friends that his greatest ambition for his family was to give his son and step-daughter the security denied him as a child.

When his patchy education ended at sixteen, Sternberg confronted the world poorly equipped to survive, let alone succeed. He took casual jobs; apprentice in a millinery store, a salesman selling cheap jewelry door to door, and stock clerk in a lace warehouse, where he gained a knowledge of if not a liking for fabrics, lace, and net that was to reappear in his films. At seventeen he adopted the christian name "Josef" and left home, wandering the United States in a search for a career that would give meaning to his life.

Paradoxically, it was his lack of education and his vagabond existence that finally provided it. For a young hobo, entertainment and enlightenment were limited. To escape from the tedium of dish-washing and farm laboring Sternberg sought galleries and libraries, reading with intense concentration, studying paintings and sculpture, assessing clinically the forces in them that attracted or repelled. His strong visual sense—he wrote later, "I can reproduce in my mind every street I have walked, each room or shop I have entered, and no face has lost its shape"—seized on these new stimuli. He looked at the world and at humanity now with the detached eye of an artist.

As yet, his interest was almost entirely in graphic art, and in the sketching and painting for which he found he had a facility. The few moving pictures he had seen, mainly in attempts to stay warm on cold nights, were grotesque and crude, but these films, for all their vulgarity, finally attracted him, and he felt the almost mystical power the medium exercises over all great directors.

His first discovery about the cinema was also his most important. There was, he saw, nothing new in the movies. All its visual problems had been solved by painters centuries before, while its obsession with story and acting seemed to him a useless complication adopted from the novel and the stage. True art, whether painting, sculpture or film, had, he sensed, little to do with story. Its duty was to expose the reality beneath the surface of life; art he defined as "the compression of infinite spiritual power into a confined space." It is a unique vision of communication that could only have sprung from an education and orientation as complex as Sternberg's. Self-taught, little read in fiction and therefore not story conscious, yet enriched with a visual memory of eidetic accuracy, he became obsessed with the elusive ambiance of the cinema, the heightened reality of the film image and the relationship it set up with the audience.

This fascination was to direct Sternberg's life, and in his single-minded pursuit of cinematic perfection he baffled or offended most of those he met. His memory for slights and gestures of goodwill was long. He never forgot the first man who helped him in his career, nor forgave the schoolmaster who mocked him. Those who offended were likely to be caricatured in his films; old teachers and employers writhe and suffer in *The Blue Angel, Blonde Venus, The Shanghai Gesture,* just as his early mentor Émile Chautard appears as an actor in sympathetic roles in *Shanghai Express* and *Morocco.* Sternberg's films were his life, mirrored and distorted, but recognizable nevertheless. For this reason he abominated critics—his autobiography is sown with biting remarks about old adversaries—and regarded criticism as his prerogative. It was a courageous friend who dared to speak against any Sternberg film.

Sternberg came alive only on the set. Normally a distant and punctilious gentleman, quietly dressed, reserved, he was transformed as the start of shooting approached into the great creator for whom all life was merely a preparation for his work. His manner, even his clothing changed. For *I Claudius* he grew a beard, ordered a heavy coat of his own design that, in the words of a friend, was "almost too heavy to lift," and wore it on the set with riding breeches, boots and a Javanese turban. For other films he adopted a velvet coat and beret, jodhpurs and a solar topee, a silk dressing gown, a boiler suit. Only his cane, the symbol of authority, remained the same. On the set his small stature, his background, his essential shyness evaporated; no actor ever entered more completely into a part.

The mythology of Sternberg the autocrat often hid the other side of his character, all that remained of the sensitive boy from Vienna. The real Sternberg was shy and acutely anxious to please. John Grierson, who knew him in the Twenties, remembers him as a retiring, modest young man; his strongest remaining impression of Sternberg is an acute humility. This ambivalence was at the core of Sternberg's mercurial nature, in which eroticism had as its darker side an interest in, even an obsession with masochism and humiliation. It is no coincidence that most of his films deal with the great humbled and the proud brought low, just as there is undoubted significance in his habit of casting in subservient roles actors dressed and made up to resemble himself.

Everybody who met Sternberg sensed this double aspect, whether in the charm that could replace his crackling animosity or in more revealing gestures suggesting that he often attacked hoping that his assertiveness would be overruled. A man who knew him well in his last years, Sydney Film Festival director David Stratton, recalls looking in on an official dinner at which Sternberg was a guest. The atmosphere was icy with tension, and it emerged that Sternberg had been offended by the failure of his hosts to collect him on time at his hotel. Although relations had to that time been strictly formal, Stratton put his hand companionably on Sternberg's shoulder and said, "Now, Jo, don't tell me you haven't been kept waiting before." Sternberg instantly beamed, indicated an empty chair and said, "David, sit down and have coffee with us." Throughout the rest of his visit, Sternberg dutifully presented himself each morning and asked "What do you require of me today?" and until his death two years later he and Stratton remained close friends.

Of Sternberg, Kevin Brownlow has commented, "No glib,

psychological summing-up can rationalize this remarkable personality.'' True. But certain insights are forced on one by the circumstances of his life and the unique subject matter of his films. It is only in the light of Sternberg's private life that the world of his films is illuminated; a world where fathers, if they appear at all, are self-interested and remote, mothers raucous harridans or dowagers of reptilian *hauteur,* children savages with the instincts of the jungle, men cowering victims who both fear and welcome the lash of contempt that their women, alone in his films retaining their individuality, can wield. There are few artists in whose work the twin currents of existence and creation are so closely, often inextricably intermingled.

If Sternberg's character is complex, his work is infinitely more so. He broke new ground in cinematography, and had enormous influence on cinema design and acting. Yet he invented nothing, not even the complex lighting that made up the so-called ''Dietrich face.'' None of his films was completely his own, in the sense that he created it from original idea to final editing, though he often tried to give this impression. His ability was to select from the work of others the elements he wished to use.

But even if his sources are observable, it is clear that in arranging the material he borrowed Sternberg was motivated by a strongly personal and original style. Ignoring the fashionable D. W. Griffith approach, with its vigorous narrative, wordy titles and often overindulged sentimentality, Sternberg took his cue from European masters like Maurice Tourneur, who combined photographic virtuosity with an insight into character, and Erich von Stroheim, a genius at suggesting psychological conflicts through details of playing and background. Stroheim became Sternberg's greatest personal and artistic influence.

Although the early work of German film and stage directors did not have an impact on the American cinema until well into the twenties, Stroheim had independently formulated theories similar to those used by Piscator, Brecht, and Max Reinhardt for the Berlin stage. All saw that drama, whether on stage or screen, had become overburdened with meretricious ''style.'' A new intimacy was needed to convey the psychological conflicts then replacing physical action as the basis of modern theater, an intimacy the Griffith style could not hope to encompass.

Reinhardt in the twenties developed new methods of acting, directing and design for modern drama. His style, and his theater, were called *Kammerspiel,* literally ''closet play.'' The *Kammerspiel* theater seated only three hundred. The stage was dimly defined and stripped of props, mood and atmosphere suggested with variations in light and texture. Unlike the Expressionists, who sought to externalize psychological conflict

the shadows. Diffusers around the lights, objects in the beam to break the line and animate the forehead, gauzes over the lens were all employed to create a dream-like atmosphere in which Sternberg's creatures flourished. He often placed or adjusted lights himself, and came up with ingenious solutions to individual problems. On *The Blue Angel*, confronted with Marlene Dietrich's lumpy nose, he mounted three additional "baby spots" on the camera platform which, while illuminating eyes and mouth, over-lapped in the center of the face to obliterate partially the offending feature, a judgment.later ratified by plastic surgery.

As a director, Sternberg was limited. Action always worried him, and his films lack the animation of contemporaries like Capra and Fleming. Fast-moving scenes such as the fight in *The Salvation Hunters* and the climax of *The Scarlet Empress* are lifeless, though with dialogue he could be effective, if wearing. In common with many directors who depend on believable expressions in close-ups to make a point, he pressured actors, forcing them to repeat scenes until exhaustion and frustration gave the desired reaction. Dietrich's scene on the spiral staircase in *The Blue Angel* took a day to shoot, Sternberg demanding continual retakes until she lost her temper, whereupon he expressed himself as satisfied. In the same film her casual pose on stage with one leg upraised was arrived at only after much experiment, with more than a dozen possible attitudes tried and discarded.

Some stars, notably, Dietrich, endured his tyranny with stoicism, but the list of those who blew up, from William Powell through Joel McCrea to Grace Moore, is a long one. Nevertheless Sternberg remained a meticulous worker even with his minor actors. Not even a featured player lacked careful direction and detailed motivations. Commenting on his role as the Mayor of Seville in *The Devil Is a Woman* Edward Everett Horton said, "I thought I was miscast—though not hopelessly—and I suggested that my accent was inappropriate for Spain, but von Sternberg gave me a long talk on the history of Spain and how it had been settled by people from all over, including England, and that my accent fitted well enough."

In technique, if not in philosophy, Sternberg had so many imitators that it is difficult to separate original and copy. Which came first, George Hill's natural sound ending for *The Secret Six* or Sternberg's for *Morocco?* With design, one can be more positive; the Sternberg visual style was unique, though its elements varied over the years, a barometer of his developing talent. Each new device was an attempt to solve what to him was the basic problem of cinema, the necessity to animate the "dead space" that separated the camera from its subject and the subject from the background, and to enliven the meaningless blankness of walls, doors and open spaces. Posters, *graffiti,* Chinese calligraphy were frequent additions to his sets; even mirrors were scrawled with slogans and messages to give them independent visual life. In the "dead space" he hung streamers, balloons, nets, veils, cardboard cut-outs and stuffed toys, until he realized that it was only by thickening the air with filters and gauzes, and by coaxing from his subjects their elusive "spiritual power" that his images could truly fill the screen with life.

Despite an instinctive desire to decorate, he was drawn to the almost mystical purity of white walls, a fascination extended after *The Devil Is a Woman* with the discovery that aluminium paint sprayed on costumes and props would suppress the natural texture and give them an additional luminosity. Again, the style had its logical basis; white walls—most Hollywood sets were painted gray to photograph evenly—reflected thirty percent more light, allowing Sternberg greater depth of focus, always desirable for precise localizing of expression and action. Among the more trivial decorative elements he employed were toys and dolls, black or white cats, masks and fans, and a recurring phallic post topped with a white globe; a shell on a pole in *The Saga of Anatahan,* a skull-crowned post in *Morocco,* a lamp against which the judge leans while sentencing "Bull" Weed in *Underworld.*

But the most consistent of Sternberg's signatures is the bird, with its rich religious, sexual, and psychological symbolism a Jungian archetype. One of the first shots in *The Salvation Hunters* is of a sea gull on a pile of flotsam, and from then on birds and feathers are given in his films a strong poetic significance: Rath's dead canary in *The Blue Angel;* the feathers on Lola's postcard portrait; the floating aigrettes of "Feathers" McCoy in *Underworld,* of "Ritzy" in *Thunderbolt,* and the feathered caps of "The Magpie" in *The Drag Net;* doves cooing to Helen Faraday in *Blonde Venus;* imperial eagles in *The Last Command,* in *The Scarlet Empress,* in *I Claudius;* twittering bird-song in Concha's house in *The Devil Is a Woman,* the plaster storks in the cabaret and her silly train-borne duck; most powerful of all, Shanghai Lily's stirring black plumes in *Shanghai Express.* Even in his last film, *The Saga of Anatahan,* Keiko waves like a trapped bird to the waiting rescue ship, and the castaways carve toy boats that will carry them away, in Sternberg's words, "on the wings of their longing."

No words can convey the atmosphere of a Sternberg film, so personal are his associations. That all his films were in some sense autobiographical cannot be doubted, but reminiscence was a passport into new worlds of artistic experiment. Contrary to popular opinion at the time, Sternberg's style was always the servant to his subject, though by choosing to examine the minute variations of emotional experience he laid himself open to charges of triviality. Certainly his work is trivial in plot. He retained always his contempt for story in the Hollywood sense; "The best source for a film is an anecdote," he remarked. But all his films explore perceptively some mood or emotional state, chart the development of an attitude, analyze the delicate evolutions of a relationship in ascendancy or decline. They have a psychological power that transcends simple plot. Under his scrutiny a reality emerges that is at once obvious and infinitely complex in its implications, the world of human emotion, of love and its dark concomitant, the desire to destroy.

# "The Blue Angel" and "Morocco"

## Andrew Sarris

### "The Blue Angel"

*The Blue Angel* occupies a paradoxical if pre-eminent place in Sternberg's career. Emil Jannings reportedly requested Sternberg as the director to guide the silent star past the sound barrier, and Sternberg agreed despite a previous clash of temperaments in *The Last Command*. The film was produced simultaneously in German and English language versions for the maximum benefit of the Paramount-Ufa combine in world markets, and thus with this one excursion into Europe all the ambiguity of Sternberg's origins reappeared as the "von" in his name was finally vindicated. After *The Blue Angel*, Sternberg would once more be treated in retrospect as a European legend corrupted by Hollywood lucre.

"Camp," declared Susan Sontag in the sixties, "is the outrageous estheticism of von Sternberg's six American movies with Dietrich, all six but especially the last, *The Devil Is a Woman* . . ." Significantly, Miss Sontag pointedly excludes *The Blue Angel* from her Camp sight. The snobbery of subtitles aside, *The Blue Angel* is undoubtedly the one Sternberg film the director's severest detractors will concede is beyond reproach and ridicule. It is worth noting, if only in passing, that Marlene Dietrich did not appear on American screens in *The Blue Angel* until after the release of *Morocco,* actually her second stint with Sternberg.

Although *The Blue Angel* may have been admired in some quarters for the wrong reasons, the film stands up today as Sternberg's most efficient achievement both emotionally and expressively. There are no hidden corners, no nagging nuances, no puzzling paradoxes. For once Sternberg is in complete rapport with his audience with a film that is at once his most brutal and least humorous. "In converting the novel into a film which would meet my standards of visual poetry,'' he recalls, ''I introduced the figure of the clown as well as all the episodes and details that led the professor to be confined in a straitjacket.''

The ultimately tragic irony of *The Blue Angel* is double-edged in a way Sternberg could not have anticipated when he undertook the project. The rise of Lola Lola and the fall of Professor Immanuel Rath in reel life is paralleled in real life by the rise of Marlene Dietrich and the fall of Emil Jannings. When *The Blue Angel* was revived in the early fifties, the critical consensus upheld the public on Dietrich's directness over Jannings' detailedness. The tedious tics of elaborately expressionistic acting have long since gone out of style, and there is still a tendency to underrate the Jannings performance. In the context of the screen's cuckolds, however, Jannings surpasses in tragic intensity even Raimu and Ake Groneberg. What he lacks in the style and stature of his Czarist general turned Hollywood extra in *The Last Command,* he more than makes up here with the nakedness of his passion.

Sternberg's sense of tragic dignity in the midst of tawdry downfall is best illustrated at that moment when Jannings hurls himself into a room to wreak vengeance on his wife and her strong-man lover. The camera remains at a discreet angle and distance from the doorway through which Dietrich escapes. The men with the straitjacket sweep past her, but we never actually see Jannings subdued by them, only Dietrich looking with ambiguous compassion at the spectacle of subjugation. Jannings has had his moment of masculine beauty on the stage by crowing like a maddened rooster at Dietrich's deception. In that soul-stirring moment Sternberg suggests through Jannings what it is to be a man, and Sternberg will not cheapen that moment by degrading a man who has been defeated.

*The Blue Angel* achieves its most electrifying effects through careful grading and construction. When Marlene Dietrich sings ''Falling in Love Again'' for the first time the delivery is playful, flirtatious, and self-consciously seductive. The final rendition is harsher, colder, and relentlessly remorseless. The difference in delivery is not related to the old stereotype of the vamp finally showing her true colors, but rather to a psychological development in Dietrich's Lola from mere sensual passivity to a more forceful fatalism about the nature of her desires. Lola's first instinct is to accept the Professor's paternal protection and her last is to affirm her natural instincts not as coquettish expedients, but as the very terms by which she expresses her existence. Thus, as the Professor has been defeated by Lola's beauty, Lola has been ennobled by the Professor's jealousy. It is in this complex interplay that *The Blue Angel* transcends the trivial genre of bourgeois male corrupted by bohemian female.

The sordid atmosphere with which Sternberg embellishes his drama emphasizes the grossness to be endured in grappling with desire. On one level of characterization, the Professor is a Lazarus resurrected from a dismal fastidiousness of death-like feelings by sniffing his way through Lola's life-drenched garments, *objets d'art* less of a symbolist than a fetishist. Fortunately, the niggling necessities of economics intervene between the drab décor and any of its frivolously sado-masochistic implications. It is not Lola who forces the Professor to peddle her gamey photos, but rather the financial realities of the situation. The shabbiness eventually engulfs the sensuality, but it is Lola's strength that she has lived with shabbiness long enough to know how to bend without breaking, and the Professor's tragic misfortune to bend first and still to break afterward.

It is not specifically Germany or the German character with which Sternberg is concerned here, but rather the spectacle of a prudent, prudish man blocked off from all means of displaying his manhood except the most animalistic. Sternberg himself has explicitly removed *The Blue Angel* from the socially significant path Siegfried Kracauer has traced *From Caligari to Hitler*. Yet the fact that *The Blue Angel* is coincidentally Sternberg's only German-made film and his most violent work may suggest that he felt the conflict between order and nature would be more violent in a German setting than in any other. This supposition, however, does not justify the judgment that Sternberg's deliberately designed drabness reflects realistically observed details of a decadent society. The world of *The Blue Angel* is as much a dream world as the world of *The Salvation Hunters*, but the illusion of reality is much stronger in *The Blue Angel* because the characters are less abstract.

Jean Renoir's *La Chienne* (1931) and Ingmar Bergman's *The Naked Night* (1953) are more profound examinations of the crisis of cuckoldry in the illusion-shattering life of man, but *The Blue Angel* is more successful dramatically. Where Renoir is more realistic and Bergman more literary, Sternberg is more effective in resolving his tragedy within the form he has postulated for it. Renoir arbitrarily ends his film as if it were a stylized spectacle of the Paris streets, but his implication is clear: life goes on, transcending pride, passion, and morality. For Bergman life is a mystery which no amount of thought can solve. Renoir and Bergman are thus concerned with ideas beyond the frames of their films, whereas Sternberg remains within his frames. For the Professor there is only his life with Lola, and deprived of Lola there is nothing but death. There is no life for Lola and the Professor beyond the running time of *The Blue Angel*. There is no world beyond the outer limits of the set. Renoir and Bergman appeal to our common sense. Sternberg appeals to our sense of spectacle.

Not that Renoir and Bergman lack mood and mannerism. Far from it. Nor can we single out *The Blue Angel* for projecting Sternberg through

Jannings. There is a great deal of Renoir in Michel Simon from *La Chienne,* and a great deal of Bergman in Ake Groneberg from *The Naked Night.* For the most part, however, *La Chienne* and *The Naked Night* open out on the world, whereas *The Blue Angel* turns in on itself. Sternberg's profundity is consequently measured less by the breadth of his vision than by the perfection of his form and by the emotional force of his characters within that form.

How much more painfully poignant, too, is the scene where Jannings helps Dietrich with her stockings than a similar Jannings maneuver with Lya da Putti in Du Pont's *Variety,* where Jannings as the dupe, pure and simple, is treated with amused contempt. By contrast, Dietrich's air of sensual complicity in *The Blue Angel* redeems the Jannings character from complete ridiculousness. There is in Sternberg a savoring of sensuality for its own sake that is both more human and more satisfying than Renoir's uncompromising humanism and Bergman's unyielding pessimism. The disassociation of Dietrich's sexuality from normal standards of dramatic psychology becomes more apparent in her later collaborations with Sternberg. In *The Blue Angel,* Dietrich is still somewhat submerged in her characterization and not yet completely possessed by her personality. She straddles a chair as she will later straddle a horse in *The Scarlet Empress,* imperiously, magisterially, fully the measurer of men in the audience, but yet she is also an organic character who finds a certain kind of maturity in marriage. If "serious" criticism of the cinema were not as puritanical as it is, the experiences of Lola and the Professor would seem more pertinent to the hidden world of domestic sexuality than is now the case. The idea that all eroticism is hopelessly exotic has made Sternbergian cinema seem much stranger than it is.

### *"Morocco"*

*Morocco* revisited is a revelation to the viewer who anticipates a heavy-breathing Sardou-like safari across the desert sands. Instead, one is treated to the paradox of characters unostentatiously impulsive, expressing the most delirious feelings with the most delicate gestures. Every bit of bric-a-brac, every shadowed shutter, every fluttering fabric conveys the characters inexorably toward an emotional decision they would resist if they could. Yet if they surrender to disastrous, even faintly ridiculous impulses, they do so as undemandingly and as unobtrusively as possible. Here again a plot synopsis cannot possibly suggest the preciseness of Sternberg's sensibility. To say that a woman gives up everything for love is to oversimplify the civilized complexity of an intrigue triangulated by a café canary, a Foreign Legionnaire, and a mustachioed man of the world, a plot less written than wired for the star voltage generated by Gary Cooper,

Marlene Dietrich, and Adolphe Menjou. On this latter level, *Morocco* is Sternberg's Hollywood movie par excellence.

For all its frenzied fabulousness, *Morocco* succeeded in its time as illusionism for the general public. The proof of this success is the long remembered disbelief in the final image of Marlene Dietrich setting out into the desert sands on spike heels in search of Gary Cooper. C. A. Lejeune of *The London Observer* has described this finale as one of the most absurd of all time. Yet to single out any one detail of a film for disbelief is to believe in the rest, and to believe in *Morocco's* California desert is to believe in Sternberg's dream décor. What Sternberg and many of his more gifted Hollywood and Ufa studio colleagues proved is that consistency of style is ultimately more convincing than documentary certification. Sternberg, in particular, creates conviction by motivating his milieu with light and shadow. In a world of illusions, his camera suggests, everything is possible and nothing is necessary. Poetry transcends plausibility when characters are too vividly depicted for common sense criteria of behavior. Again Sternberg prepares the way for his delirious dénouement with intimations of irrationality and perversity. When Dietrich materializes in top hat, white tie, and tails and is thereafter immortalized as the purveyor of pansexuality, the immediacy of impact makes Sternberg's gesture seem more gratuitous than it is. Aside from the lilting vertiginousness of vice involved in Marlene's mock seduction of a flustered female, Sternberg achieves all sorts of economies of expression in Marlene's meaningful masquerade. Her costume, for example, mocks Menjou's. Here is a representation of the civilized European male as seen from the point of view of the woman he seeks to seduce with infinite patience, but yet the effect is not one of pure parody. Neither Sternberg nor Dietrich is completely sure of all the psychological twists. There is always chance, romance, and the inspiration of improvisation. Dietrich fondles the hair of the girl she is going to outrage with a kiss, but she has none of the complacent confidence Garbo displays in a similar situation in *Queen Christina*. Dietrich's impersonation is an adventure, an act of bravado that subtly alters her conception of herself as a woman, and what begins as self-expression ends as self-sacrifice, perhaps the path also of Sternberg as an artist.

When Dietrich asks Cooper if he wants to buy her apples, this obvious double entendre is rescued from crudity by the genuine awkwardness and uncertainty of the two players. Dietrich here is in the process of discovering herself, and the awakening of self-awareness visibly delights her. Never again will she be so defenselessly charming, so personally accessible to the audience at each instant of her performance. As for Cooper, it is difficult to believe that this natural American landmark ever planted a rose behind his ear or flourished a fan behind which he stole a discreet kiss from

Dietrich. That Sternberg brings off such uncharacteristic affectations by Cooper is a mark of the director's fluency in the language of gesture.

In a limited sense, *Morocco* is a reversal of *The Blue Angel* in that a woman is humbled by a man. As in *The Blue Angel,* however, there is genuine interplay between male and female, but even more, there is a perverse interchange of masculine and feminine characteristics. If Gary Cooper's Tom Brown is Sternberg's most narcissistic hero, Marlene Dietrich is the supreme lover, male or female, and hers is the most romantic gesture in Sternberg's visual vocabulary. The complaint that a woman in high heels would not walk off into the desert is nonetheless meaningless. A dream does not require endurance, only the will to act.

When the Pasha of Marrakesh insisted to Sternberg that *Morocco* must have been shot on location, the director replied with ironic modesty that any confusion of illusion and reality "was no more than an accidental resemblance, a flaw due to my lack of talent to avoid such similarity." The real Morocco would, of course, have crushed Sternberg, Dietrich, Cooper, and Menjou under the weight of extraneous details. To make the plot fit the clime, expressiveness would have been sacrificed to the needless exposition of establishing shots. *Morocco* is the product of a period when movies could still create their own mystique, and if Sternberg's sets look less real today, his characters ring even more true. There is a delicacy of regret in Menjou's stylish suffering at the hands of Dietrich that is peculiarly modern. Sternberg did not always succeed in reconciling style with feeling, but he does with Menjou's La Bessière, part stoic, part sybarite, part satanist. Audiences sometimes laugh at him as a well-mannered masochist, particularly in the dinner scene of Dietrich's renunciation, but Sternberg has never been as close to any character as he is to this elegant expatriate who tries to maintain the decorum of his public posture as he watches the one great obsession of an otherwise ordered life disappear forever into the desert. In Menjou's pained politeness of expression is engraved the age-old tension between the Apollonian and Dionysian demands of art, between pride in restraint and passion in excess, between the formal protocol of self-control and the spontaneous eruptions of self-gratification. In the midst of his fears about Dietrich's decision, Menjou apologizes for not having listened to the babbling of a French general (played by Sternberg's old mentor, Emile Chautard). When Dietrich kisses him goodbye, Menjou clutches her wrist in one last spasmodic reflex of passion, but the other hand retains its poise at his side, the gestures of form and feeling thus conflicting to the very end of the drama. If Sternberg had been nothing more than a delirious decorator, his art would have long since faded into the limbo of fashion, but, like Menjou, Sternberg never loses his composure, and, consequently, he never sacrifices the contemplative aspect of his compositions for easy effects of parody and pathos.

# Sternberg's "Empress": The Play of Light and Shade

## Robin Wood

*A value judgment can't, we all know, be demonstratively enforced; the critic can only attempt to help other readers to an approach by which, freed from inappropriate expectations and preconceptions and adverted as to the kind of thing they have in front of them, they will be able to take the poem—take it for what it is: the judging goes with the taking.*
—*F. R. Leavis,* Scrutiny *(1943)*

Even the name is ambiguous: Joe Stern, or Josef von Sternberg? The ambiguity, in any case, is singularly appropriate to a director with insistent aspirations to high art and European culture destined to struggle to realize those aspirations within the context of the Hollywood cinema: a struggle doomed to eventual failure, but producing a series of triumphs before the inevitable defeat.

Sternberg's career is marked by an effort to dominate so extreme as to most eloquently express his terror of losing control: a dichotomy also manifested in the simultaneous arrogance and vulnerability (the former masking the latter) so characteristic of his autobiography *Fun in a Chinese Laundry*. We know that he preferred to make his films in studios, where he could control every detail; that he exercised the most meticulous control over décor, so that every leaf, every festoon, every bit of veiling, is there because he meant it to be there. These tendencies were carried to their ultimate in his last film, *The Saga of Anatahan,* for which he went out to Japan in the interests of authenticity, and then built an island—trees, creepers, and all—in a film studio.

The obsession with control stretches to all aspects of his films; apparently he not only conducted the *Scarlet Empress* score but composed it, with the help of Mendelssohn, Wagner and, especially, Tchaikovsky. It

Excerpted from *Personal Views: Explorations in Style* by Robin Wood (1976). Reprinted by permission of the publisher, Gordon Fraser Gallery Limited.

extends, of course, to his attitude toward actors, who are "puppets." Every detail of Marlene Dietrich's performance in the seven films they made together, every gesture, every movement, every expression, was created by Sternberg—according to Sternberg.

He has offered various pronouncements that, in their combination of arrogance and concealment, are profoundly typical. For *Morocco* (the first Hollywood film with Dietrich, after he had introduced her to the world in *The Blue Angel*), he purposely chose a "fatuous" subject, so that the spectators wouldn't be distracted from "the play of light and shade." He also said he would like to have his films projected upside down, for the same reason.

The motivation prompting such remarks is not difficult to guess. The films were made at a time when (even more than now) for the great mass of the public directors were "invisible" and films were experienced in terms of their stars and their plots. Sternberg was simply overcompensating, insisting on his own presence as determining force, on the phenomenon of visual style. But the consequences of such pronouncements are potentially dangerous. Taken literally, they encourage an assumption that Sternberg, in the clutches of the Hollywood machine, dwindled into an aesthete, that the films can be dismissed (as they often have been) as over-decorated "aesthetic" nothings. The dread word "camp" is not far away.

In fact, the subjects of the Dietrich films can be conclusively demonstrated, in every case, to be of the utmost importance—the true subject of a film being *created* by its style rather than existing in opposition to it. The plot lines might not look very inviting on paper, but a story only exists when it is told, and becomes a subject from the manner of the telling. The plot of *Morocco* concerns a romance between a showgirl and a foreign legionnaire; its subject is the ambiguities of free will and determinism. The "play of light and shade" is not an aesthetic abstraction but an essential factor in the film's total articulation. One feels, too, that Sternberg was perfectly aware of this: no effect in *The Scarlet Empress* appears inadvertent.

The precise character of a film is necessarily determined partly by the material circumstances of its production. *The Scarlet Empress* belongs (somewhat uneasily) to the genre of historical romance; it is also, obviously, a vehicle for its star. Its peculiar quality can be attributed to Sternberg's deliberate acceptance and manipulation of "genre," "star vehicle" and all that those terms imply: the necessity that the film be palatable to mass audiences, and that the studio heads (at least) be convinced of its commercial viability. (It was, as it happens, a flop, but that doesn't affect the point.)

It is very difficult—impossible perhaps—to distinguish clearly between Sternberg's highly idiosyncratic personal impulses and what he may have regarded cynically as commercial compromise. Would the film have been different if he had made it in complete freedom? It is unlikely that it would have been better. But its central problem and fascination—the question of tone—seems intricately bound up with its ambiguous status as art movie and pop movie, as much as with Sternberg's strange personal fusion of anguish and cynicism. . . .

The opening scene confirms the suggestion of fairy tale by presenting, in the child Sophia Frederica, an archetype of innocence, blonde and angelic, and opposing to it a mother who, bent wholly on material success, removes its toys; the child is to become a queen. Against the mother is set the humane doctor, who clearly disapproves of Mama's mercenariness, and arranges for the child eloquently to stick out her tongue at her. The simple attitudes thus elicited are swiftly undermined. The humane doctor is also the public hangman, and the angelic child's innocence is already equivocal; nothing is what it appears. "Can I become a hangman some day?" Sophia Frederica asks the kindly manservant, who responds by reading her a book about hideous tortures and executions. The word "hangman" is important. The doctor is in fact an executioner, leaving to perform an "operation" by removing a head; yet the visual image "hangman" evokes has closer relevance to the intricately interconnected imagery of the film.

From a close-up of the child's face, Sternberg dissolves to the extraordinary fantasy-sequence of horrors, which uses an editing device suggestive of turning the pages of a book: each image flattens as it gives place to the next. The technical devices and the preceding dialogue permit a three-fold implication: (1) the images represent the horrors actually perpetrated in the world, past and present—the world into which Sophia Frederica will grow up (the manservant mentions Ivan the Terrible and Peter the Great); (2) the fantastic and grotesque nature of the images suggests nightmarish illustrations in a child's storybook; and (3) the long dissolve from the child's face suggests that what we see exists inside her mind—is her visualization and perhaps partly her fantasy. Several of the images, associating torture and nudity, carry strong sado-erotic overtones. The executioner clearly enjoys his work, performing it with immense zest.

The final item in the procession of horrors has the executioner (hangman) pulling on a bell-rope, followed by the revelation that the clapper is a near-naked man, dangling upside-down by his feet, thrown helplessly from side to side of the bell-mouth. As Sternberg moved into the sequence by way of a dissolve, so another very long and slow dissolve leads us out: Sophia Frederica, now grown up, is moving joyfully to and fro on a swing. The dissolve superimposes the two images so that the movements coincide; for an instant, the human bell-clapper and the girl on the swing become one.

The fusion, in the very complexity of its suggestions, is central to the film's meaning. Such a juxtaposition can imply either comparison or contrast, likeness or unlikeness. Our first impression may well be of the contrast between the nocturnal fantasy-horrors and the blithe and carefree girl in the spring light. Yet the fantasy was partly the child's (as the return to Sophia at the end of the torture-sequence confirms), and grew out of her question, "Can I become a hangman some day?" Torture and girl are mysteriously connected, and linked to the idea of Destiny. Similarly, we may first wish to contrast the volitional movement of the girl on the swing with the helplessness of the torture-victim; yet their identification by means of the dissolve immediately qualifies this impression. The suggestion is that the girl's freedom may be only illusory, and the man's terrifying helplessness a metaphor for her inability really to control her fate.

The fusion of images also has strong sexual overtones. Sophia Frederica swings right into the camera, so that we look up into the darkness inside her skirts, which are rounded, like a bell, and this is connected with the half-nude male figure in the real bell-mouth. Power, sadism, and sexuality are thus closely associated, impotent phallus juxtaposed with flaunted and triumphant vagina. From this point on, swinging objects will recur frequently in the film, and bells will ring to announce each stage in Sophia Frederica's rise to power. The dissolve provides a germinal image-cluster from which various outgrowths of related imagery will develop. The peal of triumph will in each case carry strong overtones of irony: the marriage to a madman; the birth of the heir to the throne who is in fact a bastard. And—so unforgettable is the image—every time the bells peal out we shall remember the human bell-clapper. . . .

The end of the first movement of the film (to which the brief childhood sequence was introduction) is marked by another of the expressive dissolves that punctuate the whole—a technical device as essential to Sternberg as it is foreign to, say, Ozu, and which almost always carries meaning in his films beyond its basic usage to suggest continuity and the passing of time. Sophia is ready to depart for Russia. As she sits in the coach, her kindly and dignified but ineffectual old father delivers a brief homily, a series of conventional moral precepts that should govern her behavior (she will learn, in time, to flout all of them in order to adjust to the life into which she is thrust) and make her "worthy of her glorious destiny." As he speaks the last words, Sternberg dissolves very slowly to a shot of the coach—the whole procession—disappearing into an utterly black tunnel. The sexual symbolism is (in relation to Sophia's "glorious destiny") scarcely irrelevant. The dominant effect of a tragic-ironic pessimism is even more important if we are adequately to receive the force of the film.

The transition in the décor noted above—from the relative lightness (in both senses) of Sophia's home to the sombre and oppressive Russian court—has its parallel in the transition from Sophia's mother to the Dowager Empress. Both women are determined to bend all others to their will, with the latter a much more formidable and overpowering version of the former (who, having become redundant, is soon despatched home and disappears from the film).

Louise Dresser's performance grates on those who come to the film with prior expectations of historical authenticity, or the conventional appearance of it. Its American-ness and vulgarity, however, give the film an extra dimension. On the one hand, Sternberg clearly needed the cover of historical verisimilitude in order to smuggle past the eyes of the guardians of public morality an intrigue—not to mention his personal predilection for outrageous sexual innuendo—that flagrantly flouts the laws of the Hays Code. On the other hand, he uses Louise Dresser, the archetypal American matriarch, to establish the film's contemporary relevance. The license seems perfectly permissible within the format of legend, the court of Russia becoming a fairytale stylization of the American home, offering, like a dream, the possibility of fusing fantasy and essential psychology.

The second movement of the film culminates in the extraordinary sequences of the wedding and the ensuing banquet. The progress of the film—the progress toward the "glorious destiny"—becomes more clearly defined. Each of Sophia's natural responses is frustrated or perverted, her energies channeled into increasingly unnatural drives. On her arrival at the court—the set dominated by the Empress on her huge eagle throne—she is immediately deprived of her real name, and subjected to the humiliation of public examination by the doctor. The process begun by the removal of her toys in childhood now reaches its first major crisis in her enforced marriage to a malicious and impotent "royal half-wit" (Sam Jaffe) under the gaze of the man to whom she is tied by intense and mutual erotic impulse.

The short scene in which Sophia (now Catherine) is prepared for the wedding develops the imagery of entrapment, counterpointing and intensifying it with new motifs. It opens with the camera tracking back from Catherine as she is dressed before a mirror. In the foreground of the image elaborate veiling is lifted up, so that she is completely surrounded. When the Empress walks in, she has to pick her way among the crowd of ladies-in-waiting and obsequious courtiers: the embodiment of power who is nonetheless trapped and encumbered, as the victorious Catherine will be by flags and banners at the end of the film.

The mirror is supported by an elongated statue of the Holy Virgin, who holds it in the crook of her left arm while balancing the Christ Child in her right hand. There is another Madonna-and-Child painted on the back of the hand-mirror Catherine holds (we see it periodically reflected in the large mirror during the scene). The dialogue revolves around the need for a male heir and the Empress's sense that she should have been born a boy. "We women are too much creatures of the heart, aren't we, Catherine?" she asks, and for Catherine's assent (beautifully delivered by Dietrich with a wistful yearning), Sternberg cuts in to a closer shot of her reflected in the large mirror, framed, the living woman reduced to a "portrait."

The wedding is one of Sternberg's greatest set-pieces. It brings to a head the religious imagery that gets so much emphasis in the film, and with it the sense of desecration (epitomized succinctly in the shot of the mad groom chewing delightedly on the holy wafer as if it were a bon-bon). I don't think anyone will want to claim that the film expresses profound religious feeling, at least not in the orthodox sense. What is desecrated is natural feeling and natural response—human yearning, sexuality, motherhood—and the imagery needs to be understood in relation to this.

Before examining the wedding sequence in detail, we might pause to consider the richness and complexity of effect achieved through the décor, which the "legendary" aspect of the film permits Sternberg to develop so freely and lavishly. One may single out three distinguishable (but closely related) uses of statuary:

1. The chairs of the council chamber, above which rise huge gaunt figures, holding their hands over their eyes as if unable to bear contemplating the squalid intrigues they have eternally to witness.

2. The madonna statues: the one already referred to, holding in her right hand the infant Catherine will be denied (her child is removed from her at birth), and in her left the mirror in which Catherine is reflected—forced, increasingly, to rely upon her own resources and create an "image" of herself; and the statue that surmounts the bridal bed, presiding over its ceremonial blessing and the prayer for fruitfulness—on which Sternberg's comment is another slow dissolve from the madonna to a skeleton that holds up one of the dishes on the banquet table.

3. The statues representing martyrdom: the images of an anguished Christ on the cross and (even more striking in the use to which it is put) the St. Sebastian beside the staircase, body twisted in agony and transfixed with arrows, visually prominent in several scenes, notably that in which

Alexei endeavors to persuade Catherine to meet him clandestinely, shortly after her marriage.

Sternberg's interest in Expressionism preceded his visit to Germany to make *The Blue Angel;* the deliberately cultivated influence is visible in his silent films. In his films of the Thirties it becomes subtilized and diffused, completely assimilated into a personal style. But it is still there; and it seems legitimate to find in the St. Sebastian figure his means of giving powerful expression to all that is suppressed behind the impassive face of Alexei and the insistent insouciance of Catherine. Earlier, when Peter demonstrated his revolving soldier-toy (an extension of his madness, an expression of his militaristic fantasies), Alexei, standing by helplessly at this first stage of Catherine's disillusionment, was juxtaposed with another anguished statue.

The wedding sequence itself is marked off as a set-piece by its symmetry. It opens, as the Dowager Empress mounts the steps to her position of dominance, with the camera craning down and tracking left over the assembly; it ends with a shot that is almost a mirror-inversion of this. The symmetrical enclosing of the sequence might be felt formally to underline the stifling sense of entrapment it so powerfully creates. The décor is here at its most suffocating: the camera tracks past elaborate veiling behind which the congregation are only dimly visible, obscured; characters (especially Alexei) sit in confined compartments, hemmed in by flags and hangings; the crowns are like weights suspended above the bridal couple's heads. Two of the film's key motifs are here taken up in combination. Swinging censers insistently intrude into the foreground of the images, associated particularly with Catherine (one passes repeatedly across her face in several of the big, long-held close-ups), recalling the earlier juxtaposition of bell-clapper and swing, reminding us that the wedding is a crucial step in Catherine's rise to power.

The heart of the scene, again, is the exchange of looks between Catherine and Alexei. Their silent, and now deeply troubled, communication is again the outward sign of the only possibility of salvation; but, because it must remain silent and frustrated, it acquires equally the idea of helplessness. In the sustained close-ups of Catherine, two expressive features stand out: the pleading so eloquently conveyed by her eyes; and the physical reality of her breath as the candle before her mouth repeatedly wavers and is almost extinguished. The effect is like watching the quickened beating of her heart. . . .

The ending of the film—the murder of Peter, and Catherine's seizing of power—is the logical outcome of all that has preceded it: logical in its triumph, its tragedy and its irony, logical in the culmination of the unifying imagery. The moment that makes sense of the movement of the whole film is that when Catherine (dressed now as a man, in military uniform) ascends the stairs to ring the bell that is the signal for Peter's execution. The little girl who wanted to become a hangman has achieved her ambition; the enigma of the juxtaposed images of human bell-clapper and girl on swing is finally clarified; human energy and desire have been perverted into the brutal exercise of power. The moment also crystallizes one of the recurrent preoccupations of Sternberg's cinema: the mystery of free will and destiny. Catherine's assumption of power (like Amy Jolly's walk out into the desert at the end of *Morocco*) appears to be both a matter of deliberate choice and predestined from the beginning, both triumphant and desolating.

The disturbing power of the last sequence arises from its complexity of tone and the ambivalent feelings aroused. On the one hand, Catherine has learned how to survive in the world into which she was plunged (as Sternberg struggled to do in the commercial cinema of Hollywood); she has met it on its own terms and risen to supreme power within it (as Sternberg almost did, before the decline of his prestige). On the other, her triumph over it is won at the cost of becoming identified with it. The wondering child of the start has become Russia's "most sinister" tyrant (as the captions promised), a monstrous and dehumanized figure.

The horses gallop through the palace and up the great staircase where Alexei pleaded for a meeting, their hooves clattering deafeningly in an astonishing exhibition of energy and desecration—Sternberg tracking in at one point on the horribly contorted Christ on the cross now carried as a banner, at another allowing the agonized St. Sebastian again to dominate the foreground of the image. Catherine's face, the mouth exaggerated by make-up, has become a hideously grimacing mask, its expression recalling both the Empress's look of triumph at the end of the wedding sequence and the insane smiles at Peter, the "look" no longer directed at a human individual and no longer returned.

By associating Catherine finally not with a lover but with a magnificent white horse, Sternberg may conceivably have had in mind the legend (unsupported, apparently, by historians) of her death: that she died during attempted intercourse with a stallion which was accidentally let slip after being hauled into position. The legend's grotesqueness is quite in keeping with the figure—and the face—the film finally presents, in what is perhaps the most extraordinary of Sternberg's ironic "happy endings."

# François Truffaut

*FRANÇOIS TRUFFAUT was born in Paris in 1932. After a spotty school career, marked by hooky-playing at the movies, he took a succession of odd jobs and was arrested for stealing doorknobs to help finance a film club. André Bazin, by helping to get Truffaut released from reform school, became his adoptive father and counseled him in other youthful difficulties. After imprisonment for draft evasion during the Indochina War, Truffaut joined the staff of Bazin's newly founded magazine* Cahiers du Cinéma *and began writing film criticism for other magazines and newspapers as well.*

*Working on* Cahiers *in collaboration with critics such as Bazin, Godard, Eric Rohmer, Jacques Rivette, and others, Truffaut helped lay the foundation for a revaluation of the history and aesthetic of film unparalleled since the early writings of the first Soviet and German theorists. The main characteristics of this new criticism was an openness to the many possibilities of film style, with a special recognition of the creative potential of the American studio system and its use of such genre forms as the Western and the gangster film. Truffaut's own contribution was the first statement of the* "politique des auteurs," *or* auteur *theory, in which he argued that the directors most worthy of critical attention were those who wrote or helped write their own films; such directors, he held, were the central creative force in filmmaking.*

*In its early days the auteur theory was an attack on the official French film industry. Truffaut continued his polemic in his other writings, and as a result of these attacks he was banned from the Cannes Festival in 1958. In 1959, however, he returned in triumph: his first feature (after three shorts),* The 400 Blows, *was awarded the Grand Prize. What was to be dubbed* the New Wave *had begun—the entry into filmmaking of a generation of young French directors most of whom had started their careers as film critics.*

The 400 Blows *began Truffaut's interest in character as the center of a film's construction, a method perhaps influenced by his admiration for Renoir as well as for Rossellini, for whom he had worked on several unrealized projects in the 1950s.* Shoot the Piano Player *(1960) mingled farce and melodrama in an homage to the American gangster film and the films noirs of the 1940s and 1950s that had inspired the young Truffaut.* Jules and Jim *(1961), the story of two men in love with the same woman, once again brought Truffaut international success.*

*Truffaut's films since* Jules and Jim *have had a mixed reception as he experiments with different styles and variations of his typical themes. The Antoine Doinel films, starring Jean-Pierre Léaud and centering on the life of a character with autobiographical overtones, began with* The 400 Blows. *Truffaut elaborated this character in the* "Antoine et Colette" *sequence of* Love at Twenty *(1962) and followed his later life (still with* Léaud *as the star), in* Stolen Kisses *(1968) and* Bed and Board *(1969). But Truffaut's fascination with the anarchic impulses of youth have faded as his own career has solidified, and the satirical treatment of the literary intellectual in* The Soft Skin *(1964) has become the more worshipful attitude toward culture in* Fahrenheit 451 *(1966) and the praise of the teacher in* The Wild Child *(1970), where the teacher is played by Truffaut himself. By the time of* Small Change *(1976) the teacher delivers a final homily against child abuse, striking a didactic note foreign to the early Truffaut but increasingly present in his later films.*

*Truffaut has often played his more fluid sense of character and his lyric visual style against the enclosure of thriller plots in films such as* The Bride Wore Black *(1968) and* Mississippi Mermaid *(1969). His fascination with the actress is expressed through Jeanne Moreau in* Jules and Jim *and* The Bride Wore Black, *the double role played by Julie Christie in* Fahrenheit 451, *Catherine Deneuve in* Mississippi Mermaid, *and Isabelle Adjani in* The Story of Adèle H., *the most interesting of his recent films, in which the effects of fame upon character—a constant theme for Truffaut since* Shoot the Piano Player—*is given a complex and sympathetic treatment.*

*Truffaut's evolution from an interest in childhood to an interest in the problems of adulthood seems paralleled by his own willingness to name his artistic masters. After his apprenticeship with André Bazin, Truffaut published a long interview he had with Alfred Hitchcock (1966) and edited Bazin's writings about Jean Renoir (1971). In* Day for Night *(1974) Truffaut plays a film director (modeled in part on Buñuel) and celebrates as his subject the community of filmmakers, technicians, and performers who create that special world.*

*Published scripts include* The 400 Blows *(1969),* Jules and Jim *(1968), and a collection of all the films that feature the semi-autobiographical character Antoine Doinel (*The 400 Blows, "*Antoine et Collette,*" Stolen Kisses, Bed and Board; *1971). Full-length works about Truffaut have been written by Graham Petrie (1970), C. G. Crisp (1972), Dominique Fanne (*L'Univers de François Truffaut, in *French, 1972), and Don Allen (1974). See also James Monaco,* The New Wave *(1976). Truffaut has published a collection of his own writings on film since the early days at* Cahiers du Cinéma, *entitled* Les Films de ma vie *(1975).*

# The Books of His Life

## Dominique Fanne

Books, as privileged characters, invade the screen in the films of François Truffaut. There is the library of Fergus the painter,[1] the library in *Stolen Kisses* which Antoine sells to François Dorbön before leaving for military service.[2] There are libraries in *The Wild Child,* at Dr. Pinel's, and at Itard's home in Batignolle. When Jean Itard wants to know whether the child Victor understands the difference between good and bad, justice and injustice, he asks the boy for two objects, a key and a book. And if the boy cannot speak, he can write letters of the alphabet, scribble signs and signals; he is always there, near the library. When he practices pronouncing sounds, his candle is set upon a stack of books.

These are anonymous books, books without names like those in *Fahrenheit 451,* their titles unimportant, except for a few—*Gaspard Hauser,* for example—which are in the end saved from the incendiaries. "Behind books," says a character in *Farenheit,* "there are men." And never before have books appeared so plainly the symbol of human experience: the camera focuses upon Oskar Werner successively plunged in the dictionary, steeped in his childhood with *The Personal History of Charles Dickens,* and setting out at last in search of the free-people, the book-people. "These books," says Montag to Linda, "are my family," and he leaves on his search for the past, he rejoins Clarisse, who has metamorphosed into *The Memoirs of Saint Simon.* And indeed, it is a question of memory: Truffaut's people, so wrapped about, so overtly influenced by their past lives, can only live in the present surrounded by books. Books as the memory of the world, as necessities to mankind.

1. "The Bride Wore Black." In the novel by William Irish the painter's name is Ferguson. In the film he is called Fergus, perhaps to establish a correspondence with Balthus.
2. This was omitted from the film.

From *L'Univers de François Truffaut* by Dominique-Fanne (Paris: Éditions du Cerf, 1972). Reprinted by permission of the publisher. Translated especially for this volume by Sallie Iannotti; title supplied by the Editors.

"There will be more quotations in *Fahrenheit 451* than in all Jean-Luc's eleven films put together," Truffaut writes in his journal. *Fahrenheit*, which seems to be a filmed homage to the written word and to books, invents a living library, the book-people. Contrasted to the picture magazine that Montag reads and to the oral credits, the scores of books projected upon the screen become living objects.

> Today I saw for the first time that I cannot let the books simply fall out of the frame, it is impossible. I must follow their fall to the ground. The books, here, have become characters, and to cut them off in mid-trajectory is equivalent to filming an actor with his head cut out of the frame. I have had the feeling all along that several shots in this film had misfired, and now I see why. ("Journal de Fahrenheit," *Cahiers du Cinéma,* no. 165, p. 28)

Whether the lens is focused upon a single page of *The Brothers Karamazov* burning before our eyes or upon the book-man *The Life of Henri Brulard* greeting Montag in the forest,[3] there is no argument in the film directly in favor of books. They are quite simply filmed living and dying.

In an article for *Nouvel Observateur,* Michel Cournot complains that Truffaut has "thingified" Bradbury's novel by making little word-gags, in which all reflection and intelligence are lacking. But Truffaut is more interested in books as human memory and feeling than in books as academic statements on language. This is made very clear by the lusts and passions that come out in the book burnings in *Fahrenheit.* In contrast to the academicians, Truffaut, the autodidact, holds that a book is "the object which above all attends to memory and feeling," and he consigns to the flames a "book of the future" by Arthème Fayard.

But the books in *Fahrenheit* are ambiguous creatures. Access to human experience, yes, but at the same time they are an obstacle to communication. Montag prefers the world he finds in his books to that which he might find with his wife, Linda. The book-people at the end of the film do not talk to one another, they recite books.

### Itard's Journal

In *The Wild Child,* however, Itard's journal, which creates an essential rhythm in the film, becomes gradually less and less an obstacle to communication. In his initial script Truffaut wrote:

> The words "From Itard's Notebooks" will occur often. This form of narration should not create problems for the reader,

---

3. The actor who played this role did so for Truffaut in the style of Henri Serre.

however, since it will be shortened and tempered by what follows. This frequent, if brief, recourse to the commentary will add a rhythm to the narrative, and its final effect upon the screen will be as neutral as those connective dissolves which generally punctuate any story encompassing great stretches of time.[4]

Yet, in fact, the sequences in which Itard takes up his journal are always cut in at the very moment an important event is taking place:

> Itard writes in his journal after seeing the child: "All Paris talks of nothing but this child."
> When the boy is entrusted to his care: "I have had the child committed to my care."
> He records the emotional insensibility of the boy: "No one has ever seen the child cry."
> He records moments... The child becomes sensitive to heat and cold. The child sneezes for the first time.
> Using milk, Itard tries to make Victor speak. He realizes that he has failed to understand his pupil and that the fault is his, not Victor's.
> The child weeps for the first time.
> The child is an inventor.
> Itard decides to test Victor's understanding of injustice.

The off-screen commentaries are always spoken by Itard himself, and they are, in fact, the actual texts from his notebooks.

If the sequences of Itard writing his notes are sometimes at one with the montage—text, image, and sound woven together in a single shot—such moments are rare. Most often the commentary precedes the image of Itard and his journal, and the flow of narrative and music are cut in. Thus, when Itard is seen writing: "I have had the child committed to my care ... what excites me about this little wild creature ..." the words are spoken aloud, but the commentary continues into the following sequences, a series of traveling shots showing Victor having his nails and hair cut by Mme. Guérin. Here the spoken and the written commentaries are not in opposition.

Does the journal, then, actually bring Itard and the boy together, or does it form a barrier between them? The evidence suggests that it maintains a tight relation between doctor and child. The image of the notebook on the screen is most often preceded and followed by an image of the child, or is interposed between two shots of "Victor and Itard," or "Victor, Itard, and Mme. Guérin." What emerges, then, is a symmetrical mon-

4. Significantly, the music begins when Itard "speaks his report" for the first time and, in the script, he opens a new notebook and begins to write on the first page.

tage.[5] Yet the ambiguities of the film remain. The journal is, literally, *between* Victor and Itard.

It is the composition of the image that relieves this ambiguity. The first shots of the film serve to demonstrate the intimate link between Itard and his journal, which mars the relation between the doctor and his charge. Itard writes in his journal, the camera passes from his face to his hands, from his journal to his face. It shows the doctor sitting self-consciously in various rooms, yet always going back to his writing desk and his journal. The camera frames his hands and the paper, lingers over the act of dipping the pen in ink. If Victor sneezes and is afraid, it is only Mme. Guérin who comforts him. Itard observes, notes, writes, and praises the governess, but does not speak to Victor. The boy is merely the subject of his observations, and the montage does not link Itard, Victor, and the journal. The shots of Mme. Guérin with the boy are in counterpoint to those of Itard alone, preparing to write his notes. Similarly, after another crisis with Victor, Mme Guérin and the boy walk to the left of the screen, while Itard goes to the right, toward his writing desk, toward his journal.

Then, little by little, the camera records Itard, Victor, and the journal in the same frame; and even though, at first, it moves from the man to the boy without framing them together, the ambiguity begins to crumble. Two shots, at this moment, throw a new light upon the film. Itard returns from a trip. He goes into Victor's room and the boy takes his hand and presses it to his cheek. The man and the boy are framed together, close, and the feelings that are established in this instant of intimacy change forever the relation between Itard and his journal.

In the following shot, the scene of the dark closet at the back of the stairs (one of the longest sequences in the whole film, incidentally), Itard does not go to his writing desk until he has comforted the boy. He sets Victor to work, but places a glass of water within his reach. And for the first time the three terms—Itard, Victor, journal—are framed together in the same shot, in the same image, while the commentary itself—that is to say, the action and the commentary on that action—underscores the new bond: "Today," Itard writes, "for the first time Victor has wept."

There is no more ambiguity, the journal is no longer a barrier, it is now the boy who is the stronger force. He has, in fact, ceased to be the prisoner of the little black book where Itard has kept him enclosed. For the young doctor, the rage for observation has given way to a quieter contem-

5. Often even the movements are symmetrical. When, with the aid of a bowl of milk, Itard tries to get Victor to speak, the sequence is shot: Victor alone. Itard enters the field and the camera frames both of them. Itard writes in his journal. Victor alone. Itard enters the field—once again the camera focuses upon them together.

plation. One evening he forgets his journal altogether, and simply watches as Victor communes with the natural world. The jouranl remains indispensable to the man and to the child, a tangible symbol of their communication. Again, after the injustice sequence, Itard goes from the boy to the journal, and camera frames them together. But now this communication between man and child is no longer solely dependent upon the notebook.

Then, when Victor runs away, a fleeting shot cuts to Itard, pacing in front of his desk, not writing. A third phase of the relation is established; the absence of the child has destroyed the link between Itard and the journal, and he cannot write, he can only wait.

### The Primary Sources

Eight of Truffaut's films have their origins in books. Eight books? Not at all; many, many more than that. An astonishing tendency—to choose a book to film, and then to weave in other books by the same author. "Les Mistons," a story by Maurice Pons, appeared in the book *Virginales,* a collection devoted to childhood experiences. Perhaps by coincidence, perhaps not, another story in that book is entitled "Balzac." Now, the soundtrack from Truffaut's short picture *The Mischief Makers* [*Les Mistons,* 1957: 26 min.] is derived from three stories in *Virginales: Les Mistons* (three lines), *A bicyclette* (two lines), and *Miss Fraulein* (half a line). An unusual montage is at work here. Segments of the principal story itself are transposed and phrases drawn from the other stories are inserted, phrases that speak of a luminous, mysterious sensuality, thereby interweaving the lovers and the children.

Truffaut does much the same to all the novels he adapts. He draws his inspiration from the entire body of a writer's work, taking here and there a theme, a snatch of dialogue, and so on. Thus the conversation between Plyne and Charlie that opens *Shoot the Piano Player*[6] (a discussion of Charlie's fears and of little Lena-Martha, who has luminous blond hair, so fine and so free) is taken from *Nightfall,* another book by David Goodis. Other dialogues in the film, between the bandits Momo and Ernest, are also taken from this source.

In the same way, Jules, Jim, and Catherine of *Jules and Jim* are drawn from the book by Henri-Pierre Roché, and at the same time from another of his books, *Deux Anglaises et le continent.* Catherine is at once Lucie, Magda, and Kate of the book *Jules et Jim,* and also Muriel (her glasses, her eye problems) and Anne of *Deux Anglaises,* and even *Marie Dubois.* A number of the dialogues in the film were taken almost whole cloth from Roché's *Deux Anglaises:*

6. Adapted from *Down There,* a novel by David Goodis.—TRANS.

"I have no heart," Catherine says to Jim, "that's why I don't love you; I will never love anyone."

"I no longer suffer. . . . When you stop, then it will start for me again."

The second phrase here is joined to the preceding one in the film, but in Roché's book almost thirty pages—75 through 104—separate them. Again: "I always try to look at the nape of your neck, it is the only part of you I can study without being seen," Jim says to Catherine; and the letters between Catherine and Jim while they await the birth of their child—both are also taken from the second book.[7]

Other segments borrowed from *Deux Anglaises* appear in the film script but have disappeared from the film itself, among them the very beautiful passage Jim reads to Jules in the gymnasium ("Let me read you these lines," he says). This is the opening passage of Roché's book:

> I believe that for each man there is one woman who was created to be his mate. There can be any number of women with whom he can lead a pleasant or even a useful and happy life. But there is only one woman who is his perfect mate. Perhaps she might die, perhaps she might never find him, perhaps she will marry someone else. And in that case it would be better for that man never to marry at all. There is, also, for every woman a single man, created for her alone, who is her mate.[8]

There are other elements, too, drawn straight from *Deux Anglaises et le continent:* the fable of the wolf and the lamb, which Catherine recites, the feminine statues whose absence of sexuality appears to Jules an error in art,[9] Catherine's words to Jim about the couple and the children after their first night together, and—most important of all—the opening words of the film.[10] These are all drawn from the secondary source book. That the film does not dissipate into the jigsaw puzzle it might have been is due to the splendid screenplay composed by Jean Gruault and Truffaut. Indeed,

7. Compare this, too, with the past life of Theresa, the advice of the old professor to Jim, numerous lines spoken by Catherine to Jim about her age, the necessity of breaking off the relationship, and so on.
8. In the script the terms "man" and "woman" are reversed. [Truffaut later made a film of the book itself, *Two English Girls* (1971).—EDS.]
9. These two scenes appeared in the script, but were omitted from the film.
10. "You said, 'I love you.'
"I said, 'Wait.'
"I was going to say, 'Take me.'
"You said, 'Go away.'"

Catherine, like Marie Dubois, is enriched by the multiplicity of characters that go into her make-up.

This process which transforms the works of Pons, Goodis, and Roché is equally at work in the stories by Ray Bradbury and William Irish, even though the insertion of other elements into the films made from their works appears more in the approach to character than in the actual text and narration.

The work of these writers makes up a coherent universe, for each of their books is interlocked in some way with the others; they evoke one another, they correspond like so many memories and secret connections. Truffaut's approach to them, then, might be considered profoundly faithful. Thus, Bradbury's young girl in *Fahrenheit 451,* for example, is afraid of the children who commit suicide with the same fear that drives parents in another of his stories to take their children's places for the duration of their growth period, in order to protect them from brutalization. Similarly, William Irish writes stories, little-known stories (often, indeed, published under other names) which recall his novels.[11] "The Dancing Detective" is a story whose theme of insane revenge echoes *The Bride Wore Black* and *Rendez-vous in Black;* "I Wouldn't Be in Your Shoes" and "The Earring" evoke *I Married a Dead Man.* Irish's novels are very oddly connected sometimes; the man in *Rendez-vous in Black* is blood brother to Julie, the bride in black. Scenes in *Waltz into Darkness* (from which *Mississippi Mermaid* was adapted) in which Louis searches for Julie-Bonny resemble scenes in the story "The Light in the Window." The relationship between Louis and Marion Mahé in Truffaut's film, *Mississippi Mermaid,* is certainly that of Irish's couple, yet Louis and Marion are related also to Bill and Patricia, the protagonists of *I Married a Dead Man.* Louis-Marion, Bill-Patricia, a single couple, really, whose bond is so strong that even a name stolen from a dead woman cannot disturb it. Here, as elsewhere in Irish's work, there are transposed personalities and actions; the characters represent other characters, they destroy themselves in the place of others, they love each other in the place of others. . . .

So it appears that the approach chosen by the director for these films conveys very faithfully the worlds created by the writers. Yet at the same time another world is illuminated by it, the impassioned world of Truffaut himself.

11. Truffaut himself does this sort of thing. Before filming *The 400 Blows* he wrote a short piece, "La Fugue d'Antoine." [William Irish is the pseudonym of Cornell Woolrich, who wrote also under the name George Hopley.—TRANS.]

# "The 400 Blows": A Review

## Arlene Croce

François Truffaut's first feature, *The 400 Blows,* is one of the few master-pieces of its kind granted to the cinema in recent years. It is a sad, bitter story of a child's gradual disaffection from society. The child is tough, imaginative, exuberant; the society is dull, timid, corrupt. And the film's point of view isn't sentimental. Antoine, the hero (in a jewel of a perfor-mance by Jean-Pierre Léaud), is a completely spontaneous and engaging extrovert of thirteen or fourteen, neither more nor less remarkable or sensi-tive than his classmates. He doesn't breach the pattern in any way. He does, however, get caught. For showing a certain mild defiance, he gets a reputation as a trouble-maker, and petty-bourgeois vindictiveness does the rest. Forced out of school, betrayed by parents for whom he represents the burden of an impossible marriage, he is consigned to the police and the vice-ridden world of adults. The "good-bye to all that" gesture of the finale has some of the proud fantasy of Lamorisse's films—the suggestion that freedom lies not in the present world of corruption but in another time and place, the time and place that a child conceives of in his imagination, where he is in his element.

In a recent interview in *The New Yorker,* Truffaut dismissed the white manes and red balloons as sentimental and irrelevant additives to the child's world. But because he makes his own kind of poetry, and because he takes the path of realism, he is in no danger of being confused with Lamorisse. Unlike the Lamorisse films, *The 400 Blows* does not exist on a plane of fantasy; its premises are not allegorical. It is about the suffering an average young schoolboy must endure if he has the bad luck to be consid-ered a criminal by both his family and the state in what we can only take to be present-day Paris. Given the actualities of this situation, and a manifest talent for observation, Truffaut's approach may seem to American audiences strangely stoical. He seems to be able to accept bad luck in good grace and still move us to moral indignation.

Truffaut is not, in the political sense, engaged. He protests in terms of the transcendent values; he protests the inhumanity of man. The underlying sadness of this film is the sadness of the universal estrangement. Truffaut's beautifully oblique style of commentary is a product of poetic intuition, not, I dare say, of political evasion. In *The 400 Blows*, "new wave" technique serves to unite poetry and journalism in the powerful idiom of a particular environment—an environment, moreover, that has long supplied certain historical privileges for what an aesthetic need can make of them. On its most agreeable level, you see something of this environmental idiom in the style of an Yves Montand, and you see the difference between that and what one critic has called "the desperate strategies" of our own popular entertainers. An American filmmaker who wished to present with sympathy and truth the predicament of the young Antoines of New York and Detroit would really have to *faire les quatre cents coups*—and risk bad art as well as public indifference. What Truffaut has achieved—a genuinely un-neurotic work of public art—is something that seems at present quite beyond the capacity of American filmmakers to produce, and not only because of Hollywood. Our own tradition provides no model, no cultural precedent for the kind of radical humanism we need today—unless it be the image of Huck Finn lighting out for that territory.

The image is apolitical because the society that produced it was practically nonindustrial. To an incomparably greater degree than in the days of Mark Twain, however, politics is the way we live. You don't find many valid images of revolt today. An omnivorous society swallows the more fashionable ones whole, and the others are all bound in the pages of *Dissent* magazine. Truffaut's hero also lights out. He might be the hero of a film made thirty years ago. We Americans don't live in the past, as Richard Nixon says. We most emphatically don't. The violent flux of American life constantly revises the artist's scale of reference. Whereas even the rebellion of Holden Caulfield begins to seem like an inner-directed archaism when compared to the enormities of present-day teen-age culture, the children of *The 400 Blows* seem to be growing up in a relatively unaltered social surround. Whether or not this is part of the provincialism Truffaut is attacking, it does give the film a perennial truth, an air of timelessness, and I think the obvious allusions of *Zéro de conduite* help to point this out.

*The 400 Blows* is a film about freedom. It could, I think, convey this idea to an audience of deaf illiterates in any part of the world, because its construction is very nearly as absolutely visual as that of a silent film. Its metaphor for freedom is space, as in that other great escape film, *Grand*

*Illusion.* Notice the deceptively casual way both films gradually broaden in scope, in both the dramatic and the optical sense. To take *The 400 Blows:* who would have thought its end was in its beginning? It opens with crowded shots of a decrepit classroom packed with Vigo's grubby scholars under the tyrannical eye of a master half-demented through exhaustion; later come perambulations in and around Montmartre, a maze of architectural restrictions, reflecting a life so cramped, limited, and circular that the hero, playing hooky one day, spots his mother in *flagrante delicto;* and the wedged-in life of the tenements. . . .

Against all these things, Truffaut presses an unsparing camera. But the mood is relaxed, footling, the film moves at an even speed. We seem to be watching trivia, amusing and somewhat inconsequential. The musical score, with its jogging tunes, seems to reinforce this impression. The scene in the revolving drum injects the first disturbing note. It is, perhaps, a presentiment of brutalization. A small, blurred figure flattened on the side of an enormous whirling cylinder, and the cylinder turning in the expanse of the wide-screen—for a moment the film itself seems to be out of control. But Truffaut passes lightly over it, and things resume their old prosaic proportions. Except that now the isolation of the boy creates a new series of involvements, to which Truffaut responds with a subtle increase in momentum and an instinct for incongruities that move the film decisively out of the range of anecdote onto a level of profoundly serious narrative. By the time the boy's father hands him over to the police with all the callous piety that seems necessary to the occasion, the transition in tone is complete: this is no joke. The scenes of incarceration which follow pull you way under. The boy is flung into a cage with some routine offenders and then into a smaller one, the size of a phone booth, by himself. It is only the first of the many times we are to see children behind bars before the film comes to its close, with a great climactic letting-in of air.

The most original feature of Truffaut's beautifully oblique style of commentary is his by-now famous use of protracted sequences accomplished through the sustained single shot and through a minimum of cutting: the scene in the revolving drum; the long ride in the paddy wagon which encompasses the boy's whole descent from innocence, and which I recall as one long close-up alternated with a single reverse-field shot; the extraordinary interview with the (off-screen) psychiatrist, in which there are no cuts, merely a series of unsettling dissolves and the long tracking shot of the stupendous finale. Since cutting is a director's chief means of comment, the effects Truffaut obtains in these sequences depend on the progression of meanings within the frame. Sometimes, as in the examples cited above, the progression has the elliptical motion of fine poetry. At other times, there is little more than the amateur perpetuation of a cliché. The physical-culture outing, for all its obvious debt to Vigo, looks like

nothing so much as tired Tati (which is pretty tired), and the puppet show episode is sheer *tourisme*.

Where there is poetry in Truffaut's method, it is often graced with the kind of ambiguity cherished among the "new wave" directors. The ambiguity derives from a deliberate withholding of explicit comment, as in the interview scene—from the apparent determination of the director to express no opinions. Revelation is a matter of the direct perception of what people say and do, and what is revealed to you is your own feeling about the words and deeds of others. For example, shortly after the boy's commitment to the reformatory, a judge is seen wearily assuring the boy's mother that he will do what he can. In opposition to this paternal image, which might almost be out of some government-sponsored information film, we later see a semi-conscious young runaway being dragged back to captivity. The grown-up characters in the film may appear to us monsters of hypocrisy, but is it more correct to say that they control the world than to say that they are controlled by it? In either case, children suffer. Instead of a moral pattern in the conventional sense, you are confronted with the spectacle of unanalyzed phenomena.

Conventionally speaking, the boy's father is an amiable coward, his mother a hard-shelled Bovary ("I'm used to being criticized!")—the nearest thing to a villain in the piece. But no one can say they don't "try." Similarly, the judge, the psychiatrist, the chief of police all do their best, they "have children of their own." But, as we soon see, the caretaker locks his three little girls in a pen when the boys come running out for sports, and the runaway, accepting smuggled food, declares he would do it all again for just five more days of freedom. If Antoine judges his world, he does so through the only means that are available to him—a purehearted instinct for decency that, in the end, makes him take to his heels. Away he goes in a cross-country run that seems to take him clear across France to the sea. In the surf, liberated at last, he turns momentarily to face us; the image freezes, then slowly it fades out.

In its retention of life's ambiguity, the "new wave" technique makes unique demands on the spectator. The novelty of it is the way it can open up a film in the mind of the audience, creating an experience which is insistently problematical. This is perhaps more true of Chabrol than it is of Truffaut, but even when Truffaut seems to be putting things squarely up to you, as in the intense and disarming intimacy of the psychiatrist's interview, ambiguous sensations are evident, and there is a suspicion that, in some of the things he says, the boy may be lying. As he himself remarks, "When I tell the truth, they don't believe me." The important thing, however, is that at this moment, and at the end, you are no longer looking at the film—the film is looking at you. In Franju's words (*Cahiers du Cinéma*): "*Il parle au public, le môme, il nous parle.*" What a blessing.

# "The 400 Blows": From Scenario to Film

## C. G. Crisp

On viewing a finished film, one tends to see it as the inevitable outcome of the author's intentions. In fact, of course, changes are made continually right up to the moment of shooting and then continue under a different name—improvisation. As the final version of the scenario happens to be extant, we can see how far Truffaut was willing to adapt his ideas.

The scenario calls for the credits to unfold against a closed desk-top, which is to open for the pin-up incident, thus opening the film. Accompanying the subsequent classroom scenes, and many later ones, is a commentary spoken by an older René, recalling his schooldays and his companion Antoine. It starts: "The paradise lost of childhood is an invention of old men. How can one still believe in it at eighteen?... Our thirteenth year dragged on and on... Antoine Loinod remembers it all too well: for him it was the time of injustice." In feeling, this recalls *Les Mistons,* and is evidently a relic of the film's origin as a companion piece. The commentary was progressively eliminated, with the beneficial result (and probably the intention) of making the themes less overt. Instead of being spelled out in the commentary, themes, opinions and character traits are presented visually to the spectator in the action but not forced on him. The quote is also a reminder that Antoine's name throughout the scenario was Loinod not Doinel as it became in the film. (Doniol in reverse; Doniol-Valcroze acted under the name Etienne Loinod in Rivette's *Le Coup du berger.*)

Next come several playground scenes, with talk between masters of a possible strike, all mention of which was omitted from the final version. Then René comes home with Antoine to help with his homework; they go shopping, lose the list and buy the wrong food. Instead, the film concentrates here on Antoine alone in the house, establishing his character by the

''carefully judged mixture of good and bad.'' In the scenario, many place names are mentioned, suburb and street names being specified, even precise buildings and doorways designated—an added suggestion of the film's relevance to Truffaut's own life, as is the affectionate mention of two boulevard cinemas: ''It was there, in that atmosphere purified by night and by DDT, that the adventure began.'' The film to be seen by the children is not specified; we are simply told they are to indulge in ''dialogue appropriate to the film projected (heroism and sudden justice).'' There was also to have been an amusing incident with a passing provincial, played by Raymond Devos (who later appeared as the man on the landing stage in *Pierrot le fou*). In the fairground episode, ''the camera will emphasize the monstrous and disproportionate aspect of modern gaiety, interplay of metallic elements, whirling round abouts, rockets of steel, etc.''—a satirical element that has also disappeared.

Later, when Antoine's father tells him he should show more initiative, the directions indicate flash shots of Antoine's memories of the rotor. Similar flash shots were to accompany the reading of Balzac, but are replaced in the final version by a close-up of the page. Wandering around Paris, Antoine was to witness several odd tableaux including a man stooping to peer through a church door ''as if to watch the mass through a keyhole.'' These obsessive personal memories or references may have been filmed but were not included in the final version. Most remarkable, the time Antoine spends in René's house was fully treated in some fourteen pages (about a seventh of the scenario). There is a little girl who makes a fuss and is left at home by her parents. She creates an uproar, which disturbs all the neighbors. Antoine and René feed her and a boy who lives opposite performs a play for her. As our heroes have given her their own meal, they fabricate a new one of ''caramel'' in a saucepan. Then they go on to get the cats drunk. René's mother hides Antoine whose father has come to look for him but René's father, who is more fully delineated than in the film, tells Antoine he must leave.

All that remains of this is a fragment of the caramel-making, and the blanket-flapping scene. The rest, lovingly detailed in the scenario, has all been cut, perhaps because the girl or René's father proved inadequate as actors, but perhaps also because the film, already overlong, needed to be trimmed of personal references at this point. In contrast, the detention scenes have all been greatly expanded to give them more weight as they contribute directly to building up the climax. The material omitted would have explained the behavior of René's family and the abrupt appearance of the little girl; the film would have lost some elements of its arbitrariness at the expense of gaining others. Truffaut has had to try achieving the same effect more rapidly and with less material.

The typewriter scene is detailed minutely in the scenario, and sounds authentic. The building and firm are specified. The hat incident, however, is absent. The prosecution scenes have not merely been expanded but considerably modified: Antoine originally remained in the cell with a group of crooks and prostitutes, who treated him with a certain camaraderie. The trip to the reformatory is referred to as simply three scenes of a police van in the streets at night. No indication is given of Antoine's tears, there is no mention elsewhere of the expressionlessness of his face. Léaud's acting ability seems to have suggested wider possibilities as shooting progressed.

This hypothesis is reinforced by the scenes with the psychologist who, we are told, was to have been a young woman, quite pretty and wearing glasses. The camera was to have stayed on her, as we heard Antoine's answers "off." In the film, though, we never see her; instead there are the magnificent shots of Antoine's "explanations." Truffaut explains how this happened: he was worried that the psychologist's questions too closely resembled those in *Chiens perdus sans collier,* but didn't know what to do about it. Then he had difficulty finding an actress for the part, and realised that the characteristics he had in mind exactly fitted the scriptwriter Annette Wademant, who was not in Paris at the time—hence the decision to shoot just Léaud's side of the interview, and add her side when she became available. Truffaut discussed the interview with the boy, explaining in general what sort of questions he would ask, but left him free to answer in his own words, hoping to achieve a certain spontaneity. To make it easier for Léaud, he formulated questions which applied both to Antoine and to Léaud himself, merely asking him not to contradict the rest of the scenario. He shot the scene with no one in the room except Léaud himself and the cameraman Decaë. When they saw the rushes, Decaë suggested that they should leave it as it was, adding only the voice of the psychologist. This they did, though they retained only three of the twenty minutes shot.

There follows scenes in which Antoine's mother visits a fortune-teller. These were omitted as a possible distraction from Antoine at the climactic moment. When René tries to contact Antoine at the reformatory, Truffaut specifies that the books he brings are copies of *Cinémonde,* and that the guard tosses them away because they're not food. It is totally irrelevant, since we're never near enough to see them, yet curiously endearing, for this is precisely what Truffaut's friend Robert Lachenay would have tried to bring him.

The final escape was to involve a flight through changing countryside and a ride in the back of a truck. The film version is once again more coherent and dramatic, since it complies with the unities of time and space. The final lines of the projected scenario indicate:

107. He will stop only when the foam comes and soaks the soles of his shoes.

108. The last image of that scene, Antoine at the seaside, becomes fixed and fades into another moving image: Antoine and René walking through the streets of Paris and this image in turn becomes fixed, reminding us that it is taken by a street photographer, whilst we hear the last words of René's commentary: "Thus it was that I received a postcard from Fontenoy-sur-Mer, where I managed to contact Antoine. How are we doing now? Fine, thank you . . . and yourself? We are free, and far from the torments of adolescence, but as we wander through the streets we can't help feeling a certain complicity with our successors, too, as we watch them *recommencer Les Quatre Cents Coups*"

In the film, however, this final image and commentary have been cut, and the whole last sequence is transformed. We are no longer looking back from a safe distance, with an older René, at something that turned out satisfactorily, a cycle that will repeat with each generation. On the contrary, we see it from Antoine's viewpoint—disconcerted, unaware of what the future will bring, conditioned to expect the worst. Truffaut's later description of the final shots significantly ends on a question: "Running through the fields, he arrives at last face to face with the sea which he has never seen before. Reconciled with nature, will he soon also be reconciled with life?"

It seems safe to say that the scenario was used only for reference. Less than half of it remains in the film. Since he had never before undertaken the transformation from scenario into film on such a scale, Truffaut was willing to reject anything which, on realization turned out to be inappropriate to the actors' personalities or the precise location. Much of the scenario was certainly shot but rejected later on for various reasons. In this sense, Truffaut relied heavily on improvisation. The scenario gives no stage directions, camera movements, or décors. These would depend solely on cost and availability. Very sensibly, Truffaut approached his first film tentatively, as an experiment.

When the film was reissued in 1967 Truffaut made some changes, adding eight minutes. He says that when he made it he was afraid to exceed the magic one-and-a-half-hour limit. He managed to keep within five minutes of it only by the strictest editing. The restored material removed some ambiguities: in the 1959 version we never found out what happened to M. Loinod's *Guide Michelin;* we might reasonably have surmised that Mme. Loinod had taken it. The scenes where Antoine is seen tearing it up to make pellets remove this doubt. He also extended the early scenes establishing the boys' personalities and restored certain sections which had been unofficially censored. The boys' calling the curé "Madame" had shocked some Catholics, and had been cut out by the distributors. In some foreign versions the end had been made less pessimistic with a spoken commentary, perhaps like the one Truffaut himself had removed.

The film must have had an effect on Truffaut himself, in representing some kind of exorcism of much of his past life. Doniol-Valcroze says that "making the film reconciled Truffaut to life in somewhat the same way as reaching the sea reconciles Antoine to life"—without signifying any final resolution. A long-imagined dream had been realized, and now it was necessary to adjust to the idea of it as merely a stepping stone.

# "Shoot the Piano Player" and "Jules and Jim"

## Pauline Kael

### "Shoot the Piano Player"

The cover of David Goodis's novel *Down There,* now issued by Grove Press under the title of the film adapted from it, *Shoot the Piano Player,* carries a statement from Henry Miller—"Truffaut's film was so good I had doubts the book could equal it. I have just read the novel and I think it is even better than the film." I don't agree with Miller's judgment. I like the David Goodis book, but it's strictly a work in a limited genre, well-done and consistent; Truffaut's film busts out all over—and that's what's wonderful about it. The film is comedy, pathos, tragedy all scrambled up—much I think as most of us really experience them (surely all our lives are filled with comic horrors) but not as we have been led to expect them in films.

*Shoot the Piano Player* is about a man who has withdrawn from human experience; he wants not to care any more, not to get involved, not to *feel.* He has reduced life to a level on which he can cope with it—a revery between him and the piano. Everything that happens outside his solitary life seems erratic, accidental, unpredictable—but he can predict the pain. In a flashback we see why: when he *did* care, he failed the wife who needed him and caused her death. In the course of the film he is once more brought back into the arena of human contacts; another girl is destroyed, and he withdraws again into solitude.

Truffaut is a free and inventive director—and he fills the piano player's encounters with the world with good and bad jokes, bits from old Sacha Guitry films, clowns and thugs, tough kids, songs and fantasy and snow scenes, and homage to the American gangster films—not the classics, the socially conscious big-studio gangster films of the thirties, but the grade-B gangster films of the forties and fifties. Like Godard, who dedicated *Breathless* to Monogram Pictures, Truffaut is young, and he loves the cheap American gangster films of his childhood and youth. And like them, *Shoot the Piano Player* was made on a small budget. It was also made outside of studios with a crew that, according to witnesses, sometimes consisted of Truffaut, the actors, and a cameraman. Part of his love of cheap American movies with their dream imagery of the American gangster—the modern fairy tales for European children who go to movies—is no doubt reflected in his taking an American underworld novel and transferring its setting from Philadelphia to France.

Charles Aznavour who plays the hero is a popular singer turned actor—rather like Frank Sinatra in this country, and like Sinatra, he is an instinctive actor and a great camera subject. Aznavour's piano player is like a tragic embodiment of Robert Hutchins's Zukerkandl philosophy (whatever it is, stay out of it): he is the thinnest-skinned of modern heroes. It is his own capacity to feel that makes him cut himself off: he experiences so sensitively and so acutely that he can't bear the suffering of it—he thinks that if he doesn't do anything he won't feel and he won't cause suffering to others. The girl, Marie Dubois—later the smoky-steam-engine girl of *Jules and Jim*—is like a Hollywood forties movie type; she would have played well with Humphrey Bogart—a big, clear-eyed, crude, loyal, honest girl. The film is closely related to Godard's *Breathless;* and both seem to be haunted by the shade of Bogart.

*Shoot the Piano Player* is both nihilistic in attitude and, at the same time, in its wit and good spirits, totally involved in life and fun. Whatever Truffaut touches seems to leap to life—even a gangster thriller is transformed into the human comedy. A *comedy* about melancholia, about the hopelessness of life can only give the lie to the theme; for as long as we can joke, life is not hopeless, we can enjoy it. In Truffaut's style there is so much pleasure in life that the wry, lonely little piano player, the sardonic little man who shrugs off experience, is himself a beautiful character. This beauty is a tribute to human experience, even if the man is so hurt and defeated that he can only negate experience. The nihilism of the character—and the anarchic nihilism of the director's style—have led reviewers to call the film a surrealist farce; it isn't that strange.

When I refer to Truffaut's style as anarchic and nihilistic, I am referring to a *style,* not an absence of it. I disagree with the critics around the country who find the film disorganized; they seem to cling to the critical apparatus of their grammar-school teachers. They want unity of theme, easy-to-follow-transitions in mood, a good, coherent, old-fashioned plot, and heroes they can identify with and villains they can reject. Stanley

Kauffmann in the *New Republic* compares *Shoot the Piano Player* with the sweepings of cutting room floors; *Time* decides that "the moral, if any, seems to be that shooting the piano player might, at least, put the poor devil out of his misery." But who but *Time* is looking for a moral? What's exciting about movies like *Shoot The Piano Player, Breathless* (and also the superb *Jules and Jim,* though it's very different from the other two) is that they, quite literally, move with the times. They are full of unresolved, inexplicable, disharmonious elements, irony and slapstick and defeat all compounded—*not* arbitrarily as the reviewers claim—but in terms of the film maker's efforts to find some expression for his own anarchic experience, instead of making more of those tiresome well-made movies that no longer mean much to us.

The subject matter of *Shoot the Piano Player,* as of *Breathless,* seems small and unimportant compared to the big themes of so many films, but it only *seems* small: it is an effort to deal with contemporary experience in terms drawn out of that experience. For both Godard and Truffaut a good part of this experience has been moviegoing, but this is just as much a part of their lives as reading is for a writer. And what writer does not draw upon what he has read?

A number of reviewers have complained that in his improvisatory method, Truffaut includes irrelevancies, and they use as chief illustration the opening scene—a gangster who is running away from pursuers bangs into a telephone pole, and then is helped to his feet by a man who proceeds to walk along with him, while discussing his marital life. Is it really so irrelevant? Only if you grew up in that tradition of the well-made play in which this bystander would have to reappear as some vital link in the plot. But he's relevant in a different way here: he helps to set us in a world in which his semi-normal existence seems just as much a matter of chance and fringe behavior and simplicity as the gangster's existence—which begins to seem semi-normal also. The bystander talks; we get an impression of his way of life and his need to talk about it, and he goes out of the film, and that is that: Truffaut would have to be as stodgy and dull witted as the reviewers to bring him back and link him into the story. For the meaning of these films is that these fortuitous encounters illuminate something about our lives in a way that the old neat plots don't.

There is a tension in the method; we never quite know where we are, how we are supposed to react—and this tension, as the moods change and we are pulled in different ways, gives us the excitement of drama, of art, of *our* life. Nothing is clear-cut, the ironies crisscross and bounce. The loyal, courageous heroine is so determined to live by her code that when it's violated, she comes on too strong, and the piano player is repelled by her inability to respect the weaknesses of others. Thugs kidnaping a little boy discuss their possessions with him—a conversation worthy of a footnote in Veblen's passages on conspicuous expenditure.

Only a really carefree, sophisticated film maker could bring it off— and satisfy our desire for the unexpected that is also *right*. Truffaut is a director of incredible taste; he never carries a scene *too* far. It seems extraordinarily simple to complain that a virtuoso who can combine many moods has not stuck to one familiar old mood—but this is what the reviews seem to amount to. The modern novel has abandoned the old conception that each piece must be in place—abandoned it so thoroughly that when we read something like Angus Wilson's *Anglo-Saxon Attitudes* in which each piece does finally fit in place, we are astonished and amused at the dexterity of the accomplishment. That is the way Wilson works and it's wonderfully satisfying, but few modern novelists work that way; and it would be as irrelevant to the meaning and quality of, say, *Tropic of Capricorn* to complain that the plot isn't neatly tied together like *Great Expectations,* as to complain of the film *Shoot the Piano Player* that it isn't neatly tied together like *The Bicycle Thief.* Dwight Macdonald wrote that *Shoot the Piano Player* deliberately mixed up "three genres which are usually kept apart; crime melodrama, romance, and slapstick comedy." And, he says, "I thought the mixture didn't jell, but it was an exhilarating try." What I think is exhilarating in *Shoot the Piano Player* is that it *doesn't* "jell" and that the different elements keep *us* in a state of suspension—we react far more than we do to works that "jell." Incidentally, it's not completely accurate to say that these genres are usually kept apart: although *slapstick* rarely enters the mixture except in a far-out film like *Beat the Devil* or *Lovers and Thieves* or the new *The Manchurian Candidate,* there are numerous examples of crime melodrama-romance-comedy among well-known American films—particularly of the forties— for example *The Maltese Falcon, Casablanca, The Big Sleep, To Have and Have Not.* (Not all of Truffaut's models are cheap B pictures.)

Perhaps one of the problems that American critics and audiences may have with *Shoot the Piano Player* is a peculiarly American element in it—the romantic treatment of the man who walks alone. For decades our films were full of these gangsters, outcasts, detectives, cynics; Bogart epitomized them all—all the men who had been hurt by a woman or betrayed by their friends and who no longer trusted anybody. And although I think most of us enjoyed this romantic treatment of the man beyond the law, we rejected it intellectually. It was part of hack moviemaking—we might love it but it wasn't really intellectually respectable. And now here it is, inspired by our movies, and coming back to us via France. The heroine of *Shoot the Piano Player* says of the hero, "Even when he's with somebody, he walks alone." But this French hero carries his isolation much farther than the earlier American hero: when his girl is having a fight on his behalf and he is impelled to intervene, he says to himself, "You're out of it. Let them fight it out." He is brought into it; but where the American hero, once impelled to move, is a changed man and, redeemed by love or patriotism or a sense of fair play, he would take the initiative, save his girl, and conquer everything, this French hero simply moves into the situation when he must, when he can no longer stay out of it, and takes the consequences. He finds that the contact with people is once again defeating. He really doesn't believe in anything; the American hero only *pretended* he didn't.

*Breathless* was about active, thoughtless young people; *Shoot the Piano Player* is about a passive, melancholic character who is acted upon. Yet the world that surrounds the principal figures in these two movies is similar: the clowns in one are police, in the other gangsters, but this hardly matters. What we react to in both is the world of absurdities that is so much like our own world in which people suddenly and unexpectedly turn into clowns. But at the center is the sentimentalist—Belmondo in *Breathless*, Aznavour here—and I think there can be no doubt that both Godard and Truffaut love their heroes.

There are incidentally a number of little in-group jokes included in the film; a few of these are of sufficiently general interest to be worth mentioning, and, according to Andrew Sarris, they have been verified by Truffaut. The piano player is given the name of Saroyan as a tribute to William Saroyan, particularly for his volume of stories *The Man on the Flying Trapeze*, and also because Charles Aznavour, like Saroyan, is Armenian (and, I would surmise, for the playful irony of giving a life-evading hero the name of one of the most rambunctious of life-embracing writers). One of the hero's brothers in the film is named Chico, as a tribute to the Marx Brothers. And the impresario in the film, the major villain of the work, is called Lars Schmeel, as a disapproving gesture toward someone Truffaut does *not* admire—the impresario Lars Schmidt, known to us simply as Ingrid Bergman's current husband, but apparently known to others—and disliked by Truffaut—for his theatrical activities in Paris.

If a more pretentious vocabulary or a philosophic explanation will help: the piano player is intensely human and sympathetic, a character who empathizes with others, and with whom we, as audience, empathize; but he does not want to accept the responsibilities of his humanity—he asks only to be left alone. And because he refuses voluntary involvement, he is at the mercy of accidental forces. He is, finally, man trying to preserve his little bit of humanity in a chaotic world—it is not merely a world he never made but a world he would much rather forget about. But schizophrenia cannot be willed and so long as he is sane, he is only partly successful: crazy accidents happen—and sometimes he must deal with them. That is to say, no matter how far he retreats from life, he is not completely safe. And Truffaut himself is so completely engaged in life that he pleads for the piano player's right to be left alone, to live in his withdrawn state, *to be out of it*. Truffaut's plea is, of course, "Don't shoot the piano player."

### *"Jules and Jim"*

When the Legion of Decency condemned *Jules and Jim,* the statement read: the story has been developed "in a context alien to Christian and traditional natural morality." It certainly has. The Legion went on to say: "If the director has a definite moral viewpoint to express, it is so obscure that the visual amorality and immorality of the film are predominant and consequently pose a serious problem for a mass medium of entertainment." It would be possible to make a fraudulent case for the film's morality by pointing out that the adulterous individuals suffer and die, but this is so specious and so irrelevant to the meanings and qualities of the work that surely the Legion, expert in these matters, would recognize that it was casuistry. The Legion isn't wrong about the visual amorality either, and yet, *Jules and Jim* is not only one of the most beautiful films ever made, and the greatest motion picture of recent years, it is also, viewed as a work of art, exquisitely and impeccably *moral*. Truffaut does not have "a definite moral viewpoint to express" and he does not use the screen for messages or special pleading or to sell sex for money; he uses the film medium to express his love and knowledge of life as completely as he can.

The film is adapted from Henri-Pierre Roché's autobiographical novel, written when he was seventy-four, with some additional material from his even later work, *Deux Anglaises et le continent*. If some of us have heard of Roché, it's probably just the scrap of information that he was the man who introduced Gertrude Stein to Picasso—but this scrap shouldn't be discarded, because both Stein and Picasso are relevant to the characters and period of *Jules and Jim*. Roché is now dead, but the model for Catherine, the Jeanne Moreau role, is a German literary woman who is still alive; it was she who translated *Lolita* into German. Truffaut has indicated, also, that some of the material which he improvised on location was suggested by Apollinaire's letters to Madeleine—a girl whom he had met for a half-hour on a train.

The film begins in Paris before the First World War. Jules the Austrian (Oskar Werner) and Jim the Frenchmen (Henri Serre) are Mutt and Jeff, Sancho Panza and Don Quixote, devoted friends, contentedly arguing about life and letters. Catherine enters their lives, and Jules and Jim try to have both the calm of their friendship and the excitement of her imperious, magical presence. She marries Jules who can't hold her, and in despair he encourages Jim's interest in her—"That way she'll still be *ours.*" But Catherine can't subjugate Jim: he is too independent to be dominated by her whims. Not completely captivated, Jim fails to believe in her love when she most desperately offers it. She kills herself and him.

The music, the camera and editing movement, the rhythm of the film carry us along without pauses for reflection. Truffaut doesn't linger; nothing is held too long, nothing is overstated or even *stated.* Perhaps that's why others besides the Legion of Decency have complained: Stanley Kauffmann in the *New Republic* says that *Jules and Jim* "loses sight of purposes. . . . It is a confusion of the sheer happiness of being in the studio . . . with the reason for being there." Truffaut, the most youthfully alive and abundant of all the major film directors, needs a *reason* for making movies about as much as Picasso needs a reason for picking up a brush or a lump of clay. And of what film maker could a reference to a *studio* be less apt? He works everywhere and with anything at hand. Kauffmann says of *Jules and Jim,* "There is a lot less here than meets the eye," and Dwight Macdonald, who considers Kauffmann his only peer, is reassured: "one doesn't want to be the only square," he writes. If it gives him comfort to know there are two of them . . .

What is the film about? It's a celebration of life in a great historical period, a period of ferment and extraordinary achievement in painting and music and literature. Together Jules and Jim have a peaceful friendship (and Jim has a quiet love affair with Gilberte) but when Jules and Jim are with Catherine they feel alive. Anything may happen—she's the catalyst, the troublemaker, the source of despair as well as the source of joy. She is the enchantress who makes art out of life.

At the end, Jules, who has always given in to everything in order to keep Catherine, experiences relief at her death, although he has always delighted in the splendor she conferred on his existence. (Don't we all experience this sort of relief when we say goodbye to a particularly brilliant house guest?) The dullness in Jules, the bourgeois under the Bohemian, the passivity is made clear from the outset: it is why the girls don't fall in love with him. At the end, the excitements and the humiliations are over. He will have peace, and after a lifetime with Catherine he has earned it.

Catherine is, of course, a little crazy, but that's not too surprising. Pioneers can easily become fanatics, maniacs. And Catherine is part of a new breed—the independent, intellectual modern woman, so determined to live as freely as a man that while claiming equality she uses every feminine wile to gain extra advantages, to demonstrate her superiority, and to increase her power position. She is the emerging twentieth-century woman satirized by Strindberg, who also adored her; she is the woman with rights and responsibilities who entered Western literature after the turn of the century and has almost always been seen by the male authors as demanding the rights but refusing the responsibilities. This is the traditional male view of the feminist, and the film's view is not different. Don't we now hear complaints that Negroes are so sensitive about their rights that you can't treat them casually and equally as you would anybody else, you can't disagree on a job or question their judgment, you have to defer to their sensitivities and treat them as if they were super-whites—always in the right? So it is with Catherine.

Catherine, in her way, compensates for the homage she demands. She has, despite her need to intrude and to dominate, the gift for life. She holds nothing in reserve; she lives out her desires; when she can't control the situation, she destroys it. Catherine may be wrong-headed, as those who aspire to be free spirits often are (and they make this wrongness more visible than pliable, amiable people do), but she is devoid of hypocrisy and she doesn't lie. In one of the most upsetting and odd little scenes in the film she takes out a bottle which she says is "vitriol for lying eyes"—and Jim doesn't react any more than if it were aspirin. Catherine the free spirit has the insanity of many free spirits—she believes that she knows truth from lies, right from wrong. Her absolutism is fascinating, but it is also rather clearly *morally insane*. She punishes Jim because he has not broken with Gilberte, though she has not broken with Jules. Only the relationships *she* sets and dominates are *right*. Catherine suffers from the fatal ambivalence of the "free and equal" woman toward sex: she can leave men, but if they leave her, she is as abandoned and desolate, as destroyed and helpless as any clinging vine (perhaps *more* destroyed—she cannot even ask for sympathy). *Jules and Jim* is about the impossibility of freedom, as it is about the many losses of innocence.

All these elements are elliptical in the film—you catch them out of the corner of your eye and mind. So much happens in the span of an hour and three quarters that even if you don't take more than a fraction of the possible meanings from the material, you still get far more than if you examined almost any other current film, frame by frame, under a microscope. *Jules and Jim* is as full of character and wit and radiance as *Marienbad* is empty, and the performance by Jeanne Moreau is so vivid that the bored, alienated wife of *La Notte* is a faded monochrome. In *Jules and Jim* alienation is just one aspect of her character and we see how Catherine got there: she *becomes* alienated when she can't get her own way, when she is blocked. It is not a universal condition as in *La Notte* (neither Jules nor Jim shares in it): it is her developing insanity as she is cut off from what she wants and no longer takes pleasure in life.

Jules and Jim are portraits of artists as young men, but they are the kind of artists who grow up into something else—they become specialists in some field, or journalists; and the dedication to art of their youth becomes the *civilizing* influence in their lives. The war blasts the images of Bohemian life; both Jules and Jim are changed, but not Catherine. She is the unreconstructed Bohemian who does *not* settle down. She needed more strength, more will than they to live the artist's life—and this determination is the *un*civilizing factor. Bohemianism has made her, underneath all the graces, a moral barbarian: freedom has come to mean whatever she says it is. And when she loses what she believes to be freedom—when she can no longer dictate the terms on which Jim will live—she is lost, isolated. She no longer makes art out of life: she makes life hell.

She chooses death, and she calls on Jules to observe her choice, the last demonstration of her power over life and death, because Jules by a lifetime of yielding his own freedom to her has become, to her, a witness. He can only observe grand gestures; he cannot *make* them. In the last moment in the car, when self-destruction is completely determined, she smiles the smile of the statue: this was the mystery that drew them to her—the smile that looks so easy and natural but which is self-contained and impenetrable.

*Jules and Jim* ends after the burning of the books in Germany, the end of an epoch, as Truffaut has said, for intellectual Bohemians like Jules and Jim. The film is, in a way, a tribute to the books that were burned; I can't think of another movie so full of books, and of references to books and of writing and translating books. Books were the blood of these characters: they took their ideas of life from books, and writing books was their idea of living.

*Jules and Jim* is, among other things, the best movie ever made about what I guess most of us think of as the Scott Fitzgerald period (though it begins much earlier). Catherine jumping into the waters of the Seine to demonstrate her supremacy over Jules and Jim, who are discussing the weaknesses of women, is not unlike Zelda jumping over that balustrade. This film treatment of the period is a work of lyric poetry and a fable of the world as playground, a work of art as complex and suggestive in its way as the paintings and poetry and novels and music of the period that it is based on. It is a tribute to the school of Paris when art and Paris were synonymous; filmically it is a new school of Paris—and the new school of Paris is cinema. You go to movies, you talk movies, and you make movies. The young French painters don't compare with the Americans, and French literature is in a fancy trance, but oh, how the young French artists can make movies!

Several of the critics, among them Kauffmann, have complained that the song Jeanne Moreau sings is irrelevant to the action of the film. It's embarrassing to have to point out the obvious, that the song is the theme and spirit of the film: Jules and Jim and Catherine are the ones who "make their way in life's whirlpool of days—round and round together bound." And, in the film, the song is an epiphany: when Catherine sings, the story is crystallized, and the song, like Jim and the child rolling on the hill, seems to belong to memory almost before it is over. In the same way, the still shots catch for us, as for the characters, the distillation, the beauty of the moment. Throughout the film, Georges Delerue's exquisite music— simple and fragrant, popular without being banal—is part of the atmosphere; it is so evocative that if you put the music on the phonograph, like the little phrase from Vinteuil's sonata, it brings back the images, the emotions, the experience. Though emotionally in the tradition of Jean Renoir, as a work of film craftsmanship *Jules and Jim* is an homage to D. W. Griffith. Truffaut explores the medium, plays with it, overlaps scenes, uses fast cutting in the manner of *Breathless* and leaping continuity in the manner of *Zero for Conduct,* changes the size and shape of the images as Griffith did, and in one glorious act of homage he recreates a frame out of *Intolerance,* the greatest movie ever made. *Jules and Jim* is the most exciting movie made in the West since *L'Avventura* and *Breathless* and Truffaut's earlier *Shoot the Piano Player;* because of the beauty and warmth of its images, it is a richer, a more satisfying film than any of them. I think it will rank among the great lyric achievements of the screen, right up there with the work of Griffith and Renoir.

# "Jules and Jim": A Masculine Couple

## Dominique Fanne

There is a saying that love is destroyed by familiarity; Truffaut has explored this thesis in the concept of friendship, with the story of Jules and Jim. Jules and Jim, a masculine couple in the grand style of Laurel and Hardy, Bourvil and de Funès—a pair of opposites, one tall and thin, the other small and solid, Henri Serre and Oskar Werner. They are accomplices, they exchange ideas and hats; together they enjoy trivial pleasures, they explore their differences with tenderness. From the beginning of their friendship, they fall into the pattern of Don Quixote and Sancho Panza. Then, all at once, the smile of a statue appears—Catherine. The threesome, the couple *à trois,* is born. Is such a thing possible? Will this new morality permit the friendship to survive?

### Composition with a Young Girl

Beside Jules, Jim, and Catherine appears a little girl, Sabine. Sabine is the daughter of Catherine and Jules, but she is as familiar with Jim as she is with her father. Daughter of Jules, she resembles him not a whit. Daughter of Catherine, she has only her gesture of rubbing at her eyes. Her birth was difficult because "her parents were not in a state of grace."

When Catherine visits Jim in the chalet, Jules, outside, plays horse-and-rider with Sabine. Then the camera draws them all together, united and happy.[1] Jim rolls in the grass with Sabine and the music of the soundtrack mingles with Sabine's laughter. Jim plays with Sabine, the child, but the physical contact with her brings him close once more to the mother. And when the game is over, Jim and Catherine each take one of Sabine's hands. Only Jules walks alone, framed at the right of the image, as if the couple

1. Jean Renoir said: "There are certain shots in *Jules and Jim* that make me die of envy. I say to myself: *I* should have done these things, not Truffaut."

From *L'Univers de François Truffaut* by Dominique Fanne (Paris: Les Éditions du Cerf, 1972). Reprinted by permission of the publisher. Translated especially for this volume by Sallie Iannotti; title supplied by the editors.

were, at that moment, Catherine and Jim, with Sabine. Throughout the film the placement of the little girl in the compositions is filled with meaning.[2] She is the one, for example, who takes the guitar to Albert. Most often she is framed with either Jules or Jim depending upon which is most separated from Catherine. After Jim and Catherine have spent their night together, Sabine takes Jim's place in the domino game with Jules; and when the four of them are walking together, as in the scene when the train pulls out, Jules and Sabine are side by side. When Albert threatens the solidity of their foursome, it is Jim who takes Sabine upon his bicycle.

### An Unattainable Maternity

All eyes meet—and three madcaps collapse in laughter—over this little girl, who is, in fact, another aspect of Catherine, an alter ego. The camera focuses upon her happily dozing in a hammock, and Truffaut takes her off the screen after her mother's death and the funerals, so that she will never be seen except when she is happy and at one with the world. She is the symbol of realized maternity; in her, Catherine achieves the motherhood lacking earlier in the film. *Jules and Jim* is the story of a mother. "My daughter," Catherine says to Jim, "draws me to her like a lover." And the last line (not in the film but in the book), "I am first of all a mother." Thus, in addition to the pairing of man and woman, there are three other pairs: man and man, man and child, and woman and child.

Truffaut has put on film the theme of birth—it is even more in evidence in the script—a theme of equally great moment to Roché, especially in the book, *Deux Anglaises et le continent*. For Catherine, love makes no sense except for the creation of new life. This is true for Jim, too, who says to her: "We talk of nothing but love. And what is love's aim? The creation of children. . . ." Catherine compares the beginning of their friendship to a newborn baby, and they exist as a couple only through their desire for a child. Because Albert becomes Catherine's lover, Jim and Catherine must give up for a time the idea of having a child; and without that mutual goal, tension visibly mounts between them. They even seek medical advice when they see at last that Catherine is not going to become pregnant. Roché has a marvelous passage: "They walked together into the deep woods, and there under the big trees they made love. Jim lifted Kate up by her feet and swung her gently back and forth as if he were shaking down a little sack of walnuts, in the hope of increasing their chances of having a baby." As a couple, they cannot survive without that hope, and they break up when the child does not appear. As Catherine leaves Jim she says: "Every night I have the feeling I am being tested. I think of the child we do not have . . .

---

2. Such as the shot of the rocking chair and its occupant.

and I love you less." They are reconciled when Catherine discovers she is pregnant. She writes him:

> There are so many things on earth we do not understand, and so many unbelievable things that are true. At last I am pregnant, Jim—thank God, bow down and thank Him. I am sure, absolutely sure, that you are the father of this child, I beg you to believe me—your love is part of my life; you live inside me, Jim; for three months you have lived in me. This paper is your flesh, this ink my blood. I am pressing hard so that it will penetrate—write to me quickly.

They break off once more when the fetus dies, and Jules writes to Jim: "The child died in the first trimester of the pregnancy. Catherine wants no further contact with you."

The film is centered, always, around the child, and the commentary continues: "The two of them had created nothing. Jim thought: It is a marvelous thing to want to rediscover the laws of humanity, but how convenient it must be to conform to existing laws. We played with the very source of life. And we lost."

From this moment on, the die is cast. Jules puts the children he has always dreamed of out of his mind and turns back to his books and his insects. Jim decides to marry Gilberte because "we can still have children."

> "A beautiful story, Jim," says Catherine, "but what of me, Jim, of me and those little ones I wanted so badly. You didn't want them, Jim... "
> "But Catherine, I did ..."
> "They would have been so beautiful, Jim ..."

Catherine in her despair resembles Muriel, in *Deux Anglaises,* who writes in her journal: "Sometimes there is a chamber of horrors in my brain. My past is filled with the dead. Our dead children, Claude's and mine. He has no idea—but I look at them. Here is one, so small, lying across the bed, his head tilted back and his hands like ice. And here, here, are all of them, all the others.... Oh, I would have loved them so.

In the script of *Jules and Jim* Catherine reads the passage of the child's death in *Elective Affinities* and begins to cry.[3] And in the film a brief shot after the war shows "the military cemetery which school children already come to visit."

3. Roché quotes a different passage from Goethe's book. Truffaut's switch is interesting, even if it did not appear in the film itself.

### An Inherent Division

Thus, in *Jules and Jim* the child holds the most important place, the center of both understanding and dislocation between the couples. From the celebration of the statue on the island to the words which Jules and Jim speak of Catherine: "Image-woman for all men, not a woman, perhaps, for anyone," there is an expressed incompatibility between men and women, an inherent division, an original schism. Jim is separated from Catherine, after having loved her, when their child dies. Jules, for whom love is an absolute (as it is for Lena) loses Catherine. Catherine commits suicide. Once again, then, death, suicide, and the world of nature, more symbolic here than ever: the characters plunge into the forest, fleeing civilization, but it is all in vain.

Jules, too, is destroyed: "Thus, for Jules, their love became relative, even as his own was absolute"—because, while he can meditate upon Catherine, he cannot possess her. His tender gestures misfire; adjusting her wrap as they leave the Ursulines, the unexpected cut to a tracking shot of Catherine in the monk's cell where she has taken refuge, the close-up of their faces and the tale of the Chinese Emperor, the fleeting shot of Jule's contorted features after Catherine slaps him—all these indicate a disjointedness, which nothing will heal. And the threesome, too, like Truffaut's earlier couples, is a failure. Jules gives Catherine to Jim, largely in order not to lose her completely himself:

> Jim, Catherine doesn't love me any longer. I'm terrified that I will lose her, that she will go out of my life entirely. Love her, Jim, marry her, only let me see her—what I am trying to say is, if you love her, don't think of me as an obstacle any more.

But little by little he must give her up. Neither the couples nor the friendship of the two men can survive, and Jim and Catherine die.

Once again, then, in spite of this new attempt, in spite of the "feeling of their innocence" which Catherine holds on to, the bond between man and woman is broken. No rule of living, no ethic, seems to support this bond. Jim and Catherine are not even united in death, and Jules is unable to mingle their ashes. "Left to himself, Jules would have mingled them; Catherine had always wanted to have hers strewn to the winds from the crest of a hill, but this was not permitted."

Truffaut was thinking, perhaps, of Renoir's words: "In this day and age we are not ripe enough to converse intimately with Venus." The fairy tale that Jim was writing ends on a sour note. Between man and woman, alas, intimacy is always tragic. Theresa, that shooting star, a momentary flicker in Jules's life, illustrates it clearly; repulsing all these destructions, she runs away from love when she feels the first rough touches of the ties which begin to bind her life with that of another.

# "The Story of Adèle H."

## Stanley Kauffmann

There are three good reasons to see *The Story of Adèle H*. Two of them are familiar: the direction of François Truffaut and the cinematography of Nestor Almendros. The third is a very welcome new reason: the acting of Isabelle Adjani, who plays Adèle. At the last the film is one more of Truffaut's conscious/unconscious deceptions, but these three talents are splendid.

Romance in its lushest sense—the adoration of the adoration of woman by man or vice versa—has always been a strong trait in Truffaut. It begins in his first short film *Les Mistons,* where some 12-year-old boys are jealously enraptured by an older couple's rapture, and it continues here. His new script, by himself and two previous collaborators, Jean Gruault and Suzanne Schiffman, comes from the journals of Adèle Hugo, the younger daughter of Victor Hugo, and it tells a passionate tale.

It begins in 1863 with the arrival of Adèle in Nova Scotia. She is in pursuit of a young English officer, Lieutenant Pinson, with whom she has had an affair on the island of Guernsey, where she was sharing her father's political exile. When Pinson was transferred, Adèle followed him, via England and New York, without invitation or encouragement. Now he makes very clear that he is no longer interested in her and wishes her to leave, certainly to leave him alone. She remains, persists in pursuit, and is always rebuffed; soon the eccentricities that have been apparent in her from the start deepen into dementia.

She writes to her father, on whom she depends for money, that she is married to Pinson, and Hugo announces it in a Guernsey newspaper. (It's only about halfway through the film that her father's identity is revealed, but few will not know it beforehand through the publicity and reviews.) She pretends pregnancy by Pinson. She is so slavishly devoted to him that she even engages a prostitute and sends her to Pinson because this marvelous man must have all the women in the world. Adèle spies on his meetings

From *The New Republic,* January 24, 1976. Copyright © 1976 by Stanley Kauffmann. Reprinted by permission of Brandt & Brandt.

with his mistress but doesn't interfere. At last, to his relief, he is transferred to Barbados. But she follows, now unmistakably psychotic. The
climax comes when Pinson, who has married, seeks out Adèle in pity. She
is now a homeless vagrant. The distraught, ragged girl walks right past him
in a Barbados street, staring-eyed, unrecognizing. She collapses soon after.
A sympathetic black woman, who has learned her identity, writes to her
father and escorts Adèle back to him.

What a relief, right after Kubrick's *Barry Lyndon* which plasters us
with gobs of gorgeousness, to see filmmaking as deft as Truffaut's. He
knows exactly what to show and what to leave out, how to create substance
by ellipsis (something he learned from his master Renoir). His film
*courses,* without hurrying. (It's only 97 minutes.) And although its essence
is loneliness and waiting, a pulse of action beats in it. From the very first
shot, of Adèle landing in a long boat at night, Truffaut provides the flavor
of romance, a girl pursuing her love across the sea. The whole account of
her devotion, of her quasi adoption by her landlady, of the affection of an
old cabbie and of the quiet affection of a young bookseller from whom she
buys paper for her journal, the narrow streets, the threatening skies—all
this is very Brontë.

Truffaut has always had a feeling for panache, and he makes the most
here of military costumes (appearing briefly in one himself), of cavalry
maneuvers, of regimental discipline. He handles dreams, both sleeping and
waking, beautifully: Adèle's dreams of her sister Leopoldine, who had
drowned twenty years earlier, in which she feels herself to be drowning; or
a moment in a bank when a little boy asks her name and she says "Leopoldine." Even the fact that she comes back to tell the boy the truth is part of
the daytime dream—why would the boy care? This matter of who she is *to
herself,* in relation to the towering father who was nearly maddened by her
sister's death, in relation to Pinson who denies her the role of wife, is
central to the story.

Almendros' camera understands everything perfectly. He photographed *Two English Girls* for Truffaut, as well as several Eric Rohmer
films, and it's indisputable that by now he ranks with Sven Nykvist as one
of the world princes of cinematography. What's especially noteworthy is
that, unlike John Alcott's recent work for Kubrick, Almendros doesn't
impose gorgeousness: he *finds* the right color—finding romance, if he
needs to, in gray wet stone.

Isabelle Adjani, the Adèle, is lovely, exciting, fine-spirited and true.
Her face—dark-eyed, high-cheekboned but soft—is perfect nineteenth-
century. It's probably perfect for any century, but being a good actress, she
makes us think here of daguerrotypes. And there is never any space between her and the role, not a sliver. From the first moment we never even

think about whether she will fill the part; the only question is sometimes the other way around—is there enough size in the role as written for the being she brings to it? We're certainly going to see more of Adjani.

And in the deserved fuss about her, let's not overlook Bruce Robinson, the Pinson. He has the always-uncomfortable job of being a credible object of mad devotion; he does it, and he gives a good performance as well.

But is *The Story of Adèle H.* what it says it is? A prefatory note states, very emphatically, that the film is entirely true. It is not. First, Adjani looks, at most, 20. The gravestone that Truffaut himself shows us says that she was born in 1830; so she was 33 at the time the story begins. Immediately this fact converts the real Adèle at least from a Nina in *The Sea Gull* to a Sonia in *Uncle Vanya* and makes it a story of quite different colors.

There are other distortions, pointed out in recent letters to the *Times Literary Supplement* (Dec. 26, 1975) from Shirley Jones of the University of London and Joanna Richardson of Oxford. It's a very open question whether Adèle and Pinson ever had an affair at all. Truffaut uses a deep voice on the soundtrack, representing Hugo, to read letters from the father to Adèle, but Hugo was so outraged by her behavior that he deputed his son François-Victor to write to her. One would never know from the film that it was nine years before Adèle returned to France, to spend the rest of her life in a mental asylum. There are more falsifications.

Now the interest in these matters is not academic nicety but why Truffaut chose to falsify and felt it necessary, in advance, to deny it. Clearly he has compulsions. He wanted, he needed, a fragile young nineteenth-century romantic figure, in a romantic relation to her famous father and her dead sister, not a woman past first youth, suffering from the anger of her famous father and driven by sex frustrations into insanity.

Truffaut's romantic blurring of psychopathy in women is prominent in many of his films. Catherine in *Jules and Jim* is, under the *belle époque* glamor, a crazy killer. The "other woman" in *The Soft Skin* murders the man with horrible brutality. The heroine of *The Bride Wore Black* is a cold-blooded revenger luring men to their deaths with her sex. The heroine of *Mississippi Mermaid* is a criminal trickster. The heroine of *Such A Gorgeous Kid like Me* uses sex to dupe a man into prison. After this list of varyingly abnormal women, dangerous only to men, it's interesting to note that in Truffaut's first feature film *The 400 Blows,* which is autobiographical, the boy's mother is unfaithful to his father and has mixed feelings toward her son.

Although Adèle is not a killer, she is certainly dangerous to Pinson. Although she is clinically unstable from the start, Truffaut sees her through lyrical-melancholy eyes. And in addition to this temperamental distortion, Truffaut adds distortion of fact. And in addition to all these distortions, he insists on protesting that the film is true. Up to now one could think that his sentiment about mad and dangerous women was at least partly uncon-scious; but how can one think so here?

# Orson Welles

ORSON WELLES *was born George Orson Welles in 1915 in Kenosha, Wisconsin. Already a precocious actor, director, and adapter of plays as a schoolboy, at age sixteen he convinced the founders of the Gate Theatre in Dublin that he was a famous New York actor. As a result he worked at the Gate and also at the Abbey Theatre for a year. After scattered free-lance work in literature and publishing in New York, he took the recommendation of Thornton Wilder and joined Katherine Cornell's acting company, playing in Shakespeare, Shaw, and Chekhov. In 1936 he joined John Houseman on the Negro Theater Project, directing most notably a* Macbeth *set in Henri Christophe's Haiti. Houseman and Welles then formed another Federal Theater group, Project #891, to put on classic plays. (Welles was meanwhile working also on radio, furnishing voices for* commercials, The March of Time, *and* The Shadow.)*

During the next two years Welles and Houseman co-produced (Welles directing), nine productions, including* Doctor Faustus, *in which Welles starred, and* The Cradle Will Rock, *concerning Sacco and Vanzetti, which caused the Works Progress Administration to close down the company. In 1937 Welles and Houseman formed the Mercury Theatre and began their repertory with a modern-dress* Julius Caesar *(Welles playing Brutus), complete with overtones of Mussolini and contemporary Fascism. The radio version of* The War of the Worlds *in 1938 caused a short-lived panic with its mixture of documentary and science fiction. It was part of a weekly Mercury Theatre of the Air series produced for CBS.*

*Buoyed by his New York notoriety as a boy wonder, Welles arrived in Hollywood in 1939 to make movies for RKO, with a contract guaranteeing him a control over production that few Hollywood directors had ever had. His first film was the celebrated* Citizen Kane *(1941). Controversy has recently arisen over the relative contributions of Welles, Herman Mankiewicz, the scriptwriter, and Gregg Toland, the cameraman, to the overall effect of* Kane. *But Welles's impress is everywhere in the film, and the production is hardly conceivable apart from his direction or his performance as the central character.*

*Much of* Kane's *visual style can be traced to its origins in the expressionist social realism of German and Soviet films, as well as the films of John Ford, whom Welles acknowledged as his master. (Welles claims to have screened* Stagecoach *more than forty times before starting* Kane.) *But the force of* Kane *then and now rests in Welles's unparalleled ability to push every detail and conjuring device to its utmost, like the magician who reveals the secret life of objects and the invisible connections of the universe. The intricately articulated space of Ford's stagecoach interior expands in* Kane *to encompass, in deep focus, the layer upon layer of Kane's complex life.*

*After* Kane, *Welles's reputation as filmmaker was secure, but his career became subject to a series of stops and starts, until he became almost the archetype of the genius unappreciated or thwarted by the "industry." In part because of adverse publicity from the Hearst press,* Kane *did poorly at the box office, and RKO breached its contract, refusing to allow Welles to finish editing his second film* The Magnificent Ambersons *(1942) and taking him off* Journey into Fear, *a parodic thriller written and acted by Welles and Joseph Cotten (an old Mercury Theatre associate who had starred in* Kane *and* Ambersons). *Norman Foster finished the film but the result still seems heavily under Welles's influence.*

*Following this brief period with RKO, Welles never again found secure financing and facilities within Hollywood. His next two films,* The Stranger *(1946) and* The Lady From Shanghai *(1948), were made as independent projects, with Hollywood sufferance. After their unsatisfactory financial performance, Welles produced a shoestring film of* Macbeth *in Haiti and then went to Europe, where he made* Othello *(1951) and* Mr. Arkadin *(1955). His difficulties in getting funding for projects and in completing them once started are shown by the amount of time between films—*Touch of Evil *(1958),* The Trial *(1962),* Chimes at Midnight *(1966),* Immortal Story *(1968)—each a fascinating work, but, because of the long-drawn-out production periods, often uneven in quality. In between, Welles raised money by acting and by again applying his sonorous voice to commercials.*

*Welles has remained a tremendous influence on filmmakers, not only because of his stature and his commitment to his own art and vision, but also because of his eagerness to experiment with the accepted storytelling methods and the visual techniques of films. Different as his films are, his signature is an often fractured, discontinuous narrative of great force, generally focusing on a powerful and enigmatic central character, played by Welles himself. Welles's stamp is visible on all his films, whether the source is a detective thriller, like* Touch of Evil, *or Shakespeare. In part perhaps because Welles's acting has been a more steady source of income and artistic growth than his filmmaking, his films themselves often seem to be testaments to the conflicting claims of actor and director in Welles's artistic nature. Their spectacular visual and narrative effects, which are assertions of the filmmaker's shaping power, are often qualified by the Faustian ironies of their plots, where grandiose assertion turns out to be an empty illusion. Like Fellini, Welles, who is a brilliant amateur magician, is fascinated by the con man, although in Welles's films such characters are drawn on a larger scale or have higher cultural aspirations than Fellini's.* F for Fake *(1974), a tale of art forgery, only makes this central theme more apparent and thereby less persuasive.*

*The critical literature on Welles is large but often skewed by a fascination with Welles's personality apart from his films. Significant works are those by André Bazin (1977; in French, 1950); Charles Higham (1970); Pauline Kael (1971); Joseph McBride (1972); and Peter Cowie (1973). See also the section on* Kane *in Peter Bogdanovich's* Pieces of Time *(1973) and the reminiscences in John Houseman's autobiography,* Run-Through *(1972). Ronald Gottesman has edited two anthologies dealing with Welles, on* Citizen Kane *(1971) and on Welles's career (1976). Pauline Kael includes the shooting script of Kane as part of* The Citizen Kane Book *(1971). William Johnson surveys the whole oeuvre in "Orson Welles: Of Time and Loss"* (Film Quarterly, *1967), reprinted in Gottesman's earlier volume.*

# "Citizen Kane":
# The American Baroque

## Andrew Sarris

Within the maze of its own aesthetic, *Kane* develops two interesting themes: the debasement of the private personality of the public figure and the crushing weight of materialism. Taken together, these two themes comprise the bitter irony of an American success story that ends in futile nostalgia, loneliness, and death. The fact that the personal theme is developed verbally while the materialistic theme is developed visually creates a distinctive stylistic counterpoint. Against this counterpoint, the themes unfold within the structure of a mystery story.

Charles Foster Kane dies in a lonely castle. His last word is "Rosebud." Who or what is "Rosebud?" This is the mystery of *Citizen Kane*. The detective is a reporter for a news service which produces *March of Time*-like newsreels. The suspects are all the persons and objects Kane encountered in his cluttered life. The clues are planted in the film on three occasions, but unlike the conventional-mystery key, "Rosebud" is the answer to a man's life rather than his death. And since the intangible meanings of life end in the mystery of death, "Rosebud" is not the final solution but only the symbolic summation.

"Rosebud" is the means through which the past history of Charles Foster Kane is penetrated by the reporter-detective and the omniscient camera. Time is thrown back and brought forward in the four major movements of the film, the flashback-recollections of, respectively, Kane's banker-guardian, his business manager, his best friend, and his second wife. Each major flashback begins at a later point in time than its predecessor, but each flashback overlaps with at least one of the others so that the same event or period is seen from two or three points of view.

There is a fifth flashback—a newsreel of Kane's public career—which establishes the identity of Charles Foster Kane for the first time in the film.

Excerpted from *Film Culture*, no. 9, 1956. Reprinted by permission of *Film Culture*.

There is no transition between the opening scene of a man dying in a lonely castle with "Rosebud" on his lips and the startling appearance of the unframed newsreel. This is the first shock effect in *Citizen Kane,* and it has received undeserved abuse as a spectacularly devious method of narration. What has been generally overlooked is the great economy of this device in establishing the biographical premises of the film, without resorting to traditional montages of public reactions and telescoped historical events in the major movements of the story.

By isolating the newsreel from the main body of his film, Welles frees his flashbacks from the constricting demands of exposition, enabling his main characters to provide insights on the external outlines of the Kane biography. After the newsreel, the transitions are worked out very carefully through the logical movements of the reporter-detective. This shadowy, though thoroughly professional character links the present to the past in an interlocking jigsaw puzzle with one elusive piece—"Rosebud"—appearing only at the very end in the reporter's absence since his services are no longer needed.

The newsreel accomplishes more than a skeletal public biography of Charles Foster Kane. On a narrative level, it introduces Mr. Thatcher, Kane's banker-guardian, whose memoirs will provide the first personal flashback of Kane's life and the first significant clue to "Rosebud." The newsreel also produces a paradox that previsions the nonpolitical quality of the film. While Thatcher is telling a committee that Kane is a Communist, a speaker in Union Square attacks Kane as a Fascist. The elderly Kane tells newsreel audiences that he is and always has been an American. This is the first indication that Kane is not really committed to any cause but Kane.

The newsreel fades out; a sudden establishing shot picks up a darkened projection room. The first of the many disembodied voices in the film calls out from the darkness, and the shadow plot of *Citizen Kane* begins. A group of cynical newsmen discuss ways of pepping up the newsreel. The reporter is sent out to find the secret of "Rosebud." The semicolloquial dialogue is driven forth with relentless persistence from every direction. There is nothing profound or witty about any of it, but it moves quickly and economically.

The reporter begins his search, and the major movements of *Citizen Kane* begin. Through a hard, wide-angle lens, the reporter enters a cavernous museum, a dingy nightclub, a solidly upholstered office, a drab hospital ward, the gloomy mansion of Charles Foster Kane. The reporter's world is functional, institutional: an aging, weathered gateway to the life and time of Charles Foster Kane.

The sixth and last flashback of *Citizen Kane* offers the final clue to "Rosebud" and brings the reporter's quest to its unsuccessful conclusion.

Interestingly enough, the three clues to "Rosebud" appear at times when Kane is being treated most remotely—in the cryptic death-scene in the beginning, in the unfriendly memoirs of his banker-guardian, and in the final flashback narration of a cynical butler. The narrations of his closest acquaintances yield no clues to the symbolic truth of his life. This is the ultimate confirmation of Kane's spiritual loneliness, and it is upon this loneliness that the mystery structure of the film is based.

The mystery of "Rosebud" is solved in a memorable manner. The reporter and his entourage have departed from the Kane castle. As the cynical butler is directing the disposal of Kane's "junk" into the furnace, a workman picks up a sled in routine haste and dumps it into the flames. The camera closes in on the surface of the sled and the name "Rosebud" as the letters are dissolving in liquid fire. The audience is given the solution with the added knowledge that no one living on the screen will ever know the secret of "Rosebud."

This solution has been attacked as a trick ending unworthy of its theme. Yet without this particular resolution, the film would remain a jumbled jigsaw puzzle. The burning sled is apt not only as a symbolic summation but also as a symbolic revelation. The reporter, the butler, the workman, the friends, the enemies, the acquaintances of Kane never discover "Rosebud" because it is lost amid the "junk" of Kane's materialistic existence.

Kane's tragedy lies in the inability of the props of experience to compensate for the bare emotional stage of his human relationships. Charles Foster Kane collected valuable treasures from all over the world, but his last thoughts were of a sled he used as a boy, before great wealth came into his life. At one point in the film, he tells his banker-guardian that he might have been a great man if he had not been so wealthy. "Rosebud" became the focal point of his nostalgia for a different turning point in his life. Kane's view of his own life is deterministic, and Kane's image throughout the film is remarkably consistent with this sense of determinism.

The apparent intellectual superficiality of *Citizen Kane* can be traced to the shallow quality of Kane himself. Even when Kane is seen as a crusading journalist battling for the lower classes, overtones of stiff self-idolatry mar his actions. His clever ironies are more those of the exhibitionist than the crusader. His best friend—a detached observer functioning as a sublimated conscience—remarks to the reporter that Kane never gave anything away: "He left you a tip." His second wife complained that Kane never gave her anything that was part of him, only material possessions that he might give a dog. His business adviser and life-long admirer expressed the other side of Kane's personality, when he observed that Kane wanted something more than money.

In each case, Kane's character is described in materialistic terms. What Kane wanted—love, emotional loyalty, the unspoiled world of his boyhood symbolized by "Rosebud"—he was unable to provide to those about him or buy for himself. It is, therefore, fitting that the story of Kane should begin with his lonely death and conclude with the immolation of his life symbol.

The technique of Welles and his photographer, Gregg Toland, justifies the narrative structure. Apparently outrageous effects fall into place once the pattern of the film is discernible. *Kane* opens on a solid wire fence with a sign reading "No Trespassing." The camera moves up on a painted castle against a background of dark, brooding clouds. The same shots are repeated in reverse at the very end of the film. This initial and concluding clash of realism and expressionism flanks one of the most stylistically varied of all films.

The opening shots have been attacked as pretentious and the closing shots as anticlimactic. Yet, in a subtle way, the beginning and end of *Citizen Kane* suggest its theme. The intense material reality of the fence dissolves into the fantastic unreality of the castle and, in the end, the mystic pretension of the castle dissolves into the mundane substance of the fence. Matter has come full circle from its original quality to the grotesque baroque of its excess.

As each flashback unfolds, the visual scenario of *Citizen Kane* orchestrates the dialogue. A universe of ceilings dwarfs Kane's personal stature. He becomes the prisoner of his possessions, the ornament of his furnishings, the fiscal instrument of his collections. His booming voice is muffled by walls, carpets, furniture, hallways, stairs, and vast recesses of useless space.

Toland's camera setups are designed to frame characters in the oblique angles of light and shadow created by their artificial environment. There are no luminous close-ups in which faces are detached from their backgrounds. When characters move across rooms, the floors and ceilings move with them, altering the points of reference but never transcending them. This technique draws attention to itself both because it is so unusual and because it tends to dehumanize characters by reducing them to fixed ornaments in a shifting architecture.

Sound montage is used intensively within the flashbacks to denote the interval of time within two related scenes. A character will begin a sentence and complete it weeks, months, or years later in a different location. On occasion, one character will begin the sentence, and another will com-

plete it in the same manner. This device results in a constriction of time and
an elimination of transitional periods of rest and calm. Aside from the
aesthetic dividends of pacing and highlighting, *Kane*'s sound montage
reinforces the unnatural tension of the central character's driving, joyless
ambition. In all respects, *Kane*'s technique is a reflection and projection of
the inhuman quality of its protagonist.

One brilliant use of sound montage that has generally been ignored as
a piece of aural gargoyle is the piercing scream of a parakeet that precedes
the last appearance of Kane in the film. One flashback and several scenes
previously, Kane and his second wife are arguing in a tent surrounded by
hundreds of Kane's picnic guests. A shrill scream punctuates the argument
with a persistent, sensual rhythm. It is clear that some sexual outrage is
being committed. When the parakeet screams at the appearance of Kane,
the sound linkage in tone but not in time further dehumanizes Kane's
environment. In the baroque world that he has created, Kane is isolated
from even the most dubious form of humanity.

Kane's lack of humanity is consistently represented in the performance of Orson Welles, who alters the contours of Kane's rigidity from
youth to old age. As a young man, Kane is peculiarly joyless. A gala
occasion is recalled in which Kane threw a party for his new writers hired
away from a competing newspaper. A group of chorus girls come on the
scene. Kane is thrown in their midst and begins cutting up. The scene is
heavy with Kane's studied posturing as the life of the party.

The acting in *Kane* emerges as an elaborate arabesque of interrupted
conversations, harsh dissonances, and awkward physical confrontations.
Kane's world, peopled by Mercury Players, is tuned to the egocentric
performance of Welles. Joseph Cotten, Everett Sloane, and Dorothy Comingore, as Kane's best friend, business adviser, and second wife, respectively, and the main narrators of the film, achieve a strident rapport
with the demanding presence of Welles. The intense pitch of the acting
charges each line of dialogue with unexpected meanings. The manner of expression often alters the verbal content toward a new level of
self-conscious cynicism. In this, the acting evokes the intentional hypocrisy of the few protestations of principle that appear in the script.

Toward the end of his life, Kane reacts to the desertion of his second
wife by wrecking the furniture in her room. Again, his violent actions are
rigidly controlled by a chilling self-awareness. As he is completing his
unduly methodical havoc, he comes upon a crystal paperweight in which a
minute snow storm beats down on a miniature cottage. He speaks the name
of "Rosebud" and walks past an array of guests across the path of endless
mirrors and endless reflections of his image—mere repetitions of his ego

without magnification. This is the final arithmetic of Kane's life, the last material accounting of his greatness.

*Citizen Kane* presents an intense vision of American life, distorting and amplifying its materialistic elements at the expense of human potentialities. The implied absence of free will in the development of Kane's character is thematically consistent with the moral climate of his environment. Kane's magnitude, unchecked by limiting principles or rooted traditions, becomes the cause of his spiritual ruin. Kane emerges as an extension of the *nouveau-riche* American seeking a living culture in the dead relics of the past. Striving desperately to transcend his material worth, Kane is victimized by the power his wealth possesses to alter the moral quality of his actions. In the end, everything has been bought and paid for, but nothing has been felt.

# Welles and His Wonders

## Otis Ferguson

To make any sense about technical innovations in any one movie, one should, in an ideal state at least, have some idea of the general technique of making every movie. Before coming to the wonders of *Citizen Kane,* therefore, we will just run over a few fundamentals (we will, that is, if anyone is still around when these wandering messages of mine catch up with themselves).

The first thing necessary to a movie is a story, and the first thing necessary to stories for the screen is a writer who understands the screen and works along the line the director will take later, preferably with the director. But the most important thing in the technique of a motion picture—and here director and writer are in varying degrees inter-dependent—is its construction shot by shot, not for the effect or punch line of any one fragment, but for such devising and spacing as avoid monotony, hold the interest, and lead easily from one thing into another, *the devices for illusion being always and necessarily hidden in the natural emergence of the illusion itself.* One scene may be broken down into six or twenty camera positions, yet these shifts you are not conscious of: you follow the actor across the room and pick him up coming through the door; you may not see him when he is speaking; you may see only his face when someone else is speaking; he turns to look through a window and suddenly you are looking out the window. These are the smallest things, but they make for pace and variety—which will be the biggest things before you are through.

A scene is made, another to fit with it; there may be interscenes, or long shots covering action, establishing atmosphere; later there will be inserts, titles, the transitional devices of trick or straight cutting, dissolves, montages. At the end of maybe five, maybe ten, days' work you will have

From *The Film Criticism of Otis Ferguson,* edited by Robert Wilson (Philadelphia: Temple University Press, 1971). Reprinted by permission of Robert Wilson and Temple University Press. This essay originally appeared in *The New Republic,* June 16, 1941.

a sequence, that is, an essential incident in the story carried through from start to finish. And the next sequence should take up without jar, without confusion, and lead on again, shot by shot and scene by scene, in the right way of the story. Finally when all the sequences have been made and assembled in a rough-cut, you must study over and over this familiar work of weeks to inquire whether what you put in it is there, to study it for continuity of mood, for how well the sequences match and balance—and for where to cut, where to remake. Does it move, does it complete its circle, do characters and ideas and the express meaning come alive in action? Maybe you've got a picture, but it won't be by chance.

It is true that of all the arts, movies are farthest from being one-man shows. Actors are the most important in the public eye, and indeed they are the dramatic exposition, the writing hand, of stories on the screen; without good ones you are lost. The music and scenic departments are important, and the cutting room is the watchtower of unsung heroes who have brought a thousand bungling messes out of the hopeless into something that at least moves and has coherence. Technically, the most indispensable is the cameraman, with his crew of assistants and batteries of lights; he is a high man indeed. But it is also true that without writing and direction of intelligence, taste, and actual mastery of the craft, you just won't get a picture that is a good picture. It comes down to this: writer and director (much more the director) tell a story in movie terms, and the way they do it is the prime technique of pictures.

*Citizen Kane* in its story uses the cut-back method—which is convenient but has its drawbacks in the constant interruption of a steady line; it is quite common and I wish it were less so. For dramatic action, it shows its one big character in four main situations, supplemented by newsreel interludes here and there. This makes a pretty weak structure dramatically, so it has to be surrounded with a great deal of stationary talk, as Kane is described, analyzed, asked about, remembered, talked into existence and practically out of it. This is different from many good movies but it is not new, technically or otherwise. The mood is established or heightened by an occasional symbol: the sled and the falling-snow toy, the curtain-warning light on the stage, the bird screaming in escape, etc. Symbols are a dime a dozen and justify their use in the result achieved. I thought the fading light filament and dying sound-track at the end of the singer's career very effective; also the opening and close on the iron fence around the castle. The smoke rising to heaven at the end was trite to start with and dragged out absurdly.

As you can see, there is nothing startling in these component parts. The outstanding technical effect in the picture is in the conception of settings and the use of the camera. Gregg Toland is a trained cameraman and ace-high in his profession, and it is apparent that Welles himself was fascinated most of all by this department in movies—that many of the things done were first sketched in with the bold freehand of his dramatic imagination. (It shouldn't be forgotten that a screen-mood is more than just "photography," that it results from the collaboration, in this order, of director, cameraman, art director.)

The camera here loves deep perspectives, long rooms, rooms seen through doors and giving onto rooms through other doors, rooms lengthened out by low ceilings or made immense by high-angle shots where the ceiling seems to be the sky. Figures are widely spaced down this perspective, moving far off at will, yet kept in focus. The camera loves partial lighting or underlighting, with faces or figures blacked out, features emphasized or thrown into shadow, with one point of high light in an area of gloom or foreground figures black against brightness, with the key shifting according to mood, with every scene modeled for special effects with light batteries of varying function and power, gobos, barndoors, screens, and what not. These things are all written into the accomplished cameraman's book. There is nothing newer about shooting into lights than shooting into the sun, but there is, I suppose, something new in having the whole book thrown at you at once. Certainly there has not been such use of darkness in masses since the Russians, who simply didn't have any lights.

Sometimes all this is fine and really does the job it is put to. Along with the wide action range, it is a relief from too much closeness and light, an effect of stretching. But at other times it appears just willful dabbling: figures are in the dark for no reason—reading without the light to see, for example—or they are kept in darkness right among other clearly lighted figures (the idea is supposed to be that this shows they aren't important; the effect is to draw attention to them, as being maybe the Masked Marvel). Half real and half fish, as in the case of mermaids, is always a thing to cause vague frustration; and too often here it seems as though they were working up a feeling of omen just for the ride.

This camera also likes many of the angles so thoroughly kicked around by the experimental films—floor shots, especially, where the camera gives figures height and takes away width, makes them ominous, or at least portentous in their motions. Crane shots, too, some of them breathtaking as you move down and forward from heights or rise straight up—some of them overdone, as in the last Cook's tour of Kane's boxed accumulations. Add undercranking, to make the people in the "newsreel" clips jerk and scuttle. Add mirrors. And add the usual working tools of long, medium, and two-shots, close-ups, dolly shots, panoramas.

In the cutting there are several things noticeable. One is the long easy sweep you can get when a scene of action is covered in one long-range setup. Another lies partly in the method of treatment and partly in lack of care, and that is the time-and-place confusion which arises when you go smack from the first two-thirds of a sentence to the last third of the same sentence, spoken elsewhere years later. This is done time and again, and you might call it jump-cutting or you might call it the old shell game as far as the audience is concerned.

Another thing about the cutting that goes altogether to the fault of direction is the monotony and amateurism of handling simple dialogue. Over and over there are the two faces talking, talk, talk, talk, then close-up of the right speaker asking, then close-up of the left speaker answering, then back to two. Outside of getting your name in large letters, being a director consists exactly in knowing how to break this up, to keep interest shifting, to stress the *reaction* to a line more sharply than the face saying it. This is what gives a picture life, and it isn't done by camera ructions, however clever.

Orson Welles was naturally entranced with the marvelous things the moving camera could do for him; and while much has resulted from this preoccupation, I think his neglect of what the camera could do *to* him is the main reason why the picture somehow leaves you cold even while your mouth is still open at its excitements. There may have been the heart and belief to put into it, but there wasn't the time to learn how this might be done, or much regard for any such humdrum skill. I'll tell you about a picture which was the story of a man's life told by the cut-back method after his death, and which had the real life in it, the skill and the heart too. It was *A Man to Remember,* made in a little over two weeks for a little over $100,000 by an ex-Broadway director who was learning about pictures the hard way, and his name was Garson Kanin. And if you want to read into a story some comment on the modern man of predacious industrial power, how he got that way and what it did to him, I'll remind you of a film that told the story and made it stick, its people full-length and alive. It was made some five years ago for Sam Goldwyn and called *Come and Get It,* and the better part of its direction was done by William Wyler.

As for the contributing departments in *Citizen Kane,* Bernard Herrmann's music is an active aid; the sets are made right, both for the fantastic and for use or living; it is an all-round class-A production. But the most effective things in it are the creation of Orson Welles's drawing board, not only in whole story ideas but in plausible and adult dialogue (witty, sardonic, knowledgeable), the impression of life as it actually goes on in the big world, the ready dramatic vigor. You remember things like the kid in the snow outside the window as the hard business is transacted within; the newspaper office at night; the understatement of successive breakfasts in Kane's first marriage; the wonderful campaign-hall scene; the opera opening (there was too much ham in some of this); the trick approach through the night-club skylight and ensuing scenes; the newsreel projection-room conference as a sendoff for the story; and the newsreels themselves—excellent naturalism here.

This stuff is fine theater, technically or any other way, and along with them the film is exciting for the recklessness of its independence, even if it seems to have little to be free *for*. There is surely nothing against it as a dramatic venture that it is no advance in screen technique at all, but a retrogression. The movies could use Orson Welles. But so could Orson Welles use the movies—that is, if he wants to make pictures. Hollywood is a great field for fanfare, but it is also a field in which even Genius has to do it the hard way; and *Citizen Kane* rather makes me doubt that Orson Welles really wants to make pictures.

# Raising Kane

## Pauline Kael

James Agee, who didn't begin reviewing until later in 1941, wrote several years afterward that Welles had been "fatuously overrated as a 'genius,'" and that he himself, annoyed by all the talk, had for a while under-rated him. At the time the film was released, the most perceptive movie critic in the United States was Otis Ferguson (an early volunteer and early casualty in the Second World War), on the *New Republic*. Ferguson saw more clearly than anybody else what was specifically good and bad in *Kane*, and though he was wrong, I think, in maintaining that unobtrusive technique is the only good technique, he did perceive that *Citizen Kane* challenged this concept.

One of the games that film students sometimes play is to judge a director on whether you have the illusion that the people on the screen will go on doing what they're doing after the camera leaves them. Directors are rated by how much time you think elapsed before the actors grabbed their coats or ordered a sandwich. The longer the time, the more of a film man the director is said to be; when a director is stage-oriented, you can practi-cally see the actors walking off the set. This game doesn't help in judging a film's content, but it's a fairly reliable test of a director's film technique; one could call it a test of movie believability. However, it isn't applicable to *Citizen Kane*. You're perfectly well aware that the people won't go on doing what they're doing—that they have, indeed, completed their actions on the screen. *Kane* depends not on naturalistic believability but on our enjoyment of the very fact that those actions *are* completed, and that they all fit into place. This bravura is, I think, the picture's only true originality, and it wasn't an intentional challenge to the concept of unobtrusive tech-nique but was (mainly) the result of Welles' discovery of—and his delight in—the fun of making movies.

The best American directors in the thirties had been developing an unpretentious American naturalism; modern subjects and the advent of sound had freed them from the heavy dead hand of Germanic stage lighting and design. And so Ferguson was dismayed to see this all come back, and it *was* depressing that the critics who had always fallen for the synthetic serious were bowing and scraping and calling the picture "deep" and "realistic." Probably so many people called it realistic because the social satire made contact with what they felt about Hearst and the country; when they used the term, they were referring to the content rather than the style. But it was the "retrogressive" style that upset Ferguson—because it was when Orson Welles, an "artist" director, joined the toughness and cynicism and the verbal skills of the thirties to that incomparable, faintly absurd, wonderfully overblown style of his that people said "art." Where Ferguson went wrong was in not recognizing one crucial element: that the unconcealed—even flaunted—pleasure that Welles took in all that claptrap made it new.

And it has kept it new. Even a number of those who worked on *Kane,* such as Houseman and Dorothy Comingore, have observed that the film seems to improve with the years. At the time, I got more simple, frivolous pleasure from Preston Sturges's *The Lady Eve,* which had come out a few months earlier, and I found more excitement in John Huston's *The Maltese Falcon,* which came out a few months later. At the time (I was twenty-one), I enjoyed *Kane* for the performances and the wit, but I was very conscious of how shallow the iconoclasm was. I don't think I was wrong, exactly, but now the movie seems marvelous to me. It's an *exuberant* shallow iconoclasm, and that youthful zest for shock and for the Expressionist theatricality seems to transform the shallowness. Now the movie sums up and preserves a period, and the youthful iconoclasm is preserved in all its freshness—even the freshness of its callowness. Now that the political theme (in its specific form, that is) is part of the past, the naïveté and obviousness fade, and what remains is a great American archetype and a popular legend—and so it has a strength that makes the artificially created comic world of a movie like *The Lady Eve* disappear by comparison.

*Citizen Kane* has such energy it drives the viewer along. Though Mankiewicz provided the basic apparatus for it, that magical exuberance which fused the whole scandalous enterprise was Welles's. Works of art are enjoyed for different reasons in different periods; it may even be one of the defining characteristics of a lasting work of art that it yields up different qualities for admiration at different times. Welles' "magic," his extraordinary pleasure in playacting and illusion and in impressing an audience— what seems so charming about the movie now—was what seemed silly to me then. It was bouncy Pop Gothic in a period when the term "comic strip" applied to works of art was still a term of abuse. Now Welles's discovery of movie-making—and the boyishness and excitement of that discovery—is preserved in *Kane* the way the snow scene is preserved in the glass ball.

Seeing the movie again recently, I liked the way it looked; now that the style no longer boded a return to the aestheticism of sets and the rigidly arranged figures of the German silents, I could enjoy it without misgivings. In the thirties, Jean Renoir had been using deep focus (that is, keeping the middle range and the background as clear as the foreground) in a naturalistic way. The light seemed (and often was) "natural." You looked at a scene, and the drama that you saw going on in it was just part of the scene, and so you had the sense of discovering it for yourself, of seeing drama in the midst of life. This was a tremendous relief from the usual studio lighting, which forced your attention to the dramatic action in the frame, blurred the rest, and rarely gave you a chance to feel that the action was part of anything larger or anything continuous. In Welles's far more extreme use of deep focus, and in his arrangement of the actors in the compositions, he swung back to the most coercive use of artificial, theatrical lighting. He used light like a spotlight on the stage, darkening or blacking out the irrelevant. He used deep focus not for a naturalistic effect but for the startling dramatic effect of having crucial action going on in the background (as when Kane appears in a distant doorway).

The difference between Renoir's style and Welles's style seems almost literally the difference between day and night. Welles didn't have (nor did he, at that time, need) the kind of freedom Renoir needed and couldn't get in Hollywood—the freedom to shoot outside the studio and to depart from the script and improvise. *Kane* is a studio-made film—much of it was shot in that large room at R.K.O. where a few years earlier, Ginger Rogers and Fred Astaire had danced their big numbers. However, Welles had the freedom to try out new solutions to technical problems, and he made his theatrical technique work spectacularly. Probably it was the first time in American movies that Expressionism had ever worked for comic and satiric effects (except in bits of some of the early spoof horror films), and probably it would have been impossible to tell the *Kane* story another way without spending a fortune on crowds and set construction. Welles's method is a triumph of ingenuity in that the pinpoints of light in the darkness conceal the absence of detailed sets (a chair or two and a huge fireplace, and one thinks one is seeing a great room), and the almost treacherously brilliant use of sound conceals the absence of crowds. We see Susan at the *deserted* cabaret; we see her from the back on the opera-house stage and we imagine that she is facing an audience; we get a sense of crowds at the political rally without seeing them. It was Welles's experience both in the theater and in radio that enabled him to produce a huge historical film on a shoestring; he produced the *illusion* of a huge historical film.

But, seeing *Kane* now, I winced, as I did the first time, at the empty virtuosity of the shot near the beginning when Kane, dying, drops the glass ball and we see the nurse's entrance reflected in the glass. I noticed once again, though without being bothered by it this time, either, that there was no one in the room to hear the dying Kane say "Rosebud." I was much more disturbed by little picky defects, like the obtrusive shot up to the bridge before the reporter goes into the hospital. What is strange about reseeing a movie that one reacted to fairly intensely many years ago is that one may respond exactly the same way to so many details and *be aware* each time of having responded that way before. I was disappointed once again by the clumsily staged "cute" meeting of Kane and Susan, which seemed to belong to a routine comedy, and I thought the early scenes with Susan were weak not just because while listening to her dull, sentimental singing Welles is in a passive position and so can't animate the scenes but—and mainly—because the man of simple pleasures who would find a dumb girl deeply appealing does not tie in with the personality projected by Orson Welles. (And as Welles doesn't project any sexual interest in either Kane's first wife, Emily, or in Susan, his second wife, we don't know how to interpret Susan's claim that he just likes her voice.) Most of the newspaper-office scenes looked as clumsily staged as ever, and the first appearance of Bernstein, Kane's business manager, arriving with a load of furniture, was still confusing. (He seems to be a junk dealer—probably because an earlier scene in *American* introducing him was eliminated.)[1] I disliked again the attempt to wring humor out of the sputtering confusion of Carter, the old Dickensian editor. It's a scene like the ones Mankiewicz helped prepare for the Marx Brothers, but what was probably intended to make fun of a stuffed shirt turned into making fun of a helpless old man trying to keep his dignity, which is mean and barbarous. I still thought Susan became too thin a conception, and more shrill and shrewish than necessary, and, as Emily, Ruth Warrick was all pursed lips—a stereotype of refinement. I was still uncomfortable during the visit to Jed Leland in the hospital; Leland's character throughout is dependent on Joseph Cotten's obvious charm, and the sentimental-old-codger bit in this sequence is really a disgrace. The sequence plays all too well at a low conventional level—pulling out easy stops. I still didn't see the function of the sequence about Kane's being broke and losing control of his empire, since nothing fol-

1. *American* was the title of Mankiewicz's original script.—EDS.

lowed from it. (I subsequently discovered that things weren't going well on the set at one point, and Welles decided to go back to this scene, which had been in an earlier draft and had then been eliminated. What it coordinated with was, unfortunately, not restored.) This sequence also has the most grating bad line in the movie, when Kane says, "You know, Mr. Bernstein, if I hadn't been very rich, I might have been a really great man."

What's still surprising is how well a novice movie director handled so many of the standard thirties tricks and caricatures—the device of the alternative newspaper headlines, for example, and the stock explosive, hand-waving Italian opera coach (well played by Fortunio Bonanova). The engineering—the way the sequences are prepared for and commented on by preceding sequences, the way the five accounts tie together to tell the story—seems as ingenious as ever; though one is aware that the narrators are telling things they couldn't have witnessed, one accepts this as part of the convention. The cutting (which a reading of the script reveals to have been carried out almost exactly as it was planned) is elegantly precise, and some sequences have a good, sophomoric musical-comedy buoyancy.

What had changed for me—what I had once enjoyed but now found almost mysteriously *beautiful*—was Orson Welles's performance. An additional quality that old movies acquire is that people can be seen as they once were. It is a pleasure we can't get in theater; we can only hear and read descriptions of past fabulous performances. But here in *Kane* is the young Welles, and he seems almost embarrassed to be exposed as so young. Perhaps he *was* embarrassed, and that's why he so often hid in extravagant roles and behind those old-man false faces. He seems unsure of himself as the young Kane, and there's something very engaging (and surprisingly *human*) about Welles unsure of himself; he's a big, overgrown, heavy boy, and rather sheepish, one suspects, at being seen as he is. Many years later, Welles remarked, "Like most performers, I naturally prefer a live audience to that lie-detector full of celluloid." Maybe his spoiled-baby face was just too nearly perfect for the role, and he knew it, and knew the hostile humor that lay behind Mankiewicz's putting so much of him in the role of Hearst the braggart self-publicist and making Kane so infantile. That statement of principles that Jed sends back to Kane and that Kane then tears up must surely refer to the principles behind the co-founding of the Mercury Theatre by Welles and Houseman. Lines like Susan's "You're not a professional magician, are you?" may have made Welles flinch. And it wasn't just the writer who played games on him. There's the scene of Welles eating in the newspaper office, which was obviously caught by the camera crew, and which, to be "a good sport," he had to use. Welles is one of the most self-conscious of actors—it's part of his rapport with the audience—and this is what is so nakedly revealed in this role, in which he's playing a young man his own age and he's insecure (and with some reason) about what's coming through. Something of the young, unmasked man is revealed in these scenes—to be closed off forever after.

Welles picks up assurance and flair as Kane in his thirties, and he's also good when Kane is just a little older and jowly. I think there's no doubt that he's more sure of himself when he's playing this somewhat older Kane, and this is the Kane we remember best from the first viewing—the brash, confident Kane of the pre-election-disaster period. He's so fully—classically—American a showoff one almost regrets the change of title. But when I saw the movie again it was the younger Kane who stayed with me—as if I had been looking through a photograph album and had come upon a group of pictures of an old friend, long dead, as he had been when I first met him. I had almost forgotten Welles in his youth, and here he is, smiling, eager, looking forward to the magnificent career that everyone expected him to have.

I think what makes Welles's directorial style so satisfying in this movie is that we are constantly aware of the mechanics—that the pleasure *Kane* gives doesn't come from illusion but comes from our enjoyment of the dexterity of the illusionists and the working of the machinery. *Kane,* too, is a clock that laughs. *Citizen Kane* is a film made by a very young man of enormous spirit; he took the Mankiewicz material and he played with it, he turned it into a magic show. It is Welles's distinctive quality as a movie director—I think it is his genius—that he never hides his cleverness, that he makes it possible for us not only to enjoy what he does but to share his enjoyment in doing it. Welles's showmanship is right there on the surface, just as it was when, as a stage director, he set *Julius Caesar* among the Nazis, and set *Macbeth* in Haiti with a black cast and, during the banquet scene, blasted the audience with a recording of the "Blue Danube Waltz"—an effect that Kubrick was to echo (perhaps unknowingly?) in *2001.* There is something childlike—and great, too—about his pleasure in the magic of theater and movies. No other director in the history of movies has been so open in his delight, so eager to share with us the game of pretending, and Welles's silly pretense of having done everything himself is just another part of the game.

Welles's magic as a director (at this time) was that he could put his finger right on the dramatic fun of each scene. Mankiewicz had built the scenes to end at ironic, dramatic high points, and Welles probably had a more innocently brazen sense of melodramatic timing than any other movie director. Welles also had a special magic beyond this: he could give *élan* to scenes that were confused in intention, so that the movie seems to go from dramatic highlight to highlight without lagging in between. There doesn't appear to be any waste material in *Kane,* because he charges right through the weak spots as if they were bright, and he almost convinces you (or *does* convince you) that they're shining jewels. Perhaps these different kinds of magic can be suggested by two examples. There's the famous sequence in which Kane's first marriage is summarized by a series of breakfasts, with overlapping dialogue. The method was not new, and it's used here on a standard marriage joke, but the joke is a basic good joke, and the method is honestly used to sum up as speedily as possible the banality of what goes wrong with the marriage. This sequence is adroit, and Welles brings out the fun in the material, but there's no *special* Wellesian magic in it— except, perhaps, in his own acting. But in the cutting from the sequence of Kane's first meeting with Susan (where the writing supplies almost no clue to why he's drawn to this particular twerp of a girl beyond his finding her relaxing) to the political rally, Welles's special talent comes into play. Welles directs the individual scenes with such flourish and such *enjoyment of flourish* that the audience reacts as if the leap into the rally were clever and funny and logical, too, although the connection between the scenes isn't established until later, when Boss Jim Gettys uses Susan to wreck Kane's political career.

As a director, Welles is so ebullient that we go along with the way he wants us to feel; we're happy to let him "put it over on us." Given the subject of Hearst and the witty script, the effect is of complicity, of a shared knowingness between Welles and the audience about what the movie is about. Kane's big smile at the rally seals the pact between him and us. Until Kane's later years, Welles, in the role, has an almost total empathy with the audience. It's the same kind of empathy we're likely to feel for smart kids who grin at us when they're showing off in the school play. It's a beautiful kind of emotional nakedness—ingenuously exposing the sheer love of playacting—that most actors lose long before they become "professional." If an older actor—even a very good one—had played the role, faking youth for the young Kane the way Edward Arnold, say, sometimes faked it, I think the picture might have been routine. Some people used to say that Welles might be a great director but he was a bad actor, and his performance wrecked his pictures. I think just the opposite—that his directing style is such an emanation of his adolescent love of theater that his films lack a vital unifying element when he's not in them or when he plays only a small part in them. He needs to be at the center. *The Magnificent Ambersons* is a work of feeling and imagination and of obvious effort—and the milieu is much closer to Welles's own background than the milieu of *Kane* is—but Welles isn't in it, and it's too bland. It feels empty, uninhabited. Without Orson Welles's physical presence—the pudgy, big prodigy, who incarnates egotism—*Citizen Kane* might (as Otis Ferguson suggested) have disintegrated into vignettes. We feel that he's making it all happen. Like the actor-managers of the old theater, he's the man onstage running the show, pulling it all together.

# Welles after Kane

## William S. Pechter

More and more, the career of Orson Welles has come to take on distressing parallels to that of his creation, Charles Foster Kane, and as Welles said of Kane, in the previews of his first film, "Ladies and gentlemen, I don't know what you'll think about Mr. Kane. I can't imagine. You see, I play the part myself. Well, Kane is a hero and a scoundrel, a no-account and a swell guy . . . a great lover, a great American citizen, and a dirty guy. That depends upon who's talking about him." One hardly knows whether to laugh or cry.

And thus, depending upon who's talking about him, Welles's later failures are either treated with a doting indulgence or his earlier achievements belittled, both being instances of that form of rewriting history by which the inconveniences of fact are triumphed over by the consistency of criticism; at least one would probably have to be a film critic to be able to believe some good was served by either eulogizing the later failures or gloating over them. Well, they *are* failures, but they *were* achievements. It is possible, perhaps, to dismiss *Citizen Kane* as little more than a bag of tricks, good tricks but tricks nonetheless; yet, although much of that film's excitement derives from the sheer exuberance and audacity—real audacity—of its exploration of the medium's techniques, I think this is considerably to underestimate the work. But one may concede the case of *Citizen Kane,* and still there is *The Magnificent Ambersons,* a less perfect work, perhaps; also, I think, a finer one. Beginning with its apparently random and casual collection of nostalgic images of bygone styles in clothes and motorcars, like so many snapshots from a family album, the film quietly deepens and extends itself into an almost achingly sorrowful picture of a vanished style of life, and of irrecoverable loss; and, in so doing, manages to achieve what *Citizen Kane,* in all its brilliant eclecticism, never does: a unified style of its own. And it is style as practiced by a

From *Twenty-Four Times a Second* by William S. Pechter. Copyright © 1962 by William S. Pechter. Reprinted by permission of Harper & Row, Publishers, Inc. The title "Welles after Kane" has been provided by the Editors.

film-maker capable of raising style to the level at which it becomes indistinguishable from genius.

But it is style—as, in Welles's work, it was never again to be—pressed wholly into the service of meaning. Nothing is gratuitous; from the sleigh ride through an impossibly soft and radiant snowscape—the snow as surreal as that which floats through Kane's crystal globe, the sleigh itself thereafter to give way to fuming, sputtering automobiles—to the "last of the great, long-remembered dances" at the Amberson mansion, all of the film's imagery is darkened and complicated by a sense, an almost tragic sense, of the impermanence of all that appears solid and substantial, and of the evanescence of all that is beautiful. *The Magnificent Ambersons* is, like *Citizen Kane,* about a man's fall, but also about the fall of a house, and of a society. The film's narrative remains faithful to that of the novel by Booth Tarkington from which it was adapted, but what Welles brings to that narrative, not in the novel, above all, is mystery. It is a quality which arises, in part, from the difference between the grayish naturalism of the novel's language and the rich chiaroscuro of the imagery of the film. But the film's imagery itself seems, finally, to arise from the apprehension of some deeper kind of mystery: that mystery inherent in the way men come to be as they are, and in the way all power declines and dies.

And, when all the tricks are emptied from *Citizen Kane*'s bag of tricks, it is that sense of mystery which still remains. Although an audience conditioned to psychological explanation may suddenly grow acutely attentive when one character says that Kane wanted to be loved, and nod in perfect understanding at the closing confrontation with "Rosebud," the psychological explanation is, finally, just one of several explanations offered by the characters in the film, and this in a film everywhere filled with the implication that any single explanation, indeed, any explanation, must remain inadequate to the mystery which a person may contain. As the reporter and his staff prepare to leave the Kane mansion, a photographer asks him if he ever did find out what Rosebud means. "No," he replies, "I never did. Maybe Rosebud was something he couldn't get, or something he lost, but I don't think it would have explained anything, anyway. I don't think any word can explain a man's life. I guess Rosebud is just a piece in a jigsaw puzzle. A missing piece."[1]

---

1. Although the usual objection to *Citizen Kane* is that the character of Kane is, finally, too simple-minded in its conception, I would argue, rather, that Kane does not even exist as a character in the sense in which we conventionally construe the meaning of this. Kane is a force which we know only through its impact on various bodies; our sole "objective" glimpse of him is at the moment of his death, at which the force that he contains escapes him. Or he is an image, a fragmented image, which, unlike that of a jigsaw puzzle, cannot be put back

It is the film's final irony: we *do* discover what Rosebud is, and still do not know what it means. A burning sled . . . a sled, outside the Kanes' old cabin, gradually becoming buried in the ceaselessly falling snow . . . a line: "I was on the way to the warehouse in search of my youth"; what is it all but an evocation of the past, of irretrievable loss, retaining all its mystery, explaining nothing? And so the film ends; the sled in flames; the fire obliterating the painted word; the great castle, its lights extinguished, its chimneys billowing forth the smoke of Kane's possessions as they burn; antique statuary, mysterious wharves, silent pools; and the camera moving down a wire fence, gliding past a posted warning, ending the film with the words with which it began, now deepened in meaning, now implicating us: "No Trespassing."

If I appear to dwell on Welles's two earliest films, it is because, for all the attention that has been paid to them as works of technical brilliance, they yet remain insufficiently appreciated as works of art; that, and the fact that, among Welles's subsequent films, there is little else to dwell upon. *Citizen Kane* is not a profound work, but, aside from that, it is almost everything else one might wish a first work to be: unmistakably individual, exploratory, exuberant, charged with an excitement undiminished after twenty years; and *The Magnificent Ambersons* is, I think, one of the most mysteriously beautiful films ever made. Probably, the course of Welles's work since cannot be wholly understood without taking into account the conditions under which he has had to struggle for that work's existence. Given carte blanche to make *Citizen Kane,* he had virtually to enjoin R.K.O. to release it. *Citizen Kane* was preceded by two projects, one of them an experimental treatment for the filming of Conrad's *Heart of Darkness,* both of which the studio chose finally to reject; *The Magnificent Ambersons* followed only after two more aborted projects.

By the time *Journey into Fear,* Welles's third Mercury production, was to be filmed, Welles was replaced as director by the studio with some safe nonentity. Several hundred thousand feet—footage of sufficient length to complete a feature—of a fourth film were shot in South America before Welles was recalled, and his relations with R.K.O. terminated. Footage for the unfinished film was entombed in the studio's vaults, where it resides to this day (if, with the demise of R.K.O., these vaults themselves still exist), and both *The Magnificent Ambersons* and *Journey into Fear* were released in mutilated versions; the former shorn of some forty-five minutes, and concluding with a sequence Welles neither wrote nor directed. In fact,

---

together; for what we see of Kane, in the various evocations of him, is contradictory, and incomplete; we can never possess all the pieces, and those we have can never exactly be made to fit.

what one sees in *The Magnificent Ambersons* now is only a version of Welles's conception of the film, one onto which has been tacked the proverbial Hollywood happy ending. In the twenty-two years which elapsed between his making *Citizen Kane* and *The Trial,* Welles has directed only eight other finished films (including *Journey into Fear*), his own filmmaking usually financed by his acceptance of acting roles in the hack work of others, and, of those made since *Citizen Kane,* it was not until *The Trial* that another of his films was released in exactly the form in which he wished it. But life is not so prodigal as Hollywood with happy endings.

Yet *Journey into Fear,* despite the fact that the credit for its direction is not given to Welles, is everywhere stamped with the mark of his individuality, as are the two other melodramas which sporadically succeeded it, *The Stranger* and *The Lady from Shanghai.* All are witty, exciting, above all, enormously entertaining; and, if their brilliance seems to reside largely on their surface, well, where else should brilliance be? They are melodramas; only their enthusiasts have pretended they are more; although, at least in the case of the last, one alarming, three-dimensional character is quite indelibly created: Glenn Anders as the monstrous Mr. Grisby. Then, in 1948, Welles made his first film of Shakespeare, *Macbeth,* with himself in the leading role. It is a film easily dismissed as a production of the play, with its drastic textual rearrangement and, but for Welles and Dan O'Herlihy, generally impoverished acting; it is also by far the most interesting film made of Shakespeare to pursue the idea that an adaptation of a play into film requires as radical and complete a transformation of the original materials as does the adaptation of a play into opera.

Welles made his *Macbeth* on a slender budget in little more than three weeks—he has called it, "for better or worse . . . a kind of violently sketched charcoal drawing of a great play"—and, if he allowed most of the performances to go flagrantly awry, it was not because of any inability on his part to direct actors; it would be difficult to match the ensemble playing of Welles's Mercury Theatre company in his first two films with that in many others. Welles's preoccupation in *Macbeth* is clearly with inventing a line of visual imagery raised to the level of the language, even if, in the accomplishment, what more often resulted was a reduction of the language to the level of the visual imagery; one would really have to be, at the least, a Verdi wholly to succeed in what Welles was attempting, and Welles is not this. Still, while the achievement of Welles's film is decidedly not that of Shakespeare's *Macbeth,* the film does manage to achieve a striking, genuinely barbaric splendor of its own. And, despite the film's many failures, if one considers the respectfully dull ways that *Macbeth* has been done badly on our stages, one might be less inclined to undervalue that achievement.

What happened to Welles's great gifts as a filmmaker during the four years that elapsed between *Macbeth* and the completion of his *Othello?* I cannot pretend to be able to say. It is not that it is difficult to speculate upon the causes of so spectacular a decline; it is all too easy. But the facts are these: *Macbeth* was made in approximately three weeks, at the end of a period during which Welles may be said to have worked with some regularity as a filmmaker; *Othello* was made over a period of four years, one of only three films Welles directed between *Macbeth* in 1948 and *The Trial* in 1962. What happened, I cannot pretend to say, but I can guess, and I would guess that Welles has always been the kind of artist whose genius lies in his intuition, who is, time and again, betrayed by his premeditation; and four years is a long time to premeditate. But more important, I think, is that, unlike a Bresson, Welles is a filmmaker whose talent is necessarily impaired by disuse, being bound, as it is, less to some commanding imaginative vision than to an ardent exploration of his medium, and needing the constant renewal of a continuing contact with that medium to keep it from stagnation; for the apparent consequence of Welles's inability to work in his medium has been a virtual obsession with the medium per se.

In any case, the special badness of Welles's *Othello,* [2] with all its fussy inflation of eye-catching details, is of a kind to make the free-wheeling carelessness of his *Macbeth* seem positively invigorating by comparison. It is the details, in fact, which take over this *Othello,* crowding out character, crowding out action, almost, but not quite, crowding out everything that is the play. All is sacrificed to the *mise en scène,* but it is a *mise en scène* now become an orgy of tilted camera angles, intricate composition, and florid chiaroscuro. Concern is now exclusively for effects, and not effects directed toward the end of any total meaning but rather isolated effects, singular flashes of brilliance (and some, admittedly, brilliant), indulged in only for themselves. Each scene is invested with an impact out of all proportion to its meaning or its relevance to context; each scene played and shot as though it were climactic. Gone is the marvelous rhythmic continuity of *Citizen Kane;* given way to a monotonous fluidity (almost every transition is a quick dissolve) as discrete, supercharged images flow one into the other. There is a word for Welles's film of *Othello.* It suffers not from lack of talent; rather, from a conspicuous waste of it. All has grown

2. For a thoroughgoing autopsy of Welles's *Othello,* and one that is eminently fair, I refer the reader to Eric Bentley, "Orson Welles and Two Othellos," in *What Is Theatre?* (New York: Atheneum, 1968).

overripe; the individual cells have developed at the expense of the organism as a whole. The word is decadent.

And it is that word which best characterizes all of Welles's films since. There is little to choose from between *Mr. Arkadin* (known also by the title, *Confidential Report*) and *Touch of Evil;* of the two, I tend to prefer the former, which seems to me more willing to accept itself at its own level of preposterousness, rather than go rummaging about among half-baked profundities. But, whatever one's preference, such distinctions as may be drawn between the two are fine, and *Touch of Evil* is, I think, profoundly bad, its badness only somewhat obscured by such things as the long-take crane shot on which it opens, a virtuoso exercise which exhibits more skill in three minutes than is to be found in the life's work of most other directors.

The film is melodrama again, as was *Mr. Arkadin,* but, whereas Welles was once able to use his camera ingeniously to enhance such material, here the camera, with few exceptions, just gets in the way, intruding on the action, complicating it unnecessarily, further cluttering a film already, in its narrative, prodigally cluttered, and generally providing graphic evidence of what kind of artistic disaster may occur when a medium whose propensity is to reveal is taken in the hands of a director whose proclivity is to obscure. *Touch of Evil* probably contains more irrelevant movement per frame than anything else yet committed to film, movement finally signifying nothing so much as Welles's radical failure as a director; yet what remains glaringly apparent, despite all the camera's agitation, is Welles's corresponding failure as an actor. In *Touch of Evil,* he manages wholly to accomplish what one saw only intermittently realized in his playing of Othello: the reduction of himself to the status of a prop, a fabrication of the makeup room, a triumph of paste and putty. Even his fatness fails to exist as a human quality; it is simply another grotesque; fatness in the abstract. Among more zealous lovers of cinema, *Touch of Evil* has attained something of the status of Welles' masterpiece; and for those, not necessarily cinema enthusiasts, who just relish the spectacle of a prodigious talent recklessly exploring all possible ways to squander and parody itself, *Touch of Evil* is, indeed, highly recommended. I found it deeply depressing.

9387